# About the Cover Image

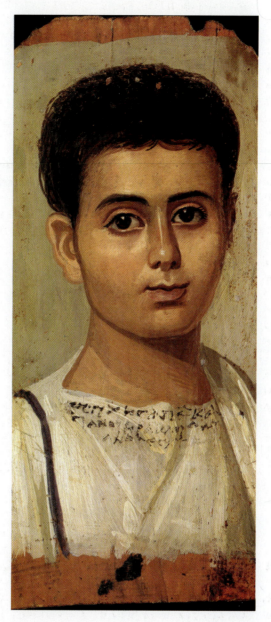

**_Portrait of the Boy Eutyches,_ encaustic on wood and paint, 100–150 C.E.**

In this lifelike portrait from Roman Egypt painted on a wood panel around 100–150 C.E., a teenage boy gazes at the viewer. He is identified in the Greek writing on his tunic as "Eutyches, freedman." Painted in encaustic, a technique in which the pigments are mixed into beeswax, the portrait is a product of the multicultural, multiethnic society that was Roman Egypt: the technique and style of the painting are Greek, the boy's clothing and hairstyle are Roman, and the purpose was Egyptian. Portrait panels like this were placed over the faces of mummies, reflecting Egyptian beliefs about the afterlife.

Metropolitan Museum of Art, New York, USA/Bridgeman Images

# A History of Western Society

## THIRTEENTH EDITION

**VOLUME 1**
From Antiquity to the Enlightenment

**Merry E. Wiesner-Hanks**
*University of Wisconsin–Milwaukee*

**Clare Haru Crowston**
*University of Illinois at Urbana-Champaign*

**Joe Perry**
*Georgia State University*

**John P. McKay**
*University of Illinois at Urbana-Champaign*

bedford/st.martin's
Macmillan Learning

Boston | New York

**FOR BEDFORD/ST. MARTIN'S**

*Vice President, Editorial, Macmillan Learning Humanities:* Edwin Hill
*Senior Program Director for History:* Michael Rosenberg
*Senior Executive Program Manager for History:* William J. Lombardo
*History Marketing Manager:* Melissa Rodriguez
*Director of Content Development, Humanities:* Jane Knetzger
*Senior Developmental Editor:* Heidi L. Hood
*Senior Content Project Manager:* Christina M. Horn
*Senior Workflow Project Manager:* Jennifer Wetzel
*Production Coordinator:* Brianna Lester
*Advanced Media Project Manager:* Sarah O'Connor Kepes
*Media Editor:* Mary Starowicz
*Editorial Assistant:* Carly Lewis
*Copy Editor:* Susan Zorn

*Indexer:* Leoni Z. McVey
*Editorial Services:* Lumina Datamatics, Inc.
*Composition:* Lumina Datamatics, Inc.
*Cartographer:* Mapping Specialists, Ltd.
*Text Permissions Manager:* Kalina Ingham
*Text Permissions Editor:* Mark Schaefer
*Photo Permissions Editor:* Robin Fadool
*Photo Researcher:* Bruce Carson
*Director of Design, Content Management:* Diana Blume
*Text Design:* Boynton Hue Studio
*Cover Design:* William Boardman
*Cover Image:* Metropolitan Museum of Art, New York, USA/Bridgeman Images
*Printing and Binding:* LSC Communications

Manufactured in the United States of America.

1   2   3   4   5   6        24   23   22   21   20   19

*For information, write:* Bedford/St. Martin's, 75 Arlington Street, Boston, MA 02116

ISBN 978-1-319-10963-9 (Combined Edition)
ISBN 978-1-319-10956-1 (Volume 1)
ISBN 978-1-319-10913-4 (Volume 2)
ISBN 978-1-319-21840-9 (Since 1300)

**ACKNOWLEDGMENTS**

*Acknowledgments and copyrights appear on the same page as the text and art selections they cover; these acknowledgments and copyrights constitute an extension of the copyright page.*

*A History of Western Society* grew out of the initial three authors' desire to infuse new life into the study of Western Civilization. The three current authors, Merry E. Wiesner-Hanks, Clare Haru Crowston, and Joe Perry, who first used the book as students or teachers and took over full responsibilities with the eleventh edition, continue to incorporate the latest and best scholarship in the field and to give special attention to the history of daily life, which has long been a popular distinction of this text. All three of us regularly teach introductory history courses and thus bring insights into the text from the classroom, as well as from new secondary works and our own research in archives and libraries.

In this new thirteenth edition we continue to add tools to help students think historically and master the material. Because our colleagues and current adopters say they like to teach with primary sources in a variety of ways, we have added more variety to the book's primary source program. Every chapter now includes a new **"Viewpoints"** feature that pairs two written or visual primary sources on the same issue, as well as the popular feature **"Thinking Like a Historian"** (one per chapter), which groups at least five sources around a central question, plus **"Evaluating Visual Evidence"** (one per chapter) and **"Evaluating Written Evidence"** (one per chapter), each of which features an individual primary source. Along with broadening the primary source features, we have shortened and tightened the main chapter narratives to make the overall reading experience more manageable for students. We have also focused on ways to help students think about the big picture as they read. To help students look for and understand the most important points conveyed in each chapter, **section heading questions now drive the narrative** and replace traditional section titles. To help students see how developments are related to each other, we have also replaced the chronology tables with **new visual timelines** at the start of each chapter, which provide an appealing and engaging way to foster the development of chronological reasoning skills.

## The Story of *A History of Western Society*: Bringing the Past to Life for Students

When *A History of Western Society* was first conceptualized, social history was dramatically changing the ways we understood the past, and the original authors decided to create a book that would re-create the lives of ordinary people in appealing human terms, while also giving major economic, political, cultural, and intellectual developments the attention they unquestionably deserve. The current authors remain committed to advancing this vision for today's classroom, with a broader definition of social history that brings the original vision into the twenty-first century.

History as a discipline never stands still, and over the last several decades cultural history has joined social history as a source of dynamism. Because of its emphasis on the ways people made sense of their lives, *A History of Western Society* has always included a large amount of cultural history, ranging from foundational works of philosophy and literature to popular songs and stories. We have enhanced this focus on cultural history in recent editions in a way that highlights the interplay between men's and women's lived experiences and the ways men and women reflect on these experiences to create meaning. The joint social and cultural perspective requires — fortunately, in our opinion — the inclusion of objects as well as texts as important sources for studying history, which has allowed us to incorporate the growing emphasis on material culture in the work of many historians. We know that engaging students' interest in the past is often a challenge, but we also know that the text's hallmark approach — the emphasis on daily life and individual experience in its social and cultural dimensions — connects with students and makes the past vivid and accessible.

## Chapters and Features That Humanize the Past

Because students often have trouble engaging with the past, we seek to make it more approachable in human terms. One way we do this is by discussing social and cultural history, particularly in the acclaimed **"Life" chapters**, which emphasize daily life in a particular time period. The five chapters are Chapter 4: *Life* in the Hellenistic World, 338–30 B.C.E.; Chapter 10: *Life* in Villages and Cities of the High Middle Ages, 1000–1300; Chapter 18: *Life* in the Era of Expansion, 1650–1800; Chapter 22: *Life* in the Emerging Urban Society, 1840–1914; and Chapter 30: *Life* in an Age of Globalization, 1990 to the Present.

To make the past even more discernible and memorable, we give students a chance to see it through individual people's lives in the popular **"Individuals in Society" biographical essays**. Appearing in each chapter, these essays offer brief studies of individuals and the societies in which they lived. We have found that students empathize with these human beings as they themselves seek to define their own identities. The spotlighting of individuals, from the master artist Leonardo da Vinci to the former slave and Moravian missionary Rebecca Protten to security analyst and fugitive Edward Snowden, perpetuates the book's continued attention to cultural and intellectual developments and highlights human agency. These essays reflect changing interests within the historical profession as well as the development of "microhistory." New biographical essays include "King Taharqa of Kush and Egypt" (Chapter 2); "Abelard and Heloise" (Chapter 10); "Catarina de San Juan" (Chapter 14); "Mary Shelley" (Chapter 21); and "Sigmund Freud" (Chapter 26).

## Primary Sources and Historical Thinking

Because understanding the past requires that students engage directly with sources on their own, this edition features an expansive primary source program within its covers. These primary source assignments help students master a number of key learning outcomes, among them **critical thinking**, **historical thinking**, **analytical thinking**, and **argumentation**. Foremost among these assignments is **"Thinking Like a Historian"** (one in each chapter), which groups at least five sources around a central question, with additional questions to guide students' analysis of the evidence and suggestions for essays that will allow them to put these sources together with what they have learned in class. Topics include "Land Ownership and Social Conflict in the Late Republic" (Chapter 5); "Humanist Learning" (Chapter 12); "The Rights of Which Men?" (Chapter 19); "The Republican Spirit in 1848" (Chapter 21); "Normalizing Eugenics and 'Racial Hygiene' in Nazi Germany" (Chapter 27); and "The Conservative Reaction to Immigration and Islamist Terrorism" (Chapter 30).

To encourage comparative analysis, our **new "Viewpoints"** feature pairs two written or visual sources that show contrasting or complementary perspectives on a particular issue. We hope that teachers will use these passages to get students thinking about diversity within and across societies, as well as across cultures. The thirty "Viewpoints" assignments — one in each chapter — introduce students to working with sources, encourage critical analysis, and extend the narrative while giving voice to the people of the past. Each includes a brief introduction and questions for analysis. Carefully chosen for accessibility, each pair of documents presents views on a diverse range of topics, such as "Greek Playwrights on Families, Fate, and Choice" (Chapter 3); "Roman and Byzantine Views of Barbarians" (Chapter 7); "Italian and English Views of the Plague" (Chapter 11); "Rousseau and Wollstonecraft Debate Women's Equality" (Chapter 16); "Contrasting Visions of the Sans-Culottes" (Chapter 19); "The White Man's Versus the Brown Man's Burden" (Chapter 24); and "Cold War Propaganda" (Chapter 28).

The final types of original source features, **"Evaluating Visual Evidence"** (one per chapter) and **"Evaluating Written Evidence"** (one per chapter), supply an individual visual or written source, which are often more substantial in length than in other features, with headnotes and questions that help students understand the source and connect it to the information in the rest of the chapter. Selected for their interest and carefully integrated into their historical context, these sources provide students with firsthand encounters with people of the past and should, we believe, help students "hear" and "see" the past. With twenty-four written and visual sources new to this edition, students can evaluate evidence such as "Homer's *Iliad*" (Chapter 3); "Charlemagne and His Second Wife Hildegard" (Chapter 8); "Apprenticeship Contract for a Money-Changer" (Chapter 10); "Lucas Cranach's *The True Church and the False Church*, ca. 1546" (Chapter 13); "Depictions of Africans in European Portraiture" (Chapter 14); "Gonzales Coques, *The Young Scholar and His Wife*, 1640" (Chapter 15); "Mixed Races" (Chapter 17); "Hogarth's Satirical View of the Church" (Chapter 18); "Trench Warfare on the Western Front" (Chapter 25); "De-Stalinization and Khrushchev's 'Secret Speech'" (Chapter 28); "The 'May Events' in Paris, 1968" (Chapter 29); and more.

To give students abundant opportunities to hone their textual and visual analysis skills, as well as a sense of the variety of sources on which historians rely, the primary source program includes a mix of canonical and lesser-known sources; a diversity of perspectives representing ordinary and prominent individuals alike; and a wide variety of source types, from tomb inscriptions, diaries, sermons, letters, and poetry, to artifacts, paintings, architecture, and propaganda posters. In addition, we have quoted extensively from a wide range of primary sources in the narrative, demonstrating that such quotations are the "stuff" of history. We believe that our extensive use of primary source extracts as an integral part of the narrative as well as in extended form in the primary source boxes will give students ample practice in thinking critically and historically.

Finally, the thoroughly revised companion reader, *Sources for Western Society*, Thirteenth Edition, provides a rich selection of documents to complement each chapter of the text and is FREE when packaged with the textbook.

## New Coverage and Updates to the Narrative

This edition is enhanced by the incorporation of a wealth of new scholarship and subject areas that immerse students in the dynamic and ongoing work of history. Revisions to the thirteenth edition include updated coverage of the domestication of plants and animals in Chapter 1; an expanded discussion of Kush and Assyria in Chapter 2; more analysis and attention to causation in sections on epics, warfare between city-states, gender, and philosophers in Chapter 3; and more analysis of Alexander the Great's legacy, Hellenistic commerce, mystery religions, and science in Chapter 4.

Chapters 5 and 6 have been substantially revised to reflect a wealth of recent scholarship. Chapter 5 now emphasizes that Rome's greatest achievement and basis for its success was its ability to incorporate conquered peoples as Roman citizens, an insight historians of Rome have increasingly stressed in the last several decades. Chapter 5 also devotes more attention to how the Roman army was organized and how conquered land was distributed. This chapter offers more analysis of the sources for Roman history; adds a discussion of aristocratic snobbery and attitudes toward "new men"; expands coverage of the patron-client system; de-emphasizes the role of Cato in the Third Punic War; presents an entirely new view of activity in the countryside in the late republic; broadens the analysis of patterns in Roman expansion and political challenges; provides new coverage of the Marian military reforms and the Catiline conspiracy; and supplies a revised discussion of the *populares* and *optimates*. Substantial changes in Chapter 6 reflect new scholarship as well. It emphasizes the continuing role of the Senate and other Roman elites in running the empire and adds more coverage of the auxiliary forces provided by Rome's allies, cultural blending in the provinces, and the diverse nature of early Christianity.

Chapter 8 offers revised coverage of Muslims in Europe as well as Carolingian royal politics. Coverage of the Black Death in Chapter 11 has been updated to reflect recent research, including exciting insights that have come from science. Chapter 14 contains more about Portuguese exploration and settlement; new discussion of the role of Islam in the Indian Ocean world; an updated account of the Spanish conquest; and revised coverage of European ideas about race.

Chapter 16 contains an updated discussion of Muslim and Arab scientific scholarship and of how patterns of education, trade, and patronage led the Scientific Revolution to take place in Europe rather elsewhere in the world. Chapter 17 includes information about important changes in financial systems and in thinking about governmental regulation of the economy, as well as an expanded section about Adam Smith and the emergence of the discipline of "political economy" in this period. Chapter 18 supplies new material on contraception methods in the eighteenth century and on attitudes toward miscarriage and abortion. Chapter 21 includes expanded coverage of Utopian socialism, Tories and Whigs, the Peterloo Massacre, and the Irish famine.

The reorganization of Chapters 22 and 23 made room for new and expanded coverage. Chapter 22 supplies a new and updated discussion of middle-class professionalization, an expanded discussion of the advent of the public health movement in London, and additional information about religion among the working classes. Chapter 23 includes more about the costs and benefits for ordinary people of the newly established responsive national states; new coverage of Florence Nightingale in the Crimean War; and new material and updated scholarship on Louis Napoleon and the Second Empire, the emergence of the British Liberal Party, Karl Lueger and anti-Semitism in Vienna, and pogroms in the Pale of Settlement.

A new section in Chapter 24 offers extended material about the immigrant experience in the United States. It also includes an expanded discussion of King Leopold's Congo Free State and updated material on British intervention in Egypt before World War I, Asian immigration and passport controls, the Berlin Conference, and German colonial war. Chapter 25 includes new material and updated scholarship on Wilhelm II's character, the First and Second Moroccan Crises, and Austro-Hungarian occupation of Serbia. Chapter 26 adds a new title and additional material to explain the changes associated with the consolidation of modernism and modernity in the decades around 1900. Chapter 30 includes updates and new information about populism, Russian interference in U.S. elections, the politics of Internet privacy, and American relations with the European Union under the Trump administration.

## Helping Students Understand and Engage with the Narrative

We know firsthand and take seriously the challenges students face in understanding, retaining, and mastering so much material that is often unfamiliar. With the goal of making this the most student-centered edition yet, we have enhanced the text with new pedagogy and tools designed to prompt active reading and comprehension of the continuities and changes that are the driving forces of historical development. Our book now has a wealth of pedagogical aids that help students understand where they are going in their reading and where they have been. To focus students' reading, questions now drive the narrative. Not only does each chapter open with **a chapter preview that poses questions**, but **each major heading is now one of these questions**. These questions are repeated again in the "Review & Explore" section at the end of each chapter.

We also provide tools that anchor the narrative in the big picture. Today's students are visually oriented, and we have replaced our chapter chronology tables with **new visual timelines** that assist them in developing chronological reasoning skills and making connections among events. To help students understand the bigger picture, each chapter includes **"Looking Back, Looking Ahead" conclusions** that provide an insightful synthesis of the chapter's main developments, while connecting to events that students will encounter in the chapters to come. In this way students are introduced to history as an ongoing process of interrelated events. These conclusions are followed by **"Make Connections" questions** that prompt students to assess larger developments across chapters, thus allowing them to develop skills in evaluating change and continuity, making comparisons, and analyzing context and causation.

To help students prepare for exams, in addition to repeating the major section heading questions in **"Review the Main Ideas,"** each "Review & Explore" section includes an **"Identify Key Terms"** prompt. For students who wish to know more, this section concludes with a **"Suggested Resources"** listing that supplies up-to-date readings on the vast amount of new work being done in many fields, as well as recommended documentaries, feature films, television programs, and websites.

To promote clarity and comprehension, boldface **key terms** in the text are defined in the margins and listed in the chapter review. **Phonetic spellings** are located directly after terms that readers are likely to find hard to pronounce. The topic-specific **thematic chronologies** that appear in many chapters provide a more focused timeline of certain developments. Once again, we also provide a **unified timeline** at the end of the text. Comprehensive and easy to locate, this timeline allows students to compare developments over the centuries. We are also proud of the text's high-quality art and map program, which has been thoroughly revised and features hundreds of **contemporaneous illustrations** (20 percent new). To make the past tangible, and as an extension of our attention to cultural history, we include images of numerous **artifacts**—from swords and fans to playing cards and record players. As in earlier editions, all illustrations have been carefully selected to complement the text, and all include captions that inform students while encouraging them to read the text more deeply. High-quality **full-size maps** contextualize major developments in the narrative, and helpful spot maps are embedded in the narrative to locate areas under discussion. We recognize students' difficulties with geography, and the new edition includes the popular **"Mapping the Past" map activities**. Included in each chapter, these activities give students valuable skills in reading and interpreting maps by asking them to analyze the maps and make connections to the larger processes discussed in the narrative.

In addition, whenever an instructor assigns the **LaunchPad e-book** (which is free when bundled with the print book), students get full access to **LearningCurve**, an online adaptive learning tool that promotes mastery of the book's content and diagnoses students' trouble spots. With this adaptive quizzing, students accumulate points toward a target score as they go, giving the interaction a game-like feel. Feedback for incorrect responses explains why the answer is incorrect and directs students back to the text to review before they attempt to answer the question again. The end result is a better understanding of the key elements of the text. Instructors who actively assign LearningCurve report that their students come to class prepared for discussion and their students enjoy using it. In addition, LearningCurve's reporting feature allows instructors to quickly diagnose which concepts students are struggling with so they can adjust lectures and activities accordingly.

For instructors who need a mobile-ready and fully accessible option for delivering LearningCurve's adaptive quizzing with the narrative alone, Macmillan Learning's new **Achieve Read & Practice e-book** platform offers an exceptionally easy-to-use and affordable option. This simple product pairs the Value Edition e-book—a two-color narrative-only text (no boxed features or sources and fewer visuals)—with the power of LearningCurve's quizzing, all in a format that is mobile-friendly, allowing students to complete their assignments at home, in the library, or on the go.

## Helping Instructors Teach with Digital Resources

As noted, *A History of Western Society* is offered in Macmillan Learning's premier learning platform, **LaunchPad**, an intuitive, interactive e-book and course space. Free when packaged with the print book or available at a low price when used on its own, LaunchPad grants students and teachers access to a wealth of online tools and resources built specifically for this text to enhance reading comprehension and promote in-depth study. LaunchPad's course space and interactive e-book are ready to use "as is," or they can be edited and customized with the instructor's own materials and assigned right away.

Developed with extensive feedback from history instructors and students, **LaunchPad for *A History of Western Society*** includes the complete narrative and special features of the print book plus the companion reader, *Sources for Western Society*; and **LearningCurve**, an adaptive learning tool that is designed to get students to read before they come to class. With **source-based questions in the test bank and in LearningCurve**, instructors now have multiple ways to test students on their understanding of sources and narrative in the book.

This edition also includes **Guided Reading Exercises** that prompt students to be active readers of the chapter narrative and auto-graded **primary source quizzes** to test comprehension of written and visual sources. These features, plus **additional primary source documents, video sources and tools for making video assignments, map activities, flashcards, and customizable test banks**, make LaunchPad a great asset for any instructor who wants to enliven the history of Western Civilization for students.

For instructors who simply want an auto-graded tool that will ensure that students read the narrative before they come to class, mobile-ready and accessible **Achieve Read & Practice for *A History of Western Society*** offers an exceptionally easy-to-use and affordable option. This simple product pairs the Value Edition e-book—a two-color narrative-only text (no boxed features or sources and fewer visuals)—with the power of **LearningCurve** quizzing, all in a format that is mobile-friendly, allowing students to read and take quizzes on the reading on the device of their choosing.

These new directions have not changed the central mission of the book, which is to introduce students to the broad sweep of Western Civilization in a fresh yet balanced manner. Every edition has incorporated new research to keep the book up-to-date and respond to the changing needs of readers and instructors, and we have continued to do this in the thirteenth edition. As we have made these changes, large and small, we have sought to give students and teachers an integrated perspective so that they can pursue—on their own or in the classroom—the historical questions that they find particularly exciting and significant. To learn more about the benefits of LearningCurve and LaunchPad, see the "Versions and Supplements" section on page xi.

## Acknowledgments

It is a pleasure to thank the instructors who read and critiqued the book in preparation for its revision:

Lisa Balabanlilar, *Rice University*
Peter Robert Dear, *Cornell University*
Fred M. Donner, *University of Chicago*
Alex d'Erizans, *Borough of Manhattan Community College*
Jacqueline deVries, *Augsburg University*
Arthur Eckstein, *University of Maryland*
Antonio Feros, *University of Pennsylvania*
Michelle Llyn Ferry, *Coastline Community College*
Jennifer L. Foray, *Purdue University*
Linda Frey, *University of Montana*
Peter Fritzsche, *University of Illinois at Urbana-Champaign*
Jane Hathaway, *Ohio State University*
Toby Huff, *Harvard University*
Robert L. Janda, *Cameron University*
Julie Langford, *University of South Florida*
Leslie S. Leighton, *Georgia State University*
J. Michael Long, *Front Range Community College*
John F. Lyons, *Joliet Junior College*
Joseph Manning, *Yale University*
Tim Myers, *Butler County Community College*
Graham Oliver, *Brown University*
Gesche Peters, *Dawson College*
Julie M. Powell, *Ohio State University*
Sheila A. Redmond, *Algoma University*
Matthew Restall, *Pennsylvania State University*
William B. Robison, *Southeastern Louisiana University*
Annette Timm, *University of Calgary*
Sherry Hardin Turille, *Cape Fear Community College*
Luke Yarbrough, *St. Louis University*

It is also a pleasure to thank the many editors who have assisted us over the years, first at Houghton Mifflin and now at Bedford/St. Martin's (Macmillan Learning). At Bedford/St. Martin's these include senior development editor Heidi Hood, senior content project manager Christina Horn, media editor Mary Starowicz, editorial assistant Carly Lewis, senior executive program manager William Lombardo, and senior program director Michael Rosenberg. Other key contributors were photo researcher Bruce Carson, text permissions researcher Mark Schaefer, text designer Cia Boynton, copy editor Susan Zorn, proofreader Angela Morrison, indexer Leoni McVey, and cover designer William Boardman.

Many of our colleagues at the University of Illinois, the University of Wisconsin–Milwaukee, and Georgia State University continue to provide information and stimulation, often without even knowing it. We thank them for it. We also thank the many students over the years with whom we have used earlier editions of this book. Their reactions and opinions helped shape the revisions to this edition, and we hope it remains worthy of the ultimate praise that they bestowed on it: that it's "not boring like most textbooks." Merry Wiesner-Hanks would, as always, also like to thank her husband, Neil, without whom work on this project would not be possible. Clare Haru Crowston thanks her husband, Ali, and her children, Lili, Reza, and Kian, who are a joyous reminder of the vitality of life that we try to showcase in this book. Joe Perry thanks his colleagues and students at Georgia State for their intellectual stimulation and is grateful to Joyce de Vries for her unstinting support and encouragement.

Each of us has benefited from the criticism of our coauthors, although each of us assumes responsibility for what he or she has written and revised. Merry Wiesner-Hanks takes responsibility for Chapters 1–13; Clare takes responsibility for Chapters 14–20; and Joe Perry takes responsibility for Chapters 21–30.

We'd especially like to thank the founding authors, John P. McKay, Bennett D. Hill, and John Buckler, for their enduring contributions and for their faith in each of us to carry on their legacy.

MERRY E. WIESNER-HANKS
CLARE HARU CROWSTON
JOE PERRY

# VERSIONS AND SUPPLEMENTS

Adopters of *A History of Western Society* and their students have access to abundant print and digital resources and tools, the acclaimed *Bedford Series in History and Culture* volumes, and much more. The LaunchPad course space for *A History of Western Society* provides access to the narrative as well as a wealth of primary sources and other features, along with assignment and assessment opportunities at the ready. Achieve Read & Practice supplies adaptive quizzing and our mobile, accessible Value Edition e-book in one easy-to-use, affordable product. See below for more information, visit the book's catalog site at **macmillanlearning.com**, or contact your local Bedford/St. Martin's representative.

## Get the Right Version for Your Class

To accommodate different course lengths and course budgets, *A History of Western Society* is available in several different versions and formats to best suit your course needs. The comprehensive *A History of Western Society* includes a full-color art program and a robust set of features. *A History of Western Society,* Concise Edition, also provides the full narrative, with a streamlined art and feature program, at a lower price. *A History of Western Society,* Value Edition, offers a trade-sized two-color option with the full narrative and selected art and maps at a steep discount. The Value Edition is also offered at the lowest price point in loose-leaf format, and all of these versions are available as e-books. To get the best values of all, package a new print book with Launch-Pad or Achieve Read & Practice at no additional charge to get the best each format offers. LaunchPad users get a print version for easy portability with an interactive e-book for the full-feature text and course space, along with Learning-Curve and loads of additional assignment and assessment options; Achieve Read & Practice users get a print version with a mobile, interactive Value Edition e-book plus LearningCurve adaptive quizzing in one exceptionally affordable, easy-to-use product.

- **Combined Edition** (Chapters 1–30): available in paperback, Concise Edition, Value Edition, loose-leaf, and e-book formats and in LaunchPad and Achieve Read & Practice

- **Volume 1, From Antiquity to the Enlightenment** (Chapters 1–16): available in paperback, Concise Edition, Value Edition, loose-leaf, and e-book formats and in LaunchPad and Achieve Read & Practice

- **Volume 2, From the Age of Exploration to the Present** (Chapters 14–30): available in paperback, Concise Edition, Value Edition, loose-leaf, and e-book formats and in LaunchPad and Achieve Read & Practice

- **Since 1300** (Chapters 11–30): available in paperback and e-book formats and in LaunchPad and Achieve Read & Practice

As noted below, any of these volumes can be packaged with additional titles for a discount. To get ISBNs for discount packages, visit **macmillanlearning.com** or contact your Bedford/St. Martin's representative.

## Assign LaunchPad — an Assessment-Ready Interactive E-book with Sources and Course Space

Available for discount purchase on its own or for packaging with new survey books at no additional charge, LaunchPad is a breakthrough solution for history courses. Intuitive and easy to use for students and instructors alike, LaunchPad is ready to use as is and can be edited, customized with your own material, and assigned quickly. LaunchPad for *A History of Western Society* includes Bedford/St. Martin's high-quality content all in one place, including the full interactive e-book and the companion reader *Sources for Western Society*, plus LearningCurve adaptive quizzing, guided reading activities designed to help students read actively for key concepts, auto-graded quizzes for each primary source, and chapter summative quizzes. Through a wealth of formative and summative assessments, including the adaptive learning program of LearningCurve (see the full description ahead), students gain confidence and get into their reading before class. These features, plus additional primary source documents, video sources and tools for making video assignments, map activities, flashcards, and customizable test banks, make LaunchPad an invaluable asset for any instructor.

LaunchPad easily integrates with course management systems, and with fast ways to build assignments, rearrange chapters, and add new pages, sections, or links, it lets teachers build the courses they want to teach and hold students accountable. For more information, visit **launchpadworks.com**, or to arrange a demo, contact us at **historymktg@macmillan.com**.

## Assign LearningCurve So Your Students Come to Class Prepared

Students using LaunchPad or Achieve Read & Practice receive access to LearningCurve for *A History of Western Society*. Assigning LearningCurve in place of reading quizzes is easy for instructors, and the reporting features help instructors track overall class trends and spot topics that are giving students trouble so they can adjust their lectures and class activities. This online learning tool is popular with students because it was designed to help them rehearse content at their own pace in a nonthreatening, game-like environment. The feedback for wrong answers provides instructional coaching and sends students back to the book for review. Students answer as many questions as necessary to reach a target score, with repeated chances to revisit material they haven't mastered. When LearningCurve is assigned, students come to class better prepared.

## Assign Achieve Read & Practice So Your Students Can Read and Study Wherever They Go

Available for discount purchase on its own or for packaging with new survey books at no additional charge, Achieve Read & Practice is Bedford/St. Martin's most affordable digital solution for history courses. Intuitive and easy to use for students and instructors alike, Achieve Read & Practice is ready to use as is and can be assigned quickly. Achieve Read & Practice for *A History of Western Society* includes the Value Edition interactive e-book, LearningCurve adaptive quizzing, assignment tools, and a gradebook. All this is built with an intuitive interface that can be read on mobile devices and is fully accessible, easily integrates with course management systems, and is available at a discounted price so anyone can use it. Instructors can set due dates for reading assignments and LearningCurve quizzes in just a few clicks, making it a simple and affordable way to engage students with the narrative and hold students accountable for course reading so they will come to class better prepared. For more information, visit macmillanlearning.com/ReadandPractice, or to arrange a demo, contact us at historymktg@macmillan.com.

## Tailor Your Text to Match Your Course with Bedford Select for History

Create the ideal textbook for your course with only the chapters you need. Starting from the Value Edition version of the text, you can delete and rearrange chapters, select chapters of primary sources from *Sources for Western Society*, and add additional primary sources, curated skills tutorials, or your own original content to create just the book you're looking for. With Bedford Select, students pay only for material that will be assigned in the course, and nothing more. It is easy to build your customized textbook, without compromising the quality and affordability you've come to expect from Bedford/St. Martin's. For more information, talk to your Bedford/St. Martin's representative or visit macmillanlearning.com/bedfordselect.

## iClicker

### iClicker, Active Learning Simplified

iClicker offers simple, flexible tools to help you give students a voice and facilitate active learning in the classroom. Students can participate with the devices they already bring to class using our iClicker Reef mobile apps (which work with smartphones, tablets, or laptops) or iClicker remotes. iClicker Reef access cards can also be packaged with LaunchPad or your textbook at a significant savings for your students. To learn more, talk to your Macmillan Learning (Bedford/St. Martin's) representative or visit www.iclicker.com.

## Take Advantage of Instructor Resources

Bedford/St. Martin's has developed a rich array of teaching resources for this book and for this course. They range from lecture and presentation materials and assessment tools to course management options. Most can be found in LaunchPad or can be downloaded or ordered at macmillanlearning.com.

**Bedford Coursepack for Blackboard, Canvas, Brightspace by D2L, or Moodle.** We can help you integrate our rich content into your course management system. Registered instructors can download coursepacks that include our popular free resources and book-specific content for *A History of Western Society*. Visit macmillanlearning.com to find your version or download your coursepack.

**Instructor's Resource Manual.** The instructor's manual offers both experienced and first-time instructors tools for presenting textbook material in engaging ways. It includes content learning objectives, annotated chapter outlines, and strategies for teaching with the textbook, plus suggestions on how to get the most out of LearningCurve and a survival guide for first-time teaching assistants.

**Guide to Changing Editions.** Designed to facilitate an instructor's transition from the previous edition of *A History of Western Society* to this new edition, this guide presents an overview of major changes as well as of changes in each chapter.

**Online Test Bank.** The test bank includes a mix of fresh, carefully crafted multiple-choice, matching, short-answer, and essay questions for each chapter. Many of the multiple-choice questions feature a map, an image, or a primary source excerpt as the prompt. All questions appear in Microsoft Word format and in easy-to-use test bank software that allows instructors to add, edit, re-sequence, filter by question type or learning objective, and print questions and answers. Instructors can also export questions into a variety of course management systems.

***The Bedford Lecture Kit: Lecture Outlines, Maps, and Images.*** Look good and save time with *The Bedford Lecture Kit*. These presentation materials include fully customizable multimedia presentations built around chapter outlines that are embedded with maps, figures, and images from the textbook and are supplemented by more detailed instructor notes on key points and concepts.

## Print, Digital, and Custom Options for More Choice and Value

For information on free packages and discounts up to 50%, visit macmillanlearning.com, or contact your local Bedford/ St. Martin's representative.

***Sources for Western Society,*** **Thirteenth Edition.** This primary source collection — available in Volume 1, Volume 2, and Since 1300 versions — provides a revised selection of sources to accompany *A History of Western Society*, Thirteenth Edition. Each chapter features five or six written and visual sources by well-known figures and ordinary individuals alike. With over thirty new selections — including several new visual sources — and enhanced pedagogy throughout, this book gives students the tools to engage critically with canonical and lesser-known sources and prominent and ordinary voices. Each chapter includes a "Sources in Conversation" feature that presents differing views on key topics. This companion reader is an exceptional value for students and offers plenty of assignment options for instructors. Available free when packaged with the print text and included in the LaunchPad e-book with auto-graded quizzes for each source. Also available on its own as a downloadable e-book.

**Bedford Select for History.** Create the ideal textbook for your course with only the chapters you need. Starting from a Value Edition history text, you can rearrange chapters, delete unnecessary chapters, select chapters of primary sources from the companion reader and add primary source document projects from the Bedford Document Collections, or choose to improve your students' historical thinking skills with the Bedford Tutorials for History. In addition, you can add your own original content to create just the book you're looking for. With Bedford Select, students pay only for material that will be assigned in the course, and nothing more. Order your textbook every semester, or modify from one term to the next. It is easy to build your customized textbook, without compromising the quality and affordability you've come to expect from Bedford/St. Martin's.

**Bedford Document Collections.** These affordable, brief document projects provide 5 to 7 primary sources, an introduction, historical background, and other pedagogical features. Each curated project — designed for use in a single class period and written by a historian about a favorite topic — poses a historical question and guides students through analysis of the sources. Examples include: "Premodern Trade: Doing Business in the Land of Pepper," "The Spread of Christianity in the Sixteenth and Early Seventeenth Centuries," "Absolutism in Practice: Louis XIV, Versailles, and the Art of Personal Kingship," "Pirates and Empire in the Seventeenth-Century Atlantic World," and "Living through Perestroika: The Soviet Union in Upheaval, 1985–1991." These primary source projects are available in a low-cost, easy-to-use digital format or can be combined with other course materials in Bedford Select to create an affordable, personalized print product.

**Bedford Tutorials for History.** Designed to customize textbooks with resources relevant to individual courses, this collection of brief units, each 16 pages long and loaded with examples, guides students through basic skills such as using historical evidence effectively, working with primary sources, taking effective notes, avoiding plagiarism and citing sources, and more. Up to two tutorials can be added to a Bedford/St. Martin's history survey title at no additional charge, freeing you to spend your class time focusing on content and interpretation. For more information, visit macmillanlearning.com/historytutorials.

**The Bedford Series in History and Culture.** More than 100 titles in this highly praised series combine first-rate scholarship, historical narrative, and important primary documents for undergraduate courses. Each book is brief, inexpensive, and focused on a specific topic or period. Revisions of several popular titles, such as *Spartacus and the Slave Wars: A Brief History with Documents*, by Brent D. Shaw; *The Scientific Revolution: A Brief History with Documents*, by Margaret C. Jacob; THE COMMUNIST MANIFESTO *by Karl Marx and Frederick Engels with Related Documents*, edited by John E. Toews; and *The Nuremberg War Crimes Trial, 1945–46: A Brief History with Documents*, by Michael R. Marrus, are now available. For a complete list of titles, visit macmillanlearning.com. Package discounts are available.

***Rand McNally Atlas of World History.*** This collection of almost 70 full-color maps illustrates the eras and civilizations in world history from the emergence of human societies to the present. Free when packaged.

***The Bedford Glossary for World History.*** This handy supplement for the survey course gives students historically contextualized definitions for hundreds of terms — from *abolitionism* to *Zoroastrianism* — that they will encounter in lectures, reading, and exams. Free when packaged.

**Trade Books.** Titles published by sister companies Hill and Wang; Farrar, Straus and Giroux; Henry Holt and Company; St. Martin's Press; Picador; and Palgrave Macmillan are available at a 50% discount when packaged with Bedford/St. Martin's textbooks. For more information, visit macmillanlearning.com/tradeup.

*A Pocket Guide to Writing in History.* Updated to reflect changes made in the 2017 *Chicago Manual of Style* revision, this portable and affordable reference tool by Mary Lynn Rampolla provides reading, writing, and research advice useful to students in all history courses. Concise yet comprehensive advice on approaching typical history assignments, developing critical reading skills, writing effective history papers, conducting research, using and documenting sources, and avoiding plagiarism — enhanced with practical tips and examples throughout — has made this slim reference a bestseller. Package discounts are available.

*A Student's Guide to History.* This complete guide to success in any history course provides the practical help students need to be successful. In addition to introducing students to the nature of the discipline, author Jules Benjamin teaches a wide range of skills, from preparing for exams to approaching common writing assignments, and explains the research and documentation process with plentiful examples. Package discounts are available.

# BRIEF CONTENTS

# CONTENTS

photo: Deir el-Medina, Thebes, Egypt/Bridgeman Images

photo: British Museum, London, UK/De Agostini Picture Library/Bridgeman Images

photo: National Archeological Museum, Athens, Greece/De Agostini Picture Library/G. Dagli/Orti/Bridgeman Images

# 4  *Life* in the Hellenistic World

# 5  The Rise of Rome

photo: Museo Archeologico, Ostia, Italy/De Agostini Picture Library/A. Dagli Orti/Bridgeman Images

photo: akg-images/Newscom

# 8 Europe in the Early Middle Ages
## 600–1000                                    200

# 9 State and Church in the High Middle Ages
## 1000–1300                                    230

photo: Musée de la Tapisserie, Bayeux, France/Bridgeman Images

# 12 European Society in the Age of the Renaissance

## 1350–1550                                     324

# 13 Reformations and Religious Wars

## 1500–1600                                     356

photo: Nativity of the Virgin, lunette from the Lotto Chapel, 1525 (fresco)/Lorenzo Lotto (ca. 1480–1556)/Church of San Michele al Pozzo Bianco, Bergamo, Italy/photo © Mauro Ranzani/Bridgeman Images

photo: "Procession of the Holy League" by François Bunel, 1590/Musée des Beaux-Arts, Valenciennes, France/Bridgeman Images

# 14 European Exploration and Conquest
## 1450–1650                                              390

photo: Museu Nacional de Soares dos Reis, Porto, Portugal/Bridgeman Images

# 15 Absolutism and Constitutionalism
## ca. 1589–1725                                          424

photo: By Charles Le Brun (1619–1690), 1678/Museum of Fine Arts, Budapest, Hungary/Erich Lessing/Art Resource, NY)

# 16   Toward a New Worldview

photo: *An Experiment on a Bird in the Air Pump*, 1768/National Gallery, London/Bridgeman Images

# MAPS, FIGURES, AND TABLES

## Maps

# Figures and Tables

# SPECIAL FEATURES

## EVALUATING VISUAL EVIDENCE

## EVALUATING WRITTEN EVIDENCE

## VIEWPOINTS

## THINKING LIKE A HISTORIAN

## INDIVIDUALS IN SOCIETY

## MAPPING THE PAST

# A History of
# Western Society

# 1
# Origins

## TO 1200 B.C.E.

**For most of their time on the earth,** humans were foragers moving through the landscape, inventing ever more specialized tools. Previous generations of historians have generally tended to view that long foraging past not as "history," but as "prehistory." History only began, for them, when writing began. This leaves out most of the human story, however, and today historians no longer see writing as such a sharp dividing line. They explore all eras of the human past using many different types of sources, sometimes using technologies that were unavailable until recently, such as DNA analysis and radiocarbon dating, although they do still tend to pay more attention to written sources.

About 11,000 years ago, people in some places domesticated plants and animals and began to live in permanent villages, some of which grew into cities. They created structures of governance to control their more complex societies, and some invented writing to record taxes, inventories, and payments; later writing was put to other uses. These new technologies and systems were first introduced in the Tigris and Euphrates River Valleys of southwest Asia and the Nile Valley of northeast Africa, areas that became linked through trade connections, military conquests, and migrations. ■

# CHAPTER PREVIEW

- What do we mean by "the West" and "Western civilization"?

- How did early human societies create new technologies and cultural forms?

- What kind of civilization did the Sumerians build in Mesopotamia?

- How did the Akkadian and Old Babylonian empires develop in Mesopotamia?

- How did the Egyptians establish a prosperous and long-lasting society?

**Life in New Kingdom Egypt, ca. 1500–1300 B.C.E.**
In this wall painting from the tomb of an official, a man guides a wooden ox-drawn plow through the soil, while the woman walking behind throws seed in the furrow. The painting was designed not to show real peasants working but to depict the servants who would spring to life to serve the deceased in the afterlife. Nevertheless, the gender division of labor and the plow itself are probably accurate. (Deir el-Medina, Thebes, Egypt/ Bridgeman Images)

# What do we mean by "the West" and "Western civilization"?

Human groups have long made distinctions between themselves and others. Some of these distinctions are between small groups such as neighboring tribes, some between countries and civilizations, and some between vast parts of the world. Among the most enduring of the latter are the ideas of "the West" and "the East."

## Describing the West

Ideas about the West and the distinction between West and East derived originally from the ancient Greeks. Greek civilization grew up in the shadow of earlier civilizations, especially Egypt and Mesopotamia. The Greeks defined themselves in relation to these more advanced cultures, which they saw as "Eastern." They were also the first to use the word *Europe* for a geographic area, taking the word from the name of a minor goddess. They set Europe in opposition to "Asia" (also named for a minor goddess), by which they meant both what we now call western Asia and what we call Africa.

The Greeks passed these ideas on to the Romans, who saw themselves clearly as part of the West. To Romans, the East was more sophisticated and more advanced, but also decadent and somewhat immoral. Roman value judgments have continued to shape preconceptions, stereotypes, and views of differences between the West and the East to this day.

Greco-Roman ideas about the West were passed on to people who lived in western and northern Europe, who saw themselves as the inheritors of this classical tradition and thus as the West. When these Europeans established colonies outside Europe beginning in the late fifteenth century, they regarded what they were doing as taking Western culture with them. With colonization, *Western* came to mean those cultures that included significant numbers of people of European ancestry, no matter where on the globe they were located.

In the early twentieth century, educators and other leaders in the United States became worried that many people, especially young people, were becoming cut off from European intellectual and cultural traditions. They encouraged the establishment of college and university courses focusing on "Western civilization," the first of which was taught at Columbia University in 1919. In designing the course, the faculty included cultures that, as far back as the ancient Greeks, had been considered Eastern, such as Egypt and Mesopotamia. This conceptualization and the course spread to other colleges and universities, developing into what became known as the introductory Western civilization course, a staple of historical instruction for generations of college students.

After World War II, divisions between the West and the East changed again, with *Western* coming to imply a capitalist economy and *Eastern* the Communist Eastern bloc. Thus, Japan was considered Western, and some Greek-speaking areas of Europe became Eastern. The collapse of communism in the Soviet Union and eastern Europe in the 1980s brought yet another refiguring, with much of eastern Europe joining the European Union, originally a Western organization.

In the early twenty-first century, *Western* still suggests a capitalist economy, but it also has certain cultural connotations, such as individualism and competition. Islamist radicals often describe their aims as an end to Western cultural, economic, and political influence, though Islam itself is generally described, along with Judaism and Christianity, as a Western monotheistic religion. Thus, throughout its long history, the meaning of "the West" has shifted, but in every era it has meant more than a geographical location.

## What Is Civilization?

Just as the meaning of the word *Western* is shaped by culture, so is the meaning of the word *civilization*. In the ancient world, residents of cities generally viewed themselves as more advanced and sophisticated than rural folk. They saw themselves as more "civilized," a word that comes from the Latin adjective *civilis*, which refers to a citizen, either of a town or of a larger political unit.

This depiction of people as either civilized or uncivilized was gradually extended to whole societies. Beginning in the eighteenth century, European scholars described any society in which political, economic, and social organizations operated on a large scale, not primarily through families and kin groups, as a **civilization**. Civilizations had cities; laws that governed human relationships; codes of manners and social conduct that regulated how people were to behave; and scientific, philosophical, and theological beliefs that explained the larger world. Civilizations also had some form of political organization through which one group was able to coerce resources out of others to engage in group endeavors,

■ **civilization**  A large-scale system of human political, economic, and social organizations; civilizations have cities, laws, states, and often writing.

■ **Paleolithic era**  The period of human history up to about 9000 B.C.E., when tools were made from stone and bone and people gained their food through foraging.

# TIMELINE

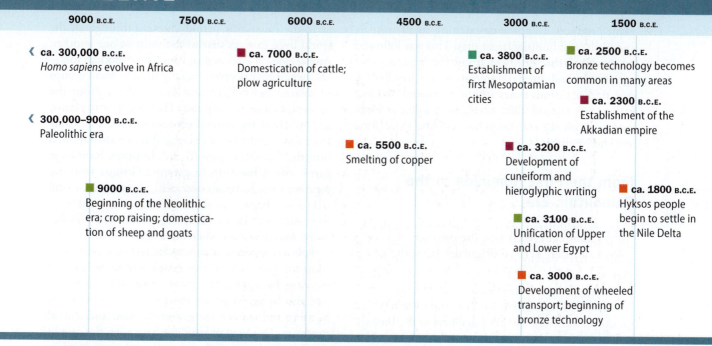

| 9000 B.C.E. | 7500 B.C.E. | 6000 B.C.E. | 4500 B.C.E. | 3000 B.C.E. | 1500 B.C.E. |
|---|---|---|---|---|---|

**‹ ca. 300,000 B.C.E.**
*Homo sapiens* evolve in Africa

**ca. 7000 B.C.E.**
Domestication of cattle; plow agriculture

**ca. 3800 B.C.E.**
Establishment of first Mesopotamian cities

**ca. 2500 B.C.E.**
Bronze technology becomes common in many areas

**‹ 300,000–9000 B.C.E.**
Paleolithic era

**ca. 2300 B.C.E.**
Establishment of the Akkadian empire

**ca. 5500 B.C.E.**
Smelting of copper

**ca. 3200 B.C.E.**
Development of cuneiform and hieroglyphic writing

**ca. 1800 B.C.E.**
Hyksos people begin to settle in the Nile Delta

**9000 B.C.E.**
Beginning of the Neolithic era; crop raising; domestication of sheep and goats

**ca. 3100 B.C.E.**
Unification of Upper and Lower Egypt

**ca. 3000 B.C.E.**
Development of wheeled transport; beginning of bronze technology

**A note on dates:** This book generally uses the terms B.C.E. (Before the Common Era) and C.E. (Common Era) when giving dates, a system of chronology based on the Christian calendar and now used widely around the world.

such as building large structures or carrying out warfare. States established armies, bureaucracies, and taxation systems. Generally only societies that used writing were judged to be civilizations.

Until the middle of the twentieth century, historians often referred to the places where writing and cities developed as "cradles of civilization," proposing a model of development for all humanity patterned on that of an individual life span. However, the idea that all human societies developed (or should develop) in a uniform process from a "cradle" to a "mature" civilization has now been largely discredited, and some historians choose not to use the term *civilization* at all because it could imply that some societies are superior to others.

Just as the notion of "civilization" has been questioned, so has the notion of "Western civilization."

Ever since the idea of "Western civilization" was first developed, people have debated what its geographical extent and core values are. Are there certain beliefs, customs, concepts, and institutions that set Western civilization apart from other civilizations, and, if so, when and how did these originate? How were these values and practices transmitted over space and time, and how did they change? No civilization stands alone, and each is influenced by its neighbors. Whatever Western civilization was—and is—it has been shaped by interactions with other societies, cultures, and civilizations. Even so, the idea that there are basic distinctions between the West and the rest of the world in terms of cultural values has been very powerful for thousands of years, and it still shapes the way many people view the world.

## How did early human societies create new technologies and cultural forms?

Scientists who study the history of the earth use a variety of systems to classify and divide time. Geologists and paleontologists divide time into periods that last many millions of years and that are determined by the movements of continents and the evolution and extinction of plant and animal species. During the nineteenth century, European archaeologists coined labels for eras of the human past according to the primary material out of which surviving tools had been made. Thus the earliest human era became the Stone Age, the next era the Bronze Age, and the next the Iron Age. They further divided the Stone Age into the Paleolithic and Neolithic eras. During the **Paleolithic era**, people used stone and other natural products to make tools and gained food largely by foraging, that is, by gathering plant products, trapping or catching small animals and birds, and hunting larger prey. This was followed by the **Neolithic era**, which saw the beginning of agriculture and animal domestication; this change occurred at various times around the world, but the earliest was around 9000 B.C.E., so this date is often used to mark the transition between the Paleolithic and the Neolithic.

## From the First Hominids to the Paleolithic Era

Using many different pieces of evidence from all over the world, archaeologists, paleontologists, and other scholars have developed a view of human evolution that has a widely shared basic outline, though there are disagreements about details. Sometime between 7 and 6 million years ago in southern and eastern Africa, groups of human ancestors (members of the biological "hominid" family) began to walk upright, which allowed them to carry things. About 3.4 million years ago, some hominids began to use naturally occurring objects as tools, and around 2.5 million years ago, one group in East Africa began to make simple tools, a feat that was accompanied by, and may have spurred, brain development. Groups migrated into much of Africa and then into Asia and Europe; by about 600,000 years ago, there were hominids throughout much of Afro-Eurasia.

About 300,000 years ago, again in East Africa, some of these early humans evolved into *Homo sapiens* ("thinking humans"), which had still larger and more complex brains that allowed for symbolic language and better social skills. *Homo sapiens* invented highly specialized tools made out of a variety of materials. They made regular use of fire for heat, light, and cooking. They also migrated, first across Africa, and by 130,000 years ago, and perhaps earlier, out of Africa into Eurasia. Eventually they traveled farther still, reaching Australia using rafts about 50,000 years ago and the Americas by about 15,000 years ago, or perhaps earlier. They moved into areas where other types of hominids lived, interacting with them and in some cases interbreeding with them. Gradually other types of hominids became extinct, leaving *Homo sapiens* as the only survivors and the ancestors of all modern humans.

In the Paleolithic period, humans throughout the world lived in ways that were similar to one another. Archaeological evidence and studies of modern foragers suggest that people generally lived in small groups of related individuals and moved throughout the landscape in search of food. They ate mostly plants, and much of the animal protein in their diet came from foods gathered or scavenged rather than hunted directly. Paleolithic peoples did, however, hunt large game, often hunting in groups. Groups working together forced animals over cliffs, threw spears to kill them, and, beginning about 15,000 B.C.E., used bows to shoot projectiles so that they could stand farther away from their prey while hunting.

Paleolithic people were not differentiated by wealth. Most foraging societies that exist today, or did so until recently, have some type of division of labor by sex and also by age. Men are more often responsible for hunting and women for gathering plant and animal products. This may or may not have been the case in the Paleolithic era, or there may have been a diversity of patterns in different areas around the world.

Beginning in the Paleolithic era, human beings have expressed themselves through what we would now term the arts or culture: painting and decorating walls and objects, making music, telling stories, dancing alone or in groups. Paleolithic evidence of culture, particularly from after about 50,000 years ago, includes flutes, carvings, jewelry, and amazing paintings done on cave walls and rock outcroppings that depict animals, people, and symbols. Burials, paintings, and objects suggest that people may have developed ideas about supernatural forces that controlled some aspects of the natural world and the humans in it, what we now term spirituality or religion. Spiritually adept men and women communicated with that unseen world, and objects such as carvings or masks were probably thought to have special healing or protective powers. (See "Evaluating Visual Evidence: Paleolithic Venus Figures," page 7.)

Total human population grew very slowly during the Paleolithic. One estimate proposes that there were perhaps 500,000 humans in the world about 30,000 years ago. By about 10,000 years ago, this number had grown to 5 million — ten times as many people. This was a significant increase, but it took twenty thousand years. The low population density meant that human impact on the environment was relatively small, although still significant.

## Domestication

Foraging remained the basic way of life for most of human history, and for groups living in extreme environments, such as tundras or deserts, it was the only possible way to survive. In a few especially fertile areas,

---

■ **Neolithic era** The period after 9000 B.C.E., when people developed agriculture, domesticated animals, and used tools made of stone and wood.

■ **Fertile Crescent** An area of mild climate and abundant wild grain where agriculture first developed, in present-day Lebanon, Israel, Jordan, Turkey, and Iraq.

■ **pastoralism** An economic system based on herding flocks of goats, sheep, cattle, or other animals beneficial to humans.

# Paleolithic Venus Figures

(Museo Civico Palazzo Chiericati, Vicenza, Italy/De Agostini Picture Library/A. Dagli Orti/Bridgeman Images)

Written sources provide evidence about the human past only after the development of writing, allowing us to read the words of people long dead. For most of human history, however, there were no written sources, so we "read" the past through objects. Interpreting written documents is difficult, and interpreting archaeological evidence is even more difficult and often contentious. For example, small stone statues of women with enlarged breasts and buttocks dating from the later Paleolithic period (roughly 33,000–9000 B.C.E.) have been found in many parts of Europe. These were dubbed "Venus figures" by nineteenth-century archaeologists, who thought they represented Paleolithic standards of female beauty just as the goddess Venus represented classical standards. A reproduction of one of these statues, the six-inch-tall Venus of Lespugue made from a mammoth tusk about 25,000 years ago in southern France, is shown here.

## EVALUATE THE EVIDENCE

1. As you look at this statue, does it seem to link more closely with fertility or with sexuality? How might your own situation as a twenty-first-century person shape your answer to this question?
2. Some scholars see Venus figures as evidence that Paleolithic society was egalitarian or female dominated, but others point out that images of female deities or holy figures are often found in religions that deny women official authority. Can you think of examples of the latter? Which point of view seems most persuasive to you?

however, the natural environment provided enough food that people could become more settled. About 15,000 years ago, the earth's climate entered a warming phase, and more parts of the world were able to support people who did not move very much or at all. Archaeological sites in many places begin to include storage pits and grindstones, evidence that people were intensifying their work to get more food from the surrounding area, becoming sedentary or semi-sedentary rather than nomadic. They also acquired more objects and built more permanent housing.

In several of these places, along with gathering wild grains, roots, and other foodstuffs, people began planting seeds in the ground and selected the seeds they planted in order to get crops that had favorable characteristics, such as larger edible parts. Through this human intervention, certain crops became domesticated, that is, modified by selective breeding so as to serve human needs. Scholars used to think that crop raising was the cause of sedentism, or a sedentary way of life, but they now know that in many places villages preceded intentional crop raising by thousands of years, so the primary line of causation runs the other way: people began to raise crops because they were living in permanent communities. Thus people were "domesticated," meaning settled down, before plants and animals were.

Intentional crop planting first developed around 9000 B.C.E., in the area archaeologists call the **Fertile Crescent**, which runs from present-day Lebanon, Israel, and Jordan north to Turkey and then south and east to the Iran-Iraq border. Over the next two millennia, a similar process—first sedentism, then domestication—happened elsewhere as well, in the Nile River Valley, western Africa, China, India, Papua New Guinea, and Mesoamerica.

Along with domesticating certain plants, people also domesticated animals. Dogs were the first to be domesticated, and in about 9000 B.C.E., at the same time they began to raise crops, people in the Fertile Crescent domesticated wild goats and sheep. They began to breed the goats and sheep selectively for qualities that they wanted. Sheep and goats allow themselves to be herded, and people developed a new form of living, **pastoralism**, based on herding and raising livestock. Eventually other grazing animals, including cattle, camels, horses, yak, and reindeer, also became the basis of pastoral economies in Central and West Asia, many parts of Africa, and far northern Europe.

The domestication of certain large animals had a significant impact on human ways of life. Cattle, water buffalo, donkeys, and horses can be trained to carry people or burdens on their backs and pull against loads dragged behind them. Their use dramatically increased the power available to humans to carry out their tasks, which had both an immediate effect in the societies in which this happened and a long-term effect when these societies later encountered other societies in which human labor remained the only source of power. Domesticated animals eventually far outnumbered their wild counterparts and were used for destruction in war as well as food production and transport.

The shift from hunting and gathering to the domestication of plants and animals grew out of a combination of demographic, social, and cultural changes. In terms of demographic factors, populations may have slowly grown beyond the readily available food supply, despite the warming climate that had boosted the supply of foraged foods and allowed sedentary villages to develop. This increase in population resulted from lower child mortality and longer life spans, and perhaps also from higher fertility rates resulting from a sedentary village lifestyle. Naturally occurring foods often included grains or other crops that could be ground and cooked into a mush soft enough for

babies to eat. This mush—for which there is widespread archaeological evidence—allowed women to decide to stop nursing their children at a younger age and instead put their energies elsewhere. In so doing, women lost the contraceptive effects of breast-feeding, and children were born at more frequent intervals. But instead of moving to a new area—the solution that foragers relied on when faced with the problem of food scarcity—people chose to stay with or near the physical and social structures of the sedentary villages they had built. So they developed a different way to increase the food supply to keep up with population growth—plant and animal domestication. Thus began cycles of expanding population and intensification of land use that have continued to today.

A very recent archaeological find at Göbekli Tepe (guh-BEK-lee TEH-peh) in present-day Turkey suggests that cultural factors may have played a role in the development of agriculture as well, interweaving with demographic and social factors. Here around 9000 B.C.E. hundreds of people came together to build rings of massive, multi-ton, elaborately carved limestone pillars, and then covered them with dirt and built more. Archaeological remains indicate that the people who created this site ate wild game and plants, not crops. Once these pillars were carved and raised in place, however, their symbolic, cultural, or perhaps religious importance may have made people decide to adopt a subsistence strategy that would allow them to stay nearby. Indeed, it is very near here that evidence of the world's oldest domesticated wheat has been discovered. So while the people who built Göbekli Tepe were foragers, their descendants who decided to stay nearby became crop raisers. Archaeologists speculate that, at least in this case, the symbolic, cultural, or perhaps religious importance of the structure can help explain why the people who built it changed from foraging to agriculture.

**Pillar at Göbekli Tepe**   The huge limestone pillars arranged in rings at the Paleolithic site Göbekli Tepe are somewhat humanoid in shape, and the carvings are of dangerous animals, including lions, boars, foxes, snakes, vultures, and scorpions. The structure required enormous skill and effort of the people who built it, and clearly had great importance to them. (Vincent J. Musi/National Geographic Creative)

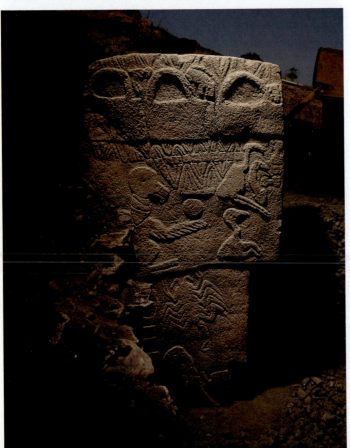

## Implications of Agriculture

Whatever the reasons for the move from foraging to agriculture, within several centuries of initial crop planting, people in the Fertile Crescent, parts of China, and the Nile Valley were relying primarily on domesticated food products. Some historians view this change as the most important development in human history, as it made everything else possible. They term it the "Agricultural Revolution" or sometimes the "Neolithic Revolution," because according to the periodization of the human past developed in the nineteenth century, agriculture marked the transition from Paleolithic to Neolithic.

A field of planted and weeded crops yields ten to one hundred times as much food—measured in calories—as the same area of naturally occurring plants. It also requires much more labor, however, which was provided both by the greater number of people in the community and by those people working longer hours. In contrast to the twenty hours a week foragers spent on obtaining food, farming peoples were often in the fields from dawn to dusk. Some scientists, in fact, describe the development of agriculture as a process of codependent domestication: humans domesticated crops, but crops also "domesticated" humans so that they worked long hours spreading particular crops around the world, especially wheat, rice, and later corn. Early farmers were also less healthy than foragers were; their narrower range of foodstuffs made them more susceptible to disease and nutritional deficiencies. They did have the consolation of alcohol, which should perhaps be added to the list of reasons for the development and spread of crop raising, as planted crops provided a reliable supply of raw material people could transform into this high-energy substance that also became their principal painkiller. Alcohol became part of social events, and its consumption was often ritualized, with beer and wine among the offerings given to spirits and deities, or consumed by shamans, priests, and worshippers.

Sometime in the seventh millennium B.C.E., people attached wooden sticks to frames that animals dragged through the soil, thus breaking it up and allowing seeds to sprout more easily. These simple scratch plows, pulled by cattle and water buffalo, allowed Neolithic people to produce a significant amount of surplus food. Some people in the community could now spend their days performing other tasks, thus increasing the division of labor. Some people specialized in making tools, houses, and other items needed in village life, or in producing specific types of food. Families and households became increasingly interdependent, trading food for other commodities or services.

The division of labor allowed by plow agriculture contributed to the creation of social hierarchies based on wealth and power, which have been a central feature of human society since the Neolithic period. Although no written records were produced during this era, archaeological evidence provides some clues about how the hierarchies might have developed. Compared to foragers, villagers needed more complex rules about how food was to be distributed and how different types of work were to be valued. Certain individuals must have begun to specialize in the determination and enforcement of these rules, and informal structures of power gradually became more formalized. Religious specialists probably developed more elaborate rituals to celebrate life passages and to appeal to the gods for help in times of difficulty, such as illness.

Individuals who were the heads of large families or kin groups had control over the labor of others, and this power became more significant when that labor brought material goods that could be stored. Material goods—plows, sheep, cattle, sheds, pots, carts—gave one the ability to amass still more material goods, and the gap between those who had them and those who did not widened. Through violence, purchase, and other processes, some individuals came to own other people as well. Slavery predates written records, but it developed in almost all agricultural societies. Like animals, slaves were a source of physical power for their owners, allowing them to amass still more wealth and influence. In the long era before the invention of fossil fuel technology, the ability to exploit animal and human labor was the most important mark of distinction between elites and the rest of the population. Such social hierarchies were reinforced over generations as children inherited goods and status from their parents. By the time writing was invented, social distinctions between elites—the nobles, hereditary priests, and other privileged groups—and the rest of the population were already in existence.

Along with hierarchies based on wealth and power, the development of agriculture was intertwined with a hierarchy based on gender. In many places, plow agriculture came to be a male task. Men's responsibility for plowing and other agricultural tasks took them outside the household more often than women's duties did, enlarging their opportunities for leadership. As a result, they may have been favored as inheritors of family land and of the right to farm communally held land. Accordingly, over generations, women's independent access to resources decreased. The system in which men have more power and access to resources than women of the same social level, and in which some men are dominant over other men, is called **patriarchy** and is found in every society in the world with written records, although the level of inequality varies. Men's control of property was rarely absolute, because the desire to keep wealth and property within a family or kin group often resulted in women's inheriting, owning, and in some cases managing significant amounts of wealth. Hierarchies of wealth and power thus intersected with hierarchies of gender in complex ways.

## Trade and Cross-Cultural Connections

By 7000 B.C.E. or so, some agricultural villages in the Fertile Crescent may have had as many as ten thousand residents. One of the best known of these, Çatal Hüyük (CHAH-tahl-huh-yuk) in what is now Turkey, which existed from about 7500 to about 5700 B.C.E., shows evidence of trade as well as specialization of labor. Çatal Hüyük's residents lived in densely packed

■ **patriarchy** A social system in which men have more power and access to resources than women of the same social level, and in which some men are dominant over other men.

mud-brick houses with walls covered in white plaster that had been made with burned lime. Along with planting crops and raising sheep, Çatal Hüyük's residents made textiles, pots, figurines, baskets, carpets, copper and lead beads, and other goods, and they decorated their houses with murals showing animal and human figures. They gathered, sharpened, and polished obsidian, a volcanic rock that could be used for knives, blades, and mirrors, and then traded it with neighboring towns to obtain seashells and flint. From here the obsidian was exchanged still farther away, for Neolithic societies slowly developed local and then regional networks of exchange and communication.

Among the goods traded in some parts of the world was copper, which people hammered into shapes for jewelry and tools. Like most metals, in its natural state copper usually occurs mixed with other materials in a type of mixed rock material called ore, and by about 5500 B.C.E., people in the Balkans had learned that copper could be extracted from ore by heating it in a smelting process. Smelted copper was poured into molds and made into spear points, axes, chisels, beads, and other objects. Pure copper is soft, but through experimentation artisans learned that it would become harder if they mixed it with other metals during heating, creating an alloy called bronze.

Because it was stronger than copper, bronze had a far wider range of uses, so much so that later historians decided that its adoption marked a new period in human history: the **Bronze Age**. The Bronze Age began about 3000 B.C.E., and by about 2500 B.C.E., bronze technology was having an impact in many parts of the world. The end of the Bronze Age came with the adoption of iron technology, which occurred from 1200 B.C.E. to 300 B.C.E. (see Chapter 2). All metals were expensive and hard to obtain, however, so stone, wood, and bone remained important materials for tools and weapons long into the Bronze and even Iron Age. Metals were not available at all in many parts of the world, so in some places stone, wood, and bone tools never lost their importance.

Objects were not the only things traded over increasingly long distances during the Neolithic period, for people also carried ideas as they traveled. Knowledge about the seasons and the weather was vitally important for those who depended on crop raising, and agricultural peoples in many parts of the world began to calculate recurring patterns in the world around them, slowly developing calendars. Using their own observations and ideas that came from elsewhere, they built earth and stone structures to help them predict the movements of the sun and stars. These included Nabta Playa, erected about 4500 B.C.E. in the desert west of the Nile Valley in Egypt, and Stonehenge, erected about 2500 B.C.E. in southern England.

The rhythms of the agricultural cycle and patterns of exchange also shaped religious beliefs and practices. In many places multiple gods came to be associated with patterns of birth, growth, death, and regeneration in a system known as **polytheism**. Like humans, the gods came to have a division of labor and a social hierarchy. There were rain gods and sun gods, sky goddesses and moon goddesses, gods that ensured the health of cattle or the growth of corn, and goddesses of the hearth and home.

## What kind of civilization did the Sumerians build in Mesopotamia?

The origins of Western civilization are generally traced to an area that is today not seen as part of the West: Mesopotamia (mehs-oh-puh-TAY-mee-uh), the Greek name for the land between the Euphrates (yoo-FRAY-teez) and Tigris (TIGH-grihs) Rivers (Map 1.1), which today is in Iraq. The earliest agricultural villages in Mesopotamia were in the northern, hilly parts of the river valleys, where there is abundant rainfall for crops. By about 5000 B.C.E., farmers had brought techniques of crop raising southward to the southern part of Mesopotamia, called Sumer. In this arid climate farmers developed irrigation on a large scale, which demanded organized group effort but allowed the population to grow. By about 3800 B.C.E., one of the agricultural villages, Uruk (OO-rook), had expanded significantly, becoming what many historians view as the world's first city, with a population that eventually numbered more than fifty thousand.

People living in Uruk built large temples to honor their chief god and goddess, and also invented the world's first system of writing. Over the next thousand years, other cities also grew in Sumer, trading with one another and adopting writing.

### Environment and Mesopotamian Development

From the outset, geography had a profound effect on Mesopotamia because here agriculture is possible only with irrigation. Consequently, the Sumerians and later civilizations built their cities along the Tigris and Euphrates Rivers and their branches. They used the rivers to carry agricultural and trade goods, and also to provide water for vast networks of irrigation channels. The Tigris and Euphrates flow quickly at certain times of the year and carry silt down from the mountains

**MAP 1.1 Spread of Cultures in the Ancient Near East, ca. 3000–1640 B.C.E.** This map illustrates the spread of the Mesopotamian and Egyptian cultures through the semicircular stretch of land often called the Fertile Crescent. From this area, the knowledge and use of agriculture spread throughout western Asia, North Africa, and Europe.

and hills, causing floods. To prevent major floods, the Sumerians created massive hydraulic projects, including reservoirs, dams, and dikes as well as canals. In stories written later, they described their chief god, Enlil, as "the raging flood which has no rival" and believed that at one point there had been a massive flood, a tradition that also gave rise to the biblical story of Noah:

> A flood will sweep over. . . . A decision that the seed of mankind is to be destroyed has been made. The verdict, the word of the divine assembly, cannot be revoked.[1]

Judging by historical records, however, actual destructive floods were few.

In addition to water and transport, the rivers supplied fish, a major element of the Sumerian diet, and reeds, which were used for making baskets and writing implements. The rivers also provided clay, which was hardened to create bricks, the Sumerians' primary building material in a region with little stone. Clay was fired into pots, and inventive artisans developed the potter's wheel so that they could make pots that were stronger and more uniform than those made by earlier methods of coiling ropes of clay. The potter's wheel in turn appears to have led to the introduction of wheeled vehicles sometime in the fourth millennium B.C.E. Wheeled vehicles, pulled by domesticated

donkeys, led to road building, which facilitated settlement, trade, and conquest, although travel and transport by water remained far easier.

Cities and villages in Sumer and farther up the Tigris and Euphrates traded with one another, and even before the development of writing or kings, it appears that colonists sometimes set out from one city to travel hundreds of miles to the north or west to found a new city or to set up a community in an existing center. These colonies might well have provided the Sumerian cities with goods, such as timber and metal ores, that were not available locally. The cities of the Sumerian heartland continued to grow and to develop governments, and each one came to dominate the surrounding countryside, becoming city-states independent from one another, though not very far apart.

The city-states of Sumer continued to rely on irrigation systems that required cooperation and at least some level of social and political cohesion. The authority to run this system was, it seems, initially assumed by Sumerian priests. Encouraged and directed by their religious leaders, people built temples on tall platforms in the center of their cities. Temples grew into elaborate complexes of buildings with storage space for grain and other products and housing for animals. (Much later, by about 2100 B.C.E., some of

■ **Bronze Age** The period in which the production and use of bronze implements became basic to society.

■ **polytheism** The worship of many gods and goddesses.

**Clay Letter Written in Cuneiform and Its Envelope, ca. 1850 B.C.E.**    In this letter from a city in Anatolia, located on the northern edge of the Fertile Crescent in what is now Turkey, a Mesopotamian merchant complains to his brother at home, hundreds of miles away, that life is hard and comments on the trade in silver, gold, tin, and textiles. Correspondents often enclosed letters in clay envelopes and sealed them by rolling a cylinder seal across the clay, leaving the impression of a scene, just as you might use a stamped wax seal today. Here the very faint impression of the sender's seal at the bottom shows a person, probably the owner of the seal, being led in a procession toward a king or god. (© The Trustees of the British Museum/Art Resource, NY)

the major temple complexes were embellished with a huge stepped pyramid, called a ziggurat, with a shrine on the top.) The Sumerians believed that humans had been created to serve the gods, who lived in the temples. To support the needs of the gods, including the temple constructions, and to support the religious leaders, temples owned large estates, including fields and orchards. Temple officials employed individuals to work the temple's land.

By 2500 B.C.E. there were more than a dozen city-states in Sumer. Each city developed religious, political, and military institutions, and judging by the fact that people began to construct walls around the cities and other fortifications, warfare between cities was quite common. Presumably their battles were sometimes sparked by disputes over water, as irrigation in one area reduced or altered the flow of rivers in other areas.

## The Invention of Writing and the First Schools

The origins of writing probably go back to the ninth millennium B.C.E., when Near Eastern peoples used clay tokens as counters for record keeping. By the fourth millennium, people had realized that impressing the tokens on clay, or drawing pictures of the tokens on clay, was simpler than making tokens. This breakthrough in turn suggested that more information could be conveyed by adding pictures of still other objects. The result was a complex system of pictographs in which each sign pictured an object. These pictographs were the forerunners of the Sumerian form of writing known as **cuneiform** (kyou-NEE-uh-form) (Figure 1.1), from the Latin term for "wedge shaped," used to describe the indentations

made by a sharpened stylus in clay, which was invented about 3200 B.C.E.

Pictographs were initially limited in that they could not represent abstract ideas, but the development of ideograms — signs that represented ideas — made writing more versatile. Thus the sign for star could also be used to indicate heaven, sky, or even god. The development of the Sumerian system of writing was piecemeal, with scribes making changes and additions as they were needed. Over time, the system became so complicated that scribal schools were established; by 2500 B.C.E., these schools flourished throughout Sumer. Students at the schools were all male, and most came from families in the middle range of urban

| | MEANING | PICTOGRAPH | IDEOGRAM | PHONETIC SIGN |
|---|---|---|---|---|
| A | Star | | | |
| B | Woman | | | |
| C | Mountain | | | |
| D | Slave woman | | | |
| E | Water In | | | |

**FIGURE 1.1  Sumerian Writing**
(Source: S. N. Kramer, *The Sumerians: Their History, Culture and Character.* Copyright © 1963 by The University of Chicago Press.)

■ **cuneiform**  Sumerian form of writing; the term describes the wedge-shaped marks made by a stylus.

society. Each school had a master, teachers, and monitors. Discipline was strict, and students were caned for sloppy work and misbehavior. One graduate of a scribal school had few fond memories of the joy of learning:

> My headmaster read my tablet, said:
> "There is something missing," caned me.
> . . .
> The fellow in charge of silence said:
> "Why did you talk without permission," caned me.
> The fellow in charge of the assembly said:
> "Why did you stand at ease without permission," caned me.[2]

Scribal schools were primarily intended to produce individuals who could keep records of the property of temple officials, kings, and nobles. Thus writing first developed as a way to enhance the growing power of elites, not to record speech, although it later came to be used for that purpose, and the stories of gods, kings, and heroes were also written down. Hundreds of thousands of hardened clay tablets have survived from ancient Mesopotamia, and from them historians have learned about many aspects of life, including taxes and wages. Sumerians wrote numbers as well as words on clay tablets, and some surviving tablets show multiplication and division problems.

## Religion in Mesopotamia

To Sumerians, and to later peoples in Mesopotamia as well, the world was controlled by gods and goddesses, who represented cosmic forces such as the sun, moon, water, and storms. The king of the gods was Enlil, who was believed to rule over the gods just as the king of a city-state ruled his population. Almost as powerful were the gods of the sun, of storms, and of freshwater. Each city generally had a chief god or goddess, or sometimes several, with a large temple built in his or her honor. In Uruk, for example, one of the central temples was dedicated to the goddess Inanna, the goddess of love and sexuality, who was also associated with the planet Venus. In one widely told myth, Inanna descends to the underworld, setting off a long struggle among her worshippers to find a replacement. Another deity is found to take her place, but then Inanna returns, just as Venus sets and rises.

People believed that humans had been created to serve the gods and generally anticipated being well treated by the gods if they served them well. The best way to honor the gods was to make the temple as grand and impressive as possible because the temple's size demonstrated the strength of the community and the power of its chief deity. Once it was built, the temple itself was often off-limits to ordinary people, who did not worship there as a spiritual community. Instead the temple was staffed by priests and priestesses who carried out rituals to honor the god or goddess. Kings and other political leaders might also visit the temple and carry out religious ceremonies from time to time, particularly when they thought the assistance of the gods was especially needed.

**Sacrificial Procession Scene**   In this fragment from a wall painting from the palace of King Zimri-Lim of Mari on the middle Euphrates from about 1800 B.C.E., a giant deity in a scalloped robe strides in front of priests, one of whom is leading a bull to be sacrificed. Mari was an important city-state in Mesopotamia, and the public rooms of its palace were decorated with scenes showing the close link between kings and deities. (Musée du Louvre, Paris, France/Bridgeman Images)

The peoples of Mesopotamia had many myths to account for the creation of the universe. According to one told by the Babylonians, in the beginning was the primeval sea, known as the goddess Tiamat, who gave birth to the gods. When Tiamat tried to destroy the gods, Marduk, the chief god of the Babylonians, proceeded to kill her and divide her body and thus created the sky and earth. These myths are the earliest known attempts to answer the question, how did it all begin? They traveled with people when they moved and were eventually written down, but not until long after they had first been told, and they often had many variations. Written texts were not an important part of Sumerian religious life, nor were they central to the religious practices of most of the other peoples in this region.

In addition to stories about gods, the Sumerians told stories about heroes and kings, many of which were eventually reworked into the world's first epic poem, the *Epic of Gilgamesh* (GIL-guh-mesh). An epic poem is a narration of the achievements, the labors, and sometimes the failures of heroes that embodies peoples' ideas about themselves. Historians can use epic poems to learn about various aspects of a society, and to that extent epics can be used as historical sources. This epic recounts the wanderings of Gilgamesh — the semihistorical king of Uruk — and his search for eternal life, and it grapples with enduring questions about life and death, friendship, humankind and deities, and immortality.

## Sumerian Politics and Society

Exactly how kings emerged in Sumerian society is not clear. Scholars have suggested that during times of emergencies, a chief priest or perhaps a military leader assumed what was supposed to be temporary authority over a city. Temporary power gradually became permanent kingship, and sometime before 2450 B.C.E. kings in some Sumerian city-states began transferring their kingship to their sons, establishing patriarchal hereditary dynasties in which power was handed down through the male line. This is the point at which written records about kingship began to appear. The symbol of royal status was the palace, which came to rival the temple in grandeur.

Kings made alliances with other powerful individuals, often through marriage. Royal family members were depended upon for many aspects of government. Kings worked closely with religious authorities and relied on ideas about the kings' connections with the gods, as well as the kings' military might, for their power. Acting together, priests, kings, and officials in Sumerian cities used force, persuasion, and taxation to maintain order, keep the irrigation systems working, and keep food and other goods flowing.

The king and his officials held extensive tracts of land, as did the temple; these lands were worked by the palace's or the temple's clients, free men and women who were dependent on the palace or the temple. They received crops and other goods in return for their labor. Some individuals and families owned land outright and paid their taxes in the form of agricultural products or items they made. At the bottom rung of society were slaves. Some Sumerian slaves were most likely prisoners of war and criminals who had lost their freedom as punishment for their crimes; others perhaps came into slavery to repay debts. Compared to many later societies, slaves were not widely used in Sumer, where most agricultural work was done by dependent clients. Slaves in Sumer also engaged in trade and made profits. They could borrow money, and many slaves were able to buy their freedom.

Sumerian society made distinctions based on gender. Most elite landowners were male, but women who held positions as priestesses or as queens ran their own estates, independently of their husbands and fathers. Some women owned businesses and took care of their own accounts. They could own property and distribute it to their offspring. Sons and daughters inherited from their parents, although a daughter received her inheritance in the form of a dowry, which technically remained hers but was managed by her husband or husband's family after marriage. The Sumerians established the basic social, economic, and intellectual patterns of Mesopotamia, and they influenced their neighbors to the north and east.

**Mesopotamian Harpist**
This small clay tablet, carved between 2000 B.C.E. and 1500 B.C.E., shows a seated woman playing a harp. Her fashionable dress and hat suggest that she is playing for wealthy people, perhaps at the royal court. Images of musicians are common in Mesopotamian art, indicating that music was important in Mesopotamian culture and social life. (Musée du Louvre, Paris, France/Erich Lessing/Art Resource, NY)

# How did the Akkadian and Old Babylonian empires develop in Mesopotamia?

The wealth of Sumerian cities also attracted non-Sumerian conquerors from the north, beginning with the Akkadians and then the Babylonians. Both of these peoples created large states in the valley of the Tigris and Euphrates, and Hammurabi, one ruler of Babylon, proclaimed an extensive law code. Merchants traveled throughout the Fertile Crescent and beyond, carrying products and facilitating cultural exchange.

## The Akkadians and the Babylonians

In 2331 B.C.E., Sargon, the king of a city to the north of Sumer, conquered a number of Sumerian cities with what was probably the world's first permanent army and created a large state. The symbol of his triumph was a new capital, the city of Akkad (AH-kahd). Sargon also expanded the Akkadian empire westward to north Syria. He encouraged trading networks that brought in goods from as far away as the Indus River and what is now Turkey. Sargon spoke a different language than did the Sumerians, one of the many languages that scholars identify as belonging to the Semitic language family, which includes modern-day Hebrew and Arabic. However, Akkadians adapted cuneiform writing to their own language, and Akkadian became the diplomatic language used over a wide area.

Sargon tore down the defensive walls of Sumerian cities and appointed his own sons as their rulers to help him cement his power. He also appointed his daughter, Enheduana (2285–2250 B.C.E.), as high priestess in the city of Ur. Here she wrote a number of hymns, especially those in praise of the goddess Inanna, becoming the world's first author to put her name to a literary composition. (See "Thinking Like a Historian: Addressing the Gods," page 16.) For hundreds of years Enheduana's works were copied on clay tablets, which have been found in several cities in the area, indicating that people may have recited or read them.

Sargon's dynasty appears to have ruled Mesopotamia for about 150 years, during which time the Tigris and Euphrates Valleys attracted immigrants from many places. Then his empire collapsed, in part because of a period of extended drought, and the various city-states became independent again. One group of immigrants into Mesopotamia were the Amorites (AM-uh-rites), who migrated from the west. The Amorites were initially nomadic pastoralists, not agriculturalists, but they began to raise crops when they settled throughout Mesopotamia. They founded several city-states after Sargon's dynasty ended, one of which was Babylon along the middle Euphrates, where that river runs close

**Sargon of Akkad**   This bronze head, with elaborately worked hair and beard, might portray the great conqueror Sargon of Akkad (though his name does not appear on it). The eyes were originally inlaid with jewels, which have since been gouged out. Produced around 2300 B.C.E., this head was found in the ruins of the Assyrian capital of Nineveh, where it had been taken as loot. (INTERFOTO/Alamy)

to the Tigris. Babylon became more than a city-state, growing to include smaller territories whose rulers recognized the king of Babylon as their overlord.

## Life Under Hammurabi

Hammurabi of Babylon (r. 1792–1750 B.C.E.) was initially a typical king of his era, but late in his reign he conquered several other kingdoms, uniting most of Mesopotamia under his rule. The era from his reign to around 1595 B.C.E. is called the Old Babylonian period. As had earlier rulers, Hammurabi linked his success with the will of the gods. He encouraged the spread of myths that explained how Marduk, the primary god of Babylon, had been elected king of the gods by the other deities in Mesopotamia. Marduk later became widely regarded as the chief god of Mesopotamia, absorbing the qualities and powers of other gods.

Hammurabi's most memorable accomplishment was the proclamation of an extensive law code, introduced about 1755 B.C.E. Like the codes of the earlier lawgivers, **Hammurabi's law code** proclaimed that he issued his laws on divine authority "to establish law and justice in

■ **Hammurabi's law code**   A proclamation issued by Babylonian king Hammurabi to establish laws regulating many aspects of life.

## Addressing the Gods

Hymns and incantations to the gods are among the earliest written texts in Mesopotamia and Egypt, and sculpture and paintings also often show people addressing the gods. The sources here are examples of such works. What ideas about the gods and the way humans should address them are shared in all these sources, and how do ideas in Egypt differ from those in Mesopotamia?

**1** **Enheduana's "Exaltation of Inanna."** Enheduana (2285–2250 B.C.E.), the daughter of Sargon of Akkad, was appointed by her father as high priestess in the Sumerian city of Ur, where she wrote a number of literary and religious works that were frequently recopied long after her death, including this hymn to the goddess Inanna.

~ Your divinity shines in the pure heavens.... Your torch lights up the corners of heaven, turning darkness into light. The men and women form a row for you and each one's daily status hangs down before you. Your numerous people pass before you, as before Utu [the sun-god], for their inspection. No one can lay a hand on your precious divine powers; all your divine powers.... You exercise full ladyship over heaven and earth; you hold everything in your hand. Mistress, you are magnificent, no one can walk before you. You dwell with great An [the god of the heavens] in the holy resting-place. Which god is like you in gathering together ... in heaven and earth? You are magnificent, your name is praised, you alone are magnificent!

I am En-hedu-ana, the high priestess of the moon god.... Mercy, compassion, care, lenience and homage are yours, and to cause flood storms, to open hard ground and to turn darkness into light. My lady, let me proclaim your magnificence in all lands, and your glory! Let me praise your ways and greatness! Who rivals you in divinity? Who can compare with your divine rites? ... An and Enlil [the chief god of Sumer] have determined a great destiny for you throughout the entire universe. They have bestowed upon you ladyship in the assembly chamber. Being fitted for ladyship, you determine the destiny of noble ladies. Mistress, you are magnificent, you are great! Inanna, you are magnificent, you are great! My lady, your magnificence is resplendent. May your heart be restored for my sake! Your great deeds are unparalleled, your magnificence is praised! Young woman, Inanna, your praise is sweet!

(British Museum, London, UK/Werner Forman Archive/Bridgeman Images)

**2** **Babylonian cylinder seal showing a man addressing the deities.** Dating from the Old Babylonian period (1800–1600 B.C.E.), this seal shows a man (left) addressing two deities, the one on the right holding the rod and ring, symbols of authority. The cuneiform inscription reads, "Ibni-Amurru, son of Ilima-ahi, servant of the god Amurru."

**3** **Pyramid text of King Unas.** This incantation, designed to assist the king's ascent to the heavens after his death, was inscribed on a wall of the royal burial chambers in the pyramid of the Egyptian king Unas (r. 2375–2345) at Saqqara, a burial ground near the Nile.

Re-Atum [the sun-god], this Unas comes to you,
A spirit indestructible
Who lays claim to the place of the four pillars!
Your son comes to you, this Unas comes to you
May you cross the sky united in the dark,

### ANALYZING THE EVIDENCE

1. In Source 1 from Mesopotamia, what powers and qualities of the goddess Inanna does Enheduana praise? In Source 2, what qualities do the deities in the cylinder seal exhibit?
2. In Sources 3–5 from Egypt, what powers and qualities does the sun-god exhibit?
3. What common features do you see across all the sources in the powers ascribed to the gods and the proper attitude of humans in addressing them?
4. Continuing to think about similarities, bear in mind that Enheduana was a member of the ruling dynasty of Akkad, and Unas and Akhenaton were kings of Egypt. How did their social position shape their relationship to the gods?
5. The pharaohs of Egypt were also regarded as gods; how does this make the relationship of Unas and Akhenaton to the sun-god distinctive?

May you rise in lightland, the place in which you
    shine!
Osiris, Isis, go proclaim to Lower Egypt's gods
And their spirits:
"This Unas comes, a spirit indestructible,
Like the morning star above Hapy [the god of the
    flooding of the Nile],
Whom the water-spirits worship;
Whom he wishes to live will live,
Whom he wishes to die will die!"
. . .

Thoth [the god of law and science], go proclaim
    to the gods of the west
And their spirits:
"This Unas comes, a spirit indestructible,
Decked above the neck as Anubis
Lord of the western height
He will count hearts, he will claim hearts,
Whom he wishes to live will live,
Whom he wishes to die will die!"

**5** **Relief depicting Akhenaton, Nefertiti, and their daughter, Meritaton, making an offering to Aton.** This carved alabaster relief comes from the royal palace at Tell el-Amarna.

(Egyptian National Museum, Cairo, Egypt/Bridgeman Images)

**4** **Hymn to Aton.** When the pharaoh Akhenaton (r. 1351–1334 B.C.E.) promoted the worship of the sun-god Aton instead of older Egyptian gods, new hymns were written for the pharaoh to sing in honor of the god.

Thou appearest beautifully on the horizon of heaven
Thou living Aton, the beginning of life!
When thou art risen on the eastern horizon,
Thou hast filled every land with thy beauty.
Thou art gracious, great, glistening, and high over every land;
Thy rays encompass the lands to the limit of all that thou hast made
. . .
Thy rays suckle every meadow.
When thou risest, they live, they grow for thee.
Thou makest the seasons in order to rear all that thou hast made,
The winter to cool them,
And the heat that they may taste thee.
Thou hast made the distant sky in order to rise therein,
In order to see all that thou dost make.
While thou wert alone,
Rising in thy form as the living Aton,

Appearing, shining, withdrawing or approaching,
Thou madest millions of forms of thyself alone.
Cities, towns, fields, road, and river —
Every eye beholds thee over against them,
For thou art the Aton of the day over the earth . . .
Thou art in my heart,
And there is no other that knows thee
Save thy son Nefer-kheperu-Re Wa-en-Re [Akhenaton],
For thou hast made him well versed in thy plans and in thy
    strength . . .
Since thou didst found the earth
And raise them up for thy son
Who came forth from thy body:
The king of Upper and lower Egypt, . . . Akhenaton . . . and the Chief
    Wife of the King . . . Nefertiti, living and youthful forever and ever.

**PUTTING IT ALL TOGETHER**

Using the sources above, along with what you have learned in class and in this chapter, write a short essay that compares ideas about the gods in Mesopotamia and Egypt. How do these ideas reflect the physical environment in which these two cultures developed, and how do they reflect their social and political structures?

Sources: (1) J. A. Black et al., *Electronic Text Corpus of Sumerian Literature* (http://etcsl.orinst.ox.ac.uk/), Oxford 1998–2006. Reprinted by permission of the University of Oxford Oriental Studies Faculty; (3) Miriam Lichtheim, *Ancient Egyptian Literature: A Book of Readings*, vol. 1, *The Old and Middle Kingdoms* (Berkeley: University of California Press, 1973), p. 31. © 2006 by the Regents of the University of California. Republished by permission of the University of California Press; permission conveyed through Copyright Clearance Center, Inc.; (4) John A. Wilson, trans., in James B. Pritchard, ed., *Ancient Near Eastern Texts Relating to the Old Testament — Third Edition with Supplement*, pp. 370–371. Copyright © 1969 by Princeton University Press; permission conveyed through Copyright Clearance Center, Inc.

the language of the land, thereby promoting the welfare of the people." Its 282 laws set a variety of punishments, primarily fines, but also physical punishment such as mutilation, whipping, and burning. It is unknown whether its provisions were always or even generally followed, but it influenced other law codes of the area, including those later written down in Hebrew Scripture.

Hammurabi's code began with legal procedure. There were no public prosecutors or district attorneys, so individuals brought their own complaints before the court. Each side had to produce witnesses to support its case. In cases of murder, the accuser had to prove the defendant guilty; any accuser who failed to do so was put to death. Another procedural regulation declared that once a judge had rendered a verdict, he could not change it.

Hammurabi's code provides a wealth of information about daily life in Mesopotamia. Because of farming's fundamental importance, the code dealt extensively with agriculture. Tenants faced severe penalties for neglecting the land or not working it at all. Because irrigation was essential to grow crops, tenants had to keep the canals and ditches in good repair. Anyone whose neglect of the canals resulted in damaged crops had to bear all the expense of the lost crops. Those tenants who could not pay the costs were forced into slavery. Those who helped slaves escape from their owners were to be put to death.

Babylon was a society in which business was important, so many of the laws are about contracts and what happens if someone breaks them. Those who defrauded others were to pay back ten times the amount, and a merchant who tried to increase the interest rate on a loan forfeited the entire amount. Laws about business indicate that many women carried out trade on their own; provisions about wine sellers refer to them as "she," and women were specifically allowed to sell property. There was also a form of consumer protection: a boat builder who did sloppy work had to repair the boat at his own expense.

About one-third of the laws relate to marriage and the family. As elsewhere in southwest Asia, marriage had aspects of a business agreement. The groom or his father offered the prospective bride's father a gift, called a marriage settlement, and if this was acceptable, the bride's father provided his daughter with a dowry. As in Sumer, after marriage the dowry belonged to the woman and was a means of protecting her rights and status. Expectations for how husbands and wives should behave were embedded in the law code, with differential treatment of cases depending on whether the spouses had lived up to these. (See "Evaluating Written Evidence: Hammurabi's Code on Marriage and Divorce," page 19.) Reproduction was clearly important: a man was specifically allowed to bring a concubine into the household or have children with servants or slaves if his wife could not bear children.

The penalty for adultery, defined as sex between a married woman and a man not her husband, was death. A husband had the power to spare his wife by obtaining a pardon for her from the king. He could, however, accuse his wife of adultery even if he had not caught her in the act. In such a case she could try to clear herself, and if she was found innocent, she could take her dowry and leave her husband.

Norms about how parents and children should behave toward one another were also embedded in the code. A father could not disinherit a son without just cause, and the code ordered the courts to forgive a son for his first offense. Men could adopt children into their families and include them in their wills, which artisans sometimes did to teach them the family trade, or wealthy landowners sometimes did to pass along land to able younger men, particularly if they had no children of their own.

The Code of Hammurabi demanded that the punishment fit the crime, calling for "an eye for an eye, and a tooth for a tooth," at least among equals. However, a higher-ranking man who physically hurt a commoner or slave, perhaps by breaking his arm or putting out his eye, could pay a fine to the victim instead of having his arm broken or losing his own eye. As long as criminal and victim shared the same social status, however, the victim could demand exact vengeance.

## Cultural Exchange in the Fertile Crescent

Law codes, preoccupied as they are with the problems of society, provide a bleak view of things, but other Mesopotamian documents give a happier glimpse of life. Wills and financial documents reveal couples who respected one another and women who were engaged in business. The Mesopotamians enjoyed a vibrant and creative culture that left its mark on the entire Fertile Crescent, as other groups adopted Mesopotamian practices. Mesopotamian writing, mathematics, merchandise, and other aspects of the culture spread far beyond the Tigris and Euphrates Valleys. Overland trade connected Sumer, Akkad, and Babylon with the eastern Mediterranean coast, where cities flourished under local rulers. (See "Viewpoints: Faulty Merchandise in Babylon and Egypt," page 20.) These cities were mercantile centers rich not only in manufactured goods but also in agricultural produce, textiles, and metals. People in Syria and elsewhere in the Middle East used Akkadian cuneiform to communicate in writing with their more distant neighbors.

Southern and central Anatolia (modern Turkey) presented a similar picture of extensive contact between cultures. Major Anatolian cities with large local populations were also home to colonies of traders from Mesopotamia. Thousands of cuneiform tablets testify to centuries of commercial and cultural exchanges with Mesopotamia, and eventually with Egypt, which rose to power in the Nile Valley.

# Hammurabi's Code on Marriage and Divorce

Most of the provisions in Hammurabi's law code concern what we today term civil law rather than criminal law, including a great many on the family. The following are only some of many that concern marriage and the relationship between husbands and wives.

~

128. If a man take a wife and do not arrange with her the (proper) contracts, that woman is not a (legal) wife. . . .

137. If a man set his face to put away a concubine who has borne him children or a wife who has presented him with children, he shall return to that woman her dowry and shall give to her the income of field, garden and goods and she shall bring up her children; from the time that her children are grown up, from whatever is given to her children they shall give to her a portion corresponding to that of a son and the man of her choice may marry her.

138. If a man would put away his wife who has not borne him children, he shall give her money to the amount of her marriage settlement and he shall make good to her the dowry which she brought from her father's house and then he may put her away.

139. If there were no marriage settlement, he shall give to her one mana of silver for a divorce.

140. If he be a freeman [i.e., a freed slave], he shall give her one-third mana of silver.

141. If the wife of a man who is living in his house, set her face to go out and play the part of a fool, neglect her house, belittle her husband, they shall call her to account; if her husband say "I have put her away," he shall let her go. On her departure nothing shall be given to her for her divorce. If her husband say: "I have not put her away," her husband may take another woman. The first woman shall dwell in the house of her husband as a maid servant.

142. If a woman hate her husband, and say: "Thou shalt not have me," they shall inquire into her reasons for this; and if she have been a careful mistress and be without reproach and her husband have been going about and greatly belittling her, that woman has no blame. She shall receive her dowry and shall go to her father's house.

143. If she have not been a careful mistress, have gadded about, have neglected her house and have belittled her husband, they shall throw that woman into the water.

## EVALUATE THE EVIDENCE

1. According to the law code, what must a husband who wants to divorce his wife do, and what factors shape the consequences?
2. According to the law code, what must a wife who wants to divorce her husband do, and what factors shape the consequences?
3. What do these laws reveal about norms for male and female behavior in ancient Babylon, that is, what people thought made a good husband and a good wife?

Source: *The Code of Hammurabi, King of Babylon*, translated by Robert Francis Harper (Chicago: University of Chicago Press, 1904), pp. 62, 63–64.

# How did the Egyptians establish a prosperous and long-lasting society?

At about the same time that Sumerian city-states expanded and fought with one another in the Tigris and Euphrates Valleys, a more cohesive state under a single ruler grew in the valley of the Nile River in North Africa. This was Egypt, which for long stretches of history was prosperous and secure behind desert areas on both sides of the Nile Valley. At various times groups migrated into Egypt seeking better lives or invaded and conquered Egypt. Often these newcomers adopted aspects of Egyptian religion, art, and politics, and the Egyptians also carried their traditions with them when they established an empire and engaged in trade.

## The Nile and the God-King

No other single geographical factor had such a fundamental and profound impact on the shaping of

# VIEWPOINTS

## Faulty Merchandise in Babylon and Egypt

Goods of all sorts were bought, sold, and transported throughout the ancient world, and, as happens today, some were not of the quality those receiving them expected. The following documents discuss faulty merchandise. The first is from an inscribed clay tablet from Babylon, sent about 1750 B.C.E. by a copper merchant named Nanni to a copper smelter named Ea-nasir. Nanni complains about the copper received and the rude treatment given to his agent. It is probably the world's oldest customer-service complaint. The second is a letter written on papyrus in hieratic script, sent about 1200 B.C.E. by Khay, an official at the temple for the god Harakhti (Horus), to Montuhi, the mayor of Elephantine, a city on an island in the Nile. Khay comments about the poor-quality honey Montuhi had sent.

### Nanni's Letter

Tell Ea-nasir Nanni sends the following message:

When you came, you said to me as follows: "I will give Gimil-Sin (when he comes) fine quality copper ingots." You left then but you did not do what you promised me. You put ingots which were not good before my messenger (Sit-Sin) and said: "If you want to take them, take them; if you do not want to take them, go away!"

What do you take me for, that you treat somebody like me with such contempt? I have sent as messengers gentlemen like ourselves to collect the bag with my money (deposited with you) but you have treated me with contempt by sending them back to me empty-handed several times, and that through enemy territory. Is there anyone among the merchants who trade with Telmun [a trading center on the Persian Gulf] who has treated me in this way? You alone treat my messenger with contempt! On account of that one (trifling) mina of silver which I owe (?) you, you feel free to speak in such a way, while I have given to the palace on your behalf 1,080 pounds of copper. . . . How have you treated me for that copper? You have withheld my money bag from me in enemy territory; it is now up to you to restore (my money)

to me in full. Take cognizance that (from now on) I will not accept here any copper from you that is not of fine quality. I shall (from now on) select and take the ingots individually in my own yard, and I shall exercise against you my right of rejection because you have treated me with contempt.

### Khay's Letter

The [title lost] of the chapel of Harakhti, Khay, greets [the mayor] of Elephantine Montuhi [prosperity] and health and in the favor of Amon-Re, King of the Gods! . . .

I opened the jar of honey which you had procured for the god and proceeded to draw out ten *hin*-measures of honey from it for the divine offering, but I found it was all full of lumps of (congealed) ointment. So I resealed it and sent it back south to you. If it is someone else who gave it to you, let him inspect it. And you shall see whether you might locate a good (jar of honey) and send it on to me. Then shall Pre [a god] keep you healthy. But if there isn't any, you shall send the *menet*-jar of incense by the hand of the priest Netjermose until you locate some honey.

And you shall send me the timbers of seasoned sycamore wood. Then shall Amon-Re keep you healthy, and Harakhti let you achieve a long lifetime.

### QUESTIONS FOR ANALYSIS

1. In Nanni's letter, along with the poor-quality copper Ea-nasir offered, why else is he upset? What does he threaten to do?
2. Nanni is a merchant, and Khay a priest. How do their occupations shape what they suggest will be the consequences for bad merchandise?
3. How does the information in these letters provide evidence for the economic and cultural developments discussed in this chapter?

Sources: Nanni's letter: A. Leo Oppenheim, ed., *Letters from Mesopotamia: Official, Business, and Private Letters on Clay Tablets from Two Millennia* (Chicago: University of Chicago Press, 1967), pp. 82–83; Khay's letter: Edward Wente, ed., *Letters from Ancient Egypt* (Athens, Ga.: Scholars Press, 1990), pp. 128–129.

Egyptian life, society, and history as the Nile River. The Nile flooded once a year for a period of several months, bringing fertile soil and moisture for farming, and agricultural villages developed along its banks by at least 6000 B.C.E. Although the Egyptians worried at times that these floods would be too high or too low, they also praised the Nile as a creative and comforting force:

Hail to thee, O Nile, that issues from the earth
  and comes to keep Egypt alive! . . .
He that waters the meadows which Re [Ra] created,
He that makes to drink the desert . . .
He who makes barley and brings emmer [wheat]
  into being . . .
He who brings grass into being for the cattle . . .
He who makes every beloved tree to grow . . .
O Nile, verdant art thou, who makest man and
  cattle to live.[3]

The Egyptians based their calendar on the Nile, dividing the year into three four-month periods: *akhet* (flooding), *peret* (growth), and *shemu* (harvest).

Through the fertility of the Nile and their own hard work, Egyptians produced an annual agricultural surplus, which in turn sustained a growing and prosperous population. The Nile also unified Egypt. The river was the region's principal highway, promoting communication and trade throughout the valley.

Egypt was fortunate in that it was nearly self-sufficient. Besides having fertile soil, Egypt possessed enormous quantities of stone, which served as the raw material of architecture and sculpture, and abundant clay for pottery. Moreover, the raw materials that Egypt lacked were close at hand. The Egyptians could obtain copper from Sinai (SIGH-nigh) and timber from Lebanon, and they traded with peoples farther away to obtain other materials that they needed.

The political power structures that developed in Egypt came to be linked with the Nile. Somehow the idea developed that a single individual, a king, was responsible for the rise and fall of the Nile. This belief came about before the development of writing in Egypt, so, as with the growth of priestly and royal power in Sumer, the precise details of its origins have been lost. The king came to be viewed as a descendant of the gods, and thus as a god himself. (See "Thinking Like a Historian: Addressing the Gods," page 16.)

Political unification most likely proceeded slowly, but stories told about early kings highlighted one who had united Upper Egypt—the upstream valley in the south—and Lower Egypt—the delta area of the Nile that empties into the Mediterranean Sea—into a single kingdom around 3100 B.C.E. Historians later divided Egyptian history into dynasties, or families of kings, and modern historians divide Egyptian history into periods (see the chronology "Periods of Egyptian History"). The political unification of Egypt in the Archaic Period (3100–2660 B.C.E.) ushered in the period known as the Old Kingdom (2660–2180 B.C.E.), an era remarkable for prosperity and artistic flowering.

The focal point of religious and political life in the Old Kingdom was the king, who commanded wealth, resources, and people. The king's surroundings had to be worthy of a god, and only a magnificent palace was suitable for his home; in fact, the word **pharaoh**, which during the New Kingdom came to be used for the king, originally meant "great house." Just as the kings occupied a great house in life, so they reposed in great pyramids after death. Built during the Old Kingdom, these massive stone tombs contained all the things needed by the king in his afterlife. The pyramid also symbolized the king's power and his connection with the sun-god. After burial the entrance was blocked and concealed to ensure the king's undisturbed peace, although grave robbers later found the tombs fairly easy to plunder.

**Pharaoh Khafre**   This statue from around 2570 B.C.E. shows Pharaoh Khafre seated on his throne, with the wings of the falcon-god Horus wrapped around his head, a visual depiction of the connections between the Egyptian rulers and the gods. Khafre built the second-largest of the great pyramids at Giza as his tomb. (Egyptian National Museum, Cairo, Egypt/De Agostini Picture Library/A. Dagli Orti/Bridgeman Images)

To ancient Egyptians, the king embodied the concept of **ma'at**, a cosmic harmony that embraced truth, justice, and moral integrity. Ma'at gave the king the right, authority, and duty to govern. To the people, the king personified justice and order—harmony among themselves, nature, and the divine.

Kings did not always live up to this ideal, of course. The two parts of Egypt were difficult to hold together, and several times in Egypt's long history, there were periods of disunity, civil war, and chaos. During the First Intermediate Period (2180–2080 B.C.E.), rulers of various provinces asserted their independence from the king, and Upper and Lower Egypt were ruled by rival dynasties. There is evidence that the Nile's floods were

■ **pharaoh** The title given to the king of Egypt in the New Kingdom, from a word that meant "great house."

■ **ma'at** The Egyptian belief in a cosmic harmony that embraced truth, justice, and moral integrity; it gave the kings the right and duty to govern.

unusually low during this period because of drought, which contributed to instability just as it helped bring down the Akkadian empire. Warrior-kings reunited Egypt in the Middle Kingdom (2080–1640 B.C.E.) and expanded Egyptian power southward into Nubia.

## Egyptian Religion

Like the Mesopotamians, the Egyptians were polytheistic, worshipping many gods of all types, some mightier than others. They developed complex ideas of their gods that reflected the world around them, and these views changed over the many centuries of Egyptian history as gods took on new attributes and often merged with one another. During the Old Kingdom, Egyptians considered the sun-god Ra the creator of life. He commanded the sky, earth, and underworld. Ra was associated with the falcon-god Horus, the "lord of the sky," who served as the symbol of divine kingship.

Much later, during the New Kingdom (see the chronology "Periods of Egyptian History"), the pharaohs of a new dynasty favored the worship of a different sun-god, Amon, whom they described as creating the entire cosmos by his thoughts. Amon brought life to the land and its people, they wrote, and he sustained both. Because he had helped them overthrow their enemies, Egyptians came to consider Amon the champion of fairness and justice, especially for the common people. As his cult grew, Amon came to be identified with Ra, and eventually the Egyptians combined them into one sun-god, Amon-Ra.

The Egyptians likewise developed views of an afterlife that reflected the world around them and that changed over time. During the later part of the Old Kingdom, the walls of kings' tombs were carved with religious texts that provided spells; these spells would bring the king back to life and help him ascend to Heaven, where he would join his divine father, Ra. Toward the end of the Old Kingdom, the tombs of powerful nobles also contained such inscriptions, an indication that more people expected to gain everlasting life. In the Middle Kingdom, new types of spells appeared on the coffins of even more people, a further expansion in admission to the afterlife.

During the New Kingdom, a time when Egypt came into greater contact with the cultures of the Fertile

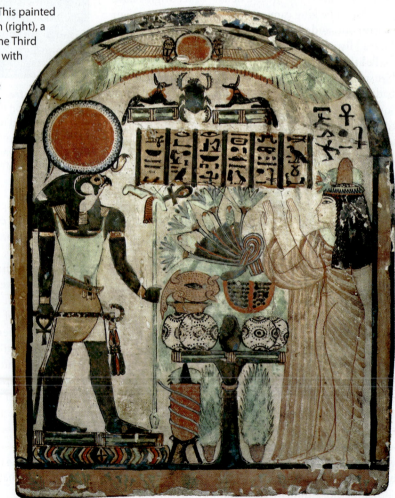

**Funeral Stele of a Wealthy Woman**    This painted wooden stele shows Djed-amon-iu-ankh (right), a wealthy Egyptian woman who lived in the Third Intermediate Period, in a thin gown and with a cone of ointment on her head, and the sun-god Ra (left) in the form of Horus the falcon-god. Ra-Horus is holding a scepter in one hand and the ankh, the Egyptian symbol of life, in the other. Djed-amon-iu-ankh offers food and lotus flowers to the god, and the hieroglyphs above them describe the offering. Steles were erected in Egypt for funeral purposes and depicted the person memorialized in an attitude of reverence. (© The Trustees of the British Museum/ Art Resource, NY)

Crescent, Egyptians developed more complex ideas about the afterlife, recording these in funerary manuscripts that have come to be known as the *Book of the Dead*, written to help guide the dead through the difficulties of the underworld. These texts explained that the soul left the body to become part of the divine after death, and they told of the god Osiris (oh-SIGH-ruhs) who died each year and was then brought back to life by his wife, Isis (IGH-suhs), when the Nile flooded. Osiris eventually became king of the dead, weighing dead humans' hearts to determine whether they had lived justly enough to deserve everlasting life. (See "Thinking Like a Historian: The Moral Life," in Chapter 2 on page 40.) Egyptians also believed that proper funeral rituals, in which the physical body was mummified, were essential for life after death, so Osiris was assisted by Anubis, the jackal-headed god of mummification.

New Kingdom pharaohs came to associate themselves with both Horus and Osiris, and they were regarded as avatars of Horus in life and Osiris in death. The pharaoh's wife was associated with Isis, for both the queen and the goddess were regarded as protectors.

## Egyptian Society and Work

Egyptian society reflected the pyramids that it built. At the top stood the king, who relied on a sizable circle of nobles, officials, and priests to administer his kingdom. All of them were assisted by scribes, who used a writing system perhaps adapted from Mesopotamia and perhaps developed independently. Egyptian scribes actually created two writing systems: one called hieroglyphic, which was used for important religious or political texts and inscriptions, and a much simpler system called hieratic, which allowed scribes to write more quickly. Hieratic writing was used for the documents of daily life, such as letters, contracts, and accounts, and also for medical and literary works. (See "Viewpoints: Faulty Merchandise in Babylon and Egypt," page 20.) Students learned hieratic first, and only those from well-off families or whose families had high aspirations took the time to learn hieroglyphics. In addition to scribes, the cities of the Nile Valley were home to artisans of all types, along with merchants and other tradespeople. A large group of farmers made up the broad base of the social pyramid.

For Egyptians, the Nile formed an essential part of daily life. During the season of its flooding, from June to October, farmers worked on the pharaoh's building programs and other tasks away from their fields. When the water began to recede, they diverted some of it into ponds for future irrigation and began planting wheat and barley for bread and beer, using plows pulled by oxen or people to part the soft mud. From October to February farming families planted

| PERIODS OF EGYPTIAN HISTORY | | |
|---|---|---|
| **Dates** | **Period** | **Significant Events** |
| 3100–2660 B.C.E. | Archaic | Unification of Egypt |
| 2660–2180 B.C.E. | Old Kingdom | Construction of the pyramids |
| 2180–2080 B.C.E. | First Intermediate | Political disunity |
| 2080–1640 B.C.E. | Middle Kingdom | Recovery and political stability |
| 1640–1570 B.C.E. | Second Intermediate | Hyksos migrations; struggles for power |
| 1570–1070 B.C.E. | New Kingdom | Creation of an Egyptian empire; growth in wealth |
| 1070–712 B.C.E. | Third Intermediate | Political fragmentation and conquest by outsiders (see Chapter 2) |

and tended crops, and then from February until the next flood they harvested them.

As in Mesopotamia, common people paid their obligations to their superiors in products and in labor, and many faced penalties if they did not meet their quota. One scribe described the scene at harvest time:

> And now the scribe lands on the river bank and is about to register the harvest-tax. The janitors carry staves and the Nubians rods of palm, and they say, Hand over the grain, though there is none. The farmer is beaten all over, he is bound and thrown into a well, soused and dipped head downwards. His wife has been bound in his presence and his children are in fetters.[4]

Peoples' labor obligations in the Old Kingdom may have included forced work on the pyramids and canals, although recent research suggests that most people who built the pyramids were paid for their work. Some young men were drafted into the pharaoh's army, which served as both a fighting force and a labor corps.

## Egyptian Family Life

The lives of all Egyptians centered around the family. Just as in Mesopotamia, first marriages were generally arranged by the couples' parents, and they seem to have taken place at a young age. Once couples were married, having children, especially sons, was a high priority, as indicated by surviving charms to promote fertility and prayers for successful childbirth. Boys continued the family line, and only they could perform the proper burial rites for their father. Second marriages, resulting from divorce or the death of a spouse, were common and were more often determined by the spouses themselves.

Wealthy Egyptians lived in spacious homes with attractive gardens and walls for privacy. For them, life included a daily bath and clean clothes, along with perfumes as deodorants. Poorer people lived in cramped quarters, with narrow rooms for living, including two small rooms for sleeping and cooking. These small houses suggest that most Egyptians lived in small family groups, not as large extended families. The very poor lived in small buildings with their animals. Egyptians of all classes generally wore linen clothes made from fibers of the flax plant.

Marriage was a family matter, not a religious ritual, and a woman brought some of her family's property to the marriage, which continued to belong to her, though her husband had the right to manage it. Both spouses could initiate divorce, and if they divorced, the woman took her marriage portion with her and could also claim a share of the profits made during her marriage. Women could own land in their own names, operate businesses, testify in court, and bring legal action against men. Some wealthy Egyptian men had several wives or concubines, but most men had only one wife. Information from literature and art depicts a world in which ordinary husbands and wives enjoyed each other's company alone and together with family and friends. Egyptian tomb monuments often show the couple happily standing or sitting together.

## The Hyksos and New Kingdom Revival

While Egyptian civilization flourished in the Nile Valley, various groups migrated throughout the Fertile Crescent and then accommodated themselves to local cultures (Map 1.2). Some settled in the Nile Delta, including a group the Egyptians called Hyksos, which means "rulers of the uplands." Although they were later portrayed as a conquering horde, the Hyksos were actually migrants looking for good land, and their entry into the delta, which began around 1800 B.C.E., was probably gradual and generally peaceful.

The Hyksos brought with them the methods of making bronze and casting it into tools and weapons that became standard in Egypt. The Hyksos also brought inventions that revolutionized Egyptian warfare, including bronze armor and weapons as well as horse-drawn chariots and the composite bow made of laminated wood and horn, which was far more powerful than the simple wooden bow.

The migration of the Hyksos, combined with a series of famines and internal struggles for power, led Egypt to fragment politically in what later came to be known as the Second Intermediate Period (1640–1570 B.C.E.). During this time, the Egyptians adopted bronze technology and new forms of weaponry from the Hyksos, while the newcomers began to worship Egyptian deities and modeled their political structure on that of the Egyptians.

In about 1570 B.C.E., a new dynasty of pharaohs arose, pushing the Hyksos out of the delta, subduing Nubia in the south, and conquering parts of Canaan in the northeast. In this way, these Egyptian warrior-pharaohs inaugurated what scholars refer to as the New Kingdom — a period in Egyptian history characterized by not only enormous wealth and conscious imperialism but also a greater sense of insecurity because of new contacts and military engagements. By expanding Egyptian power beyond the Nile Valley, the pharaohs created the first Egyptian empire, and they

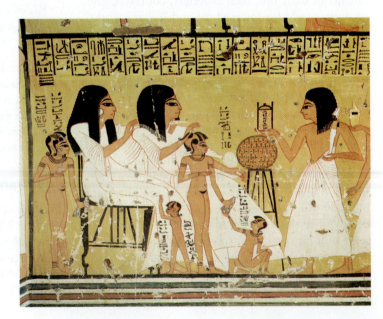

**An Egyptian Family**    This painting from the tomb of the Egyptian official Inherkau, who lived and worked during the reign of Ramesses III (r. 1184–1153), toward the end of the New Kingdom, shows the deceased and his wife Wabet (left) receiving offerings from their two sons (only one of whom is visible in this image, at the right). Their grandchildren play around their feet with birds or bird toys, in a scene that combines family life and religious rituals. Inherkau oversaw artisans and workers on the royal tombs at Thebes, as had his father and grandfather before him. Most of the people who worked on the tombs at Thebes were not slaves but were paid for their labor. Many craftsmen and officials such as Inherkau built their own underground tombs near Thebes, with burial chambers with vaulted ceilings and wall decorations. (© From the Tomb of Ankerkhe, Workmen's Tombs, Deir el-Medina, Thebes, Egypt/Bridgeman Images)

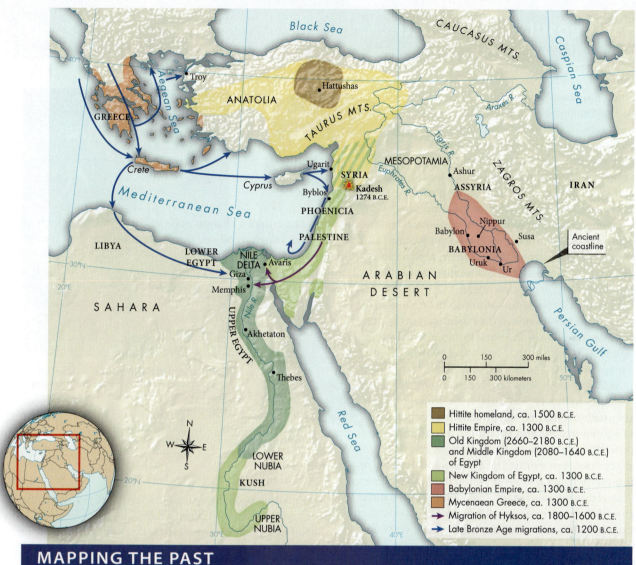

## MAPPING THE PAST

### MAP 1.2 Empires and Migrations in the Eastern Mediterranean

The rise and fall of empires in the eastern Mediterranean were shaped by internal developments, military conflicts, and the migration of peoples to new areas.

**ANALYZING THE MAP**  At what point was the Egyptian empire at its largest? The Hittite Empire? What were the other major powers in the eastern Mediterranean at this point?

**CONNECTIONS**  What were the major effects of the migrations of the Hyksos? Of the late Bronze Age migrations? What clues does the map provide about why the late Bronze Age migrations had a more powerful impact than those of the Hyksos?

celebrated their triumphs with monuments on a scale unparalleled since the pyramids of the Old Kingdom. Even today the colossal granite statues of these pharaohs and the rich tomb objects testify to the might and splendor of the New Kingdom.

The New Kingdom pharaohs include a number of remarkable figures. Among these was Hatshepsut (r. ca. 1479–ca. 1458 B.C.E.), one of the few female pharaohs in Egypt's long history, who seized the throne for herself and used her reign to promote building and trade.

Amenhotep III (r. ca. 1388–ca.1350 B.C.E.) corresponded with other powerful kings in Babylonia and other kingdoms in the Fertile Crescent, sending envoys, exchanging gifts, and in some cases marrying their daughters. The kings promised friendship and active cooperation. They made alliances for offensive and defensive protection and swore to uphold one another's authority. Hence, the greatest powers of the period maintained peace, which facilitated the movement of gifts between kings and trade between ordinary people.

The Egyptian pharaoh's connection with the divine stretched to members of his family, so that his siblings and children were also viewed as divine in some ways. Because of this, a pharaoh often took his sister or half-sister as one of his wives. This concentrated divine blood set the pharaonic family apart from other Egyptians (who did not generally marry close relatives) and allowed the pharaohs to imitate the gods, who in Egyptian mythology often married their siblings. A pharaoh chose one of his wives, often a relative, to be the "Great Royal Wife," or principal queen.

The familial connection with the divine allowed a handful of women to rule in their own right in Egypt's long history. We know the names of four female pharaohs, of whom the most famous was Hatshepsut (r. 1479–1458 B.C.E.), the sister and wife of Thutmose II. After he died, she served as regent — adviser and co-ruler — for her young stepson Thutmose III. Hatshepsut sent trading expeditions and sponsored artists and architects, ushering in a period of artistic creativity and economic prosperity. She oversaw the building of an elaborate terraced temple at Deir el Bahri, which eventually served as her mortuary temple. Hatshepsut's status as a powerful female ruler was difficult for Egyptians to conceptualize, and she is often depicted in male dress or with a false beard, thus looking more like a male ruler. After her death, Thutmose III tried to destroy all evidence that she had ever ruled, smashing statues and scratching her name off inscriptions, perhaps because of personal animosity or because he wanted to erase the fact that a woman had once been pharaoh. Only within recent decades have historians and archaeologists begun to (literally) piece together her story.

Though female pharaohs were very rare, many royal women had power through their position as "Great Royal Wives." The most famous was Nefertiti, the wife of Akhenaton. Her name means "the perfect (or beautiful) woman has come," and inscriptions also give her many other titles. Nefertiti used her position to spread the new religion of the sun-god Aton.

Together Nefertiti and Akhenaton built a new capital city at Akhetaton, the present Amarna, away from the old centers of power. There they developed the cult of Aton to the exclusion of the traditional deities. Nearly the only literary survival of their religious belief is the "Hymn to Aton," which declares Aton to be the only god. It describes Nefertiti as "the great

**Granite head of Hatshepsut.** (bpk Bildagentur/ Aegyptisches Museum und Papyrussammlung, Staatliche Museen, Berlin, Germany/Margarete Buesing/Art Resource, NY)

**Painted limestone bust of Nefertiti.**
(Aegyptisches Museum, SMPK, Berlin, Germany/ Bridgeman Images)

royal consort whom he, Akhenaton, loves. The mistress of the Two Lands, Upper and Lower Egypt."

Nefertiti is often shown as being the same size as her husband, and in some inscriptions she is performing religious rituals that would normally have been carried out only by the pharaoh. The exact details of her power are hard to determine, however. Her husband may have removed her from power, though there is also speculation that after his death she may have ruled secretly in her own right under a different name. Her tomb has long since disappeared. In the last decade, individual archaeologists have claimed that several different mummies were Nefertiti, but most scholars dismiss these claims. Because her parentage is unknown, DNA testing such as that done on Tutankhamon's corpse would not reveal whether any specific mummy was Nefertiti.

## QUESTIONS FOR ANALYSIS

1. Why might it have been difficult for Egyptians to accept a female ruler?
2. What opportunities do hereditary monarchies such as that of ancient Egypt provide for women? How does this fit with gender hierarchies in which men are understood as superior?

Amenhotep III was succeeded by his son, who took the name Akhenaton (ah-keh-NAH-tuhn) (r. 1351–1334 B.C.E.). He renamed himself as a mark of his changing religious ideas. Egyptians had long worshipped various sun-gods and aspects of the sun — Ra, Amon, Amon-Ra — but Akhenaton favored instead the worship of the god Aton (also spelled Aten), the visible disk of the sun. He was not a monotheist (someone who worships only one god), but he did order that the names of other sun-gods be erased from the walls of buildings, transferred taxes from the traditional priesthood of Amon-Ra, and built huge new temples to Aton, especially at his new capital in the area now known as Amarna. In these temples Aton was to be worshipped in bright sunlight. Akhenaton also had artists portray him in more realistic ways than they had portrayed earlier pharaohs; he is depicted interacting with his children and especially with his wife Nefertiti (nehf-uhr-TEE-tee), who supported his new religious ideas. (See "Individuals in Society: Hatshepsut and Nefertiti," page 26.)

Akhenaton's new religion, imposed from above, failed to find a place among the people, however. After his death, traditional religious practices returned and the capital was moved back to Thebes. The priests of Amon-Ra led this restoration, but it was also supported by Akhenaton's son Tutankhamon (r. 1333–1323 B.C.E.), whose short reign was not particularly noteworthy and whose name would probably not be remembered except for the fact that his was the only tomb of an Egyptian king to be discovered nearly intact. Study of Tutankhamon's mummy also revealed that he suffered from malaria and a malformed foot, and had broken his leg shortly before he died. His high status did not make him immune to physical ailments. The wealth of "King Tut's tomb," assembled for a boy-king who died unexpectedly at nineteen, can only suggest what must have originally been in the tomb of a truly powerful pharaoh.

Tutankhamon's short reign was also marked by international problems, including warfare on several of the borders of the Egyptian empire. His grandfather and father had engaged in extensive diplomatic relations with rulers of states dependent on Egypt and with other powerful kings, but Tutankhamon was less successful at these diplomatic tasks. He also died childless. His successors were court officials, and in 1298 B.C.E. one of them established a new dynasty whose members would reassert Egypt's imperial power and respond to new challenges.

## Conflict and Cooperation with the Hittites

One of the key challenges facing the pharaohs after Tutankhamon was the expansion of the kingdom of the Hittites. At about the same time that the Sumerians were establishing city-states, speakers of Indo-European languages migrated into Anatolia. Indo-European is a large family of languages that includes English, most of the languages of modern Europe, Persian, and Sanskrit. It also includes Hittite, the language of a people who seem to have migrated into this area about 2300 B.C.E.

Surviving records indicate that in the sixteenth century B.C.E. the Hittite king Hattusili I led his forces against neighboring kingdoms. Hattusili's grandson and successor, Mursili I, extended the Hittite conquests as far as Babylon. On his return home, the victorious Mursili was assassinated by members of his own family, which led to dynastic warfare. This pattern of expansion followed by internal conflict was repeated frequently, but when they were united behind a strong king, the Hittites were extremely powerful.

As the Hittites expanded southward, they came into conflict with the Egyptians, who were re-establishing their empire. The pharaoh Ramesses II engaged in numerous campaigns to retake Egyptian territory in Syria. He assembled a large well-equipped army with thousands of chariots and expected to defeat the Hittites easily, but he and his army were ambushed by them at the Battle of Kadesh in 1274 B.C.E. Returning to Egypt, Ramesses declared that he had won and had monuments carved commemorating his victory. In reality, neither side gained much by the battle, though both sides seem to have recognized the impossibility of defeating the other.

In 1258, Ramesses II and the Hittite king Hattusili III concluded a peace treaty, which was recorded in both Egyptian hieroglyphics and Hittite cuneiform. Returning to the language of cooperation established in earlier royal diplomacy, each side promised not to invade the other and to come to the other's aid if attacked. Each promised peace and brotherhood, and the treaty ended with a long oath to the gods, who would curse the one who broke the treaty and bless the one who kept it.

## NOTES

1. J. A. Black et al., *Electronic Text Corpus of Sumerian Literature* (http://etcsl.orinst.ox.ac.uk/), Oxford 1998–2006. Reprinted by permission of the University of Oxford Oriental Studies Faculty.

2. Quoted in S. N. Kramer, *The Sumerians: Their History, Culture, and Character*, p. 238. Copyright © 1963 by The University of Chicago. All rights reserved. Used by permission of the publisher.

3. James B. Pritchard, ed., *Ancient Near Eastern Texts Relating to the Old Testament — Third Edition with Supplement*, p. 372. © 1950, 1955, 1969, renewed 1978 by Princeton University Press; permission conveyed through Copyright Clearance Center, Inc.

4. Quoted in A. H. Gardiner, "Ramesside Texts Relating to the Taxation and Transport of Corn," *Journal of Egyptian Archaeology* 27 (1941): 19–20.

# LOOKING BACK  LOOKING AHEAD

The political and military story of waves of migrations, battles, and the rise and fall of empires can mask striking continuities across the Neolithic and Bronze Ages. The social patterns that were set in early agricultural societies—with most of the population farming the land and a small number of elite who lived off their labor—lasted for millennia. Disrupted peoples and newcomers shared practical concepts of agriculture and metallurgy with one another, and wheeled vehicles allowed merchants to transact business over long distances. Merchants, migrants, and conquerors carried their gods and goddesses with them, and religious beliefs and practices blended and changed. Cuneiform tablets, wall inscriptions, and paintings testify to commercial exchanges and cultural accommodation, adoption, and adaptation.

The treaty of Ramesses II and Hattusili III brought peace between the Egyptians and the Hittites for a time, which was further enhanced by Ramesses II's marriage to a Hittite princess. This stability was not to last, however. Within several decades of the treaty, new peoples were moving into the eastern Mediterranean, disrupting trade and in some cases looting and destroying cities. There is evidence of drought, and some scholars have suggested that a major volcanic explosion in Iceland cooled the climate for several years, leading to a series of poor harvests. Both the Egyptian and Hittite Empires shrank dramatically. All of these developments are part of a general "Bronze Age Collapse" that historians see as a major turning point.

## Make Connections

Think about the larger developments and continuities within and across chapters.

1. What basic elements of Mesopotamian and Egyptian society can be traced back to the Neolithic period, and why do you think there were these continuities?

2. How were the societies that developed in Mesopotamia and Egypt similar to one another, and how were they different?

3. The civilizations discussed in this chapter developed in parts of the world not usually seen today as part of "the West." What customs, concepts, institutions, or other aspects of Mesopotamian and Egyptian civilization have continued in parts of the world understood today as "the West" that would explain why they are viewed as foundational?

# 1  REVIEW & EXPLORE

## Identify Key Terms

Identify and explain the significance of each item below.

civilization ( p. 4)

Paleolithic era (p. 5)

Neolithic era (p. 6)

Fertile Crescent (p. 7)

pastoralism (p. 7)

patriarchy (p. 9)

Bronze Age (p. 10)

polytheism (p. 10)

cuneiform (p. 12)

Hammurabi's law code (p. 15)

pharaoh (p. 21)

ma'at (p. 21)

## Review the Main Ideas

Answer the section heading questions from the chapter.

1. What do we mean by "the West" and "Western civilization"? (p. 4)

2. How did early human societies create new technologies and cultural forms? (p. 5)

3. What kind of civilization did the Sumerians build in Mesopotamia? (p. 10)

4. How did the Akkadian and Old Babylonian empires develop in Mesopotamia? (p. 15)

5. How did the Egyptians establish a prosperous and long-lasting society? (p. 19)

## Suggested Resources

### BOOKS

- Fagan, Brian M. *People of the Earth: An Introduction to World Prehistory*, 14th ed. 2013. A thorough survey that presents up-to-date scholarship, designed for students.

- Harding, A. F. *European Societies in the Bronze Age*. 2000. A comprehensive survey of developments in Europe during the Bronze Age.

- Hawass, Zahi. *Silent Images: Women in Pharaonic Egypt*. 2000. Blends text and pictures to draw a history of ancient Egyptian women.

- Kriwaczek, Paul. *Babylon: Mesopotamia and the Birth of Civilization*. 2012. Traces Mesopotamia from the first settlements to the fall of Babylon.

- Leick, Gwendolyn. *The Babylonians*. 2002. An introduction to all aspects of Babylonian life and culture.

- McCarter, Susan Foster. *Neolithic*. 2007. An introductory survey of the development and impact of agriculture, with many illustrations.

- Podany, Amanda. *Brotherhood of Kings: How International Relations Shaped the Ancient Near East*. 2010. Examines a thousand years of diplomacy among rulers.

- Scott, James C. *Against the Grain: A Deep History of the Earliest States*. 2017. A critical view of the development of agriculture.

- Tattersall, Ian. *Masters of the Planet: The Search for Our Human Origins*. 2012. An up-to-date survey of how humans evolved, in a lively narrative written for general readers.

- Van de Mieroop, Marc. *A History of the Ancient Near East, 3000–332 B.C.E.* 2010. A concise history from Sumerian cities to Alexander the Great.

- Visicato, Giuseppe. *The Power and the Writing: The Early Scribes of Mesopotamia*. 2000. Studies the practical importance of early Mesopotamian scribes.

### MEDIA

- *Ancient Mesopotamia and Egypt*. Two interactive websites from the British Museum with objects in the museum's fabulous collection, with maps, essays, and other resources. **http://www.mesopotamia.co.uk/ http://www.ancientegypt.co.uk/**

- *Ancient Worlds: Come Together* (BBC, 2010). Archaeologist and historian Richard Miles explores the beginning of civilization in the cities of Mesopotamia in this documentary.

- *Cave of Forgotten Dreams* (Werner Herzog, 2010). Renowned director Werner Herzog goes inside the newly discovered Chauvet caves of southern France to film the oldest-known human artwork from around 32,000 years ago.

- *Egypt's Golden Empire* (PBS, 2002). This three-part series on the era of the New Kingdom examines the lives of pharaohs, nobles, and ordinary people in Egypt's expanding empire.

- *Eternal Egypt*. A multimedia website with over fifteen hundred examples of Egyptian art and artifacts, along with articles, maps, and animations. Run by the Egyptian Supreme Council of Antiquities, Egyptian Center for Documentation of Cultural and Natural Heritage, and IBM. **www. eternalegypt.org/ EternalEgyptWebsiteWeb/HomeServlet**

- *The Kings: From Babylon to Baghdad* (History Channel, 2004). This feature-length History Channel special surveys the rulers of Mesopotamia from Sargon of Akkad to Saddam Hussein, with special attention to military matters.

- *Theban Mapping Project*. An interactive website run by a scholar from the American University in Cairo that highlights the excavations of palaces, tombs, and temples in the Valley of the Kings, with maps, videos, articles, and thousands of photos. **www .thebanmappingproject.com/**

# 2

# Small Kingdoms and Mighty Empires in the Near East

## 1200–510 B.C.E.

**The migrations, drought, and destruction** of what scholars call the Bronze Age Collapse in the late thirteenth century B.C.E. ended the Hittite Empire and weakened the Egyptians. Much was lost, but the old cultures of the ancient Near East survived to nurture new societies. The technology for smelting iron, which developed in Anatolia as well as other places in the world, improved and spread, with iron weapons and tools becoming stronger and thus more important by about 1000 B.C.E. In the absence of powerful empires, the Phoenicians, Kushites, Hebrews, and many other peoples carved out small independent kingdoms until the Near East was a patchwork of states. The Hebrews created a new form of religious belief with a single god and wrote down their religious ideas and traditions in what later became the most significant written document from this period.

In the tenth century B.C.E. this jumble of small states gave way to an empire that for the first time embraced the entire Near East: the empire of the Assyrians. The Assyrians assembled a huge army that used sophisticated military technology and brutal tactics, and they also developed effective administrative techniques and stunning artistic works. The Assyrian Empire lasted for about three hundred years and then broke apart with the rise of a new empire centered in Babylon. Then, beginning in 550 B.C.E., the Persians conquered the Medes—nomadic peoples who had settled in Iran—and then the Babylonians and Assyrians, creating the largest empire yet seen, stretching from Anatolia in the west to the Indus Valley in the east. The Persians established effective methods of governing their diverse subjects and built roads for conquest, trade, and communication. ◼

## CHAPTER PREVIEW

- How did iron technology shape new states after 1200 B.C.E.?

- How did the Hebrews create an enduring religious tradition?

- How did the Assyrians and Neo-Babylonians gain and lose power?

- How did the Persians conquer and rule their extensive empire?

**Life in the Persian Empire**

Two men dressed in clothing of the Medes, one of the groups conquered by the Persians, drive a four-horse chariot in this small model made entirely of gold. In the nineteenth century a huge collection of silver and gold objects from the fifth and fourth centuries B.C.E. was found on the banks of the Oxus River in what is now Tajikistan. Most likely, the spot had been a ferry crossing and the objects had been buried long ago. (British Museum, London, UK/De Agostini Picture Library/Bridgeman Images)

# How did iron technology shape new states after 1200 B.C.E.?

If the Bronze Age Collapse was a time of massive political and economic disruption, it was also a period when new technologies spread, especially iron. Even though empires shrank, many small kingdoms survived that shared a common culture across a wide area while also following their own local traditions.

## Iron Technology

Along with migration and drought, another significant development in the centuries around 1200 B.C.E. was the spread of iron tools and iron technology. Iron is the most common element in the earth, but most iron found on or near the earth's surface occurs in the form of ore, which must be smelted to extract the metal. This is also true of the copper and tin that are used to make bronze, but these can be smelted at much lower temperatures than iron. As artisans perfected bronze metalworking techniques, they also experimented with iron. They developed a long and difficult process for smelting iron, using charcoal and a bellows (which raised the temperature of the fire significantly) to extract the iron from the ore. This procedure was performed in an enclosed furnace, and the process was repeated a number of times as the ore was transformed into wrought iron, which could be hammered into shapes.

Iron smelting was developed independently in several different places, including western Africa in what is now Nigeria, Anatolia (modern Turkey), and most likely India. In Anatolia, the earliest smelted weapon has been dated to about 2500 B.C.E., but there may have been some smelting earlier. Most of the iron produced was too brittle to be of much use until about 1100 B.C.E., when techniques improved and iron weapons gradually became stronger and cheaper than their bronze counterparts. Thus, in the schema of dividing history into periods according to the main material out of which tools are made (see Chapter 1), the **Iron Age** began in about 1100 B.C.E. Iron weapons became

important items of trade around the Mediterranean and throughout the Tigris and Euphrates Valleys, and the technology for making them traveled as well. From Anatolia, iron objects were traded west into Greece and central Europe, and north into western Asia. By 500 B.C.E., knowledge of smelting had traveled these routes as well.

Ironworkers continued to experiment and improve their products. Near Eastern ironworkers discovered that if the relatively brittle wrought iron objects were placed on a bed of burning charcoal and then cooled quickly, the outer layer would form into a layer of much harder material, steel. Goods made of cast or wrought iron were usually traded locally, but fine sword and knife blades of steel traveled long distances, and the knowledge of how to make them followed. Because it was fairly plentiful and relatively cheap when compared with bronze, iron has been called the "democratic metal." The transition from bronze to iron happened over many centuries, but iron (and even more so, steel) would be an important factor in history from this point on.

## The Decline of Egypt and the Emergence of Kush

Although the treaty between the Egyptians and Hittites in 1258 B.C.E. (see Chapter 1) seemed to indicate a future of peace and cooperation, this was not to be. Groups of seafaring peoples whom the Egyptians called Sea Peoples migrated and marauded in the eastern Mediterranean. Just who these people were and

**Nubian Cylinder Sheath** This small silver sheath made about 520 B.C.E., perhaps for a dagger, depicts a winged goddess and the Egyptian god Amon-Ra (not shown in photograph). It and others like it were found in the tombs of Kushite kings who ruled from Meroë, and they suggest ways that kings even long after Taharqa adopted and adapted Egyptian artistic styles and religious ideas. (Cylinder sheath of Amani-natake-lebte. Napatan Period, reign of King Amani-natake-lebte, 538–519 B.C [gilded silver and colored paste]/Nubian/Museum of Fine Arts, Boston, Massachusetts, USA/Harvard University–Boston Museum of Fine Arts Expedition/Photograph provided by Bridgeman Images/Photograph © 2019 Museum of Fine Arts, Boston. All Rights Reserved.)

■ **Iron Age** Period beginning about 1100 B.C.E., when iron became the most important material for tools and weapons.

■ **Kush** Kingdom in Nubia that adopted hieroglyphics and pyramids, and later conquered Egypt.

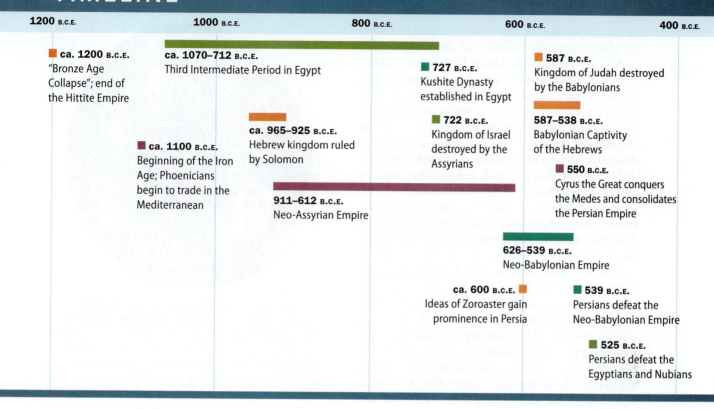

1200 B.C.E.  1000 B.C.E.  800 B.C.E.  600 B.C.E.  400 B.C.E.

- **ca. 1200 B.C.E.**
"Bronze Age Collapse"; end of the Hittite Empire

- **ca. 1070–712 B.C.E.**
Third Intermediate Period in Egypt

- **ca. 1100 B.C.E.**
Beginning of the Iron Age; Phoenicians begin to trade in the Mediterranean

- **ca. 965–925 B.C.E.**
Hebrew kingdom ruled by Solomon

- **911–612 B.C.E.**
Neo-Assyrian Empire

- **727 B.C.E.**
Kushite Dynasty established in Egypt

- **722 B.C.E.**
Kingdom of Israel destroyed by the Assyrians

- **ca. 600 B.C.E.**
Ideas of Zoroaster gain prominence in Persia

- **587 B.C.E.**
Kingdom of Judah destroyed by the Babylonians

- **587–538 B.C.E.**
Babylonian Captivity of the Hebrews

- **550 B.C.E.**
Cyrus the Great conquers the Medes and consolidates the Persian Empire

- **626–539 B.C.E.**
Neo-Babylonian Empire

- **539 B.C.E.**
Persians defeat the Neo-Babylonian Empire

- **525 B.C.E.**
Persians defeat the Egyptians and Nubians

where they originated are much debated among scholars. They may have come from Greece, or islands in the Mediterranean such as Crete and Sardinia, or Anatolia, or from all of these places. Wherever they came from, their movements and their raids, combined with the expansion of the Assyrians (see "Assyria's Long Road to Power"), led to the collapse of the Hittite Empire.

In Egypt, the pharaoh Ramesses III (r. 1186–1155 B.C.E.) defeated the Sea Peoples in both a land and sea battle, but these were costly struggles, as were other military engagements. Egypt entered into a long period of political fragmentation and conquest by outsiders that scholars of Egypt refer to as the Third Intermediate Period (ca. 1070–712 B.C.E.). The long wars against invaders weakened and impoverished Egypt, causing political upheaval and economic decline. Scribes created somber portraits that no doubt exaggerated the negative, but they were effective in capturing the mood:

> The land of Egypt was abandoned and every man was a law to himself. During many years there was no leader who could speak for others. Central government lapsed, small officials and headmen took over the whole land. Any man, great or small, might kill his neighbor. In the distress and vacuum that followed . . . men banded together to plunder one another. They treated the gods no better than men, and cut off the temple revenues.[1]

The decline of Egypt allowed new powers to emerge. South of Egypt was a region called Nubia, mostly in present-day Sudan, which, as early as 2000 B.C.E., served as a conduit of trade through which ivory, gold, ebony, animal skins, and eventually iron flowed north from sub-Saharan Africa, with wine, olive oil, papyrus, and other products flowing south. Small kingdoms arose in this area. As Egypt expanded during the New Kingdom (see Chapter 1), it took over northern Nubia, incorporating it into the growing Egyptian empire. The Nubians adopted many features of Egyptian culture, many Nubians became officials in the Egyptian bureaucracy and officers in the army, and there was significant intermarriage between the two groups.

Later, with the contraction of the Egyptian empire in the Third Intermediate Period, an independent kingdom, **Kush**, rose in power in Nubia, with its capital at Napata. Kush had a rich supply of iron, which it used for weapons, tools, personal adornments, and other products. Researchers in archaeo-metallurgy (the study

**The Kingdom of Kush, 1000 B.C.E.–300 C.E.**

of ancient metals) are now using advanced technologies that detect magnetic fields and electrical resistance underground to locate and study Kushite iron production centers. The Kushites conquered southern Egypt, and in 727 B.C.E., the Kushite king Piye (r. ca. 747–716 B.C.E.) swept through the Nile Valley to the delta in the north. United once again, Egypt enjoyed a period of peace and prosperity. The Kushite rulers understood themselves to be a new dynasty of pharaohs and were devoted to Egyptian gods such as Amon-Ra. Piye's son Taharqa (r. 690–664 B.C.E.) launched the biggest building campaign since the New Kingdom, with temples, monuments, and pyramids throughout the Nile Valley. (See "Individuals in Society: King Taharqa of Kush and Egypt," page 35.)

Late in Taharqa's reign, invading Assyrians (see "Assyria's Long Road to Power") pushed the Kushites out of Egypt, and the Kushite rulers moved their capital slightly farther up the Nile to Meroë, which was surrounded by iron ore deposits and forests for producing the charcoal needed to smelt iron. Meroë became a center for the production of iron, which the Kushite kings may have controlled. Iron products from Meroë were the best in the world and were traded to much of Africa and across the Red Sea and the Indian Ocean to India.

**Phoenician Coin**    This silver Phoenician coin shows an animal-headed ship containing soldiers with shields and helmets above the waves, and a hippocampus, a mythical beast, below. Phoenician gold and silver coins have been found throughout the Mediterranean, evidence of the Phoenicians' extensive trading network. This particular coin was most likely not used very often, as the images on it are still sharp; silver is soft, and frequent handling would have rubbed off the edges of the images. (Erich Lessing/Art Resource, NY)

## The Rise of Phoenicia

While Kush expanded in the southern Nile Valley, another group rose to prominence along the Mediterranean coast of modern Lebanon, the northern part of the area called Canaan in ancient sources. These Canaanites established the prosperous commercial centers of Tyre, Sidon, and Byblos and were master shipbuilders. Between about 1100 and 700 B.C.E., the residents of these cities became the seaborne merchants of the Mediterranean. Their most valued products were purple and blue textiles that were dyed with a compound made from the secretions of murex sea snails, especially prized because the brilliant color did not fade. From this originated their Greek name, **Phoenicians** (fih-NEE-shuhnz), meaning "Purple People."

The trading success of the Phoenicians brought them prosperity. In addition to textiles and purple dye, they began to manufacture goods for export, such as tools, weapons, and cookware. They worked bronze and iron, which they shipped as processed objects or as ores, and made and traded glass products. Phoenician ships often carried hundreds of jars of wine, and the Phoenicians introduced grape growing to new regions around the Mediterranean, dramatically increasing the wine available for consumption and trade. They imported rare goods and materials, including hunting dogs, gold, and ivory, from Persia in the east and their neighbors to the south. They also expanded their trade to Egypt, where they mingled with other local traders.

Moving beyond Egypt, the Phoenicians struck out along the coast of North Africa to establish new markets in places where they encountered little competition. The Phoenicians planted trading posts and small farming communities along the coast, founding colonies in Spain, Sicily, and North Africa. Their trade routes eventually took them to the far western Mediterranean and beyond to the Atlantic coast of modern-day Portugal. The Phoenicians' voyages brought them into contact with the Greeks, to whom they introduced many aspects of the older and more urbanized cultures of Mesopotamia and Egypt.

In the ninth century B.C.E., the Phoenicians founded, in modern Tunisia, the city of Carthage, which prospered to become the leading city in the western Mediterranean; by the sixth century B.C.E., it was the center of an empire that controlled many other Phoenician colonies. Here ironsmiths began smelting and smithing wrought iron and steel on a large scale for use and export, specializing in transforming partially worked ore into finished products. They developed new technologies to improve their products; for

■ **Phoenicians**  Seafaring people from Canaan who traded and founded colonies throughout the Mediterranean and spread the phonetic alphabet.

Like his father Piye, who conquered and united Egypt after a long period of political disruption, Taharqa (r. 690–664 B.C.E.) was the king of Kush who was also the pharaoh of Egypt, ruling for twenty-six years after being crowned in 690 B.C.E. in the Egyptian capital of Memphis in what was termed Egypt's Twenty-Fifth Dynasty. An able military commander, he ensured peace for the first part of his reign and used the time to build and expand temples and monuments to the gods throughout the Nile Valley, especially to Amon-Ra, a powerful Egyptian god whom the Kushite kings also especially revered. These buildings were filled with statues, busts, paintings, and plaques with Taharqa's name or image, showing the black-skinned king as a sphinx or warrior, or as worshipping the gods or being protected by them. He presented himself as heir to the powerful New Kingdom pharaohs who had ruled eight centuries earlier, another period during which rulers had expanded their territories and built monuments and temples. Taharqa's construction boom included pyramids, the first built since the Middle Kingdom. Ultimately there were more pyramids in Kush (modern-day Sudan) than there were in Egypt.

During the sixth year of his rule, the Nile swelled the perfect amount from spring rains: enough to ensure excellent harvests, but not so much that any villages were flooded. Taharqa ordered this fortunate event recorded on tall columns called stelae, which noted that the floods had killed the snakes and rats, but no people, and thanked the gods for favoring Egypt and its king.

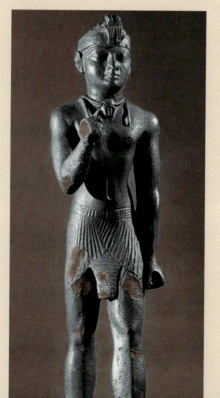

**Bronze life-size statue of King Taharqa.**
(State Hermitage Museum, St. Petersburg, Russia/ Werner Forman Archive/ Shutterstock)

While he was a young man, Taharqa had apparently led Kushite troops against the Assyrians, who were expanding their empire in Lebanon and Judah. In 701 B.C.E. the Assyrians under King Sennacherib initially defeated the Kushites and their allies, and then turned against Jerusalem, the capital of Judah. According to biblical accounts, the Jewish king Hezekiah asked the Egyptian and Kushite troops for assistance, and there is a brief mention in the Bible (2 Kings 19:9; Isaiah 37:9) of "King Tirhakah of Kush" (older translations use "Ethiopia," a translation of the Greek word for this area) whom scholars have identified with Taharqa, setting out to fight the Assyrians. There is also a longer discussion of God sending an angel who slew thousands of Assyrians. Whatever happened to cause the death of Sennacherib's troops (and some modern scholars think this might have been a plague), he abandoned his siege and left, and the city was spared.

In 679 B.C.E., during the middle of Taharqa's reign, the Assyrians under Sennacherib's son Esarhaddon began expanding again, occupying Judah and Lebanon. When they invaded Egypt, Taharqa's forces initially defeated them, but on a second attempt the Assyrian forces captured and sacked Memphis, killing many members of the royal family or taking them away as prisoners to Assyria. Esarhaddon ordered a commemorative pillar showing Taharqa's son kneeling in front of him with a rope piercing his lips. Taharqua himself escaped south, however, and the Kushites held to their Egyptian territories south of Memphis until he died. For several more decades Kushites, Assyrians, and others fought in the Nile Valley, and gradually a native Egyptian dynasty reasserted control. Both they and the Assyrians attempted to destroy any record of Kushite rule, erasing inscriptions and records and destroying art and artifacts. Much of what we know about Egypt's black pharaohs has only emerged in the last several decades, as statues and stelae long buried have been excavated.

### QUESTIONS FOR ANALYSIS

1. In what ways is Taharqa similar to earlier Egyptian pharaohs? In what ways is he different?
2. Why would the Egyptian dynasty that succeeded Taharqa's Kushite Dynasty be eager to destroy the record of its existence?

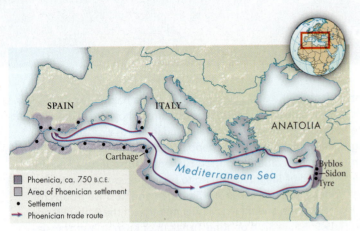

**Phoenician Settlements in the Mediterranean**

example, they recycled the shells of murex sea snails left over from purple dye production into a flux, a chemical compound that helped rid the iron of impurities. As in Meroë, the iron industry was controlled by the state and was a source of power that would help Carthage continue to expand its empire. In the third century B.C.E. this empire was brought into conflict with an expanding Rome (see Chapter 5).

The Phoenicians made many technological advances, and their overwhelming cultural achievement was the spread of a completely phonetic system of writing—that is, an alphabet. Writers of both cuneiform and hiero-glyphics had developed signs that were used to represent sounds, but these were always used with a much larger number of ideograms. Sometime around 1800 B.C.E., workers in the Sinai Peninsula, which was under Egyptian control, began to write only with phonetic signs, with each sign designating one sound. This system vastly simplified writing and reading, and it spread among common people as a practical way to record ideas and communicate. The Phoenicians adopted the simpler system for their own language and spread it around the Mediterranean. The Greeks modified this alphabet and then used it to write their own language, and the Romans later based their alphabet—the script we use to write English today—on Greek. Alphabets based on the Phoenician alphabet were also created in the Persian Empire and formed the basis of Hebrew, Arabic, and various alphabets of South and Central Asia. The system invented by ordinary people and spread by Phoenician merchants is the origin of most of the world's phonetic alphabets today.

## How did the Hebrews create an enduring religious tradition?

The legacy of another people who took advantage of Egypt's collapse to found an independent state may have been even more far-reaching than that of the Phoenicians. For a period of several centuries, a people known as the Hebrews controlled first one and then two small states on the western end of the Fertile Crescent, Israel and Judah. Politically unimportant when compared with the Egyptians or Babylonians, the Hebrews created a new form of religious belief called **monotheism**, or worship of a single god. They called their all-powerful god **Yahweh** (YAH-way), spelled YHWH in ancient Hebrew because the written language had no vowels. (In the Middle Ages, different vowels were added by Christian scholars, first in Latin and then in other languages, which resulted in "Jehovah." Most English-language Bibles now translate YHWH as "LORD.") Beginning in the late 600s B.C.E., the Hebrews began to write down their religious ideas, traditions, laws, advice literature, prayers, hymns, history, and prophecies in a series of books. These were gathered together centuries later to form the Hebrew Bible, which Christians later adopted and termed the "Old Testament." These writings later became the core of the Hebrews' religion, *Judaism*, a word taken from the kingdom of Judah, the southern of the two Hebrew kingdoms and the one that was the primary force in developing religious traditions. (The word *Israelite*, often used as a synonym for *Hebrew*, refers to all people in this group, and not simply the residents of the northern kingdom of Israel.) Jews today revere these texts, as do many Christians, and Muslims respect them, all of which gives them particular importance.

### The Hebrew State

Most of the information about the Hebrews comes from the Bible, which, like all ancient documents, must be used with care as a historical source. Archaeological evidence has supported many of its details, and because it records a living religious tradition, extensive textual and physical research into everything it records continues, with enormous controversies among scholars about how to interpret findings. The Hebrews were nomadic pastoralists who may have migrated into the Nile Delta from the east, seeking good land for their herds of sheep and goats. According to the

■ **monotheism**   Worship of a single god.

■ **Yahweh**   The sole god in the Jewish religion.

Hebrew Bible, they were enslaved by the Egyptians but were led out of Egypt by a charismatic leader named Moses. The biblical account is very dramatic, and the events form a pivotal episode in the history of the Hebrews and the later religious practices of Judaism. Moses conveyed God's warning to the pharaoh that a series of plagues would strike Egypt, the last of which was the threat that all firstborn sons in Egypt would be killed. He instructed the Hebrews to prepare a hasty meal of a sacrificed lamb eaten with unleavened bread. The blood of the lamb was painted over the doors of Hebrew houses. At midnight Yahweh spread death over the land, but he passed over the Hebrew houses with the blood-painted doors. This event became known as the Passover and later became a central religious holiday in Judaism. The next day a terrified pharaoh ordered the Hebrews out of Egypt. Moses then led them in search of what they understood to be the Promised Land, an event known as the Exodus, which was followed by forty years of wandering.

Possible route of the Exodus, ca. 1250 B.C.E.

Solomon's kingdom, ca. 950 B.C.E.

Israel, ca. 800 B.C.E.

Judah, ca. 800 B.C.E.

**The Hebrew Exodus and State, ca. 1250–800 B.C.E.**

According to scripture, the Hebrews settled in the area between the Mediterranean and the Jordan River known as Canaan. They were organized into tribes, each tribe consisting of numerous families who thought of themselves as all related to one another and having a common ancestor. At first, good farmland, pastureland, and freshwater sources were held in common by each tribe. Common use of land was—and still is—characteristic of nomadic peoples. The Bible divides up the Hebrews at this point into twelve tribes, each named according to an ancestor.

In Canaan, the nomadic Hebrews encountered a variety of other peoples, whom they both learned from and fought. They slowly adopted agriculture and, not surprisingly, at times worshipped the agricultural gods of their neighbors, including Baal, an ancient fertility god. Like the Hyksos in Egypt, this was an example of the common historical pattern of newcomers adapting themselves to the culture of an older, well-established people.

The Bible reports that the greatest danger to the Hebrews came from a group known as the Philistines, who were most likely Greek-speaking people who had migrated to Canaan as part of the movement of the Sea Peoples and who established a kingdom along the Mediterranean coast. The Philistines' superior technology and military organization at first made them invincible, but the Hebrews found a champion and a spirited leader in Saul. In the biblical account, Saul and his men battled the Philistines for control of the land, often without success. In the meantime, Saul established a monarchy over the Hebrew tribes, becoming their king, an event conventionally dated to about 1025 B.C.E.

**A Golden Calf** According to the Hebrew Bible, Moses descended from Mount Sinai, where he had received the Ten Commandments, to find the Hebrews worshipping a golden calf, which was against Yahweh's laws. In July 1990 an American archaeological team found this model of a gilded calf inside a pot. The figurine, which dates to about 1550 B.C.E., is strong evidence for the existence in Canaan of religious traditions that involved animals as divine symbols. (www.BibleLandPictures.com/Alamy)

The Bible includes detailed discussion of the growth of the Hebrew kingdom. It relates that Saul's work was carried on by David of Bethlehem (r. ca. 1005–965 B.C.E.), who pushed back the Philistines and waged war against his other neighbors. To give his kingdom a capital, he captured the city of Jerusalem, which he enlarged, fortified, and made the religious and political center of his realm. David's military successes enlarged the kingdom and won the Hebrews unprecedented security, and his forty-year reign was a period of vitality and political consolidation.

David's son Solomon (r. ca. 965–925 B.C.E.) launched a building program that the biblical narrative describes as including cities, palaces, fortresses, and roads. The most symbolic of these projects was the Temple of Jerusalem, which became the home of the Ark of the Covenant, the chest that contained the holiest of Hebrew religious articles. The temple in Jerusalem was intended to be the religious heart of the kingdom, a symbol of Hebrew unity and Yahweh's approval of the kingdom built by Saul, David, and Solomon.

Evidence of this united kingdom may have come to light in August 1993 when an Israeli archaeologist found an inscribed stone slab in northern Israel probably dating from the second half of the ninth century B.C.E. that refers to a "king of Israel" and also to the "House of David." This discovery has been regarded by most scholars as the first mention of King David's dynasty outside of the Bible. The nature and extent of this kingdom continue to be disputed among archaeologists, who offer divergent datings and interpretations for the finds that are continuously brought to light.

Along with discussing expansion and success, the Bible also notes problems. Solomon's efforts were hampered by strife. The financial demands of his building program drained the resources of his people, and his use of forced labor for building projects also fanned popular resentment.

A united Hebrew kingdom did not last long. At Solomon's death, his kingdom broke into political halves. The northern part became Israel, with its capital at Samaria, and the southern half became Judah, with Jerusalem remaining its center. War soon broke out between them, as recorded in the Bible, which weakened both kingdoms. The Assyrians wiped out the northern kingdom of Israel in 722 B.C.E. Judah survived numerous calamities until the Babylonians crushed it in 587 B.C.E. The survivors were forcibly relocated to Babylonia, a period commonly known as the Babylonian Captivity. In 539 B.C.E., the Persian king Cyrus the Great (see "Consolidation of the Persian Empire") conquered the Babylonians and permitted some forty thousand exiles to return to Jerusalem. They rebuilt the temple, although politically the area was simply part of the Persian Empire.

## The Jewish Religion

During and especially after the Babylonian Captivity, the most important legal and ethical Hebrew texts were edited and brought together in the **Torah**, the first five books of the Hebrew Bible. Here the exiles redefined their beliefs and practices, thereby establishing what they believed was the law of Yahweh. Fundamental to an understanding of the Jewish religion is the concept of the **Covenant**, an agreement that people believed to exist between themselves and Yahweh. According to the Bible, Yahweh appeared to the tribal leader Abraham, promising him that he would be blessed, as would his descendants, if they followed Yahweh. (Because Judaism, Christianity, and Islam all regard this event as foundational, they are referred to as the "Abrahamic religions.") Yahweh next appeared to Moses during the time he was leading the Hebrews out of Egypt, and Yahweh made a Covenant with the Hebrews: if they worshipped Yahweh as their only god, he would consider them his chosen people and protect them from their enemies. The Covenant was understood to be made with the whole people, not simply a king or an elite, and was renewed again several times in the accounts of the Hebrew people in the Bible. Individuals such as Abraham and Moses who acted as intermediaries between Yahweh and the Hebrew people were known as prophets; much of the Hebrew Bible consists of writings in their voices, understood as messages from Yahweh to which the Hebrews were to listen.

**Jewish Blessing on Silver Scroll**   This tiny silver scroll, dating from about 600 B.C.E. and found in rock-hewn burial chambers near Jerusalem, contains the oldest known citation of texts also found in the Hebrew Bible: "May Yahweh bless you and keep you, and make [his face] shine upon you." It was worn as an amulet to provide protection against evil. (Ketef Hinnom, Jerusalem [silver]/The Israel Museum, Jerusalem, Israel/Bridgeman Images)

Worship was embodied in a series of rules of behavior, the Ten Commandments, which Yahweh gave to Moses. (See "Thinking Like a Historian: The Moral Life," page 40.) These required certain kinds of religious observances and forbade the Hebrews to steal, kill, lie, or commit adultery, thus creating a system of ethical absolutes. From the Ten Commandments a complex system of rules of conduct was created and later written down as Hebrew law, most likely influenced by Hammurabi's code (see Chapter 1). This code often called for harsh punishments, but later tradition, largely the work of the prophets who lived from the eighth to the fifth centuries B.C.E., put more emphasis on righteousness than on retribution.

Like the followers of other religions in the ancient Near East, Jews engaged in rituals through which they showed their devotion. They were also expected to please Yahweh by living up to high moral standards and by worshipping him above all other gods. The first of the Ten Commandments expresses this obligation: "I am the Lord your God . . . you shall have no other gods besides me" (Exodus 20:23). Increasingly this was understood to be a commandment to worship Yahweh alone. The later prophets such as Isaiah created a system of ethical monotheism, in which goodness was understood to come from a single transcendent god, and in which religious obligations included fair and just behavior toward other people as well as rituals. They saw Yahweh as intervening directly in history and also working through individuals—both Hebrews and non-Hebrews—that he had chosen to carry out his aims. (See "Viewpoints: Rulers and Divine Favor: Views of Cyrus the Great," page 42.) Judging by the many prophets (and a few prophetesses) in the Bible exhorting the Hebrews to listen to Yahweh, honor the Covenant, stop worshipping other gods, and behave properly, adherence to this system was a difficult challenge.

Like Mesopotamian deities, Yahweh punished people, but the Hebrews also believed he was a loving and forgiving god who would protect and reward all those who obeyed his commandments. A hymn recorded in the book of Psalms captures this idea:

> Blessed is every one who fears the Lord, who
>   walks in his ways!
> You shall eat the fruit of the labor of your hands;
> you shall be happy, and it shall be well with you.
> Your wife will be like a fruitful vine within your house;
> your children will be like olive shoots around
>   your table.
> Lo, thus shall the man be blessed who fears the
>   Lord. (Psalms 128:1–4)

The religion of the Hebrews was thus addressed to not only an elite but also the individual. Because kings or other political leaders were not essential to its practice, the rise or fall of a kingdom was not crucial to the religion's continued existence. Religious leaders were important in Judaism, but personally following the instructions of Yahweh was the central task for observant Jews in the ancient world.

## Hebrew Family and Society

The Hebrews were originally nomadic, but they adopted settled agriculture in Canaan, and some lived in cities. The shift away from pastoralism affected more than just how people fed themselves. Communal use of land gave way to family or private ownership, and devotion to the traditions of Judaism came to replace tribal identity.

Family relationships reflected evolving circumstances. Marriage and the family were fundamentally important in Jewish life; celibacy was frowned upon, and almost all major Jewish thinkers and priests were married. Polygamy was allowed, but the typical marriage was probably monogamous. In the codes of conduct written down in the Hebrew Bible, sex between a married woman and a man not her husband was an "abomination," as were incest and sex between men. Men were free to have sexual relations with concubines, servants, and slaves, however.

As in Mesopotamia and Egypt, marriage was a family matter, too important to be left to the whims of young people. (See "Evaluating Written Evidence: A Jewish Family Contract," page 43.) Although specific rituals may have been expected to ensure ritual purity in sexual relations, sex itself was understood as part of Yahweh's creation, and the bearing of children was seen in some ways as a religious function. Sons were especially desired because they maintained the family bloodline, while keeping ancestral property in the family. As in Mesopotamia, land was handed down within families, generally from father to son. A firstborn son became the head of the household at his father's death. Mothers oversaw the early education of the children, but as boys grew older, their fathers gave them more of their education. Both men and women were expected to know religious traditions so that they could teach their children and prepare for religious rituals and ceremonies. Women worked in the fields alongside their husbands in rural areas, and in shops in the cities. According to biblical

■ **Torah** The first five books of the Hebrew Bible, containing the most important legal and ethical Hebrew texts; later became part of the Christian Old Testament.

■ **Covenant** An agreement that the Hebrews believed to exist between themselves and Yahweh, in which he would consider them his chosen people if they worshipped him as their only god.

## The Moral Life

Ancient peoples developed various codes of behavior and morality, which included how they were to treat other humans and often also how they were to act toward the gods. What similarities and differences do you see in the ideas of a moral life for New Kingdom Egyptians, Hebrews, and Zoroastrian Persians?

**1** **The Egyptian *Book of the Dead*.**   During the New Kingdom and afterward, well-to-do Egyptians were buried with papyrus scrolls on which were written magical and religious texts, now known as the *Book of the Dead*, designed to help the deceased make the crossing to the afterlife. These included a standardized list of things the deceased had not done during life, what modern scholars have called a "negative confession."

To be said on reaching the Hall of the Two Truths so as to purge N [here the name of the deceased was written] of any sins committed and to see the face of every god:

Hail to you, great God, Lord of the Two Truths!
I have come to you, my Lord,
I was brought to see your beauty. . . .

I have not done crimes against people,
I have not mistreated cattle,
I have not sinned in the Place of Truth.
I have not known what should not be known,
I have not done any harm.
I did not begin a day by exacting more than my due,
My name did not reach the bark of the mighty
   ruler.
I have not blasphemed a god,
I have not robbed the poor.
I have not done what the god abhors,
I have not maligned a servant to his master.
I have not caused pain,
I have not caused tears.
I have not killed,

I have not ordered to kill,
I have not made anyone suffer.
I have not damaged the offerings in the temples,
I have not depleted the loaves of the gods,
I have not stolen the cakes of the dead [food left
   for the deceased].
I have not copulated nor defiled myself.
I have not increased nor reduced the measure,
I have not diminished the arura [arable land],
I have not cheated in the fields.
I have not added to the weight of the balance,
I have not falsified the plummet of the scales.
I have not taken milk from the mouth of
   children,
I have not deprived cattle of their pasture.
I have not snared birds in the reeds of the gods,
I have not caught fish in their ponds.
I have not held back water in its season,
I have not dammed a flowing stream,
I have not quenched a needed fire.
I have not neglected the days of meat offerings,
I have not detained cattle belonging to the god,
I have not stopped a god in his procession.
I am pure, I am pure, I am pure, I am pure!

**2** **The Ten Commandments.**   According to Hebrew Scripture, where they appear twice, the Ten Commandments were given by Yahweh to Moses. HaShem (which means "the Name") is one of the names of God in Judaism, used as a sign of reverence and respect, as is writing "G-d."

**Exodus 20**
1: And G-d spoke all these words, saying:
2: I am HaShem thy G-d, who brought thee out of the land of Egypt, out of the house of bondage.
3: Thou shalt have no other gods before Me.
4: Thou shalt not make unto thee a graven image, nor any manner of likeness, of any thing that is in heaven above, or that is in the earth beneath, or that is in the water under the earth;
5: thou shalt not bow down unto them, nor serve them; for I HaShem thy G-d am a jealous G-d, visiting the iniquity of the fathers upon the children unto the third and fourth generation of them that hate Me;

### ANALYZING THE EVIDENCE

1. In Source 1, what religious duties and personal actions does the negative confession suggest were important to Egyptians?
2. In Source 2, the Ten Commandments, what actions were required of or forbidden to Hebrews?
3. What does Zoroaster call on believers to do in Source 3?
4. In these moral codes, what will be the rewards of those who do what they are supposed to do? What will be the fate of those who do not?
5. What seems to be the most important moral duty in each of these codes?

6: and showing mercy unto the thousandth generation of them that love Me and keep My commandments.

7: Thou shalt not take the name of HaShem thy G-d in vain; for HaShem will not hold him guiltless that taketh His name in vain.

8: Remember the sabbath day, to keep it holy.

9: Six days shalt thou labour, and do all thy work;

10: but the seventh day is a sabbath unto HaShem thy G-d, in it thou shalt not do any manner of work, thou, nor thy son, nor thy daughter, nor thy man-servant, nor thy maid-servant, nor thy cattle, nor thy stranger that is within thy gates;

11: in six days HaShem made heaven and earth, the sea, and all that in them is, and rested on the seventh day; wherefore HaShem blessed the sabbath day, and hallowed it.

12: Honour thy father and thy mother, that thy days may be long upon the land which HaShem thy G-d giveth thee.

13: Thou shalt not murder; Thou shalt not commit adultery; Thou shalt not steal; Thou shalt not bear false witness against thy neighbour.

14: Thou shalt not covet thy neighbour's house; thou shalt not covet thy neighbour's wife, nor his man-servant, nor his maid-servant, nor his ox, nor his ass, nor any thing that is thy neighbour's.

**3** **Zoroaster's teachings in the Avesta.** The sacred texts of the Zoroastrians, collected in the Avesta, include some written by Zoroaster himself as liturgical poems that priests were to recite during divine services. This one tells believers about aspects of Ahuramazda they should understand, such as Right and Good Thought, as they decide what to do in their lives.

Now I will speak, O proselytes, of what ye may bring to the
attention even of one who knows,
praises for the Lord [Ahuramazda] and Good Thought's acts of
worship
well considered, and for Right; the gladness beheld by the daylight.
Hear with your ears the best message, behold with lucid mind
the two choices in the decision each man makes for his own person
before the great Supplication, as ye look ahead to the declaration
to Him.
They are the two Wills, the twins who in the beginning made
themselves heard through dreaming,
those two kinds of thought, of speech, of deed, the better and
the evil;
and between them well-doers discriminate rightly, but ill-doers
do not.
Once those two Wills join battle, a man adopts
life or non-life, the way of existence that will be his at the last:
that of the wrongful the worst kind, but for the righteous one,
best thought.
Of these two Wills, the Wrongful one chooses to do the worst
things,
but the most Bounteous Will (chooses) Right, he who clothes
himself in adamant;
as do those also who committedly please the Lord with genuine
actions, the Mindful One.

Between those two the very Daevas [the traditional gods of Iran]
fail to discriminate rightly, because delusion
comes over them as they deliberate, when they choose worst thought;
they scurry together to the violence with which mortals blight the
world.
But suppose one comes with dominion for Him, with good
thought and right,
then vitality informs the body, piety the soul:
their ringleader Thou wilt have as if in irons:
and when the requital comes for their misdeeds,
for Thee, Mindful One [Ahuramazda], together with Good
Thought, will be found dominion
to proclaim to those, Lord, who deliver Wrong into the hands of
Right.
May we be the ones who will make this world splendid,
Mindful One and Ye Lords, bringers of change, and Right,
as our minds come together where insight is fluctuating.
For then destruction will come down upon Wrong's prosperity,
and the swiftest (steeds) will be yoked from the fair dwelling of
Good Thought,
of the Mindful One, and of Right, and they will be the winners in
good repute.
When ye grasp those rules that the Mindful One lays down,
O mortals,
through success and failure, and the lasting harm that is for the
wrongful
as furtherance is for the righteous, then thereafter desire will be
fulfilled.

## PUTTING IT ALL TOGETHER

Using the sources above, along with what you have learned in class and in Chapters 1 and 2, write a short essay that discusses similarities and differences in ideas about the moral life for New Kingdom Egyptians, Hebrews, and Zoroastrian Persians. What is the basis of morality for these three groups, and how does this shape how people are supposed to act?

Sources: (1) Miriam Lichtheim, *Ancient Egyptian Literature: A Book of Readings,* vol. 2, *The New Kingdom* (Berkeley: University of California Press, 1976), pp. 124–126. © 2006 by the Regents of the University of California. Published by the University of California Press. Reprinted by permission; (2) *The Tanakh,* JPS Electronic Edition, based on the 1917 JPS translation, https://www.jewishvirtuallibrary.org/jsource/Bible/Exodus20.html; (3) M. L. West, *The Hymns of Zoroaster: A New Translation of the Most Ancient Sacred Texts of Iran.* Copyright © M. L. West, (London: I. B. Tauris, 2010), used by permission of Bloomsbury Publishing Plc.

In Mesopotamia — and elsewhere in the ancient world — individuals who established large empires through conquest often later proclaimed that their triumph was the result of divine favor, and they honored the gods of the regions they conquered. King Cyrus the Great of Persia appears to have followed this tradition. A text written in cuneiform on a sixth-century B.C.E. Babylonian clay cylinder presents Cyrus describing the way in which the main Babylonian god Marduk selected him to conquer Babylon and restore proper government and worship. Cyrus is also portrayed as divinely chosen in the book of Isaiah in Hebrew Scripture, which was probably written sometime in the late sixth century B.C.E. after Cyrus allowed the Jews to return to Jerusalem. Because Cyrus was not a follower of the Jewish God, however, the issue of divine favor was more complicated for Jews than it was for Babylonians.

## The Cyrus Cylinder

I am Cyrus, king of the universe, the great king, the powerful king, king of Babylon, king of Sumer and Akkad, king of the four quarters of the world. . . .

When I went as harbinger of peace i[nt]o Babylon I founded my sovereign residence within the palace amid celebration and rejoicing. Marduk, the great lord, bestowed on me as my destiny the great magnanimity of one who loves Babylon, and I every day sought him out in awe. My vast troops marched peaceably in Babylon, and the whole of [Sumer] and Akkad had nothing to fear. I sought the welfare of the city of Babylon and all its sanctuaries. As for the population of Babylon, . . . [w]ho as if without div[ine intention] had endured a yoke not decreed for them, I soothed their weariness, I freed them from their bond. . . . Marduk, the great lord, rejoiced at [my good] deeds, and he pronounced a sweet blessing over me, Cyrus, the king who fears him, and over Cambyses, the son [my] issue, [and over] all my troops, that we might proceed further at his exalted command.

## The Book of Isaiah, Chapter 45

Thus said the Lord to Cyrus, His anointed one — whose right hand He has grasped, Treading down nations before him, Ungirding the loins of kings, Opening doors before him, and letting no gate stay shut: I will march before you, and level the hills that loom up; I will shatter doors of bronze and cut down iron bars. I will give you treasures concealed in the dark and secret hoards — So that you may know that it is I the LORD, the God of Israel, who call you by name. For the sake of My servant Jacob, Israel My chosen one, I call you by name, I hail you by title, though you have not known Me. I am the LORD, and there is none else; beside Me, there is no God. I engird you, though you have not known Me. . . .

It was I who roused him [that is, Cyrus] for victory, and who level all roads for him. He shall rebuild My city, and let My exiled people go, without price and without payment — said the LORD of hosts.

### QUESTIONS FOR ANALYSIS

1. How would you compare the portrayal of Cyrus in the two texts?
2. The Babylonians worshipped many gods, and the Hebrews were monotheistic. How does this shape the way divine actions and favor are portrayed in the texts?
3. Both of these texts have been very influential in establishing the largely positive historical view of Cyrus. What limitations might there be in using these as historical sources?

Sources: Cylinder inscription translation by Irving Finkel, curator of Cuneiform Collections at the British Museum, www.britishmuseum.org. Used by permission of The British Museum; "The Book of Isaiah" in *Tanakh: A New Translation of The Holy Scriptures According to the Traditional Hebrew Text.* Copyright © 1985 by The Jewish Publication Society. Used by permission of the Jewish Publication Society.

codes, menstruation and childbirth made women ritually impure, but the implications of this belief in ancient times are contested by scholars.

Children, according to the book of Psalms, "are a heritage of the lord, and the fruit of the womb is his reward" (Psalms 128:3), and newly married couples were expected to begin a family at once. The desire for children to perpetuate the family was so strong that if a man died before he could sire a son, his brother was legally obliged to marry the widow. The son born of the brother was thereafter considered the offspring of the dead man. If the brother refused, the widow had her revenge by denouncing him to the elders and publicly spitting in his face.

The development of urban life among the Jews created new economic opportunities, especially in crafts and trades. People specialized in certain occupations and, as in most ancient societies, these crafts were family trades. Sons worked with their father, daughters with their mother. If the business prospered, the family

# A Jewish Family Contract

During the time of Persian rule in Egypt, Jewish soldiers were stationed in Elephantine, a military post on the Nile. Historians have since recovered papyrus documents from that location, known as the Elephantine papyri, which provide information on all sorts of everyday social and economic matters, including marriage, divorce, property, slavery, and borrowing money. The text below is an agreement by a Jewish father regarding a house he had given to his daughter, probably as part of her dowry. It was written in Aramaic, the language of business in the Persian Empire.

∼

On the 21st of Chisleu, that is the 1st of Mesore, year 6 of King Artaxerxes,* Mahseiah b. Yedoniah, a Jew of Elephantine, of the detachment of Haumadata, said to Jezaniah b. Uriah of the said detachment as follows: There is the site of 1 house belonging to me, west of the house belonging to you, which I have given to your wife, my daughter Mibtahiah, and in respect of which I have written her a deed. The measurements of the house in question are 8 cubits and a handbreadth by 11, *by the measuring-rod.*[†] Now do I, Mahseiah, say to you, Build and equip that site . . . and dwell thereon with your wife. But you may not sell that house or give it as a present to others; only your children by my daughter Mibtahiah shall have power over it after you two. If tomorrow or

some other day you build upon this land, and then my daughter divorces you and leaves you, she shall have no power to take it or give it to others; only your children by Mibtahiah shall have power over it, in return for the work which you shall have done. If, on the other hand, she recovers from you [in other words, if Jezaniah divorces *her*], she [may] take half the house, and [the] othe[r] half shall be at your disposal in return for the building which you will have done on that house. And again as to that half, your children by Mibtahiah shall have power over it after you. If tomorrow or another day I should institute suit or process against you and say I did not give you this land to build on and did not draw up this deed for you, I shall give you a sum of 10 *karshin* by royal weight, at the rate of 2 *R* to the ten, and no suit or process shall lie. This deed was written by 'Atharshuri b. Nabuzeribni in the fortress of Syene at the dictation of Mahseiah.

Witnesses hereto (signatures)

## EVALUATE THE EVIDENCE

1. How does Mahseiah seek to assist his daughter and his future grandchildren?
2. What does this contract reveal about the movement and mixtures of peoples in the Persian Empire, and about Persian methods of governing?

*This is the date of the document. Chisleu was a month in the Hebrew calendar, Mesore a seasonal period in the Egyptian calendar. Artaxerxes is most likely Artaxerxes I, king of Persia from 465 to 424 B.C.E., which means that the year this agreement was drafted was 459 B.C.E.

[†]A cubit was the length of a forearm, roughly 20 inches; the house site was thus about 15 by 18 feet.

Source: James B. Pritchard, ed., *Ancient Near Eastern Texts Relating to the Old Testament — Third Edition with Supplement.* © 1950, 1955, 1969, renewed 1978 by Princeton University Press; permission conveyed through Copyright Clearance Center, Inc.

might be assisted by a few paid workers or slaves. The practitioners of a craft usually lived in a particular section of town. Commerce and trade developed later than crafts. Trade with neighboring countries was handled by foreigners, usually Phoenicians. Jews dealt mainly in local trade, and in most instances craftsmen and farmers sold directly to their customers.

The Torah set out rules about many aspects of life. Among these was the set of dietary laws known as *kashrut* (from which we derive the English word *kosher*), setting out what plants and animals Jews were forbidden to eat and how foods were to be prepared properly. Later commentators sought to explain these laws as originating in concerns about health or hygiene, but the biblical text simply gives them as rules coming from Yahweh, sometimes expressed in terms

of ritual purity or cleanliness. It is not clear how these rules were followed during the biblical period, because detailed interpretations were written down only much later, during the time of the Roman Empire. As with any law code, from Hammurabi's to contemporary ones, it is much easier to learn about what people were supposed to do according to the laws of the Torah than what they actually did.

Beliefs and practices that made Jews distinctive endured, but the Hebrew states did not. Small states like those of the Phoenicians and the Hebrews could exist only in the absence of a major power, and the beginning of the ninth century B.C.E. saw the rise of such a power: the Assyrians of northern Mesopotamia. They conquered the kingdom of Israel, the Phoenician cities, and eventually many other states as well.

# How did the Assyrians and Neo-Babylonians gain and lose power?

The **Assyrian Empire** originated in northern Mesopotamia, from where it expanded to encompass much of the Near East in the tenth through the seventh centuries B.C.E. After building up their military, the Assyrians conquered many of their neighbors, including Babylonia, and took over much of Syria all the way to the Mediterranean. They then moved into Anatolia, where the pressure they put on the Hittite Empire was one factor in its collapse. Assyria's success allowed it to become the leading power in the Near East, with an army that at times numbered many tens of thousands. Internal strife and civil war led to its decline, allowing the Neo-Babylonians to build a somewhat smaller empire.

## Assyria's Long Road to Power

The Assyrians had inhabited northern Mesopotamia since the third millennium B.C.E., forming a kingdom that grew and shrank in size and power over the centuries. During the time of Sargon of Akkad (r. ca. 2334–2279 B.C.E.), they were part of the Akkadian empire, then independent, then part of the Babylonian empire under Hammurabi, then independent again (see Chapter 1). Warfare with the Babylonians and other Near Eastern states continued off and on, and in the thirteenth century B.C.E., the Assyrians slowly began to create a larger state.

The eleventh century B.C.E.—the time of the Bronze Age Collapse—was a period of instability and retrenchment in southwest Asia. The Assyrians did not engage in any new wars of conquest but remained fairly secure within their borders. Under the leadership of King Adad-nirari II (r. 911–892 B.C.E.), Assyria began a campaign of expansion and domination, creating what scholars have termed the Neo-Assyrian Empire. The next several turbulent centuries were marked by Assyrian military campaigns, constant efforts by smaller states to maintain or recover their independence, and eventual further Assyrian conquest.

Assyrian history is often told as a story of one powerful king after another, but among the successful Assyrian rulers there was one queen, Shammuramat, whose name in Greek became Semiramis. She ruled with her husband and then as regent for her young son in 810–806 B.C.E. Although not much can be known for certain about the historical Queen Semiramis, many legends grew up about her. Some emphasized her wisdom, beauty, and patronage of the arts, while others portrayed her as a sex-crazed sorceress. These stories cannot be used as evidence for the lives

of women in the Assyrian Empire, but like the stories of Queen Cleopatra of Egypt (see Chapter 5), they can be used as evidence for the continuing fascination with the few women who held political power in the ancient world.

Eighth-century kings continued the expansion of Assyria, which established its capital at Nineveh (NIHN-uh-vuh) on the Tigris River. In 717 B.C.E. Sargon II (r. 721–705 B.C.E.) led his army in a sweeping attack along the coast of the eastern Mediterranean south of Phoenicia, where he defeated the armies of the Egyptian pharaoh. His successor king Sennacherib (r. 705–681 B.C.E.) besieged many cities in Judah, which was under the leadership of King Hezekiah (r. ca. 715–686 B.C.E.). Sennacherib's account of his siege of Jerusalem in 701 B.C.E. provides a vivid portrait of the Assyrian war machine:

> As to Hezekiah, the Jew, he did not submit to my yoke, I laid siege to 46 of his strong cities, walled forts and to the countless small villages in their vicinity, and conquered them by means of well-stamped earth-ramps, and battering rams brought thus near to the walls combined with the attack by foot soldiers, using mines, breaches as well as sapper work. . . . Himself I made prisoner in Jerusalem, his royal residence, like a bird in a cage. I surrounded him with earthwork in order to molest those who were leaving his city's gate.[2]

What he does not mention is that the siege of Jerusalem was not successful, a fact he also left out of the carvings and artwork that he ordered for his palace. (See "Evaluating Visual Evidence: Assyrians Besiege a City," page 45.) Although they had conquered many cities in Judah, the Assyrian armies gave up their attempts to conquer the entire kingdom and went home.

Sennacherib's campaign is also recorded several times in the Hebrew Bible. The biblical accounts attribute Judah's ability to withstand the Assyrian siege to an angel sent by Yahweh, but they also describe Hezekiah as taking practical measures to counter the Assyrian invasion, including making weapons and ordering the building of a tunnel that would divert water from the springs outside the walls of Jerusalem into the city, thus both limiting the water available for Assyrian troops and assuring the city of a steady supply. The tunnel was completed and worked as planned and is now a major tourist attraction, with water still flowing in it at certain times of the year. In addition to weapons, water, and possible divine favor, there appear to have been other

■ **Assyrian Empire** An empire that originated in northern Mesopotamia and expanded to encompass much of the Near East in the tenth through the seventh centuries B.C.E.

# Assyrians Besiege a City

In this Assyrian carving made about 700 B.C.E., from the palace of King Sennacherib at Nineveh, troops attack the Jewish fortified town of Lachish using a variety of siege machinery. On the right, defending soldiers crowd a tower, while men and women carry sacks away from the city. This attack was part of Sennacherib's campaign to conquer Judah, which he described in written accounts as well as carvings ordered for his palace. Lachish was one of the cities that Sennacherib was able to overpower and subjugate.

### EVALUATE THE EVIDENCE

1. What means of attack do the Assyrians use against the besieged city in the carving?
2. How does the artist convey the idea that Assyrian military might was overwhelming?
3. Why might Sennacherib have chosen to have the siege of Lachish rather than that of the more important city of Jerusalem portrayed in his palace? What does that suggest about the purpose of art such as this?

(De Agostini Picture Library/G. Nimatallah/Bridgeman Images)

reasons as well for the Assyrian withdrawal. The biblical texts also mention attacks on the Assyrians by Kushite and Egyptian troops (see "Individuals in Society: King Taharqa of Kush and Egypt," page 35), and modern scholars also suggest that there may have been a plague among the Assyrian troops.

Despite this one loss, in general by means of almost constant warfare, the Assyrians created an empire that stretched from east and north of the Tigris River to central Egypt (Map 2.1). Revolt against the Assyrians inevitably promised the rebels bloody battles and cruel sieges followed by surrender, accompanied by systematic torture and slaughter, or by deportations. Like many conquerors, the Assyrians recognized that relocated peoples were less likely to rebel because they were forced to create new lives for themselves far from their original homelands and that simply relocating leaders might be enough to destroy opposition.

Assyrian methods were certainly harsh, but in practical terms Assyria's success was actually due primarily to the size of its army and the army's sophisticated and effective military organization. By Sargon II's time, the Assyrians had invented the mightiest military machine the ancient Near East had ever seen, with perhaps seventy thousand men in the field, armed with iron spears and swords, in an era that typically saw armies of under ten thousand.

Assyrian military genius was remarkable for the development of a wide variety of siege machinery and techniques, including excavation to undermine city walls and battering rams to knock down walls and gates. Never before in the Near East had anyone

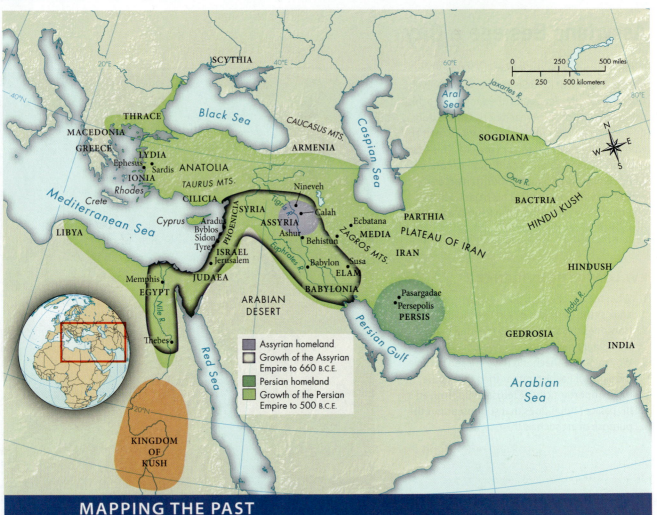

## MAPPING THE PAST

### MAP 2.1 The Assyrian and Persian Empires, ca. 1000–500 B.C.E.

At its height around 650 B.C.E., the Assyrian Empire included almost all of the old centers of power in the ancient Near East. By 513 B.C.E., however, the Persian Empire was far larger.

**ANALYZING THE MAP** How does the Persian Empire compare in size to the Assyrian Empire? What other differences can you identify between the two?

**CONNECTIONS** Compare this map to Map 1.2. What changes and continuities do you see in the centers of power in the ancient Near East?

applied such technical knowledge to warfare. The Assyrians even invented the concept of a corps of engineers, who bridged rivers with pontoons or provided soldiers with inflatable skins for swimming. And the Assyrians knew how to coordinate their efforts, both in open battle and in siege warfare.

### Assyrian Rule and Culture

The Assyrians won most of their battles, and they also knew how to use their victories to consolidate their power. The key to success in all empires is to get cooperation from some people in the regions you wish to dominate, and the Assyrians did this well. Although the lands closest to Assyria became provinces governed by Assyrian officials, kingdoms that were farther away were not annexed but became dependent states that followed Assyria's lead and also paid Assyria a hefty tribute. The Assyrian king chose these states' rulers either by regulating the succession of native kings or by supporting native kings who appealed to him.

In the seventh century B.C.E., Assyrian power seemed firmly established, yet the downfall of Assyria came swiftly and completely. Conflicts among various claimants to the throne, generals, and governors led to civil war, which weakened Assyria's ability to withstand opponents. Babylon won its independence from Assyria in 626 B.C.E. and joined forces with the Medes, an Indo-European-speaking people from Persia (modern Iran). Together the Babylonians and the Medes destroyed the Assyrian Empire in 612 B.C.E., paving the way for the rise of the Neo-Babylonian and then the Persian Empire. The Hebrew prophet Nahum (NAY-uhm) spoke for many when he asked, "Nineveh is laid waste: who will bemoan her?" (Nahum 3:7). Their cities destroyed and their power shattered, the Assyrians disappeared from history, remembered only as a cruel people of the Old Testament who oppressed the Hebrews. Two hundred years later, when the Greek adventurer and historian Xenophon (ZEH-nuh-fuhn) passed by the ruins of Nineveh, he marveled at the extent of the former city but knew nothing of the Assyrians. The glory of their empire was forgotten.

Modern archaeology has brought the Assyrians out of obscurity. In 1839, the English archaeologist and traveler A. H. Layard began excavations at Nineveh. His findings electrified the world. Layard's workers unearthed masterpieces, including monumental sculpted figures—huge winged bulls, human-headed lions, and sphinxes—as well as brilliantly sculpted friezes. Among the most renowned of Layard's finds were the Assyrian palace reliefs, whose number was increased by the discoveries of twentieth-century archaeologists. For the kings' palaces, Assyrian artists carved reliefs that showed scenes of war as a series of episodes that progressed from the time the army marched out until the enemy was conquered. In doing so, they created a visual narrative of events, a form still favored by comic-book artists and the authors of graphic novels.

Equally valuable were the numerous Assyrian cuneiform documents, which ranged from royal accounts of mighty military campaigns to simple letters by common people. The biggest find was the library of King Ashurbanipal (r. 668–627 B.C.E.), the last major Assyrian king, in the city of Nineveh. Like many Assyrian kings, Ashurbanipal was described as extremely cruel, but he was also well educated and deeply interested in literary and religious texts, especially those from what was already to him the ancient Mesopotamian past. Included in the tens of thousands of texts in his library were creation accounts from ancient Babylon (some most likely simply confiscated from the city of Babylon, which was part of the Assyrian Empire), the *Epic of Gilgamesh*, and many other mythological and religious texts, as well as word lists, chronicles, and

royal documents. Some texts relate to medicine and astronomy, and others to foretelling the future or practicing magic. The clay tablets on which these were written are harder than normal, which many scholars think may have happened as a result of a fire that destroyed the city of Nineveh shortly after the end of Ashurbanipal's reign.

## The Neo-Babylonian Empire

The decline of Assyria allowed a new dynasty of kings to create a somewhat smaller empire centered at Babylon, which historians call the Neo- (or new) Babylonian empire to distinguish it from the earlier Babylonia Empire of Hammurabi. With the help of the Medes, who had established themselves in modern western Iran, people living in southern Mesopotamia overthrew Assyrian rule in 626 B.C.E. The Neo-Babylonian empire they created was marked by an attempt to restore past Babylonian greatness. Their most famous king, Nebuchadnezzar II (neh-buh-kuhd-NEH-zuhr)

**Assyrian Winged Human-Headed Bull**   This giant alabaster human-headed bull, from the palace of King Ashurnasirpal II (r. 888–859 B.C.E.) in Nimrud (now in Iraq), represents an Assyrian protective deity called a lamassu. Assyrians often placed pairs of lamassu at the entrance to palaces, where they stood as sentinels. This one was destroyed by the Islamic State in Iraq and the Levant (ISIL) in 2015, when they bulldozed and blew up the palace because they judged the artifacts idolatrous. (Nimrud, Iraq/Bridgeman Images)

(r. 604–562 B.C.E.), thrust Babylonian power into Syria and Judah, destroying Jerusalem and forcibly deporting the residents to Babylonia.

The Neo-Babylonian rulers focused on solidifying their power and legitimizing their authority. Kings and priests consciously looked back to the great days of Hammurabi and other earlier kings. They instituted a religious revival that included restoring old temples and sanctuaries, as well as creating new ones in the same tradition. Part of their aim was commercial: they sought to resurrect the image of Babylonian greatness in order to revive the economy and attract new people to the area. In their hands, the city of Babylon grew and gained a reputation for magnificence and luxury. The city, it was said by later Greek and

Roman writers, even housed hanging gardens, one of the "wonders of the ancient world." No contemporary written or archaeological sources confirm the existence of the hanging gardens, but they do confirm that Babylon was a bustling, thriving city.

The Neo-Babylonian empire preserved many basic aspects of older Babylonian law, literature, and government, yet it failed to bring peace and prosperity to Mesopotamia. Loss of important trade routes to the north and northeast reduced income, and additional misfortune came in the form of famine and plague. The Neo-Babylonian empire was weakened and ultimately conquered in 539 B.C.E. by their former allies, the Medes, who had themselves found new allies, the Persians.

# How did the Persians conquer and rule their extensive empire?

The Assyrians rose to power from a base in the Tigris and Euphrates River Valleys of Mesopotamia, which had seen many earlier empires. They were defeated by a coalition that included a Mesopotamian power — Babylon — but also a people with a base of power in a part of the world that had not been the site of earlier urbanized states: Persia (modern-day Iran), a stark land of towering mountains and flaming deserts, with a broad central plateau in the heart of the country (see Map 2.1). Beginning in the sixth century B.C.E., the Persians created an even larger empire than the Assyrians did, and one that stretched far to the east. Though as conquerors they willingly used force to accomplish their ends, they also used diplomacy to consolidate their power and generally allowed the peoples that they conquered to practice their existing customs and religions. Thus the **Persian Empire** was one of political unity and cultural diversity.

## Consolidation of the Persian Empire

Iran's geographical position and topography explain its traditional role as the highway between western and eastern Asia. Nomadic peoples migrating south from the broad steppes of Russia and Central Asia have streamed into Iran throughout much of history. Confronting the uncrossable salt deserts, most have turned either westward or eastward, moving on until they reached the advanced and wealthy urban centers of Mesopotamia and India. Cities did emerge along these routes, however, and Iran became the area where nomads met urban dwellers.

Among the nomadic groups were Indo-European-speaking peoples who migrated into this area about 1000 B.C.E. with their flocks and herds. They were also horse breeders, and the horse gave them a decisive military advantage over those who already lived in the area. One of the Indo-European groups was the Medes, who settled in a part of northern Iran later called Media. The Medes united under one king and joined the Babylonians in overthrowing the Assyrian Empire. With the rise of the Medes, the balance of power in western Asia shifted for the first time to the area east of Mesopotamia.

In 550 B.C.E., Cyrus the Great (r. 559–530 B.C.E.), king of the Persians and one of the most remarkable statesmen of antiquity, conquered the Medes. Cyrus's conquest of the Medes resulted not in slavery and slaughter but in the union of the two peoples. Having united Persia and Media, Cyrus set out to achieve two goals. First, he wanted to win control of the shore of the Mediterranean and thus of the terminal ports of the great trade routes that crossed Iran and Anatolia. Second, he strove to secure eastern Iran from the pressure of nomadic invaders.

In a series of major campaigns, Cyrus achieved his goals. He conquered various kingdoms of the Tigris and Euphrates Valleys, and then swept into western Anatolia. Here his forces met those of the young kingdom of Lydia, a small state where gold may have first been minted into coins. Croesus (KREE-suhs) (r. 560?–546?), the Lydian king at the time, was reputed to have been fabulously wealthy, giving rise to the phrase "richer than Croesus" for someone with enormous wealth. Croesus considered Cyrus an immediate threat and planned to attack his territory. Greek legends later related that Croesus consulted the oracle at Delphi, that is, the priestess of the temple to the god Apollo at Delphi, who was understood to convey the words of the god when she spoke. Speaking through the priestess, Apollo said of the invasion, "If you make war on the Persians, you will destroy a mighty empire" (Herodotus 1.53.3). Thinking that the oracle meant the Persian Empire, Croesus went ahead and was defeated; the oracle meant that he would destroy his own kingdom.

Cyrus's generals subdued the Greek cities along the coast of Anatolia, thus gaining him important ports on the Mediterranean. From there, Cyrus marched to the far eastern corners of Iran and conquered the regions of Parthia and Bactria in Central Asia, though he ultimately died on the battlefield there.

After his victories, Cyrus made sure that the Persians were portrayed as liberators, and in some cases he was more benevolent than most conquerors were. According to his own account, he freed all of the captive peoples who were living in forced exile in Babylonia, including the Hebrews. He returned their sacred objects to them and allowed those who wanted to return to Jerusalem to do so, and he paid for the rebuilding of their temple. (See "Viewpoints: Rulers and Divine Favor: Views of Cyrus the Great," page 42.)

Cyrus's successors continued Persian conquests, creating the largest empire the world had yet seen. In 525 B.C.E. Cyrus's son Cambyses (r. 530–522 B.C.E.) subdued the Egyptians and the Nubians. At Cambyses's death (the circumstances of which are disputed), Darius I (r. 521–486 B.C.E.) took over the throne and conquered Scythia in Central Asia, along with much of Thrace and Macedonia, areas north of the Aegean Sea. By 510, the Persians also ruled the western coast of Anatolia and many of the islands of the Aegean. Thus, within forty years, the Persians had transformed themselves from a subject people to the rulers of a vast empire that included all of the oldest kingdoms and peoples of the region, as well as many outlying areas (see Map 2.1). Unsurprisingly, Darius began to call himself "King of Kings." Invasions of Greece by Darius and his son Xerxes were unsuccessful, but the Persian Empire lasted another two hundred years, until it became part of the empire of Alexander the Great (see Chapter 4).

The Persians also knew how to preserve the empire they had won on the battlefield. Learning from the Assyrians, they created an efficient administrative system to govern the empire based in their newly built capital city of Persepolis near modern Shiraz, Iran. Under Darius, they divided the empire into districts and appointed either Persian or local nobles as administrators called **satraps** to head each one. The satrap controlled local government, collected taxes, heard

**Archers in the King's Palace**   In this colorful decorative frieze made of glazed brick, men wearing long Persian robes and laced ankle boots carry spears, bows, and quivers. This reconstruction in the Louvre Museum in Paris was made from material found in the palace of King Darius I of Persia in Susa, built about 510 B.C.E. Enough bricks were found there to suggest that there were originally many archers, perhaps representing Darius's royal guards or symbolizing the entire Persian people. (Musée du Louvre, Paris, France/Erich Lessing/Art Resource, NY)

legal cases, and maintained order. He was assisted by a council, and also by officials and army leaders sent from Persepolis who made sure that the satrap knew the will of the king and that the king knew what was going on in the provinces. This system lessened opposition to Persian rule by making local elites part of the system of government, although sometimes satraps used their authority to build up independent power.

Communication and trade were eased by a sophisticated system of roads linking the empire from the coast of Asia Minor to the valley of the Indus River. On the roads were way stations where royal messengers could get food and horses, a system that allowed messages to be communicated quickly, much like the famed pony express in the American West. These roads meant that the king was usually in close touch

■ **Persian Empire**   A large empire centered in today's Iran that used force and diplomacy to consolidate its power and that allowed cultural diversity.

■ **satraps**   Administrators in the Persian Empire who controlled local government, collected taxes, heard legal cases, and maintained order.

with officials and subjects. The roads also simplified the defense of the empire by making it easier to move Persian armies. In addition, the system allowed the easy flow of trade, which Persian rulers further encouraged by building canals, including one that linked the Red Sea and the Nile.

## Persian Religion

Iranian religion was originally tied to nature, with many gods. Ahuramazda (ah-HOOR-uh-MAZ-duh), the chief god, was the creator of all living creatures. Mithra, the sun-god whose cult would later spread throughout the Roman Empire, saw to justice and redemption. Fire was a particularly important god, and fire was often part of religious rituals. A priestly class, the Magi, developed among the Medes to officiate at sacrifices, chant prayers to the gods, and tend the sacred flame.

Around 600 B.C.E., the ideas of Zoroaster, a thinker and preacher whose dates are uncertain, began to gain prominence. Zoroaster is regarded as the author of key religious texts, later gathered together in a collection of sacred texts called the Avesta. (See "Thinking Like a Historian: The Moral Life," page 40.) He introduced new spiritual concepts to the Iranian people, stressing devotion to Ahuramazda alone instead of many gods, and emphasizing the individual's responsibility to choose between the forces of creation, truth, and order and those of nothingness, chaos, falsehood, and disorder. Zoroaster taught that people possessed the free will to decide between these and that they must rely on their own conscience to guide them through an active life in which they focused on "good thoughts, good words, and good deeds." Their decisions were crucial, he warned, for there would come a time of reckoning. At the end of time, the forces of order would win, and the victorious Ahuramazda, like the Egyptian god Osiris (see "Egyptian Religion" in Chapter 1), would preside over a last judgment to determine each person's eternal fate. Those who had lived according to good and truth would enter a divine kingdom. Liars and the wicked, denied this blessed immortality, would be condemned to eternal pain, darkness, and punishment. Thus Zoroaster preached a last judgment that led to a heaven or a hell.

Scholars — and contemporary Zoroastrians — debate whether Zoroaster saw the forces of disorder as a malevolent deity named Angra Mainyu who was co-eternal with and independent from Ahuramazda, or whether he was simply using this term to mean "evil thoughts" or "a destructive spirit." Later

forms of **Zoroastrianism** followed each of these lines of understanding. Most Zoroastrians believed that the good Ahuramazda and the evil Angra Mainyu were locked together in a cosmic battle for the human race, a religious conceptualization that scholars call dualism, which was rejected in Judaism and Christianity. Some had a more monotheistic interpretation, however, and saw Ahuramazda as the only uncreated god.

Whenever he actually lived, Zoroaster's writings were spread by teachers, and King Darius began to use Zoroastrian language and images. Under the protection of the Persian kings, Zoroastrian ideas spread throughout Iran and the rest of the Persian Empire, and then beyond this into central China. Zoroastrianism became the official religion of the later Persian Empire ruled by the Sassanid dynasty, and much later Zoroastrians migrated to western India, where they became known as Parsis and still live today. Zoroastrianism survived the fall of the Persian Empire to influence Christianity, Islam, and Buddhism, largely because of its belief in a just life on earth and a happy afterlife. Good behavior in the world, even though unrecognized at the time, would receive ample reward in the hereafter. Evil, no matter how powerful in life, would be punished after death. In some form or another, Zoroastrian concepts still pervade many modern religions, and Zoroastrianism still exists as a religion.

## Persian Art and Culture

The Persians made significant contributions to art and culture. They produced amazing works in gold and silver, often with inlaid jewels and semiprecious stones. They transformed the Assyrian tradition of realistic monumental sculpture from one that celebrated gory details of slaughter to one that showed both the Persians and their subjects as dignified. They noted and carved the physical features of their subjects: their hair, their clothing, their tools and weapons. Because they depicted both themselves and non-Persians realistically, Persian art serves as an excellent source for learning about the weapons, tools, clothing, and even hairstyles of many peoples of the area.

These carvings adorned temples and other large buildings in cities throughout the empire, and the Persians also built new cities from the ground up. The most spectacular of these was Persepolis, designed as a residence for the kings and an administrative and cultural center. The architecture of Persepolis combined elements found in many parts of the empire. Underneath the city was a system of closed water pipes, drainage canals, and conduits that allowed water from nearby mountains to flow into the city without flooding it, provided water for households and plantings inside the city, and carried away sewage and waste from the city's

■ **Zoroastrianism**  Religion based on the ideas of Zoroaster that stressed devotion to the god Ahuramazda alone and that emphasized the individual's responsibility to choose between good and evil.

**Gold Staff Handle**
Roaring lions made from lapis lazuli decorate this golden socket from the seventh to sixth century B.C.E. Persia. Then, as now, lions were a symbol of royalty and strength. Fragments of bone in the socket indicate that this was the handle of a long staff, like that seen held by Assyrian and Persian kings. (British Museum, London, UK/Bridgeman Images)

many residents. The Persians thus further improved the technology for handling water that had been essential in this area since the time of the Sumerians.

The Persians allowed the peoples they conquered to maintain their own customs and beliefs, as long as they paid the proper amount of taxes and did not rebel. Persian rule resulted in an empire that brought people together in a new political system, with a culture that blended older and newer religious traditions and ways of seeing the world. Even the Persians' opponents, including the Greeks who would eventually conquer the Persian Empire, admired their art and institutions.

## NOTES

1. James H. Breasted, *Ancient Records of Egypt*, vol. 4 (Chicago: University of Chicago Press, 1907), para. 398.
2. James B. Pritchard, ed., *Ancient Near Eastern Texts Relating to the Old Testament—Third Edition with Supplement*, p. 288. © 1950, 1955, 1969, renewed 1978 by Princeton University Press; permission conveyed through Copyright Clearance Center, Inc.

**King Darius Defeats His Enemies**    King Darius of Persia proclaimed victory over his enemies with a written inscription and sculpture high on a cliff near Mount Behistun so all could see. He attributed his victory to Ahuramazda, the god of Zoroastrianism, whose symbol is carved above the chained prisoners. The proclamation itself was inscribed in three different cuneiform script languages, and it has been a vital tool for scholars as they have deciphered these ancient languages. (Vivienne Sharp/Heritage Images/Newscom)

# LOOKING BACK LOOKING AHEAD

During the centuries following the Bronze Age Collapse, natives and newcomers brought order to life across the ancient Near East. As Egypt fell, small kingdoms, including those of the Nubians, Phoenicians, and Hebrews, grew and prospered. Regular trade and communication continued, and new products and ideas were transported by sea and land. Beginning about 900 B.C.E., the Assyrians created a large state through military conquest that was often brutal, though they also developed effective structures of rule through which taxes flowed to their leaders. The Persians, an Iranian people whose center of power was east of Mesopotamia, then established an even larger empire, governing through local officials and building beautiful cities.

The lands on the northern shore of the Mediterranean were beyond the borders of the urbanized cultures and centralized empires of the ancient Near East but maintained contact with them through trade and migration. As the Persian Empire continued to expand, it looked further westward toward these lands, including Greece, as possible further conquests. Greek-speaking people living in Anatolia and traveling more widely throughout the area had also absorbed numerous aspects of Persian and other more urbanized cultures they had encountered. They learned of Near Eastern religions and myths, and of the sagas of heroic wars. They also acquired many of the advanced technologies developed by their eastern neighbors, including the use of bronze and later iron, the phonetic alphabet, wine making, and shipbuilding. The Greeks combined these borrowings with their own traditions, ideas, and talents to create a distinct civilization, one that fundamentally shaped the subsequent development of Western society.

## Make Connections

Think about the larger developments and continuities within and across chapters.

1. How were the Assyrian and Persian Empires similar to earlier river valley civilizations? How were they different? What might explain the pattern of similarities and differences?

2. The Persians and Assyrians became significant in history through military conquest and the establishment of empires, and the Phoenicians and Hebrews through cultural creations. Which of these were longer-lasting, and why?

3. What lessons and insights might the Persian Empire have to offer future diverse states and empires, including those of the modern world?

# 2   REVIEW & EXPLORE

## Identify Key Terms

Identify and explain the significance of each item below.

Iron Age (p. 32)

Kush (p. 33)

Phoenicians (p. 34)

monotheism (p. 36)

Yahweh (p. 36)

Torah (p. 38)

Covenant (p. 38)

Assyrian Empire (p. 44)

Persian Empire (p. 48)

satraps (p. 49)

Zoroastrianism (p. 50)

## Review the Main Ideas

Answer the section heading questions from the chapter.

**1.** How did iron technology shape new states after 1200 B.C.E.? (p. 32)

**2.** How did the Hebrews create an enduring religious tradition? (p. 36)

**3.** How did the Assyrians and Neo-Babylonians gain and lose power? (p. 44)

**4.** How did the Persians conquer and rule their extensive empire? (p. 48)

## Suggested Resources

### BOOKS

- Briant, Pierre. *From Cyrus to Alexander*. 2002. A superb treatment of the entire Persian Empire.

- Clark, Peter. *Zoroastrianism: An Introduction to an Ancient Faith*. 1998. The best introduction to the essence of Zoroastrianism.

- Edwards, David N. *The Nubian Past*. 2004. Studies the history of Nubia and the Sudan, incorporating archaeological evidence to supplement historical sources.

- Foster, Benjamin R. *Civilizations of Ancient Iraq*. 2009. Discusses the development of cities and the empires of Babylonia and Assyria.

- Gates, Charles. *Ancient Cities: The Archaeology of Urban Life in the Ancient Near East and Egypt, Greece, and Rome*. 2003. Provides a survey of ancient life primarily from an archaeological point of view, but also includes cultural and social information.

- Goldenberg, Robert. *The Origins of Judaism: From Canaan to the Rise of Islam*. 2007. Examines the development of Jewish ideas and traditions.

- Kriwaczek, Paul. *In Search of Zarathustra: Across Iran and Central Asia to Find the World's First Prophet*. 2002.

An award-winning BBC journalist follows the legacy of Zoroaster back through time.

- Kugel, James. *The God of Old: Inside the Lost World of the Bible*. 2004. A noted biblical scholar surveys the way the ancient Israelites understood God.

- Markoe, Glenn E. *The Phoenicians*. 2000. A fresh investigation of the Phoenicians at home and abroad in the western Mediterranean over their long history, with many illustrations.

- Meyers, Carol. *Rediscovering Eve: Ancient Israelite Women in Context*. 2012. A brief study designed for general readers that draws on archaeology and ethnography along with biblical texts.

- Morkot, Robert G. *The Black Pharaohs: Egypt's Nubian Rulers*. 2000. Examines the growth of the Kushite kingdom and its rule over pharaonic Egypt in the eighth century B.C.E.

- Provan, Iain, V. Philips Long, and Tremper Longman III. *A Biblical History of Israel*. 2003. A history of ancient Israel that relies primarily on the biblical text.

### MEDIA

- *Ancient Sudan-Nubia*. An informative website with information and visual material on Kush, Nubia, and Meroë. **www.ancientsudan.org/**

- *The Bible's Buried Secrets* (*Nova*, 2008). In this two-hour documentary, *Nova* examines the ancient Israelites through biblical and other ancient texts and archaeological artifacts.

- *Engineering an Empire: The Persians* (History Channel, 2006). This hour-long documentary focuses on the engineering of the Persian Empire, especially its canals and roads.

- *Israel Antiquities Authority*. Official website of the Israel Antiquities Authority, with a huge collection of artifacts from many periods in the "National Treasures" section. **www.antiquities.org.il/home_eng.asp**

- *Nubia: The Forgotten Kingdom* (Discovery Channel, 2003). Archaeologists excavate temples and markets of the ancient city of Dangeil and examine Nubia's links with Egypt.

- *Phoenicia: The Phoenician Ship Expedition*. Traces the building and voyage of a reconstruction of a Phoenician trading vessel that in 2008–2010 retraced the Phoenicians' route around Africa and in 2012 sailed to London for the Olympics. **phoenicia.org .uk/index.htm**

- *Quest for the Phoenicians* (National Geographic, 2004). Scientists use DNA analysis and other modern technologies to examine the migrations and the sailing routes of the ancient Phoenicians.

# 3

# The Development of Greek Society and Culture

## ca. 3000–338 B.C.E.

**The people of ancient Greece** built on the traditions and ideas of earlier societies to develop a culture that fundamentally shaped the intellectual and cultural traditions of Western civilization. Humans came into Greece over many thousands of years, in waves of migrants whose place of origin and cultural characteristics have been the source of much scholarly debate. The first to arrive were foragers, but techniques of agriculture and animal domestication had spread into Greece from Turkey by about 6500 B.C.E., after which small farming communities worked much of the land. Early settlers to Greece brought skills in making bronze weapons and tools, which became more common around 3000 B.C.E.

Drawing on their day-to-day experiences as well as human reason, people in Greece developed ways of questioning, understanding, and explaining the world around them and the place of humans in it, which grew into modern philosophy and science. They also created new political forms such as the polis and new types of literature and art. The history of the Greeks is divided into three broad periods, two of which are covered in this chapter: the Helladic period of the Bronze Age, roughly 3000 B.C.E. to 1100 B.C.E.; and the Hellenic period, from 1100 B.C.E. to 338 B.C.E., when Greece was conquered by Macedonia. The later Hellenistic period is covered in Chapter 4. ■

## CHAPTER PREVIEW

- How did the geography of Greece shape its earliest kingdoms?

- What was the role of the polis in Greek society?

- How did the wars of the classical period shape Greek history?

- What ancient Greek ideas and ideals have had a lasting influence?

**Life and Death in Ancient Greece**
This painting on the side of a large jar, made in the sixth century B.C.E. and used for mixing wine and water, shows warriors in the Trojan War arguing over the body of Patroclus, a Greek warrior beloved by Achilles, after he was killed by the Trojan prince Hektor. Scenes from myths and epics surrounded the ancient Greeks in their homes and public spaces, communicating cultural values.
(National Archeological Museum, Athens, Greece/De Agostini Picture Library/G. Dagli Orti/ Bridgeman Images)

# How did the geography of Greece shape its earliest kingdoms?

During the Bronze Age, which for Greek history is called the Helladic period, early settlers in Greece began establishing small communities contoured by the mountains and small plains that shaped the land. These communities sometimes joined together to form kingdoms, most prominently the Minoan kingdom on the island of Crete and the Mycenaean kingdom on the mainland. The Minoan and Mycenaean societies flourished for centuries until the Bronze Age Collapse, when Greece entered a period of decline known as the Dark Age (ca. 1100–800 B.C.E.). Epic poems composed by Homer and Hesiod after the Dark Age provide the poets' versions of what life may have been like in these early Greek kingdoms.

## Geography and Settlement

Hellas, as the Greeks still call their land, encompassed the Greek peninsula, the islands of the Aegean (ah-GEE-uhn) Sea, and the lands bordering the Aegean, an area known as the Aegean basin (Map 3.1). Geography acts as an enormously divisive force in Greek life; mountains divide the land, and although there are good harbors on the sea, there are no navigable rivers. Much of the land is rocky and not very fertile, which meant that food availability was a constant concern.

The major regions of Greece were Thessaly and Macedonia in the north, and Boeotia (bee-OH-shuh) and the large island of Euboea (YOU-boh-ee-ah) in the center, lands marked by fertile plains that helped

**MAP 3.1 Classical Greece, 500–338 B.C.E.** In antiquity, the home of the Greeks included the islands of the Aegean and the western shore of Turkey as well as the Greek peninsula itself. Crete, the home of Minoan civilization, is the large island at the bottom of the map.

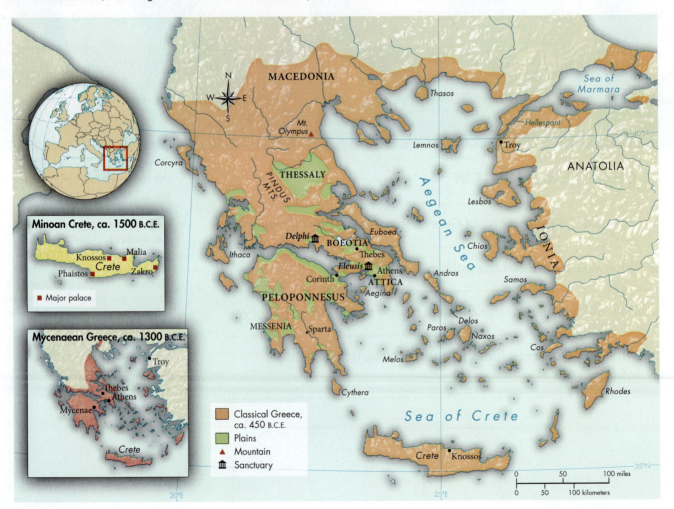

# TIMELINE

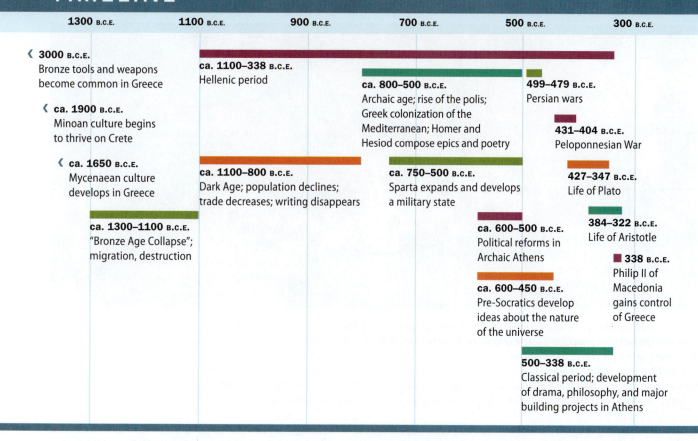

| 1300 B.C.E. | 1100 B.C.E. | 900 B.C.E. | 700 B.C.E. | 500 B.C.E. | 300 B.C.E. |
|---|---|---|---|---|---|

**‹ 3000 B.C.E.**
Bronze tools and weapons become common in Greece

**‹ ca. 1900 B.C.E.**
Minoan culture begins to thrive on Crete

**‹ ca. 1650 B.C.E.**
Mycenaean culture develops in Greece

**ca. 1300–1100 B.C.E.**
"Bronze Age Collapse"; migration, destruction

**ca. 1100–338 B.C.E.**
Hellenic period

**ca. 1100–800 B.C.E.**
Dark Age; population declines; trade decreases; writing disappears

**ca. 800–500 B.C.E.**
Archaic age; rise of the polis; Greek colonization of the Mediterranean; Homer and Hesiod compose epics and poetry

**ca. 750–500 B.C.E.**
Sparta expands and develops a military state

**ca. 600–500 B.C.E.**
Political reforms in Archaic Athens

**ca. 600–450 B.C.E.**
Pre-Socratics develop ideas about the nature of the universe

**500–338 B.C.E.**
Classical period; development of drama, philosophy, and major building projects in Athens

**499–479 B.C.E.**
Persian wars

**431–404 B.C.E.**
Peloponnesian War

**427–347 B.C.E.**
Life of Plato

**384–322 B.C.E.**
Life of Aristotle

**338 B.C.E.**
Philip II of Macedonia gains control of Greece

---

to sustain a strong population capable of serving as formidable cavalry and infantry. Immediately to the south of Boeotia was Attica, with plains for wheat and hillier areas where olives and wine grapes flourished. Attica's harbors looked to the Aegean, which invited its inhabitants, the Athenians, to concentrate on maritime commerce. Still farther south, the Peloponnesus (peh-luh-puh-NEE-suhs), a large peninsula connected to the rest of mainland Greece by a very narrow isthmus at Corinth, was a patchwork of high mountains and small plains that divided the area into several regions. Beyond the coast, the islands of the Aegean served as stepping-stones to Anatolia, present-day Turkey.

The geographical fragmentation of Greece encouraged political fragmentation. Communications were poor, with rocky tracks far more common than roads. Early in Greek history, several kingdoms did emerge, but the rugged terrain prohibited the growth of a great empire like those of Mesopotamia or Egypt. Instead tiny states became the most common form of government.

## The Minoans

On the large island of Crete, Bronze Age farmers and fishermen began to trade their surpluses with their neighbors, and cities grew, housing artisans and merchants. Beginning about 2000 B.C.E., Cretan traders voyaged throughout the eastern Mediterranean and the Aegean. Social hierarchies developed, and in many

cities certain individuals came to hold power. The Cretans began to use writing about 1900 B.C.E., in a form later scholars called Linear A. This has not been deciphered, but scholars know that the language of Crete was not related to Greek, so they do not consider the Cretans "Greek."

What we can know about the culture of Crete depends on archaeological and artistic evidence, and of this there is a great deal. At about the same time that writing began, rulers in several cities of Crete began to build large structures with hundreds of interconnected rooms. The largest of these, at Knossos (NOH-suhs), has over a thousand rooms, with pipes for bringing in drinking water and sewers to get rid of waste. The archaeologists who discovered these huge structures called them "palaces," and they named the flourishing and vibrant culture of this era **Minoan**, after a mythical king of Crete, Minos.

Few specifics are known about Minoan political life except that a king and a group of nobles stood at its head. Minoan life was long thought to have been relatively peaceful, but new excavations are revealing more and more walls around cities, which has called the peaceful nature of Minoan society into question. In terms of their religious life, Minoans appear to have worshipped goddesses far more than gods. Whether this translated into more egalitarian gender roles for real people is unclear, but surviving Minoan art shows women as well as men

---

**■ Minoan** A wealthy and vibrant culture on Crete from around 1900 B.C.E. to 1450 B.C.E., ruled by a king with a large palace at Knossos.

**Minoan Bull-Leaping**   A colorful fresco dating from around 1600 B.C.E. found at the palace of Knossos on Crete shows three people in a scene of bull-leaping. The outside figures are women, who are generally portrayed with light skin to represent women's association with the household, and the figure leaping over the bull is a man, whose reddish skin associates him with the outdoors. Bulls were venerated in Minoan culture, and this may be a scene of an actual ritual sport done at the palace, a spectacle celebrating human athletic prowess and mastery of nature. (National Archaeological Museum, Athens, Greece/Bridgeman Images)

leading religious activities, watching entertainment, and engaging in athletic competitions.

Beginning about 1700 B.C.E. Minoan society was disrupted by a series of earthquakes and volcanic eruptions on nearby islands, some of which resulted in large tsunamis. The largest of these was a huge volcanic eruption that devastated the island of Thera to the north of Crete, burying the Minoan town there in lava and causing it to collapse into the sea. This eruption, one of the largest in recorded history, may have been the origin of the story of the mythical kingdom of Atlantis, a wealthy kingdom with beautiful buildings that had sunk under the ocean. The eruption on Thera was long seen as the most important cause of the collapse of Minoan civilization, but scholars using radiocarbon and other types of scientific dating have called this theory into question, as the eruption seems to have occurred somewhat earlier than 1600 B.C.E., and Minoan society did not collapse until more than two centuries later. In fact, new settlements and palaces were often built on Crete following the earthquakes and the eruption of Thera.

## The Mycenaeans

As Minoan culture was flourishing on Crete, a different type of society developed on the mainland. This society was founded by groups who had migrated there after 2000 B.C.E. By about 1650 B.C.E., one group of these

immigrants had raised palaces and established cities at Thebes, Athens, Mycenae (migh-SEE-nee), and elsewhere. These palace-centers ruled by local kings formed a loose alliance under the authority of the king of Mycenae, and the archaeologists who first discovered traces of this culture called it **Mycenaean** (migh-see-NEE-an).

As in Crete, the political unit in Mycenaean Greece was the kingdom, and the king and his warrior aristocracy stood at the top of society. The seat and symbol of the king's power was his palace, which was also the economic center of the kingdom. Within the palace's walls, royal artisans fashioned gold jewelry and rich ornaments, made pottery, forged weapons, prepared hides and wool for clothing, and manufactured the other goods needed by the king and his supporters. The Mycenaean economy was marked by an extensive division of labor, and at the bottom of the social scale were male and female slaves.

Palace scribes kept records with a script known as Linear B, which scholars realized was an early form of Greek and have learned to read. Thus, they consider the Mycenaeans the first truly "Greek" culture to emerge in this area. Information on Mycenaean culture comes through inscriptions and other forms of written records as well as buildings and other objects. All of these point to a society in which war was common. Mycenaean cities were all fortified by thick stone walls, and graves contain bronze spears, javelins, swords, helmets, and the first examples of metal armor known in the world. Mycenaean kingdoms appear to have fought regularly with one another.

■ **Mycenaean**   A Bronze Age culture that flourished in Greece from about 1650 B.C.E. to 1100 B.C.E., building fortified palaces and cities.

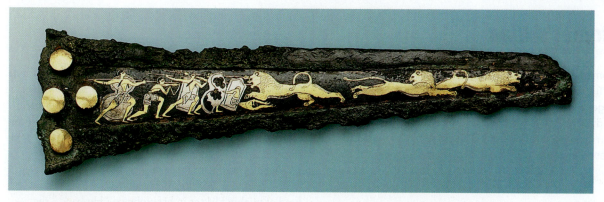

**Mycenaean Dagger Blade**   This scene in gold and silver on the blade of an iron dagger depicts hunters armed with spears and protected by shields defending themselves against charging lions. Judging by the number of hunting scenes in surviving Mycenaean art, the Mycenaeans seemed to enjoy the thrill and the danger of hunting. (National Archaeological Museum, Athens, Greece/Bridgeman Images)

Contacts between the Minoans and Mycenaeans were originally peaceful, and Minoan culture and trade goods flooded the Greek mainland. But most scholars think that around 1450 B.C.E., possibly in the wake of another earthquake that left Crete vulnerable, the Mycenaeans attacked Crete, destroying many towns and occupying Knossos. For about the next fifty years, the Mycenaeans ruled much of the island. The palaces at Knossos and other cities of the Aegean became grander as wealth gained through trade and tribute flowed into the treasuries of various Mycenaean kings. Linear B replaced Linear A as a writing system, a further sign of Mycenaean domination.

Prosperity did not bring peace, however; between 1300 and 1100 B.C.E., various kingdoms in and beyond Greece ravaged one another in a savage series of wars that destroyed both the Minoan and Mycenaean civilizations. Among these wars was perhaps one that later became known as the Trojan War, fought by Greeks in Ionia, the coastal area of Anatolia.

The fall of the Minoans and Mycenaeans was part of what scholars see as a general collapse of Bronze Age civilizations in the eastern Mediterranean (see Chapters 1 and 2). This collapse appears to have had a number of causes: internal economic and social problems; invasions and migrations by outsiders, who destroyed cities and disrupted trade and production; changes in warfare and weaponry, particularly the adoption of iron weapons, which made foot soldiers the most important factor in battles and reduced the power of kings and wealthy nobles fighting from chariots; and natural disasters, which reduced the amount of food and contributed to famines.

These factors worked together to usher in a period of poverty and disruption that historians of Greece have traditionally called the Dark Age (ca. 1100–800 B.C.E.). Cities were destroyed, population declined, villages were abandoned, and trade decreased. Pottery became simpler, and jewelry and other grave goods became less ornate. Even writing, which had not been widespread previously, was a casualty of the chaos, and Linear A and B inscriptions were no longer produced.

The Bronze Age Collapse led to the widespread and prolonged movement of Greek peoples, both within Greece itself and beyond. They dispersed beyond mainland Greece farther south to the islands of the Aegean and in greater strength across the Aegean to the shores of Anatolia, arriving at a time when traditional states and empires had collapsed. By the conclusion of the Dark Age, the Greeks had spread their culture throughout the Aegean basin and, like many other cultures around the Mediterranean and the Near East, they had adopted iron.

## Homer, Hesiod, and the Epic

Archaeological sources from the Dark Age are less rich than those from the periods that came after, and so they are often used in conjunction with literary sources written in later centuries to give us a more complete picture of the era. Unlike the Hebrews, the Greeks had no sacred book that chronicled their past. Instead they had epics, poetic tales of legendary heroes and of the times when people believed the gods still walked the earth. Of these, the *Iliad* and the *Odyssey* are the most important. Most scholars think they were composed in the eighth or seventh century B.C.E. By the fifth century B.C.E. they were attributed to a poet named Homer, though whether Homer was an actual historical individual is debated. What is not debated is their long-lasting impact, both on later Greek culture and on the Western world.

The *Iliad* recounts the tale of the Trojan War of the late Bronze Age. As Homer tells it, the Achaeans (uh-KEE-uhnz), the name he gives to the Mycenaeans, sent an expedition to besiege the city of Troy and

## Homer's *Iliad*

Homer's *Iliad* unfolds during the tenth year of the siege of Troy by the Greeks. It opens with lines about Achilles's anger and closes with Priam, the king of Troy, bringing the body of his son Hektor back to Troy after Achilles has killed him in revenge for Hektor's killing of Achilles's beloved friend Patroclus.

### Book 1

Sing, O goddess, the anger of Achilles son of Peleus, that brought countless ills upon the Achaeans. Many a brave soul did it send hurrying down to Hades [underworld], and many a hero did it yield a prey to dogs and vultures, for so was the will of Zeus fulfilled from the day on which the son of Atreus, king of men [i.e., Agamemnon], and great Achilles, first fell out with one another.

### Book 24

[Priam goes to Achilles's tent, asking him for Hektor's body.] "Think of your father, O Achilles like unto the gods, who is such even as I am, on the sad threshold of old age. It may be that those who dwell near him harass him, and there is none to keep war and ruin from him. Yet when he hears of you being still alive, he is glad, and his days are full of hope that he shall see his dear son come home to him from Troy; but I, wretched man that I am, had the bravest in all Troy for my sons, and there is not one of them left. I had fifty sons when the Achaeans came here. . . . The greater part of them has fierce Ares [the god of war] laid low, and Hektor, him who was alone left, him who was the guardian of the city and ourselves, him have you lately slain; therefore I am now come to the ships of the Achaeans to ransom his body from you. . . ."

[Achilles answers.] "Unhappy man, you have indeed been greatly daring; how could you venture to come alone to the ships of the Achaeans, and enter the presence of him who has slain so many of your brave sons? You must have iron courage: sit now upon this seat, and for all our grief we will hide our sorrows in our hearts, for weeping will not avail us. The immortals know no care, yet the lot they spin for man is full of sorrow. . . ."

[Achilles lets Priam take the body of Hektor.] Andromache [Hektor's wife] led their wailing as she clasped the head of mighty Hektor in her embrace. "Husband," she cried, "you have died young, and leave me in your house a widow; he of whom we are the ill-starred parents is still a mere child, and I fear he may not reach manhood. Ere he can do so our city will be razed and overthrown. . . . Our women will be carried away captives to the ships, and I among them; while you, my child, who will be with me will be put to some unseemly tasks, working for a cruel master. Or, may be, some Achaean will hurl you (O miserable death) from our walls, to avenge some brother, son, or father whom Hektor slew. . . . You have left, O Hektor, sorrow unutterable to your parents, and my own grief is greatest of all."

### EVALUATE THE EVIDENCE

1. Achilles is generally seen as the hero of the *Iliad*. Do the first lines of the epic present him in a heroic light?
2. How does Homer portray the relationship between the gods and humans?
3. How do the exchange between Achilles and Priam and Andromache's lament in the last book of the poem portray death in war? Does the search for battlefield glory seem worth it?

Source: Homer, *The Iliad of Homer*, trans. Samuel Butler (Longmans, Green and Co.: London, 1898), http://www.perseus.tufts.edu/hopper/text?doc=Perseus%3Atext%3A1999.01.0217%3Abook%3D1%3Acard%3D1 and http://www.perseus.tufts.edu/hopper/text?doc=Perseus:text:1999.01.0217:-book=24.

to retrieve Helen, the wife of one of the Mycenaean kings, who was abducted by Paris, the Trojan king's son. The epic is full of bloody battles, duels between individual warriors, surprise attacks, revenge killings, desperate grief, noble speeches, and interventions by the gods, who also fight among themselves. At its heart is the quarrel between the Mycenaean king, Agamemnon, and the stormy hero of the poem, Achilles (uh-KIHL-eez), whose uncontrolled anger brings suffering to all. (See "Evaluating Written Evidence: Homer's *Iliad*," above.) Ancient Greeks and Romans believed that the Trojan War was a real event

embellished by poetic retelling, but by the modern era most people regarded it as a myth until the ruins of Troy were discovered in the late nineteenth century. Today most scholars think that the core of the story was a composite of many conflicts, although the characters are not historical.

Homer's *Odyssey* recounts the adventures of Odysseus (oh-DIH-see-uhs), a wise and fearless hero of the war at Troy, during his ten-year voyage home. He encounters many dangers, storms, and adventures, but he finally reaches his home and unites again with Penelope, the ideal wife, dedicated to her husband and family.

Both of Homer's epics portray engaging but flawed characters who are larger than life yet human. The men and women at the center of the stories display the quality known as *arête* (ah-reh-TAY), that is, excellence and living up to one's fullest potential. Homer also portrays the gods and goddesses as Greeks understood them, not perfect beings but instead much like humans, with emotions, needs, and desires. They generally sit on Mount Olympus in the north of Greece and watch the fighting at Troy, although they sometimes participate in the action.

Greeks also learned about the gods and goddesses of their polytheistic system from another poet, Hesiod (HEH-see-uhd), who most scholars think lived sometime between 750 and 650 B.C.E. In his poem, the *Theogony*, Hesiod combined Mesopotamian myths with a variety of Greek oral traditions to forge a coherent story of the origin of the gods. In another of his poems, *Works and Days*, the gods watch over the earth, looking for justice and injustice, while leaving the great mass of men and women to live lives of hard work and endless toil.

# What was the role of the polis in Greek society?

Homer and Hesiod both lived in the era after the Dark Age, which later historians have termed the Archaic age (800–500 B.C.E.). The most important political change in this period was the development of the **polis** (PAH-luhs; plural *poleis*), a word generally translated as "city-state." With the polis, the Greeks established a new type of political structure. During the Archaic period, poleis established colonies throughout much of the Mediterranean, spreading Greek culture. Two particular poleis, each with a distinctive system of government, rose to prominence on the Greek mainland: Sparta and Athens.

## Organization of the Polis

The Greek polis was not the first form of city-state to emerge. The earliest states in Sumer were also city-states, as were many of the small Mycenaean kingdoms. What differentiated the new Greek model from older city-states is the fact that the polis was more than a political institution; it was a community of citizens with their own customs and laws. With one exception, the poleis that emerged after 800 did not have kings but instead were self-governing. The physical, religious, and political forms of the polis varied from place to place, but everywhere the polis was relatively small, reflecting the fragmented geography of Greece. The very smallness of the polis enabled Greeks to see how they fit individually into the overall system—and how the individual parts made up the social whole. This notion of community was fundamental to the polis and was the very badge of Greekness.

Poleis developed from Dark Age towns. When fully developed, each polis normally shared a surprisingly large number of features with other poleis. Physically a polis was a society of people who lived in a city (*asty*) and cultivated the surrounding countryside (*chora*). The countryside was essential to the economy of the polis and provided food to sustain the entire population. By the fifth century B.C.E., the city was generally surrounded by a wall. The city contained a point, usually elevated, called the acropolis, and a public square or marketplace called the agora (ah-guh-RAH). On the acropolis, people built temples, altars, public monuments, and various dedications to the gods of the polis. The agora was the political center of the polis. In the agora were shops, public buildings, and courts.

All poleis, with one exception, did not have standing armies. Instead they largely relied on their citizens for protection. Wealthy aristocrats often served as cavalry. The backbone of the army, however, was the heavily armed infantry, or **hoplites**, middle-class and upper-middle-class propertied citizens who could afford leather and bronze armor and helmets, shields, and iron-tipped weapons, which they purchased themselves. They marched and fought in a close rectangular formation known as a *phalanx*, holding their shields together to form a solid wall, with the spears of the front row sticking out over the tops of the shields. As long as the phalanx stayed in formation, the hoplites presented an enemy with an impenetrable wall. This meant that commanders preferred to fight battles on open plains, where the hoplites could more easily maintain the phalanx, rather than in the narrow mountain passes that were common throughout much of Greece.

For naval battles, cities also relied on citizens as rowers for their warships, though these citizens were usually paid. An experienced rower was valuable because he had learned how to row in rhythm with many other men, and some rowers became professionals who hired themselves out to any military leader. In times of intense warfare cities also used slaves as rowers because there were not enough free men available.

- **polis**  Generally translated as "city-state," it was the basic political and institutional unit of Greece in the Hellenic period.

- **hoplites**  Heavily armed citizens who served as infantry troops and fought to defend the polis.

## Governing Structures

Each Greek polis had one of several different types of government. Monarchy, rule by a king, had been prevalent during the Mycenaean period but declined thereafter. Sporadic periods of violent political and social upheaval often led to the seizure of power by one man, a type of government the Greeks called **tyranny**. Tyrants generally came to power by using their wealth or by negotiating to win a political following that toppled the existing legal government. In contrast to its contemporary meaning, however, tyranny in ancient Greece did not necessarily mean oppressive rule. Some tyrants used their power to benefit average citizens by helping to limit the power of the landowning aristocracy, which made them popular.

Other types of government in the Archaic age were democracy and oligarchy. **Democracy** translates as "the power of the people" but was actually rule by citizens, not the people as a whole. Almost all Greek cities defined a citizen as an adult man with at least one or, at some times and places, two citizen parents. Women were citizens for religious and reproductive purposes, but their citizenship did not give them the right to participate in government. Free men who were not children of a citizen, resident foreigners, and slaves were not citizens and had no political voice. Thus ancient Greek democracy did not reflect the modern concept that all people are created equal, but it did permit male citizens to share equally in determining the diplomatic and military policies of the polis, without respect to wealth. This comparatively broad basis of participation made Greek democracy an appealing model to some political thinkers across the ages, although others feared direct democracy and viewed it as "mob rule."

**Oligarchy**, which literally means "the rule of the few," was government by citizens who met a minimum property requirement. Many Greeks preferred oligarchy because it provided more political stability than democracy did. (Many of the Founding Fathers of the United States agreed, and they established a system in which the most important elections were indirect and only property owners had the right to vote.) Although oligarchy was the government of the prosperous, it left the door open to political and social advancement. If members of the polis obtained enough wealth to meet property or money qualifications, they could enter the governing circle.

## Overseas Expansion

The development of the polis coincided with the growth of the Greek world in both wealth and numbers, which brought new problems. The increase in population created more demand for food than the land could supply. The resulting social and political tensions drove many people to seek new homes outside Greece. In some cases the losers in a conflict within a polis were forced to leave.

Greeks from the mainland and Ionia traveled throughout the Mediterranean, sailing in great numbers to Sicily and southern Italy (Map 3.2). Here they conquered local peoples, though also later intermarried with them, and established prosperous cities. Some adventurous Greeks sailed farther west to Sardinia, France, Spain, and perhaps even the Canary Islands. In Sardinia they first established trading stations and then permanent towns. From these new outposts Greek influence extended to southern France.

Colonization changed the entire Greek world, both at home and abroad. In economic terms the expansion of the Greeks created a much larger market for agricultural and manufactured goods. From the east, especially from the northern coast of the Black Sea, came wheat. In return flowed Greek wine and olive oil, which could not be produced in the harsher climate of the north. Greek-manufactured goods, notably rich jewelry and fine pottery, circulated from southern Russia to Spain. During the same period the Greeks adopted the custom of minting coins from metal, first developed in the kingdom of Lydia in Anatolia. Coins provided many advantages

**Golden Comb** This golden comb, produced about 400 B.C.E. in Scythia (see Map 3.2), shows a battle between three warriors, perhaps the three brothers who are the legendary founders of Scythia. Their dress shows a combination of Greek and Eastern details; the mounted horseman is clothed with largely Greek armor, while the warriors on foot are wearing Eastern dress. The comb may have been made by a Greek craftsman who had migrated to the Black Sea area, as the Greeks had established colonies there, but it was buried in a Scythian burial mound. (State Hermitage Museum, St. Petersburg, Russia/Bridgeman Images)

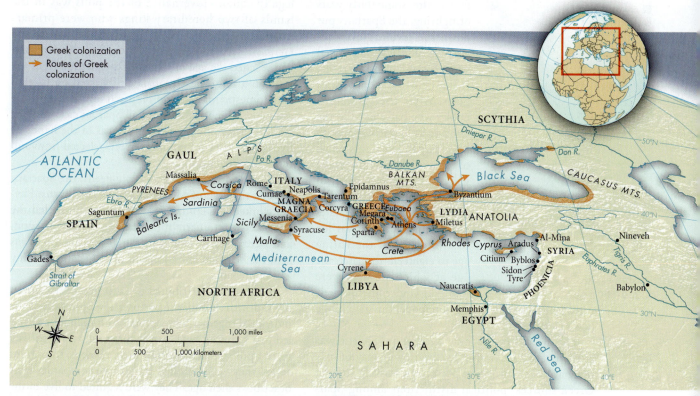

**MAP 3.2 Greek Colonization, ca. 750–550 B.C.E.** The Greeks established colonies along the shores of the Mediterranean and the Black Sea, spreading Greek culture and creating a large trading network.

over barter: they allowed merchants to set the value of goods in a determined system, they could be stored easily, and they allowed for more complex exchanges than did direct barter.

New colonies were planned and initially supplied by the *metropolis*, or "mother city." Once founded, however, they were independent of the metropolis, a pattern that was quite different from most later systems of colonization. Colonization spread the polis and its values far beyond the shores of Greece.

## The Growth of Sparta

Many different poleis developed during the Archaic period, but Sparta became the leading military power in Greece. To expand their polis, the Spartans did not establish colonies but set out in about 750 B.C.E. to conquer Messenia (muh-SEE-nee-uh), a rich, fertile region in the southwestern Peloponnesus. This conflict, called the First Messenian War by later Greek historians, lasted for twenty years and ended in a Spartan triumph. The Spartans appropriated Messenian land and turned the Messenians into **helots** (HEH-luhts), unfree residents forced to work state lands.

In about 650 B.C.E., Spartan exploitation and oppression of the Messenian helots, along with Sparta's defeat at the hands of a rival polis, led to a massive helot revolt that became known as the Second Messenian War. The Spartan poet Tyrtaeus, a contemporary of these events, vividly portrays the violence of the war:

For it is a shameful thing indeed
When with the foremost fighters
An elder falling in front of the young men
Lies outstretched,
Having white hair and grey beard,
Breathing forth his stout soul in the dust,
Holding in his hands his genitals
stained with blood.[1]

■ **tyranny** Rule by one man who took over an existing government, generally by using his wealth to gain a political following.

■ **democracy** A type of Greek government in which all citizens administered the workings of government.

■ **oligarchy** A type of Greek government in which citizens who owned a certain amount of property ruled.

■ **helots** Unfree residents of Sparta forced to work state lands.

**Spartan Expansion,
ca. 750–500 B.C.E.**

Finally after some thirty years of fighting, the Spartans put down the revolt. Nevertheless, the political and social strain it caused led to a transformation of the Spartan polis. After the war, non-nobles who had shared in the fighting as hoplites appear to have demanded rights equal to those of the nobility and a voice in the government. (In more recent history, similar demands in the United States during the Vietnam War led to a lowering of the voting age to eighteen, to match the age at which soldiers were drafted.) Under intense pressure, the aristocrats agreed to remodel the state into a new system.

The plan for the new system in Sparta was attributed to the lawgiver Lycurgus, who may or may not have been an actual person. According to later Greek sources, political distinctions among Spartan men were eliminated, and all citizens became legally equal. Governance of the polis was in the hands of two hereditary kings who were primarily military leaders. The kings were also part of the *Gerousia* (jeh-roo-SEE-ah), a council of men who had reached the age of sixty and thus retired from the Spartan army. The Gerousia deliberated on foreign and domestic matters and prepared legislation for the assembly, which consisted of all Spartan citizens. The real executive power of the polis was in the hands of five ephors (EH-fuhrs), or overseers, elected from and by all the citizens.

To provide for their economic needs, the Spartans divided the land of Messenia among all citizens. Helots worked the land, raised the crops, provided the Spartans with a certain percentage of their harvest, and occasionally served in the army. The Spartans kept the helots in line by means of systematic brutality and oppression.

In the system attributed to Lycurgus, every citizen owed primary allegiance to Sparta. Suppression of the individual together with emphasis on military prowess led to a barracks state. Family life itself was sacrificed to the polis. Once Spartan boys reached the age of seven, they were enrolled in separate companies with other boys their age. They were required to live in the barracks and eat together in a common mess hall until age thirty. They slept outside on reed mats and underwent rugged physical and military training until they were ready to become frontline soldiers. For the rest of their lives, Spartan men kept themselves prepared for combat. In battle Spartans were supposed to stand and die rather than retreat. Because men often did not see their wives or other women for long periods, not only in times of war but also in peace, their most meaningful relations were same-sex ones. The Spartan military leaders may have viewed such relationships as militarily advantageous because they believed that men would fight even more fiercely for lovers and comrades.

Spartans expected women in citizen families to be good wives and strict mothers of future soldiers. They were prohibited from wearing jewelry or ornate clothes. They, too, were supposed to exercise strenuously in the belief that hard physical training promoted the birth of healthy

**Spartan Hoplite** This bronze figurine portrays an armed foot soldier about to strike an enemy. His massive helmet with its full crest gives his head nearly complete protection, while a metal corselet covers his chest and back, and greaves (similar to today's shin guards) protect his lower legs. In his right hand he carries a thrusting spear (now broken off), and in his left a large, round shield. (bpk, Bildagentur/Antikensammlung, Staatliche Museen, Berlin, Germany/Photo: Johannes Laurentius/Art Resource, NY)

children. Xenophon (ca. 430–354 B.C.E.), a later Athenian admirer of the Spartans, commented:

> [Lycurgus had] insisted on the training of the body as incumbent no less on the female than the male; and in pursuit of the same idea instituted rival contests in running and feats of strength for women as for men. His belief was that where both parents were strong their progeny would be found to be more vigorous.[2]

An anecdote frequently repeated about one Spartan mother sums up Spartan military values. As her son was setting off to battle, the mother handed him his shield and advised him to come back either victorious, carrying the shield, or dead, being carried on it. Yet Spartan women were freer than many other Greek women. With men in military service much of their lives, women in citizen families owned land and ran the estates and were not physically restricted or secluded.

Along with the emphasis on military values for both sexes, the Spartan system served to instill in society the civic virtues of dedication to the state and a code of moral conduct. These aspects of Spartan society, along with Spartan military successes, were generally admired throughout the Greek world.

## The Evolution of Athens

Like Sparta, Athens faced pressing social, economic, and political problems during the Archaic period, but the Athenian response was far different from that of the Spartans. Instead of creating a state devoted to the military, the Athenians created a state that became a democracy.

For Athens, the late seventh century B.C.E. was a time of turmoil, the causes of which are unclear. In 621 B.C.E., Draco (DRAY-koh), an Athenian aristocrat, under pressure from small landholders and with the consent of the nobles, published the first law code of the Athenian polis. His code was harsh — and for this reason his name is the origin of the word *draconian* — but it embodied the ideal that the law belonged to all citizens. The aristocracy still governed Athens oppressively, however, and the social and economic situation remained dire. Despite Draco's code, noble landholders continued to force small farmers and artisans into economic dependence. Many families were sold into slavery because of debt; others were exiled, and their land was mortgaged to the rich.

One person who recognized these problems clearly was Solon (SOH-luhn), an aristocrat and poet. Reciting his poems in the Athenian agora, where anyone could hear his call for justice and fairness, Solon condemned his fellow aristocrats for their greed and dishonesty. According to later sources, Solon's sincerity and good sense convinced other aristocrats that he was no crazed revolutionary. He also gained the trust of the common people, whose problems provoked them to demand access to political life, much as commoners in Sparta had. Around 594 B.C.E., the nobles elected Solon chief *archon* (AHR-kahn), or magistrate of the Athenian polis, with authority over legal, civic, and military issues.

Solon immediately freed all people enslaved for debt, recalled all exiles, canceled all debts on land, and made enslavement for debt illegal. He allowed non-nobles into the old aristocratic assembly, where they could take part in the election of magistrates, including the annual election of the city's nine archons.

Although Solon's reforms solved some immediate problems, they did not satisfy either the aristocrats or the common people completely, and they did not bring peace to Athens. During the sixth century B.C.E., the successful general Pisistratus (pih-SIHS-trah-tuhs) declared himself tyrant. Under his rule, Athens prospered, and his building program began to transform the city into one of the splendors of Greece. He raised the civic consciousness and prestige of the polis by instituting new cultural festivals that brought people together. Although he had taken over control of the city by force, his reign as tyrant weakened the power of aristocratic families and aroused rudimentary feelings of equality in many Athenian men.

Athens became more democratic under the leadership of Cleisthenes (KLIE-thuh-neez), a wealthy and prominent aristocrat who had won the support of lower-status men and became the leader of Athens in 508 B.C.E. Cleisthenes created the *deme* (deem), a unit of land that kept the roll of citizens, or *demos*, within its jurisdiction. Men enrolled as citizens through their deme instead of through their family group, which brought people of different families together and promoted community and democracy. The demes were grouped into ten tribes, which thus formed the link between the demes and the central government. Each tribe elected a military leader, or *strategos* (plural *strategoi*).

The democracy functioned on the idea that all full citizens were sovereign. In 487 B.C.E., the election of the city's nine archons was replaced by reappointment by lot, which meant that any citizen with a certain amount of property had a chance of becoming an archon. This system gave citizens prestige, although the power of the archons gradually dwindled as the strategoi became the real military leaders of the city. Legislation was in the hands of two bodies, the *boule* (boo-LAY), or council, composed of five hundred members, and the *ecclesia* (ek-lay-SEE-yah), the assembly of all citizens. By supervising the various committees of government and proposing bills to the ecclesia, the boule guided Athenian political life. Nonetheless, the ecclesia had the final word. Open to all male citizens over eighteen years of age, it met at a specific place to vote on matters presented to it.

# How did the wars of the classical period shape Greek history?

From the time of the Mycenaeans, violent conflict was common in Greek society, and this did not change in the fifth century B.C.E., the beginning of what scholars later called the classical period of Greek history, which they date from about 500 B.C.E. to the conquest of Greece by Philip of Macedon in 338 B.C.E. First, the Greeks beat back the armies of the Persian Empire. Then, turning their spears against one another, they destroyed their own political system in a century of warfare culminating in the Peloponnesian War. There was no enforceable international law, very little diplomacy, and each polis maintained a substantial military force and a culture of militarism. Constant armed conflicts allowed the rise of a dominant new power: the kingdom of Macedonia.

## The Persian Wars

In 499 B.C.E., the Greeks who lived in Ionia rebelled unsuccessfully against the Persian Empire, which had ruled the area for fifty years (see Chapter 2). The Athenians had provided half-hearted help to the Ionians in this failed rebellion, and in 490 B.C.E., the Persians retaliated against Athens, only to be surprisingly defeated by the Athenian hoplites at the Battle of Marathon. (According to legend, a Greek runner carried the victory message to Athens. When the modern Olympic games were founded in 1896, they included a long-distance running race between Marathon and Athens, a distance of about twenty-five miles, designed to honor the ancient Greeks. The marathon was set at its current distance of 26.2 miles for the London Olympics of 1908, so that the finish would be in front of the royal box in the stadium.)

In 480 B.C.E., the Persian king Xerxes I (r. 485–465 B.C.E.) personally led a massive invasion of Greece. Under the leadership of Sparta, many, though not all, Greek poleis joined together to fight the Persians. The first confrontations between the Persians and the Greeks occurred at the pass of Thermopylae (thuhr-MAWP-uh-lee), where an outnumbered Greek army, including three hundred top Spartan warriors, held off a much larger Persian force for several days. The

■ Areas of Persian control
■ Greek states at war with Persia
■ Neutral Greek states

Thermopylae 480 B.C.E.
Artemisium 480 B.C.E.
Plataea 479 B.C.E.
Marathon 490 B.C.E.
Salamis 480 B.C.E.
Crete

**The Persian Wars, 499–479 B.C.E.**

Greeks at Thermopylae fought heroically, but the Persians won the battle and subsequently occupied and sacked Athens.

At the same time as the land battle of Thermopylae, Greeks and Persians fought one another in a naval battle at Artemisium off Boeotia. The Athenians, led by the general Themistocles, provided the heart of the naval forces with their fleet of triremes, large oar-propelled warships that could carry nearly two hundred rowers, along with soldiers for battles. Storms had wrecked many Persian ships, and neither side won a decisive victory. Only a month or so later, the Greek fleet met the Persian armada at Salamis, an island across from Athens. Though outnumbered, the Greek navy won an overwhelming victory by outmaneuvering the Persians. The remnants of the Persian fleet retired, and in 479 B.C.E., the Greeks overwhelmed the Persian army at Plataea. By defeating the Persians, the Greeks ensured that they would not be ruled by a foreign power.

## Growth of the Athenian Empire

The defeat of the Persians created a power vacuum in the Aegean, and the Athenians took advantage of the situation. Led by Themistocles, the Athenians and their allies formed the **Delian League**, a military alliance aimed at protecting the Aegean Islands, liberating Ionia from Persian rule, and keeping the Persians out of Greece. The Delian (DEE-lee-uhn) League was intended to be a free alliance under the leadership of Athens, but as the Athenians drove the Persians out of the Aegean, they also became increasingly imperialistic. Instead of treating its allies as equals, Athens treated them like subjects, collecting tribute by force and attempting to control the economic resources of the entire Delian League. Major allies revolted, and they were put down brutally. Athenian ideas of freedom and democracy did not extend to the citizens of other cities.

The aggressiveness of Athenian rule

■ Delian League
■ Allied with Delian League, 446 B.C.E.
● Athenian military settlement

Thasos
Corcyra
PERSIAN EMPIRE
BOEOTIA
Megara   Athens
Corinth        Delos
Sparta

**The Delian League, ca. 478–431 B.C.E.**

also alarmed Sparta and its allies. Relations between Athens and Sparta grew more hostile, particularly when Pericles (PEHR-uh-kleez) (ca. 494–429 B.C.E.), an ambitious aristocrat, became the leading statesman in Athens by gaining support among ordinary citizens through measures that broadened democracy. Like the democracy he led, Pericles was aggressive and imperialistic. In 459 B.C.E., Sparta and Athens went to war over conflicts between Athens and some of Sparta's allies. The war ended in 445 B.C.E with a treaty promising thirty years of peace, and no serious damage to either side. The treaty divided the Greek world between the two great powers, with each agreeing to respect the other and its allies.

Peace lasted about thirteen years instead of thirty. Athens continued its severe policies toward its subject allies and came into conflict with Corinth, one of Sparta's leading supporters. In this climate of anger and escalation, Pericles decided to punish the city of Megara, which had switched allegiance from Sparta to Athens and then back again. In 433/2 B.C.E., Pericles persuaded the Athenians to pass a law that excluded the Megarians from trading with Athens and its empire. In response the Spartans and their allies declared war.

## The Peloponnesian War

The Peloponnesian War lasted a generation and brought in its wake disease, famine, civil wars, widespread destruction, and huge loss of life (Map 3.3). During the first Spartan invasion of Attica, which began in 431 B.C.E., cramped conditions within the walls of Athens nurtured a dreadful plague that killed huge numbers, eventually claiming Pericles himself. The charismatic and eloquent Cleon became the leader of Athens and urged a more aggressive war strategy, doubling the tribute of Athens's allies to pay for it. Both Cleon and the leading Spartan general were killed in battle. Recognizing that ten years of war had resulted only in death, destruction, and stalemate, Sparta and Athens concluded the Peace of Nicias (NIH-shee-uhs) in 421 B.C.E.

The Peace of Nicias resulted in a cold war, in which hostility and threats continued but there was no open warfare between Sparta and Athens. But even cold war can bring horror and misery, especially to those caught in the middle. Such was the case when, in 416 B.C.E., the Athenians sent a fleet to the largely neutral island of Melos with an ultimatum: the Melians could surrender or perish. The Melians resisted. The Athenians conquered them, killed the men of military age, and sold the women and children into slavery.

**Replica of the Greek trireme *Olympia***   This replica of a Greek trireme slices through the water as the crew pulls on the three rows of long oars, from which the ship gets its name. In battle, a bronze battering ram would have capped the front of the ship, and rowers rowed as hard as possible to smash an enemy ship, then jumped on the other ship to engage in hand-to-hand combat. (Private Collection/Photo © Mike Andrews/Bridgeman Images)

The cold war grew hotter, thanks to the ambitions of Alcibiades (al-suh-BIE-uh-dees) (ca. 450–404 B.C.E.), an aristocrat and a kinsman of Pericles. A shameless opportunist, Alcibiades widened the war to further his own career and increase the power of Athens. He convinced the Athenians to attack Syracuse, the leading polis in Sicily. Conquering Syracuse would bring Athens an immense amount of resources, and also cut off the grain supply from Sicily to Sparta and its allies, allowing Athens to end the war and become the greatest power in Greece. The undertaking was vast, requiring an enormous fleet and thousands of sailors and soldiers, and it ended in disaster in 413 B.C.E., with nearly the entire fleet captured or destroyed by Syracusan forces. The Athenian historian Thucydides (thoo-SIHD-ih-dees) (ca. 460–ca. 399 B.C.E.), who saw action in the war himself and later tried to understand its causes, wrote the epitaph for the Athenians: "Infantry, fleet, and everything else were utterly destroyed, and out of many few returned home."[3]

The disaster in Sicily ushered in the final phase of the war. Sparta immediately declared war on Athens, and many of Athens's allies broke their ties with Athens. The Persians threw their support behind Sparta and built a fleet of ships for them; in exchange they expected Ionia to be returned to them once the Spartans were successful. In Athens, a coup in 411 B.C.E.

■ **Delian League**   A military alliance led by Athens whose aims were to protect the Aegean Islands, liberate Ionia from Persian rule, and keep the Persians out of Greece.

## MAPPING THE PAST

### MAP 3.3 The Peloponnesian War, 431–404 B.C.E.

This map shows the alignment of states during the Peloponnesian War.

**ANALYZING THE MAP** How would you compare the area controlled by Sparta and its allies to that of Athens and its allies? How would you expect these similarities and/or differences to affect the way that each side chose to conduct its military campaigns?

**CONNECTIONS** What does the location of the major battles and sieges suggest about the impact of the war throughout Greece?

led by wealthy men angry at the handling of the war overthrew the democratic government, briefly replacing it with an oligarchic one.

Now equipped with a fleet, the Spartans challenged the Athenians in the Aegean, and a long series of inconclusive naval battles followed. In 405 B.C.E., Spartan forces destroyed the last Athenian fleet at the Battle of Aegospotami, after which the Spartans blockaded Athens until it was starved into submission. In 404 B.C.E., after twenty-seven years of fighting, the Peloponnesian War was over.

### The Struggle for Dominance

The decades after the end of the Peloponnesian War were turbulent ones, with warfare continuing. Democracy was restored in Athens, but it and its chief rivals Sparta and Thebes each continued to try to create a political system in which it would dominate. When Athens surrendered to Sparta in

404 B.C.E., the Spartans used their victory to build an empire. Their decision brought them into conflict with Persia, which demanded the return of Ionia to its control. From 400 to 386 B.C.E., the Spartans fought the Persians for Ionia, a conflict that eventually engulfed Greece itself. After years of stalemate the Spartans made peace with Persia and their own Greek enemies. The result was a treaty, the King's Peace of 386 B.C.E., in which the Greeks and Persians pledged themselves to live in harmony. This agreement cost Sparta its empire but not its position of dominance in Greece.

The Spartans were not long content with this situation, however, and decided to punish cities that had opposed Sparta during the war. In 378 B.C.E., the Spartans launched an unprovoked attack on Athens. Together the Thebans and the Athenians created what was called the Second Athenian Confederacy, a federation of states to guarantee the terms of the peace treaty. The two fought Sparta until 371 B.C.E., when, due to growing fear of Theban might, Athens made a separate peace with Sparta. Left alone, Thebes defended itself until later that year, when the Thebans routed the Spartan army on the small plain of Leuctra and, in a series of invasions, eliminated Sparta as a major power.

## Philip II and Macedonian Supremacy

While the Greek states exhausted themselves in endless conflicts, the new power of Macedonia arose in the north. The land, extensive and generally fertile, nurtured a large population. Macedonia had strong ties to the Greek poleis, but the government there developed as a kingdom, not a democracy or oligarchy.

The kings of Macedonia slowly built up their power over rival states, and in 359 B.C.E., the brilliant and cultured Philip II ascended to the throne. With decades of effort he secured the borders of Macedonia against invaders from the north, and he then launched a series of military operations in the northwestern Aegean. By clever use of his wealth and superb army, he gained control of the area, and in 338 B.C.E., he won a decisive victory over Thebes and Athens that gave him command of Greece. Because the Greeks could not put aside their quarrels, they fell to an invader, and 338 B.C.E. is often seen as marking the end of the classical period.

After his victory, Philip led a combined army of soldiers from Macedonia and from many Greek states in an attempt to liberate the Ionian Greeks from Persian rule. Before he could launch this campaign, however, Philip fell to an assassin's dagger in 336 B.C.E. His young son Alexander vowed to carry on Philip's mission. He would succeed beyond all expectations.

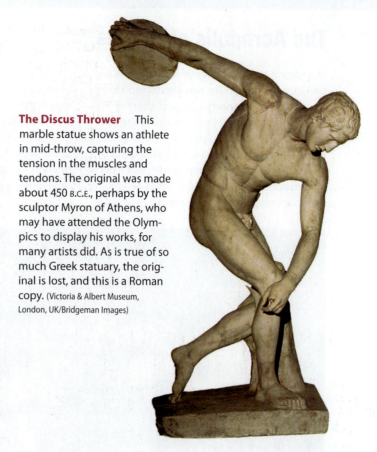

**The Discus Thrower** This marble statue shows an athlete in mid-throw, capturing the tension in the muscles and tendons. The original was made about 450 B.C.E., perhaps by the sculptor Myron of Athens, who may have attended the Olympics to display his works, for many artists did. As is true of so much Greek statuary, the original is lost, and this is a Roman copy. (Victoria & Albert Museum, London, UK/Bridgeman Images)

# What ancient Greek ideas and ideals have had a lasting influence?

Despite the violence that dominated Greece for nearly two centuries beginning in 500 B.C.E., or to some degree because of it, playwrights and thinkers pondered the meaning of the universe and the role of humans in it, and artists and architects created new styles to celebrate Greek achievements. Although warfare was one of the hallmarks of the classical period, intellectual and artistic accomplishments were as well.

## Athenian Arts in the Age of Pericles

In the midst of the warfare of the fifth century B.C.E., Pericles turned Athens into the showplace of Greece. He appropriated Delian League funds to pay for a huge building program. Workers erected temples and other buildings as patriotic memorials housing statues and carvings, often painted in bright colors, showing the gods in human form and celebrating the Greek victory over the Persians. (The paint later washed away, leaving the generally white sculpture that we think of as "classical.") Many of the temples were built on the high, rocky Acropolis that stood in the center of the city, on top of the remains of temples that had been burned by the Persians, and sometimes incorporating these into their walls.

The Athenians normally hiked up the long approach to the Acropolis only for religious festivals, of which the most important and joyous was the Great Panathenaea, held every four years to honor the virgin goddess Athena and perhaps offer sacrifices to older deities as well. (See "Evaluating Visual Evidence: The Acropolis of Athens," page 70.) For this festival, Athenian citizens and legal noncitizen residents formed a huge procession to bring the

# The Acropolis of Athens

The natural rock formation of the Acropolis probably had a palace on top as early as the Mycenaean period, when the palace was also surrounded by a defensive wall. Temples were constructed beginning in the sixth century B.C.E., and after the Persian wars Pericles ordered the reconstruction and expansion of many of these, as well as the building of new and more magnificent temples and an extension of the defensive walls. The largest building is the Parthenon, a temple dedicated to the goddess Athena, which originally housed a forty-foot-tall statue of Athena made of ivory and gold sheets attached to a wooden frame. Much of the Parthenon was damaged when it was shelled during a war between Venice and the Ottoman Empire in the seventeenth century C.E., and air pollution continues to eat away at the marble.

(Klaas Lingbeek-van Kranen/Getty Images)

**EVALUATE THE EVIDENCE**

1. Imagine yourself as an Athenian walking up the hill toward the Parthenon. What impression would the setting and the building itself convey?
2. What were the various functions of the Acropolis?

statue of Athena in the Parthenon an exquisite robe, richly embroidered by the citizen women of Athens with mythological scenes. The marchers first saw the Propylaea, the ceremonial gateway whose columns appeared to uphold the sky. On the right was the small temple of Athena Nike, built to commemorate the victory over the Persians. As visitors walked on, they obtained a full view of the Parthenon, the chief temple dedicated to Athena at the center of the Acropolis, with a huge painted ivory and gold statue of the goddess inside. After the religious ceremonies, all the people joined in a feast.

The development of drama was tied to the religious festivals of the city, especially those celebrating the god of wine, Dionysus (see "Public and Personal Religion"). Drama was as rooted in the life of the polis as were the architecture and sculpture of the Acropolis. The polis sponsored the production of plays and required wealthy citizens to pay the expenses of their production. At the beginning of the year, dramatists submitted their plays to the chief archon of the polis. He chose those he considered best and assigned a theatrical troupe to each playwright. Many plays were highly controversial, containing overt political and social commentary, but the archons neither suppressed nor censored them.

Not surprisingly, given the incessant warfare, conflict was a constant element in Athenian drama, and

The plays of Aeschylus and Sophocles often involve one family member killing another, which sets off a cycle of further violence, and through these actions the playwrights address issues of fate, the will of the gods, and human moral responsibility when faced with a choice. Aeschylus's *Agamemnon*, produced in 458 B.C.E., traces the homecoming of King Agamemnon from the Trojan War, an expedition that had begun with his sacrificing his daughter Iphigenia to the goddess Artemis so the winds would shift and the Greek fleet could sail to Troy. (His wife Clytemnestra plots his murder in revenge, and she stabs him.) In Sophocles's *Antigone* (an-TIH-guh-nee), produced about 441 B.C.E., two sons of King Oedipus have killed each other in a war over who would rule. The current king Creon forbids them to be buried, but their sister Antigone disobeys him and carries out the proper funeral rituals. Creon condemns her to be walled up, so she kills herself, as does her fiancé (who is also Creon's son) and Creon's wife.

## Agamemnon

Meanwhile his armed men moped along the shores,
And cursed the wind, and ate his dwindling stores . . .
Then Calchas [a soothsayer] spoke again. The wind, he said,
Was sent by Artemis; and he revealed
Her remedy — a thought to crush like lead
The hearts of Atreus' sons, who wept, as weep they must,
And speechless ground their scepters in the dust.
The elder king [Agamemnon] then spoke: "What can I say?
Disaster follows if I disobey;
Surely yet worse disaster if I yield
And slaughter my own child, my home's delight,
In her young innocence, and stain my hand
With blasphemous unnatural cruelty,
Bathed in the blood I fathered! Either way,
Ruin! Disband the fleet, sail home, and earn
The deserter's badge — abandon my command,
Betray the alliance — now? The wind must turn,
There must be sacrifice, a maid must bleed —
Their chafing rage demands it — they are right!
May good prevail, and justify my deed!"
Then he put on
The harness of Necessity.
The doubtful tempest of his soul
Veered, and his prayer was turned to blasphemy,
His offering to impiety . . .
Heedless of her tears,
Her cries of "Father!" and her maiden years,

Her judges valued more
Their glory and their war.

## Antigone

**Creon** *(to Antigone):*
You — tell me not at length but in a word.
You knew the order not to do this thing?

**Antigone:**
I knew, of course I knew. The word was plain.

**Creon:**
And still you dared to overstep these laws?

**Antigone:**
For me it was not Zeus who made that order.
Nor did that Justice who lives with the gods below
mark out such laws to hold among mankind.
Nor did I think your orders were so strong
that you, a mortal man, could over-run
the gods' unwritten and unfailing laws.
Not now, nor yesterday's, they always live,
and no one knows their origin in time.
So not through fear of any man's proud spirit
would I be likely to neglect these laws,
draw on myself the gods' sure punishment.
I knew that I must die; how could I not?
even without your warning. If I die
before my time, I say it is a gain.
Who lives in sorrows many as are mine
how shall he not be glad to gain his death?
And so, for me to meet this fate, no grief.
But if I left that corpse, my mother's son,
dead and unburied I'd have cause to grieve
as now I grieve not.
And if you think my acts are foolishness
The foolishness may be in a fool's eye.
. . .
Look what I suffer, at whose command,
Because I respected the right.

### QUESTIONS FOR ANALYSIS

1. How do Agamemnon and Antigone justify what they have done?
2. Does Aeschylus or Sophocles seem more approving of the choice made by the title character of his play?
3. Given what was going on in Athens at the time that these plays were performed, how can these plays be seen as political commentary?

playwrights used their art in attempts to portray, understand, and resolve life's basic conflicts. The Athenian dramatists examined questions about the relationship between humans and the gods, the demands of society on the individual, and the nature of good and evil. Aeschylus (EHS-kuh-lihs) (525–456 B.C.E.), the first of the great Athenian dramatists, was also the first to express the agony of the individual caught in conflict. In his trilogy of plays, *The Oresteia* (ohr-eh-STEE-uh), Aeschylus deals with the themes of betrayal, murder, and reconciliation, urging that reason and justice be applied to reconcile fundamental conflicts. The final play concludes with a prayer that civil dissension never be allowed to destroy the city and that the life of the city be one of harmony and grace.

Sophocles (SOF-uh-klees) (496–406 B.C.E.) also dealt with matters personal and political. He wrote over one hundred plays, of which only seven survive. Among these is *Antigone* (an-TIH-guh-nee), in which the title character chooses to bury the body of her brother though the king has forbidden this because her brother had led foreign troops against the city. (See "Viewpoints: Greek Playwrights on Families, Fate, and Choice," page 71.) Sophocles later wrote *Oedipus* (EHD-uh-puhs) *the King* and its sequel, *Oedipus at Colonus*, which tell the story of Antigone's father Oedipus, doomed by the gods to kill his father and marry his mother. Try as he might to avoid his fate, his every action brings him closer to its fulfillment. When at last he realizes that he has unwittingly carried out the decree of the gods, Oedipus blinds himself and flees into exile. In *Oedipus at Colonus*, Sophocles dramatizes the last days of the broken king, whose patient suffering and uncomplaining piety win him the praise of the gods.

With Euripides (you-RIHP-uh-dees) (ca. 480–406 B.C.E.), drama entered a new and, in many ways, more personal phase. To him the gods were far less important than human beings. The essence of Euripides's tragedy is the flawed character—men and women who bring disaster on themselves and their loved ones because their passions overwhelm reason. Among these were the leaders of Athens, against whom Euripedes directed his antiwar play *The Trojan Women*, produced in the spring after the slaughter and subjugation of the Melians.

Writers of comedy treated the affairs of the polis and its politicians bawdily and often coarsely. Even so, their plays were also performed at religious festivals. Best known are the comedies of Aristophanes (eh-ruh-STAH-fuh-neez) (ca. 445–386 B.C.E.), an ardent lover of his city and a merciless critic of cranks and quacks. (See "Individuals in Society: Aristophanes," page 73.) Like Aeschylus, Sophocles, and Euripides, Aristophanes used his art to dramatize his ideas on the right conduct of the citizen and the value of the polis.

## Households and Work

In sharp contrast with the rich intellectual and cultural life of Periclean Athens stands the simplicity of its material life. The Athenians, like other Greeks, lived with comparatively few material possessions in houses that were rather simple. Well-to-do Athenians lived in houses consisting of a series of rooms opening onto a central courtyard. Artisans often set aside a room to use as a shop or work area. Larger houses often had a dining room at the front where the men of the family ate and entertained guests at drinking parties called *symposia*, and a **gynaeceum** (also spelled *gynaikeion*), a room or section at the back where the women of the family and the female slaves worked, ate, and slept. Other rooms included the kitchen and bathroom. By modern standards there was not much furniture.

Cooking, done over a hearth in the house, provided welcome warmth in the winter. Baking and roasting were done in ovens. Meals consisted primarily of various grains, especially wheat and barley, as well as lentils, olives, figs, grapes, fish, and a little meat, foods that are now part of the highly touted "Mediterranean diet." The Greeks used olive oil for cooking, and also as an ointment and as lamp fuel. The only Greeks who consistently ate meat were the Spartan warriors. They received a small portion of meat each day, together with the infamous Spartan black broth, a concoction of pork cooked in blood, vinegar, and salt. One Athenian, after tasting the broth, commented that he could easily understand why the Spartans were so willing to die.

In the city a man might support himself as a craftsman—a potter, bronze-smith, sailmaker, or tanner—or he could contract with the polis to work on public buildings. Certain crafts, including spinning and weaving, were generally done by women, who produced cloth for their own families and sold it. Men and women without skills worked as paid laborers but competed with slaves for work.

Slavery was commonplace in Greece, as it was throughout the ancient world. Slaves were usually foreigners and often "barbarians," people whose native language was not Greek. Most citizen households in Athens owned at least one slave. Slaves in Athens ranged widely in terms of their type of work and opportunities for escaping slavery. Some male slaves were skilled workers or well-educated teachers and tutors of writing, while others were unskilled laborers in the city, agricultural workers in the countryside, or laborers in mines. Female slaves worked in agriculture or as domestic servants and nurses for children.

■ **gynaeceum** Women's quarters at the back of an Athenian house where the women of the family and the female slaves worked, ate, and slept.

## Aristophanes

I n 424 B.C.E., in the middle of the Peloponnesian War, citizens of Athens attending one of the city's regular dramatic festivals watched *The Knights*, in which two slaves complain about their fellow slave's power over their master Demos ("the people" in Greek) and everyone else around him. They run into a sausage seller and tell him that an oracle has predicted he will become more influential than their fellow slave and will eventually dominate the city, becoming what in ancient Greece was called a demagogue. He doesn't think this possible, as he is only a sausage seller, but the men tell him he is the perfect candidate: "Mix and knead together all the state business as you do for your sausages. To win the people, always cook them some savoury that pleases them. Besides, you possess all the attributes of a demagogue; a screeching, horrible voice, a perverse, crossgrained nature and the language of the market-place. In you all is united which is needful for governing."* This leads to a series of shouted debates between the influential slave and the sausage maker, each one accusing the other of corruption and indecent behavior, and making ever more elaborate promises to the citizens of Athens. Ultimately the sausage seller wins, and the formerly domineering slave becomes a lowly sausage seller.

Although the forceful slave's name is never mentioned in the play, everyone knew he represented Cleon, at that point the leader of Athens, who had risen to power through populist speeches. The real Cleon may well have been among the thousands in the audience, as front-row seats at festivals were a reward he had just been given by the citizens of Athens for a military victory. Cleon had taken legal action against the playwright two years earlier for another play, accusing him of slandering the polis, but in this case he did nothing.

That playwright was Aristophanes, the only comic playwright in classical Athens from whom whole plays survive. Not much is known about Aristophanes's life, other than a few ambiguous clues in the plays. His first play, now lost, was produced in 427 B.C.E., and his last datable play, also now lost, in 386 B.C.E. (The dates of his life are inferred from these, as there is a comment in one play suggesting he was only eighteen when his first play was produced.) He directed some of his own plays, won the theater competition several times, and had sons who were also comic playwrights. Even in his early plays, Aristophanes seems to have opposed anything

**Roman copy of a Hellenistic bust depicting what Aristophanes might have looked like.** (Musée du Louvre, Paris, France/De Agostini Picture Library/Bridgeman Images)

that was new in Athens: new types of leaders (like Cleon), new styles in drama (Euripides was a standard target), new kinds of educators (such as the Sophists), new philosophy (especially that of Socrates). Everything and everyone except the people of Athens themselves was open to ridicule, and the more obscene the better: poets throw turds at each other, politicians collapse drunk and vomiting in the streets, military leaders walk around with huge erections when their wives refuse to have sex with them until they call off the war. Aristophanes combined kinds of comedy that today are often separated — political satire, complicated wordplay, celebrity slamming, cross-dressing, slapstick, dirty jokes, silly props, absurdity, audience taunting — and was a master at all of these.

### QUESTIONS FOR ANALYSIS

1. How might political satires such as those of Aristophanes have both critiqued and reinforced civic values in classical Athens?
2. Can you think of more recent parallels to Aristophanes's political satires? What has been the response to these?

*Aristophanes, *The Knights,* ed. Eugene O'Neill, Jr. (New York: Random House, 1938), lines 215–219. Available at Perseus Digital Library: http://www.perseus.tufts .edu/hopper/text?doc=Perseus%3Atext%3A1999.01.0034%3Acard%3D213.

Slaves received some protection under the law, and those who engaged in skilled labor for which they were paid could buy their freedom.

## Gender and Sexuality

Citizenship was the basis of political power for men in ancient Athens and was inherited. After the middle of the fifth century B.C.E., people were considered citizens only if both parents were citizens, except for a few men given citizenship as a reward for service to the city. Adult male citizens were expected to take part in political decisions and be active in civic life, no matter what their occupation. They were also in charge of relations between the household and the wider community. Women in Athens and elsewhere in Greece, like those in Mesopotamia, brought dowries to their husbands upon marriage, which became the husband's to invest or use, though he was supposed to do this wisely.

Women did not play a public role in classical Athens. We know the names of no female poets, artists, or philosophers, and the names of very few women at all. The Athenian ideal for the behavior of a citizen's wife was a

**Young Man and Hetaera**   In this scene painted on the inside of a drinking cup, a hetaera holds the head of a young man who has clearly had too much to drink. Sexual and comic scenes were common on Greek pottery, particularly on objects that would have been used at a private dinner party hosted by a citizen, known as a symposium. Wives did not attend symposia, but hetaerae and entertainers were often hired to perform for the male guests. (Painter: Makron, drinking cup [kylix], Greek, Late Archaic Period, about 490–480 B.C.E./Place of manufacture: Greece, Attica, Athens; ceramic, Red Figure, Height: 12.8 cm. [5¼ in.]; Diameter: 33.2 cm. [13⅛ in.]/Museum of Fine Arts, Boston, Massachusetts, U.S.A./Henry Lillie Pierce Fund, 01.8022/Photograph provided by Bridgeman Images/Photograph © 2019 Museum of Fine Arts, Boston. All Rights Reserved.)

domestic one: she was to stay at home, bearing and raising children, spinning and weaving cloth, and overseeing the household and its servants and slaves. (See "Thinking Like a Historian: Gender Roles in Classical Athens," page 76.) This physical seclusion kept citizen women away from men who were not family members, assuring citizen men that their children were theirs. How much this ideal was followed is debated by historians, but women in wealthier citizen families probably spent most of their time at home in the gynaeceum, leaving the house only to attend some religious and city festivals, and perhaps occasionally plays. They did visit temples to ask the gods for help in childbirth and other rituals specific to women.

Women from noncitizen families lived freer lives than citizen women, although they worked harder and had fewer material comforts. They performed manual labor in the fields or sold goods or services in the agora, going about their affairs much as men did.

Among the services that some women and men sold was sex. Women who sold sexual services ranged from poor streetwalkers known as *pornai* to middle-status hired mistresses known as *palakai,* to sophisticated courtesans known as *hetaerae,* who added intellectual accomplishments to physical beauty. Hetaerae accompanied men at dinner parties and in public settings where their wives would not have been welcome, serving men as social as well as sexual partners.

Same-sex relations were generally accepted in all of ancient Greece, not simply in Sparta. In classical Athens part of a male adolescent citizen's training might entail a hierarchical sexual and tutorial relationship with an adult man, who most likely was married and may have had female sexual partners as well. These relationships between young men and older men were often celebrated in literature and art, in part because Athenians regarded perfection as possible only in the male. Women were generally seen as inferior to men, dominated by their bodies rather than their minds. The perfect body was that of the young male, and perfect love was that between a young man and a slightly older man. The extent to which perfect love was sexual or spiritual was debated among the ancient Greeks. In one of his dialogues, the philosopher Plato (see "The Flowering of Philosophy") argues that the best kind of love is one in which contemplation of the beloved leads to contemplation of the divine, an intellectualized love that came to be known as "platonic." Plato was suspicious of the power of sexual passion because it distracted men from reason and the search for knowledge.

Along with praise of intellectualized love, Greek authors also celebrated physical sex and desire. The soldier-poet Archilochus (d. 652 B.C.E.) preferred "to light upon the flesh of a maid and ram belly to belly and thigh to thigh."[4] The lyric poet Sappho, who lived on the island of Lesbos in the northern Aegean Sea in the sixth century B.C.E., wrote often of powerful desire. One of her poems describes her reaction on seeing her beloved talking to someone else:

He appears to me, that one, equal to the gods,
the man who, facing you,
is seated and, up close, that sweet voice of yours
he listens to

And how you laugh your charming laugh. Why it
makes my heart flutter within my breast,
because the moment I look at you, right then, for me,
to make any sound at all won't work any more.

My tongue has a breakdown and a delicate
— all of a sudden — fire rushes under my skin.
With my eyes I see not a thing, and there is a roar
that my ears make.
Sweat pours down me and a trembling
seizes all of me; paler than grass
am I, and a little short of death
do I appear to me.[5]

Sappho's description of the physical reactions caused by love — and jealousy — reaches across the centuries. The Hellenic and even more the Hellenistic Greeks regarded Sappho as a great lyric poet, although because some of her poetry is directed toward women, over the last century she has become better known for her sexuality than her writing. Today the English word *lesbian* is derived from Sappho's home island of Lesbos.

Same-sex relations did not mean that people did not marry; Athenians saw the continuation of the family line as essential. Sappho, for example, appears to have been married and had a daughter. Sexual desire and procreation were both important aspects of life, but ancient Greeks did not necessarily link them.

## Public and Personal Religion

Like most peoples of the ancient world, the Greeks were polytheists, worshipping a variety of gods and goddesses who were immortal but otherwise acted just like people. Migration, invasion, and colonization brought the Greeks into contact with other peoples and caused their religious beliefs to evolve. How much these contacts shaped Greek religion and other aspects of culture has been the subject of a fierce debate since the late 1980s, when in *Black Athena: The Afroasiatic Roots of Classical Civilization*, Martin Bernal proposed that the Greeks owed a great deal to the Egyptians and Phoenicians, and that scholars since the nineteenth century had purposely tried to cover this up to make the Greeks seem more European and less indebted to cultures in Africa and Asia.[6] Bernal's ideas are highly controversial, and most classicists do not accept his evidence, but they are part of a larger tendency among scholars in the last several decades — including those who vigorously oppose Bernal — to see the Greeks less in isolation from other groups and more in relation to the larger Mediterranean world.

Greek religion was primarily a matter of ritual, with rituals designed to appease the divinities believed to control the forces of the natural world. Processions, festivals, and sacrifices offered to the gods were frequently occasions for people to meet together socially, for times of cheer or even drunken excess.

By the classical era, the primary gods were understood to live metaphorically on Mount Olympus, the highest mountain in Greece. Zeus was the king of the gods and the most powerful of them, and he was married to Hera, who was also his sister. Zeus and Hera had several children, including Ares, the god of war.

**Religious Procession**　This painted wooden slab from about 540 B.C.E., found in a cave near Corinth, shows adults and children about to sacrifice a sheep to the deities worshipped in this area. The participants are dressed in their finest clothes and crowned with garlands. Music adds to the festivities. Rituals such as this were a common part of religious life throughout Greece. (National Archaeological Museum, Athens, Greece/De Agostini Picture Library/G. Dagli Orti/Bridgeman Images)

## Gender Roles in Classical Athens

Athenian men's ideas about the proper roles for men and women, conveyed in written and visual form, became one of the foundations of Western notions of gender for millennia. How do the qualities they view as ideal and praiseworthy for men compare with those they view as ideal for women?

**1** **Pericles's funeral oration, from Thucydides's *History of the Peloponnesian War*, 430** B.C.E. In this speech given in honor of those who had died in the war, the Athenian leader Pericles glorifies the achievements of Athenian men and women.

If we look to the laws, they afford equal justice to all in their private differences; if to social standing, advancement in public life falls to reputation for capacity, class considerations not being allowed to interfere with merit; nor again does poverty bar the way; if a man is able to serve the state, he is not hindered by the obscurity of his condition. . . . Further, we provide plenty of means for the mind to refresh itself from business. We celebrate games and sacrifices all the year round, and the elegance of our private establishments forms a daily source of pleasure. . . . [I]n education, where our rivals from their very cradles by a painful discipline seek after manliness, at Athens we live exactly as we please, and yet are just as ready to encounter every legitimate danger. . . . We cultivate refinement without extravagance and knowledge without effeminacy; wealth we employ more for use than for show. . . . Again, in our enterprises we present the singular spectacle of daring and deliberation, each carried to its highest point, and both united in the same persons. . . . In short, I say that as a city we are the school of Hellas; while I doubt if the world can produce a man, who where he has only himself to depend upon, is equal to so many emergencies, and graced by so happy a versatility as the Athenian. . . .

If I must say anything on the subject of female excellence to those of you who will now be in widowhood, it will be all comprised in this brief exhortation: Great will be your glory in not falling short of your natural character; and greatest will be hers who is least talked of among the men whether for good or for bad.

**2** **Xenophon, *Oeconomicus*, ca. 360** B.C.E. In a treatise on household management, the historian, soldier, and philosopher Xenophon creates a character, Isomachus, who provides his much younger wife with advice and informs her about ideal gender roles. "God" in this selection means all of the gods, personified as male; "law" is personified as female ("law gives her consent").

ISOMACHUS: "God made provision from the first by shaping, as it seems to me, the woman's nature for indoor and the man's for outdoor occupations. Man's body and soul He furnished with a greater capacity for enduring heat and cold, wayfaring and military marches; or, to repeat, He laid upon his shoulders the outdoor works. While in creating the body of woman with less capacity for these things," I continued, "God would seem to have imposed on her the indoor works; and knowing that He had implanted in the woman and imposed upon her the nurture of new-born babies, He endowed her with a larger share of affection for the new-born child than He bestowed upon man. And since He imposed on woman the guardianship of the things imported from without, God, in His wisdom, perceiving that a fearful spirit was no detriment to guardianship, endowed the woman with a larger measure of timidity than He bestowed on man. Knowing further that he to whom the outdoor works belonged would need to defend them against malign attack, He endowed the man in turn with a larger share of courage. . . . Law, too, gives her consent—law and the usage of mankind, by sanctioning the wedlock of man and wife; and just as God ordained them to be partners in their children, so the law establishes their common ownership of house and estate. Custom, moreover, proclaims as beautiful those excellences of man and woman with which God gifted them at birth. Thus for a woman to bide tranquilly at home rather than roam abroad is no dishonour; but for a man to remain indoors, instead of devoting himself to outdoor pursuits, is a thing discreditable."

### ANALYZING THE EVIDENCE

1. In Sources 1–3, what qualities do the authors see as praiseworthy in men? In women?
2. In Sources 2 and 3, what do Xenophon and Aristotle view as the underlying reasons for gender differences?
3. The two paintings in Sources 4 and 5 show scenes that were normal parts of real Athenian life, but how do they also convey ideals for men and women? What are these ideals?
4. Because no writing or art by Athenian women has survived, we have to extrapolate women's opinions from works by men. What do the body language and expression of the young woman in Source 4 suggest she thought about her situation?

**4** **Vase painting showing Athenian woman at home, fifth century B.C.E.** A well-to-do young woman sits on an elegant chair inside a house, spinning and weaving. The bed piled high with coverlets on the left was a symbol of marriage.

(Musée du Louvre, Paris, France/Erich Lessing/Art Resource, NY)

**3** **Aristotle, *The Politics*.** In *The Politics,* one of his most important works, Aristotle examines the development of government, which he sees as originating in the power relations in the family and household.

〜 The city belongs among the things that exist by nature, and man is by nature a political animal. . . . The family is the association established by nature for the supply of men's everyday wants. . . .

It is clear that the rule of the soul over the body, and of the mind and the rational element over the passionate, is natural and expedient; whereas the equality of the two or the rule of the inferior is always hurtful. The same holds good of animals in relation to men; for tame animals have a better nature than wild, and all tame animals are better off when they are ruled by man; for then they are preserved. Again, the male is by nature superior, and the female inferior; and the one rules, and the other is ruled; this principle, of necessity, extends to all mankind. . . .

A similar question may be raised about women and children, whether they too have virtues: ought a woman to be temperate and brave and just, and is a child to be called temperate, and intemperate, or not? . . . Here the very constitution of the soul has shown us the way; in it one part naturally rules, and the other is subject, and the virtue of the ruler we maintain to be different from that of the subject; the one being the virtue of the rational, and the other of the irrational part. Now, it is obvious that the same principle applies generally, and therefore almost all

things rule and are ruled according to nature. . . . For the slave has no deliberative faculty at all; the woman has, but it is without authority, and the child has, but it is immature. So it must necessarily be supposed to be with the moral virtues also; all should partake of them, but only in such manner and degree as is required by each for the fulfillment of his duty. . . . Clearly, then, moral virtue belongs to all of them; but the temperance of a man and of a woman, or the courage and justice of a man and of a woman, are not, as Socrates maintained, the same; the courage of a man is shown in commanding, of a woman in obeying. . . . All classes must be deemed to have their special attributes; as the poet says of women, "Silence is a woman's glory," but this is not equally the glory of man.

**5** **Lekythos (oil flask), with a wedding scene, attributed to the Amasis Painter, ca. 550 B.C.E.** In this early representation of an Attic wedding procession, the bearded groom drives the cart to his home, while the bride (right) pulls her veil forward in a gesture associated with marriage in Greek art.
(Lekythos, ca. 550–530 B.C.E. [terracotta]/Amasis Painter [fl. ca. 560–515 B.C.E.]/Metropolitan Museum of Art, New York, New York, U.S.A./Bridgeman Images)

## PUTTING IT ALL TOGETHER

Using the sources above, along with what you have learned in class and this chapter, write a short essay that compares ideals for men and women in classical Athens. How did these ideas about gender roles both reflect and shape Athenian society and political life?

Sources: (1) Thucydides, *The Peloponnesian War* (London: J. M. Dent; New York, E. P. Dutton, 1910), at Perseus Digital Library; (2) Xenophon, *The Economist,* trans. H. G. Dakyns, at http://www.gutenberg.org/files/1173/1173-h/1173-h.htm; (3) Aristotle, *Politics,* Book One, translated by Benjamin Jowett, at http://classics.mit.edu/Aristotle/politics.1.one.html.

Zeus was also the father of the god Apollo, who represented the epitome of youth, beauty, and athletic skill, and who served as the patron god of music and poetry. Apollo's half-sister Athena was a warrior-goddess who had been born from the head of Zeus.

The Greeks also honored certain heroes. A hero was born of the union of a god or goddess and a mortal, and was considered an intermediary between the divine and the human. A hero displayed his divine origins by performing deeds beyond the ability of human beings. Herakles (or Hercules, as the Romans called him), the son of Zeus and the mortal woman Alcmene, was the most popular of the Greek heroes, defeating mythical opponents and carrying out impossible (or "Herculean") tasks. Devotees to Hercules believed that he, like other heroes, protected mortals from supernatural dangers and provided an ideal of vigorous masculinity.

The polis administered cults and festivals, and everyone was expected to participate in these events, comparable to today's patriotic parades or ceremonies. Much religion was local and domestic, and individual families honored various deities privately in their homes. Many people also believed that magic rituals and spells were effective and sought the assistance of individuals reputed to have special knowledge or powers. Even highly educated Greeks sought the assistance of fortune-tellers and soothsayers, from the oracle at Delphi to local figures who examined the flights of birds or the entrails of recently slaughtered chickens for clues about the future.

Along with public and family forms of honoring the gods, some Greeks also participated in what later historians have termed **mystery religions**, in which participants underwent an initiation ritual and gained secret knowledge that they were forbidden to reveal to the uninitiated. The Eleusinian mysteries, held at Eleusis in Attica, are one of the oldest of these. They centered on Demeter, the goddess of the harvest, whose lovely daughter Persephone (per-SEH-foh-nee) as the story goes, was taken by the god Hades to the underworld. In mourning, Demeter caused drought, and ultimately Zeus allowed Persephone to return to her, though she had to spend some months of the year in Hades. There is evidence of an agrarian ritual celebrating this mythological explanation for the cycle of the seasons as early as the Bronze Age, and in the sixth century B.C.E., the rulers of nearby Athens made the ritual open to all Greeks, women and slaves included. Many people flocked to the annual ceremonies and learned the mysteries, which by the fourth century B.C.E. appear to have promised life after death to those initiated into them.

Another somewhat secret religion was that of Dionysus (die-uh-NIE-suhs), the god of wine and powerful emotions, who was killed and then reborn, which is why he, like Persephone, became the center of mystery religions offering rebirth. As the god of wine, he also represented freedom from the normal constraints of society, and his worshippers were reported to have danced ecstatically and even to have become a frenzied and uncontrolled mob. Whether or how often this actually happened is impossible to know, as contemporary Athenian writers who did not approve may have embellished their accounts of these wild rituals, and later scholars sometimes regarded them simply as fiction because chaotic orgies did not fit with their notions of the rational and orderly Greeks.

Greeks also shared some public Panhellenic festivals, the chief of which were sports festivals held every four years at Olympia in honor of Zeus. Their origins were attributed to the gods, though they most likely actually grew out of athletic competitions held in honor of a recently deceased person, which had been common since Mycenaean times. They included foot and chariot races, javelin throwing, wrestling, and boxing, all except chariot racing performed nude. Open to male athletes from around the Greek world, contestants won only a wreath, so had to be fairly wealthy or find a rich patron to pay for training, transportation, and other expenses. Athletes might also receive rewards from the polis that sponsored them, as the games became a tool through which cities asserted their superiority over their rivals. The modern Olympic games, first held in 1896, have continued this pattern of mixing politics and sports.

## The Flowering of Philosophy

Just as the Greeks developed rituals to honor the gods, they spun myths and epics to explain the origin of the universe. Over time, however, as Greeks encountered other peoples with different beliefs, some of them began to question their old gods and myths, and they sought rational rather than supernatural explanations for natural phenomena. These Greek thinkers, based in Ionia, are called the Pre-Socratics because their rational efforts preceded those of the Athenians. They took individual facts and wove them into general theories that led them to conclude that, despite appearances, the universe is actually simple and subject to natural laws. The Pre-Socratics began an intellectual revolution with their idea that nature was predictable, creating what we now call philosophy and science.

Drawing on their observations, the Pre-Socratics speculated about the basic building blocks of the universe. Thales (THAY-leez) (ca. 600 B.C.E.) thought the basic element of the universe was water, and Heraclitus (hehr-uh-KLIE-tuhs) (ca. 500 B.C.E.) thought it was fire. Democritus (dih-MAH-kruh-tuhs) (ca. 460 B.C.E.) broke this down further and created the atomic theory, the idea that the universe is made up of invisible, indestructible particles. The culmination of Pre-Socratic thought was the theory that four simple substances make up the universe: fire, air, earth, and water.

The stream of thought started by the Pre-Socratics branched into several directions. Hippocrates (hih-PAH-kruh-teez) (ca. 470–400 B.C.E.) became the most prominent physician and teacher of medicine of his time.

Hippocrates sought natural explanations for diseases and seems to have advocated letting nature take its course and not intervening too much. Illness was caused not by evil spirits, he asserted, but by physical problems in the body, particularly by imbalances in what he saw as four basic bodily fluids: blood, phlegm, black bile, and yellow bile. In a healthy body, these fluids, called humors, were in perfect balance, and the goal of medical treatment of the ill was to help the body bring them back into balance.

The **Sophists** (SOF-ihsts), a group of thinkers in fifth-century-B.C.E. Athens, applied philosophical speculation to politics and language, questioning the beliefs and laws of the polis to understand their origin. They believed that excellence in both politics and language could be taught, and they provided lessons for the young men of Athens who wished to learn how to persuade others. Their later opponents criticized them for charging fees and also accused them of using rhetoric to deceive people instead of presenting the truth. (Today the word *sophist* is usually used in this sense, describing someone who deceives people with clever-sounding but false arguments.)

Socrates (SOK-ruh-teez) (ca. 469–399 B.C.E.), whose ideas are known only through the works of others, also applied philosophy to politics and to people. He seemed, to many Athenians, to be a Sophist because he also questioned Athenian traditions, although he never charged fees. His approach when exploring ethical issues and defining concepts was to start with a general topic or problem and to narrow the matter to its essentials. He did so by continuously questioning participants in a discussion or argument through which they developed critical-thinking skills, a process known as the **Socratic method**.

Socrates was viewed with suspicion by many because he challenged the traditional beliefs and values of Athens, including its democracy. One of his students had headed the bloody oligarchical coup in 411 B.C.E., and one of the people he insulted had been a fighting hero in the restoration of democracy after the coup. Charges were brought against Socrates for corrupting the youth of the city and for impiety, that is, for not believing in the gods honored in the city. Thus, he was essentially charged with being unpatriotic because he criticized the traditions of the city and the decisions of government leaders. He was tried and imprisoned, and though he had several opportunities to escape, in 399 B.C.E., he drank the poison ordered as his method of execution and died.

Most of what we know about Socrates, including the details of his trial and death, comes from his student Plato (427–347 B.C.E.), who wrote dialogues in which Socrates asks questions. Plato also founded the Academy, a school dedicated to philosophy. He developed the theory that there are two worlds: the impermanent, changing world that we know through our senses, and the eternal, unchanging realm of "forms" that constitute the essence of true reality. According to Plato, true knowledge and the possibility of living a virtuous life

come from contemplating ideal forms—what later came to be called **Platonic ideals**—not from observing the visible world. Thus if you want to understand justice, asserted Plato, you should think about what would make perfect justice, not study the imperfect examples of justice around you. Although it is hard to separate Plato's thought from Socrates's, in his major work *The Republic,* Plato has Socrates argue that the best form of government is rule by enlightened individuals, what he called "philosopher-kings." Democracy is far too undisciplined and would lead to anarchy, so the role of the people is simply to choose a wise ruler.

Plato's student Aristotle (384–322 B.C.E.) also thought that true knowledge was possible, but he believed that such knowledge came from observation of the world, analysis of natural phenomena, and logical reasoning, not contemplation. Aristotle thought that everything had a purpose so that, to know something, one also had to know its function. Excellence—*arête* in Greek—meant performing one's function to the best of one's ability, whether one was a horse or a person. The range of Aristotle's thought is staggering. His interests embraced logic, ethics, natural science, physics, politics, poetry, and art. He studied the heavens as well as the earth and judged the earth to be the center of the universe, with the stars and planets revolving around it.

Plato's idealism profoundly shaped Western philosophy, but Aristotle came to have an even wider influence; for many centuries in Europe, the authority of Aristotle's ideas was second only to the Bible's. His works—which are actually a combination of his lecture notes and those of his students, copied and recopied many times—were used as the ultimate proof that something was true, even if closer observation of the phenomenon indicated that it was not. Thus, ironically, Aristotle's authority was sometimes invoked in a way that contradicted his own ideas. Despite these limitations, the broader examination of the universe and the place of humans in it that Socrates, Plato, and Aristotle engaged in is widely regarded as Greece's most important intellectual legacy.

**NOTES**

1. J. M. Edmonds, *Greek Elegy and Iambus* (Cambridge, Mass.: Harvard University Press, 1931), I.70, frag. 10.
2. *The Works of Xenophon*, trans. Henry G. Dakyns (London: Macmillan and Co., 1892), p. 296.

■ **mystery religions** Belief systems that were characterized by secret doctrines, rituals of initiation, and sometimes the promise of rebirth or an afterlife.

■ **Sophists** A group of thinkers in fifth-century-B.C.E. Athens who applied philosophical speculation to politics and language and were accused of deceit.

■ **Socratic method** A method of inquiry used by Socrates based on asking questions, through which participants developed their critical-thinking skills and explored ethical issues.

■ **Platonic ideals** According to Plato, the eternal unchanging ideal forms that are the essence of true reality.

3. Thucydides, *History of the Peloponnesian War*, 7.87.6.

4. G. Tarditi, *Archilochus Fragmenta* (Rome: Edizioni dell'Ateno, 1968), frag. 112.

5. Gregory Nagy, *The Ancient Greek Hero in 24 Hours* (Cambridge, Mass.: Harvard University Press, 2013), p. 119. Used by permission of Gregory Nagy, Center for Hellenic Studies.

6. Martin Bernal, *Black Athena: The Afroasiatic Roots of Classical Civilization* (New Brunswick, N.J.: Rutgers University Press, 1991). Essays by classical scholars refuting Bernal can be found in Mary R. Lefkowitz and Guy Maclean Rogers, eds., *Black Athena Revisited* (Durham: University of North Carolina Press, 1996).

# LOOKING BACK  LOOKING AHEAD

The ancient Greeks built on the endeavors of earlier societies in the eastern Mediterranean, but they also added new elements, including drama, philosophy, science, and naturalistic art. They created governments that relied on the participation of citizens. These cultural and political achievements developed in a society that, for many centuries, was almost always at war with the Persians and with each other. Those conflicts led many to wonder whether democracy was really a good form of government and to speculate more widely about abstract ideals and the nature of the cosmos. The Greeks carried these ideas with them as they colonized much of the Mediterranean, in migrations that often resulted from the conflicts that were so common in Greece.

The classical Greeks had tremendous influence not only on the parts of the world in which they traveled or settled, but also on all of Western civilization from that point on. As you will see in Chapter 5, Roman art, religion, literature, and many other aspects of culture relied on Greek models. And as you will see in Chapter 12, European thinkers and writers made conscious attempts to return to classical ideals in art, literature, and philosophy during the Renaissance. In the new United States, political leaders from the Revolutionary era on decided that important government buildings should be modeled on the Parthenon or other temples, complete with marble statuary of their own heroes. In some ways, capitol buildings in the United States are perfect symbols of the legacy of Greece — gleaming ideals of harmony, freedom, democracy, and beauty that (as with all ideals) do not always correspond with realities.

## Make Connections

Think about the larger developments and continuities within and across chapters.

1. How did division and conflict within and among city-states shape Greek history from the Bronze Age through the classical period?

2. How were Greek understandings of the role of the gods in public and private life similar to those of the Egyptians and Sumerians? How were they different?

3. Looking at your own town or city, what evidence do you find of the cultural legacy of ancient Greece?

# 3   REVIEW & EXPLORE

## Identify Key Terms

Identify and explain the significance of each item below.

Minoan (p. 57)

Mycenaean (p. 58)

polis (p. 61)

hoplites (p. 61)

tyranny (p. 62)

democracy (p. 62)

oligarchy (p. 62)

helots (p. 63)

Delian League (p. 66)

gynaeceum (p. 72)

mystery religions (p. 78)

Sophists (p. 79)

Socratic method (p. 79)

Platonic ideals (p. 79)

## Review the Main Ideas

Answer the section heading questions from the chapter.

**1.** How did the geography of Greece shape its earliest kingdoms? (p. 56)

**2.** What was the role of the polis in Greek society? (p. 61)

**3.** How did the wars of the classical period shape Greek history? (p. 66)

**4.** What ancient Greek ideas and ideals have had a lasting influence? (p. 69)

## Suggested Resources

### BOOKS

- Beard, Mary. *The Parthenon.* 2010. A cultural history of Athens's most famous building, including the many controversies that surround it.
- Cartledge, Paul. *The Spartans: The World of the Warrior Heroes of Ancient Greece.* 2002. A solid general book on the history and legacy of Sparta.
- Eckstein, Arthur M. 2006. *Mediterranean Anarchy, Interstate Warfare and the Rise of Rome.* Examines the long-term impact of endemic conflict in Mediterranean politics.
- Fisher, N. R. E. *Slavery in Classical Greece.* 2001. A brief study that puts slavery into its social, political, and intellectual contexts.
- Hansen, Mogens Herman. *Polis: An Introduction to the Ancient Greek City-State.* 2006. The authoritative study of the polis.
- Holland, Tom. *Persian Fire: The First World Empire and the Battle for the West.* 2007. Designed for general audiences, a dramatic retelling of conflict between the Greeks and the Persians.

- Kagan, Donald. *The Peloponnesian War.* 2003. A comprehensive yet accessible study that focuses on leaders and battles, but also the human costs.
- Maclachlan, Bonnie. *Women in Ancient Greece: A Sourcebook.* 2012. Source materials in translation, with texts from literary, rhetorical, philosophical, and legal sources, as well as papyri and inscriptions.
- Osborne, Robin. *Greece in the Making, 1200–479 B.C.* 2d ed. 2009. Traces the evolution of Greek communities from villages to cities and the development of their civic institutions.
- Rhodes, P. J. *Periclean Athens.* 2018. A concise introduction, designed for students, to the major political and cultural developments of Pericles's time.
- Roochnik, David. *Retrieving the Ancients: An Introduction to Greek Philosophy.* 2004. A sophisticated and well-written narrative of ancient Greek thought designed for students.
- Worthington, Ian. *Philip II of Macedonia.* 2010. Examines Philip's life and legacy, based on literary and archaeological sources.

### MEDIA

- *Ancient Apocalypse: Mystery of the Minoans* (BBC, 2008). Explores the role of the volcanic eruption on the nearby island of Thera in ending Minoan civilization; shot on location in Crete.
- *Athens: The Truth About Democracy* (BBC, 2007). Historian Bettany Hughes takes a critical look at classical Athens, with attention to slavery, imperialism, the flow of money, and restrictions on women.
- *Diotima: Materials for the Study of Women and Gender in the Ancient World.* Contains an extensive anthology of translated Greek, Latin, Egyptian, and Coptic texts, along with articles, book reviews, databases, and images. **www.stoa.org/diotima/**
- *The Greeks* (PBS 2016). Three-part series made by National Geographic that explores ancient Greek history from the Bronze Age through the classical period, and considers its impact on today's world.

- *The Odyssey* (Andrey Konchalovskiy, 1997). Originally made as a television miniseries, this film portrays many of Odysseus's adventures much as Homer wrote them, as they need no enhancing. Shot on location in the Mediterranean and with an international cast.
- *Perseus Digital Library.* The premier website for accessing the literature and archaeology of ancient Greek culture and now Roman as well, with hundreds of primary texts in Greek, Latin, and English translation, and thousands of images from museum collections and archaeological sites. **www.perseus.tufts.edu/hopper/**
- *The Rise and Fall of the Spartans* (History Channel, 2003). Examines the creation, maintenance, and end of Sparta's distinctive military/political system.
- *Troy* (Wolfgang Petersen, 2004). A fairly decent Hollywood film that focuses, as did Homer in his epic, on the personalities and motivations of the characters as well as on the Trojan War itself.

# 4

# *Life* in the Hellenistic World

## 338–30 B.C.E.

**When his father Philip was assassinated in 336 B.C.E.,** two years after he conquered Greece, twenty-year-old Alexander inherited not only his crown but also his determination to lead a united Greek force in fighting Persia. Alexander's invasion of the Persian Empire led to its downfall, but he died while planning his next campaign, only a little more than a decade after he had started. He left behind a huge empire that quickly broke into slightly smaller kingdoms, but more important, his death ushered in an era, the Hellenistic, in which Greek culture, the Greek language, and Greek thought spread as far as India, blending with local traditions. The end of the Hellenistic period is generally set at 30 B.C.E., the year of the death of Cleopatra VII—a Greek ruler—and the Roman conquest of her kingdom of Egypt. The Romans had conquered much of what had been Alexander's empire long before this, but many aspects of Hellenistic culture continued to flourish under Roman governance, adapting to Roman ways of life. Thus rather than coming to an abrupt end in one specific year, the Hellenistic world gradually evolved into the Roman.

In many ways, life in the Hellenistic world was not much different from life in Hellenic Greece or from that in any other Iron Age agricultural society: most people continued to be farmers, raising crops and animals for their own needs and for paying rents and taxes to their superiors. Those who lived in cities, however, often ate foods and drank wine that came from far away, did business with people who were quite unlike them, and adopted religious practices and ways of thinking unknown to their parents. Hellenistic cities thus offer striking parallels to those of today. ■

## CHAPTER PREVIEW

- How and why did Alexander the Great create an empire, and how did it evolve?

- How did Greek ideas and traditions spread to create a Hellenized society?

- What characterized the Hellenistic economy?

- How did religion, philosophy, and the arts reflect and shape Hellenistic life?

- How did science and medicine serve the needs of Hellenistic society?

**Hellenistic Married Life** This small terra-cotta figurine from Myrina in what is now Turkey, made in the second century B.C.E., shows a newly married couple sitting on a bridal bed. The groom is drawing back the bride's veil, and she is exhibiting the modesty that was a desired quality in young women. Figurines representing every stage of life became popular in the Hellenistic period and were used for religious offerings in temples and sacred places. This one was found in a tomb. (Musée du Louvre, Paris, France/Erich Lessing/Art Resource, NY)

# How and why did Alexander the Great create an empire, and how did it evolve?

Fully intending to carry out Philip's designs to lead the Greeks against the Persians, Alexander (r. 336–323 B.C.E.) proclaimed to the Greek world that the invasion of Persia was to be a mighty act of revenge for Xerxes's invasion of Greece in 480 B.C.E. (see "The Persian Wars" in Chapter 3) and more recent Persian interference in Greek affairs. Although he could not foresee this, Alexander's invasion ended up being much more. His campaign swept away the Persian Empire, which had ruled the area for over two hundred years. In its place Alexander established a Macedonian monarchy, and although his rule over these vast territories was never consolidated due to his premature death, he left behind a legacy of political and cultural influence, as well as a long period of war. Macedonian kings established dynasties and Greek culture spread in this Hellenistic era.

## Military Campaigns

Despite his youth, Alexander was well prepared to invade Persia. Philip had groomed his son to become king and had given him the best education possible, hiring the Athenian philosopher Aristotle to be his tutor. In 334 B.C.E. Alexander led an army of Macedonians and Greeks into Persian territory in Asia Minor. With him went a staff of philosophers to study the people of these lands, poets to write verses praising Alexander's exploits, scientists to map the area and study strange animals and plants, and a historian to write an account of the campaign. Alexander intended not only a military campaign but also an expedition of discovery.

In the next three years Alexander moved east into the Persian Empire, winning major battles at the Granicus River and Issus (Map 4.1). He moved into Syria and took most of the cities of Phoenicia and the eastern coast of the Mediterranean without a fight. His army

**MAP 4.1 Alexander's Conquests, 334–324 B.C.E.** This map shows the course of Alexander's invasion of the Persian Empire. More important than the great success of his military campaigns were the founding of new cities and the expansion of existing ones by Alexander and the Hellenistic rulers who followed him.

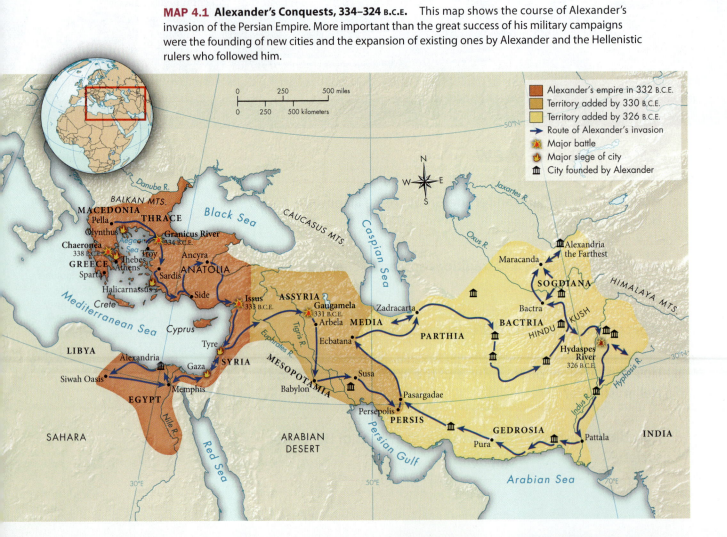

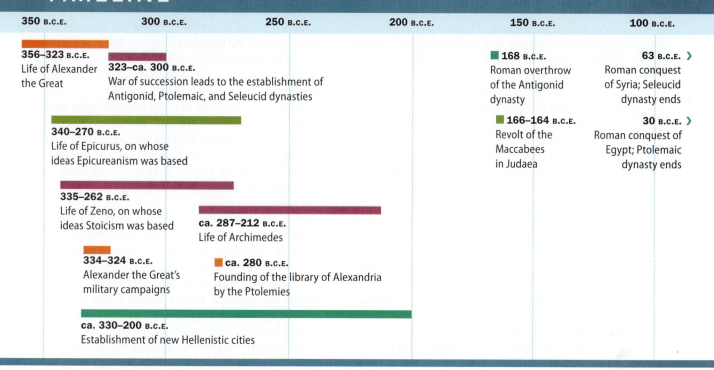

| 350 B.C.E. | 300 B.C.E. | 250 B.C.E. | 200 B.C.E. | 150 B.C.E. | 100 B.C.E. |
|---|---|---|---|---|---|

**356–323 B.C.E.**
Life of Alexander
the Great

**323–ca. 300 B.C.E.**
War of succession leads to the establishment of
Antigonid, Ptolemaic, and Seleucid dynasties

**340–270 B.C.E.**
Life of Epicurus, on whose
ideas Epicureanism was based

**335–262 B.C.E.**
Life of Zeno, on whose
ideas Stoicism was based

**ca. 287–212 B.C.E.**
Life of Archimedes

**334–324 B.C.E.**
Alexander the Great's
military campaigns

**ca. 280 B.C.E.**
Founding of the library of Alexandria
by the Ptolemies

**ca. 330–200 B.C.E.**
Establishment of new Hellenistic cities

**168 B.C.E.**
Roman overthrow
of the Antigonid
dynasty

**63 B.C.E.** ❯
Roman conquest
of Syria; Seleucid
dynasty ends

**166–164 B.C.E.**
Revolt of the
Maccabees
in Judaea

**30 B.C.E.** ❯
Roman conquest of
Egypt; Ptolemaic
dynasty ends

successfully besieged the cities that did oppose him, including Tyre and Gaza, executing the men of military age afterwards and enslaving the women and children. He then turned south toward Egypt, which had earlier been conquered by the Persians. The Egyptians saw Alexander as a liberator, and he seized it without a battle. After honoring the priestly class, Alexander was proclaimed pharaoh, the legitimate ruler of the country. He founded a new capital, Alexandria, on the coast of the Mediterranean, which would later grow into an enormous city. He next marched to the oasis of Siwah, west of the Nile Valley, to consult the famous oracle of Zeus-Amon, a composite god who combined qualities of the Greek Zeus and the Egyptian Amon-Ra (see "Egyptian Religion" in Chapter 1). No one will ever know what the priest told him, but henceforth Alexander called himself the son of Zeus.

Alexander left Egypt after less than a year and marched into Assyria, where at Gaugamela he defeated the Persian army, and then conquered the principal

**Amphora with Alexander and Darius at the Battle of Issus** Alexander, riding bareback, charges King Darius III, who is standing in a chariot. This detail from a jug was made within a decade after the battle in a Greek colony in southern Italy, beyond the area of Alexander's conquests, a good indication of how quickly Alexander's fame spread. (Apulian amphora, ca. 330–320 B.C.E., by Darius Painter, red-figure pottery from Ruvo in Magna Graecia, Italy/Museo Archeologico Nazionale, Naples, Italy/De Agostini Picture Library/A. Dagli Orti/Bridgeman Images)

Persian capital of Persepolis. There he performed a symbolic act of retribution by burning the royal buildings of King Xerxes, the invader of Greece during the Persian wars 150 years earlier. Without success Alexander pursued Persia's King Darius III (r. 336–330 B.C.E.), who appears to have been killed by Persian conspirators.

The Persian Empire had fallen and the war of revenge was over, but Alexander had no intention of stopping. Many of his troops had been supplied by Greek city-states that had allied with him; he released these troops from their obligations of military service, but then rehired them as mercenaries. Alexander then began his personal odyssey. With his Macedonian soldiers and Greek mercenaries, he set out to conquer more of Asia. He plunged deeper into the East, into lands completely unknown to the Greek world. It took his soldiers four additional years to conquer Bactria (in today's Afghanistan) and the easternmost parts of the now-defunct Persian Empire, but still Alexander was determined to continue his march.

In 326 B.C.E. Alexander crossed the Indus River and entered India (in the area that is now Pakistan). There, too, he saw hard fighting, and finally at the Hyphasis (HIH-fuh-sihs) River his troops refused to go farther. Alexander was enraged by the mutiny, for he believed he was near the end of the world. Nonetheless, the army stood firm, and Alexander relented. (See "Viewpoints: Greek Historians on Alexander the Great," page 87.) Still eager to explore the limits of the world, Alexander turned south to the Arabian Sea, and he waged a bloody and ruthless war against the people of the area. After reaching the Arabian Sea and turning west, he led his army through the grim Gedrosian Desert (now part of Pakistan and Iran). The army and those who supported the troops with supplies suffered fearfully, and many soldiers died along the way. Nonetheless, in 324 B.C.E. Alexander returned to Susa in the Greek-controlled region of Assyria, and in a mass wedding that symbolized both his conquest and his aim to unite Greek and Persian cultures, he married the daughter of Darius as well as the daughter of a previous Persian king, and at his order his high officers all married Persian wives. He gave wedding presents to Macedonian soldiers who married Persian women as well, a number reported to be 10,000. How many of these marriages of ordinary

soldiers survived is unknown, but of the high officers, only Seleucus, the founder of the vast Seleucid Empire (see "The Political Legacy"), kept his Persian wife; his son and successor in 280, Antiochus I, was thus half-Persian.

His mission was over, but Alexander never returned to his homeland of Macedonia. He died the next year in Babylon from fever, wounds, and excessive drinking. He was only thirty-two, but in just thirteen years he had created an empire that stretched from his homeland of Macedonia to India, gaining the title "the Great" along the way.

Alexander so quickly became a legend that he still seems superhuman. That alone makes a reasoned interpretation of his goals and character very difficult. His contemporaries from the Greek city-states thought he was a bloody-minded tyrant, but later Greek and Roman writers and political leaders admired him and even regarded him as a philosopher interested in the common good. That view influenced many later European and American historians, but this idealistic interpretation has generally been rejected after a more thorough analysis of the sources. The most common view today is that Alexander was a brilliant leader who sought personal glory through conquest and who tolerated no opposition.

## The Political Legacy

The main question at Alexander's death was whether his vast empire could be held together. Although he fathered a successor, the child was not yet born when Alexander died, and was thus too young to assume the duties of kingship. (Later he and his mother, Roxana, were murdered by one of Alexander's generals, who viewed him as a threat.) This meant that Alexander's empire was a prize for the taking. Several of the chief Macedonian generals aspired to become sole ruler, which led to a civil war lasting for decades that tore Alexander's empire apart. By the end of this conflict, the most successful generals had carved out their own smaller though still vast monarchies, each in competition for power with the others, as were their successors. As in the classical period, there was no enforceable international law, and the shifting and unstable balances of power combined with the ruthlessness and ambitions of leaders led to frequent war.

Alexander's general Ptolemy (ca. 367–ca. 283 B.C.E.) claimed authority over Egypt, and after fighting off rivals, established a kingdom and dynasty there, called the Ptolemaic (TAH-luh-MAY-ihk). In 304 B.C.E. he took the title of pharaoh, and by the end of his long life he had a relatively stable realm to pass on to his son. The **Ptolemaic dynasty** would rule Egypt for nearly three hundred years, until the death of the last Ptolemaic ruler, Cleopatra VII, in 30 B.C.E. (see Chapter 5). Seleucus (ca. 358–281 B.C.E.), another of Alexander's

■ **Ptolemaic dynasty** Dynasty of rulers established by General Ptolemy in Egypt after Alexander's conquests, which ruled until 30 B.C.E.

■ **Seleucid Empire** Large empire established in the Near East by General Seleucus after Alexander's conquests, which remained in power until 63 B.C.E.

■ **Antigonid dynasty** Dynasty of rulers established by General Antigonus in Macedonia after Alexander's conquests, which ruled until 168 B.C.E.

■ **Hellenistic** A term that literally means "like the Greek," used to describe the period after the death of Alexander the Great, when Greek culture spread.

# VIEWPOINTS

## Greek Historians on Alexander the Great

The works of only four ancient writers about Alexander the Great survive, all from three centuries or more after Alexander's death, though they make use of now-lost much older primary sources. Diodorus was a first-century-B.C.E. Greek historian, born in Sicily, and Arrian (ca. 86–160 C.E.) was a Greek military leader and historian. Both excerpts describe Alexander's troops' refusal to go farther east in India.

### Diodorus

Alexander observed that his soldiers were exhausted with their constant campaigns. They had spent almost eight years among toils and dangers, and it was necessary to raise their spirits by an effective appeal if they were to undertake an expedition against the Gandaridae [people who lived across the Hyphasis River]. There had been many losses among the soldiers, and no relief from fighting was in sight. The hooves of the horses had been worn thin by steady marching. The arms and armour were wearing out, and Greek clothing was quite gone. They had to clothe themselves in foreign materials, recutting the garments of the Indians. This was the season also, as luck would have it, of the heavy rains. They had been going on for seventy days, to the accompaniment of continuous thunder and lightning . . . he saw only one hope of gaining his wish, if he might gain the soldiers' great goodwill though gratitude. Accordingly he allowed them to ravage the enemy's country, which was full of every good thing. During these days when the army was busy foraging, he called together the wives of the soldiers and their children; to the wives he undertook to give a monthly ration, to the children he delivered a service bonus in proportion to the military records of their fathers. When the soldiers returned laden with wealth from their expedition, he brought them together for a meeting. He delivered a carefully prepared speech about the expedition against the Gandaridae but the Macedonians did not accept it, and he gave up the undertaking.

### Arrian

The spirit of the Macedonians now began to flag, when they saw the king [Alexander] raising one labour after another, and incurring one danger after another. Conferences were held throughout the camp, in which those who were the most moderate bewailed their lot, while others resolutely declared that they would not follow Alexander any farther, even if he should lead the way. When he heard of this, before the disorder and pusillanimity [cowardice] of the soldiers should advance to a great degree, he called a council of the officers of the brigades and addressed them: — "Macedonians and Grecian allies, seeing that you no longer follow me into dangerous enterprises with a resolution equal to that which formerly animated you, I have collected you together into the same spot, so that I may either persuade you to march forward with me, or may be persuaded by you to return. . . . But, O Macedonians and Grecian allies, stand firm! Glorious are the deeds of those who undergo labour and run the risk of danger; and it is delightful to live a life of valour and to die leaving behind immortal glory. . . . For the land is yours, and you act as its viceroys [rulers]. The greater part also of the money now comes to you. . . ." Having said this, he retired into his tent . . . waiting to see if any change would occur in the minds of the Macedonians. . . . But on the contrary, when there was a profound silence throughout the camp, and the soldiers were evidently annoyed at his wrath, without being at all changed by it . . . he made known to the army that he had resolved to march back again.

### QUESTIONS FOR ANALYSIS

1. What do the two authors say that Alexander did to try to persuade his troops to go further? What do these actions suggest about the authors' views of Alexander's character as a leader?
2. What other aspects of Alexander's campaigns do these sources reveal?

Sources: *Diodorus of Sicily*, with an English translation by C. Bradford Welles (Cambridge: Harvard University Press 1961), vol. 8, pp. 391–393; Arrian, *The Anabasis of Alexander*, translated by E. J. Chinook (London: Hodder and Stoughton, 1884), pp. 307–308, 314.

officers, carved out a large state, the **Seleucid Empire** (SUH-loo-suhd), that stretched from the coast of Asia Minor to India. He was assassinated in 281 B.C.E. on the order of the ruler of the Ptolemaic kingdom, but his son succeeded him, founding a dynasty that also lasted for centuries, although the kingdom itself shrank as independent states broke off in Pergamum, Bactria, Parthia, and elsewhere. Antigonus I (382–301 B.C.E.), a third general, became king of Macedonia and established the **Antigonid** (an-TIH-guh-nuhd) **dynasty**, which lasted until it was overthrown by the Romans in 168 B.C.E. The remains of the Seleucid Empire were also conquered by the Romans, in 63 B.C.E., and the Ptolemaic kingdom ended with Roman conquest in 30 B.C.E. (see Chapters 5 and 6).

**Hellenistic** rulers amassed an enormous amount of wealth from their large kingdoms, and royal patronage provided money for the production of literary works and the research and development that allowed discoveries in science and engineering. To encourage

**Royal Couple Cameo** This Hellenistic cameo, designed to be worn as a necklace, probably portrays King Ptolemy II and his sister Arsinoe II, rulers of the Ptolemaic kingdom of Egypt. During the Hellenistic period portraits of queens became more common because of the increased importance of hereditary monarchies. (Kunthistorisches Museum, Vienna, Austria/Erich Lessing/Art Resource, NY)

obedience and support for their militaristic ambitions, Hellenistic kings often created ruler cults that linked the king's authority with that of the gods, or they adopted ruler cults that already existed, as Alexander did in Egypt. These deified kings were not considered gods as mighty as Zeus or Apollo, and the new ruler cults probably had little religious impact on the people being ruled. The kingdoms never won the deep emotional loyalty that Greeks had once felt for the polis, but the ruler cult was an easily understandable symbol of unity within the kingdom.

Hellenistic kingship was hereditary, which gave women who were members of royal families more power than any woman had in democracies such as Athens, where citizenship was limited to men. Wives and mothers of kings had influence over their husbands and sons, and a few women ruled in their own right when there was no male heir.

Greece itself changed politically during the Hellenistic period. To enhance their joint security, many poleis organized themselves into leagues of city-states, of which the two most extensive were the Aetolian (ee-TOH-lee-uhn) League in western and central Greece and the Achaean (uh-KEE-uhn) League in southern Greece. These leagues also became involved in the frequent warfare of the Hellenistic period, contributing to the anarchy of the eastern Mediterranean.

# How did Greek ideas and traditions spread to create a Hellenized society?

Alexander's most important legacy was clearly not political unity. Instead it was the spread of Greek ideas and traditions across a wide area, a process scholars later called **Hellenization**. To maintain contact with the Greek world as he moved farther eastward, Alexander founded new cities and military colonies and expanded existing cities, settling Greek and Macedonian troops and veterans in them. Besides keeping the road back to Greece open, these settlements helped secure the countryside around them. This practice continued after his death, with more than 250 new cities founded in North Africa, West and Central Asia, and southeastern Europe. These cities and colonies became powerful instruments in the spread of Hellenism and in the blending of Greek and other cultures.

## Urban Life

In many respects the Hellenistic city resembled a modern city. It was a cultural center with theaters, temples, and libraries. It was a seat of learning, a home of poets,

writers, teachers, and artists. City dwellers could find amusement through plays, musical performances, animal fights, and gambling. The Hellenistic city was also an economic center that provided a ready market for grain and produce raised in the surrounding countryside. In short, the Hellenistic city offered cultural and economic opportunities for rich and poor alike.

To the Greeks, civilized life was unthinkable outside of a city, and Hellenistic kings often gave cities all the external trappings of a polis. Each had an assembly of citizens, a council to prepare legislation, and a board of magistrates to conduct political business. Yet, however similar to the Greek polis it appeared, such a city could not engage in diplomatic dealings, make treaties, pursue its own foreign policy, or wage its own wars. The city was required to follow royal orders, and the king often placed his own officials in it to see that his decrees were followed.

A Hellenistic city differed from a Greek polis in other ways as well. The Greek polis had one body of law and one set of customs. In the Hellenistic city Greeks represented an elite class. Natives and non-Greek foreigners who lived in Hellenistic cities usually

■ **Hellenization** The spread of Greek ideas, culture, and traditions to non-Greek groups across a wide area.

possessed lesser rights than Greeks and often had their own laws. In some instances this disparity spurred natives to assimilate Greek culture in order to rise politically and socially.

The city of Pergamum in northwestern Anatolia is a good example of an older city that underwent changes in the Hellenistic period. Previously an important strategic site, Pergamum was transformed by its new Greek rulers into a magnificent city complete with all the typical buildings of the polis, including gymnasia, baths, and one of the finest libraries in the entire Hellenistic world. The new rulers erected temples to the traditional Greek deities, but they also built imposing temples to other gods. There was a Jewish population in the city, who may have established a synagogue. Especially in the agora, the public marketplace in the center of town, Greeks

and indigenous people met to conduct business and exchange goods and ideas. Greeks felt as though they were at home, and the evolving culture mixed Greek and local elements.

The Bactrian city of Ay Khanoum on the Oxus River, on the border of modern Afghanistan, is a good example of a brand-new city where cultures met. Bactria and Parthia had been part of the Seleucid kingdom, but in the third century B.C.E. their governors overthrew the Seleucids and established independent kingdoms in today's Afghanistan and Turkmenistan (Map 4.2). Bactria became an outpost of Hellenism, from which the rulers of China and India learned of sophisticated societies other than their own. It had Greek temples and administration buildings, and on a public square was a long inscription in Greek verse carved in stone, erected by a man who may have been

## MAPPING THE PAST

### MAP 4.2 The Hellenistic World, ca. 263 B.C.E.

This map depicts the Hellenistic world after Alexander's death.

**ANALYZING THE MAP** Compare this map to Map 4.1. After Alexander's death, were the Macedonians and Greeks able to retain control of most of the land he had conquered? What areas were lost?

**CONNECTIONS** What does this map suggest about the success or failure of Alexander's dreams of conquest?

# Bactrian Disk with Religious Figures

This spectacular metal disk, about 10 inches across, was made in the Bactrian city of Ay Khanoum in the second century B.C.E. It probably depicts Cybele, a Greek earth mother goddess, and Nike, the Greek winged goddess of victory, being pulled in a chariot by lions with the sun-god Helios above. A priest holds a sun parasol—a royal symbol—above them, and a priestess is standing on a stepped altar at the right. Worship of Cybele spread into Greece from the east, and was then spread by her Greek followers as they conquered, traveled, and migrated.

## EVALUATE THE EVIDENCE

1. Looking at the disk along with the other illustrations of divine and human figures in this chapter and Chapter 3, what elements of the imagery seem typically Greek? Which appear different, so are perhaps of Asian origin?
2. Why do you think the artist who made this might have combined Greek and non-Greek elements to create a hybrid image on this luxury item?

(Pictures from History/Bridgeman Images)

---

a student of Aristotle and taken from a saying of the Oracle at Delphi:

> In childhood, learn good manners
> In youth, control your passions
> In middle age, practice justice
> In old age, be of good counsel
> In death, have no regrets.[1]

Along with this very public display of Greek ideals, the city also had temples to local deities and artwork that blended Greek and local styles (for an example, see the metal disk in "Evaluating Visual Evidence: Bactrian Disk with Religious Figures," above).

## Greeks in Hellenistic Cities

Like Alexander himself, the ruling dynasties of the Hellenistic world were Macedonian, and Macedonians and Greeks filled all the important political, military, and diplomatic positions. Besides building Greek cities, Hellenistic kings offered Greeks land and money as lures to further immigration.

The Hellenistic monarchy, unlike the Greek polis, did not depend solely on its citizens to fulfill its political needs, but instead relied on professionals. Talented Greek men had the opportunity to rise quickly in the government bureaucracy. Appointed by the king, these administrators did not have to stand for election each year, unlike many officials of Greek poleis. Since they held their jobs year after year, they had ample time to create new administrative techniques, and also time to develop ways to profit personally from their positions.

Greeks also found ready employment in the armies and navies of the Hellenistic monarchies. Alexander had proved the Greco-Macedonian style of warfare to be far superior to that of other peoples, and Alexander's successors, themselves experienced officers, realized the importance of trained soldiers in their campaigns for dominance. Hellenistic kings were reluctant to arm the local populations or to allow them to serve in the army, fearing military rebellions among their conquered subjects. The result was the emergence of paid professional armies and navies consisting primarily of Greeks, although drawn from many areas of Greece and Macedonia, not simply from one polis. Unlike the citizen hoplites of classical Greece, these men were full-time soldiers. Hellenistic kings paid them well, often giving them land or leasing it to them as an incentive to remain loyal.

Greeks were able to dominate other professions as well. Hellenistic kingdoms and cities recruited Greek writers and artists to create Greek literature, art, and culture. Greek architects, engineers, and skilled craftsmen found themselves in great demand to produce the Greek-style buildings commissioned by the Hellenistic monarchs. Architects and engineers would sometimes design and build whole cities, which they laid out in checkerboard fashion and filled with typical Greek buildings. An enormous wave of construction took place during the Hellenistic period.

Increased physical and social mobility benefited some women as well as men. More women learned to read than before, and they engaged in occupations in which literacy was beneficial, including care of the sick. During the Hellenistic period women still had to have male guardians to buy, sell, or lease land; to borrow money; and to represent them in other commercial transactions. (The requirement of a male guardian was later codified in Roman law and largely maintained in Europe into the nineteenth century.) Yet often such a guardian was present only to fulfill the letter of the law. The woman was the real agent and handled the business being transacted.

Because of the opportunities the Hellenistic monarchies offered, many people moved frequently. These were generally individual decisions, not part of organized colonization efforts such as those that had been common earlier in Greek history (see Chapter 3). Once a Greek man had left home to take service with, for instance, the army or the bureaucracy of the Ptolemies, he had no incentive beyond his pay and the comforts of life in Egypt to keep him there. If the Seleucid king offered him more money or a promotion, he might well accept it and take his talents to Asia Minor. Thus professional Greek soldiers and administrators were very mobile and were apt to look to their own interests, not their kingdom's. Linguistic changes further facilitated the ease with which people moved. Instead of the different dialects spoken in Greece itself, a new Greek dialect called the *koine* (koy-NAY), which means "common," became the spoken language of traders, the royal court, the bureaucracy, and the army across the Hellenistic world.

As long as Greeks continued to migrate, the kingdoms remained stable and strong. In the process they drew an immense amount of talent from the Greek peninsula. However, the Hellenistic monarchies could not keep recruiting Greeks forever, in spite of their wealth and willingness to spend lavishly, as the population of Greece was not boundless. In time the huge surge of immigration slowed greatly.

## Greeks and Non-Greeks

Across the Hellenistic world the prevailing institutions and laws became Greek. Everyone, Greek or non-Greek, who wanted to find an official position or

compete in business had to learn Greek. Those who did gained an avenue of social mobility, and as early as the third century B.C.E. local people in some Hellenistic cities began to rise in power and prominence. They adopted a Greek name and, if they were male, went to Greek educational institutions or sent their sons there. Hoping to impress the Greek elite, priests in Babylon and Alexandria composed histories of their areas in Greek. Once a man knew Greek, he could move more easily to another area for better opportunities, and perhaps even hide his non-Greek origins. He could also join a military unit and perhaps be deployed far from his place of origin. Thus learning Greek was an avenue of geographic mobility as well.

Cities granted citizenship to Hellenized local people and sometimes to Greek-speaking migrants, although there were fewer political benefits of citizenship than there had been in the classical period, because real power was held by monarchs, not citizens. Even a few women received honorary citizenship in Hellenistic cities because of aid they had provided in times of crisis. Being Greek became to some degree a matter of culture, not bloodlines.

Cultural influences in the other direction occurred less frequently, because they brought fewer advantages. Few Greeks learned a non-Greek language, unless they were required to because of their official position. Greeks did begin to worship local deities, but often these were somewhat Hellenized and their qualities blended with those of an existing Greek god or goddess. (See "Evaluating Visual Evidence: Bactrian Disk with Religious Figures," page 90.) Greeks living in Egypt generally cremated their dead while Egyptians continued to mummify them, although by the first century B.C.E. Greeks and Romans sometimes mummified their dead as well, attaching realistic portraits painted on wooden panels to the mummies. These portraits have served as important sources about clothing and hairstyles.

Yet the spread of Greek culture was wider than it was deep. Hellenistic kingdoms were never entirely unified in language, customs, and thought. The principal reason for this phenomenon is that Greek culture generally did not extend far beyond the reaches of the cities. Many urban residents adopted the aspects of Hellenism that they found useful, but people in the countryside generally did not embrace it, nor were they encouraged to.

Ptolemaic Egypt provides an excellent example of this situation. The Ptolemies maintained separate legal systems for Greeks and Egyptians. The indigenous people were the foundation of the kingdom: they fed it by their labor in the fields and financed its operations with their taxes. For this reason, the Ptolemies tied local people to the land more tightly than they had been before, making it nearly impossible for them to leave their villages. The bureaucracy of the Ptolemies was relatively efficient, and the indigenous population was viciously and cruelly exploited. Even in times of hardship, the king's taxes came first, even though payment might mean starvation. The people's desperation was summed up by one Egyptian, who scrawled the warning, "We are worn out; we will run away."[2] To many Egyptians, revolt or a life of banditry was preferable to working the land under the harsh Ptolemies.

The situation was somewhat different in the booming city of Alexandria, founded by Alexander to be a new seaport, where there had been a small village earlier. Within a century of its founding, it was probably the largest city in the world, with a population numbering in the hundreds of thousands. The ruling elite was primarily Greek, and the Ptolemies tried to keep the Greek and Egyptian populations apart, but this was not always possible. Although the Ptolemies encouraged immigration from Greece, the number

**Head of a Young Nubian**   This bust, carved in black porphyry rock, was most likely made in Alexandria in the second or first century B.C.E. Hellenistic sculptors depicted the wide range of migrants to the city in stone, bronze, and marble. (Private Collection/De Agostini Picture Library/G. Dagli Orti/ Bridgeman Images)

of immigrants was relatively low, so intermarriage increased. And the Ptolemies themselves gave privileges to local priests, building temples and sponsoring rituals honoring the local gods. Priestly families became owners of large landed estates and engaged in other sorts of business as well, becoming loyal supporters of the Ptolemaic regime. Even the processions honoring local gods still celebrated Greekness, however, and sometimes became a flash point sparking protests by Egyptians.

In about 280 B.C.E. the Ptolemies founded a library in Alexandria that both glorified Greek culture and sponsored new scholarship. It came to contain hundreds of thousands of papyrus scrolls of Greek writings, including copies of such classic works as the poems of Homer, the histories of Herodotus and Thucydides, and the philosophical works of Plato and Aristotle, as well as newer accounts of scientific discoveries. The Ptolemies sent representatives to Greece to buy books, paid for copies made of any Greek books that were brought to Alexandria, and supported scholars who edited multiple versions of older books into a single authoritative version. The library became one of the foremost intellectual centers of the ancient world, pulling in Greek-speaking writers, scholars, scientists, and thinkers from far away and preserving Greek writings.

Greek culture spread more deeply in the Seleucid kingdom than in Egypt, although this was not because the Seleucids had an organized plan for Hellenizing the local population. The primary problem for the Seleucids was holding on to the territory they had inherited. To do this, they established cities and military colonies throughout the region to nurture a vigorous and large Greek-speaking population and to defend the kingdom from their Persian neighbors. Seleucid military colonies were generally founded near existing villages, thus exposing even rural residents to all aspects of Greek life. Many local people found Greek political and cultural forms attractive and imitated them. In Asia Minor and Syria, for instance, numerous villages and towns developed along Greek lines, and some of them grew into Hellenized cities.

The kings of Bactria and Parthia spread Greek culture even further. Some of these rulers converted to Buddhism, and the Buddhist ruler of the Mauryan Empire in northern India, Ashoka (ca. 269–233 B.C.E.), may have ordered translations of his laws into Greek for the Greek-speaking residents of Bactria and Parthia. In the second century B.C.E., after the collapse of the Mauryan Empire, Bactrian armies conquered part of northern India, establishing several small Indo-Greek states where the mixing of religious and artistic traditions was particularly pronounced.

# What characterized the Hellenistic economy?

Alexander's conquest of the Persian Empire not only changed the political face of the ancient world and led to a shared urban culture, but also brought the Near East and Egypt fully into the sphere of Greek economics. The Hellenistic period, however, did not see widespread improvements in the way most people lived and worked. The majority of people were farmers who lived in the countryside, and their lives continued to be dominated by hard work. There were relatively few advances in agricultural or production methods, and many people who lived in rural areas were actually worse off than they had been before, because of higher levels of rents and taxes. Wealthy and middling-status people in cities flourished, but poorer people in cities who depended on wages were hurt by inflation. Alexander and his successors did link East and West in a broad commercial network, however, and the spread of Greeks throughout the Near East and Egypt created new markets and stimulated trade.

## Rural Life

As in every ancient society, the vast majority of people in the Hellenistic world were subsistence farmers who lived in the countryside. For them, the most important event of the 330s B.C.E. may have been a long-lasting drought, not Alexander's conquests. Most people in this period worked on small family farms that they owned or rented, or on larger farms owned by wealthy absentee landlords. The mainstays of Hellenistic agriculture remained the triad of grain, grapevines, and olive trees, which had been the core of Mediterranean crop raising since the Bronze Age, so prominent that "grain, new wine, and olive oil" are frequently mentioned together in Hebrew Scripture.

Farmers relied on a simple plow pulled by oxen to break the ground and prepare the soil for planting. Plowing also controlled weeds and preserved soil moisture. Farmers further broke up the land with mattocks, a tool similar to a pickax. At harvest time they reaped the grain with sickles. Barley was more common than wheat because it was hardier and could grow in poorer soil; it was generally eaten as a cooked grain. Wheat, on the other hand, was the preferred grain for making bread. Lentils and beans served as food for both people and animals, and as fertilizer for the soil. Olive trees grew even in poor earth, and fruit trees added welcome sweets to the family diet. Whenever possible, farmers grew grapevines, as wine was a common drink in the Hellenistic world, where it was generally drunk mixed with water because the wine was so rough. Protein came from cheese, fish — fresh, dried, salted, and smoked — and very occasionally meat.

Men tended to do the plowing, while women and children hoed and weeded. Plowing and seeding were

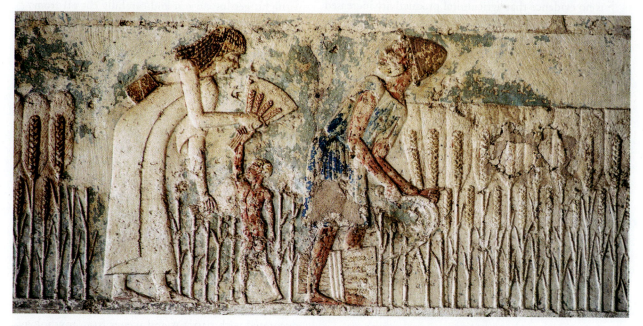

**Harvesting Grain in Hellenistic Egypt**　In this scene from the outer court of the tomb of Petosiris in Egypt, a man cuts grain with a sickle and a woman and child bind it into sheaves, a standard division of labor throughout the ancient world. Petosiris was a high priest who lived in the fourth century B.C.E., but his tomb was made later, after Egypt had been conquered by Alexander the Great. It was decorated in a style that mixed Greek and Egyptian elements, as was true of so much of Hellenistic culture. (Relief from vestibule of tomb of Petosiris, necropolis of Khmun [or Hermopolis], Tuna el-Gebel, Egypt/De Agostini Picture Library/S. Vannini/Bridgeman Images)

usually done in the autumn. Winter rains encouraged growth, and farmers harvested their crops in early summer. After the harvest, grain was spread over a circular threshing floor, where donkeys harnessed to a pole crushed the kernels. Grapes were harvested in early fall and left sitting for two weeks before being crushed into wine.

At harvest time people offered some of their crops to the gods in thanks and set aside another — no doubt larger — portion for paying their rents and taxes. Another portion was saved as seed for the next year, but the largest portion was stored to be eaten over the next months. With what was left, farmers treated themselves to a festive meal, enjoyed along with music and dancing as a short break from work. Government intervened in rural people's lives primarily in the collection of taxes, as much of the revenue for the Hellenistic kingdoms was derived from taxing land and agricultural products. Egypt had a strong tradition of central authority dating back to the pharaohs, which the Ptolemies inherited and tightened. They had the power to mobilize local labor into the digging and maintenance of canals and ditches, and they even attempted to decree what crops Egyptian farmers would plant and what animals would be raised. Such centralized planning was difficult to enforce at the local level, however, especially because the officials appointed to do so switched positions frequently and concentrated most on extracting taxes. Thus, despite some royal interest in agriculture, there is no evidence that agricultural productivity increased or that practices changed. Technology was applied to military needs, but not to those of food production.

Diodorus of Sicily, a Greek historian who apparently visited Ptolemaic Egypt around 60 B.C.E., was surprised that Egyptians could feed all their children instead of resorting to the selective exposure of infants practiced in Greece. He decided that this was because of their less formal child-rearing habits:

They feed their children in a sort of happy-go-lucky fashion that in its inexpensiveness quite surpasses belief; for they serve them with stews made of any stuff that is ready to hand and cheap, and give them such stalks as the byblos plant [the reeds from which papyrus is made] as can be roasted in the coals and the roots and the stems of marsh plants, either raw or boiled or baked. And since most of the children are reared without shoes or clothing because of the mildness of the climate of the country, the entire expense incurred by the parents of a child until it comes to maturity is not more than twenty drachmas. These are the leading reasons why Egypt has such an extraordinarily large population.[3]

Egyptian parents would probably have given other reasons, such as rents and taxes, for why their children had simple food and no shoes.

## Production of Goods

As with agriculture, although demand for goods increased during the Hellenistic period, no significant new techniques of production appear to have developed. Manual labor, not machinery, continued to turn out the raw materials and manufactured goods the Hellenistic world used.

Diodorus gives a picture of this hard labor, commenting about life in the gold mines owned by the kings:

At the end of Egypt is a region bearing many mines and abundant gold, which is extracted with great pain and expense. . . . For kings of Egypt condemn to the mines criminals and prisoners of war, those who were falsely accused and those who were put into jail because of royal anger, not only them but sometimes also all of their relatives. Rounding them up, they assign them to the gold mines, taking revenge on those who were condemned and through their labors gaining huge revenues. The condemned — and they are very many — all of them are put in chains; and they work persistently and continually, both by day and throughout the night, getting no rest and carefully cut off from escape. For the guards, who are barbarian soldiers and who speak a different language, stand watch over them so that no man can either by conversation or friendly contact corrupt any of them.[4]

Apart from gold and silver, which were used primarily for coins and jewelry, bronze continued to be used for shields. Iron was utilized for weapons and tools.

Pottery remained an important commodity, and most of it was produced locally. The coarse pottery used in the kitchen for plates and cups changed little. Fancier pots and bowls, decorated with a shiny black glaze, came into use during the Hellenistic period. This ware originated in Athens, but potters in other places began to imitate its style, heavily cutting into the Athenian market. In the second century B.C.E. a red-glazed ware, often called Samian, burst on the market and soon dominated it. Pottery was often decorated with patterns and scenes from mythology, legend, and daily life. Potters often portrayed heroic episodes, such as battles from the *Iliad*, or gods, such as Dionysus at sea. Pots journeyed with Greek merchants, armies, and travelers, so these images spread knowledge of Greek religion and stories west as far as

Portugal and east as far as Southeast Asia. Pottery thus served as a means of cultural exchange — of ideas as well as goods — among people scattered across huge portions of the globe.

## Commerce

Alexander's conquest of the Persian Empire had immediate effects on trade and prices. In the conquered Persian capitals Alexander had found vast sums of gold, silver, and other treasure. This wealth financed the creation of new cities, the building of roads, and the development of harbors. It also provided the thousands who participated in his expeditions with booty, with which they could purchase commodities. The release of this vast Persian horde of money into the Greek world led to inflation, however, and prices on basic commodities such as flour and olive oil doubled or more. After a high point in about 300 B.C.E., prices gradually sank, but they never returned to prices of the earlier period. Those who depended on wages for a living were badly hurt by this inflation, and they did what poor people often do as they search for a better life: migrate, which in this case meant to the new cities of the East.

Greek merchants eagerly took advantage of new opportunities for trade, which was facilitated by the coining of money. Most of the great monarchies coined their money according to a uniform system, which meant that much of the money used in Hellenistic kingdoms had the same value. Traders were less in need of money changers than in the days when each major power coined money on a different standard.

Overland trade was conducted by caravan, and the backbone of this caravan trade was the camel — a shaggy, ill-tempered, but durable animal ideally suited to the harsh climate of the caravan routes. Luxury goods that were light, rare, and expensive traveled over the caravan routes to Alexandria or to the harbors of Phoenicia and Syria, from which they were shipped to Greece, Italy, and Spain. In time these luxury items, including ivory, precious stones, and spices, became more commonplace, in part because of an increased volume of trade. Perhaps the most prominent good in terms of volume was silk, and the trade in silk later gave the major east-west route its name: the Silk Road. In return the Greeks and Macedonians sent east manufactured goods, especially metal weapons, cloth, wine, and olive oil. Although these caravan routes can trace their origins to earlier times, they became far more prominent in the Hellenistic period. Business customs and languages of trade developed and became standardized, so that merchants from different nationalities could communicate in a way understandable to all of them.

The durability and economic importance of the caravan routes are amply demonstrated by the fact that the death of Alexander, the ensuing wars of his successors, and later regional conflicts had little effect on trade. Numerous mercantile cities grew up along these routes, and commercial contacts brought people from far-flung regions together, even if sometimes indirectly. The merchants and the caravan cities were links in a chain that reached from the Mediterranean Sea to India and beyond to China, along which ideas as well as goods were passed.

More economically important than the trade in luxury goods were commercial dealings in essential commodities like raw materials and grain and such mass-produced items as pottery. The Hellenistic monarchies usually raised enough grain for their own needs as well as a surplus for export. This trade in grain was essential for the cities of Greece and the Aegean, many of which could not grow enough. Fortunately for them, abundant wheat supplies were available nearby in Egypt and in the area north of the Black Sea (see Map 4.2). Cities in Greece often paid for their grain by exporting olive oil and wine.

Most trade in bulk commodities was seaborne, and the Hellenistic merchant ship was the workhorse of the day. The merchant ship had a broad beam and relied on sails for propulsion. It was far more seaworthy than the contemporary warship, the trireme (see Chapter 3), which was long, narrow, and built for speed. A small crew of experienced sailors could handle the merchant vessel easily. Maritime trade provided opportunities for workers in other industries and trades: sailors, shipbuilders, dockworkers, accountants, teamsters, and pirates. Piracy was always a factor in the Hellenistic world, so ships' crews had to be ready to defend their cargoes as well as transport them.

Much maritime trade was shipped in large two-handled pottery jars called amphoras, which protected contents from water and rodents. They were easy and cheap to produce, were surprisingly durable, and could easily be reused. Amphoras contained all sorts of goods — wine, olive oil, spices, unguents, dried fish, olives, grapes, salt, and the pine pitch used to caulk ships so that they would not leak. Like modern containers, amphoras often had stamps, inscriptions, or other markings indicating where they were made, where they were going, and what their contents were. These markings and the remains of the amphoras' contents have provided marine archaeologists and historians with much of their information about trade in the Hellenistic world. Amphoras made specifically for wine seem to have been standardized in size and shape so that they could fit on racks in ships, making long-distance shipping of wine cheaper and easier, just as standardized steel containers have made the shipping of breakable wine bottles — and every other commodity — cheaper and easier today.

Slaves were a staple of Hellenistic trade, traveling in all directions on both land and sea routes. A few lists of slaves owned by a single individual have survived, and these indicate that slaves in one area often came from far away and from many different regions. Ancient authors cautioned against having too many slaves from one area together, as this might encourage them to revolt. War provided prisoners for the slave market; to a lesser extent, so did kidnapping and capture by pirates, although the origins of most slaves are unknown. Both old Greek states and new Hellenistic kingdoms were ready slave markets, and throughout the Mediterranean world slaves were almost always in demand. Slaves were to be found in the cities and temples of the Hellenistic world; in the shops, fields, armies, and mines; and in the homes of wealthier people. Their price varied depending on their age, sex, health, and skill level, and also—as with any commodity—on market conditions. Large-scale warfare increased the number of slaves available, so the price went down; during periods of relative peace, fewer people were enslaved through conquest, so the price went up.

# How did religion, philosophy, and the arts reflect and shape Hellenistic life?

The mixing of peoples in the Hellenistic era influenced religion, philosophy, and the arts. The Hellenistic kings built temples to the old Olympian gods and promoted rituals and ceremonies like those in earlier Greek cities, but new deities also gained prominence. More people turned to mystery religions, which blended Greek and non-Greek elements. Others turned to practical philosophies that provided advice on how an individual should live a good life. Themes of individualism emerged in Hellenistic art and literature as well.

## Religion and Magic

When Hellenistic kings founded cities, they also built temples, staffed by priests and supported by taxes, for the Olympian gods of Greece. The transplanted religions, like those in Greece itself, sponsored literary, musical, and athletic contests, which were staged in beautiful surroundings among impressive new Greek-style buildings. These festivities offered bright and lively entertainment, both intellectual and physical. They fostered Greek culture and traditional sports and were attractive to socially aspiring individuals who adopted Greek culture.

Along with the traditional Olympian gods, Greeks and non-Greeks in the Hellenistic world also honored and worshipped deities that had not been important in the Hellenic period or that were a blend of imported Greek and indigenous gods and goddesses. Tyche (TIGH-kee), for example, the goddess and personification of luck, fate, chance, and fortune, became increasingly prominent during the chaotic years following Alexander's death. Contemporaries commented that when no other cause could be found for an event, Tyche was responsible. Temples to her were built in major cities of the eastern Mediterranean, including Antioch and Alexandria, and her image was depicted on coins and bas-reliefs.

Tyche could be blamed for bad things that happened, but Hellenistic people did not simply give in to fate. Instead they honored Tyche with public rituals and more-private ceremonies, and they also turned to professionals who offered spells for various purposes. We generally make a distinction between religion and magic, but for Greeks there was not a clear line. Thus they would write spells using both ordinary Greek words and special "magical" language known only to the gods, often instructing those who purchased them to carry out specific actions to accompany their words. Thousands

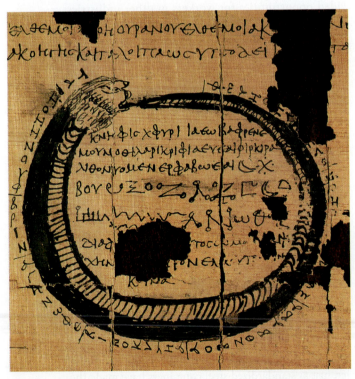

**Hellenistic Magical Text**    This text, written in Greek and Egyptian on papyrus, presents a magical incantation surrounded by a lion-headed snake. Both Hellenic and Hellenistic Greeks sought to know the future through various means of divination and to control the future through rituals and formulas that called on spirits and gods. (Papyrus 121 f.3r/British Library, London, UK/© British Library Board. All rights reserved/Bridgeman Images)

of such spells survive, many of which are curse tables, intended to bring bad luck to a political, business, or athletic rival; or binding spells, meant to force a person to do something against his or her will. These binding spells included hundreds intended to make another person love the petitioner. They often invoke a large number of deities to assist the petitioner, reflecting the mixture of gods that was common in Hellenistic society. (See "Evaluating Written Evidence: A Hellenistic Spell of Attraction," page 98.)

Hellenistic kings generally did not suppress indigenous religious practices. Some kings limited the power of existing priesthoods, but they also subsidized them with public money. Priests continued to carry out the rituals that they always had, perhaps now adding the name *Zeus* to that of the local deity or composing their hymns in Greek.

Some Hellenistic kings intentionally sponsored new deities that mixed Egyptian and Greek elements. When Ptolemy I Soter established the Ptolemaic dynasty in Egypt, he thought that a new god was needed who would appeal to both Greeks and Egyptians. Working together, an Egyptian priest and a Greek priest combined elements of the Egyptian god Osiris (god of the afterlife) with aspects of the Greek gods Zeus, Hades (god of the underworld), and Asclepius (god of medicine) to create a new god, Serapis. Like Osiris, Serapis came to be regarded as the judge of souls, who rewarded virtuous and righteous people with eternal life. Like Asclepius, he was also a god of healing. Ptolemy I's successors made Serapis the protector and patron of Alexandria and built a huge temple in the god's honor in the city. His worship spread as intentional government policy, and he was eventually adopted by Romans as well, who blended him with their own chief god, Jupiter.

Many people were attracted to mystery religions, so called because at the center of each was an inexplicable event that brought union with a god and was not to be divulged to anyone not initiated into them. Mystery religions incorporated aspects of both Greek and non-Greek religions and provided an element of personal control in an unstable world by claiming to save their adherents from the worst that fate could do. Most taught that by the rites of initiation, in which the secrets of the religion were shared, devotees became united with a deity who had also died and risen from the dead. The sacrifice of the god and his victory over death saved the devotee from eternal death. Similarly, mystery religions demanded a period of preparation in which the converts strove to become pure and holy, that is, to live by the religion's precepts. Once aspirants had prepared themselves, they went through the initiation, usually a ritual of great emotional intensity symbolizing the entry into a new life.

The Egyptian cult of Isis became the most widespread of the mystery religions in the Hellenistic world, and later spread to Rome. She herself had not died and been reborn, but instead had brought her husband Osiris (now merged with Serapis) back to life (see "Egyptian Religion" in Chapter 1). Some of her followers believed she would provide them with a better afterlife, while others worshipped Isis more for benefits she might offer in *this* life: fertility in crops and animals, protection during childbirth, safety during voyages. People saw her as embodying exotic ancient wisdom, just as some people today believe that Egyptian *ankh* symbols or pyramid shapes bring good luck or have power. Her priests asserted that she had bestowed on humanity the gift of civilization and founded law and literature. The worship of Isis was

**Isis and Horus**   In this small statue from Egypt, the goddess Isis is shown suckling her son Horus. Worship of Isis spread throughout the Hellenistic world; her followers believed that Isis offered them life after death, just as she had brought Horus's father, Osiris, back to life. (Musée du Louvre, Paris, France/Peter Willi/Bridgeman Images)

# A Hellenistic Spell of Attraction

Spells that have survived from the Hellenistic world include hundreds that are intended to make another person love the petitioner. Most of these are heterosexual, but a few involve men seeking men or women seeking women. This spell, inscribed on a lead tablet, is directed toward Anubis, the Egyptian dog-headed god of the underworld, and mentions a number of Egyptian and Greek deities associated with the underworld. Through this spell a woman named Sophia seeks to attract a woman named Gorgonia, although the spell itself is formulaic and was most likely written by a professional.

Fundament of the gloomy darkness, jagged-toothed dog, covered with coiling snakes, turning three heads, traveler in the recesses of the underworld, come, spirit-driver, with the Erinyes [or Furies, Greek goddesses of vengeance, often shown with snake hair and whips], savage with their stinging whips; holy serpents, maenads [frenzied female followers of Dionysus], frightful maidens, come to my wroth incantations. Before I persuade by force this one and you, render him immediately a fire-breathing daemon. Listen and do everything quickly, in no way opposing me in the performance of this action; for you are the governors of the earth. . . . By means of this corpse-daemon inflame the heart, the liver [which people also saw as a location of emotions], the spirit of Gorgonia, whom Nilogenia bore, with love and affection for Sophia, whom Isara bore. Constrain Gorgonia, whom Nilogenia bore, to cast herself into the bath-house for the sake of Sophia, whom Isara bore; and you, become a bath-woman.* Burn, set on fire, inflame her soul, heart, liver, spirit with love for Sophia, whom Isara bore. Drive Gorgonia, whom Nilogenia bore, drive her, torment her body night and day, force her to rush forth from every place and every house, loving Sophia, whom Isara bore, she, surrendered like a slave, giving herself and all her possessions to her, because this is the will and command of the great god. . . . Blessed lord of the immortals, holding the scepters of Tartaros and of terrible, fearful Styx (?) and of life-robbing Lethe, the hair of Kerberos trembles in fear of you, you crack the loud whips of the Erinyes; the couch of Persephone delights you, when you go to the longed bed, whether you be the immortal Serapis, whom the universe fears, whether you be Osiris, star of the land of Egypt; your messenger is the all-wise boy; yours is Anubis, the pious herald of the dead. Come hither, fulfill my wishes, because I summon you by these secret symbols.

## EVALUATE THE EVIDENCE

1. In the spell, what feelings does Sophia direct Anubis to create in Gorgonia, and what behavior is the expected result of these feelings?
2. What aspects of this spell appear distinctively Hellenistic? What aspects fit with modern understandings of sexual attraction?

*Public baths were common in Hellenistic and Roman society as places where people went for recreation and relaxation as well as cleansing, much like today's spas. Here Sophia wants Gorgonia to meet her in a public bath, and Anubis wants to change himself into a female bath attendant so he can cast his spell on her more easily.

Source: Bernadette J. Brooten, *Love Between Women: Early Christian Responses to Female Homoeroticism* (Chicago: University of Chicago Press, 1996), pp. 83–87. Copyright © 1966 by The University of Chicago. All rights reserved. Used by permission of the publisher.

spread by merchants and others moving around the Mediterranean, with temples springing up in ports and other cities, offering her devotees a community as well as a place of worship.

## Hellenism and the Jews

Jews in Hellenistic cities were generally treated the same as any other non-Greek group. At first they were seen as resident aliens. As they grew more numerous, they received permission to form a political corporation, a *politeuma* (pah-lih-TOO-mah), which gave them a great deal of autonomy. The Jewish politeuma, like the rest of the Hellenistic city, was expected to obey the king's commands, but there was virtually no royal interference with the Jewish religion. The Seleucid king Antiochus III (ca. 242–187 B.C.E.), for instance, recognized that most Jews were loyal subjects, and in his efforts to solidify his empire he endorsed their religious customs and ensured their autonomy.

Antiochus IV Epiphanes (r. 175–ca. 164 B.C.E.) broke with this pattern. He expanded the Seleucid kingdom and nearly conquered Egypt, but while he was there a revolt broke out in Judaea, led by Jews who opposed the Hellenized Jewish leader he had designated for them. Antiochus attacked Jerusalem, killing many, and restored his leader. According to Hebrew Scripture, he then banned Jewish practices and worship, ordered copies of the Torah burned, and set up altars to the Greek gods in Jewish temples. This sparked a widespread Jewish revolt that began in 166 B.C.E., called the Revolt of the Maccabees after the name of one of its leaders. Using guerrilla tactics, the Maccabees fought Syrian troops who were fighting under Seleucid commanders, retook Jerusalem, and set up a semi-independent state in 164 B.C.E. This state lasted for about a century, until it was conquered by the Romans. (The rededication of the temple in Jerusalem after the Maccabee victory is celebrated in the Jewish holiday of Hanukkah.)

Jews living in Hellenistic cities often embraced many aspects of Hellenism. The Revolt of the Maccabees is seen by some historians, in fact, as primarily a dispute between Hellenized Jews and those who wanted to retain traditional practices. So many Jews learned Greek, especially in Alexandria, that the Hebrew Bible was translated into Greek and services in the synagogue there came to be conducted in Greek. Jews often took Greek names, participated in Greek political institutions such as citizens' assemblies, adopted Greek practice by forming their own trade associations, and put inscriptions on graves as the Greeks did. Some Jews were given the right to become full citizens of Hellenistic cities, although relatively few appear to have exercised that right. Citizenship would have allowed them to vote in the assembly and serve as magistrates, but it would also have obliged them to worship the gods of the city—a practice few Jews chose to follow.

## Philosophy and the People

Philosophy during the Hellenic period was the exclusive province of the wealthy and educated, for only they had leisure enough to pursue philosophical studies (see "The Flowering of Philosophy" in Chapter 3). During the Hellenistic period, however, although philosophy was still directed toward the educated elite, it came to touch the lives of more men and women than ever before. There were several reasons for this development. First, much of Hellenistic life, especially in the new cities of the East, seemed unstable and without venerable traditions to the Greeks who migrated to these cities. Greeks were far more mobile than they had ever been before, but their very mobility left them feeling uprooted. Second, traditional religions had declined and there was a growing belief that one could do relatively little to change one's fate. One could honor Tyche, the goddess of fortune, through rituals in the hope that she would be kind, but to protect against the worst that Tyche could do, many Greeks also looked to philosophy. Philosophers themselves became much more numerous, and several new schools of philosophical thought caught the minds and hearts of many contemporary Greeks and some non-Greeks.

One of these was **Epicureanism** (eh-pih-kyou-REE-uh-nih-zuhm), a practical philosophy of serenity in an often-tumultuous world. Epicurus (eh-pih-KYOUR-uhs) (340–270 B.C.E.) was influenced by the atomic theory developed by the Pre-Socratic philosopher Democritus (see "The Flowering of Philosophy" in Chapter 3). Like Democritus, he

thought that the world was made up of small pieces of matter that move in space and that determine the events of the world. Although he did not deny the existence of the gods, Epicurus taught that they had no effect on human life. Epicurus used observation and logic to study the world, and also to examine the human condition. He decided that the principal goods of human life were contentment and pleasure, which he defined as the absence of pain, fear, and suffering. By encouraging the pursuit of pleasure, he was not advocating drunken revels or sexual excess, which he thought caused pain, but moderation in food, clothing, and shelter.

The writings of Epicurus survive only in fragments, but the third-century-C.E. biographer Diogenes Laertes quotes several of his letters. It is impossible to know if these are actual letters or not, but they express sentiments that fit with Epicurus's ideas, including these from a letter written at the end of his life, when he apparently suffered from kidney stones:

> I have written this letter to you on a happy day to me, which is also the last day of my life. For I have been attacked by a painful inability to urinate, and also dysentery, so violent that nothing can be added to the violence of my sufferings. But the cheerfulness of my mind, which comes from the recollection of all my philosophical contemplation, counterbalances all these afflictions. And I beg you to take care of the children of Metrodorus, in a manner worthy of the devotion shown by the young man to me, and to philosophy.[5]

Epicurus also taught that individuals could most easily attain peace and serenity by ignoring the outside world and looking into their personal feelings and reactions. This ideal was one to which anyone could aspire, no matter what their social standing. Epicurus is reported to have allowed slaves and even women to attend his school, a sharp contrast with the earlier philosopher Plato. Epicureanism taught its followers to ignore politics and issues, for politics led to tumult, which would disturb the soul. Although the Epicureans thought that the state originated through a social contract among individuals, they did not care about the political structure of the state. They were content to live under a democracy, oligarchy, monarchy, or any other form of government, and they never speculated about the ideal state.

Zeno (335–262 B.C.E.), a philosopher from Cyprus, advanced a different concept of human beings and the universe. Zeno first came to Athens to form his own school, the Stoa, named after the

■ **Epicureanism** A system of philosophy based on the teachings of Epicurus, who viewed a life of contentment, free from fear and suffering, as the greatest good.

## Hellenistic Medicine

Hellenistic medical specialists based their ideas about the body and their handling of illness on observation, and also on the writings ascribed to the Greek physician Hippocrates and his followers. These were copied, recopied, edited, and expanded over the centuries, so it is impossible to say who wrote any specific work, but they contain ideas that were widely shared. How did Hellenistic physicians view the healthy body, and what did they recommend to maintain good health and treat sickness?

**1** **Hippocratic Writings, *The Nature of Man*.** This treatise discusses the structure of the human body and the causes of disease.

〜 The human body contains blood, phlegm, yellow bile and black bile. These are the things that make up its constitution and cause its pains and health. Health is primarily that state in which these constituent substances are in the correct proportion to each other, both in strength and quantity, and are well mixed. Pain occurs when one of the substances presents either a deficiency or an excess, or is separated in the body and not mixed with the others. . . .

Now the quantity of the phlegm in the body increases in winter because it is that bodily substance most in keeping with the winter, seeing that it is the coldest. . . . The following signs show that winter fills the body with phlegm: people spit and blow from their noses the most phlegmatic mucus in winter; swellings become white especially at that season and other diseases show phlegmatic signs. . . .

And just as the year is governed at one time by winter, then by spring, then by summer, and then by autumn; so at one time in the body phlegm predominates, at another time blood, at another time yellow bile and this is followed by a preponderance of black bile. In these circumstances it follows that the diseases which increase in winter should decrease in summer and vice versa. . . .

Some diseases are produced by the manner of life that is followed; others by the life-giving air that we breathe. That there are these two types must be demonstrated in the following way. When a large number of people all catch the same disease at the same time, the cause must be ascribed to something common to all and which they all use; in other words to what they all breathe. In such a disease, it is obvious that individual bodily habits cannot be responsible because the malady attacks one after another, young and old, men and women alike.

**2** **Hippocratic Writings, *Prognosis*.** This treatise provides guidance about how to examine a patient and determine if a disease will be fatal or not.

〜 It seems to be highly desirable that a physician pay much attention to prognosis. If he is able to tell his patients when he visits them not only about their past and present symptoms, but also to tell them what is going to happen, as well as to fill in the details they have omitted, he will increase his reputation as a medical practitioner and people will have no qualms in putting themselves in his care. . . .

The signs to watch for in acute diseases are as follows: First, study the patient's face; whether it has a healthy look and in particular whether it is exactly as it normally is. If the patient's normal appearance is preserved, this is best; just as the more abnormal it is, the worse it is. . . .

Rapid breathing indicates either distress or inflammation of the organs above the diaphragm. Deep breaths taken at long intervals are a sign of delirium. If the expired air from the mouth and nostrils is cold, death is close at hand. . . .

The most helpful kinds of vomiting is that in which the matter consists of phlegm and bile, as well-mixed as possible, and is neither thick nor particularly great in quantity. If it is not well-mixed, it is less good. The vomiting of dark green, livid or dark material, no matter which of these colours, must be considered a bad sign.

In all disease of the lungs, running at the nose and sneezing is bad.

### ANALYZING THE EVIDENCE

1. In Source 1, what are the basic substances in the body, and how do they create pain and illness? How is health shaped by the seasons and by people's actions? By things in the air (which we would call germs, though the Greeks thought of them as poisons)?
2. In Source 2, what does the author suggest that a physician pay attention to when diagnosing illness, and why is prognosis important? How does the technique of the physician in Source 3 fit with this advice?
3. How does the author of Source 4 suggest infections in the pleural cavity be handled?
4. What does the author of Source 5 recommend for people who want to stay healthy, and how does this advice differ for different types of individuals?
5. Taking the sources together, what do these authors see as the most important role of physicians in preventing and treating illness? What do they see as the most important role of people themselves in maintaining their own health?

(Hulton Archive/Getty Images)

**3** **Physician with young patient**. This plaster cast from ca. 350 B.C.E. shows a physician examining a child, while Asclepius, the god of healing, observes.

**4** **Hippocratic Writings, *Diseases.*** In this section of a long treatise, the author discusses treatment of people who have pus in the pleural cavity surrounding the lungs, which today is often linked with emphysema.

First cut the skin between the ribs with a knife with a rounded blade. Then take a sharp-pointed knife wrapped in a strip of cloth with its tip exposed a thumb-nail's length and make an incision. Next, having drained away as much pus as seems appropriate, drain the wound with a drain of raw linen, attached to a cord. Let out the pus once a day. On the tenth day, after having let out all the pus, drain the wound with a piece of fine linen. Then inject warm wine and oil through a small tube, so that the lung accustomed to being moistened by the pus might not suddenly be dried out. Let out the morning's infusion toward evening, and the evening one in the morning. When the pus becomes thick like water, sticky to the finger when touched, and scanty, insert a hollow tin drainage tube. When the [pleural] cavity is completely drained, gradually cut the drain shorter, and allow the wound to heal until you finally take out the drain.

**5** **Hippocratic Writings, *A Regimen for Health.*** In this treatise the author provides suggestions for preventing illness.

People with a fleshy, soft, or ruddy appearance are best kept on a dry diet for the greater part of the year as they are constitutionally moist. Those with firm and tight-drawn skins, and those with tawny and dark complexions should keep to a diet containing plenty of fluids most of the time, as such people are naturally dry. The softest and most moist diets suit young bodies best as at that age the body is dry and has set firm. Older people should take a drier diet most of the time, for at that age bodies are moist, soft, and cold. Diets then must be conditioned by age, the time of year, habit, country and constitution. They should be opposite in character to the prevailing climate, whether winter or summer. Such is the best road to health. . . .

Fat people who want to reduce should take their exercise on an empty stomach and sit down to their food out of breath. . . . [T]hey should take only one meal a day, go without baths, sleep on hard beds and walk about with as little clothing as may be. Thin people who want to get fat should do exactly the opposite. . . . A wise man ought to realize that health is his most valuable possession and learn how to treat his illnesses by his own judgment.

## PUTTING IT ALL TOGETHER

Using the sources above, along with what you have learned in class and in the chapters in this book, write a short essay that analyzes ideas about health and illness in the Hellenistic world, and the treatments that resulted from these ideas. What characterized a healthy body, and how was good health to be regained in the case of illness? Many of the ideas and treatments may seem strange, given how we understand the body today, but do any sound familiar?

Sources: (1) *Hippocratic Writings*, edited with an introduction by G. E. R. Lloyd (Penguin Classics, 1983). Introduction copyright © G. E. R. Lloyd, 1978. Translation of "Fractures" copyright © Loeb Classical Library (Harvard University Press, 1928). Translations of "The Seed," "The Nature of the Child," and "The Heart" copyright © I. M. Lonie, 1978. All other translations copyright © J. Chadwick and W. N. Mann, 1950. Reproduced by permission of Penguin Books Ltd.; (2) *Hippocratic Writings*, pp. 170–171, 172, 177; (4) James Longrigg, *Greek Medicine: From the Heroic to the Hellenistic Age: A Source Book* (London: Duckworth, 1998), 139; (5) *Hippocratic Writings*, p. 274.

**NOTES**

1. Ahmad Hasan Dani et al., *History of Civilizations of Central Asia* (Paris: UNESCO, 1992), p. 107.
2. Quoted in W. W. Tarn and G. T. Griffith, *Hellenistic Civilizations*, 3d ed. (Cleveland and New York: Meridian Books, 1961), p. 199.
3. All quotations from Diodorus are reprinted by permission of the publishers and the Trustees of the Loeb Classical Library from Diodorus of Sicily, *Biblioteca historica* 1.80–36, Loeb Classical Library Volume 279, with an English translation by C. H. Old-father, pp. 275, 277. Cambridge, Mass.: Harvard University Press. First published 1933. Loeb Classical Library® is a registered trademark of the President and Fellows of Harvard College.
4. Diodorus of Sicily, *Biblioteca historica* 3.12.1–3.
5. Diogenes Laertius, *Lives of Eminent Philosophers* 10.22, trans. C. D. Yonge, at Attalus (http://www.attalus.org/old/diogenes10a.html#22).
6. Diodorus of Sicily, *Biblioteca historica* 3.12.2–3.

# LOOKING BACK LOOKING AHEAD

The conquests of Philip and Alexander broadened Greek and Macedonian horizons, but probably not in ways that they had intended. The empire that they created lasted only briefly, but the Hellenistic culture that developed afterwards took Greeks even beyond the borders of Alexander's huge empire as conquerors, merchants, artists, and sailors. Throughout the Mediterranean and western Asia, they interacted with Egyptians, Persians, Bactrians, Jews, and countless others, influencing them and being shaped in return.

The most deeply Hellenized non-Greek people were, ironically, those who conquered much of what had been Alexander's empire: the Romans. The Romans derived their alphabet from the Greek alphabet, though they changed the letters somewhat. Roman statuary was modeled on Greek statuary and was often, in fact, made by Greek sculptors, who found ready customers among wealthy Romans. Furthermore, the major Roman gods and goddesses were largely the same as the Greek ones, though they had different names. Although the Romans did not seem to have been particularly interested in the speculative philosophy of Socrates and Plato, they were drawn to the more practical philosophies of the Epicureans and Stoics. And like the Hellenistic Greeks, many Romans turned from traditional religions to mystery religions that offered secret knowledge and promised eternal life. Among these was Christianity, a new religion that grew in the Roman Empire and whose most important early advocate was Paul of Tarsus, a well-educated Hellenized Jew who wrote in Greek. Significant aspects of Greek culture thus lasted long after the Hellenistic monarchies and even the Roman Empire were gone, shaping all subsequent societies in the Mediterranean and Near East.

## Make Connections

Think about the larger developments and continuities within and across chapters.

1. How was Greek society in the Hellenistic era similar to that of the earlier Hellenic era examined in Chapter 3? How was it different? What would you judge to be more significant, the continuities or the changes?

2. Cities had existed in the Tigris and Euphrates Valleys and the Near East long before Alexander's conquests. What would residents of Sumer (Chapter 1), Babylon (Chapters 1 and 2), and Pergamum find unusual about one another's cities? What would seem familiar?

3. How would you compare religion in Egypt in the Old and New Kingdoms (Chapter 1) with religion in Hellenistic Egypt? What provides the best explanation for the differences you have identified?

# 4   REVIEW & EXPLORE

## Identify Key Terms

Identify and explain the significance of each item below.

Ptolemaic dynasty (p. 86)

Seleucid Empire (p. 87)

Antigonid dynasty (p. 87)

Hellenistic (p. 87)

Hellenization (p. 88)                          Stoicism (p. 100)
Epicureanism (p. 99)                           natural law (p. 100)

## Review the Main Ideas

Answer the section heading questions from the chapter.

**1.** How and why did Alexander the Great create an empire, and how did it evolve? (p. 84)

**2.** How did Greek ideas and traditions spread to create a Hellenized society? (p. 88)

**3.** What characterized the Hellenistic economy? (p. 93)

**4.** How did religion, philosophy, and the arts reflect and shape Hellenistic life? (p. 96)

**5.** How did science and medicine serve the needs of Hellenistic society? (p. 101)

## Suggested Resources

### BOOKS

- Adamson, Peter. *Philosophy in the Hellenistic and Roman World.* 2015. A history of philosophy designed for nonspecialists that began life as a series of podcasts.
- Bowden, Hugh. *Mystery Cults of the Ancient World.* 2010. Examines the main mystery religions of the ancient Mediterranean, using artistic and literary evidence.
- Chaniotis, Angelos. *War in the Hellenistic World.* 2005. Covers the wars of this period, the reasons behind them, and how they were waged.
- Connelly, Joan. *Portrait of a Priestess: Women and Ritual in Ancient Greece.* 2009. A survey of the important public roles of priestesses, with many illustrations.
- Errington, R. Malcolm. *A History of the Hellenistic World, 323–30 B.C.* 2008. Easily the best coverage of the period: full, scholarly, and readable.

- Freeman, Philip. *Alexander the Great.* 2010. Designed for general readers, this excellent biography portrays Alexander as both ruthless and cultured.
- Jaeger, Mary. *Archimedes and the Roman Imagination.* 2008. Puts the discovery of the new manuscript into the context of Archimedes's other scientific works.
- Manning, J. G. *The Last Pharaohs: Egypt Under the Ptolemies, 305–30 B.C.* 2009. Examines the impact of the Ptolemies on Egyptian society and the way their state blended Greek and Egyptian elements.
- Shipley, Graham. *The Greek World After Alexander, 323–30 B.C.* 2000. A very thorough discussion of political, socioeconomic, intellectual, and cultural developments.
- Waterfield, Robin. *Dividing the Spoils: The War for Alexander the Great's Empire.* 2011. A cultural and political narrative of this turbulent period based on up-to-date research.

### MEDIA

- *Ancient History Sourcebook.* Well-organized website of ancient Mediterranean texts and art and archaeological sources. Organized chronologically and topically, with materials from 2000 B.C.E. to 500 C.E. **www.fordham.edu/Halsall/ancient/asbook.html**
- *Ancient Mysteries: The Lost Treasures of the Alexandria Library* (History Channel, 2004). Documentary presenting the building of the library and its collection, the research undertaken there, and the destruction of the library at the hands of a Christian mob in the fourth century C.E.
- *Brought to Life: Exploring the History of Medicine.* Interactive website from the Science Museum in London offering a thematic approach to the past three thousand years in the history of medicine that

foregrounds objects and material culture. Includes many items from the ancient Mediterranean. **www.sciencemuseum.org.uk/broughttolife**
- *Infinite Secrets: The Genius of Archimedes* (*Nova*, 2004). Excellent *Nova* special that explores Archimedes's ideas, theories, and writings, and tells the story of the lost manuscript featured in this chapter.
- *In the Footsteps of Alexander the Great* (BBC, 2010). Michael Wood follows Alexander's two-thousand-mile journey from Greece to India in this documentary, tracing his conquests and the meaning these have for the peoples of these areas today.
- *Pothos.* Long-standing user-generated website with articles, debates, a blog, and visual materials about Alexander the Great. **www.pothos.org/content/**

# 5

# The Rise of Rome

## ca. 1000–27 B.C.E.

**The Hellenistic monarchies that arose after Alexander's conquests** extended eastward and southward from Greece. The Greek colonies that had been established in southern Italy were not part of these monarchies, but culturally they became part of the Hellenistic world. To the north of the Greek city-states in the Italian peninsula, other people built their own societies. Among these were the people who later became the Romans, who settled on hills along the Tiber River in central Italy. Beginning in the sixth century B.C.E., the Romans gradually took over more and more territory in Italy through conquest and annexation. At about the same time, a group of aristocrats revolted against the kings ruling Rome and established a republican government in which the main institution of power was a political assembly, the Senate. Under the direction of the Senate, the Romans continued their political and military expansion, first to all of Italy, then throughout the western Mediterranean basin, and then to areas in the east that had been part of Alexander's empire. As they did, they learned about and incorporated Greek art, literature, philosophy, and religion, but the wars of conquest also led to serious problems that the Senate proved unable to handle.

Roman history is generally divided into three periods: the monarchical period, traditionally dated from 753 B.C.E. to 509 B.C.E., in which the city of Rome was ruled by kings; the republic, traditionally dated from 509 B.C.E. to 27 B.C.E., in which it was ruled by the Senate and expanded its power first to all of Italy and then beyond; and the empire, from 27 B.C.E. to 476 C.E., in which the vast Roman territories were ruled by an emperor. This chapter covers the first two of these periods. The Roman Empire will be discussed in Chapters 6 and 7. ■

## CHAPTER PREVIEW

■ How did the Romans become the dominant power in Italy?

■ What were the key institutions of the Roman Republic?

■ How did the Romans build a Mediterranean empire?

■ How did expansion affect Roman society and culture?

■ What led to the fall of the Roman Republic?

**Etruscan Dancers**
A fresco from an Etruscan tomb, painted about 470 B.C.E., shows dancers in an idyllic setting with olive trees, while other walls depict musicians and a banquet. The scenes are based on similar scenes on Greek pottery, evidence of the connections between the Etruscans and their Greek neighbors to the south. This tomb is one among many thousands in the Necropolis of Monterozzi in Tarquinia, just north of Rome, now a UNESCO World Heritage Site. (Pictures from History/Bridgeman Images)

## How did the Romans become the dominant power in Italy?

The colonies established by Greek poleis (city-states) in the Hellenic era (see "Overseas Expansion" in Chapter 3) included a number along the coast of southern Italy and Sicily. Although Alexander the Great (see Chapter 4) created an empire that stretched from his homeland of Macedonia to India, his conquests did not reach as far as southern Italy and Sicily. Thus the Greek colonies there remained politically independent. They became part of the Hellenistic cultural world, however, and they transmitted much of that culture to people who lived farther north in the Italian peninsula. These people included the Etruscans, who built the first cities north of the Greek colonies, and then the Romans, who eventually came to dominate the peninsula.

### The Geography of Italy

The Italian peninsula occupies the center of the Mediterranean basin (Map 5.1). Italian winters are rainy,

**MAP 5.1 Roman Italy and the City of Rome, ca. 218 B.C.E.** As Rome expanded, it built roads linking major cities and offered various degrees of citizenship to the territories it conquered or with which it made alliances. The territories outlined in green that are separate from the Italian peninsula were added by 218 B.C.E., largely as a result of the Punic Wars.

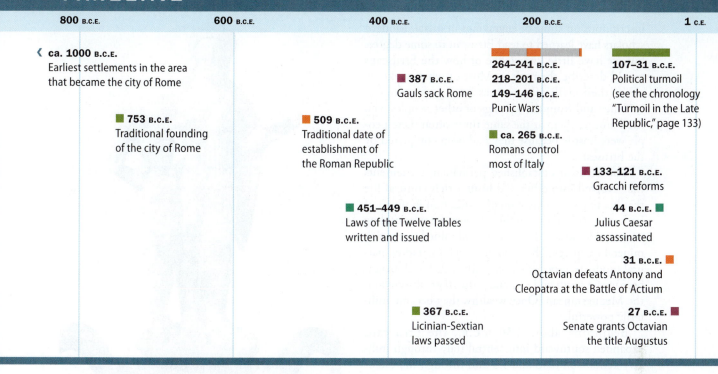

❮ **ca. 1000 B.C.E.**
Earliest settlements in the area that became the city of Rome

■ **753 B.C.E.**
Traditional founding of the city of Rome

■ **509 B.C.E.**
Traditional date of establishment of the Roman Republic

■ **451–449 B.C.E.**
Laws of the Twelve Tables written and issued

■ **367 B.C.E.**
Licinian-Sextian laws passed

■ **387 B.C.E.**
Gauls sack Rome

**264–241 B.C.E.**
**218–201 B.C.E.**
**149–146 B.C.E.**
Punic Wars

■ **ca. 265 B.C.E.**
Romans control most of Italy

**107–31 B.C.E.**
Political turmoil (see the chronology "Turmoil in the Late Republic," page 133)

■ **133–121 B.C.E.**
Gracchi reforms

**44 B.C.E.** ■
Julius Caesar assassinated

**31 B.C.E.** ■
Octavian defeats Antony and Cleopatra at the Battle of Actium

**27 B.C.E.** ■
Senate grants Octavian the title Augustus

---

but the summer months are dry. Because of the climate, the rivers of Italy usually carry little water during the summer. Most of Italy's rivers are unsuitable for regular, large-scale shipping and never became major thoroughfares for commerce and communications. Yet the rivers nourished a bountiful agriculture that could produce enough crops for a growing population.

Geography encouraged Italy to look to the Mediterranean. In the north, Italy is protected by the Alps, which form a natural barrier. From the north the Apennine Mountains run southward along the east coast for the entire length of the Italian boot, cutting off access to the Adriatic Sea for those to their west. This barrier induced Italy to look west to Spain and Carthage rather than east to Greece, but it did not carve up the land in a way that would prevent the development of political unity.

In their southward course, the Apennines leave two broad and fertile plains to their west: Latium and Campania. These plains attracted settlers and invaders from the time that peoples began to move into Italy. Among these peoples were those who would found Rome on the Tiber River in Latium.

This site enjoyed several advantages. The Tiber provided Rome with a constant source of water. Located at an easy crossing point on

the Tiber, Rome thus stood astride the main avenue of communications between northern and southern Italy. Positioned amid seven hills, Rome was defensible, and it was relatively close to the sea through the port of Ostia seventeen miles away. Thus, Rome was in an excellent position to develop the resources of Latium and maintain contact with the rest of Italy.

## The Etruscans

Before Rome rose to power, the dominant group in northern Italy was the culture that is now called Etruscan, which developed in north-central Italy about 800 B.C.E. Recent studies of DNA evidence have indicated that the Etruscans most likely originated in Turkey or elsewhere in the Near East, but they migrated to Italy by at least 3000 B.C.E. and developed their culture there. The Etruscans spoke a language that was very different from Greek and Latin, although they adopted the Greek alphabet to write it. We know they wrote letters, records, and literary works, but once the Romans conquered them, knowledge of how to read and write Etruscan died out. Also, the writings themselves largely disappeared because many were written on linen books that did not survive; what remain are

**The Etruscans, ca. 500 B.C.E.**

111

inscriptions on stone or engravings in metal. Modern scholars have learned to read Etruscan to some degree, but we have little knowledge of how the Etruscans would describe themselves. Most of what we know about their civilization comes from archaeological evidence and from the writings of other peoples who lived around them at the same time; often these people were hostile because they had been conquered by the Etruscans.

The Etruscans established permanent settlements that evolved into cities and built a rich cultural life that became the foundation of civilization in much of Italy. They spread their influence over the surrounding countryside, which they farmed and mined for its rich mineral resources. They also grew rich by trading natural products, especially iron, with their Greek neighbors to the south and east and with others throughout the Mediterranean. Once wealthy, they became militarily powerful.

Beginning about 750 B.C.E., the Etruscans expanded southward into central Italy through military actions on land and sea and through the establishment of colony cities. Written records of battles all come from the side of the Etruscans' opponents, but objects found in graves indicate that military values were important in their society, as wealthy men were buried with bronze armor and shields and iron weapons. In the process of expansion, the Etruscans encountered a small collection of villages subsequently called Rome and for several centuries engaged in a series of wars with the Romans, which also involved other groups that lived in northern and central Italy.

## The Founding of Rome

Archaeological evidence indicates that the ancestors of the Romans began to settle on the hills east of the Tiber during the early Iron Age, around 1000 to 800 B.C.E. Archaeological sources provide the most important information about this earliest period of Roman history, but later Romans told a number of stories about the founding of Rome. These stories mix legend and history, as Roman historians were more concerned with telling a good story than with precision about details and dates, but mythical or not, they illustrate the traditional ethics, morals, and ideals of Rome.

The Romans' foundation myths were told in a number of different versions. In the most common of these, Romulus and Remus founded the city of Rome, an event later Roman authors dated precisely to 753 B.C.E. These twin brothers were the sons of the war-god Mars, and their mother, Rhea Silvia, was a descendant of Aeneas, a brave and pious Trojan who left Troy after it was destroyed by the Greeks in the Trojan War (see "Homer, Hesiod, and the Epic" in Chapter 3). The brothers, who were left to die by a

**Etruscan Figure of a Mother and Son**    This bronze Etruscan sculpture from the sixth to fourth century B.C.E. shows a mother and child. The influence of Hellenistic Greek art is evident in the musculature of the little boy and the drape of the woman's clothing. The holders at the sides may have held candles. (Museo Civico Archeologico, Bologna, Italy/De Agostini Picture Library/akg-images)

jealous uncle, were raised by a female wolf. When they were grown, they decided to build a city in the hills that became part of Rome, but they quarreled over which hill should be the site of the city. In the end, Romulus killed Remus and named the city after himself. He also established a council of advisers later called the Senate. Romulus and his mostly male followers expanded their power over the neighboring Sabine peoples, in part by abducting and then marrying their women. The Sabine women then arranged a peace by throwing themselves between their brothers and their husbands, convincing them that killing kin would make the men cursed. The Romans, favored by the gods, continued their rise to power.

Despite its tales of murder, rape, and kidnapping, this founding myth ascribes positive traits to the Romans: they are descended from gods and heroes, can thrive in wild and tough settings, and will defend their boundaries at all costs. The story also portrays women who were ancestors of Rome as virtuous and brave, and it highlights what would become Rome's greatest achievement, marveled at by ancient Greek authors and emphasized by historians today: its ability to include conquered peoples within its fold. In contrast to Athens, where newcomers could never become citizens and were always excluded from full political participation, in most of Rome's history Rome regularly offered citizenship to the elite members of newly conquered territories. Even freed slaves were endowed with citizenship immediately upon receiving their freedom, something that was also never possible in Athens. Rome was thus a multiethnic society from the start, able to inspire loyalty to Rome in many different peoples.

Later Roman historians continued the story by describing a series of kings after Romulus, each elected by the Senate. According to tradition, the last three kings were Etruscan, and another tale about female virtue was told to explain why the Etruscan kings were overthrown, for ancient historians often attributed major government upheavals to the possession or loss of women. In this story, the son of King Tarquin, the Etruscan king who ruled Rome, raped Lucretia, a virtuous Roman wife, in her own home. Lucretia summoned her husband and father to the house, told them what had happened, and demanded they seek vengeance. She then committed suicide by plunging a knife into her heart.[1] Her father and husband and the other Roman nobles swore on the bloody knife to avenge Lucretia's death by throwing out the Etruscan kings, and they did. Whether any part of this story is true can never be known, but Romans generally accepted it as history and dated the expulsion of the Etruscan kings to 509 B.C.E. They saw this year as marking the end of the monarchical period and the dawn of the republic.

Most historians today view the idea that Etruscan kings ruled in the city of Rome as legendary, but fighting with groups that came from the north, such as the Etruscans, was a major early Roman experience and would shape Rome's later policies. Historians also stress the influence of the Etruscans on Rome. The Etruscans transformed Rome from a relatively large town to a real city. The Romans adopted the Etruscan alphabet, which the Etruscans themselves had adopted from the Greeks. They also adopted an Etruscan symbol, a bundle of rods tied together with an ax emerging from the center, which symbolized the Etruscan king's power. This ceremonial object was called the fasces (FAS-eez), and was carried first by Etruscan officials and then by Romans. (It was also used by later governments: in the twentieth century Mussolini would use the fasces as the symbol of his political party, the Fascists, and fasces are on the speaker's platform of the U.S. House of Representatives and form the armrests of Abraham Lincoln's chair in the Lincoln Memorial in Washington, D.C.) Even the toga, the white woolen robe worn by citizens, came from the Etruscans, as did

gladiatorial combat honoring the dead. In engineering and architecture as well, the Romans adopted some design elements and the basic plan of their temples, along with paved roads, from the Etruscans.

In this early period, the city of Rome does appear to have been ruled by kings, as were most territories in the ancient world. A hereditary aristocracy also developed — again, an almost universal phenomenon; it advised the kings and may have played a role in choosing them. And sometime in the sixth century B.C.E., a group of aristocrats revolted against these kings and established a government in which the main institution of power was in the **Senate**, an assembly of aristocrats, rather than a single monarch. Rome thereby became a republic. Executive power was in the hands of two members of the Senate called **consuls**, but they were elected for one-year terms only and rejoined the ranks of the Senate after their term in office.

Under kings and then the Senate, the villages along the Tiber gradually grew into a single city, whose residents enjoyed contacts with the larger Mediterranean world. Temples and public buildings began to grace Rome, and the Forum, a large plaza between two of Rome's hills, became a public meeting place similar to the Greek agora (see "Organization of the Polis" in Chapter 3). In addition, trade in metalwork became common, and wealthier Romans began to import fine Greek vases and other luxuries.

## The Roman Conquest of Italy

In the period from 509 to 264 B.C.E., referred to by historians as the early republic, the Romans fought numerous wars with their neighbors on the Italian peninsula, with an army initially made up primarily of citizens of Rome who volunteered or were conscripted for short terms by ballots, essentially a lottery among all male citizens ages sixteen to forty-six. Only those citizens with a certain amount of property were eligible for army service, and the units were organized by how much money a soldier could spend on arms and armor; the wealthiest citizens formed the cavalry, as only they could afford horses. Conquered territories were often turned into allies, and other territories became allies of Rome without fighting. Alliances with the towns around them in Latium gave the Romans a large population that could be tapped for military needs, though allied armies were led by Romans. Wealth gained from victories using troops from Rome's allies was split between Rome itself and

■ **Senate** The assembly that was the main institution of power in the Roman Republic, originally composed only of aristocrats.

■ **consuls** Primary executives in the Roman Republic, elected for one-year terms in the Senate, who commanded the army in battle, administered state business, and supervised financial affairs.

all her allies, a strategy that encouraged loyalty to Rome. Rome often declared conquered territory public land, sometimes settling Roman colonists in it or selling it to private landholders, but often allowing conquered or allied people to continue to inhabit and farm it. The Romans also ensured good behavior by threatening to reassign lands if the allies rebelled.

These wars of the early republic later became the source of legends that continued to express Roman values. One of these involved the aristocrat Cincinnatus, who had been expelled from the Senate and forced to pay a huge fine because of the actions of his son. As the story goes, in 458 B.C.E. he was plowing the fields of his small farm when the Senate asked him to return and assume the office of dictator. This position, which had been created very early in the republic, was one in which one man would be given ultimate powers for six months in order to handle a serious crisis such as an invasion or rebellion. (Like the word *tyrant* in ancient Greece, *dictator* did not have its current negative meaning in the early Roman Republic.) At this point the armies of the Aequi, a neighboring group, had surrounded Roman forces commanded by both consuls, and Rome was in imminent danger of catastrophe. Cincinnatus, wiping his sweat, listened to the appeal of his countrymen and led the Roman infantry in victory over the Aequi. He then

returned to his farm, becoming a legend among later Romans as a man of simplicity who put his civic duty to Rome before any consideration of personal interest or wealth, and who willingly gave up power for the greater good. The Roman Senate actually chose many more men as dictator in the centuries after Cincinnatus, but no subsequent dictator achieved his legendary reputation. For George Washington and other leaders of the American War of Independence, he became the symbolic model of a leader who had performed selfless service but then stepped down from power, which Washington himself did.

In 387 B.C.E., the Romans suffered a major setback when the Celts—or Gauls, as the Romans called them—invaded the Italian peninsula from the north, destroyed a Roman army, and sacked the city of Rome. (For more on the Gauls, who lived in present-day France, see Chapter 7.) More intent on loot than on conquest, the Gauls agreed to abandon Rome in return for a thousand pounds of gold. As the story was later told, when the Gauls provided their own scale and weights to measure the gold, the Romans howled in indignation, claiming these were rigged. The Gallic chieftain Brennus then threw his sword on the scale, exclaiming "*Vae victis*" (woe to the conquered), implying that those who were defeated were at the mercy of their conquerors. The Romans then had to put more gold on the scale to balance the added sword. These words, though legendary, were used by later Romans as an explanation for why they would not surrender to other groups that sought to conquer Rome, and the city of Rome was not sacked again until 410 C.E.

The Romans rebuilt their city and continued their campaign of conquest and annexation through alliances. They brought Latium and their Latin allies fully under their control and conquered Etruria and the Etruscans (see Map 5.1). Starting in 343 B.C.E., they turned south and grappled with the Samnites in a series of bitter wars for the possession of Campania. The Samnites were a formidable enemy and inflicted serious losses on the Romans, but the Romans won in the end and continued their expansion southward.

Alarmed by Roman expansion, as were all the Greek cities in southern Italy, the city of Tarentum in southern Italy called for help from Pyrrhus (PIHR-uhs), king of Epirus in western Greece. He came to Italy with a large army, and in 280 B.C.E. he won two furious battles but suffered heavy casualties—thus the phrase "Pyrrhic victory" is still used today to describe a victory involving severe losses.

Pyrrhus then received an offer from the Greek cities in Sicily to help them drive out the Carthaginians, who were expanding their holdings throughout the Mediterranean (see "The Rise of Phoenicia" in Chapter 2 and "The Punic Wars" later in this chapter). He initially defeated Carthaginian armies and was

**Fresco of a Campanian Foot Soldier**   This fresco from the sixth century B.C.E. shows a soldier wearing a gilded helmet with a large feather. Campania is an area in southern Italy around the present-day city of Naples, first settled by Italic people, then colonized by Greeks, and then conquered by Romans in their expansion southward. (Museo Archeologico Nazionale, Naples, Italy/De Agostini Picture/Bridgeman Images)

proclaimed king of Sicily, but his demands for money and manpower to continue fighting led the Greeks in Sicily to turn against him, and he decided to go back to Italy, where in his absence the Romans had rebuilt their army and conquered or made alliances with almost all of the Greek cities. After an inconclusive battle, Pyrrhus and his army returned to Epirus, leaving almost all of southern Italy in Roman hands. The Romans then turned north again, and by about 265 B.C.E. they had conquered or taken into their sphere of influence most of Italy.

These campaigns meant that an army made up of wealthier citizens serving for short terms was no longer enough, and soldiers gradually served for longer and longer terms. They were organized into legions of about five thousand men, armed with iron swords and iron-tipped spears, and wearing chest plates and helmets.

Along with military conquest and diplomatic alliances, the Romans enlisted religion in their expansion. Victorious generals made sure to honor the gods of the people they had conquered and to invite those gods to settle in Rome. By doing so they transformed them into gods they could also call on for assistance in their future campaigns. In this way Greek deities and mythical heroes were absorbed into the Roman pantheon. Their names were changed to Roman names, so that Zeus (the king of the gods), for example, became Jupiter, and Herakles (the semidivine hero) became Hercules, but their personal qualities and powers were similar. (See "Evaluating Visual Evidence: The Temple of Hercules Victor," page 116.)

Religion for the Romans was largely a matter of honoring the state and the family, not developing a close relationship with a deity or worshipping with a congregation of fellow believers. The main goal of religion was to secure the peace of the gods, what was termed *pax deorum*, and to harness divine power for public and private enterprises. Religious rituals were an important way of expressing common values, which for Romans meant those evident in their foundation myths: bravery, morality, seriousness, family, and home. The sacred fire at the shrine of the goddess Vesta in the city of Rome, for example, was attended by the vestal virgins, young women chosen from aristocratic families. Vesta was the goddess of hearth and home, whose protection was regarded as essential to Roman well-being. The vestal virgins were important figures at major public rituals, though at several times of military loss and political crisis they were also charged with negligence of duty or unchastity, another link between female honor and the Roman state.

Along with the great gods, the Romans believed in spirits who inhabited fields, forests, crossroads, and even the home itself. These spirits were to be honored with rituals and gifts so that they would be appeased instead of becoming hostile. Family and individual religious practices varied considerably, and every household had its own guardian deities.

Once they had conquered an area, the Romans built roads. These roads provided an easy route for communication between the capital and outlying areas, allowed for the quick movement of armies, and offered an efficient means of trade. Many were marvels of engineering, as were the stone bridges the Romans built over Italy's many rivers.

In politics the Romans shared full Roman citizenship with the elites of many of their oldest allies, particularly the inhabitants of the cities of Latium. In other instances they granted citizenship without the right to vote or hold Roman office. These allies were subject to Roman taxes and calls for military service but ran their own local affairs. The extension of Roman citizenship strengthened the state and increased its population and wealth, although limitations on this extension would eventually become a source of conflict (see "The Countryside and Land Reforms" later in this chapter).

## What were the key institutions of the Roman Republic?

Along with citizenship, the republican government was another important institution of Roman political life. Roman institutions were not static; they changed over time to address problems as they emerged.

### The Roman State

Most of our written sources about Roman government and history in the republican period come from upper-class authors whose families were members of the Senate, many from the late republican period (147–30 B.C.E.), so they were looking backward. They shaped their narratives to both explain and help maintain the privileges of their social, political, and economic status, and were thus critical of change, which they generally saw as decline. They viewed the Senate favorably, and emphasized its leadership in a phrase describing the Roman government: *senatus populusque Romanus*, "the Senate and the Roman people," abbreviated SPQR. That phrase shows up in legal, political, and historical writings, and its abbreviation is on coins and inscriptions, including those from the imperial period. By that point the Senate no longer had much power, and the Senate and the

# The Temple of Hercules Victor

(Justin Kase z12z/Alamy)

This round temple, dating from the second century B.C.E., is the oldest surviving marble building in Rome, made in a Greek style of materials that were partly imported from Greece. The columns that form the colonnade are built in a style later art historians called "Corinthian," with very ornate tops. It once contained a statue of the mythical hero Hercules and was dedicated to him at this spot, where legend told he killed a monster who had stolen some cattle. The temple may have been built by Mummius Achaicus, the consul and general who defeated Greek forces and destroyed the city of Corinth. Like many successful military commanders, when he returned to Rome after his military campaign, he was celebrated with a triumphal parade through the streets of the city. He rode in a chariot, wearing a laurel wreath and a purple toga, at the head of a procession of his soldiers, captives, and objects

taken from Greece. Roman triumphs ended at the temple of Jupiter, where generals offered tokens of victory to the gods.

## EVALUATE THE EVIDENCE

1. Looking at the picture of the temples on the Acropolis in Athens in "Evaluating Visual Evidence" in Chapter 3 on page 70, what stylistic similarities do you see between those buildings and this temple?
2. How do those similarities, and the fact that this temple was dedicated to Hercules, provide evidence for Roman adoption of Greek religion and culture?
3. What do temples such as this, and triumphal parades, suggest about the links between religion, the state, and military conquest for Romans during this time of expansion?

people (embodied in other assemblies) were often hostile to one another, so the phrase had become a traditional patriotic motto, not a description of political reality. Recent historians have used evidence left by ordinary people, along with more critical readings of the literary sources, to get a clearer picture of the development of the Roman state.

All types of sources indicate that in the early republic, social divisions determined the shape of politics. Political power was in the hands of a hereditary

**Coin Showing a Voter**   This coin from 63 B.C.E. shows a citizen wearing a toga dropping a voting tablet into a voting urn, the Roman equivalent of today's ballot box. The tablet has a *V* on it, meaning a yes vote, and the coin has an inscription giving the name of the moneyer, the official who controlled the production of coins and decided what would be shown on them. Here the moneyer, Lucius Cassius Longinus, depicted a vote held fifty years earlier regarding whether an ancestor of his should be named prosecutor in a trial charging three vestal virgins with unchastity. As was common among moneyers, Longinus chose this image as a means to advance his political career, in this case by suggesting his family's long history of public office. (Bibliothèque Nationale de France [BNF]/Snark/Art Resource, NY)

aristocracy—the **patricians**, whose privileged legal status was determined by their birth as members of certain families. Once a patrician, always a patrician, though belonging to a family whose members had been in the Senate did not guarantee entrance. If a patrician couldn't finance a campaign, he couldn't get elected. Aristocratic families rose and fell in power over Rome's long history, and some important leaders were what the Romans called *novi homines* (new men), the first in their families to serve in the Senate or as consul. Families that had long held power snobbishly regarded these new men with disdain or suspicion.

The common people of Rome, the **plebeians** (plih-BEE-uhns), were free citizens with a voice in politics, but initially they had few of the patricians' political and social advantages. Most plebeians were poor artisans, small farmers, and landless urban dwellers, though some increased their wealth in the course of Roman expansion and came to rival the patricians economically. Plebeians were later allowed to obtain the highest offices in Rome, but even the most powerful among them were derided (though sometimes in whispers) as novi homines.

The Romans created several assemblies through which men elected high officials and passed legislation. The earliest was the Centuriate Assembly, in which citizens were organized into groups called centuries. Each citizen was assigned to a century depending on his status and amount of wealth, and the patricians possessed the majority of centuries. When an election was ordered, each century met separately and voted as a bloc, which meant that the patricians could easily outvote the plebeians. In 471 B.C.E., plebeian men won the right to meet in an assembly of their own, the Plebeian Assembly, and to pass ordinances.

The highest officials of the republic were the two consuls, who were elected for one-year terms by the Centuriate Assembly. The consuls commanded the army in battle, administered state business, presided over the Senate and assemblies, and supervised

financial affairs. In effect, they ran the state. The consuls appointed quaestors (KWEH-stuhr) to assist them in their duties, and in 421 B.C.E. the quaestorship became an elective office open to plebeian men. In 366 B.C.E., the Romans created a new office, that of praetor (PREE-tuhr). When the consuls were away from Rome, the praetors could act in their place; they could also command armies, act as governors in the provinces, interpret law, and administer justice.

The most important institution was the Senate, which during the republic grew to several hundred members. Senate membership was a lifetime position, and all senators had previously been elected to one of the high positions, which automatically conferred Senate membership. Because the Senate sat year after year with the same members, it provided stability and continuity. It passed formal decrees that were technically "advice" to the magistrates, who were not bound to obey them but usually did. The Senate directed the magistrates on the conduct of war and had the power over the expenditure of public money. In times of emergency, it could name a dictator.

Within the city of Rome itself, the Senate's powers were limited by laws and traditions, but as Rome expanded, the Senate had greater authority in the outlying territories. The Romans divided the lands that they conquered into provinces, and the Senate named the governors, most of whom were former consuls or praetors, for each province. Another responsibility of the Senate was to handle relations between Rome and other powers.

A lasting achievement of the Romans was their development of civil law. Roman civil law, the *ius civile*, consisted of statutes, customs, and procedures that regulated the lives of citizens, especially in matters of concern to those who owned property, such

■ **patricians**  The Roman hereditary aristocracy; they held most of the political power in the republic.

■ **plebeians**  The common people of Rome; they were free but had few of the patricians' advantages.

as ownership, inheritance, and contracts. It became increasingly complex over the centuries, and later emperors would try to develop uniform codes that brought what was a bewildering group of statutes and rulings together (see Chapter 7). By contrast, Roman criminal law was brutally simple, and often harsh. As the Romans came into more frequent contact with foreigners, the consuls and praetors applied a broader *ius gentium*, the "law of the peoples," to matters such as peace treaties, the treatment of prisoners of war, and the exchange of diplomats. In the ius gentium, all sides were to be treated the same regardless of their nationality. By the late republic, Roman jurists had widened this principle still further into the concept of *ius naturale*, "natural law," based in part on Stoic beliefs (see "Philosophy and the People" in Chapter 4). Natural law, according to these thinkers, is made up of rules that govern human behavior and that come from applying reason rather than customs or traditions, and so apply to all societies. In reality, Roman officials generally interpreted the law to the advantage of Rome, of course, at least to the extent that the strength of Roman armies allowed them to enforce it. But Roman law came to be seen as one of the most important contributions Rome made to the development of Western civilization.

## Social Conflict in Rome

Inequality between plebeians and patricians led to a conflict known as the **Struggle of the Orders**, which lasted for the entire early republican period. In this conflict the plebeians sought to increase their power by taking advantage of the fact that Rome's survival depended on its army, which needed plebeians to fill the ranks of the infantry. According to tradition, in 494 B.C.E. the plebeians literally walked out of Rome and refused to serve in the army. Their general strike worked, and the patricians grudgingly made important concessions. They allowed the plebeians to elect their own officials, the **tribunes**, who presided over the Plebeian Assembly, brought plebeian grievances to the Senate for resolution, could stop debate in the Senate, and could veto the decisions of the consuls if they wished. The tribunes were regarded as being

legally inviolate, and if anyone harmed them, the Plebeian Assembly pledged to avenge them immediately.

The law itself was the plebeians' primary target during the Struggle of the Orders. Only the patricians knew what the law was, and only they could argue cases in court. All too often they used the law for their own benefit. According to ancient Greek and Roman historians, after much struggle, in 449 B.C.E., the patricians surrendered their legal monopoly and codified and published the Laws of the Twelve Tables, so called because they were inscribed on twelve bronze plaques. The Laws of the Twelve Tables covered many legal issues, including property ownership, guardianship, inheritance, procedure for trials, and punishments for various crimes. With legal procedures now made public, plebeians could argue cases in court. Later, in 445 B.C.E., the patricians passed a law, the *lex Canuleia*, that for the first time allowed patricians and plebeians to marry one another.

Licinius and Sextius were plebeian tribunes in the fourth century B.C.E. who mounted a sweeping assault on patrician privilege. They proposed a series of laws, which the Senate passed in 367 B.C.E. Though historians continue to debate exactly what these Licinian-Sextian laws were, they apparently gave wealthy plebeians access to all the offices of Rome, including the right to hold one of the two consulships. Once plebeians could hold the consulship, they could also sit in the Senate and advise on policy. The laws also limited the amount of conquered land any single individual could hold, though this was frequently ignored. Though decisive, this victory did not end the Struggle of the Orders, which happened only in 287 B.C.E. with the passage of the *lex Hortensia*. This law gave the resolutions of the Plebeian Assembly the force of law for patricians and plebeians alike.

The long Struggle of the Orders had resulted in an expansion of power to wealthy plebeians, and by 200 B.C.E. the majority of the consuls were plebeian. This did not mean they were concerned with the problems of average people. Political power had been expanded only slightly and still resided largely in a group of wealthy families, some of whom happened to be plebeian. Access to the highest political offices was still difficult for any plebeian, who often had to get the support of patrician families if he wanted a political career.

Networks of support were actually important for all Romans involved in public life, not simply aspiring plebeians. Roman politics operated primarily through a **patron-client system** whereby free men promised their votes to a more powerful man in exchange for his help in legal or other matters. The more powerful patron looked after his clients, and his clients' support helped the patron advance his career. This system held Roman society together even as it was undergoing political upheavals.

---

■ **Struggle of the Orders** A conflict in which the plebeians sought political representation and safeguards against patrician domination.

■ **tribunes** Plebeian-elected officials; tribunes brought plebeian grievances to the Senate for resolution and protected plebeians from the arbitrary conduct of patrician magistrates.

■ **patron-client system** An informal system of patronage in which free men promised their votes to a more powerful man in exchange for his help in legal or other matters.

■ **Punic Wars** A series of three wars between Rome and Carthage in which Rome emerged the victor.

The patron-client system even extended to foreign affairs. As Rome expanded, along with conquered territories and allies (and conquered territories turned allies), Rome also developed a number of client kingdoms along its borders, such as the Bosporan kingdom on the north shore of the Black Sea and the Votadini people in northeast England. Client kings conducted their own internal business according to their own laws and customs, but gave up their rights to independent foreign affairs. The client kingdoms enjoyed the protection of Rome while defending Rome's borders, but they were not relationships between equals: Rome always remained the senior partner. In time many of these states became provinces of the Roman Empire (see Chapters 6 and 7).

## How did the Romans build a Mediterranean empire?

As the republican government was developing, Rome continued to expand its holdings beyond the Italian peninsula. Unlike Alexander the Great, the Romans did not map out grandiose strategies to conquer the world, but they became masters of the Mediterranean in a relatively short period of time, amazing their contemporaries. Historians debate the reasons they were so successful. Some view them as pathological predators among more peaceful neighbors, but the many wars in the Hellenistic period suggest that Rome's neighbors were also quite militaristic. A newer view is that Rome was one warlike state among many, successful primarily because it incorporated allies as citizens, thus maintaining a large population base despite losses in war.

### The Punic Wars

As they pushed southward, incorporating the southern Italian peninsula into their growing territory, the Romans confronted another great power in the western Mediterranean, the Carthaginians. The city of Carthage had been founded by Phoenicians as a trading colony in the eighth century B.C.E. (see "The Rise of Phoenicia" in Chapter 2). By the fourth century B.C.E., the Carthaginians began to expand their holdings. They had one of the largest navies in the Mediterranean and were wealthy enough to hire mercenaries to do much of their fighting. At the end of a long string of wars, the Carthaginians had created and defended a mercantile empire that stretched from western Sicily to the western end of the Mediterranean (see Map 5.1).

Beginning in the fifth century B.C.E., the Romans and the Carthaginians made a series of treaties with one another that defined their spheres of influence, and they worked together in the 270s B.C.E. to defeat Pyrrhus. But the Greek cities that became Roman allies in southern Italy and Sicily saw Carthage as a competitor in terms of trade. This competition led to the first of the three **Punic Wars** between Rome and Carthage. The First Punic War lasted for twenty-three years (264–241 B.C.E.) and ended with the Romans in possession of Sicily, which became their first real province.

The peace treaty between Rome and Carthage brought no peace because both powers had their sights set on dominating the western half of the Mediterranean. In 238 B.C.E., the Romans took advantage of Carthaginian weakness to seize Sardinia and Corsica. The Carthaginians responded by expanding their holdings in Spain under the leadership of the commander Hamilcar Barca. With him he took his ten-year-old son, Hannibal, whom he had earlier led to an altar where he had made the boy swear to be an enemy to Rome forever. In the following years, Hamilcar and his son-in-law Hasdrubal (HAHZ-droo-buhl) subjugated much of southern Spain and in the process rebuilt Carthaginian power. Rome first made a treaty with Hasdrubal, setting the boundary between Carthaginian and Roman interests at the Ebro River, and then began to extend its own influence in Spain.

In 221 B.C.E., Hamilcar's son Hannibal became the Carthaginian commander in Spain and laid siege to Saguntum (suh-GUHN-tum), a Roman-allied city that lay within the sphere of Carthaginian interest and was making raids into Carthaginian territories. The Romans declared war, claiming that Carthage had attacked a city friendly to Rome. So began the Second Punic War. In 218 B.C.E., Hannibal marched an army of tens of thousands of troops — and, more famously, several dozen war elephants — from Spain across what is now France and over the Alps into Italy. Once there, he defeated one Roman army after another and, in 216 B.C.E., he won his greatest victory at the Battle of Cannae (KAH-nee). Hannibal also made alliances with other enemies of Rome, including King Philip V of Macedonia and the king of Syracuse. He then spread devastation throughout the Italian peninsula, and he also sowed dissension among the Roman-allied cities in central and southern Italy by exposing Rome's inequitable treatment of her allies. A number rebelled. Yet Hannibal was not able to win areas near Rome in central Italy because Roman allies there, who had been extended citizenship rights, remained loyal.

Despite Hannibal's successes, his allies did not supply him with enough food and supplies to sustain his troops. The Senate of Carthage did not reinforce

Hannibal with additional troops because it wanted to use these troops to retake Sicily and Sardinia from Rome, and also because it feared that Hannibal could pose a threat to it if he were too successful.

Rome also fought back, and in 210 B.C.E. it found a counterpart to Hannibal in the young commander Scipio Africanus (SKIP-ee-oh af-rih-KAHN-us).

Scipio copied Hannibal's methods of mobile warfare and guerrilla tactics and made more extensive use of cavalry than had earlier Roman commanders. He battled first in Spain, which in 207 B.C.E. he wrested from the Carthaginians. That same year, the Romans sealed Hannibal's fate at the Battle of Metaurus, where they destroyed a major Carthaginian army coming

## MAPPING THE PAST

### MAP 5.2 Roman Expansion During the Republic, ca. 282–44 B.C.E.

Rome expanded in all directions, first west and then east, eventually controlling every shore of the Mediterranean.

**ANALYZING THE MAP** Which years saw the greatest expansion of Roman power during the republic? How might the different geographic features have helped or hindered the expansion into certain areas?

**CONNECTIONS** What allowed the Romans to maintain their power across such a wide and diverse area?

to reinforce Hannibal. Scipio then struck directly at Carthage itself, prompting the Carthaginians to recall Hannibal from Italy to defend their homeland.

In 202 B.C.E., at the town of Zama near Carthage (Map 5.2), Scipio defeated Hannibal in a decisive battle. The Carthaginians sued for peace and in 201 B.C.E. the Roman Senate agreed, on terms that were very favorable to the Romans. Hannibal himself later served as a military adviser at the Seleucid court in its battle with Rome.

The Second Punic War and the treaty that ended it contained the seeds of still other wars. Rome regarded the treaty as making Carthage permanently subordinate to Rome, unable to wage war against its neighbors without Roman approval. But Carthage did just that in 151 B.C.E., after Numidia, a kingdom in North Africa that bordered Carthage and was a client state of Rome, launched a border raid on Carthaginian territory. In response, Rome declared war on Carthage in 149 B.C.E., which became the Third Punic War. After a three-year siege, led by Scipio Aemilianus, the grandson by adoption of Scipio Africanus, the Roman army took the city in 146 B.C.E. and destroyed it. The Romans sold the remaining residents into slavery and annexed Carthage's territory, which became an important source of grain to feed the city of Rome.

During the war with Hannibal, the Romans had invaded the Iberian Peninsula, an area rich in material resources and the home of fierce warriors. They met with bloody and determined resistance. Not until 133 B.C.E., after years of brutal and ruthless warfare, did Scipio Aemilianus finally conquer Spain. Scipio's victory meant that Roman language, law, and culture would in time permeate this entire region, although it would be another century before the Iberian Peninsula was completely pacified.

The Punic Wars required huge numbers of troops, and Rome was forced to ignore its official requirement that soldiers be citizens with a certain amount of property. Although it still maintained the lottery for drafting wealthier citizens, Rome devised other ways as well to increase the number of troops. Rome's allies in the Italian peninsula were required to provide more soldiers, and poor volunteers were recruited from Rome itself with modest amounts of pay and the promise of war booty. The Roman state began providing standardized weapons and armor, as many soldiers were too poor to afford these on their own, and army service increased from six years to about twenty.

## Rome Turns East

During the Second Punic War, King Philip V of Macedonia made an alliance with Hannibal against Rome. The Romans, in turn, allied themselves with the Aetolian League of city-states in central Greece.

The cities of the league bore the brunt of the fighting on the Greek peninsula until after the Romans had defeated Hannibal in 202 B.C.E. Then the Roman legions were deployed against the Macedonians, who were defeated in a series of wars. Roman armies also won significant victories against the forces of the Seleucid emperors, and that empire shrank, with parts becoming Roman client kingdoms. In 148 B.C.E., Rome made Macedonia into a Roman province. Another decisive victory came in 146 B.C.E., when the Romans attacked the city of Corinth. Just as they had at Carthage earlier that year, the Romans destroyed the city, killing the men and sending the women and children into slavery, and looting it for treasure. Statues, paintings, and other works of art were shipped to Rome. (See "Evaluating Visual Evidence: The Temple of Hercules Victor," page 116.) In 133 B.C.E., the king of Pergamum bequeathed his kingdom to the Romans. The Ptolemies of Egypt retained formal control of their kingdom, but they obeyed Roman wishes in terms of trade policy.

Once the Romans had conquered the Hellenistic world, they faced the formidable challenge of governing it, which they met by establishing the first Roman provinces in the East. Declaring the Mediterranean *mare nostrum*, "our sea," the Romans began to create political and administrative machinery to hold the Mediterranean together under a political system of provinces ruled by governors sent from Rome. Not all Romans were joyful over Rome's conquest of the Mediterranean world; some considered the victory a misfortune. The historian Sallust (86–34 B.C.E.), for example, writing from hindsight, complained that the acquisition of an empire was the beginning of Rome's troubles:

> But when through labor and justice our Republic grew powerful, great kings defeated in war, fierce nations and mighty peoples subdued by force, when Carthage the rival of the Roman people was wiped out root and branch, all the seas and lands lay open, then — fortune began to be harsh and to throw everything into confusion. The Romans had easily borne labor, danger, uncertainty, and hardship. To them leisure, riches — otherwise desirable — proved to be burdens and torments. So at first money, then desire for power grew great. These things were a sort of cause of all evils.[2]

Sallust was one of the voices creating a narrative of decline that became very powerful in the tumultuous late republic, and that influenced historians for long afterwards.

# How did expansion affect Roman society and culture?

By the second century B.C.E., the Romans ruled much of the Mediterranean world, and tremendous wealth poured into Rome, especially from the East, though holding on to Roman provinces was also costly because of military expenditures. Roman institutions, social patterns, and ways of thinking changed to meet the new era. Some looked nostalgically back at what they fondly considered the good old days and idealized the traditional agrarian and family-centered way of life. Others embraced the new urban life and eagerly accepted Greek culture.

## Roman Families

The core of traditional Roman society was the family, and the word *family* (*familia*) in ancient Rome actually meant all those under the authority of a male head of household, including nonrelated slaves, freedmen, and servants. In poor families, this group might be very small, but among the wealthy, it could include hundreds of slaves and servants.

The male head of household was called the **paterfamilias**. Just as slave owners held power over their slaves, fathers held great power over their children, which technically lasted for their children's whole lives. Initially this seems to have included power over life and death, but by the second century B.C.E., that had been limited by law and custom. Fathers continued to have the power to decide how family resources should be spent, however, and sons did not inherit until after their fathers had died.

In the early republic, legal authority over a woman generally passed from her father to her husband on marriage, but the Laws of the Twelve Tables allowed it to remain with her father even after marriage. That was advantageous to the father, and could also be to the woman, because her father might be willing to take her side in a dispute with her husband, and she could return to her birth family if there was quarreling or abuse. By the late republic, more and more marriages were of this type, and during the time of the empire (27 B.C.E.–476 C.E.), almost all of them were.

To marry, both spouses had to be free Roman citizens. Most citizens did marry, with women of wealthy families marrying in their midteens and non-elite women in their late teens. Grooms were generally somewhat older than their brides. Marital agreements, especially among the well-to-do, were stipulated with contracts between the families involved. According to Roman law, marriage required a dowry, a payment of money, property, and/or goods that went from the bride's family to the groom. If their owner allowed it, slaves could enter a marriage-like relationship called *contubernium*, which benefited their owner because any children produced from it would be his. People who were not slaves or citizens certainly lived together in marriage-like relationships, but these had no standing before the law and their children could not legally inherit.

Weddings were central occasions in a family's life, with spouses chosen carefully by parents, other family members, or marriage brokers. Professional fortune-tellers were frequently consulted to determine whether a match was good or what day would be especially lucky or auspicious for a couple to marry. The ceremony typically began with the bride welcoming the groom and the wedding party to her home for a feast, and then later the whole group progressed with much noise to the groom's household. It would be very unlucky if the bride tripped while going into the house, so the groom often carried her across the doorstep. The bride's entrance into the groom's house marked the point at which the two were married. As elsewhere in the ancient world, no public officials or priests were involved.

Women could inherit and own property under Roman law, though they generally received a smaller portion of any family inheritance than their brothers did. A woman's inheritance usually came as her dowry on marriage. In the earliest Roman marriage laws, men could divorce their wives without any grounds, and women could not divorce their husbands. By the second century B.C.E., however, these laws had changed, and both men and women could initiate divorce. By then, women had also gained greater control over their dowries and other family property, perhaps because Rome's military conquests meant that many husbands were away for long periods of time and women needed some say over family finances.

Although marriages were arranged by families primarily for the handing down of property, preserving wealth, and legitimizing children, the Romans, in something of a contradiction, viewed the model marriage as one in which husbands and wives were loyal to one another and shared interests and activities. The Romans praised women who were virtuous and loyal to their husbands and devoted to their children. (See "Viewpoints: Praise of Good Women in the Eulogy for Murdia and the Turia Inscription," page 124.)

Traditionally minded Romans thought that mothers should nurse their own children and personally see

■ **paterfamilias** The oldest dominant male of the Roman family, who held great power over the lives of family members.

**Household Shrine to the Gods and Ancestors** Two protector deities (*lares*), each holding a container for liquid, flank an ancestor-spirit (which the Romans called the "genius"), his head covered as a sign of reverence, who holds a box for incense and a bowl for offerings. At the bottom a snake, symbol of fertility and prosperity, approaches an altar. This elaborate shrine in the entryway of the house of two wealthy freedmen in Pompeii was a symbol of their prosperity and upward mobility, but even poor families had a designated space for protective lares figures. (House of the Vettii, Pompeii, Italy/Werner Forman Archive/Bridgeman Images)

to their welfare. Non-elite Roman women did nurse their own children, although wealthy women increasingly employed slaves as wet nurses and to help them with child rearing. Very young children were under their mother's care, and most children learned the skills they needed from their own parents. For children from wealthier urban families, opportunities for formal education increased in the late republic. Boys and girls might be educated in their homes by tutors, who were often Greek slaves, and boys also might go to a school run by a private teacher and paid for by their parents.

Most people in the expanding Roman Republic lived in the countryside. Farmers used oxen and donkeys to plow their fields, collecting the dung of the animals for fertilizer. Along with crops raised for local consumption and to pay their rents and taxes, many farmers raised crops to be sold. These included wheat, flax for making linen cloth, olives, and wine grapes.

Until the late republic most Romans, rich and poor, ate the same plain meals of bread, olives, vegetables, and a little meat or fish, with fruit for dessert. They used fingers and wooden spoons to serve themselves from simple pottery or wooden bowls and plates. They usually drank water or wine mixed with water from clay cups. Drinking unmixed wine was considered a sign of degeneracy. The Romans took three meals a day: an early breakfast, a main meal or dinner in the middle of the day, and a light supper in the evening. Dinner was also a social event, the main time for Romans to visit, chat, and exchange news. Afterward everyone who could afford the time took a long nap, especially during the hot summer months.

Most Romans worked long days, and an influx of slaves from Rome's wars and conquests provided additional labor for the fields, mines, and cities. To the Romans, slavery was a misfortune that befell some people, but it did not entail any racial theories. Slave boys and girls were occasionally formally apprenticed in trades such as leatherworking, weaving, or metalworking. Well-educated slaves served as tutors or accountants, ran schools, and designed and made artwork and buildings. For loyal slaves, the Romans always held out the possibility of freedom, and manumission, the freeing of individual slaves by their masters, was fairly common, especially for household

Tombstones in Rome, like those of today, provide information about what those who erected them thought was important for later generations to know about the deceased. Those for women were often erected by their husbands or sons, including those below, both dating from the first century B.C.E. The first, a eulogy for a woman named Murdia, was erected by a son from her first marriage. The second, erected by a husband, is traditionally called the "Turia inscription," although we do not know the identity of the woman or her husband with certainty.

### The Eulogy for Murdia

. . . of my mother Murdia, daughter of Lucius. . . . She made all her sons heirs in equal proportion, and gave her daughter a share as a legacy. Her maternal love was expressed by her concern for her children, and the equal shares she gave to each of them.

She left a specified sum of money to her husband so that the dowry, to which he was entitled, should be enhanced by her good opinion of him. . . . This behavior was typical of her. Her parents gave her in marriage to worthy men. Her obedience and honour preserved her marriages; as wife she endeared herself by her virtues, was beloved for her loyalty and was left the more honoured because of her judgement, and after her death to be praised in the estimation of her fellow citizens. . . .

For these reasons, praise for all good women is simple and similar, since their native goodness and the trust they have maintained do not require a diversity of words. Sufficient is the fact that they have all done the same good deeds that deserve fine reputation, and since their lives fluctuate with less diversity, by necessity we pay tribute to values they hold in common, so that nothing may be lost from fair precepts and harm what remains.

Still, my dearest mother deserved greater praise than all others, since in modesty, propriety, chastity, obedience, woolworking, industry, and loyalty she was on an equal level with other good women, nor did she take second place to any woman in virtue, work and wisdom in times of danger.

### The Turia Inscription

You became an orphan suddenly before the day of our wedding, when both your parents were murdered together in the solitude of the countryside. It was mainly due to your efforts that the death of your parents was not left unavenged. . . . Then pressure was brought to bear on you and your sister to accept the view that your father's will, by which you and I were heirs, had been invalidated by his having contracted a [fictitious purchase] with his wife. . . . You defended our common cause by asserting the truth, namely, that the will had not in fact been broken. . . . They gave way before your firm resolution and did not pursue the matter any further. . . .

You provided abundantly for my needs during my flight [into political exile] and gave me the means for a dignified manner of living, when you took all the gold and jewelry from your own body and sent it to me and over and over again enriched me in my absence with servants, money and provisions, showing great ingenuity in deceiving the guards posted by our adversaries.

You begged for my life when I was abroad—it was your courage that urged you to this step—and because of your entreaties I was shielded by the clemency of those against whom you marshalled your words. But whatever you said was always said with undaunted courage.

Meanwhile when a troop of men collected by Milo, whose house I had acquired by purchase when he was in exile, tried to profit by the opportunities provided by the civil war and break into our house to plunder, you beat them back successfully and were able to defend our home.

### QUESTIONS FOR ANALYSIS

1. What qualities do both men praise in their female relatives, and how might they describe the ideal Roman woman?
2. Murdia's son comments that "praise for all good women is simple and similar." Do the actions Turia's husband highlights support this, or did the unrest of the late Roman Republic shape what were regarded as admirable qualities in Roman women?

Sources: Eulogy for Murdia: Jane F. Gardner and Thomas Wiedemann, eds., *The Roman Household: A Sourcebook* (New York: Routledge, 1991), pp. 132–133; Turia inscription: Mary R. Lefkowitz and Maureen B. Fant, eds., *Women's Life in Greece and Rome: A Source Book in Translation*, 2d ed., pp. 135–137. © 1982, 1992 M. B. Fant and M. R. Lefkowitz. Reprinted with permission of Johns Hopkins University Press and Bloomsbury Publishing.

slaves, who remained part of the *familia*. Because they also became citizens, freedmen were part of wealthy men's networks of patronage and clientage. Nonetheless, slaves rebelled from time to time, sometimes in large-scale revolts put down by Roman armies (see "Civil War and the Rise of Julius Caesar").

Membership in a family did not end with death; the spirits of the family's ancestors were understood to remain with the family and were venerated. They and other gods regarded as protectors of the household—collectively these were called the *lares* and *penates*—were represented by small statues that stood in a special cupboard or a niche in the wall. The statues were taken out at meals and given small bits of food, or food was thrown into the household's hearth for them. The lares and penates represented the gods at family celebrations such as weddings, and families took the statues with them when they moved. They were honored in special rituals and ceremonies, although the later Roman poet Ovid (43 B.C.E.–17 C.E.) commented that these did not have to be elaborate:

> The spirits of the dead ask for little.
> They are more grateful for piety than for an
>     expensive gift —
> Not greedy are the gods who haunt the Styx [the
>     river that bordered the underworld] below.
> A rooftile covered with a sacrificial crown,
> Scattered kernels, a few grains of salt,
> Bread dipped in wine, and loose violets —
> These are enough.[3]

## New Social Customs and Greek Influence

Many aspects of life did not change greatly during the Roman expansion. Most people continued to marry and form families and to live in the countryside, with the rhythm of their days and years determined by the needs of their crops. But the conquest of the Mediterranean world and the wealth it brought gave the Romans leisure, especially in cities. The spoils of war went to build theaters, stadiums, and other places of amusement. This new urban culture reflected Hellenistic Greek influences. Some Romans, especially younger people, developed a liking for Greek literature, and it became common for an educated Roman to speak both Latin and Greek. The new Hellenism profoundly stimulated the growth and development of Roman art and literature. Roman artists copied many aspects of Greek art, but used art, especially portraiture, to communicate Roman values. Portrait busts in stone were a favored art form. Those who commissioned them wanted to be portrayed as individuals, but also as representing certain admirable qualities, such as wisdom or dignity.

Greek influence was also strong in literature. Roman authors sometimes wrote histories and poetry in Greek, or translated Greek classics into Latin. The poet Ennius (EHN-ee-uhs) (239–169 B.C.E.), the father of Latin poetry, studied Greek philosophy, wrote comedies in Latin, and adapted many of Euripides's tragedies for the Roman stage. Plautus (ca. 254–184 B.C.E.) brought a bawdy humor to his reworkings of Greek plays. The Roman dramatist Terence (ca. 195–159 B.C.E.) wrote comedies of refinement and grace that owed their essential elements to Greek models. All early Roman literature was derived from that of the Greeks, but it flourished because it also spoke to Roman ways of thinking.

Many rich urban dwellers changed their eating habits by consuming elaborate meals of exotic dishes and vintage wines drawn from all over the empire. Metal spoons took the place of wooden ones, and silver and bronze platters took the place of pottery. In the early first century B.C.E. artisans in Syria developed glassblowing, a technique they took to Rome when Syria was conquered by the Romans in 64 B.C.E. Glassblowing revolutionized glass production, and glass drinking cups could soon be seen on nearly every Roman table. By the late republic and early empire, many wealthy Romans dined formally on couches around a circular table. The Romans built status recognition into their dining rooms with the order in which people were seated, how they were seated, and differences in the meals they were served.

During the second century B.C.E., the Greek custom of bathing also gained popularity in the Roman world. The Romans built more and more large public buildings containing pools and exercise rooms, and by the period of the early empire, baths had become an essential part of any Roman city. The baths were socially important places where men and women went to see and be seen. Social climbers tried to talk to the right people and wangle invitations to dinner; politicians took advantage of the occasion to discuss the affairs of the day; marriages were negotiated by wealthy fathers. Baths were also places where people could buy sex; the women and men who worked in bathhouses often made extra income through prostitution. Because of this, conservative moralists portrayed them as dens of iniquity, but they were seen by most Romans as a normal part of urban life.

**Roman Bath**    This Roman bath in Bath, England (a city to which it gave its name), was built beginning in the first century C.E. around a natural hot spring. The Romans spread the custom of bathing, which they had adopted from the Greeks, to the outer reaches of their empire. In addition to hot water, bathers used oil for massage and metal scrapers to clean and exfoliate their skin. Many Roman artifacts have been unearthed at Bath, including a number of curse tablets, small tablets made of lead calling on the gods to harm someone, which were common in the Greco-Roman world. Not surprisingly, many of the curse tablets found at Bath relate to the theft of clothing while people were bathing. (bath: Photo © Neil Holmes/Bridgeman Images; artifact: © The Trustees of the British Museum/Art Resource, NY)

## Opposing Views: Cato the Elder and Scipio Aemilianus

Romans differed greatly in their opinions about the new social customs and about Greek influence. Two men, Marcus Cato (234–149 B.C.E.) and Scipio Aemilianus (185–129 B.C.E.), both of whom were military commanders and consuls, the highest office in the Roman Republic, can serve as representatives of these opposing views.

Marcus Cato was born a plebeian and owned a small rural estate, but his talent and energy caught the eye of high patrician officials and he became their client. He fought in the Second Punic War under Scipio Africanus and then returned to Rome, where he worked his way up through various offices. In 195 B.C.E., he was elected consul. A key issue facing Cato was the heated debate over the repeal of the Oppian Law, which had been passed twenty years earlier, right after Rome's disastrous loss to Carthage at the Battle of Cannae. Rome had needed money to continue the war, and the law decreed that no woman was to own more than a small amount of gold, or wear clothing

trimmed in purple, or drive a chariot in the city of Rome itself. These were all proclaimed to be luxuries that wasted money and undermined the war effort. The law was passed in part for financial reasons, but it also had gendered social implications, as there was no corresponding law limiting men's conspicuous consumption. By 195 B.C.E., the war was over and this restriction on women's spending had lost its economic rationale. Roman women publicly protested against it, and Cato led the battle to prevent its repeal, arguing that women's desire to spend money was a disease that could never be cured and that women were like wild animals and would engage in an orgy of shopping if the law were lifted. The women's political actions were more effective than Cato's speeches, however, and the law was lifted, although later in his political career Cato pushed for other laws forbidding women from wearing fancy clothing or owning property.

Women's spending was not the only thing destroying Roman society, according to Cato. He made speeches in the Senate decrying Greek influence, and set himself up as the defender of what he saw as traditional Roman values: discipline, order, morality, frugality, and an agrarian way of life. He was also practical, however, and made certain his older son learned Greek as an essential tool in Roman society, though he instructed the boy not to take Greek ideas too seriously. Cato held the office of censor, and he attempted to remove from the lists of possible officeholders anyone who did not live up to his standards. He even criticized his superior Scipio Africanus for being too lenient toward his troops and spending too much money. Cato proclaimed his views through his decisions when acting as a military commander, and also in his written works, which were all in Latin.

Late in life Cato was a diplomat to Carthage, and, according to later Roman historians, after he saw that the city had recovered economically from the war with Rome, he came home declaring, "Carthage must be destroyed." Cato's words were traditionally seen as a major reason for the Third Punic War, though more recently historians have emphasized differences of opinion between Rome and Carthage about the terms of the peace treaty that had ended the Second Punic War.

The military campaign against Carthage was led by Scipio Aemilianus, in contrast to Cato an avid devotee of Hellenism. Like his grandfather, Scipio believed that broader views had to replace the old Roman narrowness. Rome was no longer a small city; it was the capital of the world, and Romans had to adapt themselves to that fact. Scipio became an innovator in both politics and culture. He developed a more personal style of politics that looked unflinchingly at the broader problems that the success of Rome brought to its people. He embraced Hellenism wholeheartedly and promoted its spread in Roman society. Perhaps more than anyone else of his day, Scipio represented the new Roman—imperial, cultured, and independent.

In his education and interests, too, Scipio broke with the past. As a boy he had received the traditional Roman training, learning to read and write Latin and becoming acquainted with the law. He mastered the fundamentals of rhetoric and learned how to throw the javelin, fight in armor, and ride a horse. But as a young man he formed a lasting friendship with his tutor, the Greek historian Polybius, who had been brought to Rome as a war hostage during Rome's long fight with the Antigonid dynasty in Macedonia and the leagues of city-states in Greece. Polybius actively encouraged him in his study of Greek and in his intellectual pursuits. In later life Scipio's love of Greek learning, rhetoric, and philosophy became legendary. Scipio also promoted the spread of Hellenism in Roman society, and his views became more widespread than those of Cato. In general, Rome absorbed and added what it found useful from Hellenism, just as earlier it had absorbed aspects of Etruscan culture.

# What led to the fall of the Roman Republic?

The wars of conquest created serious problems for the Romans. Ever-larger armies had to be recruited to defend Rome's larger territory, with more extensive systems of administration and tax collection needed to support these. Roman generals, who commanded huge numbers of troops for long periods of time, acquired great power and ambition and were becoming too mighty for the Senate to control. Ordinary citizens who fought in those armies and paid taxes to support them thought the Senate paid no attention to their concerns, and supported alternatives to Senatorial control. Another problem was that proposals to redistribute land seized from conquered people to poor citizens led those conquered people—who were often officially allies of Rome—to demand full Roman citizenship. The spoils of war seemed to many people to be unevenly distributed, with military contractors and those who collected taxes profiting greatly, while average soldiers gained little. These complex and explosive problems largely account for the turmoil of the late republic (133–27 B.C.E.) and the gradual transformation of government into one in which one man held the most power.

## The Countryside and Land Reforms

Following a narrative of decline that began during the late republican period itself, historians traditionally saw the long-lasting foreign wars as devastating for the Roman countryside, with the prolonged fighting drawing men away from their farms for long periods, and the farms falling into wrack and ruin. There were not enough free men to keep the land under full cultivation, and women were not skilled enough to do so. Veterans and their families sold their land cheaply to wealthy landowners, who created huge estates, which the Romans called latifundia (lah-tuh-FUHN-dee-uh), worked by slave labor. Many veterans migrated to the cities, especially to Rome, leaving the countryside depopulated. According to this view, once they lost their land and property, men became ineligible for military service, even if they were veterans of major battles and numerous campaigns, and they were willing to support any leader who would allow them to serve again, with the pay that military service brought.

This understanding of what was going on the countryside and its causes and consequences has been

**Tomb of a Roman Baker**   Marcus Vergilius Eurysaces, a prosperous baker and freedman in late republican Rome, had this 30-foot-tall tomb built for himself and his wife Atistia sometime between 50 and 20 b.c.e. Over columns crammed together are odd circular openings, thought to represent basins for measuring grain or kneading dough. At the top a carved frieze shows scenes from bread production, some on a very large scale, which accounts for Eurysaces's wealth. Some of the many rural residents and former slaves who flocked to Rome became rich and celebrated their new wealth and its sources ostentatiously, upsetting the traditional elites. (Schtze/Rodemann/Bildarchiv Monheim/AGE Fotostock)

challenged in the twenty-first century by historians using archaeological, demographic, genetic, and other sources rather than primarily relying on the written works of elite men. Despite the losses due to foreign wars, the countryside was not depopulated, because the birthrate went up as families adjusted to meet the needs for agricultural labor over their life cycles. Families were able to maintain small and medium-sized family farms even when several of their men were away at war, with women or other male family members running them quite successfully. There were large slave-staffed estates in some places, and sometimes the rich may have owned many small farms that became one of their sources of income, but this was not a universal pattern, and the number of slaves in the countryside was much lower than previously thought. In this newer interpretation, landlessness was largely the

result of overpopulation rather than simply a concentration of landholding into large estates, as when men returned from war there were too many people in the countryside. Many then did migrate to Rome, becoming urban poor who were unhappy with the way the Senate ran things. The city of Rome grew dramatically, but this did not leave the countryside empty. Thus as with many issues in history, new evidence has made the story more complex and open to debate.

There is no debate that there were many landless poor in the city of Rome who could vote in the citizens' assemblies because they were citizens, and they tended to back anyone who offered them better prospects than the Senate did. One of these was Tiberius Gracchus (tigh-BEER-ee-uhs GRAK-uhs) (163–133 b.c.e.), an army officer in the Third Punic War who was elected tribune in 133 b.c.e. Tiberius proposed that public land in the territories of Roman allies in Italy be redistributed to the poor of the city of Rome, and that the limit to the amount of land allowed to each individual set by the Licinian-Sextian laws be enforced. Although his reform enjoyed the support of some distinguished and popular members of the Senate, it angered those who had taken large tracts of public land for their own use, and also upset Rome's allies, whose citizens were farming the land he proposed to give to Rome's urban poor. Tiberius also acted in a way that was unprecedented, introducing his land bill in the Plebeian Assembly without officially consulting the Senate. When King Attalus III of Pergamum died and left his wealth and kingdom to the Romans in his will, Tiberius used his powers as a tribune to take the money for his reforms without asking the Senate for approval—another affront to its power, as the Senate was responsible for managing the finances of the provinces.

Many powerful Romans became suspicious of Tiberius's growing influence with the people, and Tiberius put himself forward as the champion of the people opposed to the elites of the Senate, a populist message that many leaders since have also used to gain power. The Senate could not act against him while he was tribune; however, when he sought re-election after his term was over, riots erupted among his opponents and supporters, and a group of senators beat Tiberius to death in cold blood. The death of Tiberius was the beginning of an era of political violence.

Although Tiberius was dead, his land bill became law, and his brother Gaius (GAY-uhs) Gracchus (153–121 b.c.e.) took up the cause. The name later given to the laws championed by the brothers, the

**Gracchi reforms**, reflects the fact that more than one Gracchus brother advocated them. (*Gracchi* is the Latin plural of *Gracchus*.) Gaius was also a veteran soldier with an enviable record, and when he became tribune in 123 B.C.E. he demanded even more extensive reform than had his brother. To help the urban poor, Gaius pushed legislation to provide them with cheap grain for bread, and he revived the program to send poor and propertyless people from Rome out to form colonies. To address the concerns of Rome's allies about this, he proposed making all non-Roman Italians citizens so that they would be eligible for these benefits as well. This was not popular with many Roman citizens, rich and poor, who turned against him.

When Gaius failed in 121 B.C.E. to win the tribunate for the third time, he feared for his life. In desperation, Gaius armed his staunchest supporters, whereupon the Senate gave the consuls the license to kill him. On learning this, Gaius committed suicide, and many of his supporters died in the turmoil. (See "Thinking Like a Historian: Land Ownership and Social Conflict in the Late Republic," page 130.)

## Political Violence

The death of Gaius brought little peace, and trouble came from two sources: the outbreak of new wars in the Mediterranean basin and further political unrest in Rome, problems that operated together to encourage the rise of military strongmen. In 112 B.C.E., Rome declared war against the rebellious Jugurtha (joo-GUHR-thuh), king of Numidia in North Africa, one of Rome's client kingdoms whose actions had led to the Third Punic War.

The Roman legions made little headway against Jugurtha until 107 B.C.E., when Gaius Marius (MEHR-ee-uhs) (157–86 B.C.E.), a politician not from the traditional Roman aristocracy, became consul. He had no army, as the Roman troops were all fighting on Rome's northern border, and he decided to further expand the group of those eligible to be recruited to include all Roman citizens, even the poorest. He offered them armor, weapons, and most important, pay and retirement benefits in the form of land grants in conquered territory. Terms of service were extended to sixteen years, and training was to be all year round. Thus he completed the transformation of the Roman legions from a part-time citizens' force into a professional standing army, a process that had been going on gradually for some time. Marius also granted citizens of Rome's Italian allies full Roman citizenship if they completed a period of service in the Roman army. These Marian reforms increased the size and improved the military capabilities of the army, but they also meant that troops were loyal to the commanders who paid and rewarded them, and not the Senate.

Marius was unable to defeat Jugurtha directly, but his assistant and brother-in-law Sulla bribed Jugurtha's father-in-law to betray him, and Jugurtha was captured and executed in 104 B.C.E. in Rome. Marius later claimed this as a victory, and he was elected consul again, ultimately being elected an unprecedented seven times for the one-year term of the consul.

Fighting was also a problem on Rome's northern border, where two Germanic peoples, the Cimbri and Teutones, were moving into Gaul (present-day France) and later into northern Italy. After the Germans had defeated Roman armies sent to repel them, Marius as consul successfully led the campaign against them in 102 B.C.E., for which he was elected consul again, against the wishes of the Senate.

Rome was dividing into two political factions, both of whom wanted political power; contemporaries termed these factions the *populares* and the *optimates*. These were not political parties or consistent ideologies, but represented differences of opinion about the best way to get things done. In general the populares advocated for greater authority for the Citizens' Assembly and the tribunes and spoke in language stressing the welfare of the Roman people, and the optimates upheld the leadership role of the Senate and spoke in the language of Roman traditions. Individual politicians shifted their rhetoric and tactics depending on the situation; however, both of these factions were represented in the Senate.

This division is one of many in the turmoil of the late republic, and both groups had their favored general. Marius was the general backed by the populares, who from 104 B.C.E. to 100 B.C.E. elected him consul every year, although this was technically illegal and put unprecedented power into a Roman military commander's hands.

The favored general of the optimates was Sulla, who was Marius's brother-in-law and had earlier been his assistant. In 91 B.C.E. many Roman allies in the Italian peninsula rose up against Rome because they were expected to pay taxes and serve in the army but had no voice in political decisions because they were not full citizens. This revolt became known as the Social War, so named from the Latin word *socius*, or "ally." Sulla's armies gained a number of victories over the Italian allies, and Sulla gained prestige through his success in fighting them. In the end, however, the Senate agreed to give many allies Roman citizenship in order to end the fighting.

Sulla's military victories led to his election as consul in 88 B.C.E., and he was given command of the Roman army in a campaign against Mithridates, the king of a state that had gained power and territory

---

■ **Gracchi reforms**  Land reforms proposed by the Gracchi brothers to distribute public land to the poor of the city of Rome.

## Land Ownership and Social Conflict in the Late Republic

Landless poor who migrated to Rome were a serious social problem and a hot-button political issue in the late republic. Landless citizens could vote in the citizens' assemblies, and tended to back anyone who offered them better opportunities, especially land and the means to farm it. How did political leaders of the late republic seek to solve the problem, and why did this remain an issue?

**1 Speech by Tiberius Gracchus.** The general and tribune Tiberius Gracchus gave an eloquent public speech outlining the problem in 133 B.C.E., as related by the later Roman biographer Plutarch.

He took his place and spoke on behalf of the poor. "The wild beasts that roam over Italy have their dens, each has a place of repose and refuge. But the men who fight and die for Italy enjoy nothing but the air and light. Without house or home they wander about with their wives and children. Their commanders lie when they exhort the soldiers in their battles to defend sepulchres and shrines from the enemy, for not one of these many Romans has either hereditary altar or ancestral tomb; they fight and die to protect the wealth and luxury of others; they are styled masters of the world, and have not a single clod of earth they can call their own." About this time King Attalus Philometor [of Pergamum] died, and Eudemus of Pergamum brought to Rome his last will, in which the Roman people was named the king's heir. Tiberius proposed a law of popular appeal providing that the king's money, when brought to Rome, should be distributed among those of the citizens receiving allotments of public land, to provide them with equipment and give them a start in farming. As for cities that were in the kingdom of King Attalus, he declared that the disposal of them was not the senate's business, but that he himself would put a resolution before the people. By this he offended the senate more than ever.

**2 Reforms proposed by Tiberius Gracchus.** Along with the small allotments of land for veterans paid for by King Attalus's money, Tiberius Gracchus proposed other measures, as reported by the Roman historian Appian.

After speaking thus he again brought forward the existing law providing that nobody should hold more than 500 *iugera* [about 300 acres] of public domain. But he added a provision to the former law that two sons of the occupiers might each hold one half of that amount [in addition to that held by their father] and that the remainder should be divided among the poor. This was extremely disturbing to the rich because . . . they could no longer disregard the law as they had done before. . . . They collected together in groups, and made lamentation, and accused the poor of appropriating their fields of long standing, their vineyards, and their buildings. Some said they had paid the price of the land to their neighbors. Were they to lose the money with the land? . . . Others said that their wives' dowries had been expended on these estates, or that the land had been given to their own daughters as dowry. Moneylenders could show loans made on their security. All kinds of wailing and expressions of indignation were heard at once. On the other side were heard the lamentations of the poor — that they were being reduced from competence to extreme poverty, because they were unable to rear their offspring. They recounted the military services they had rendered, by which this very land had been acquired, and were angry that they should be robbed of their share of the common property. [The law was passed through procedures that many senators regarded as illegal.] Gracchus, immensely popular

### ANALYZING THE EVIDENCE

1. In Sources 1–3, what measures do Tiberius and Gaius Gracchus propose to provide land for the poor? Where would this land come from, and who might be living on it?
2. Who opposes the reforms of the Gracchi, and what do they give as their reasons?
3. In Source 4, how does the Senate seek to assure landowners they will retain their property?
4. In Source 5, what does the Flavian Bill propose, and why does the Senate oppose it? How and why is Cicero attempting to play both sides of the issue? Given what you have learned in the chapter about overpopulation in Italy, do you think there were many "deserted parts" into which people could be moved, as Cicero comments?
5. These sources stretch over more than seventy years. Why do you think this issue persisted over this long period?

by reason of the law, was escorted home by the multitude as though he were the founder, not of a single city or people, but of all the nations of Italy. . . . The defeated ones remained in the city and talked the matter over, feeling aggrieved and saying that as soon as Gracchus should become a private citizen he would be sorry that he had done outrage to the sacred and inviolable office of tribune, and had sown in Italy so many seeds of future strife.

## 3  The reforms of Gaius Gracchus.  Tiberius Gracchus was assassinated by a group of senators, but his brother Gaius became tribune and continued reforms, as related by Plutarch.

Of the laws which he now proposed with the object of gratifying the people and destroying the power of the senate, the first concerned public lands, which were to be divided among the poor citizens; another provided that common soldiers were to be clothed at public expense without any reduction in pay, and that no one under seventeen years of age should be conscripted into military service; another concerned the allies, giving the Italians equal suffrage rights with the citizens of Rome; a fourth related to grain, lowering the market price for the poor; a fifth, dealing with the courts of justice, was the greatest blow to the power of the senators, for hitherto they alone could sit on juries, and were therefore much feared by the plebs and *equites* [wealthy commoners]. . . . He also proposed measures for sending out colonies, for constructing roads, and for building public granaries.

## 4  The Agrarian Law of 111 B.C.E.  After Gaius Gracchus committed suicide in 121 B.C.E., the Senate passed several laws overturning the Gracchi reforms.

With respect to the public land belonging to the Roman people within Italy . . . whatever portion of such public land or ground within Italy, or outside the city of Rome, or in a city, town, or village a land commissioner has granted or assigned and any individual shall hold or possess at the time when this measure becomes law . . . excluding such land or ground specially excepted as aforesaid, shall be private land, and for all such land, ground, or buildings there shall be the same right of purchase or sale as for other private lands, grounds, or buildings. . . . Nor shall any person take steps whereby an individual who rightfully holds or shall hold the said land, ground, or building in accordance with the law or plebiscite shall be prevented from using, enjoying, holding, or possessing the said land, ground, or building . . . nor shall any person make a proposal to that effect in the senate.

## 5  Cicero discusses the Flavian Bill, 60 B.C.E.  After the law of 111 B.C.E. made almost all land in Italy private property, land for soldiers or veterans could only be found by turning to the newly conquered provinces or by using state funds to buy private land in Italy to distribute to them. In a private letter, Cicero (see "Civil War and the Rise of Julius Caesar") discusses a bill proposed by Pompey to do this.

[The bill proposed] that land be purchased with the windfall which will come in from the new foreign revenues in the next five years. The senate was opposed to this whole agrarian scheme, suspecting that Pompey was aimed at getting some new powers. Pompey set his heart on carrying the law through. I, with the full approval of the applicants for land, was for confirming the holdings of all private persons — for, as you know, our strength lies in the rich landed gentry; at the same time I satisfied Pompey and the populace — which I also wanted to do — by supporting the purchase of land, thinking that if it were faithfully carried out, the dregs of the city population could be drained off and the deserted parts of Italy peopled.

## PUTTING IT ALL TOGETHER

Using the sources above, along with what you have learned in class and in this chapter, write a short essay that analyzes land reform and social conflict in the later Roman Republic. How did political leaders of the late republic seek to solve the problem of increasing landlessness and a concentration of wealth, and why were their measures unsuccessful? How did this issue play into the power struggle between the Senate and charismatic military leaders during this period?

Sources: (1) Plutarch, *Life of Tiberius Gracchus*, 4.1–2; (2) Appian, *Civil Wars*, 1.i.9–2.16. Loeb Classical Library. Cambridge, Mass.: Harvard University Press. Loeb Classical Library® is a registered trademark of the President and Fellows of Harvard College.; (3) Plutarch, *Life of Gaius Gracchus*, 3–9; (4) The Agrarian Law of 111 B.C., *Corpus Inscriptionum Latinarum*, 2d ed., vol. 1 (Berlin, 1865– ), no. 585; (5) Cicero, *Letters to Atticus*, book 1, no. 29. Loeb Classical Library. Cambridge, Mass.: Harvard University Press. Loeb Classical Library® is a registered trademark of the President and Fellows of Harvard College.

**Cavalry Soldier from Gaius Marius's First Legion**    This funeral stele shows a cavalry soldier from Gaius Marius's first legion holding a shield and lance. At the bottom right are nine *phalera*, sculpted metal disks awarded to soldiers for distinguished conduct in action, and two *armilla*, metal armbands similarly awarded as military decorations. As with military honors today, these were not worn as part of everyday wear, but on dress uniform occasions such as triumphal parades and religious ceremonies. (Museum of Roman Civilization, Rome, Italy/De Agostini Picture Library/A. Dagli Orti/Bridgeman Images)

in what is now northern Turkey and was expanding into Greece. Before he could depart, however, the populares gained the upper hand in the Citizens' Assembly, revoked his consulship, and made Marius the commander of the troops against Mithridates. Riots broke out. Sulla fled the city and returned at the head of an army, an unprecedented move by a Roman general. He quelled the riots, put down his opponents, made some political changes that reduced the power of the assembly, and left again, this time to fight Mithridates.

Sulla's forces were relatively successful against Mithridates, but meanwhile Marius led his own

troops into Rome in 86 B.C.E., undid Sulla's changes, and killed many of his supporters. Although Marius died shortly after his return to power, those who supported him continued to hold Rome. Sulla returned in 83 B.C.E., and after a brief but intense civil war he entered Rome and ordered a ruthless butchery of his opponents. He then returned all power to the Senate and restored the conservative constitution as it had been before the Gracchi reforms. In 81 B.C.E., he was granted the office of dictator, a position he used to enhance his personal power. Dictators were supposed to step down after six months—many had done so in Roman history—but Sulla held this position for two years. In 79 B.C.E., Sulla abdicated his dictatorship because he was ill and believed his policies would last. Yet civil war was to be the constant lot of Rome for the next forty-eight years, and Sulla's abuse of political office became the blueprint for later leaders.

## Civil War and the Rise of Julius Caesar

The history of the late republic is the story of power struggles among many famous Roman figures against a background of unrest at home and military campaigns abroad. This led to a series of bloody civil wars that raged from Spain across northern Africa to Egypt. Sulla's political heirs were Pompey, Crassus, and Julius Caesar, all of them able military leaders and brilliant politicians. Pompey (106–48 B.C.E.) began a meteoric rise to power as a successful commander of troops for Sulla against Marius in Italy, Sicily, and Africa. He then suppressed a rebellion in Spain, led naval forces against pirates in the Mediterranean, and defeated Mithridates and the forces of other rulers as well, transforming their territories into Roman provinces and providing wealth for the Roman treasury.

Crassus (ca. 115–53 B.C.E.) also began his military career under Sulla and became the wealthiest man in Rome through buying and selling land. In 73 B.C.E., a major slave revolt broke out in Italy, led by Spartacus, a former gladiator. The slave armies defeated several Roman units sent to quash them. Finally Crassus led a large army against them and put down the revolt. Spartacus was apparently killed on the battlefield, and the slaves who were captured were crucified, with thousands of crosses lining the main road to Rome.

Pompey and Crassus then made an informal agreement with the populares in the Senate. Both were elected consuls in 70 B.C.E. and began to dismantle Sulla's constitution and initiate economic and political reforms. They and the Senate moved too slowly for some people, however, and several politicians who had been losing out in the jockeying for power, especially Catiline (108–62 B.C.E.), planned a coup, attracting people to their cause with the promise of

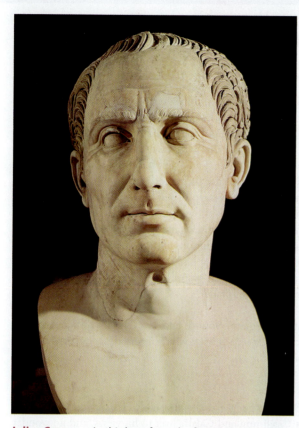

**Julius Caesar**    In this bust from the first century B.C.E., the sculptor portrays Caesar as a man of power and intensity. Showing individuals as representing certain virtues was common in Roman portraiture. (Museo e Gallerie Nazionali di Capodimonte, Naples, Italy/Bridgeman Images)

| TURMOIL IN THE LATE REPUBLIC | |
|---|---|
| 104 B.C.E. | Marius and Sulla defeat Jugurtha |
| 107, 104–100, 86 B.C.E. | Marius is elected consul |
| 91–88 B.C.E. | Social War |
| 88 B.C.E. | Sulla is elected consul |
| 86 B.C.E. | Marius leads his own troops into Rome and kills Sulla's supporters |
| 81 B.C.E. | Sulla is elected dictator |
| 79 B.C.E. | Sulla abdicates |
| 73–71 B.C.E. | Spartacus leads major slave revolt |
| 70 B.C.E. | Pompey and Crassus are elected consuls |
| 60 B.C.E. | Pompey, Crassus, and Caesar form the First Triumvirate; Caesar is elected consul |
| 49 B.C.E. | Caesar crosses the Rubicon and takes Rome |
| 48 B.C.E. | Caesar defeats Pompey at the Battle of Pharsalus |
| 44 B.C.E. | Caesar is killed by a group of senators |

debt relief. They planned to organize unrest in the countryside and in Rome, but the Catiline conspiracy was discovered, and Cicero (106–43 B.C.E.), who was one of the consuls in 63 B.C.E. when all this happened, denounced the conspirators on the floor of the Senate. Catiline—who was in attendance during Cicero's speech—fled Rome, and Cicero had several of the other leaders condemned to death without a trial and executed.

The man who cast the longest shadow over these troubled years was Julius Caesar (100–44 B.C.E.). Born of a noble family, he received an excellent education, which he furthered by studying in Greece with some of the most eminent teachers of the day. He had serious intellectual interests and immense literary ability. His account of his military operations in Gaul, the *Commentaries on the Gallic Wars*, became a classic of Western literature. Caesar was a superb orator, and his personality and wit made him popular. Military service was an effective stepping-stone to politics, and Caesar was a military genius who knew how to win battles and turn victories into permanent gains. He was also a shrewd politician of unbridled ambition, who knew how to use the patron-client system to his

advantage. He became a protégé of Crassus, who provided cash for Caesar's needs, and at the same time helped the careers of other politicians, who in turn looked after Caesar's interests in Rome when he was away from the city. Caesar launched his military career in Spain, where his courage won the respect and affection of his troops.

In 60 B.C.E., Caesar returned to Rome from Spain, where Pompey had been sitting for three years after military victories in the East, losing some of his popularity as a conquering general as he could not convince the Senate to give his veterans land. Together with Crassus, the three concluded an informal political alliance later termed the **First Triumvirate** (trigh-UHM-veh-ruht). Crassus's money helped Caesar be elected consul, and Pompey married Caesar's daughter Julia. Crassus was appointed governor of Syria, Pompey of Hispania (present-day Spain), and Caesar of Gaul.

Personal ambitions undermined the First Triumvirate. While Caesar was away from Rome fighting in Gaul, supporters of Caesar and Pompey formed gangs

■ **First Triumvirate**  The name later given to an informal political alliance among Caesar, Crassus, and Pompey in which they agreed to advance one another's interests.

# Cicero and the Plot to Kill Caesar

Marcus Tullius Cicero (106 B.C.E.–43 B.C.E.) was a lawyer, orator, senator, and statesman who served as consul in 63 B.C.E. He tended to favor Pompey in the conflict between generals, as he thought Caesar was a greater danger to traditional republican institutions. He was not involved in the plot to assassinate Caesar, but he was involved in the jockeying for power that followed, as evidenced by the following letters and speeches.

After learning of the murder, Cicero gave this frank opinion of the events in a letter to one of the assassins:

Would to heaven you had invited me to that noble feast that you made on the ides of March: no remnants, most assuredly, should have been left behind. The part you unluckily spared gives us so much perplexity that we find something to regret, even in the godlike service that you and your illustrious associates have lately rendered to the republic.*

By the "part you unluckily spared" he meant Mark Antony, Caesar's firm supporter, whom Cicero feared. Still undecided about what to do after the assassination, Cassius, one of the leaders of the plot, wrote to Cicero asking for advice. Cicero responded:

*To Trebonius, in T. de Quincy, *Cicero: Offices, Essays, and Letters* (New York: Everyman's Library), pp. 328–329.

Where to advise you to begin to restore order I must acknowledge myself at a loss. To say the truth, it is the tyrant alone, and not the tyranny, from which we seem to be delivered: for although the man [Caesar] is destroyed, we still servilely maintain all his despotic ordinances. We do more: and under the pretence of carrying his designs into execution, we approve of measures which even he himself would never have pursued. . . . This outrageous man [Antony] represents me as the principal advisor and promoter of your glorious efforts. Would to heaven the charge were true! For had I been a party in your councils, I should have put it out of his power thus to bother and embarrass our plans.†

At this stage the young Octavian, Caesar's designated heir, sought Cicero's advice, which Cicero described in a series of letters:

Octavian has great schemes afoot. He has won the veterans at Casilinum and Calatia over to his views, and no wonder since he gives them 500 denarii apiece. He plans to make a round of the other colonies. His object is plain: war with

†To Cassius, in de Quincy, *Cicero*, pp. 324–325.

that attacked each other, and there were riots in the streets of Rome. The First Triumvirate disintegrated. Crassus died in battle while trying to conquer Parthia, and Caesar and Pompey accused each other of treachery. Fearful of Caesar's popularity and growing power, the Senate sided with Pompey and ordered Caesar to disband his army. He refused, and instead in 49 B.C.E. he crossed the Rubicon River in northern Italy—the boundary of his territorial command—with soldiers. ("Crossing the Rubicon" is still used as an expression for committing to an irreversible course of action.) Although their forces outnumbered Caesar's, Pompey and the Senate fled Rome, and Caesar entered the city and took control without a fight.

Caesar then led his army against those loyal to Pompey and the Senate in Spain and Greece. In 48 B.C.E., despite being outnumbered, he defeated Pompey and his army at the Battle of Pharsalus in central Greece. Pompey fled to Egypt, which was embroiled in a battle for control not between two generals but between a brother and a sister, Ptolemy XIII and Cleopatra VII (69–30 B.C.E.). Caesar followed Pompey to Egypt, Cleopatra allied herself with

Caesar, and Caesar's army defeated Ptolemy's army, ending the power struggle. Pompey was assassinated in Egypt, Cleopatra and Caesar became lovers, and Caesar brought Cleopatra to Rome. (See "Individuals in Society: Queen Cleopatra," page 136.) Caesar put down a revolt against Roman control by the king of Pontus in northern Turkey, then won a major victory over Pompey's army—now commanded by his sons—in Spain.

In the middle of defeating his enemies in battles all around the Mediterranean (see Map 5.2), Julius Caesar returned to Rome several times and was elected or appointed to various positions, including consul and dictator. He was acclaimed imperator, a title given to victorious military commanders and a term that later gave rise to the word *emperor*. Sometimes these elections happened when Caesar was away fighting; they were often arranged by his chief supporter and client in Rome, Mark Antony (83–30 B.C.E.), who was himself a military commander. Whatever Caesar's official position, after he crossed the Rubicon he simply made changes on his own authority, though often with the approval of the Senate, which he packed with

Antony and himself as commander-in-chief. So it looks to me as though in a few days' time we shall be in arms. . . . [H]e proffers himself as our leader and expects me to back him up. For my part I have recommended him to go to Rome. I imagine he will have the city rabble behind him, and the honest men too if he convinces them of his sincerity. Ah Brutus, where are you? What a golden opportunity you are losing! I could not foretell this, but I thought something of the kind would happen. . . . I'm nervous of Antony's power and don't want to leave the coast. . . . Varro [an enemy of Antony] doesn't think much of the boy's [i.e., Octavian's] plan, I take a different view. He has a strong force at his back and can have Brutus.[‡]

Even though he contemptuously called him a "boy," Cicero decided to openly side with Octavian, and in 43 B.C.E. he denounced Antony in a speech to the Senate:

Do you not remember, in the name of the immortal gods, what resolutions you have made against these men [Antony and his supporters]? You have repealed the acts of Antony. You have taken down his law. You have voted that they were carried by violence and with a disregard of the auspices. You have called out the troops throughout all Italy. You have pronounced that colleague and ally of

all wickedness [Antony] a public enemy. What peace can there be with this man? . . . But these men will stick to your eyes, and when they can to your very throats; for what fences will be strong enough for us to restrain savage beasts? Oh, but the result of war is uncertain. It is at all events in the power of brave men such as you ought to be to display your valor, for certainly brave men can do that, and not fear the caprice of fortune.[§]

Antony and Octavian briefly reconciled and formed the Third Triumvirate. An ill and aging Cicero was declared an enemy of the state and sought to leave Italy, but was intercepted by Antony's men and killed.

### EVALUATE THE EVIDENCE

1. What can you infer from these letters about how well prepared the conspirators and other leaders in the Senate such as Cicero were to take control of the government after Caesar's death?
2. Given Cicero's words and actions here and his earlier ones in the Catiline conspiracy and the debate about land reform (both discussed in this chapter), does he seem to be motivated more by a consistent ideology or by personal ambition?

[‡]*To Atticus*, 16.8.1–2 in D. R. Shackleton-Bailey, *Cicero's Letters to Atticus*, vol. 6 (Cambridge: Cambridge University Press, 1967), pp. 185–187, 189.

[§]*The Fourteenth Phillipic*, in C. D. Yonge, *Cicero, Select Orations* (New York: Harper and Brothers, 1889), p. 499.

his supporters. The Senate transformed his temporary positions as consul and dictator into ones he would hold for life.

Caesar began to make a number of legal and economic reforms. He issued laws about debt, the collection of taxes, and the distribution of grain and land. Families who had many children were to receive rewards, and Roman allies in northern Italy were to have full citizenship. He reformed the calendar, which had been based on the cycles of the moon, by replacing it with one based on the sun, adapted from the Egyptian calendar. He sponsored celebrations honoring his victories, had coins struck with his portrait, and founded new colonies, which were to be populated by veterans and the poor. He planned even more changes, including transforming elected positions such as consul, tribune, and provincial governor into ones that he appointed.

Caesar was wildly popular with most people in Rome for his generosity, and even with many senators. Other senators, led by Brutus and Cassius, favored the traditional republic and opposed Caesar's rise to what was becoming absolute power. In 44 B.C.E., they conspired to kill him and did so on March 15 — the

date called the "Ides of March" in the Roman calendar — stabbing him multiple times on the steps of the theater of Pompey, where the Senate was meeting that day. (See "Evaluating Written Evidence: Cicero and the Plot to Kill Caesar," above.)

The result of Caesar's assassination was yet another round of civil war. Caesar had named his eighteen-year-old grandnephew and adopted son, Octavian, as his heir. In 43 B.C.E., Octavian joined forces with two of Caesar's lieutenants, Mark Antony and Lepidus (LEH-puh-duhs), in a formal pact known later as the **Second Triumvirate**. Together they hunted down Caesar's killers and defeated the military forces loyal to Pompey's sons and to the conspirators. They agreed to divide the provinces into spheres of influence, with Octavian taking most of the west, Antony the east, and Lepidus the Iberian Peninsula and North Africa. The three came into conflict, however, and Lepidus was forced into exile by Octavian, leaving the other two to confront one another.

■ **Second Triumvirate** A formal agreement in 43 B.C.E. among Octavian, Mark Antony, and Lepidus to defeat Caesar's murderers.

# INDIVIDUALS IN SOCIETY

## Queen Cleopatra

Cleopatra VII (69–30 B.C.E.) was a member of the Ptolemy dynasty, the Hellenistic rulers of Egypt who had established power in the third century B.C.E. Although she was Greek, she was passionately devoted to her Egyptian subjects and was the first in her dynasty who could speak Egyptian in addition to Greek. Just as ancient pharaohs had linked themselves with the gods, she had herself portrayed as the goddess Isis and may have seen herself as a reincarnation of Isis (see "Religion and Magic" in Chapter 4).

At the time civil war was raging in the late Roman Republic, Cleopatra and her brother Ptolemy XIII were in a dispute over who would be supreme ruler in Egypt. Julius Caesar captured the Egyptian capital of Alexandria, Cleopatra arranged to meet him, and the two became lovers, although Cleopatra was much younger and Caesar was married. The two apparently had a son, Caesarion, and Caesar's army defeated Ptolemy's army, ending the power struggle. In 46 B.C.E., Cleopatra arrived in Rome, where Caesar put up a statue of her as Isis in one of the city's temples.

After Caesar's assassination, Cleopatra returned to Alexandria, where she became involved in the continuing Roman civil war that now pitted Octavian, Caesar's grandnephew and heir, against Mark Antony, who commanded the Roman army in the East. Cleopatra invited Antony to come to Egypt in 41 B.C.E., and though Antony was married to the powerful Roman aristocrat Fulvia, the two became lovers and Cleopatra had twins, whom Antony acknowledged as his. When Fulvia died, Antony married Octavian's sister Octavia, an attempt to cement an alliance between the two men, but he divorced her in 32 B.C.E. and married Cleopatra. Antony's wedding present to Cleopatra was a huge grant of territory, much of it territory that officially belonged to the Roman people, which greatly increased her power and that of all her children, including Caesarion. Antony also declared Caesarion to be Julius Caesar's rightful heir.

Octavian used the wedding gift as the reason to declare Antony a traitor. He and other Roman leaders described Antony as a romantic fool captivated by the seductive Cleopatra, whom they portrayed as a decadent Eastern queen and a threat to what were considered traditional Roman values. Roman troops turned against Antony and joined with Octavian, and at the Battle of Actium in 31 B.C.E., Octavian defeated the army and navy of Antony and Cleopatra. Antony committed suicide, as did Cleopatra shortly afterward. Octavian ordered the teenage Caesarion killed, but the young children of Antony and Cleopatra were allowed to go back to Rome, where they were raised by Antony's ex-wife Octavia, as were Antony's children by Fulvia. Another consequence of Octavian's victory was that Egypt became a Roman province.

Roman sources are openly hostile to Cleopatra, and she became the model of the alluring woman whose sexual attraction led men to their doom. Stories about her beauty, sophistication, lavish spending, desire for power, and ruthlessness abounded and were retold for centuries. The most dramatic story was that she committed suicide through the bite of a poisonous snake, which may have been true and which has been the subject of countless paintings. Her tumultuous relationships with Caesar and Antony have been portrayed in plays, novels, movies, and television programs.

### QUESTIONS FOR ANALYSIS

1. How did Cleopatra benefit from her relationships with Caesar and Antony? How did they benefit from their relationships with her?
2. How did ideas about gender and Roman suspicion of the more sophisticated Greek culture combine to shape Cleopatra's fate and the way she is remembered?
3. In Chapter 1, "Individuals in Society: Hatshepsut and Nefertiti" (see page 26) also focuses on leading female figures in Egypt, but these two women lived more than a thousand years before Cleopatra. How would you compare their situation with hers?

The only portraits of Cleopatra that date from her own lifetime are on the coins that she issued. This one, made at the mint of Alexandria, shows her as quite plain, reinforcing the point made by Cicero that her attractiveness was based more on intelligence and wit than on physical beauty. The reverse of the coin shows an eagle, a symbol of rule. (© The Trustees of the British Museum/Art Resource, NY)

Both Octavian and Antony set their sights on gaining more territory. Cleopatra had returned to rule Egypt after Caesar's death, and she supported Antony. In 31 B.C.E., Octavian's forces defeated the combined forces of Antony and Cleopatra at the Battle of Actium in Greece, but the two escaped. Octavian pursued them to Egypt, and they committed suicide rather than fall into his hands. Octavian's victory at Actium put an end to an age of civil war. For his success, the Senate in 27 B.C.E. gave Octavian the name Augustus, meaning "revered one." The Senate did not mean this to be a decisive break with tradition, but because Octavian survived and began to transform the Roman government (see Chapter 6), that date is generally used to mark the end of the Roman Republic and the start of the Roman Empire.

## NOTES

1. Plutarch, *Pyrrhos* 21.14. In this chapter, works in Latin with no translator noted were translated by John Buckler.
2. Sallust, *War with Catiline* 10.1–3.
3. Ovid, *Fasti* 2.535–539.

# LOOKING BACK  LOOKING AHEAD

As the Greeks were creating urban culture and spreading it around the Mediterranean, other peoples, including the Etruscans and the people who later became the Romans, built their own societies on the Italian peninsula. The Romans spread their way of life throughout Italy by means of conquest and incorporation. After wars in which they defeated the wealthy city of Carthage, they expanded their political dominance throughout the western Mediterranean basin. Then they conquered in the East until they came to view the entire Mediterranean as *mare nostrum*, "our sea." As a result of these successes, Roman society and culture became Hellenized.

Yet Roman successes also brought war and civil unrest. The final days of the republic were filled with war and chaos, and the republican institutions did not survive. Rome became an empire ruled by one man. The laws and administrative practices of the republic shaped those of the empire, however, as well as those of later states in Europe and beyond. When the American constitution was drafted in 1787, its authors—well read in Roman history and law—favored a balance of powers like those they idealized in the Roman Republic, and they chose to call the smaller and more powerful deliberative assembly the Senate. They, too, were divided into those who favored rule by traditional elites and those who favored broader political power. That division is reflected in the fact that the U.S. Congress has two houses, the House of Representatives elected directly by voters, and the Senate, originally elected indirectly by state legislatures.

## Make Connections

Think about the larger developments and continuities within and across chapters.

1. How would you compare ideals for male and female behavior in republican Rome with those of classical Sparta and classical Athens in Chapter 3? What are some possible reasons for the differences and similarities you have identified?

2. The Phoenicians, the Greeks, and the Romans all established colonies around the Mediterranean. How did these colonies differ, and how were they the same, in terms of their economic functions and political situations?

3. Looking over the long history of the Roman Republic, do interactions with non-Romans or conflicts among Romans themselves appear to be the most significant drivers of change, and why? How were these related to one another?

# 5    REVIEW & EXPLORE

## Identify Key Terms

Identify and explain the significance of each item below.

Senate (p. 113)

consuls (p. 113)

patricians (p. 117)

plebeians (p. 117)

Struggle of the Orders (p. 118)

tribunes (p. 118)

patron-client system (p. 118)

Punic Wars (p. 119)

paterfamilias (p. 122)

Gracchi reforms (p. 129)

First Triumvirate (p. 133)

Second Triumvirate (p. 135)

## Review the Main Ideas

Answer the section heading questions from the chapter.

**1.** How did the Romans become the dominant power in Italy? (p. 110)

**2.** What were the key institutions of the Roman Republic? (p. 115)

**3.** How did the Romans build a Mediterranean empire? (p. 119)

**4.** How did expansion affect Roman society and culture? (p. 122)

**5.** What led to the fall of the Roman Republic? (p. 127)

## Suggested Resources

### BOOKS

- Boatwright, Mary T., et al. *The Romans: From Village to Empire*, 2d ed. 2012. An excellent survey of Roman history that emphasizes everyday life as well as political developments.

- Canfora, Luciano. *Julius Caesar: The Life and Times of the People's Dictator*. 2007. Provides a new interpretation of Caesar that puts him fully into the context of his times.

- Eckstein, Arthur M. *Mediterranean Anarchy, Interstate War, and the Rise of Rome*. 2006. Places the rise of the Roman Republic in the context of the wars of contemporary Hellenistic states.

- Evans, J. K. *War, Women, and Children in Ancient Rome*. 2000. Provides a concise survey of how war affected the home front in wartime.

- Everitt, Anthony. *The Rise of Rome: The Making of the World's Greatest Empire*. 2012. An engaging and thorough narrative written for general readers.

- Forsythe, Gary A. *A Critical History of Early Rome from Prehistory to the First Punic War*. 2005. Uses archaeological findings as well as written sources to examine the political, social, and religious developments of early Rome.

- Haynes, Sybille. *Etruscan Civilization: A Cultural History*. 2005. Deals with cultural history, giving special emphasis to Etruscan women.

- Holland, Tom. *Rubicon: The Last Years of the Roman Republic*. 2005. A dramatic account of the disintegration of the republic from the Gracchi to Caesar's death.

- Matz, David. *Daily Life of the Ancient Romans*. 2008. A brief but valuable account of the ordinary things in Roman life.

- Miles, Richard. *Carthage Must Be Destroyed: The Rise and Fall of a Civilization*. 2011. A lively narrative of the rise and fall of Carthage, based on early sources and archaeological evidence.

- Murell, John. *Cicero and the Roman Republic*. 2008. Looks at the late republic through Cicero's life and political career.

- Rosenstein, Nathan. *Rome at War: Farms, Families and Death in the Middle Republic*. 2004. Detailed analysis of what was actually going on in the countryside, based on a huge range of sources.

- Warrior, Valerie. *Roman Religion*. 2006. A relatively brief study that examines the actual practices of Roman religion in their social contexts.

## MEDIA

- *Ancient Rome: The Rise and Fall of an Empire* (BBC, 2006). A six-part docudrama; each part focuses on a turning point, with one on the Gracchi and another on Julius Caesar.

- *Great Generals of the Ancient World: Alexander the Great, Hannibal, Julius Caesar* (History Channel, 2006). Three-part set examining the military careers, battles, and personalities of the most successful generals in the ancient world.

- *LacusCurtius: Into the Roman World.* Website with primary and secondary resources on ancient Rome, including photographs, inscriptions, maps, and links to other Roman websites. **penelope.uchicago.edu/ Thayer/E/Roman/home.htm**

- *Mysterious Etruscans.* Informative, well-illustrated website with information on Etruscan language, art, religion, and lifestyle. **www.mysteriousetruscans.com/**

- *Rome* (HBO and BBC, 2005, 2007). British-American historical-drama television series set in the transition from republic to empire, with real historical figures and invented characters.

- *Spartacus* (Stanley Kubrick, 1960). Oscar-winning epic tells the story of the slave revolt led by Spartacus; starring and produced by Kirk Douglas, who considered the movie in part a response to McCarthy-era blacklisting.

# 6

# The Roman Empire

## 27 B.C.E.–284 C.E.

**In 27 B.C.E. the civil wars were largely over,** at least for a time. With peace came prosperity, stability, and a new vision of Rome's destiny. In his epic poem the *Aeneid* celebrating the creation of the Roman people out of many different ancestors, the Roman poet Virgil expressed this vision:

> You, Roman, remember—these are your arts:
> To rule nations, and to impose the ways of peace,
> To spare the humble and to conquer the proud.[1]

This was an ideal, of course, but Augustus, now the ruler of Rome, recognized that ideals and traditions were important to Romans. Instead of creating a new form of government, he left the republic officially intact, but increasingly held more power himself. The rulers that followed him attempted to assert their power as well, though some were more successful than others and all relied on the help of the Senate and other traditional elites to run the empire. The boundaries of the Roman Empire expanded in all directions, and the army became an important means of Romanization through its forts, camps, and cities, where Roman culture mixed with local traditions. A new religion, Christianity, developed in the eastern Roman province of Judaea, and spread on the roads and sea-lanes used by Roman traders and troops. By the third century C.E. civil wars had returned, however, and it seemed as if Augustus's creation would collapse.  ■

# CHAPTER PREVIEW

- How did Augustus and Roman elites create a foundation for the Roman Empire?

- How did the Roman state develop after Augustus?

- What was life like in the city of Rome and in the provinces?

- How did Christianity grow into a major religious movement?

- What political and economic problems did Rome face in the third century C.E.?

**Life in Imperial Rome**
In this terra-cotta relief from the third century C.E., a woman sells fruit and poultry from a shop while customers line up in front of her. Women were public merchants in imperial Rome, and some controlled their own finances, something that would have been unthinkable in ancient Athens. (Museo Archeologico, Ostia, Italy/De Agostini Picture Library/A. Dagli Orti/Bridgeman Images)

# How did Augustus and Roman elites create a foundation for the Roman Empire?

After Augustus (r. 27 B.C.E.–14 C.E.) ended the civil wars that had raged off and on for decades, he faced the monumental problems of reconstruction. He first had to reconstruct a functioning government. Next he had to pay his armies for their services, and care for the welfare of the provinces. Then he had to address the danger of various groups on Rome's European frontiers. Augustus was highly successful in meeting these challenges, creating a system of government in which he ruled together with the Senate and other members of the Roman elite.

## Augustus and His Allies

Augustus claimed that he was restoring the republic, but he actually transformed the government into one in which he held increasing amounts of power. Historians used to see this transformation as the sole creation of Augustus and his family, but they increasingly recognize that Augustus was assisted in this by senators and other members of the Roman elite who wanted to play an active role in governance. Augustus and his successors turned for advice to a circle of trusted friends. Many of these were from senatorial families or those just beneath them in Rome's social hierarchy, who were called *equites,* a word meaning "horsemen" in Latin because this class had originally formed the cavalry of the Roman army.

Together the senators and equites formed a tiny elite of under ten thousand members who held almost all military, political, and economic power in Rome's expanding territory, a pattern that had started during the republican period and continued under Augustus's successors. An ambitious young man from a senatorial or equestrian family who wished to gain power and wealth generally first served as an official somewhere in the Italian peninsula. He then spent time as a high military officer, and if he was successful, he gained a post as a governor, high official, or military leader in the provinces, taking the Roman legal system and Roman culture with him. He then might try to gain a seat in the Senate, though Augustus limited these seats to around six hundred and set high minimum property requirements, so competition was fierce. Sons of sitting senators did not just inherit their fathers' seats but had to serve in the administration or high in the army first, and then run a campaign.

Although Augustus curtailed the power of the Senate, it continued to exist as the chief deliberative body of the state, and it continued to act as a court of law. Augustus and the Senate ruled together, as both needed the other to rule effectively, and the relationship between them was fluid. Augustus intentionally pursued a policy of conciliation with some of his former enemies. Toward the end of his reign, he closed the popular assemblies, so ordinary Romans could make their opinions known to him only when they saw him in person at games or during his speeches. At these times vast crowds of thousands organized themselves to clap, stomp, and shout their opinions, but these were never as important in determining policy as the opinions of Augustus's intimates.

**Augustus as Imperator** In this marble statue, found in the villa of Augustus's widow, Augustus is depicted in a military uniform and in a pose usually used to show leaders addressing their troops. This portrayal emphasizes his role as imperator, the head of the army. The figures on his breastplate show various peoples the Romans had defeated or with whom they had made treaties, along with assorted deities. Although Augustus did not declare himself a god — as later Roman emperors would — this statue shows him barefoot, just as gods and heroes were in classical Greek statuary, and accompanied by Cupid riding a dolphin, both symbols of the goddess Venus, whom he claimed as an ancestor. (Vatican Museums and Galleries, Vatican State/Bridgeman Images)

# TIMELINE

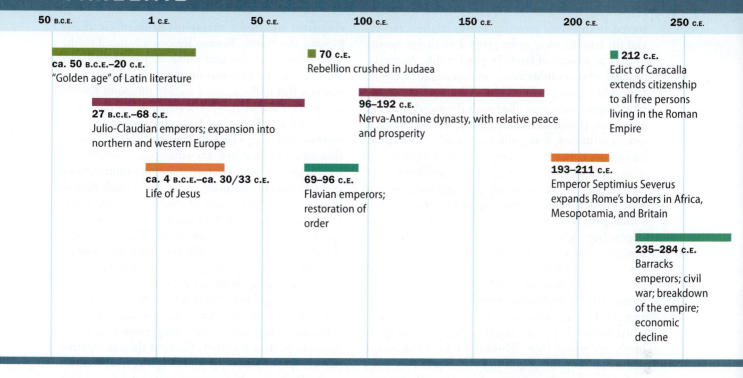

| 50 B.C.E. | 1 C.E. | 50 C.E. | 100 C.E. | 150 C.E. | 200 C.E. | 250 C.E. |
|---|---|---|---|---|---|---|

**ca. 50 B.C.E.–20 C.E.**
"Golden age" of Latin literature

**27 B.C.E.–68 C.E.**
Julio-Claudian emperors; expansion into northern and western Europe

**ca. 4 B.C.E.–ca. 30/33 C.E.**
Life of Jesus

**70 C.E.**
Rebellion crushed in Judaea

**96–192 C.E.**
Nerva-Antonine dynasty, with relative peace and prosperity

**69–96 C.E.**
Flavian emperors; restoration of order

**212 C.E.**
Edict of Caracalla extends citizenship to all free persons living in the Roman Empire

**193–211 C.E.**
Emperor Septimius Severus expands Rome's borders in Africa, Mesopotamia, and Britain

**235–284 C.E.**
Barracks emperors; civil war; breakdown of the empire; economic decline

---

Augustus fit his own position into the republican constitution not by creating a new office for himself but by gradually taking over many of the offices that traditionally had been held by separate people. He was elected consul, which gave him the right to call the Senate into session and present legislation to the citizens' assemblies. As a patrician, Augustus was ineligible to be a tribune, but the Senate gave Augustus the powers of a tribune anyway, such as the right to preside over the *concilium plebis* (see Chapter 5). Recognizing the importance of religion, he had himself named *pontifex maximus*, or chief priest. An additional title that the Senate bestowed on Augustus was *princeps civitatis* (prihn-KEHPS cih-vee-TAH-tees), "first citizen of the state," and because of this his government is called the **principate**. This title had no official powers attached to it and had been used as an honorific for centuries, so it was inoffensive to Roman ears. One of the cleverest tactics of Augustus and his allies among the Roman elite was to use noninflammatory language for the changes they were making. Only later would *princeps civitatis* become the basis of the word *prince*, meaning "sovereign ruler."

Augustus was also named **imperator**, another traditional title often given to a general by his troops after a major victory, derived from the Latin word *imperium*, which means "power to command." In the late republic more than one military commander sometimes held this title at the same time, but gradually it was restricted to the man who ruled Rome,

given to him when he acceded to power, and became one of his titles. (The English word *emperor* comes from *imperator* in this more exclusive sense, and the rulers of Rome after Augustus are conventionally called emperors.) Here again Augustus and his successors used familiar language to make change seem less dramatic. They never adopted the title "king" (*rex* in Latin), as this would have been seen as too great a break with Roman traditions.

Augustus's title of imperator reflects the source of most of his power: his control and command of the army. He could declare war, he controlled deployment of the Roman army, and he paid the soldiers' wages. He granted bonuses and gave veterans retirement benefits. He could override any governor's decision about military matters in a province. Building on the earlier military reforms of Marius and Julius Caesar, Augustus further professionalized the military, making the army a recognized institution of government.

Soldiers who were Roman citizens were organized into legions, units of about five thousand men. These legionaries were generally volunteers; they received a salary and training under career officers who advanced in rank according to experience, ability, valor, and length of service. Legions were often transferred from place to place as the need arose. Soldiers

---

■ **principate** Official title of Augustus's form of government, taken from *princeps*, meaning "first citizen."

■ **imperator** Title originally given to a Roman general after a major victory that came to mean "emperor."

served twenty-year terms, plus five in the reserves, and on retiring were to be given a discharge bonus of cash or a piece of land. To pay for this, Augustus ordered a tax on inheritance and on certain types of sales. The legions were backed up by auxiliaries, military forces from cities allied with Rome, which were obliged to provide a certain number of recruits each year, a situation many allies resented. Allies often had to use conscription to gain enough soldiers for what were often very long terms. Auxiliaries were paid—though at a lower rate than legionaries—and were granted Roman citizenship when they retired, which gave them legal, social, and economic privileges, but this was still not always an attractive position. Auxiliaries sometimes stayed near the area where they had been recruited, but often they served far away from home as well. They specialized in different fighting techniques than did Roman legions, and the Romans often sent the auxiliaries into the worst battles first, reserving their legions until absolutely necessary. (See "Thinking Like a Historian: Army and Empire," page 146.)

Grants of land to veterans had originally been in Italy, but by Augustus's time there was not enough land to continue this practice. Instead he gave veterans land in the frontier provinces that had been taken from the people the Romans conquered, usually near camps with active army units. Some veterans objected, and at Augustus's death they briefly revolted, but these colonies of veterans continued to play an important role in securing the Roman Empire's boundaries and controlling its newly won provinces. Augustus's veterans took abroad with them their Latin language and Roman culture, becoming important agents of Romanization and part of the cultural mixing that occurred in border areas.

Like the armies of Marius and Julius Caesar, the army that Augustus developed was loyal to him as a person, not as the head of the Roman state. This would lead to trouble later, but the basics of the political and military system that Augustus created lasted fairly well for almost three centuries.

## Roman Expansion

One of the most significant aspects of Augustus's reign was Roman expansion into central and eastern Europe and consolidation of holdings in western Europe (Map 6.1). Augustus began his work in the west by completing the conquest of Spain begun by Scipio Africanus in the third century B.C.E. In Gaul he founded twelve new towns, and the Roman road system linked new settlements with one another and with Italy. The German frontier along the Rhine River was the scene of hard fighting. In 12 B.C.E.

Augustus ordered a major invasion of Germany beyond the Rhine. Roman legions advanced to the Elbe River, and the area north of the Main River and west of the Elbe was on the point of becoming Roman. But in 9 C.E. some twenty thousand Roman troops were annihilated at the Battle of the Teutoburg Forest by an alliance of Germanic tribes led by a Germanic officer who had acquired Roman citizenship and a Roman military education. Military historians see this major defeat as an important turning point in Roman expansion, because although Roman troops penetrated the area of modern Austria, southern Bavaria, and western Hungary, the Romans never again sent a major force east of the Rhine. Hereafter the Rhine and the Danube remained the Roman frontier in central Europe, and the Romans used these rivers to supply their garrisons.

The Romans began to build walls, forts, and watchtowers to firm up their defenses, especially in the area between the two rivers, where people could more easily enter Roman territory. Romans then conquered the regions of modern Serbia, Bulgaria, and Romania in the Balkans, which gave them a land-based link between the eastern and western Mediterranean. After all the conquests under his rule, Augustus left explicit instructions in his will that Roman territory not be expanded any further, as there was plenty to do trying to subdue, Romanize, and properly govern the huge territory Rome had. Most of his successors paid no attention to his wishes.

Within the area along the empire's northern border the legionaries and auxiliaries built fortified camps. Roads linked the camps with one another, and settlements grew up around the camps. Traders began to frequent the frontier and to do business with the people who lived there. Thus Roman culture—the rough-and-ready kind found in military camps—gradually spread into the north, blending with local traditions through interactions and intermarriage. As a result, for the first time central and northern Europe came into direct and continuous contact with Mediterranean culture. Many Roman camps eventually grew into cities of several thousand people, transforming the economy of the area around them. Roman cities were the first urban developments in most parts of central and northern Europe.

As a political and religious bond between the provinces and Rome, Augustus encouraged the cult of *Roma et Augustus* (Rome and Augustus) as the guardians of the state and the source of all benefits to society. The cult spread rapidly, especially in the eastern Mediterranean, where local people already had traditions of divine kingship developed in the Hellenistic monarchies (see Chapter 4) or even earlier. Numerous temples to Rome and Augustus or just to Augustus

**MAP 6.1 Roman Expansion Under the Empire, 44 B.C.E.–180 C.E.** Following Roman expansion during the republic, Augustus added vast tracts of Europe to the Roman Empire, which the emperor Trajan later enlarged by assuming control over parts of central Europe, the Near East, and North Africa.

were built throughout Roman territory. The temple at Caesarea—a new city in Judaea, built as a port and named in honor of Augustus by King Herod, ruler of the Jewish client state of Rome—was huge, as big as the Jewish temple in Jerusalem. For later emperors as well, Roman officials and provincial elites who acted as patrons for their cities built celebratory arches, altars, temples, columns, and other structures to honor and show their loyalty and devotion to the ruler. (See "Evaluating Visual Evidence: Ara Pacis Augustae," page 148.)

Many of these structures were decorated with texts as well as images, chosen by those who set up the monument. For example, Augustus wrote an official account of his long career, which he included with his will, and told the Senate to set it up as a public inscription after his death. The original document, which no longer survives, was engraved on two bronze columns

in front of the Mausoleum of Augustus, a large tomb erected in Rome by Augustus that is still standing. In many other places throughout the Roman Empire copies were carved into monuments on the order of provincial elites, some of which survive, and the text became known as the *Res Gestae Divi Augusti* (The deeds of the divine Augustus).

In the late eighteenth century the English historian Edward Gibbon dubbed the stability and relative peace within the empire that Augustus created the **pax Romana**, the "Roman peace," which he saw as lasting about two hundred years, until the end of the reign of Marcus Aurelius in 180 C.E. Gibbon's term has been an influential description of this period ever since he invented it, but those

■ **pax Romana** The "Roman peace," a term invented by the historian Edward Gibbon in the eighteenth century to describe the first and second centuries C.E., which he saw as a time of political stability and relative peace.

## Army and Empire

Military might made it possible for the Romans to conquer and hold a huge empire. As the empire grew, it needed to recruit Romans into its legions as well as troops from allied and conquered areas into its auxiliary forces. It then needed to make these soldiers effective, loyal, and dependable. How did the Romans assemble, train, organize, and use soldiers from diverse cultures to conquer and hold their empire?

**1** **Julius Caesar, *The Gallic War*, 50 B.C.E.** Writing of his successful campaigns in Gaul and presenting himself as the consummate Roman military leader, Caesar (using the third person) describes his efforts to rally his wavering troops.

Such a terrible panic suddenly seized our whole army as severely affected everyone's courage and morale. Our men started asking questions, and the Gauls and traders replied by describing how tall and strong the Germans were, how unbelievably brave and skillful with weapons. . . . The panic began among the military tribunes and prefects, and the other men who, having no great military experience, had followed Caesar from Rome to court his friendship. . . . They hid themselves away in their tents and bemoaned their fate. . . . As soon as Caesar was aware of the situation he called a council, ordered centurions of all ranks to attend, and severely reprimanded them. . . . Why did they despair of their own courage, or of his anxious concern for their well-being? The danger posed by this enemy had already been experienced in the time of our fathers, when the Cimbri and Teutoni were expelled by Gaius Marius. On that occasion it was clear that the army had deserved as much credit as its commander. . . . From all this, said Caesar, they could see how crucial was firmness of purpose. . . . The Germans were the same people who had often clashed with the Helvetii—and the Helvetii had frequently beaten them, not only within their own borders but also in Germany itself—and yet the Helvetii had proved no match for our army. . . . And so, Caesar concluded, he would do at once what he had intended to put off till a later date. The very next night, during the fourth watch, they would strike camp. Then he would know as soon as possible whether their sense of shame and duty was stronger than their fear. . . . At the end of this speech the change of attitude was quite remarkable, and there arose an immense enthusiasm and eagerness to start the campaign.

**2** **Augustus, *Res Gestae Divi Augusti*, ca. 14 C.E.** In his account of his career, written at the end of his life, Augustus describes some of the actions he took regarding the army.

Wars, both civil and foreign, I undertook throughout the world, on sea and land, and when victorious I spared all citizens who sued for pardon. The foreign nations which could with safety be pardoned I preferred to save rather than to destroy. The number of Roman citizens who bound themselves to me by military oath was about 500,000. Of these I settled in colonies or sent back into their own towns, after their term of service, something more than 300,000, and to all I assigned lands, or gave money as a reward for military service. . . .

I settled colonies of soldiers in Africa, Sicily, Macedonia, both Spains, Achaia, Asia, Syria, Gallia Narbonensis, Pisidia. Moreover, Italy has twenty-eight colonies founded under my auspices which have grown to be famous and populous during my lifetime.

**3** **Titus Flavius Josephus, *The Jewish War*, ca. 75 C.E.** Josephus was a commander in the Jewish revolt against the Romans in 66 C.E. who after he was taken prisoner went over to the Roman side. Here he describes how he used the Romans as a model for the Jewish army. Like Caesar in Source 1, he writes of himself in the third person.

Josephus knew that the invincible might of Rome was chiefly due to unhesitating obedience and to practice in arms. He despaired of providing similar instruction, demanding as it did a long period of training; but he saw that the habit of obedience resulted from the number of their officers, and he now reorganized his

### ANALYZING THE EVIDENCE

1. How does Julius Caesar use history and tradition in Source 1 to convince his troops to fight, and what do you think his purpose was in relating this incident as he did?
2. Why would the promise of eventual citizenship and land, as described by Augustus in Source 2 and recorded in military diplomas like the one in Source 4, have been an effective recruiting tool? How would this practice have helped maintain the empire?
3. What aspects of the Roman military does Josephus use as a model for his own forces in Source 3, and how do these compare with the qualities Vegetius identifies in Source 5 as ideal in the perfect recruit? Why would these have been important to Roman military success?
4. Julius Caesar and Augustus were military generals and rulers of Rome, Josephus was an opponent of Rome, and Vegetius was a Roman looking back at the past. How do you think their positions shaped their perspectives on the Roman army and the reasons for its success?

**4  Roman military diploma, 71 C.E.**
Military diplomas were bronze sheets, wired together, that certified that a former soldier in the auxiliary forces had been honorably discharged and granted Roman citizenship by the emperor as a reward for service. They are dated, and as on this one, they often recorded the former soldier's units, tours of duty, commanders, and the names of his father, wife, and children. One copy stayed in Rome, and one was sent to the soldier himself to take to the province where he intended to live, much as members of the military today receive discharge papers.

(The Israel Museum, Jerusalem/Acquired in memory of Chaim Herzog, Sixth President of the State of Israel, by his family and Yad Chaim Herzog: the Carmen and Louis Warschaw Fund of Archeological Acquisitions; and David and Genevieve Hendin, New York/Bridgeman Images)

**5  Vegetius, *Epitome of Military Science*, ca. 380–390 C.E.** Vegetius seems to have been a Roman imperial bureaucrat who described what he saw as ideal military recruitment and training at a point when the Roman Empire was in decline and the army faced many challenges.

In every battle it is not numbers and untaught bravery so much as skill and training that generally produce the victory. For we see no other explanation of the conquest of the world by the Roman People than their drill-at-arms, camp-discipline and military expertise. . . . But what succeeded against all [enemies] was careful selection of recruits, instruction in the rules, so to speak, of war, toughening in daily exercises, prior acquaintance in field practice with all possible eventualities in war and battle, and strict punishment of cowardice. Scientific knowledge of warfare nurtures courage in battle. No one is afraid to do what he is confident of having learned well. A small force which is highly trained in the conflicts of war is more apt to victory: a raw and untrained horde is always exposed to slaughter. . . . The rural populace is better suited for arms. They are nurtured under the open sky in a life of work, enduring the sun, careless of shade, unacquainted with bathhouses, ignorant of luxury, simple souled, content with a little, with limbs toughened to endure every kind of toil. . . . If ancient custom is to be retained, everyone knows that those entering puberty should be brought to the levy. For those things are taught not only more quickly but even more completely which are learned from boyhood. Secondly military alacrity, jumping and running should be attempted before the body stiffens with age. . . . You need not greatly regret the absence of tall stature. It is more useful that soldiers be strong than big. . . . The youth in whose hands is to be placed the defence of provinces, the fortune of battles, ought to be of outstanding breeding if numbers suffice, and morals. Decent birth makes a suitable soldier, while a sense of shame prevents flight and makes him a victor.

army on the Roman model, appointing more junior commanders than before. He divided the soldiers into different classes, and put them under decurions and centurions, those being subordinate to tribunes, and the tribunes to commanders of larger units. He taught them how to pass on signals, how to sound the advance and the retreat, how to make flank attacks and encircling movements, and how a victorious unit could relieve one in difficulties and assist any who were hard pressed. He explained all that contributed to toughness of body or fortitude of spirit. Above all he trained them for war by stressing Roman discipline at every turn: they would be facing men who by physical prowess and unshakable determination had conquered almost the entire world.

## PUTTING IT ALL TOGETHER

Using the sources above, along with what you have learned in class and in Chapters 5 and 6, write a short essay that analyzes the military's role in the empire's expansion. How did the Romans assemble, train, organize, and use soldiers from diverse cultures to conquer and hold their empire? How would you assess the relative importance of various factors in this process, and why might your assessment be different from those of the authors cited here?

Sources: (1) Julius Caesar, *Seven Commentaries on the Gallic War*, trans. Carolyn Hammond (New York: Oxford University Press, 1998), pp. 24–27. By permission of Oxford University Press; (2) *Velleius Paterculus*, Loeb Classical Library, Volume 152, translated by Frederick W. Shipley; pp. 347, 383. Cambridge, Mass.: Harvard University Press. First published 1924. The Loeb Classical Library® is a registered trademark of the President and Fellows of Harvard College; (3) Josephus, *The Jewish War*, trans. G. A. Williamson (Baltimore, Md.: Penguin Books, 1972), p. 172; (5) N. P. Milner, trans., *Vegetius: Epitome of Military Science* (Liverpool: Liverpool University Press, 1996), pp. 2–8.

## Ara Pacis Augustae

In the middle years of Augustus's reign, the Roman Senate ordered a huge altar, the Ara Pacis Augustae (Altar of Augustan Peace), built to honor his return to Rome after three years in Hispania and Gaul. It was dedicated on the birthday of his wife Livia, shortly after the death of her son Drusus. The altar was decorated with life-size reliefs of Augustus and members of his family, prominent members of the Senate, and other people and deities. One side, shown here, depicts a goddess figure, most likely the goddess Peace herself, with twin babies on her lap, flanked by nymphs representing land and sea, and surrounded by plants and animals.

(DEA/G. Dagli Orti/De Agostini/Getty Images)

### EVALUATE THE EVIDENCE

1. What do the elements depicted here most likely symbolize?
2. How did the senators who commissioned this choose to portray Augustus's reign, and why would it be in their best interests to do so?
3. The Ara Pacis Augustae and the *Res Gestae Divi Augusti* (see "Thinking Like a Historian: Army and Empire," page 146) were both works of public art designed to commemorate the deeds of Augustus. Why might the Senate and the provincial elites who set up monuments inscribed with the *Res Gestae* have commissioned such works? Can you think of contemporary parallels?

the Romans conquered might not have agreed that Roman rule was so harmonious (see "Viewpoints: The *Pax Romana*," page 149).

Although the pax Romana was not peaceful for everyone, under Augustus and many of his successors the Romans were often able to continue doing what they had under the republic: create a sense of loyalty in conquered people by granting at least some of them citizenship and other privileges. Augustus also respected local customs and ordered his governors to do the same. Roman governors applied Roman law to Romans living in their territories, but they let local people retain their own laws. As long as they provided taxes, did not rebel, and supplied a steady stream of recruits for Roman armies, people could continue to run their political and social lives as they had before

In 70 C.E., Roman forces under a general named Cerialis defeated groups in Gaul that had revolted against Rome and proclaimed their own kingdoms. After his victory, Cerialis apparently gave a speech to the assembled troops, proclaiming the benefits brought by Rome. The Romans continued their expansion northward into Britain, where one of their opponents was the Scottish chieftain Calgacus, who also apparently gave a speech. Both of these speeches appear in the writings of Tacitus (ca. 56–ca. 120 C.E.), a Roman official, senator, and historian.

## Speech of Cerialis, from Tacitus, *History*

Cerialis then convoked an assembly of the Trevai and Lingones [two Gallic tribes] and thus addressed them: "I have never cultivated eloquence; it is by my sword that I have asserted the excellence of the Roman people. . . . Roman generals and emperors entered your territory, as they did the rest of Gaul, with no ambitious purposes, but at the solicitation of your ancestors, who were wearied to the last extremity by intestine strife, while the Germans, who they had summoned to their help, had imposed their yoke alike on friend and foe. How many battles have we fought against the Cimbri and Tuetones [two German tribes], at the cost of what hardships to our armies, and with what result have we waged our German wars, is perfectly well known. It is not to defend Italy that we occupied the borders of the Rhine, but to insure that no second Ariovistus [a Germanic leader] should seize Gaul. . . . Gaul has always had its petty kingdoms and intestine wars, till you submitted to our authority. We, though so often provoked, have used the right of conquest to burden you only with the cost of maintaining peace. For the tranquility of nations cannot be preserved without armies; armies cannot exist without pay; pay cannot be furnished without tribute; all else is common among us. . . .

Should the Romans be driven out (which God forbid) what can result but wars between all these nations? By the prosperity and order of eight hundred years has this fabric of empire been consolidated, nor can it be overthrown without destroying those who overthrow it. Yours will be the worst peril, for you have gold and wealth, and these are the chief incentives to war. Give therefore your love and respect to the cause of peace, and to that capital [i.e., Rome] in which we, conquerors and conquered, claim an equal right. Let the lessons of fortune in both its forms teach you not to prefer rebellion and ruin to submission and safety." With words to this effect he quieted his audience, who feared harsher treatment.

## Speech of Calgacus, from Tacitus, *Agricola*

Now, however, the furthest limits of Britain are thrown open . . . there are no tribes beyond us, nothing indeed but waves and rocks, and the yet more terrible Romans, from whose oppression escape is sought by obedience and submission. Robbers of the world, having by their universal plunder exhausted the land, they rifle the deep [i.e., the oceans]. If the enemy be rich, they are rapacious; if he be poor, they lust for domination; neither East nor West has been able to satisfy them. Alone among men they covet with equal eagerness the poor and the rich. To robbery, slaughter, plunder they give the lying name of empire; they create a desert and call it peace.

Nature has willed that every man's children and kindred should be his dearest objects. Yet these are torn from us by conscriptions to be slaves in foreign lands. Our wives and our sisters, even though they may escape being raped by the enemy, are seduced under the names of friendship and hospitality. Our goods and fortunes they collect for their tribute, our harvests for their granaries. Our very hands and bodies, under the lash and in the midst of insult, are worn down by the toil of clearing forests and swamps.

### QUESTIONS FOR ANALYSIS

1. How do Cerialis and Calgacus differ in their opinions about Roman domination? On what aspects of Roman conquest do the two agree?
2. Tacitus was born in the provinces, and like many ancient historians, he uses speeches to make points in his narrative, even though he did not speak to eyewitnesses. How might these factors have shaped these sources and what we can learn from them?

Sources: Tacitus, *The History of Tacitus*, trans. A. J. Church and W. J. Brodribb (London: Macmillan, 1864), at: http://classics.mit.edu/Tacitus/histories.mb.txt; Tacitus, *The Agricola and Germania*, trans. A. J. Church and W. J. Brodribb (London: Macmillan, 1877), pp. 25–26.

Roman conquest. This policy was crucial in holding the empire together. Although the Roman army was everywhere, historians have estimated that at its height in the second century C.E., the Roman military had no more than roughly 100,000 troops. There is no way that these few men could have managed populations of millions of rebellious subjects.

While Romans did not force their culture on local people in Roman territories, local elites with aspirations knew that the best way to rise in stature and power was to adopt aspects of Roman culture. Thus, just as ambitious individuals in the Hellenistic world embraced Greek culture and learned to speak Greek, those determined to get ahead now learned Latin, and sometimes Greek as well if they wished to be truly well educated.

## Latin Literature

Many poets and prose writers were active in the late republic and the principate, and scholars of literature later judged their work to be of such high quality that they called the period from about 50 B.C.E. to 20 C.E. the "golden age" of Latin literature. Roman poets and prose writers celebrated the physical and emotional joys of a comfortable life in works that were polished and elegant. As had Athenian playwrights, they also responded to the political turmoil going on around them, as Augustus appropriated the past, made claims about his own destiny, and promoted social change.

Rome's greatest poet was Virgil (70–19 B.C.E.), who drew on earlier traditions but gave them new twists. The *Georgics*, for example, is a poem about agriculture that used Hellenistic models to capture both the peaceful pleasures and the day-to-day harshness of rural life. Virgil's masterpiece is the *Aeneid* (uh-NEE-ihd), an epic poem that is the Latin equivalent of the Greek *Iliad* and *Odyssey*. Virgil's account of the founding of the Roman people as a hybrid created out of many different groups gave final form to the legend of Aeneas, the Trojan hero (and ancestor of Romulus and Remus) who escaped to Italy at the fall of Troy:

> I sing of warfare and a man at war,
> From the sea-coast of Troy in the early days,
> He came to Italy by destiny,
> To our Lavinian western shore,
> A fugitive, this captain, buffeted
> Cruelly on land as on the sea
> By blows from the powers of the air—behind
>    them
> Baleful Juno [the queen of the gods] in her sleep-
>    less rage.
> And cruel losses were his lot in war,
> Till he could found a city and bring home
> His gods to Latium, land of the Latin race,
> The Alban lords, and the high walls of Rome.[2]

As Virgil told it, Aeneas became the lover of Dido, the widowed queen of Carthage, but left her because his destiny called him to found Rome. Swearing the destruction of Rome, Dido committed suicide, and according to Virgil, her enmity helped cause the Punic Wars. In leaving Dido, an "Eastern" queen, Aeneas

put duty and the good of the state ahead of marriage or pleasure. The resemblances between this story and the very recent real events involving Antony and Cleopatra were not lost on Virgil's audience. Making the public aware of these parallels, and of Virgil's description of Aeneas as an ancestor of Julius Caesar, fit well with Augustus's aims. Augustus encouraged Virgil to write the *Aeneid* and made sure it was circulated widely immediately after Virgil died. It puts sexual relations as well as war at the center of the story of Rome, just as the founding myths of the rape of the Sabine women and the suicide of Lucretia had earlier (see Chapter 5).

The poet Horace (65–8 B.C.E.) rose from humble beginnings to friendship with Augustus. The son of an ex-slave and tax collector, Horace nonetheless received an excellent education, which he finished in Athens. His most important works are a series of odes, short lyric poems often focusing on a single individual or event. One of these commemorated Augustus's victory over Antony and Cleopatra at Actium in 31 B.C.E. Horace depicted Cleopatra as a frenzied queen, drunk with desire to destroy Rome, a view that has influenced opinions about Cleopatra until today.

The historian Livy (59 B.C.E.–17 C.E.) was a friend of Augustus and a supporter of the principate. He especially approved of Augustus's efforts to restore what he saw as republican virtues. Livy's 142-volume history of Rome, titled simply *Ab Urbe Condita* (From the founding of the city), began with the legend of Aeneas and ended with the reign of Augustus. Livy used the works of earlier Greek and Roman writers, as well as his own experiences, as his source material.

Augustus actively encouraged poets and writers, but he could also turn against them. The poet Ovid (AH-vuhd) (43 B.C.E.–17 C.E.) wrote erotic poetry about absent lovers and the joys of seduction, as well as other works about religious festivals and mythology. His best-known work is *The Art of Love*, a satire of the serious instructional poetry that was common in Rome at the time. *The Art of Love* provides advice to men about how to get and keep women, and for women about how to get and keep men. (See "Evaluating Written Evidence: Ovid, *The Art of Love*," page 151.) This work was so popular, Ovid relates, that shortly after completing it he felt compelled to write *The Cure for Love*, advising people how to fall out of love and forget their former lovers. Have lots of new lovers, it advises, and don't hang around places, eat foods, or listen to songs that will make you remember your former lover. In 8 B.C.E. Augustus banished Ovid to a city on the Black Sea far from Rome. Why he did so is a mystery, and Ovid himself states only that the reason was "a poem and a mistake." Some scholars argue that Augustus banished Ovid because his poetry celebrated adultery at a time when Augustus was

## Ovid, *The Art of Love*

*The Art of Love* is a humorous guide for lovers written by the Roman poet Ovid. Ovid addresses the first two parts to men, instructing them on how to seduce and keep women — look good, give them compliments, don't be too obvious. The third part is his corresponding advice for women, which in its main points is the same. The section below comes from the beginning of part one, advising men on where and how to meet women.

Now, that you still are fancy-free, now is the time for you to choose a woman and say to her: "You are the only woman that I care for." She's not going to be wafted down to you from heaven on the wings of the wind. You must use your own eyes to discover the girl that suits you. The hunter knows where to spread his nets in order to snare the stag; he knows the valley where the wild boar has his lair. The birdcatcher knows where he should spread his lime; and the fisherman, what waters most abound in fish. And thou who seekest out the object of a lasting love, learn to know the places which the fair ones most do haunt. You won't have to put to sea in order to do that, or to undertake any distant journeys. . . .

. . . But it is especially at the theatre you should lay your snares; that is where you may hope to have your desires fulfilled. Here you will find women to your taste: one for a moment's dalliance, another to fondle and caress, another to have all for your own. . . .

Forget not the arena where mettled steeds strive for the palm of Victory. This circus, where an immense concourse of people is gathered, is very favourable to Love. . . . Sit close beside her, as close as you are able; there's nothing to prevent. The narrowness of the space compels you to press against her and, fortunately for you, compels her to acquiesce. Then, of course, you must think of some means of starting the conversation. Begin by saying the sort of thing people generally do say on such occasions. Some horses are seen entering the stadium; ask her the name of their owner; and whoever she favours, you should follow suit. And when the solemn procession of the country's gods and goddesses passes along, be sure and give a rousing cheer for Venus, your protectress. If, as not infrequently befalls, a speck of dust lights on your fair one's breast, flick it off with an airy finger; and if there's nothing there, flick it off just the same; anything is good enough to serve as a pretext for paying her attention. . . .

Dinners and banquets offer easy access to women's favour, and the pleasures of the grape are not the only entertainment you may find there; Love, with rosy cheeks, often presses in her frail hands the amphora of Bacchus [the god of wine]. As soon as his wings are drenched with wine, Cupid [the god of love] grows drowsy and stirs not from his place. But anon he'll be up and shaking the moisture from his wings, and woe betide the man or woman who receives a sprinkling of this burning dew. Wine fills the heart with thoughts of love and makes it prompt to catch on fire.

### EVALUATE THE EVIDENCE

1. What metaphors and symbols does Ovid use to describe finding a lover and falling in love?
2. What does this guide indicate about leisure activities in the Rome of Ovid's day?

Source: *The Love Books of Ovid: Being the Amores, Ars Amatoria, Remedia Amoris and Medicamina Faciei Femineae of Publius Ovidius Naso*, trans. J. Lewis May (New York: Rarity Press, 1930), pp. 98, 100, 101–102, 104.

promoting marriage and childbearing, and others say it was because the poet knew about political conspiracies. Whatever its causes, the exile of Ovid became a symbol of misunderstood poetic genius for many later writers.

## Marriage and Morality

Augustus's banishing of Ovid may have simply been an excuse to get rid of him, but concern with morality and with what were perceived as traditional Roman virtues was a matter not just for literature in Augustan Rome, but also for law. Augustus promoted marriage and childbearing through legal changes that released free women and freedwomen (female slaves who had been freed) from male guardianship if they had given birth to a certain number of children. Men and women who were unmarried or had no children were restricted in the inheritance of property. Adultery, defined as sex with a married woman or with a woman under male guardianship, was made a crime, not simply the private family matter it had been.

In imperial propaganda, Augustus had his own family depicted as a model of traditional morality, with his wife Livia at his side and dressed in conservative and somewhat old-fashioned clothing rather than the more daring Greek styles that wealthy women were actually wearing in Rome at the time. In fact, Augustus's family did not live up to this ideal.

Augustus had his daughter Julia arrested and exiled for adultery and treason. Although it is impossible to tell what actually happened, she seems to have had at least one affair after her father forced her to marry a second husband—her stepbrother Tiberius.

Same-sex relationships among men were acceptable in Roman society as long as there was an age and status difference between partners and certain sexual norms were followed. Roman citizens were expected never to be sexually penetrated, for this would mean a loss of what was termed *integritas*. Thus a respectable Roman man could penetrate whomever he wished and still maintain his masculinity, but losing his integritas brought shame on himself and his family and could mean a loss of status. Men were expected to control their own bodily urges, however, and also control those under their power, including family, servants, inferiors, and soldiers. We do not know very much about same-sex relationships among women in Rome, though court gossip and criticism of powerful women, including the wives of Augustus's successors, sometimes included charges of such relationships, along with charges of heterosexual promiscuity and other sexual slander. Most of these were in fact personal attacks on the men who were supposed to control them, however, rather than statements about the women's actual behavior.

## How did the Roman state develop after Augustus?

Augustus's success in creating solid political institutions was tested by those who ruled immediately after him, a dynasty historians later called the Julio-Claudians (27 B.C.E.–68 C.E.) after the families who comprised it. The incompetence of Nero, one of the Julio-Claudians, and his failure to deal with the army generals allowed a military commander, Vespasian (veh-SPAY-zhuhn), to claim the throne and establish a new dynasty, the Flavians (69–96 C.E.), who reasserted order. The Flavians were followed by a series of relatively successful emperors, the Nerva-Antonine dynasty (96–192 C.E.), and Rome entered a period of political stability, prosperity, and relative peace that lasted until the end of the second century C.E.

### The Julio-Claudians and the Flavians

Augustus had no male children who survived, but he married his only daughter Julia to a series of male relatives and in-laws who he thought would be good heirs. Two died, but the third, Tiberius, a successful general who was the son of Augustus's wife Livia by her first marriage and thus Julia's stepbrother, survived. Adoption of an heir was a common practice among members of the elite in Rome, who used this method to pass on property to a chosen younger man—often a relative—if they had no sons. Long before Augustus's death he shared many of the powers that the Senate had given him, including the imperium over the army, with Tiberius, thus grooming him to succeed him. In his will Augustus confirmed him as heir, and left him most of his vast fortune when he died in 14 C.E. The Senate confirmed Tiberius (r. 14–37 C.E.) as princeps.

For fifty years after Augustus's death the Julio-Claudians provided the rulers of Rome. They generally followed the pattern set by Augustus and adopted a nephew or great-nephew as their sons in order to promote them, though there were also often intrigues and plots surrounding the succession. Augustus's creation of an elite unit of bodyguards known as the **Praetorian** (pree-TAWR-ee-uhn) **Guard** had repercussions for his successors. In 41 C.E. the Praetorians murdered Tiberius's successor Caligula (r. 37–41 C.E.) and forced the Senate to ratify their choice of Claudius as emperor. Such events were repeated frequently. During the first three centuries of the empire, the Praetorian Guard often murdered emperors they were supposed to protect and raised to emperor men of their own choosing.

Under Claudius (r. 41–54 C.E.), Roman troops invaded Britain, and roads, canals, and aqueducts were built across the empire. Claudius was followed by his great-nephew Nero (r. 54–68 C.E), whose erratic actions and policies led to a revolt in 68 C.E. by several generals, which was supported by the Praetorian Guard and members of the Senate. He was declared an enemy of the people and committed suicide. This opened the way to widespread disruption and civil war. In 69 C.E., the "year of the four emperors," four men claimed the position of emperor in quick succession. Roman armies in Gaul, on the Rhine, and in the east marched on Rome to make their commanders emperor. The man who emerged triumphant was Vespasian, commander of the eastern armies.

Vespasian (r. 69–79 C.E.) restored the discipline of the armies. To prevent others from claiming the throne, he designated his sons Titus (r. 79–81 C.E.) and Domitian (r. 81–96 C.E.) as his successors, thus establishing the Flavian dynasty. Although Roman policy was to rule by peaceful domination whenever possible, he used the army to suppress the rebellions that had begun erupting at the end of Nero's reign. The most famous of these was one that had burst out in Judaea in 66 C.E., sparked by long-standing popular unrest over taxes. Jewish rebels initially defeated the Roman troops stationed in Judaea, but a larger army

■ **Praetorian Guard**  Imperial bodyguard created by Augustus.

## THE JULIO-CLAUDIANS, THE FLAVIANS, AND THE NERVA-ANTONINES

| The Julio-Claudians | | The Flavians | | The Nerva-Antonines | |
|---|---|---|---|---|---|
| 27 B.C.E.–14 C.E. | Augustus | 69 C.E.–79 C.E. | Vespasian | 96 C.E.–98 C.E. | Nerva |
| 14 C.E.–37 C.E. | Tiberius | 79 C.E.–81 C.E. | Titus | 98 C.E.–117 C.E. | Trajan |
| 37 C.E.–41 C.E. | Caligula | 81 C.E.–96 C.E. | Domitian | 117 C.E.–138 C.E. | Hadrian |
| 41 C.E.–54 C.E. | Claudius | | | 138 C.E.–161 C.E. | Antoninus Pius |
| 54 C.E.–68 C.E. | Nero | | | 161 C.E.–180 C.E. | Marcus Aurelius |
| | | | | 180 C.E.–192 C.E. | Commodus |

under the leadership of Vespasian and his son Titus put down the revolt. They destroyed much of the city of Jerusalem, including the Jewish temple, in 70 C.E., and took thousands of Jews as military captives and slaves, dispersing them throughout the empire.

The Flavians carried on Augustus's work in Italy and on the frontiers. During the brief reign of Vespasian's son Titus, Mount Vesuvius in southern Italy erupted, destroying Pompeii and other cities and killing thousands of people. (See "Individuals in Society: Pliny the Elder," page 154.) Titus gave money and sent officials to organize the relief effort. His younger brother Domitian, who followed him as emperor, won additional territory in Germany, consolidating it into two new provinces. Later in life he became more autocratic, however, and he was killed in 96 C.E. in a plot that involved his own wife, ending the Flavian dynasty.

### The Nerva-Antonine Dynasty

The Flavians were succeeded by the Nerva-Antonine dynasty, which ruled from 96 C.E. to 192 C.E. In the sixteenth century the political philosopher Niccolò Machiavelli termed five of these the "five good emperors"—Nerva, Trajan, Hadrian, Antoninus Pius, and Marcus Aurelius. Machiavelli praised them because they all adopted able men as their successors during their lifetimes, thus giving Rome stability, although they may simply have been lucky, as this was a pattern set by Julius Caesar and Augustus, not something new. Eighteenth- and nineteenth-century historians generally regarded them as "good" because they were members of the Senate (thus of the class of people these historians believed should rule), and successful generals. Those people conquered by them might have had a different opinion, but they left few sources.

Dubbing emperors "good" or "bad" is not something today's historians generally do, but they view the Nerva-Antonines as able administrators and military leaders. Hadrian (r. 117–138 C.E.) is a typical example. He received a solid education in Rome and became an ardent admirer of Greek culture. He caught the attention of his elder cousin Trajan, the future emperor, who started him on a military career. At age nineteen Hadrian served on the Danube frontier, where he learned the details of how the Roman army lived and fought and saw for himself the problems of defending the frontiers. When Trajan became emperor in 98 C.E., Hadrian was given important positions in which he learned how to defend and run the empire. Although Trajan did not officially declare Hadrian his successor, at Trajan's death in 117 Hadrian assumed power.

Hadrian built or completed a number of buildings, including the circular Pantheon in Rome and new temples in Athens. He established more formal imperial administrative departments and separated civil service from military service. Men with little talent or taste for the army could instead serve the state as administrators. These innovations made for more efficient running of the empire and increased the authority of the emperor.

Under Trajan the boundaries of the Roman Empire were expanded to their farthest extent, and Hadrian worked to maintain most of these holdings, although he pulled back Roman armies from areas in the East he considered indefensible. No longer a conquering force, the army was expected to defend what had already been won. Forts and watch stations guarded the borders. Outside the forts the Romans built a system of roads that allowed the forts to be quickly supplied and reinforced in times of rebellion or unrest. Trouble for the Romans included two major revolts by Jews in the eastern part of the empire, which resulted in heavy losses on both sides and the exile of many Jews from Judaea.

Roman soldiers also built walls, of which the most famous was one across northern England built primarily during Hadrian's reign. Hadrian's Wall, as it became known, protected Romans from attacks from the north, and also allowed them to regulate immigration and trade through the many gates along the wall. Like all walls around cities or across territory, it served as a symbol and means of power and control as well as a defensive strategy.

# INDIVIDUALS IN SOCIETY

## Pliny the Elder

"My uncle was stationed at Misenum, in active command of the fleet. On 24 August, in the early afternoon, my mother drew his attention to a cloud of unusual size and appearance. . . . My uncle's scholarly acumen saw at once that it was important enough for a closer inspection, and he ordered a boat to be made ready." So begins a letter from the statesman and writer Pliny the Younger to the historian Tacitus, describing what happened when Mount Vesuvius erupted in 79 C.E. Pliny provided terrifying details of clouds of hot ash, raining pumice stones, and sheets of fire, and then sang the praises of his uncle, also named Pliny, whose actions, "begun in a spirit of inquiry, [were] completed as a hero." According to Pliny the Younger's account, his uncle "steer[ed] his course straight for the danger zone with the intention of bringing help to many more people. . . . He was entirely fearless, describing each new movement and phase of the portent to be noted down exactly as he observed them . . . and when his helmsman advised him to turn back he refused, telling him that Fortune stood by the courageous." The elder Pliny (23–79 C.E.) died on the beach near Pompeii, most likely from inhaling fumes that aggravated his asthma. His body was discovered several days later when the smoke and ash cleared.

The younger Pliny used this letter to portray his uncle as a model of traditional Roman virtues, but some of what he related was not an exaggeration. Like many young men of his social class — the equestrian — Pliny the Elder studied law and then joined the army as an officer. He was involved in several military campaigns in Germany and also found time to write books, including a volume on military tactics and several biographies. He left military service during Nero's reign and kept out of the limelight, writing noncontroversial books on grammar and rhetoric. After Nero committed suicide and Vespasian came to power, Pliny went back into government service, serving as the procurator (governor) of several different provinces. He again wrote biographies and histories, all of which are now lost, and the work that became his masterpiece, *Natural History*, an encyclopedia in which he sought to cover everything that was known to ancient Romans. In thirty-seven volumes, *Natural History* covers what we would now term biology, geology, astronomy, mineralogy, geography, ethnography, comparative anthropology, medicine, painting, building techniques, and many other subjects. Pliny's "spirit of inquiry" shines through this work, which he researched through the study of hundreds of sources (all carefully cited) and wrote while he was traveling around in government service. It is one of the largest works to have survived from the Roman Empire and served as a source of knowledge into the Renaissance, when it was one of the very first classical books to be published after the invention of the printing press in the fifteenth century. Pliny finished a first draft in about 77 C.E. and was working on revisions when he was appointed fleet commander in the Roman navy and sent to Misenum, near Naples. There the cloud of smoke from the erupting Vesuvius was too interesting for him to ignore, and he set off in a boat to investigate, with deadly results.

### QUESTIONS FOR ANALYSIS

1. What Roman ideals does the younger Pliny portray his uncle as exemplifying through his conduct during the eruption?
2. How did army and government service in the Roman Empire provide opportunities for men of broad interests like Pliny?

Source: Quotations from Pliny the Younger, *Letters* 6.16, translated with an introduction by Betty Radice, vol. 1, pp. 166, 168 (Penguin Classics 1963, reprinted 1969). Copyright © Betty Radice, 1963, 1969. Reproduced by permission of Penguin Books Ltd.

No contemporary portrait of Pliny the Elder survives, but his nephew reports that when his body was discovered, it was "still fully clothed and looking more like sleep than death." When Pompeii was excavated, archaeologists used plaster to fill the voids in layers of ash that once held human bodies, allowing us to see the exact position a person was in when he or she died. This plaster cast is not Pliny but is as close to him in death as we can come. (© SZ Photo/Manfred Storck/Bridgeman Images)

As the empire expanded, the army grew larger, and more and more troops were auxiliary forces of noncitizens. Because army service could lead to citizenship, men from the provinces and even from beyond the borders of the Roman Empire sometimes joined the army willingly to gain citizenship, receive a salary, and learn a trade, though others were drafted. The army evolved into a garrison force, with troops guarding specific areas for long periods. Soldiers on active duty had originally been prohibited from marrying, but this restriction was increasingly ignored, and some troops brought their wives and families along on their assignments. At the beginning of the third century, Emperor Septimius Severus officially recognized the marriages of active duty soldiers, which allowed their families to gain citizenship and the man to legally bequeath his property to his heirs.

# What was life like in the city of Rome and in the provinces?

The expansion and stabilization of the empire brought changes to life in the city of Rome and also to life in the provinces in the first two centuries C.E. The city grew to a huge size, bringing the problems that plague any crowded urban area but also opportunities for work and leisure. Roads and secure sea-lanes linked the empire in one vast web, creating a network of commerce and communication. Trade and production flourished in the provinces, and Romans came into indirect contact with China.

## Life in Imperial Rome

Rome was truly an extraordinary city, and with a population of over a million it may have been the largest city in the world. Although it boasted stately palaces and beautiful residential areas, most people lived in shoddily constructed houses. They took whatever work was available, producing food, clothing, construction materials, and the many other items needed by the city's residents, or selling these products from small shops or at the city's many marketplaces.

Many residents of the city of Rome were slaves, who ranged from highly educated household tutors or government officials and widely sought sculptors to workers who engaged in hard physical tasks. Slaves sometimes attempted to flee their masters, but those who failed in their escape attempts were returned to their masters and often branded on their foreheads. Others had metal collars fastened around their necks. One collar discovered near Rome read: "I have run away. Capture me. If you take me back to my master Zoninus, you will receive a gold coin."[3]

Romans used the possibility of manumission as a means of controlling the behavior of their slaves, and individual Romans did sometimes free their slaves. Often these were house slaves who had virtually become members of the family and who often stayed with their former owner's family after being freed. Manumission was limited by law, however, in part because freeing slaves made them citizens, allowing them to receive public grain and gifts of money, which some Romans thought debased pure Roman citizenship.

A typical day for the Roman family began with a modest breakfast, as in the days of the republic. Afterward came a trip to the outdoor market for the day's provisions. Seafood was a favorite item, as the Romans normally ate meat only at festivals. While poor people ate salt fish, the more prosperous dined on rare fish, oysters, squid, and eels. Wine was the common drink, and the rich often enjoyed rare vintages imported from abroad.

As in the republic, children began their education at home, where parents emphasized moral conduct, especially reverence for the gods and the law and respect for elders. Daughters learned how to manage the house, and sons learned the basics of their future calling from their fathers, who also taught them the use of weapons for military service. Boys boxed, swam, and learned to ride when possible, all to increase their strength, while giving them basic skills. Wealthy boys gained formal education from tutors or schools, generally favoring rhetoric and law for a political career.

Tombstones and sarcophagi (stone coffins) provide evidence about Roman attitudes toward work and family, and sometimes also insights into the deceased's personal philosophy. A simple tombstone reads: "To the spirits of the dead. T. Aelius Dionysius the freedman made this while he was alive both for Aelia Callitycena, his most blessed wife with whom he lived for thirty years with never a quarrel, an incomparable woman, and also for Amelius Perseus, his fellow freedman, and for their freedmen and those who come after them."[4] The more elaborate tombstone of a man named Marcus Antonius Encolpus left a blunt message for the living: "Do not pass by this epitaph, wayfarer, but stop, listen, hear, then go. There is no boat in Hades, no ferryman Charon. No caretaker Aecus, no Cerberus dog. All we dead below have become bones and ashes, nothing more. I have spoken the truth to you. Go now, wayfarer, lest even in death I seem garrulous to you."[5]

## Approaches to Urban Problems

Fire and crime were serious problems in the city, even after Augustus created urban fire and police forces. Streets were narrow, drainage was inadequate, and sanitation was poor. Numerous inscriptions record prohibitions against dumping human refuse and even cadavers on the grounds of sanctuaries and cemeteries. Private houses generally lacked toilets, so people used chamber pots.

In the second century C.E. urban planning and new construction improved the situation. For example, engineers built an elaborate system that collected sewage from public baths, the ground floors of buildings, and public latrines. They also built hundreds of miles of **aqueducts**, sophisticated systems of canals, channels, and pipes, most of them underground, that brought freshwater into the city from the surrounding hills. The aqueducts, powered entirely by gravity, required regular maintenance, but they were a great improvement and helped make Rome a very attractive place to live. Building aqueducts required thousands and sometimes tens of thousands of workers, who were generally paid out of the imperial treasury. Aqueducts became a feature of Roman cities in many parts of the empire.

Better disposal of sewage was one way that people living in Rome tried to maintain their health, and they also used a range of treatments to stay healthy and cure illness. This included treatments based on the ideas of the Greek physician Hippocrates; folk remedies; prayers and rituals at the temple of the god of medicine, Asclepius; surgery; and combinations of all of these. The most important medical researcher and physician working in imperial Rome was Galen (ca. 129–ca. 200 C.E.), a Greek born in modern-day Turkey. Like anyone hoping to rise in stature and wealth, he came to Rome. Building on the work of Hellenistic physicians, Galen wrote a huge number of treatises on anatomy and physiology, and he became the personal physician of many prominent Romans, including several emperors. He promoted the idea that imbalances among various bodily fluids caused illness and recommended bloodletting as a cure. This would remain a standard treatment in Western medicine until the eighteenth century. His research into the nervous system and the operation of muscles — most of which he conducted on animals, because the Romans forbade dissections of human cadavers — proved to be more accurate than did his ideas about the circulation of fluids. So did his practical advice on the treatment of wounds, much of which grew out of his and others' experiences with soldiers on the battlefield.

Neither Galen nor any other Roman physician could do much for infectious diseases, and in 165 C.E. troops returning from campaigns in the East brought a new disease with them that spread quickly in the city and then beyond into other parts of the empire. Modern epidemiologists think this was most likely smallpox, but in the ancient world it became known simply as the Antonine plague, because it occurred during the reigns of emperors from the Antonine family. Whatever it was, it appears to have been extremely virulent in the city of Rome and among the Roman army for a decade or so, with total deaths estimated at about 5 million.

Along with fire and disease, food was an issue in the ever-more-crowded city. Because of the danger of starvation, the emperor, following republican practice, provided the citizen population with free grain for bread and, later, oil and wine. By feeding the citizenry, the emperor prevented bread riots caused by shortages and high prices. For those who did not enjoy the rights of citizenship, the emperor provided grain at low prices. This measure was designed to prevent speculators from forcing up grain prices in times of crisis. By maintaining the grain supply, the emperor kept the favor of the people and ensured that Rome's poor did not starve.

## Popular Entertainment

In addition to supplying grain, the emperor and his family also entertained the Roman populace, often at vast expense. This combination of material support and popular entertainment to keep the masses happy is often termed "bread and circuses." The emperors gained politically from promoting public entertainment, as the arenas were places they could be seen and honored, sitting on an elevated seat next to images of the gods.

The most popular forms of public entertainment were gladiatorial contests and chariot racing. Gladiator fights were advertised on billboards, and spectators were given a program with the names and sometimes the fighting statistics of the pairs, so that they could place bets more easily.

Men came to be gladiators through a variety of ways. Some were soldiers captured in war and some were criminals, especially slaves found guilty of various crimes. By the imperial period increasing numbers were volunteers, often poor immigrants who saw gladiatorial combat as a way to support themselves. All gladiators were trained in gladiatorial schools and were legally slaves, although they could keep their winnings and a few became quite wealthy. The Hollywood portrayal of gladiatorial combat has men fighting to their death, but this was increasingly rare, as the owners of especially skilled fighters wanted them

■ **aqueducts** Canals, channels, and pipes that brought freshwater into cities.

**Roman Architecture** These three structures demonstrate the beauty, practicality, and innovation of Roman architecture. The Pont du Gard at Nîmes in France (above) is a bridge over a river carrying an aqueduct that supplied millions of gallons of water per day to the Roman city of Nîmes in Gaul; the water flowed in a channel at the very top. Although this bridge was built largely without mortar or concrete, many Roman aqueducts and bridges relied on concrete and sometimes iron rods for their strength. The Pantheon in Rome (left), a temple dedicated to all the gods, was finished in its present form around 130 C.E., after earlier temples on this site burned down. Its dome, 140 feet in diameter, remains the largest unreinforced concrete dome in the world. Romans also used concrete for more everyday purposes. The Coliseum in Rome (below), a sports arena that could seat fifty thousand spectators built between 70 and 80 C.E., was the site of gladiatorial games, animal spectacles, and executions. For a brief time it was also used for mock naval battles, but this proved to be impractical.

(Pont du Gard: Masterfile; Pantheon: Gianni Dagli Orti/Shutterstock; Coliseum: © Gerard Degeorge/Rome, Italy/Bridgeman Images)

**Gladiator Mosaic**    Made in the first half of the fourth century, this mosaic from an estate outside Rome includes the name of each gladiator next to the figure. In the back a gladiator stands in a victory pose, while the fallen gladiator in the front is marked with the symbol Ø, indicating that he has died in combat. Many of the gladiators in this mosaic, such as those at the left, appear less fit and fearsome than the gladiators depicted in movies, more closely reflecting the reality that gladiatorial combat was a job undertaken by a variety of people. (Galleria Borghese, Rome, Italy/Alinari/Bridgeman Images)

to continue to compete. Many—perhaps most—did die at a young age from their injuries or later infections, but some fought more than a hundred battles over long careers, retiring to become trainers in gladiatorial schools. Sponsors of matches sought to offer viewers ever more unusual spectacles: left-handed gladiators fighting right-handed ones, dwarf gladiators, and for a brief period even female gladiators. For a criminal condemned to die, the arena was preferable to the imperial mines, where convicts worked digging ore and died under wretched conditions. At least in the arena the gladiator might fight well enough to win freedom. Some Romans protested gladiatorial fighting, but the emperors recognized the political value of such spectacles, and most Romans enjoyed them.

The Romans were even more addicted to chariot racing than to gladiatorial shows, and watched these in large arenas such as the Circus Maximus, which could hold 150,000 spectators. Under the empire four permanent teams competed against one another. Each had its own color—red, white, green, or blue. Two-horse and four-horse chariots ran a course of seven laps, about five miles. One charioteer, Gaius Appuleius Diocles, a Greek who had Roman citizenship, raced for twenty-four years, with over 4,000 starts and nearly 1,500 wins. His admirers honored him with an inscription that proclaimed him champion of all charioteers. Other winning charioteers were also idolized, just as sports stars are today, and the demand for races was so high that they were held on more than one hundred days a year in imperial Rome.

## Prosperity in the Roman Provinces

As the empire grew and stabilized, many Roman provinces grew prosperous. Peace and security opened Britain, Gaul, and the lands of the Danube to settlers from other parts of the Roman Empire (Map 6.2). Veterans were given small parcels of land in the provinces and became tenant farmers. The rural population throughout the empire left few records, but the inscriptions that remain point to a melding of cultures, an important reason for Rome's success. One sphere where this occurred was language. People used Latin for legal and state religious purposes, but gradually Latin blended with the original language of an area and with languages spoken by those who came into the area later. Slowly what would become the Romance languages of Spanish, Italian, French, Portuguese, and Romanian evolved. Religion was another site of cultural exchange and mixture. Romans moving into an area learned about and began to venerate local gods, and local people learned about Roman ones. Gradually hybrid deities and rituals developed. At first, cultural exchange occurred more in urban than in rural areas, but the importance of cities and towns to the life of the wider countryside ensured that its effects spread far afield.

The garrison towns that grew up around provincial military camps became the centers of organized political life, and some grew into major cities, including Eburacum (modern-day York), Lutetia Parisiorum (Paris), and Londinium (London). In order to supply these administrative centers with food, land around them was cultivated more intensively. Roman merchants became early bankers, loaning money to local people and often controlling them financially. Wealthy Roman officials also sometimes built country estates in rural areas near the city, where they did grow crops but also escaped from the stresses and unhealthy conditions of city life.

During the first and second centuries C.E., Roman Gaul became more prosperous than ever before, and its prosperity attracted Roman settlers. Roman veterans mingled with the local population and sometimes married into local families. There was not much difference in many parts of the province between the original Celtic villages and their Roman successors.

In Britain, Roman influence was strongest in the south, where more towns developed. Archaeological evidence, such as coins and amphoras that held oil or wine, indicates healthy trading connections with the north, however, as Roman merchandise moved through the gates of Hadrian's Wall in exchange for food and other local products.

Across eastern Europe, Roman influence was weaker than it was in Gaul or southern Britain, and there appears to have been less intermarriage. In Illyria (ih-LIHR-ee-uh) and Dalmatia, regions of modern Albania, Croatia, and Montenegro, the local population never widely embraced either Roman culture or urban life. To a certain extent, however, Romanization occurred simply because the peoples lived in such close proximity.

The Romans were the first to build cities in northern Europe, but in the eastern Mediterranean they ruled cities that had existed before Rome itself was even a village. Here there was much continuity in urban life from the Hellenistic period. There was also less construction than in the Roman cities of northern and western Europe because existing buildings could simply be put to new uses.

**Roman Britain, ca. 130 C.E.**

The well-preserved ruins of the ancient city of Aspendos, at the mouth of the Eurymedon (now Kopru) River on the south coast of modern Turkey (see Map 6.2), give a picture of life in one of these older eastern cities. Built sometime before 500 B.C.E., the city was an important economic center in the Persian Empire and one of the earliest cities to mint coins. It was conquered by Alexander the Great and then by the Romans, but it remained prosperous. Romans and indigenous people mixed at the city's central marketplace and in temples and public buildings. The Romans built an aqueduct to bring water into the city, although this was later destroyed in an earthquake. Over the river they also built an arched stone bridge, about thirty feet wide so that carts and chariots could easily travel on it. This may have also collapsed in

**Organist and Horn Player** Games, gladiatorial contests, and other events in the cities of the Roman Empire were often accompanied by music. In this floor mosaic from a villa in Nennig, Germany, built in the third century, a horn player plays a large curved instrument known as a *cornu*, which was also used by the military to call troops. The organist plays a water organ (*hydraulis*) in which water stored in the hexagonal podium was pumped through tubes and the force of the water pushed air through the organ pipes. (Museum für Vor und Frühgeschichte, Saarbrücken, Germany/ Bridgeman Images)

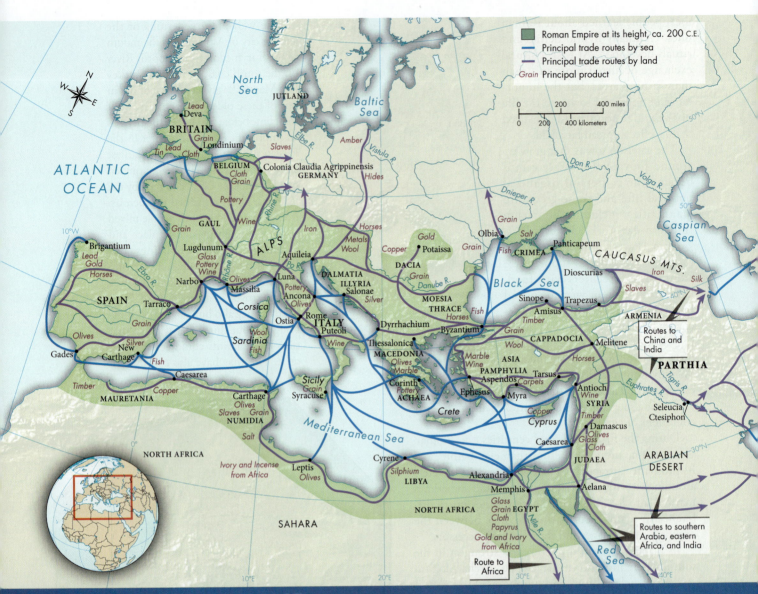

## MAPPING THE PAST

### MAP 6.2 Production and Trade in Imperial Rome, ca. 27 B.C.E.–180 C.E.

This map gives a good idea of the main products produced in various parts of the Roman Empire at its height and the trade routes connecting these regions. Map 10.2 on page 276 is a similar map that shows products and trade in roughly the same area nearly a millennium later. Examine both maps and answer the following questions.

**ANALYZING THE MAP**   What similarities and differences do you see in products during these two periods?

**CONNECTIONS**   To what extent did Roman trade routes influence later European trade routes?

an earthquake, but its foundations were so sturdy that a thousand years later the area's Turkish rulers used them to build a new bridge, which still stands. In 155 C.E. a local architect built a magnificent theater that probably held seven thousand spectators, who sat under a retractable awning that provided shade. Here men and women enjoyed plays and gladiatorial contests, for these were popular in eastern cities, as was horse racing.

More than just places to live, cities like Aspendos were centers of intellectual and cultural life. Their residents were in touch with the ideas and events of the day, in a network that spanned the entire Mediterranean and reached as far north as Britain. As long as the empire prospered and the revenues reached the imperial coffers, life in provincial cities—at least for the wealthy—could be nearly as pleasant as that in Rome.

## Trade and Commerce

The expansion of trade during the first two centuries C.E. made the Roman Empire an economic as well as a political force in the provinces (see Map 6.2). Britain and Belgium became prime grain producers, with much of their harvests going to the armies of the Rhine, and Britain's wool industry probably got its start under the Romans. Italy and southern Gaul produced huge quantities of wine, which was shipped in large pottery jugs wherever merchant vessels could carry it. Roman colonists introduced the olive to southern Spain and northern Africa, which soon produced most of the oil consumed in the western part of the empire. In the East the olive oil production of Syrian farmers reached an all-time high, and Egypt produced tons of wheat that fed the Roman populace.

The growth of industry in the provinces was another striking development of this period. Cities in Gaul and Germany eclipsed the old Mediterranean manufacturing centers. Lyons in Gaul and later Cologne in Germany became the new centers of the glassmaking industry, joining older glassmaking centers in the eastern Mediterranean. Roman glass was used for perfume, wine, and other liquids, and despite its fragility it was shipped widely. The Romans also took the manufacture of pottery to an advanced stage by introducing a wider range of vessels and making some of these on an industrial scale in kilns that were large enough to fire tens of thousands of pots at once. The most prized pottery was *terra sigillata*, reddish decorated tableware with a glossy surface. Methods for making terra sigillata spread from Italy northwards into Europe, often introduced by soldiers in the Roman army who had been trained in potterymaking in Italy. These craftsmen set up facilities to make roof tiles, amphoras, and dishes for their units, and local potters began to copy their styles and methods of manufacturing. Terra sigillata often portrayed Greco-Roman gods and heroes, so this pottery spread Mediterranean myths and stories. Local artisans added their own distinctive flourishes and sometimes stamped their names on the pots; these individual touches have allowed archaeologists to trace the pottery trade throughout the Roman Empire in great detail. Aided by all this growth in trade and industry, Europe and western Asia were linked in ways they had not been before.

As the Romans drove farther eastward, they encountered the Parthians, who had established a kingdom in what is now Afghanistan and Iran in the Hellenistic period. After the Romans tried unsuccessfully to

**Glass Beaker by Ennion** This exquisite mold-blown glass beaker from the first century C.E. with relief decorations of leaves and basketry has an inscription in Greek: "Ennion made it." Ennion came from the coastal city of Sidon in modern Lebanon and is one of a very few artisans from the ancient world whose name we know. The fine detail and precision of his work led him to have a powerful influence on the Roman glass industry. (The Israel Museum, Jerusalem, Israel/Bridgeman Images)

drive out the Parthians in the second century C.E., the Parthians came to act as a link between Roman and Chinese merchants. Chinese merchants sold their wares to the Parthians, who then carried the goods overland to Mesopotamia or Egypt, from which they were shipped throughout the Roman Empire. Silk was a major commodity traded from the East to the West, along with other luxury goods. In return the Romans traded glassware, precious gems, and slaves.

This was also an era of maritime trade. Roman ships sailed from Egyptian ports to the mouth of the Indus River, where they traded local merchandise and wares imported by the Parthians. In the late first century C.E. the Chinese emperor sent an ambassador, Gan Ying, to make contact with the Roman Empire. Gan Ying made it as far as the Persian Gulf ports, where he heard about the Romans from Parthian sailors and reported back to his emperor that the Romans were wealthy, tall, and strikingly similar to the Chinese. His report became part of a group of accounts about the Romans and other "Western" peoples that circulated widely among scholars and officials in Han China. Educated Romans did not have a corresponding interest in China, however. For them, China remained more of a mythical than a real place, and they never bothered to learn more about it.

## How did Christianity grow into a major religious movement?

During the reign of the emperor Tiberius in the Roman province of Judaea, which had been created out of the Jewish kingdom of Judah, a Jewish man named Jesus of Nazareth preached, attracted a following, and was executed on the order of the Roman prefect Pontius Pilate. At the time this was a minor event, but Christianity, the religion created by Jesus's followers, came to have an enormous impact first in the Roman Empire and later throughout the world.

### Factors Behind the Rise of Christianity

The civil wars that destroyed the Roman Republic left their mark on Judaea, where Jewish leaders had taken sides in the conflict. The turmoil created a climate of violence throughout the area, and among the Jews movements in opposition to the Romans spread. Some of the members of these movements, such as the Zealots, encouraged armed rebellion against Roman rule, which would, indeed, break out several times in the first and second centuries C.E. Many Jews came to believe that a final struggle was near, and that it would lead to the coming of a **Messiah**, a word that means one who is anointed with holy oil, as King David was (see Chapter 2), and thus the legitimate King of the Jews. This Messiah, a descendant of King David, would destroy the Roman legions and inaugurate a period of peace, happiness, and prosperity for Jews. This apocalyptic belief was an old one among Jews, but by the first century C.E. it had become more widespread than ever, with many people prophesying the imminent coming of a Messiah and readying themselves for a cataclysmic battle.

The pagan world also played its part in the story of early Christianity. The term **pagan**, derived from a Latin word with negative connotations meaning "rural dweller" (the closest English equivalent is "redneck"), came to refer to those who practiced religions other than Judaism or Christianity. Christianity was initially an urban religion, and those who lived in the countryside were less likely to be converts. What Christians would later term pagan practices included religions devoted to the traditional Roman gods of the hearth, home, and countryside; syncretistic religions that blended Roman and indigenous deities; the cult of the emperor spread through the erection of statues, temples, and monuments; and mystery religions that offered the promise of life after death (see Chapter 4). Many people in the Roman Empire practiced all of these, combining them in whatever way seemed most beneficial or satisfying to them, and some beliefs and practices from paganism became part of Christian worship.

### The Life and Teachings of Jesus

Into this climate of Messianic hope and Roman religious blending came Jesus of Nazareth (ca. 4 B.C.E.–ca. 30/33 C.E.). According to Christian Scripture, he was born to deeply religious Jewish parents and raised in Galilee, the stronghold of the Zealots and a trading center where Greeks and Romans interacted with Jews. His ministry began when he was about thirty, and he taught by preaching and telling stories.

Like Socrates, Jesus left no writings. Accounts of his sayings and teachings first circulated orally among his followers and were later written down. The principal surviving evidence for his life and deeds are the four Gospels of the Bible (Matthew, Mark, Luke, and John), books that are part of what Christians later termed the New Testament. These Gospels—the name means "good news"—are records of Jesus's life and teachings, written to build a community of faith sometime in the late first century C.E. Many different books circulated among Jesus's followers, but the Gospels were among the most widely copied and circulated early accounts of Jesus's life. By the fourth century officials in the Christian Church decided that they, along with other types of writing such as letters and prophecies, would form Christian Scripture. The four Gospels included in the Bible are called canonical, from the Greek word that means "the rule" or "the standard," as are other writings included in scripture. Other early documents were declared noncanonical, and many were lost, though some have been rediscovered in modern times. Which books would form Christian Scripture was a source of much debate in the early church, and even today different Christian groups accept different books.

The Gospels include certain details of Jesus's life, but they were not meant to be biographies. Their authors had probably heard many different people talk about what Jesus said and did, and there are discrepancies among the four accounts. These differences indicate that early followers had a diversity of beliefs about Jesus's nature and purpose, and historians today describe this period as one of "christianities" rather than a single "Christianity."

However, almost all the early sources agree on certain aspects of Jesus's teachings: He preached of a heavenly kingdom of eternal happiness in a life after death, and of the importance of devotion to God and love of others. His teachings were based on Hebrew Scripture and reflected a conception of God and morality that came from Jewish tradition. Jesus's orthodoxy enabled him to preach in the synagogue and the temple, but he deviated from orthodoxy in insisting that he taught in his own name, not in the name of Yahweh (the Hebrew name for God). The Greek translation of the Hebrew word *Messiah* is *Christos*, the origin of the English word *Christ*. Was Jesus the Messiah, the Christ? A small band of followers thought so, and Jesus claimed that he was. Yet Jesus had his own conception of the Messiah. He would establish a spiritual kingdom, not an earthly one. As recounted in one of the Gospels, he commented:

Do not lay up for yourselves treasures on earth, where moth and rust consume and where thieves break in and steal, but lay up for yourselves treasures in heaven, where neither moth nor rust consumes and where thieves do not break in and steal. For where your treasure is, there will your heart be also.[6]

The Roman official Pontius Pilate, who had authority over much of Judaea, knew little about Jesus's teachings. Like all Roman officials, he was concerned with maintaining peace and order, which was a difficult task in restive Judaea. According to the New Testament, crowds followed Jesus into Jerusalem at the time of Passover, a highly emotional time in the Jewish year that marked the Jewish people's departure from Egypt under the leadership of Moses (see Chapter 2). The prospect that these crowds would spark violence no doubt alarmed Pilate, as some Jews believed that Jesus was the long-awaited Messiah, while others thought him religiously dangerous. The four Gospels differ somewhat on exactly what actions Jesus took in the city and what Jesus and Pilate said to each other after Jesus was arrested. They agree that Pilate condemned Jesus to death by crucifixion because he claimed to be the legitimate king of the Jews, a claim that was reportedly stated in Latin above Jesus's head on the cross on which he was crucified. The only "king" the Jews had at this time was the Roman emperor Tiberius, so Jesus's claim was a political crime. Pilate's soldiers carried out the sentence. On the third day after Jesus's crucifixion, some of his followers claimed that he had risen from the dead. For his earliest followers and for generations to come, the resurrection of Jesus became a central element of faith.

## The Spread of Christianity

The memory of Jesus and his teachings survived and flourished. Believers in his divinity met in small assemblies or congregations, often in one another's homes, to discuss the meaning of Jesus's message and to celebrate a ritual (later called the Eucharist or Lord's Supper) commemorating his last meal with his disciples before his arrest. Because they expected Jesus to return to the world very soon, they regarded earthly life and institutions as unimportant. Only later did these congregations evolve into what came to be called the religion of Christianity, with a formal organization and set of beliefs.

The catalyst in the spread of Jesus's teachings and the formation of the Christian Church was Paul of Tarsus, a well-educated Hellenized Jew who was comfortable in both the Roman and the Jewish worlds. The New Testament reports that at first he persecuted members of this new Jewish sect, but then on the road to the city of Damascus in Syria he was struck blind by a vision of light and heard Jesus's voice. Once converted, he traveled all over the Roman Empire and wrote letters of advice to many groups. These letters were copied and widely circulated, transforming Jesus's ideas into more specific moral teachings. Recognizing that Christianity would not grow if it remained within Judaism, Paul connected it with the

■ **Messiah** In Jewish belief, an anointed leader who would bring a period of peace and happiness for Jews.

■ **pagan** Originally referring to those who lived in the countryside, it came to mean those who practiced religions other than Judaism or Christianity.

**Wall Painting in a Roman Catacomb**
This fresco from the Coemeterium Maius, a third-century set of catacombs in Rome, shows a woman praying with outstretched hands, flanked by two men. The cuts in the rock below are places where visitors could celebrate commemorative meals for the dead, a pre-Christian Roman practice that Christians continued. Christians brought food to catacombs and cemeteries to honor martyrs as well as deceased relatives, and the painting may represent the martyrs venerated here: a woman reputed to have been martyred while praying and two soldier-martyrs. (Photo 12/UIG via Getty Images)

non-Jewish world. As a result of his efforts, he became the most important figure in changing Christianity from a Jewish sect into a separate religion, and many of his letters became part of Christian Scripture.

The breadth of the Roman Empire was another factor behind the spread of Christianity. If all roads led to Rome, they also led outward to the provinces. This enabled early Christians to spread their faith easily throughout the world known to them. Though most of the earliest converts seem to have been Jews, or Greeks and Romans who were already interested in Jewish moral teachings, Paul urged that Gentiles, or non-Jews, be accepted on an equal basis. The earliest Christian converts included people from all social classes, though urban residents who were socially mobile were most likely to become Christian. Missionaries and others spread the Christian message through family contacts, friendships, and business networks.

The growing Christian communities differed about many things. Among these was the extent to which women should participate in the workings of the religion; some favored giving women a larger role in church affairs, while others were more restrictive, urging women to be silent on religious matters. Many women were active in spreading Christianity. Paul greeted male and female converts by name in his letters and noted that women often provided financial support for his activities.

People were attracted to Christian teachings for a variety of reasons. It was in many ways a mystery religion, offering its adherents special teachings that would give them immortality. But in contrast to traditional mystery religions, Christianity promised this immortality widely, not only to a select few.

Most early Christians believed that they would rise in body, not simply in spirit, after a final day of judgment, so they favored burial of the dead rather than the more common Roman practice of cremation. They

began to dig tunnels in the soft rock around Rome for burials, forming huge complexes of burial passageways called catacombs. Memorial services for martyrs were sometimes held in or near catacombs, but they were not regular places of worship. Instead people worshipped in the houses of more well-to-do converts.

Along with the possibility of life after death, Christianity also offered rewards in this world to adherents. One of these was the possibility of forgiveness, for believers accepted that human nature is weak and that even the best Christians could fall into sin. But Jesus loved sinners and forgave those who repented. Christianity was also attractive to many because it gave the Roman world a cause. Instead of passivity, Christians stressed the ideal of striving for a goal. By spreading the word of Christ, Christians played their part in God's plan for the triumph of Christianity on earth. Christianity likewise gave its devotees a sense of community, which was very welcome in the often highly mobile world of the Roman Empire. To stress the spiritual kinship of this new type of community, Christians often called one another "brother" and "sister." Also, many Christians took Jesus's commandment to love one another as a guide and provided support for widows, orphans, and the poor, just as they did for family members. Such material support became increasingly attractive as Roman social welfare programs broke down in the third century.

## The Growing Acceptance and Evolution of Christianity

At first most Roman officials largely ignored the followers of Jesus, viewing them simply as one of the many splinter groups within Judaism. Slowly some Roman officials and leaders came to oppose Christian practices and beliefs. They considered Christians to be subversive dissidents

**Early Christian Fresco in England**   A row of figures wearing long gowns embroidered with crosses is portrayed in this fresco from a Roman villa in Lullingston, Kent, in southern England. The villa itself was built in the first century and then expanded and remodeled; in the fourth century, one room was apparently converted into a Christian chapel or house-church. The wall paintings — some of the earliest evidence for Christianity in England — show the figures in what was the most common posture for prayer in the early Christian Church. The villa burned and collapsed in the fifth century and was excavated only in the twentieth. (© The Trustees of the British Museum, London, UK/Art Resource, NY)

because they stopped practicing traditional rituals venerating the hearth and home and they objected — often publicly or in writing — to the cult of the emperor. Some Romans thought that Christianity was one of the worst of the mystery religions, with immoral and indecent rituals. For instance, they thought that the ritual of the Lord's Supper, at which Christians said that they ate and drank the body and blood of Jesus, was an act of cannibalism involving the ritual murder of Roman boys. Many in the Roman Empire also feared that the traditional gods would withdraw their favor from the Roman Empire because of the Christian insistence that these gods either did not exist or were evil spirits. The Christian refusal to worship Roman gods, in their opinion, endangered Roman lives and society. Others worried that Christians were trying to destroy the Roman family with their insistence on a new type of kinship, and they pointed to Jesus's words in the Gospels saying that salvation was far more important than family relationships. A woman who converted, thought many Romans, might use her new faith to oppose her father's choice of marital partner or even renounce marriage itself, an idea supported by the actions of a few female converts.

Governors of Roman provinces were primarily interested in maintaining order, and they hoped that Christians and non-Christians would coexist peacefully, but conflicts arose, leading governors to carry out campaigns against Christians, including torture and executions. Most persecutions were local and sporadic in nature, however, and some of the gory stories about the martyrs are later inventions, designed to strengthen believers with accounts of earlier heroes. Christians differed in their opinions about how to respond to

persecution. Some sought out martyrdom, while others thought that doing so went against Christian teachings.

Responses to Christianity on the part of Roman emperors varied. Nero persecuted Christians, but Trajan forbade his governors to hunt them down. Though admitting that he considered Christianity an abomination, he decided it was better policy to leave Christians in peace. Later emperors increased persecutions again, ordering Christians to sacrifice to the emperor and the Roman gods or risk death. Executions followed their edicts, although estimates of how many people were actually martyred in any of these persecutions vary widely.

By the second century C.E. Christianity was also changing. The belief that Jesus was soon coming again gradually waned, and as the number of converts increased, permanent institutions were established instead of simple house churches. These included buildings and a hierarchy of officials often modeled on those of the Roman Empire. **Bishops**, officials with jurisdiction over a certain area, became especially important. They began to assert that they had the right to determine the correct interpretation of Christian teachings and to choose their successors. Councils of bishops determined which writings would be considered canonical, and lines were increasingly drawn between what was considered correct teaching and what was considered incorrect, or **heresy**.

■ **bishops** Christian Church officials with jurisdiction over certain areas and the power to determine the correct interpretation of Christian teachings.

■ **heresy** A religious practice or belief judged unacceptable by church officials.

Christianity also began to attract more highly educated individuals who developed complex theological interpretations of issues that were not clear in scripture. Often drawing on Greek philosophy and Roman legal traditions, they worked out understandings of such issues as how Jesus could be both divine and human, and how God could be both a father and a son (and later a spirit as well, a Christian doctrine known as the Trinity). Bishops and theologians often modified teachings that seemed upsetting to Romans, such as Jesus's harsh words about wealth and family ties. Given all these changes, Christianity became more formal in the second century, with power more centralized.

## What political and economic problems did Rome face in the third century C.E.?

The prosperity and political stability of the second century gave way to a period of domestic upheaval and foreign invasion. The third century saw a long series of able but ambitious military commanders who used their legions to make themselves emperors. Many tried to establish dynasties, but most failed, and those that were established were short-lived. While they were fighting each other, the generals were not able to defend against raids across Rome's borders. The nature of the army changed, and the economy weakened because of unsound policies.

**The Emperor Marcus Aurelius** This larger-than-life bronze equestrian statue, sculpted to celebrate his military victories or shortly after his death in 180 C.E., shows the emperor holding up his hand in the conventional imperial greeting. More than twenty equestrian statues could be seen in late imperial Rome, but this is the only one to survive. In the sixteenth century Michelangelo built one of the major plazas of Rome around it, although now the original has been moved to a museum for better preservation and this is a copy that stands outdoors. (UniversalImagesGroup/Getty Images)

### Civil Wars and Military Commanders

The reign of Marcus Aurelius (r. 161–180 C.E.) was marked by problems. The Tiber River flooded in 162, destroying crops and killing animals, which led to famine. Soldiers returning from wars in the East brought the Antonine plague back to Rome (see "Approaches to Urban Problems") and then carried it northward. Germanic-speaking groups attacked along the Rhine and Danube borders, and the emperor himself took over the campaign against them in 169. He spent most of the rest of his life in military camps along Rome's northern border, where in addition to leading troops he wrote a series of personal reflections in Greek. These *Meditations*, as they later came to be known, are advice to himself about doing one's duty and acting in accordance with nature, ideas that came from Stoic philosophy. He wrote:

> Take heed not to be transformed into a Caesar, not to be dipped in the purple dye [a color only the emperor could wear]. Keep yourself therefore simple, good, pure, grave, unaffected, the friend of justice, religious, kind, affectionate, strong for your proper work. Wrestle to continue to be the man Philosophy wished to make you. Reverence the gods, save men. . . . Do not act unwillingly nor selfishly nor without self-examination.[7]

The *Meditations* are a good key to Marcus Aurelius's character, but they appear not to have circulated very much during the centuries immediately after they were written. Certainly very few later emperors took this advice to heart.

After the death of Marcus Aurelius, misrule by his successors led to a long and intense spasm of fighting. Marcus Aurelius's son Commodus was strangled by a conspiracy that included his wife, and in 193 five men claimed the throne in quick succession, a repeat of what had happened in 69. Two of them were also assassinated, and Septimius Severus (r. 193–211 C.E.) emerged as the victor. He restored order, expanded the borders of the Roman Empire in Africa and western Asia, and invaded Scotland. He increased the size of the army significantly and paid the soldiers better. This made him popular with soldiers, though it also increased the taxes on civilians. Some of his policies regarding the army created additional problems in the long run. For example, changes in recruiting practices that emphasized local recruiting of non-Romans created a Roman army that became less acculturated to Roman values, and so was no longer the vehicle for Romanization that it had been in earlier centuries. In 212 Septimius Severus's son Caracalla (r. 198–217 C.E.) issued an edict making all free male residents of the Roman Empire citizens, which increased his standing with his supporters in the provinces. This edict made them eligible to serve in the legions — which may have been why Caracalla did this — but also made serving in the army less attractive, and so reduced the number of men willing to join.

In 235 the emperor Severus Alexander lost the respect of his troops by negotiating with Germanic chieftains raiding across Rome's northern border. They assassinated him and chose a different commander to be emperor, beginning a fifty-year period in which more than twenty different emperors seized power, which many historians refer to as the "crisis of the third century." These emperors were generally military commanders from the border provinces, and there were so many that the middle of the third century has become known as the age of the **barracks emperors**. Almost all were either assassinated or died in civil wars, and their preoccupation with overthrowing the ruling emperor left the borders unguarded. Non-Roman groups on the frontiers took full advantage of the chaos to overrun vast areas. When they reached the Rhine and the Danube, they often found gaping holes in the Roman defenses, and moved deep into Roman territory.

## Turmoil in Economic Life

This chaos also disrupted areas far away from the borders of the empire. Renegade soldiers and corrupt imperial officials, together with many greedy local agents, preyed on local people. In some places in the countryside, officials requisitioned villagers' livestock and compelled them to do forced labor. Farmers appealed to the government for protection so that they could cultivate the land. Although some of those in authority were unsympathetic and even violent to villagers, many others tried to maintain order. Yet even the best of them also suffered. If officials could not meet their tax quotas, which were rising to support the costs of civil war, they had to pay the deficits from their own pockets. Because the local officials were themselves so hard-pressed, they squeezed what they needed from rural families. Many farmers, unable to pay, were driven off their land, and those remaining faced ruin. As a result, agricultural productivity declined.

In response to the economic crisis, the emperors reduced the amount of silver used in coins, replacing it with less valuable metals such as copper, so that they could continue to pay their troops. This tactic, however, led to crippling inflation, which wiped out savings and sent prices soaring.

The Romans still controlled the Mediterranean, which nurtured commerce, and some parts of the empire were relatively unaffected by the uproar. The road system remained largely intact, though often roads were allowed to fall into disrepair, and unrest made it less safe for merchants to travel. Trade still flowed, but more trade became local, as did the production of food and manufactured goods.

By 284 C.E. the empire had reached a crisis that threatened its downfall. The position of emperor was gained no longer through succession ratified by the Senate but rather by victory in civil war. The empire had failed at the top, and the repercussions of the disaster had dire effects throughout the empire.

### NOTES

1. Virgil, *Aeneid*, trans. Theodore C. Williams (Boston: Houghton Mifflin, 1910), 6.851–853.
2. Virgil, *Aeneid,* trans. Robert Fitzgerald (New York: Vintage, 1990), 1.1–11.
3. Text in Mary Johnston, *Roman Life* (Chicago: Scott, Foresman, and Co., 1957), p. 172.
4. Elaine Fantham et al., eds., *Women in the Classical World* (New York: Oxford University Press, 1994), pp. 369–370.
5. Napthali Lewis and Meyer Reinhold, *Roman Civilization*, vol. 2 (New York: Harper Torchbooks, 1955), pp. 284–285.
6. Matthew 6:19–21.
7. Marcus Aurelius, *Meditations* 3.5, 6.30, trans. A. S. L. Farquharson (New York: Everyman's Library, 1961), pp. 5, 12.

■ **barracks emperors** The emperors of the middle of the third century, so called because they were military commanders.

# LOOKING BACK  LOOKING AHEAD

The first several centuries of the Roman Empire was a rich era in both economic and cultural terms. Generally working with Roman elites, rulers developed a system of government that governed vast areas of diverse people fairly effectively. The resulting stability and peace encouraged agriculture and production. Goods and people moved along roads and sea-lanes, as did ideas, including the new religion of Christianity. As they had in the republic, Romans during the empire incorporated individuals from different groups politically by granting them citizenship, and in border areas Roman and provincial culture mixed.

During a long period of internal crisis, civil war, and invasions in the third century, it seemed as if the empire would collapse, but it did not. Although emperors came and went in quick and violent succession, the basic institutions and infrastructure of the empire remained intact. Even during the worst of the ordeal, many lower-level officials and ordinary soldiers continued to do their jobs, embodying the principles of duty that Marcus Aurelius advocated. People like this would be key to passing Roman traditions on to institutions that developed later in Europe, including law courts, city governments, and nations.

## Make Connections

Think about the larger developments and continuities within and across chapters.

1. What allowed large empires in the ancient world, including the Persians (Chapter 2) and the Romans, to govern vast territories and many different peoples successfully?

2. How was slavery in the Roman Empire different from that in earlier societies? How was it similar? What might account for the continuities and changes in slavery you have identified?

3. If a male resident of Athens during the time of Pericles (Chapter 3) had time-traveled to Rome during the time of Augustus, what might he have found familiar? What might have seemed strange? How might these observations have differed if the time traveler were a female resident of Athens?

# 6  REVIEW & EXPLORE

## Identify Key Terms

Identify and explain the significance of each item below.

principate (p. 143)

imperator (p. 143)

pax Romana (p. 145)

Praetorian Guard (p. 152)

aqueducts (p. 156)

Messiah (p. 162)

pagan (p. 162)

bishops (p. 165)

heresy (p. 165)

barracks emperors (p. 167)

## Review the Main Ideas

Answer the section heading questions from the chapter.

1. How did Augustus and Roman elites create a foundation for the Roman Empire? (p. 142)

2. How did the Roman state develop after Augustus? (p. 152)

**3.** What was life like in the city of Rome and in the provinces? (p. 155)

**4.** How did Christianity grow into a major religious movement? (p. 162)

**5.** What political and economic problems did Rome face in the third century C.E.? (p. 166)

## Suggested Resources

### BOOKS

- Aldrete, Gregory S. *Daily Life in the Roman City.* 2004. Reveals the significance of ordinary Roman life in the cities of Rome, its port Ostia, and Pompeii.

- Beard, Mary. *SPQR: A History of Ancient Rome.* 2016. A best-selling survey of the grand sweep of Roman history by Britain's best-known classicist.

- Campbell, Brian. *War and Society in Imperial Rome, 31 B.C.–A.D. 284.* 2002. Shows how Roman warfare and military life influenced and was influenced by Roman society.

- Clark, Gillian. *Christianity and Roman Society.* 2004. Surveys the evolution of Christian life among Christians and with their pagan neighbors.

- D'Ambra, Eve. *Roman Women.* 2006. Treats the lives of women of all social ranks.

- Everitt, Anthony. *Augustus: The Life of Rome's First Emperor.* 2007. A lively biography that traces Augustus's rise to power.

- Freeman, Charles. *A New History of Early Christianity.* 2010. A survey of the first four centuries of Christianity, written for a general audience.

- Joshel, Sandra R. *Slavery in the Roman World.* 2010. An overview of Roman slavery, including the social and family lives of slaves, designed for students.

- Knapp, Robert. *Invisible Romans.* 2011. A view of Roman life that focuses on ordinary men and women: soldiers, slaves, laborers, housewives, gladiators, and outlaws.

- Kyle, Donald G. *Sport and Spectacle in the Ancient World.* 2007. Examines the nature and meaning of sports from Mesopotamia through Rome, including running races, fighting, and chariot racing.

- Potter, David, and David J. Mattingly. *Life, Death, and Entertainment in the Roman Empire,* 2d ed. 2010. Discusses family and gender, slavery, food, religion, and entertainment.

- Roth, Jonathan P. *Roman Warfare.* 2010. Surveys arms, tactics, strategy, and logistics from republican to imperial times.

### MEDIA

- *From Jesus to Christ: The First Christians* (PBS, 1998). A four-part documentary exploring the life and death of Jesus and the transformation of Christianity from a small group to an established church. With commentary by theologians, archaeologists, and historians on many key issues.

- *Gladiator* (Ridley Scott, 2000). The Academy Award–winning historical epic about a Roman general who becomes a gladiator and avenges the murder of his family by a power-crazy emperor.

- *I, Claudius* (BBC, 1976). A highly acclaimed fictionalized version of the political intrigue in the first century, told from the viewpoint of the emperor Claudius; with Derek Jacobi and Patrick Stewart.

- *The Roman Empire in the First Century* (PBS, 2001). A four-part documentary that examines the building of the Roman Empire, highlighting ordinary people as well as emperors.

- *Rome: The Rise and Fall of an Empire* (History Channel, 2008). A thirteen-part documentary, with re-enactments—especially of battle scenes, power struggles, and lavish banquets—that trace Rome from the second century B.C.E. to the fifth century C.E.

- *Rome Reborn: A Digital Model of Ancient Rome.* Three-dimensional digital models by an international team of scholars illustrating the urban development of ancient Rome; includes a fascinating video tour of the streets of Rome in 320 C.E. **www.romereborn.virginia.edu/**

- *Vindolanda Tablets Online.* A highly unusual find of wooden writing tablets from the second century C.E., discovered at the Roman fortress of Vindolanda behind Hadrian's Wall in Britain, that reveals many aspects of non-elite Roman society and military life. The site includes text images, transliterated texts, English translations, and historical background. **vindolanda.csad.ox.ac.uk/**

# 7

# Late Antiquity

## 250–600

**The Roman Empire, with its powerful — and sometimes bizarre** — leaders, magnificent buildings, luxurious clothing, and bloody amusements, has long fascinated people. Politicians and historians have closely studied the reasons for its successes and have even more closely analyzed the weaknesses that led to its eventual collapse. From the third century onward, the Western Roman Empire slowly disintegrated. Scholars have long seen this era as one of the great turning points in Western history, a time when the ancient world was transformed into the very different medieval world. During the past several decades, however, focus has shifted to continuities as well as changes, and what is now usually termed "late antiquity" has been recognized as a period of creativity and adaptation, not simply of decline and fall. Historians are also now more interested in why Rome lasted so long than why it fell.

The two main agents of continuity in late antiquity were the Christian Church and the Byzantine or Eastern Roman Empire. Missionaries and church officials spread Christianity within and far beyond the borders of the Roman Empire, bringing with them the Latin language and institutions based on Roman models. The Byzantine Empire lasted until 1453, a thousand years longer than the Western Roman Empire, and preserved and transmitted much of ancient Greco-Roman law, philosophy, and institutions. The main agents of change in late antiquity were groups the Romans labeled barbarians migrating into the Roman Empire. They brought different social, political, and economic structures with them, but as they encountered Roman culture and became Christian, their own ways of doing things were also transformed. ■

# CHAPTER PREVIEW

- How did Diocletian and Constantine try to reform the empire?

- How did the Christian Church become a major force in the Mediterranean and Europe?

- What were the key characteristics of barbarian society?

- How did the barbarian migrations shape Europe?

- How did the church convert barbarian peoples to Christianity?

- How did the Byzantine Empire preserve the legacy of Rome?

**Religious Life in Late Antiquity**
In this sixth-century ivory carving, a procession of people carry relics of a saint to a Christian church under construction. New churches often received holy items when they were dedicated, and processions were common ways in which people expressed community devotion.
(akg-images/Newscom)

# How did Diocletian and Constantine try to reform the empire?

In the middle of the third century, the Roman Empire faced internal turmoil and external attacks. Civil wars tore the empire apart as emperors rose and fell in quick succession, and Germanic tribes and others migrated and marauded deep within the boundaries of the empire. Wars and invasions disrupted normal commerce and agriculture, the primary sources of tax revenues. The barracks emperors of the third century dealt with economic hardship by cutting the silver content of coins until money was virtually worthless. The immediate result was crippling inflation throughout the empire, made worse by the corruption of many officials. Many Romans had become Christian, but the followers of traditional Roman religion were divided in their views of what this meant for the empire. In the early fourth century the emperor Diocletian (r. 284–305), who was born of low-status parents and had risen through the ranks of the military to become emperor, restored order, and the later emperor Constantine (r. 306–337) continued his work. How Diocletian, Constantine, and their successors responded to the problems facing the empire influenced later developments.

**MAP 7.1  The Division of the Roman World, 293**   Under Diocletian, the Roman Empire was first divided into a western and an eastern half, a development that foreshadowed the medieval division between the Latin West and the Byzantine East.

## Political Measures

Diocletian recognized that the empire had become too large for one man to handle and divided it into a western half and an eastern half (Map 7.1). Diocletian assumed direct control of the eastern part; he gave the rule of the western part to a colleague, along with the title *augustus*. Around 293 Diocletian further delegated power by appointing two men to assist the augustus and him; each of the four men was given the title *caesar*, and the system was known as the **tetrarchy** (TEH-trahr-kee), meaning "rule of four." He further divided each part of the empire into administrative units called **dioceses**, which were in turn subdivided into small provinces, all governed by an expanded bureaucracy. Although four men ruled the empire, Diocletian was clearly the senior partner and final source of authority.

Diocletian's political reforms were a momentous step. The reorganization made the empire easier to administer and placed each of the four central military commands much closer to borders or other trouble spots, so that troops could be sent more quickly when needed. Diocletian hoped that the tetrarchy would supply a clearly defined order of succession and end struggles for power over the emperorship. That did not happen, but much of Diocletian's reorganization remained.

Like Diocletian, Constantine came up through the army and took control after a series of civil wars. He eventually had authority over the entire empire, but he ruled from the East, where he established a new capital for the empire at Byzantium, an old Greek city on the Bosporus, naming it "New Rome," though it was soon called Constantinople. (Today this is Istanbul, the largest city in Turkey.) Constantine sponsored a massive building program of palaces, warehouses, public buildings, and even a hippodrome for horse racing, modeling these on Roman buildings. He built defensive works along the borders of the empire, trying hard to keep it together, and used various means to strengthen the army, as did his successors. The emperors ruling from Constantinople could not provide enough military assistance to repel invaders in the western half of the Roman Empire, however, and Roman authority there slowly disintegrated.

## Economic Issues

In response to inflation and declining tax revenues, Diocletian issued an edict that fixed maximum prices and wages throughout the empire. At the same time, taxes became payable in kind, that is, in goods such

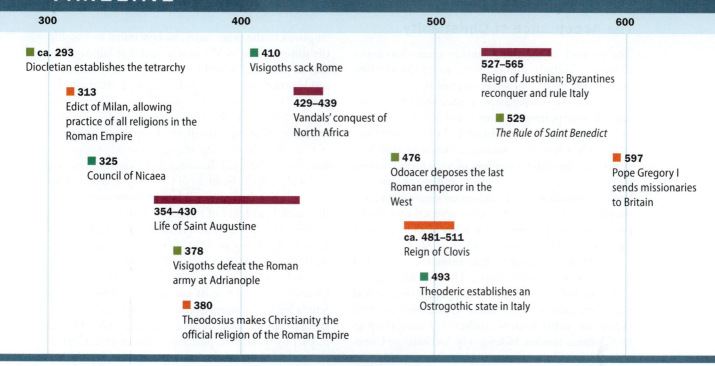

**ca. 293**
Diocletian establishes the tetrarchy

**313**
Edict of Milan, allowing practice of all religions in the Roman Empire

**325**
Council of Nicaea

**354–430**
Life of Saint Augustine

**378**
Visigoths defeat the Roman army at Adrianople

**380**
Theodosius makes Christianity the official religion of the Roman Empire

**410**
Visigoths sack Rome

**429–439**
Vandals' conquest of North Africa

**527–565**
Reign of Justinian; Byzantines reconquer and rule Italy

**529**
*The Rule of Saint Benedict*

**476**
Odoacer deposes the last Roman emperor in the West

**ca. 481–511**
Reign of Clovis

**493**
Theoderic establishes an Ostrogothic state in Italy

**597**
Pope Gregory I sends missionaries to Britain

as grain, sheep, or cloth instead of money, which made them difficult to transport to central authorities. Constantine continued these measures and also made occupations more rigid: all people involved in the growing, preparation, and transportation of food and other essentials were locked into their professions. In this period of severe depression, many individuals and communities could not pay their taxes. In such cases, local tax collectors, who were also bound to their occupations, had to make up the difference from their own funds. This system soon wiped out a whole class of moderately wealthy people and set the stage for the lack of social mobility that was a key characteristic of European society for many centuries to follow.

The emperors' measures did not really address Rome's central economic problems, however. Because of worsening conditions during the third and fourth centuries, many free farmers and their families were killed by invaders or renegade soldiers, or they abandoned farms ravaged in the fighting. Consequently, large tracts of land lay deserted. Landlords with ample resources began at once to reclaim as much of this land as they could, often hiring back the free farmers who had previously worked the land as paid labor or tenants.

**Gold Coin Showing Constantine**
In this gold coin, minted at Ticinum in northern Italy in 316, Constantine is shown with a halo, a symbol of his sacred character and connection to the sun-god. This iconography was later adopted in Christian art to signify divinity or sanctity.
(Ashmolean Museum, University of Oxford, UK/ Bridgeman Images)

The huge villas that resulted were self-sufficient and became islands of stability in an unsettled world.

Free farmers who remained on the land were exposed to raids and the tyranny of imperial officials. In return for the protection and security landlords could offer, small landholders gave over their lands and their freedom. To guarantee a supply of labor, landlords denied them freedom to move elsewhere. Henceforth they and their families worked their patrons' land, not their own. Free men and women were becoming tenant farmers bound to the land, what would later be called serfs.

■ **tetrarchy** Diocletian's four-part division of the Roman Empire.

■ **diocese** An administrative unit in the later Roman Empire; adopted by the Christian Church as the territory under the authority of a bishop.

## The Acceptance of Christianity

The turmoil of the third century seemed to some emperors, including Diocletian, to be the punishment of the gods. Diocletian stepped up persecution of Christians who would not sacrifice to Rome's traditional deities, portraying them as disloyal to the empire in an attempt to wipe out the faith. These persecutions lasted only a few years, however. Increasing numbers of Romans, including members of prominent families, were converting to Christianity, and many who followed traditional Roman religions no longer saw Christianity as un-Roman. Constantine reversed Diocletian's policy and instead ordered toleration of all religions in the Edict of Milan, issued in 313.

Whether Constantine was himself a Christian by this point is hotly debated. His later biographer, the Christian bishop Eusebius, reported that he had been converted on a battlefield in 312 after seeing a vision, and other sources attribute his conversion to his Christian mother, Helena, who had become Christian earlier. Constantine sent Helena on a journey to bring sacred relics from Jerusalem to Constantinople as part of his efforts to promote Christianity in the empire. On the other hand, he continued to worship the sun-god, and in 321 proclaimed that Sunday, "the Day of the Sun," would be the official day of rest. He was baptized only shortly before he died, although this was not uncommon for high officials. Whatever his personal beliefs at different stages of his life, there is no debate that he recognized the growing numbers of Christians in the empire and financially supported the church. He freed the clergy from imperial taxation and endowed the building of Christian churches. One of his gifts—the Lateran Palace in Rome—remained the official residence of the popes until the fourteenth century. He allowed others to make gifts to the church as well, decreeing in 321, "Every man, when dying, shall have the right to bequeath as much of his property as he desires to the holy and venerable Catholic Church. And such wills are not to be broken."[1] In return for his support, Constantine expected the assistance of church officials in maintaining order. Helped in part by its favored position in the empire, Christianity slowly became the leading religion (Map 7.2).

As they had in the first centuries of Christianity, Christians disagreed with one another about many issues,

**MAP 7.2 The Spread of Christianity, to 600**   Originating in Judaea, the southern part of modern Israel and Jordan, Christianity first spread throughout the Roman world and then beyond it in all directions.

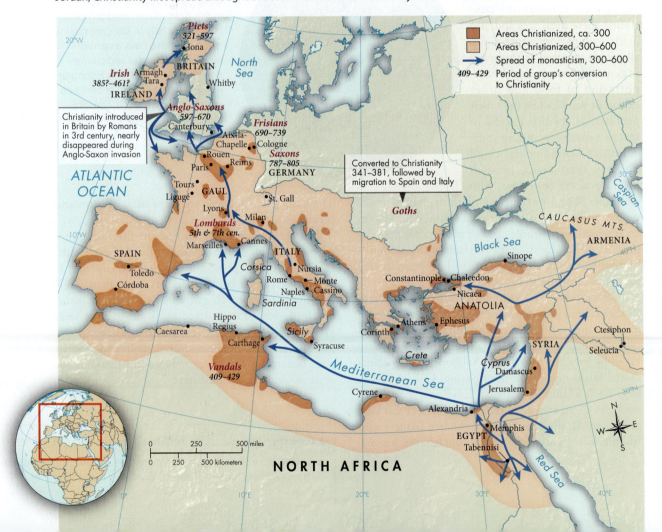

which led to schisms (SKIH-zuhms), denunciations, and sometimes violence. In the fourth and fifth centuries disputes arose over the nature of Christ. For example, **Arianism** (AI-ree-uh-nih-zuhm), developed by Arius (ca. 250–336), a priest of Alexandria, held that Jesus was created by the will of God the Father and thus was not co-eternal with him. Arian Christians reasoned that Jesus the Son must be inferior to God the Father because the Father was incapable of suffering and did not die. Arianism enjoyed such popularity and provoked such controversy that Constantine, who declared that "internal strife within the Church of God is far more evil and dangerous than any kind of war and conflict," interceded. In 325 he summoned church leaders to a council in Nicaea (nigh-SEE-uh) in Asia Minor and presided over it personally. The council produced the **Nicene Creed**, which defined the position that Christ is "eternally begotten of the Father" and of the same substance as the Father. Arius and those who refused to accept Nicene (nigh-SEEN) Christianity were banished. Their interpretation of the nature of Christ was declared a heresy, that is, a belief that contradicted the interpretation the church leaders declared was correct, which was termed orthodoxy.

These actions did not end Arianism, however. Several later emperors were Arian Christian, and Arian missionaries converted many Germanic tribes, who were attracted by the idea that Jesus was God's first-in-command, which fit well with their own warrior hierarchies and was less complicated than the idea of two persons with one substance.

The Nicene Creed says little specifically about the Holy Spirit, but in the following centuries the idea that the Father, Son, and Holy Spirit are "one substance in three persons" — the Trinity — became a central doctrine in Christianity, though again there were those who disagreed. Disputes about the nature of Christ also continued, with factions establishing themselves as separate Christian groups. The Nestorians, for example, regarded the divine and human natures in Jesus as distinct from one another, whereas the orthodox opinion was that they were united. The Nestorians split from the rest of the church in the fifth century after their position was outlawed, and settled in Persia. Nestorian Christian missionaries later founded churches in Central Asia, India, and China.

Religious and secular authorities tried in various ways to control this diversity as well as promote Christianity. In 380 the emperor Theodosius (thee-uh-DOH-shee-uhs) made Nicene Christianity the official religion of the empire. Theodosius stripped Roman pagan temples of statues, made the practice of the old Roman state religion a treasonable offense, and persecuted Christians who dissented from orthodox doctrine. Most significant, he allowed the church to establish its own courts and to use its own body of law, called canon law. The church courts, not the

**Constantine and Helena in a Nestorian Manuscript**   This fifth- to sixth-century manuscript from a Nestorian Christian community in Central Asia shows Constantine with his mother Helena, holding pieces of the True Cross, one of the many relics she is traditionally credited with bringing from Jerusalem to Constantinople. Nestorian Christians had a different view of the nature of Jesus than did Constantine, but they still viewed him and his mother as important figures in their tradition. (Pictures from History/ Bridgeman Images)

Roman government, had jurisdiction over the clergy and ecclesiastical disputes. At the death of Theodosius, the Christian Church was considerably independent of the Roman state. The foundation for later growth in church power had been laid.

Later emperors continued the pattern of active involvement in church affairs. They appointed the highest officials of the church hierarchy; the emperors or their representatives presided at ecumenical councils; and the emperors controlled some of the material resources of the church — land, rents, and dependent peasantry.

■ **Arianism**   A theological belief that originated when Arius, a priest of Alexandria, denied that Christ was co-eternal with God the Father.

■ **Nicene Creed**   A statement of belief written by a group of Christian church leaders in 325 that declared God the Father and Jesus to be of the same "substance"; other interpretations were declared heresy.

# How did the Christian Church become a major force in the Mediterranean and Europe?

As the emperors changed their policies about Christianity from persecution to promotion, the church grew, gradually becoming the most important institution in the Mediterranean and Europe. The able administrators and creative thinkers of the church developed permanent institutions and complex philosophical concepts that drew on the Greco-Roman tradition, which attracted learned Romans.

## The Church and Its Leaders

The early Christian Church benefited from the administrative abilities of church leaders. With the empire in decay, educated people joined and worked for the church in the belief that it was the one institution able to provide some stability. Bishop Ambrose of Milan (339–397) is typical of the Roman aristocrats who held high public office, were converted to Christianity, and subsequently became bishops. Like many bishops, Ambrose had a solid education in classical law and rhetoric, which he used to become an eloquent preacher. He had a strong sense of his authority and even stood up to Emperor Theodosius, who had ordered Ambrose to hand over his major church—called a basilica—to the emperor:

> At length came the command, "Deliver up the Basilica"; I reply, "It is not lawful for us to deliver it up, nor for your Majesty to receive it. By no law can you violate the house of a private man, and do you think that the house of God may be taken away? . . . But do not burden your conscience with the thought that you have any right as Emperor over sacred things. . . . It is written, God's to God and Caesar's to Caesar. The palace is the Emperor's, the churches are the Bishop's. To you is committed jurisdiction over public, not over sacred buildings."[2]

The emperor relented. Ambrose's assertion that the church was supreme in spiritual matters and the state in secular issues was to serve as the cornerstone of the church's position on church-state relations for centuries. Ambrose came to be regarded as one of the fathers of the church, that is, early Christian thinkers

whose authority was seen as second only to the Bible in later centuries.

Gradually the church adapted the organizational structure of the Roman Empire begun during the reign of Diocletian. The territory under the authority of a bishop was also called a diocese, with its center a cathedral (from the Latin *cathedra*, meaning "chair"), the church that contained the bishop's official seat of power. A bishop's jurisdiction extended throughout the diocese, and he came to control a large amount of land that was given to or purchased by the church. Bishops generally came from prominent families and had both spiritual and political power; as the Roman Empire disintegrated, they became the most important local authority on many types of issues. They claimed to trace their spiritual ancestry back to Jesus's apostles, a doctrine called **apostolic succession**. Because of the special importance of their dioceses, five bishops—those of Antioch, Alexandria, Jerusalem, Constantinople, and Rome—gained the title of *patriarch*.

After the capital and the emperor moved to Constantinople, the power of the bishop of Rome grew because he was the only patriarch in the Western Roman Empire. The bishops of Rome stressed that Rome had special significance because of its history as the capital of a worldwide empire. More significantly, they asserted, Rome had a special place in Christian history. According to tradition, Saint Peter, chief of Jesus's disciples, had lived in Rome and been its first bishop. Thus, as successors of Peter, the bishops of Rome—known as popes, from the Latin word *papa*, meaning "father"—claimed a privileged position in the church hierarchy, an idea called the **Petrine Doctrine** that built on the notion of apostolic succession. They stressed their supremacy over other Christian communities and urged other churches to appeal to Rome for the resolution of disputed doctrinal issues. Not surprisingly, the other patriarchs did not agree. They continued to exercise authority in their own regions, and local churches did as well, but the groundwork had been laid for later Roman predominance on religious matters.

Beginning in the fifth century the popes also expanded the church's secular authority, making treaties with the leaders of groups that threatened the city of Rome. One pope who did this was Gregory I (pontificate 590–604), later called "the Great," who also reorganized church lands to increase production and then distributed the additional food to the poor. He had been an official for the city of Rome before he became a church official, and his administrative and diplomatic talents helped the church expand. He sent

■ **apostolic succession** The doctrine that all bishops can trace their spiritual ancestry back to Jesus's apostles.

■ **Petrine Doctrine** A doctrine stating that the popes (the bishops of Rome) were the successors of Saint Peter and therefore heirs to his highest level of authority as chief of the apostles.

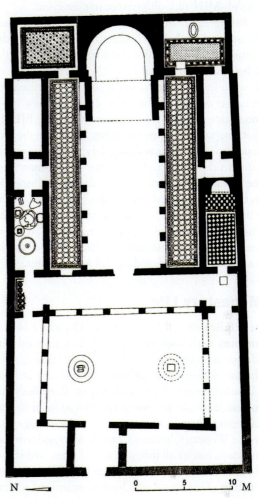

**Floor Plan and Foundation of Kursi Monastery Church**    Built on the eastern shore of the Sea of Galilee in the fifth century at a major pilgrimage site, this walled monastery had living quarters for the monks, a guesthouse, and a bath for pilgrims. It contained a church, shown here, modeled on the type of Roman public building known as a basilica, with an open courtyard with two wells (near the bottom in the pictures), mosaic floors, and a central nave separated from side aisles by rows of arched columns. In one side chapel (on the left in the pictures) was a small baptismal font, and in another a press for olive oil, a major source of income for the monastery. The skeletons of thirty monks were found in a crypt when the site was uncovered during road construction in 1970. (Private Collection/Photo © Zev Radovan/Bridgeman Images)

missionaries to the British Isles and wrote letters and guides instructing bishops on practical and spiritual matters. He promoted the ideas of Augustine, particularly those that defined church rituals as essential for salvation. The Western Christian Church headed by the pope in Rome would become the most enduring nongovernmental institution in world history.

## The Development of Christian Monasticism

Christianity began and spread as a city religion. Since the first century, however, some especially pious Christians had felt that the only alternative to the decadence of urban life was complete separation from the world. This desire to withdraw from ordinary life led to the development of the monastic life. Monasticism began in third-century Egypt, where individuals like Saint Anthony (251?–356) and small groups first withdrew from cities and from organized society to seek God through prayer in desert or mountain caves and shelters, giving up all for Christ. Gradually large colonies of monks gathered in the deserts of Upper Egypt, and Christians came to believe that monks, like the early Christian martyrs executed by Roman authorities before them, could speak to God and that their prayers had special influence. These monks were called hermits, from the Greek word *eremos*, meaning "desert." Many devout women also were attracted to this eremitical (ehr-uh-MIH-tihk-uhl) type of monasticism.

In the early fourth century, the Egyptian ascetic Pachomius (puh-KOH-mee-uhs) (290–346?) drew thousands of men and women to the monastic life at Tabennisi on the Upper Nile. There were too many for them to live as hermits, so Pachomius organized communities of men and women, creating a new type of monasticism, known as cenobitic (seh-nuh-BIH-tik), that emphasized communal living. Starting in the fourth century, information about Egyptian monasticism came to the West, and both men and women sought the monastic life. Because of the dangers of living alone in the forests of northern Europe, where wild animals, harsh climate, and marauding tribes posed ongoing threats, the eremitical form of monasticism did not take root. Most of the monasticism that developed in Gaul, Italy, Spain, England, and Ireland was cenobitic.

## Monastery Life

In 529 Benedict of Nursia (480–543), who had experimented with both eremitical and communal forms of monastic life, wrote a brief set of regulations for the monks who had gathered around him at Monte Cassino between Rome and Naples. Benedict's guide for monastic life, known as *The Rule of Saint Benedict*, came to influence all forms of organized religious life in the Western Christian Church. Men and women in monastic houses all followed sets of rules, first those of Benedict and later those written by other individuals. Because of this, men who lived a communal monastic life came to be called **regular clergy**, from the Latin word *regulus* (rule). Priests and bishops who staffed churches in which people worshipped and who were not cut off from the world were called **secular clergy**.

*The Rule of Saint Benedict* outlined a monastic life of regularity, discipline, and moderation in an atmosphere of silence. Each monk had ample food and adequate sleep. The monk spent part of each day in formal prayer, which consisted of chanting psalms and other prayers from the Bible in the part of the monastery church called the choir. The rest of the day was passed in manual labor, study, and private prayer. The monastic life as conceived by Saint Benedict struck a balance between asceticism (extreme material sacrifice, including fasting and the renunciation of sex) and activity. It thus provided opportunities for men of entirely different abilities and talents—from mechanics to gardeners to literary scholars. The Benedictine form of religious life also appealed to women, because

it allowed them to show their devotion and engage in study. Benedict's twin sister Scholastica (480–543) adapted the *Rule* for use by her community of nuns.

Benedictine monasticism also succeeded partly because it was so materially successful. In the seventh and eighth centuries monasteries pushed back forests and wastelands, drained swamps, and experimented with crop rotation. Benedictine houses thus made a significant contribution to the agricultural development of Europe.

Monasteries conducted schools for local young people, and monks and nuns copied manuscripts, preserving classical as well as Christian literature. Local and royal governments drew on the services of the literate men and able administrators the monasteries produced. This was not what Saint Benedict had intended, but perhaps the effectiveness of the institution he designed made it inevitable.

## Christianity and Classical Culture

The growth of Christianity was not simply a matter of institutions such as the papacy and monasteries, but

**Saint Jerome and Saint Ambrose**   This wood carving shows Saint Jerome and Saint Ambrose, two of the most important early church fathers, hard at work writing. Divine inspiration appears in the form of an angel and a dove. (Duomo, Modena, Italy/Photo: Ghigo Roli, 1999. Franco Cosimo Panini Editore © Management Fratelli Alinari/Alinari/Art Resource, NY)

■ **regular clergy**  Men and women who lived in monastic houses and followed sets of rules, first those of Benedict and later those written by other individuals.

■ **secular clergy**  Priests and bishops who staffed churches where people worshipped and who were not cut off from the world.

also a matter of ideas. The earliest Christian thinkers sometimes rejected Greco-Roman culture, but as Christianity grew from a tiny persecuted group to the official religion of the Roman Empire, its leaders and thinkers gradually came to terms with classical culture (see "The Growing Acceptance and Evolution of Christianity" in Chapter 6). They incorporated elements of Greek and Roman philosophy and learning into Christian teachings, modifying them to fit with Christian notions.

Saint Jerome (340–419), for example, a distinguished theologian and linguist regarded as a father of the church, translated the Old and New Testaments from Hebrew and Greek into vernacular Latin. Called the Vulgate, his edition of the Bible served as the official translation until the sixteenth century, and scholars rely on it even today. Familiar with the writings of classical authors, Saint Jerome maintained that the best ancient literature should be interpreted in light of the Christian faith.

## Christian Notions of Gender and Sexuality

Early Christians both adopted and adapted the then-contemporary views of women, marriage, and sexuality. In his plan of salvation, Jesus considered women the equal of men. Women were among the earliest converts to Christianity and took an active role in its spread, preaching, acting as missionaries, being martyred alongside men, and perhaps even baptizing believers. Because early Christians believed that the Second Coming of Christ was imminent, they devoted their energies to their new spiritual family of co-believers. Women and men joyously accepted the ascetic life, renouncing marriage and procreation to use their bodies for a higher calling. Some women, either singly or in monastic communities, declared themselves "virgins in the service of Christ." All this initially made Christianity seem dangerous to many Romans, who viewed marriage as the foundation of society and the proper patriarchal order.

Not all Christian teachings about gender were radical, however. In the first century C.E. male church leaders began to place restrictions on female believers. Women were forbidden to preach and were gradually excluded from holding official positions in Christianity other than in women's monasteries. Women who chose lives of virginity in the service of God were to be praised; Saint Jerome commented that a woman "who wishes to serve Christ more than the world . . . will cease to be a woman and will be called man," the highest praise he could bestow.[3] Even such women were not to be too independent, however. Both Jewish and classical Mediterranean culture viewed women's subordination as natural and proper, so in limiting

the activities of female believers the Christian Church was following well-established patterns, just as it did in modeling its official hierarchy after that of the Roman Empire.

Christian teachings about sexuality built on and challenged classical models. The rejection of sexual activity involved an affirmation of the importance of a spiritual life, but it also incorporated the hostility toward the body found in some Hellenistic philosophies and some of the other religions that had spread in the Roman Empire in this era. Christian teachings affirmed that God had created the material world and sanctioned marriage, but most Christian thinkers also taught that celibacy was the better life, and that anything that took one's attention from the spiritual world performed an evil function. For most clerical writers (who themselves were male) this temptation came from women, and in some of their writings women themselves are depicted as evil, the "devil's gateway." Thus the writings of many church fathers contain a strong streak of misogyny (hatred of women), which was passed down to later Christian thinkers.

## Saint Augustine on Human Nature, Will, and Sin

The most influential church father in the West was Saint Augustine of Hippo (354–430). Saint Augustine was born into an urban family in what is now Algeria in North Africa. His father, a minor civil servant, was a pagan; his mother, Monica, was a devout Christian. He gained an excellent classical education in philosophy and rhetoric and, as was normal for young Roman men, began relations with a concubine, who later had his son.

Augustine took teaching positions first in Rome and then in Milan, where he had frequent conversations with Bishop Ambrose. Through his discussions with Ambrose and his own reading, Augustine became a Christian. He returned to Africa and later became bishop of the seacoast city of Hippo Regius.

Augustine's autobiography, *The Confessions*, is a literary masterpiece and one of the most influential books in the history of Europe. Written in the rhetorical style and language of late Roman antiquity, it marks the synthesis of Greco-Roman forms and Christian thought. *The Confessions* describes Augustine's moral struggle, the conflict between his spiritual and intellectual aspirations and his sensual and material self. Many Greek and Roman philosophers had taught that knowledge would lead to virtue. Augustine came to reject this idea, claiming that people do not always act on the basis of rational knowledge. As he notes in *The Confessions*, even before he became a Christian he had decided that chastity was the best possible life, so he prayed to God for "chastity and continency," yet always added "but not yet." His education had not made him strong enough

**Adam and Eve**   This illuminated page from the book of Genesis in a ninth-century Bible tells the story of Adam and Eve; the middle of the image links their disobedience to sexual shame, an aspect of the story often highlighted in visual depictions as well as sermons and written works. Commissioned by a nobleman who was also an abbot, this Bible was presented to Charles the Bald, King of the Franks, in 846. (De Agostini Picture Library/ G. Dagli Orti/Bridgeman Images)

to avoid lust or any other evil; that would come only through God's power and grace.

Augustine's ideas on sin, grace, and redemption became the foundation of all subsequent Western Christian theology, Protestant as well as Catholic. He wrote that the basic force in any individual is the will, which he defined as "the power of the soul to hold on to or to obtain an object without constraint." The end or goal of the will determines the moral character of the individual. When Adam ate the fruit forbidden by God in the Garden of Eden (Genesis 3:6), he committed the "original sin" and corrupted the will. Adam's sin was not simply his own—it was passed on to all later humans through sexual intercourse; even infants were tainted. Original sin thus became a common social stain, in Augustine's opinion, transmitted by sexual desire. By viewing sexual desire as the result of Adam and Eve's disobedience to divine instructions, Augustine linked sexuality even more clearly with sin than had earlier church fathers. Because Adam disobeyed God and fell, all human beings have an innate tendency to sin: their will is weak. But according to Augustine, God restores the strength of the will through grace, which is transmitted in certain rituals that the church defined as **sacraments**. Grace results from God's decisions, not from any merit on the part of the individual.

When Visigothic forces captured the city of Rome in 410, horrified pagans blamed the disaster on the Christians. In response, Augustine wrote *City of God*. This original work contrasts Christianity with the secular society in which it exists. According to Augustine, history is the account of God acting in time. Human history reveals that there are two kinds of people: those who live the life of the flesh, and those who live the life of the spirit in what Augustine called the City of God. The former will endure eternal hellfire; the latter will enjoy eternal bliss. Government was a necessary evil with the power to do good by providing the peace, justice, and order that Christians need to pursue their pilgrimage to the City of God.

## What were the key characteristics of barbarian society?

Augustine's *City of God* was written in response to the conquest of Rome by an army of Visigoths, one of the many peoples the Romans—and later historians—labeled "barbarians." The word *barbarian* comes from the Greek *barbaros*, meaning someone who did not speak Greek. (To the Greeks, others seemed to be speaking nonsense syllables; *barbar* is the Greek equivalent of "blah-blah" or "yada-yada.") The Romans usually used the Latin version of *barbarian*

to mean the Germanic and other peoples who lived beyond the northeastern boundary of Roman territory, whom they regarded as unruly, savage, and primitive. That value judgment is generally also present when we use *barbarian* in English, but there really is no other word to describe the many different peoples who lived to the north of the Roman Empire. Thus historians of late antiquity use the word *barbarian* to designate these peoples, who spoke a variety of languages but had similarities in their basic social, economic, and political structures. (See "Viewpoints: Roman and Byzantine Views of Barbarians," page 181.) In contrast to most

■ **sacraments**   Certain rituals defined by the church in which God bestows benefits on the believer through grace.

The earliest written records about the barbarian groups that migrated, attacked, and sometimes conquered the more urbanized and densely populated areas of Europe and western Asia all come from the pens of educated Greeks, Romans, and Byzantines. They provide us with important information about barbarians, but always from the perspective of outsiders with a particular point of view. The selections below are typical of such commentary. The first is from the fourth-century Roman general and historian Ammianus Marcellinus, who fought in Roman armies against Germanic tribes, the Huns, and the Persians, and later wrote a history of the Roman Empire. The second is from the sixth-century Byzantine historian Agathias, describing recent encounters between the forces of the Byzantine emperor Justinian and various Germanic tribes.

### Ammianus Marcellinus on the Huns, ca. 380

The people of the Huns, but little known from ancient records, dwelling beyond the Maeotic Sea near the ice-bound ocean, exceed every degree of savagery. . . . They all have compact, strong limbs and thick necks, and are so monstrously ugly and misshapen, that one might take them for two-legged beasts or for the stumps, rough-hewn into images, that are used in putting sides to bridges. But although they have the form of men, however ugly, they are so hardy in their mode of life that they have no need of fire nor of savory food, but eat the roots of wild plants and the half-raw flesh of any kind of animal whatever, which they put between their thighs and the backs of their horses, and thus warm a little. They are never protected by any buildings, but they avoid these like tombs. . . . They are not at all adapted to battles on foot, but they are almost glued to their horses, which are hardy, it is true, but ugly. . . . They fight from a distance with missiles having sharp bone [points], instead of the usual (metal) parts, joined to the shafts with wonderful skill; then they gallop over the intervening spaces and fight hand to hand with swords, regardless of their

own lives. . . . No one in their country ever plows a field or touches a plow-handle. They are all without fixed abode, without hearth, or law, or settled mode of life, and keep roaming from place to place, like fugitives, accompanied by wagons in which they live; in wagons their wives weave for them their hideous garments, in wagons they cohabit with their husbands, bear children, and rear them to the age of puberty.

### Agathias on the Franks

The Franks are not nomads, as indeed some barbarian peoples are, but their system of government, administration and laws are modelled more or less on the Roman pattern, apart from which they uphold similar standards with regard to contracts, marriage, and religious observance. They are in fact all Christians and adhere to the strictest orthodoxy. They also have magistrates in their cities and priests and celebrate the feasts in the same way we do, and, for a barbarian people, strike me as extremely well-bred and civilized and as practically the same as ourselves except for their uncouth style of dress and peculiar language. I admire them for their other attributes and especially for the spirit of justice and harmony which prevails amongst them.

### QUESTIONS FOR ANALYSIS

1. What qualities of the Huns does Ammianus Marcellinus find admirable? What does he criticize?
2. What qualities of the Franks does Agathias praise? Why does he find these qualities admirable?
3. How does the fact that both Ammianus Marcellinus and Agathias come from agricultural societies with large cities shape their views of barbarians?

Sources: *Ammianus Marcellinus: Volume I*, Loeb Classical Library Volume 300, translated by J. C. Rolfe (Cambridge, Mass.: Harvard University Press), pp. 383, 385; Agathias, *The Histories*, trans. Joseph D. Frendo (Berlin: Walter de Gruyter, 1975), p. 10.

---

ancient Romans, many historians find much to admire in barbarian society.

Scholars have been hampered in investigating barbarian society because most groups did not write and thus kept no written records before Christian missionaries introduced writing. Greek and Roman authors did describe barbarian society, but they were not always objective observers, instead using barbarians to highlight what they thought was right or wrong about their own cultures. Thus written records must be combined with archaeological evidence to gain a more accurate picture. In addition, historians are increasingly deciphering and

using the barbarians' own written records that do exist, especially inscriptions carved in stone, bone, and wood and written in the runic alphabet. Runic inscriptions come primarily from Scandinavia and the British Isles. Most are short and limited to names, such as inscriptions on tombstones.

Barbarians included many different ethnic groups with social and political structures, languages, laws, and beliefs that developed in central and northern Europe over many centuries. Among the largest groups were Celts (whom the Romans called Gauls) and Germans; Germans were further subdivided into various groups,

**Whalebone Chest** This eighth-century chest made of whalebone, depicting warriors, other human figures, and a horse, tells a story in both pictures and words. The runes along the border are one of the varieties from the British Isles. Contact with the Romans led to the increasing use of the Latin alphabet, though runes and Latin letters were used side by side in some parts of northern Europe for centuries. (Museo Nazionale del Bargello, Florence, Italy/Erich Lessing/Art Resource, NY)

such as Ostrogoths, Visigoths, Burgundians, and Franks. Celts, Germans, and other barbarians brought their customs and traditions with them when they moved southward, and these gradually combined with classical and Christian patterns to form new types of societies.

## Village and Family Life

Barbarian groups usually resided in small villages, and climate and geography determined the basic patterns of how they lived off the land. Many groups lived in small settlements on the edges of clearings, where they raised barley, wheat, oats, peas, and beans. Men and women tilled their fields with simple wooden plows and harvested their grains with small iron sickles. The vast majority of people's caloric intake came from grain in some form; the kernels of grain were eaten as porridge, ground up for flour, or fermented into strong, thick beer.

Within the villages, there were great differences in wealth and status. Free men and their families constituted the largest class. The number of cattle a man possessed indicated his wealth and determined his social status. Free men also shared in tribal warfare. Slaves acquired through warfare worked as farm laborers, herdsmen, and household servants.

Ironworking represented the most advanced craft; much of northern Europe had iron deposits, and the dense forests provided wood for charcoal, which was used to provide the clean fire needed to make iron. The typical village had an oven and smiths who produced agricultural tools and instruments of war—one-edged swords, arrowheads, and shields. By the second century C.E. the swords produced by barbarian smiths were superior to the weapons of Roman troops.

In the first two centuries C.E. the quantity and quality of material goods increased dramatically. Goods were used locally and for gift giving, a major social custom. Gift giving conferred status on the giver, whose giving showed his higher (economic) status, cemented friendship, and placed the receiver in his debt. Goods were also traded, though commercial exchange was less important than in the Roman Empire.

Families and kin groups were the basic social units in barbarian society. Families were responsible for the debts and actions of their members and for keeping the peace in general. Barbarian law codes set strict rules of inheritance based on position in the family and often set aside a portion of land that could not be sold or given away by any family member so that the family always retained some land.

Barbarian society was patriarchal: within each household the father had authority over his wife, children, and slaves. Some wealthy and powerful men had more than one wife, a pattern that continued even after they became Christian, but polygamy was not widespread among ordinary people. Women worked alongside men in the fields and forests, and the Roman historian Tacitus reported that at times they joined men on the battlefield, urging them to fight harder. Once women were widowed, they sometimes assumed their husbands' rights over family property and held the guardianship of their children.

## Tribes and Hierarchies

The basic social and political unit among barbarian groups was the tribe or confederation, a group whose members believed that they were all descended from a common ancestor and were thus kin. Tribes were led by chieftains. The chief was the member recognized as the strongest and bravest in battle and was elected from among the male members of the most powerful family. He led the group in war, settled disputes among its members, conducted negotiations with outside powers, and offered sacrifices to the gods. The period of migrations and conquests of the Western Roman Empire witnessed the strengthening of the power of chiefs, who

**Visigothic Work and Play**   This page comes from one of the very few manuscripts from late antiquity to have survived: a copy of the first five books of the Old Testament — the Pentateuch — made around 600, perhaps in Visigothic Spain or North Africa. The top shows biblical scenes, while the bottom shows people engaged in everyday activities — building a wall, drawing water from a well, and trading punches. (Bibliothèque Nationale, Paris, France/ De Agostini Picture Library/Getty Images)

often adopted the title of king, though this title implies broader power than they actually had.

Closely associated with the chief in some tribes was the **comitatus**, or war band. These warriors swore loyalty to the chief, fought with him in battle, and were not supposed to leave the battlefield without him; to do so implied cowardice, disloyalty, and social disgrace. These oaths of loyalty were later more formalized in the development of feudalism (see Chapter 8).

Although initially a social egalitarianism appears to have existed among members of the comitatus because they regarded each other as kin, during the migrations and warfare of the third and fourth centuries, the war band was transformed into a system of stratified ranks. Among the Ostrogoths, for example, a warrior nobility evolved. Contact with the Romans stimulated demand for goods such as metal armbands, which the Romans produced for trade with barbarian groups. Armbands were of different widths and value, and they became a symbol of hierarchy among warriors, much as the insignia of military rank function today. During the Ostrogothic conquest of Italy, warrior-nobles also began to

acquire land as both a mark of prestige and a means to power. As land and wealth came into the hands of a small elite class, social inequalities within the group emerged and gradually grew stronger. These inequalities help explain the origins of the European noble class.

## Customary and Written Law

Early barbarian tribes had no written laws. Law was custom, but certain individuals were often given special training in remembering and retelling laws from generation to generation. Beginning in the late fifth century, however, some chieftains and rulers began to collect, write, and publish lists of their customs and laws. (See "Thinking Like a Historian: Slavery in Roman and Germanic Society," page 184.)

The law code of the Salian Franks, one of the barbarian tribes, included a feature common to many barbarian codes. Any crime that involved a personal injury,

---

■ **comitatus**  A war band of young men in a barbarian tribe who were closely associated with the chief, swore loyalty to him, and fought with him in battle.

## Slavery in Roman and Germanic Society

Slavery continued to be a common condition in the late Roman Empire, and the Germanic tribes were also slave-owning cultures. In both societies, slavery was based not on racial distinctions, but on one's personal status as free or unfree, which was increasingly regulated by law. How could a person cross the border between slave and free in these two societies, and what larger social values do laws regarding slavery reflect?

**1** **Theodosian Code, 435–438.** Under Emperor Theodosius II (r. 408–450), imperial decrees issued since the time of Constantine that were still in effect were brought together in a single law code.

~ If a father, forced by need, shall sell any free-born child whatsoever, the child cannot remain in perpetual slavery, but if he has made compensation by his slavery, he shall be restored to his freeborn status without the repayment of the purchase price. . . . It is established that children born from the womb of a slave woman are slaves, according to the law. . . . We have subjected the Scyrae, a barbarian nation, to Our power. Therefore We grant to all persons the opportunity to supply their own fields with men of the aforesaid race. . . . If any person should take up a boy or girl child that has been cast out of its home with the knowledge and consent of its father or owner, and if he should rear this child to strength with his own sustenance, he shall have the right to keep the said child under the same status as he wished it to have when he took charge of it, that is, as his child or as a slave, whichever he should prefer. . . . We exhort slaves, that as soon as possible they shall offer themselves for the labors of war, and if they receive their arms as men fit for military service, they shall obtain the reward of freedom. . . . [In the case of deserters] if the slave should surrender such a deserter, he shall be given his freedom.

**2** **Roman tombstone.** The tombstone at right shows a man reclining on a couch, being served a drink by a small slave boy. The inscription identifies the man as a twenty-year-old soldier and freed slave, and it gives his name simply as Victor, with no family name or patronymic.

**3** **Justinian's Code, 529–534.** The law code of Emperor Justinian includes many provisions regarding slaves.

~ Liberty is the natural power of doing whatever anyone wishes to do unless he is prevented in some way, by force or by law. Slavery is an institution of the Law of Nations by means of which anyone may subject one man to the control of another, contrary to nature. Slaves are so called for the reason that military commanders were accustomed to sell their captives, and in this manner to preserve them, instead of putting them to death. . . . Slaves are brought under our ownership either by

(Arbeia Roman Fort & Museum, © Tyne & Wear Archives & Museums, South Shields, UK/Bridgeman Images)

### ANALYZING THE EVIDENCE

1. According to the Roman laws (Sources 1 and 3), how could a person become a slave in Roman society? According to the Germanic laws (Sources 4–6), how could this happen in Germanic society? Which of these methods established more permanent conditions of servitude?
2. How could a slave become free in Roman society? In Germanic?
3. How did the man in the tombstone (Source 2) obtain his freedom?
4. According to Justinian's Code (Source 3), is slavery natural? What types of laws establish it, and how do these laws reflect Roman notions of law?
5. In Germanic society, the kin group was responsible for the actions of its members. How do the laws in Sources 4–6 reflect this principle? From Sources 1–3 and your reading in this and earlier chapters, how did family and kin shape slavery in Roman society?

the Civil Law or by that of Nations. This is done by the Civil Law where anyone who is over twenty years of age permits himself to be sold for the sake of sharing in his own price [that is, for debt]. Slaves become our property by the Law of Nations when they are either taken from the enemy, or are born of our female slaves. . . . Where a fugitive slave betakes himself to the arena [as a gladiator], he cannot escape the power of his master by exposing himself to this danger, which is only that of the risk of death; such a slave must, by all means, be restored to his master, either before or after the combat with wild beasts.

## 4 The Burgundian Code, ca. 500. King Gundobad (r. 474–516), who ruled the Burgundian kingdom in what is now southeastern France, drew up one of the earliest Germanic law codes for his subjects.

~ If anyone shall buy another's slave from the Franks [with whom the Burgundians were at war], let him prove with suitable witnesses how much and what sort of price he paid and when the witnesses have been sworn in, they shall make oath in the following manner, "We saw him pay the price in our presence, and he who purchased the slave did not do so through any fraud or connivance with the enemy." . . . If anyone wishes to manumit a slave, he may do so by giving him his liberty through a legally competent document; or if anyone wishes to give freedom to a bondservant without a written document, let the manumission thus be conferred with the witness of not less than five or seven native freemen.

## 5 Lombard laws, 643–735. The Lombards invaded Italy in 568, conquered Germanic tribes that were already there, and established a kingdom that lasted until 774. Various Lombard kings issued laws on many topics.

~ In the case of a natural son who is born to another man's woman slave, if the father purchases him and gives him his freedom by the formal procedure he shall remain free. But if the father does not free him, the natural son shall be a slave to him to whom the mother slave belongs. . . . He who renders false testimony against anyone else, or sets his hand knowingly to a false charter, and this fraud becomes evident, shall pay restitution, half to the king and half to him whose case it is. If the guilty party does not have enough to pay restitution, a public official ought to hand him over as a slave to him who was injured, and he [the offender] shall serve him as a slave. . . . If a man who is prodigal and ruined, or who has sold or dissipated his substance, or for other reasons does not have that with which to pay restitution, commits theft or adultery or a breach of the peace, or injures another man and the restitution for this is twenty solidi or more, then a public representative ought to hand him over as a slave to the man who committed such illegal acts. . . . If a freeman has a man and woman slave, or freedman and freedwoman, who are married, and inspired by hatred of the human race, he has intercourse with that woman whose husband is the slave or with the freedwoman whose husband is the freedman, he has committed adultery and we decree that he shall lose that slave or freedman with whose wife he committed adultery and the woman as well, for it is not pleasing to God that any man should have intercourse with the wife of another.

## 6 Laws of the Anglo-Saxon kings, early tenth century. The Anglo-Saxon rulers in England issued law codes; this law is from the code of Edward the Elder (r. 899–925), king of Wessex and Mercia.

~ If a man, through [being found guilty of] an accusation of stealing, forfeits his freedom and gives up his person to his lord, and his kinsmen forsake him, and he knows no one who will make legal amends for him, he shall do such servile labour as may be required and his kinsmen shall have no right to his wergeld [if he is slain].

## PUTTING IT ALL TOGETHER

Using the sources above, along with what you have learned in class and in Chapters 5, 6, and 7, write a short essay that analyzes ways in which the boundary between slave and free was established, protected, and traversed in Roman and Germanic society. How could a person cross the border between slave and free in these two societies, and what larger social values do laws regarding slavery reflect? How did the laws regarding slavery differ in Roman and Germanic society, and how were they similar?

Sources: (1) Clyde Pharr, ed., *The Theodosian Code* (Princeton, N.J.: Princeton University Press, 1952), 3.3.1, 5.6.3, 5.9.1, 7.13.16, 7.18.4; (3) S. P. Scott, trans., *The Civil Law* (Cincinnati: The Central Trust Company, 1932), vol. 2, p. 228; vol. 4, p. 82; (4) Katherine Fischer Drew, trans., *The Burgundian Code* (Philadelphia: University of Pennsylvania Press, 1972), Constitutiones Extravagantes 21.9; (5) Katherine Fischer Drew, trans., *The Lombard Laws* (Philadelphia: University of Pennsylvania Press, 1973), Rothair 156, Luitprand 63, Luitprand 140, Luitprand 152; (6) F. L. Attenborough, *Laws of the Earliest English Kings* (Cambridge: Cambridge University Press, 1922), Laws of Edward the Elder 6.

such as assault, rape, and murder, was given a particular monetary value, called the **wergeld** (WUHR-gehld) (literally "man-money" or "money to buy off the spear"), that was to be paid by the perpetrator to the victim or the family. The Salic law lists many of these:

> If any person strike another on the head so that the brain appears, and the three bones which lie above the brain shall project, he shall be sentenced to 1200 denars, which make 300 shillings. . . .
>
> If any one have killed a free woman after she has begun bearing children, he shall be sentenced to 2400 denars, which make 600 shillings.[4]

The wergeld varied according to the severity of the crime and also the social status of the victim. The fine for the murder of a woman of childbearing years was the same value as that attached to military officers of the king, to priests, and to boys preparing to become warriors, which suggests the importance of women in Frankish society, at least for their childbearing capacity.

The wergeld system aimed to prevent or reduce violence. If a person accused of a crime agreed to pay the wergeld and if the victim and his or her family accepted the payment, there was peace. If the accused refused to pay the wergeld or if the victim's family refused to accept it, a blood feud ensued.

At first, Romans had been subject to Roman law and barbarians to barbarian custom. As barbarian kings accepted Christianity and as Romans and barbarians increasingly intermarried and assimilated culturally, the distinction between the two sets of law blurred and, in the course of the seventh and eighth centuries,

disappeared. The result would be the new feudal law, to which all who lived in certain areas were subject.

## Celtic and Germanic Religion

Like Greeks and Romans, barbarians worshipped hundreds of gods and goddesses with specialized functions. They regarded certain mountains, lakes, rivers, or groves of trees as sacred because these were linked to deities. Rituals to honor the gods were held outdoors rather than in temples or churches, often at certain points in the yearly agricultural cycle. Presided over by a priest or priestess understood to have special abilities to call on the gods' powers, rituals sometimes involved animal (and perhaps human) sacrifice. Among the Celts, religious leaders called druids (DROO-ihds) had legal and educational as well as religious functions, orally passing down laws and traditions from generation to generation. Bards singing poems and ballads also passed down myths and stories of heroes and gods, which were written down much later.

The first written records of barbarian religion came from Greeks and Romans who encountered barbarians or spoke with those who had. They understood barbarian traditions through their own belief systems, often equating barbarian gods with Greco-Roman ones and adapting stories and rituals to blend the two. This assimilation appears to have gone both ways, at least judging by the names of the days of the week. In the Roman Empire the days took their names from Roman deities or astronomical bodies, and in the Germanic languages of central and northern Europe the days acquired the names of corresponding barbarian gods. Jupiter's day, for example, became Thor's day (Thursday); both of these powerful gods were associated with thunder.

**Celtic Brooch**   This magnificent silver and gold brooch, used to hold a heavy wool cape in place, is adorned with red garnets and complex patterns of interlace. Made in Ireland, the brooch has patterns similar to those found in Irish manuscripts from this era. (National Museum of Ireland, Dublin, Ireland/Photo © Boltin Picture Library/Bridgeman Images)

# How did the barbarian migrations shape Europe?

Migrating groups that the Romans labeled barbarians had moved southward and eastward off and on since about 100 B.C.E. (see Chapters 5 and 6). As their movements became more organized in the third and fourth centuries C.E., Roman armies sought to defend the Rhine-Danube border of the Roman Empire, but with troop levels low because Italians were increasingly unwilling to serve in the army, generals were forced to recruit barbarians to fill the ranks. By the fourth century barbarians made up the majority of those fighting both for and against Rome, and they climbed higher and higher in the ranks of the Roman military, often intermarrying with Roman families. Toward the end of the fifth century this barbarian assumption of authority stretched all the way to the top, and the last person with the title of emperor in the Western Roman Empire was deposed by a Gothic general.

Why did the barbarians migrate? In part they were searching for more regular supplies of food, better farmland, and a warmer climate. In part they were pushed by groups living farther eastward, especially by the Huns from Central Asia in the fourth and fifth centuries. Conflicts within and among barbarian groups also led to war and disruption, which motivated groups to move (Map 7.3).

## Celtic and Germanic People in Gaul and Britain

The Celts present a good example of both assimilation and conflict. Celtic peoples conquered by the Romans often assimilated Roman ways, adapting the Latin language and other aspects of Roman culture. In Roman Gaul and then in Roman Britain, towns were planned in the Roman fashion, with temples, public baths, theaters, and amphitheaters. In the countryside large manors controlled the surrounding lands. Roman merchants brought Eastern luxury goods and Eastern religions—including Christianity. The Romans suppressed the Celtic chieftains, and a military aristocracy made up of Romans—some of whom intermarried with Celtic families—governed. In the course of the second and third centuries, many Celts became Roman citizens and joined the Roman army. Celtic culture survived only in areas beyond the borders of the empire. (The modern Welsh, Bretons, Scots, and Irish are all peoples of Celtic descent.)

By the fourth century C.E. Gaul and Britain were under pressure from Germanic groups moving westward, and Rome itself was threatened (see Map 7.3). Imperial troops withdrew from Britain in order to defend Rome, and the Picts from Scotland and the Scots from Ireland (both Celtic-speaking peoples) invaded territory held by

the Britons. According to the eighth-century historian Bede (BEED), the Briton king Vortigern invited the Saxons from Denmark to help him against his rivals. However, Saxons and other Germanic tribes from the area of modern-day Norway, Sweden, and Denmark turned from assistance to conquest. Their goal was plunder, and at first their invasions led to no permanent settlements. As more Germanic peoples arrived, however, they took over the best lands and eventually conquered most of Britain. Historians have labeled the years 500 to 1066 (the year of the Norman Conquest) the Anglo-Saxon period of English history, after the two largest Germanic groups in England, the Angles and the Saxons.

Anglo-Saxon England was divided along ethnic and political lines. The Germanic kingdoms in the south, east, and center were opposed by the Britons in the

**Anglo-Saxon Helmet** This ceremonial bronze helmet from seventh-century England was found inside a ship buried at Sutton Hoo. The nearly 100-foot-long ship was dragged overland before being buried completely. It held one body and many grave goods, including swords, gold buckles, and silver bowls made in Byzantium. The unidentified person who was buried here was clearly wealthy and powerful. (© The Trustees of the British Museum/Art Resource, NY)

■ **wergeld** Compensatory payment for death or injury set in many barbarian law codes.

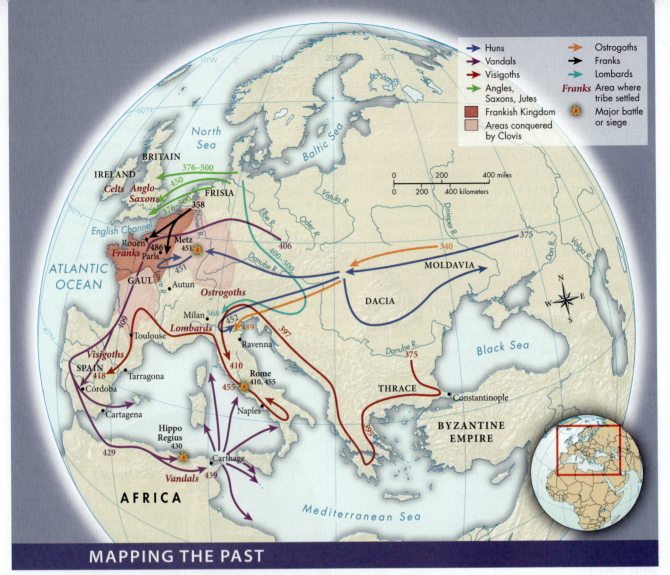

## MAPPING THE PAST

## MAP 7.3 The Barbarian Migrations, ca. 340–500

This map shows the migrations of various barbarian groups in late antiquity and can be used
to answer the following questions.

**ANALYZING THE MAP** The movements of barbarian peoples used to be labeled "invasions"
and are now usually described as "migrations." How do the dates on the map support
the newer understanding of these movements?

**CONNECTIONS** Human migration is caused by a combination of push factors—circumstances
that lead people to leave a place—and pull factors—things that attract people to a new
location. Based on the information in this and earlier chapters, what push and pull factors
might have shaped the migration patterns you see on the map?

west, who wanted to get rid of the invaders. The Anglo-
Saxon kingdoms also fought among themselves, causing boundaries to shift constantly. In the ninth century,
under pressure from the Viking invasions, King Alfred
of Wessex (r. 871–899) created a more unified state with
a reorganized army and system of fortresses for defense.

The Anglo-Saxon invasion gave rise to a rich body
of Celtic mythology, particularly legends about King
Arthur, who first appeared in Welsh poetry in the sixth
century and later in histories, epics, and saints' lives.
Most scholars see Arthur as a composite figure that
evolved over the centuries in songs and stories. In their
earliest form as Welsh poems, the Arthurian legends may

represent Celtic hostility to Anglo-Saxon invaders, but
they later came to be more important as representations
of the ideal of medieval knightly chivalry and as compelling stories whose retelling has continued to the present.

## Visigoths and Huns

On the European continent, the Germanic peoples
included a number of groups with very different cultural
traditions. The largest Germanic group was the Goths,
who were further subdivided by scholars into Ostrogoths (eastern Goths) and Visigoths (western Goths)
based on their migration patterns. Both of these groups

# Battle Between Romans and Goths

Rome's wars with the Germanic-speaking groups along its northern border come to life in this relief from a Roman sarcophagus of the third century c.e., discovered in a tomb in the city of Rome. The Romans are wearing helmets, and the soldier at the right is wearing iron or bronze chain mail, a defensive technology that the Romans adapted from the Celts.

(Terme Museum, Rome, Italy/Bridgeman Images)

## EVALUATE THE EVIDENCE

1. How would you describe this depiction of war? How does the artist show Roman superiority over the barbarians through the placement, dress, and facial features of the soldiers?
2. How does this funeral sculpture reinforce or challenge what you have learned about Roman expansion and the Romans' treatment of the peoples they conquered?

played important roles in the political developments of late antiquity. Pressured by defeat in battle, starvation, and the movement of other groups, the Visigoths moved westward from their homeland north of the Black Sea, and in 376 they petitioned the Roman emperor Valens to admit them to the empire. They offered to fight for Rome in exchange for the province of Thrace in what is now Greece and Bulgaria. Seeing in the hordes of warriors the solution to his manpower problem, Valens agreed. However, the deal fell apart when crop failures led to famine and Roman authorities exploited the Visigoths' hunger by forcing them to sell their own people as slaves. The Visigoths revolted, joined with other barbarian enemies of Rome, and defeated the Roman army at the Battle of Adrianople in 378, killing Valens and thousands of Roman soldiers in the process. This left a large barbarian army within the borders of the Roman Empire, and not that far from Constantinople.

Valens's successor made peace with the Visigoths, but relations worsened as the Visigoths continued migrating westward (see Map 7.3). The Visigothic king Alaric I, who had also been a general in one of the Roman armies in the east, invaded Italy and sacked Rome in 410. The Visigoths burned and looted the city for three days. (See "Evaluating Visual Evidence: Battle Between Romans and Goths," above.) Seeking to stabilize the situation at home, the imperial government pulled its troops from the British Isles and many areas north of the Alps, leaving these northern areas vulnerable to other migrating groups. A year later Alaric died, and his successor led his people into southwestern Gaul, where they established the Visigothic kingdom.

One significant factor in the migration of the Visigoths and other Germanic peoples was pressure from nomadic steppe peoples from Central Asia. They included the Alans, Avars, Bulgars, Khazars, and most prominently the Huns, who attacked the Black Sea area and the Byzantine Empire beginning in the fourth century.

Under the leadership of their warrior-king Attila, the Huns attacked the Byzantine Empire in 447 and then turned westward. Several Germanic groups allied with them, as did the sister of the Roman emperor, who hoped to take over power from her brother. Their troops combined with those of the Huns, and a huge army took the city of Metz, now in eastern France. A combined army of Romans and Visigoths stopped the advance of the Huns at Châlons, and they retreated. The following year they moved into the Western Roman Empire again, crossing the Alps into Italy, and a papal delegation, including Pope Leo I himself, asked Attila not to attack Rome. Though papal diplomacy was later credited with stopping the advance of the Huns, their dwindling food supplies and a plague that spread among their troops were probably much more important. The Huns retreated from Italy, and within a year Attila was dead. Later leaders were not as effective, and the Huns were never again an important factor in European history. Their conquests had pushed many Germanic groups together, however, transforming smaller bands into larger, more unified peoples who could more easily pick the Roman Empire apart.

## Germanic Kingdoms and the End of the Roman Empire

After they conquered an area, barbarians generally established states ruled by kings. The kingdoms did not have definite geographical borders, however, and their locations shifted as tribes moved. In the fifth century the Burgundians ruled over lands roughly circumscribed by the old Roman army camps in what is now central France and western Switzerland. The Visigoths exercised a weak domination over southern France and much of the Iberian Peninsula (modern Spain) until a Muslim victory in 711 ended Visigothic rule (see Chapter 8). The Vandals, another Germanic tribe whose destructive ways are commemorated in the word *vandal*, swept across Spain into North Africa in 429 and took over what had been Rome's breadbasket. In 439 they established a kingdom that included Sicily and Sardinia, and which lasted about a century, and in 455 they even sacked the city of Rome itself.

Barbarian states eventually came to include Italy itself. The Western Roman emperors were generally chosen by the more powerful successors of Constantine in the East, and they increasingly relied on barbarian commanders and their troops to maintain order. In the 470s a series of these commanders took over authority in name as well as in reality, deposing several Roman emperors. In 476 the barbarian chieftain Odoacer (OH-duh-way-suhr) deposed Romulus Augustus, the last person to have the title of Roman emperor in the West. Odoacer did not take on the title of emperor, calling himself instead the king of Italy, so this date marks the official end of the Roman Empire in the West. Emperor Zeno, the Roman emperor in the East ruling from Constantinople, worried about Odoacer's growing power and promised Theoderic (r. 471–526), the leader of the Ostrogoths who had recently settled in the Balkans, the right to rule Italy if

he defeated Odoacer. Theoderic's forces were successful, and in 493 Theoderic established an Ostrogothic state in Italy, with his capital at Ravenna.

For centuries, the end of the Roman Empire in the West was seen as a major turning point in history, the fall of the sophisticated and educated classical world to uncouth and illiterate tribes. This view was further promoted by the English historian and member of Parliament Edward Gibbon, whose six-volume *The History of the Decline and Fall of the Roman Empire*, published in 1776–1788, was required reading for university students well into the twentieth century. Over the last several decades, however, many historians have put greater stress on continuities. Not only did Rome itself last for a very long time, first as a republic and then an empire, but the Ostrogoths, for example, maintained many Roman ways. Old Roman families continued to run the law courts and the city governments, and well-educated Italians continued to study the Greek classics. Theoderic's adviser Boethius (ca. 480–524) translated Aristotle's works on logic from Greek into Latin. While imprisoned after falling out of royal favor, Boethius wrote *The Consolation of Philosophy*, which argued that philosophical inquiry was valuable for understanding God. This became one of the most widely read books in the Middle Ages, though its popularity did not prevent Boethius from being executed for treason.

In other barbarian states, aspects of classical culture also continued. Barbarian kings relied on officials trained in Roman law, and Latin remained the language of scholarly communication. Greco-Roman art and architecture still adorned the land, and people continued to use Roman roads, aqueducts, and buildings. The Christian Church in barbarian states modeled its organization on that of Rome, and many bishops were from upper-class families that had governed the empire.

Very recently some historians and archaeologists have returned to an emphasis on change. They note that people may have traveled on Roman roads, but the roads were rarely maintained, and travel itself was much less secure than during the Roman Empire. Merchants no longer traded over long distances, so people's access to goods produced outside their local area plummeted. Knowledge about technological processes such as the making of glass and roof tiles declined or disappeared. There was intermarriage and cultural assimilation among Romans and barbarians, but there was also violence and great physical destruction.

The kingdom established by the Franks is a good example of this combination of peaceful assimilation and violent conflict. The Franks were a confederation of Germanic peoples who originated in the marshy lowlands north and east of the northernmost part of the Roman Empire (see Map 7.3). In the fourth and fifth centuries they settled within the empire and allied with the Romans, some attaining high military and civil positions. The Franks believed that Merovech, a man of supernatural origins, founded their ruling dynasty, which was thus called Merovingian (mehr-uh-VIHN-jee-uhn).

The reign of Clovis (KLOH-vis) (r. ca. 481–511) marks the decisive period in the development of the Franks as a unified people. Through military campaigns, Clovis acquired the central provinces of Roman Gaul and began to conquer southern Gaul from the Burgundians and Visigoths. Clovis's conversion to Roman Christianity brought him the crucial support of the bishops of Gaul in his campaigns against tribes that were still pagan or had accepted the Arian version of Christianity. Along with brutal violence, however, the next two centuries witnessed the steady assimilation of Franks and Romans, as many Franks adopted the Latin language and Roman ways, and Romans copied Frankish customs and Frankish personal names.

From Constantinople, Eastern Roman emperors worked to hold the empire together and to reconquer at least some of the West from barbarian tribes. The emperor Justinian (r. 527–565) waged long and hard-fought wars against the Ostrogoths and temporarily regained Italy and North Africa, but his conquests had disastrous consequences. Justinian's wars exhausted the resources of the state, destroyed Italy's economy, and killed a large part of Italy's population. The wars also paved the way for the easy conquest of Italy by another Germanic tribe, the Lombards, shortly after Justinian's death. In the late sixth century the territory of the Western Roman Empire came under barbarian sway once again.

# How did the church convert barbarian peoples to Christianity?

The Mediterranean served as the highway over which Christianity spread to the cities of the Roman Empire. Christian teachings were initially carried by all types of converts, but they were often spread into the countryside and into areas beyond the borders of the empire by those who had dedicated their lives to the church, such as monks. Such missionaries were often sent by popes specifically to convert certain groups, developing new techniques to do so.

Throughout barbarian Europe, religion was not a private or individual matter; it was a social affair, and the religion of the chieftain or king determined the religion of the people. Thus missionaries concentrated their initial efforts not on ordinary people, but on kings or tribal chieftains and the members of their families, who then ordered their subjects to convert. Because they had more opportunity to spend time with missionaries, queens and other female members of the royal family were often the first converts in an area, and they influenced their husbands and brothers. Germanic kings sometimes accepted Christianity because they came to believe that the Christian God was more powerful than pagan gods and that the Christian God—in either its Arian or Roman version—would deliver victory in battle. They also appreciated that Christianity taught obedience to kingly as well as divine authority. Christian missionaries were generally literate, and they taught reading and writing to young men who became priests or officials in the royal household, a service that kings appreciated.

## Missionaries' Actions

During the Roman occupation, small Christian communities were scattered throughout Gaul and Britain. The leaders of some of these, such as Bishop Martin of Tours (ca. 316–397), who founded a monastery and established a rudimentary parish system in his diocese, supported Nicene Christianity (see "The Acceptance of Christianity"). Other missionaries were Arian Christians, who also founded dioceses and converted many barbarian groups. Bishop Ulfilas (ca. 310–383), for example, an Ostrogoth himself, translated the Bible from the Greek in which it was normally written into the Gothic language, creating a new Gothic script in order to write it down. The Ostrogoths, Visigoths, Lombards, and Vandals were all originally Arian Christians, though over the sixth and seventh centuries most of them converted to Roman Christianity, sometimes peacefully and sometimes as a result of conquest.

Tradition identifies the conversion of Ireland with Saint Patrick (ca. 385–461). Born in England to a Christian family of Roman citizenship, Patrick was captured and enslaved by Irish raiders and taken to Ireland, where he worked as a herdsman for six years. He escaped and returned to England, where a vision urged him to Christianize Ireland. In preparation, Patrick studied in Gaul and was consecrated a bishop in 432. He returned to Ireland, where he converted the Irish tribe by tribe, first baptizing the chief of each tribe. By the time of Patrick's death, the majority of the Irish people had received Christian baptism.

In his missionary work, Patrick had the strong support of Bridget of Kildare (ca. 450–528), daughter of a wealthy chieftain. Bridget defied parental pressure to marry and became a nun. She and the other nuns at Kildare instructed relatives and friends in basic Christian doctrine, made religious vestments (clothing) for churches, copied books, taught children, and above all set a religious example by their lives of prayer. In this way, in Ireland and later in the European continent, women like the nuns at Kildare shared in the process of conversion.

The Christianization of the English began in earnest in 597, when Pope Gregory I sent a delegation of monks under the Roman Augustine to Britain.

**Saint John's Crucifixion Plaque**
One of the earliest depictions of the crucifixion in Irish art, this gilt and bronze plaque from the late seventh or early eighth century shows Christ flanked by two Roman soldiers while angels hover overhead, with the figures decorated with swirls and interlace. Made by hammering a bronze sheet from behind, the plaque might have originally been on a book cover, wooden cross, or panel in a shrine. (National Museum of Ireland, Dublin, Ireland/ Photo © Boltin Picture Library/Bridgeman Images)

Augustine's approach, like Patrick's, was to concentrate on converting those who held power. When he succeeded in converting Ethelbert, king of Kent, the baptism of Ethelbert's people took place as a matter of course. Augustine established his headquarters, or *see*, at Canterbury, the capital of Kent in southern England.

In the course of the seventh century, two Christian forces competed for the conversion of the pagan Anglo-Saxons: Roman-oriented missionaries traveling north from Canterbury, and Celtic monks from Ireland and northwestern Britain. The Roman and Celtic church organizations, types of monastic life, and methods of arriving at the date of the central feast of the Christian calendar, Easter, differed completely. Through the influence of King Oswiu of Northumbria and the dynamic abbess Hilda of Whitby, the Synod (ecclesiastical council) held at Hilda's convent of Whitby in 664 opted to follow the Roman practices. The conversion of the English and the close attachment of the English Church to Rome had far-reaching consequences because Britain later served as a base for the Christianization of the continent of Europe (see Map 7.2), spreading Roman Christian teachings among both pagans and Arians.

## The Process of Conversion

When a ruler marched his people to the waters of baptism, the work of Christianization had only begun. Christian kings could order their subjects to be baptized, married, and buried in Christian ceremonies, and people complied increasingly across Europe. Churches could be built, and people could be required to attend services and belong to parishes, but the process of conversion was a gradual one.

How did missionaries and priests get masses of pagan and illiterate peoples to understand Christian ideals and teachings? They did so through preaching, assimilation, the ritual of penance, and the veneration of saints. Missionaries preached the basic teachings of Christianity in simplified Latin or translated them into the local language. In monasteries and cathedrals, men—and a few women—wrote hymns, prayers, and stories about the lives of Christ and the saints. People heard these and slowly became familiar with Christian notions.

Deeply ingrained pagan customs and practices could not be stamped out by words alone, however, or even by royal edicts. Christian missionaries often pursued a policy of assimilation, easing the conversion of pagan men and women by stressing similarities between their customs and beliefs and those of Christianity. In the same way that classically trained scholars such as Jerome and Augustine blended Greco-Roman and Christian ideas, missionaries and converts mixed pagan ideas and practices with Christian ones. Bogs and lakes sacred to Germanic gods became associated with saints, as did various aspects of ordinary life, such as traveling, planting crops, and worrying about a sick child. Aspects of existing midwinter celebrations, which often centered on the return of the sun as the days became longer, were incorporated into celebrations of Christmas. Spring rituals involving eggs and rabbits (both symbols of fertility) were added to Easter.

The ritual of penance was also instrumental in teaching people Christian ideas. Christianity taught that certain actions and thoughts were sins, meaning that they were against God's commands. Only by confessing these sins and asking forgiveness could a sinning believer be reconciled with God. Confession was initially a public ritual, but by the fifth century individual confession to a parish priest was more common. The person knelt before the priest, who questioned him or her about sins he or she might have committed. The priest then set a penance such as fasting or saying specific prayers to allow the person to atone for the sin. The priest and penitent were guided by manuals known as penitentials (peh-nuh-TEHN-shuhlz), which included lists of sins and the appropriate penance. The seventh-century English penitential of Theodore, for example, stipulated that "if a lay Christian vomits because of drunkenness, he shall do penance for fifteen days," while drunken monks were to do penance for thirty days. Those who "commit

# Gregory of Tours on the Veneration of Relics

Accounts of the miracles associated with the relics of saints were an important part of Christian preaching and writing, designed to win converts and strengthen their faith. Gregory of Tours (ca. 539–594), a highly educated bishop and historian from a wealthy Gallo-Roman family, described events surrounding relics in *Glory of the Martyrs*, a book of miracle stories about saints and martyrs.

∾

The cross of the Lord that was found by the empress Helena [Constantine's mother] at Jerusalem is venerated on Wednesday and Friday. Queen Radegund [a Merovingian Frankish queen], who is comparable to Helena in both merit and faith, requested relics of this cross and piously placed them in a convent at Poitiers that she founded out of her own zeal. . . .

A girl named Chrodigildis was punished by the loss of her eyesight . . . [and] she entered the rule of the afore-mentioned convent. With the most blessed Radegund as a guide, she bowed before the holy reliquary and there kept vigils with the other nuns. . . . In a vision it seemed to her as if someone had opened her eyes. One eye was restored to health; while she was still concerned about the other, suddenly she was awakened by the sound of a door being unlocked and regained the sight of one eye. There is no doubt that this was accomplished by the power of the cross. The possessed, the lame, and also other ill people are often cured at this place. . . .

Because he [Gregory's father] wished himself to be protected by relics of saints, he asked a cleric to grant him something from these relics, so that with their protection he might be kept safe as he set out on a long journey. He put the sacred ashes in a gold medallion and carried it with him. Although he did not even know the names of the

blessed men, he was accustomed to recount that he had been rescued from many dangers. He claimed that often, because of the powers of these relics, he had avoided the violence of bandits, the dangers of floods, the threats of turbulent men, and attacks from swords.

I will not be silent about what I witnessed regarding these relics. After the death of my father my mother carried these relics with her. It was the time for harvesting the crops, and huge piles of grain had been collected on the threshing floors. . . . The threshers kindled fires for themselves from the straw. . . . Quickly, fanned by the wind, the fire spread to the piles of grain. The fire became a huge blaze and was accompanied by the shouts of men, the wails of women, and the crying of children. This happened in our field. When my mother, who was wearing these relics around her neck, learned of this, she rushed from the meal and held the sacred relics in front of the balls of flames. In a moment the entire fire so died down that no sparks were found among the piles of burned straw and the seeds. The grain the fire had touched had suffered no harm.

## EVALUATE THE EVIDENCE

1. How do stories such as these about the veneration of relics link Christian beliefs with local and personal issues? Why would this have been important in the expansion of Christianity?

2. Gregory's father and mother were both from prominent upper-class families, and both received a good education. Why might Gregory have told stories such as these rather than ones about their learning as he sought to enhance people's commitment to the church?

Source: Gregory of Tours, *Glory of the Martyrs*, trans. Raymond Van Dam (Liverpool: Liverpool University, 1988), pp. 22, 107–108. Reproduced with permission of the Licensor through PLSclear.

---

fornication with a virgin" were to do penance for a year, as were those who perform "divinations according to the custom of the heathens."[5] Penance gave new Christians a sense of expected behavior and encouraged them to reflect on their actions, thoughts, and desires.

Most religious observances continued to be community matters, as they had been in the ancient world. People joined with family members, friends, and neighbors at their parish church to attend baptisms, weddings, and funerals presided over by a priest. The parish church often housed the **relics** of a saint, that is, bones, articles of clothing, or other objects associated with a person who had lived (or died) in a way that was spiritually heroic or noteworthy. This patron saint was understood to provide protection and assistance for those who came to worship, and the relics

served as a link between the material world and the spiritual one. (See "Evaluating Written Evidence: Gregory of Tours on the Veneration of Relics," above.)

Christians came to venerate the saints as powerful and holy. They prayed to saints or to the Virgin Mary to intercede with God, or they simply asked the saints to assist and bless them. The entire village participated in processions marking saints' days or points in the agricultural year, often carrying images of saints or their relics around the houses and fields. The decision to become Christian was often made first by an emperor or king, but actual conversion was a local matter, as people came to feel that the parish priest and the patron saint provided them with benefits in this world and the world to come.

■ **relics** Bones, articles of clothing, or other objects associated with the life of a saint.

# How did the Byzantine Empire preserve the legacy of Rome?

Barbarian migrations and Christian conversions occurred throughout all of Europe in late antiquity, but their impact was not the same in the western and eastern halves of the Roman Empire. The Western Roman Empire gradually disintegrated, but the Roman Empire continued in the East (Map 7.4). The Byzantine or Eastern Roman Empire preserved the forms, institutions, and traditions of the old Roman Empire, and its people even called themselves Romans. Byzantine emperors traced their lines back past Constantine to Augustus, and the Senate in Constantinople carried on the traditions of the old Roman Senate. Most important, however, is how Byzantium protected the intellectual heritage of Greco-Roman civilization and then passed it on to the rest of Europe.

## Sources of Byzantine Strength

While the western parts of the Roman Empire gradually succumbed to barbarian invaders, the Byzantine Empire survived attacks by Huns, Germans, Avars, Persians, and Arabs. Why didn't one or a combination of these enemies capture Constantinople as the Ostrogoths had taken Rome? The answer lies in strong military leadership and even more in the city's location and its excellent fortifications. Justinian's generals were able to reconquer much of Italy and North Africa from barbarian groups, making them part of the Eastern Roman Empire, and later generals defeated the Avars and Persians. Massive triple walls, built by the emperors Constantine and Theodosius II (r. 408–450) and kept in good repair, protected

Constantinople from sea invasion. Within the walls huge cisterns provided water, and vast gardens and grazing areas supplied vegetables and meat, so the defending people could hold out far longer than the besieging army. Attacking Constantinople by land posed greater geographical and logistical problems than a seventh- or eighth-century government could solve. The site was not absolutely impregnable, but it was almost so. For centuries the Byzantine Empire served as a bulwark for the West, protecting it against invasions from the East.

## The Law Code of Justinian

One of the most splendid achievements of the Byzantine emperors was the preservation of Roman law for the medieval and modern worlds. Roman law had developed from many sources — decisions by judges, edicts of the emperors, legislation passed by the Senate, and the opinions of jurists. By the fourth century it had become a huge, bewildering mass, and its sheer bulk made it almost unusable.

Sweeping and systematic codification took place under the emperor Justinian. He appointed a committee of eminent jurists to sort through and organize the laws. The result was the *Corpus Juris Civilis* (KAWR-puhs JOOR-uhs sih-VIH-luhs) (Body of civil law), a multipart collection of laws and legal commentary issued from 529 to 534, and often called simply the **Code of Justinian**. The first part of this work, the *Codex*, brought together all the existing imperial laws into a coherent whole, eliminated outmoded laws and contradictions, and clarified the law

**MAP 7.4  The Byzantine Empire, ca. 600**    The strategic position of Constantinople on the waterway between the Black Sea and the Mediterranean was clear to Constantine when he chose the city as the capital of the Eastern Roman Empire. Byzantine territories in Italy were acquired in Emperor Justinian's sixth-century wars and were held for several centuries.

**Greek Fire**   In this illustration from a twelfth-century manuscript, sailors shoot Greek fire toward an attacking ship from a pressurized tube that looks strikingly similar to a modern flamethrower. The exact formula for Greek fire has been lost, but it was probably made from a petroleum product because it continued burning on water. Greek fire was particularly important in Byzantine defenses of Constantinople from Muslim forces in the late seventh century. (Prado, Madrid, Spain/Bridgeman Images)

itself. It began with laws ordering the interpretation of Christian doctrine favored by the emperor in opposition to groups such as the Arians and Nestorians, and affirming the power of the emperor in matters of religion, such as this decree first issued by the emperor Theodosius:

> We desire that all peoples subject to Our benign Empire shall live under the same religion that the Divine Peter, the Apostle, gave to the Romans, and which the said religion declares was introduced by himself . . . that is to say, in accordance with the rules of apostolic discipline and the evangelical doctrine, we should believe that the Father, Son, and Holy Spirit constitute a single Deity, endowed with equal majesty, and united in the Holy Trinity.
>
> We order all those who follow this law to assume the name of Catholic Christians, and consider others as demented and insane. We order that they shall bear the infamy of heresy; and when the Divine vengeance which they merit has been appeased, they shall afterwards be punished in accordance with our resentment, which we have acquired from the judgment of Heaven.[6]

The rest of the *Codex* was structured by topic and included provisions on every aspect of life, including economic issues, social concerns, and family life. (See "Thinking Like a Historian: Slavery in Roman and Germanic Society," page 184.)

The second part of Justinian's Code, the *Digest*, is a collection of the opinions of foremost Roman jurists on complex legal problems, and the third part, the *Institutes*, is a handbook of civil law designed for students and beginning jurists. All three parts were given the force of law and formed the backbone of Byzantine jurisprudence from that point on. Like so much of classical culture, the *Corpus Juris Civilis* was lost in western Europe with the end of the Roman Empire, but it was rediscovered in the eleventh century and came to form the foundation of law for nearly every modern European nation.

## Byzantine Learning and Science

The Byzantines prized education; because of them, many masterpieces of ancient Greek literature have survived to influence the intellectual life of the modern world. The literature of the Byzantine Empire was predominantly Greek, although politicians, scholars, and lawyers also spoke and used Latin. Justinian's Code was first written in Latin. More people could read in Byzantium than anywhere else in Christian Europe at the time, and history was a favorite topic.

The most remarkable Byzantine historian was Procopius (ca. 500–562), who left a rousing account praising Justinian's reconquest of North Africa and Italy, but also wrote the *Secret History*, a vicious and uproarious attack on Justinian and his wife, the empress Theodora. (See "Individuals in Society: Theodora of Constantinople," page 196.)

■ **Code of Justinian**   A collection of laws and legal commentary issued by the emperor Justinian that brought together all existing imperial laws into a coherent whole.

# INDIVIDUALS IN SOCIETY

## Theodora of Constantinople

The most powerful woman in Byzantine history was the daughter of a bear trainer for the circus. Theodora (ca. 497–548) worked as a dancer and burlesque actress, both dishonorable occupations in the Roman world. Despite her background, she caught the eye of Justinian, who was then a military leader and whose uncle (and adoptive father) Justin had himself risen from obscurity to become the emperor of the Byzantine Empire. Under Justinian's influence, Justin changed the law to allow an actress who had left her disreputable life to marry whom she liked, and Justinian and Theodora married in 525. When Justinian was proclaimed co-emperor with his uncle Justin on April 1, 527, Theodora received the rare title of *augusta*, or empress. Thereafter her name was linked with Justinian's in the exercise of imperial power.

Most of our knowledge of Theodora's early life comes from the *Secret History*, a tell-all description of the vices of Justinian and his court written around 550 by Procopius (pruh-KOH-pee-uhs), who was the official court historian and thus spent his days praising those same people. In the *Secret History* he portrays Theodora and Justinian as demonic, greedy, and vicious. In scene after detailed scene, Procopius portrays Theodora as particularly evil, sexually insatiable, depraved, and cruel, a temptress who used sorcery to attract men, including the hapless Justinian.

In one of his official histories, *The History of the Wars of Justinian*, Procopius presents a very different Theodora. Riots between the supporters of two teams in chariot races — who formed associations somewhat like both street gangs and political parties — had turned deadly, and Justinian wavered in his handling of the perpetrators. Both sides turned against the emperor, besieging the palace while Justinian was inside it. Shouting "N-I-K-A" (victory), the rioters swept through the city, burning and looting, and destroyed half of Constantinople. Justinian's counselors urged flight, but, according to Procopius, Theodora made a speech urging him to stay. Justinian rallied, had the rioters driven into the hippodrome, and ordered between thirty thousand and thirty-five thousand men and women executed. The revolt was crushed and Justinian's authority was restored, an outcome approved by Procopius.

Other sources also describe or suggest Theodora's influence on imperial policy. Justinian passed a number of laws that improved the legal status of women, such as allowing women to own property the same way that men could and to be guardians over their own children. Justinian is reputed to have consulted her every day about all aspects of state policy, including religious policy regarding the doctrinal disputes that continued throughout his reign. Institutions that she established, including hospitals, orphanages, houses for the rehabilitation of prostitutes, and churches, continued to be reminders of her charity and piety.

Theodora has been viewed as a symbol of the manipulation of beauty and cleverness to attain position and power, and also as a strong and capable co-ruler who held the empire together during riots, revolts, and deadly epidemics. Just as Procopius expressed both views, the debate has continued to today among writers of science fiction and fantasy as well as biographers and historians.

The empress Theodora (center) shown with a halo, symbolizing piety, and a crown, symbolizing power, in an intricate mosaic of thousands of cubes of colored glass and stone, created in Ravenna, Italy, in the sixth century. Like Justinian, Theodora had power over secular and religious institutions, much to the dismay of many at Justinian's court. (Universal History Archive/UIG via Getty Images)

### QUESTIONS FOR ANALYSIS

1. How would you assess the complex legacy of Theodora?
2. Since the official and unofficial views of Procopius are so different regarding the empress, should he be trusted at all as a historical source?

---

Although the Byzantines discovered little that was new in mathematics and geometry, they made advances in terms of military applications. For example, they invented an explosive liquid that came to be known as "Greek fire." The liquid was heated and propelled by a pump through a bronze tube, and as the jet left the tube, it was ignited — somewhat like a modern flamethrower. Greek fire saved Constantinople from Arab assault in 678 and was used in both

■ **Orthodox Church** Eastern Christian Church in the Byzantine Empire.

land and sea battles for centuries, although modern military experts still do not know the exact nature of the compound. In mechanics Byzantine scientists improved and modified artillery and siege machinery.

The Byzantines devoted a great deal of attention to medicine, and the general level of medical competence was far higher in the Byzantine Empire than in western Europe. Yet their physicians could not cope with the terrible disease, often called the "Justinian plague," that swept through the Byzantine Empire and parts of western Europe between 542 and about 560. Probably originating in northwestern India and carried to the Mediterranean region by ships, the disease was similar to what was later identified as the bubonic plague. Characterized by high fever, chills, delirium, and enlarged lymph nodes, or by inflammation of the lungs that caused hemorrhages of black blood, the Justinian plague claimed the lives of tens of thousands of people. The epidemic had profound political as well as social consequences: it weakened Justinian's military resources, thus hampering his efforts to restore unity to the Mediterranean world.

By the ninth or tenth century most major Greek cities had hospitals for the care of the sick. The hospitals might be divided into wards for different illnesses, and hospital staff included surgeons, practitioners, and aids with specialized responsibilities. The imperial Byzantine government bore the costs of these medical facilities.

## The Orthodox Church

The continuity of the Roman Empire in the East meant that Christianity developed differently there than it did in the West. The emperors in Constantinople were understood to be Christ's representative on earth; their palace was considered holy and was filled with relics and religious images, called icons. Emperors convened councils, appointed church officials, and regulated the income of the church. As in Rome, there was a patriarch in Constantinople, but he did not develop the same powers that the pope did in the West because there was never a similar power vacuum into which he needed to step. The **Orthodox Church**, the name generally given to the Eastern Christian Church, was more subject to secular control than the Western Christian Church.

Monasticism in the Orthodox world differed in fundamental ways from the monasticism that evolved in western Europe. First, while *The Rule of Saint Benedict*

gradually became the universal guide for all western European monasteries, each individual house in the Byzantine world developed its own set of rules for organization and behavior. Second, education never became a central feature of Orthodox monasteries. Monks and nuns had to be literate to perform the appropriate rituals, but no Orthodox monastery assumed responsibility for the general training of the local young.

There were also similarities between Western and Eastern monasticism. As in the West, Eastern monasteries became wealthy property owners, with fields, pastures, livestock, and buildings. Since bishops and patriarchs of the Orthodox Church were recruited only from the monasteries, these religious leaders also exercised cultural influence.

Like their counterparts in the West, Byzantine missionaries traveled far beyond the boundaries of the empire in search of converts. In 863 the emperor Michael III sent the brothers Cyril (826–869) and Methodius (815–885) to preach Christianity in Moravia (a region in the modern Czech Republic). Cyril invented a Slavic alphabet using Greek characters, later termed the Cyrillic (suh-RIH-lihk) alphabet in his honor. In the tenth century other missionaries spread Christianity, the Cyrillic alphabet, and Byzantine art and architecture to Russia. The Byzantines were so successful that the Russians would later claim to be the successors of the Byzantine Empire. For a time Moscow was even known as the "Third Rome" (the second Rome being Constantinople).

## NOTES

1. Maude Aline Huttman, ed. and trans., *The Establishment of Christianity and the Proscription of Paganism* (New York: AMS Press, 1967), p. 164.
2. R. C. Petry, ed., *A History of Christianity: Readings in the History of Early and Medieval Christianity* (Englewood Cliffs, N.J.: Prentice Hall, 1962), p. 70.
3. Saint Jerome, *Commentaries on the Letter to the Ephesians*, book 16, cited in Vern Bullough, *Sexual Variance in Society and History* (Chicago: University of Chicago Press, 1976), p. 365.
4. E. F. Henderson, ed., *Select Historical Documents of the Middle Ages* (London: G. Bell and Sons, 1912), pp. 176–189.
5. John McNeill and Helena M. Gamer, *Medieval Handbooks of Penance: A Translation of the Principal Libri Poenitentiales and Selections from Related Documents* (New York: Columbia University Press, 1938).
6. Justinian's Code 1.1.1, in S. P. Scott, trans., *The Civil Law*, vol. 12 (Cincinnati: The Central Trust Company, 1932), p. 9.

# LOOKING BACK LOOKING AHEAD

The Christian Church and the barbarian states absorbed many aspects of Roman culture, and the Roman Empire continued to thrive in the East as the Byzantine Empire, but western Europe in 600 was very different than it had been in 250. The

Western Roman Empire had slowly disintegrated under pressure from barbarian groups. Barbarian kings ruled small states from Italy to Norway, while churches and monasteries rather than emperors and wealthy individuals took on the role of constructing new buildings and providing education. The city of Rome no longer attracted a steady stream of aspiring immigrants and had shrunk significantly, as had many other cities, which were no longer centers of innovation. As the vast network of Roman urban centers dissolved, economies everywhere became more localized. Commentators such as Augustine advised people to put their faith in the eternal City of God rather than in worldly cities, because human history would always bring great change. People who lived with Augustine in Hippo would have certainly understood such counsel, for they watched the Vandals besiege their city in 430, move swiftly across North Africa, and bring an end to Roman rule there. Although Justinian's Byzantine forces reclaimed the area a little over a century later, the culture that survived was as much barbarian as Roman, with smaller cities, less trade, and fewer schools.

Two hundred years after the Vandal attack, the residents of Byzantine North Africa confronted another fast-moving army of conquest, Arabian forces carrying a new religion, Islam. This Arabic expansion dramatically shaped the development of Western civilization. Though the end of the Roman Empire in 476 has long been seen as a dramatic break in European history, the expansion of Islam two centuries later may have been even more significant. Many of the patterns set in late antiquity continued, however. Warrior values such as physical prowess, bravery in battle, and loyalty to one's lord remained central and shaped the development of the political system known as feudalism. The Frankish kingdom established by Clovis continued to expand, becoming the most important state in Europe. The economic and political power of the Christian Church expanded as well, with monasteries and convents providing education for their residents. The vast majority of people continued to live in small villages, trying to raise enough grain to feed themselves and their families, and asking the saints for help to overcome life's difficulties.

## Make Connections

Think about the larger developments and continuities within and across chapters.

1. The end of the Roman Empire in the West in 476 has long been viewed as one of the most important turning points in history. Do you agree with this idea? Why or why not?

2. In what ways was the role of the family in barbarian society similar to that of the family in classical Athens (Chapter 3) and republican Rome (Chapter 5)? In what ways was it different? What might account for the similarities and differences that you identify?

3. How did the Christian Church adapt to Roman and barbarian society? How was it different in 600 from how it had been in 100?

## 7   REVIEW & EXPLORE

### Identify Key Terms

Identify and explain the significance of each item below.

tetrarchy (p. 172)

diocese (p. 172)

Arianism (p. 175)

Nicene Creed (p. 175)

apostolic succession (p. 176)

Petrine Doctrine (p. 176)

regular clergy (p. 178)

secular clergy (p. 178)

sacraments (p. 180)

comitatus (p. 183)

wergeld (p. 186)

relics (p. 193)

Code of Justinian (p. 194)

Orthodox Church (p. 197)

## Review the Main Ideas

Answer the section heading questions from the chapter.

1. How did Diocletian and Constantine try to reform the empire? (p. 172)

2. How did the Christian Church become a major force in the Mediterranean and Europe? (p. 176)

3. What were the key characteristics of barbarian society? (p. 180)

4. How did the barbarian migrations shape Europe? (p. 187)

5. How did the church convert barbarian peoples to Christianity? (p. 191)

6. How did the Byzantine Empire preserve the legacy of Rome? (p. 194)

## Suggested Resources

### BOOKS

- Brown, Peter. *Augustine of Hippo*, rev. ed. 2000. The definitive biography of Saint Augustine, who is viewed here as a symbol of change.

- Burns, Thomas S. *Rome and the Barbarians, 100 B.C.–A.D. 400*. 2003. Argues that Germanic and Roman cultures assimilated with each other more than they conflicted.

- Burrus, Virginia. *Late Ancient Christianity*. 2010. A volume in the People's History of Christianity series, which focuses on the beliefs and practices of ordinary men and women.

- Clark, Gillian. *Late Antiquity: A Very Short Introduction*. 2011. A compact survey of the era, portraying it as a period of great transformation rather than simply decline.

- Clark, Gillian. *Women in Late Antiquity: Pagan and Christian Lifestyles*. 1994. Explores law, marriage, and religious life.

- Dunn, Marilyn. *The Emergence of Monasticism: From the Desert Fathers to the Early Middle Ages*. 2003. A thorough study of the beginnings of monasticism.

- Goldsworthy, Adrian. *How Rome Fell: Death of a Superpower*. 2009. A detailed narrative that emphasizes internal weaknesses caused by civil war and struggles for power.

- Heather, Peter. *The Fall of the Roman Empire: A New History of Rome and the Barbarians*. 2006. A masterful analysis that asserts the centrality of barbarian military actions in the end of the Roman Empire.

- Herrin, Judith. *Byzantium: The Surprising Life of a Medieval Empire*. 2008. Written for a general audience, this book portrays a tradition-based yet dynamic empire and discusses its significance for today.

- Todd, Malcolm. *The Early Germans*, 2d ed. 2004. Uses archaeological and literary sources to analyze Germanic social structure, customs, and religion and to suggest implications for an understanding of migration and ethnicity.

- Ward-Perkins, Bryan. *The Fall of Rome and the End of Civilization*. 2006. Uses material evidence to trace the physical destruction and economic dislocation that accompanied the barbarian migrations.

- Wells, Peter S. *The Barbarians Speak: How the Conquered Peoples Shaped Roman Europe*. 1999. Presents extensive evidence of Celtic and Germanic social and technical development.

### MEDIA

- *Barbarians II* (History Channel, 2007). A four-part documentary with many battle re-enactments that views the Vandals, Saxons, Franks, and Lombards as warrior barbarian hordes with savage tactics that "drove the empire to its knees."

- *Christian Classics Ethereal Library*. Hosted by Calvin College, this website has hundreds of primary sources in the public domain on all aspects of the history of Christianity and is especially strong in the writings of the church fathers, including Jerome, Ambrose, Augustine, and Benedict. **www.ccel.org**

- *The Germanic Tribes: The Complete Four-Part Saga* (Kultur, 2003). Using computer graphics and re-enactments, this documentary examines the settlements and religion of the German tribes as well as their warfare and argues that they actually preserved much of the Roman legacy.

- *Terry Jones' Barbarians* (BBC, 2007). A witty and lively four-part documentary by a member of the Monty Python comedy troupe that sees the barbarians as less important for Rome's fall than other factors.

# 8

# Europe in the Early Middle Ages

## 600–1000

**By the fifteenth century, scholars in the growing cities of northern Italy** began to think that they were living in a new era, one in which the glories of ancient Greece and Rome were being reborn. What separated their time from classical antiquity, in their opinion, was a long period of darkness, to which a seventeenth-century professor gave the name *Middle Ages*. In this conceptualization, Western history was divided into three periods—ancient, medieval, and modern—an organization that is still in use today.

For a long time the end of the Roman Empire in the West was seen as the division between the ancient period and the Middle Ages, but, as we saw in the last chapter, there was continuity as well as change. The transition from ancient to medieval was also a slow process, not a single event. The agents in this process included not only Christian officials and missionaries and the barbarian migrations that broke the Roman Empire apart, but also the new religion of Islam, which deeply influenced Western civilization.

The first several centuries in this new era (ca. 600–1000), conventionally known as the "early Middle Ages," was a time of disorder and destruction, but it also marked the creation of a new type of society and a cultural revival that influenced later intellectual and literary traditions. While agrarian life continued to dominate Europe, political and economic structures that would influence later European history began to form, and Christianity continued to spread. People at the time did not know that they were living in an era that would later be labeled "middle" or sometimes even "dark," and we can wonder whether they would have shared this negative view of their own times. ■

## CHAPTER PREVIEW

- What were the origins of Islam, and what impact did it have on Europe as it spread?

- How did the Franks build and govern a European empire?

- What were the significant intellectual and cultural developments in Charlemagne's era?

- How did the ninth-century invasions and migrations shape Europe?

- How and why did Europe become politically and economically decentralized in this period?

# What were the origins of Islam, and what impact did it have on Europe as it spread?

In the seventh century C.E. two empires dominated the area today called the Middle East: the Byzantine Empire with its capital at Constantinople and the Persian Sassanid empire with its capital at Baghdad. Between the two lay the Arabian peninsula, where a merchant called Muhammad began to have religious visions around 610. By the time he died in 632, all Arabia had accepted his creed of Islam. A century later his followers controlled what is now Syria, Palestine, Egypt, North Africa, Spain, and part of France. This expansion profoundly affected the development of Western civilization as well as the history of Africa and Asia.

## The Culture of the Arabian Peninsula

In Muhammad's time Arabia was inhabited by various tribes, many of them Bedouins (BED-oo-wins). These nomadic peoples grazed goats and sheep on the sparse patches of grass that dotted the vast semiarid peninsula. The power of the Bedouins came from their fighting skills, toughness, ability to control trade, and possession of horses and camels. Other people in the Arabian peninsula lived more settled lives in the southern valleys and coastal towns and cities along the Red Sea, such as Yemen, Mecca, and Medina, supporting themselves by agriculture and trade. Caravan routes crisscrossed Arabia and carried goods to Byzantium, Persia, and Syria, producing wealth for merchants.

For all people in the Arabian peninsula, the basic social unit was the clan—a group of blood relations connected through the male line. Clans expected loyalty from their members and in turn provided support and protection. Arabians of all types respected certain aspects of one another's customs and had some religious rules and rituals in common. For example, people throughout Arabia kept three months of the year as sacred; during that time any fighting stopped so that everyone could attend holy ceremonies in peace. The city of Mecca was the major religious and economic center of western Arabia. For centuries before the rise of Islam, many people in the Arabian peninsula prayed at the Ka'ba (KAH-buh), a temple in Mecca containing a black stone thought to be the dwelling place of a god, as well as objects connected to other gods. Economic links also connected Arabian peoples, but what eventually molded the diverse Arabian tribes into a powerful political and social unity was a new religion based on the teachings of Muhammad.

## The Prophet Muhammad

Except for a few vague remarks in the **Qur'an** (kuh-RAHN), the sacred book of Islam, Muhammad (ca. 571–632) left no account of his life. Muslim tradition

accepts some of the sacred stories that developed about him as historically true, but those accounts were not written down until about a century after his death. (Similarly, the earliest accounts of the life of Jesus, the Christian Gospels, were not written until forty to sixty years after his death.) Orphaned at the age of six, Muhammad was raised by his grandfather. As a young man he became a merchant in the caravan trade. Later he entered the service of a wealthy widow, and their subsequent marriage brought him financial independence.

The Qur'an reveals Muhammad to be an extremely devout man, ascetic, self-disciplined, and literate, but not formally educated. He prayed regularly, and when he was about forty he began to experience religious visions. Unsure for a time about what he should do, Muhammad discovered his mission after a vision in which the angel Gabriel instructed him to preach. Muhammad described his visions in a stylized and often rhyming prose and used this literary medium as his *Qur'an*, or "prayer recitation." Muhammad's revelations were written down by his followers during his lifetime and organized into chapters, called *sura*, shortly after his death. In 651 Muhammad's third successor arranged to have an official version published. The Qur'an is regarded by Muslims as the direct words of God to his Prophet Muhammad and is therefore especially revered. (When Muslims around the world use translations of the Qur'an, they do so alongside the original Arabic, the language of Muhammad's revelations.) At the same time, other sayings and accounts of Muhammad, which gave advice on matters that went beyond the Qur'an, were collected into books termed *hadith* (huh-DEETH). Muslim tradition (*Sunna*) consists of both the Qur'an and the hadith.

Muhammad's visions ordered him to preach a message of a single God and to become God's prophet, which he began to do in his hometown of Mecca. He gathered followers slowly, but also provoked a great deal of resistance because he urged people to give up worship of the gods whose sacred objects were in the Ka'ba and also challenged the power of the local elite. In 622 he migrated with his followers to Medina, an event termed the *hijra* (HIJ-ra) that marks the beginning of the Muslim calendar. At Medina, Muhammad was much more successful, gaining converts, especially from urban areas, and working out the basic principles of the faith. That same year, through the Charter of Medina, Muhammad formed the first *umma*, a community that united his followers from different tribes and set religious ties above clan loyalty. The charter also extended rights to others living in Medina,

# TIMELINE

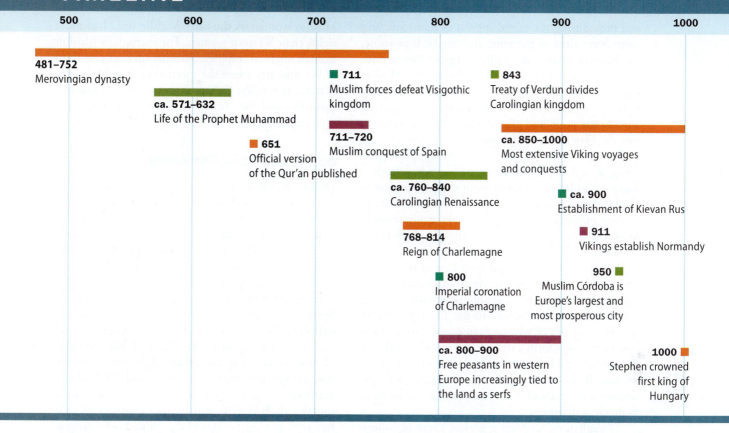

**500** **600** **700** **800** **900** **1000**

**481–752**
Merovingian dynasty

**ca. 571–632**
Life of the Prophet Muhammad

**651**
Official version
of the Qur'an published

**711**
Muslim forces defeat Visigothic
kingdom

**711–720**
Muslim conquest of Spain

**ca. 760–840**
Carolingian Renaissance

**768–814**
Reign of Charlemagne

**800**
Imperial coronation
of Charlemagne

**843**
Treaty of Verdun divides
Carolingian kingdom

**ca. 850–1000**
Most extensive Viking voyages
and conquests

**ca. 900**
Establishment of Kievan Rus

**911**
Vikings establish Normandy

**950**
Muslim Córdoba is
Europe's largest and
most prosperous city

**ca. 800–900**
Free peasants in western
Europe increasingly tied to
the land as serfs

**1000**
Stephen crowned
first king of
Hungary

including Jews and Christians, which set a precedent for the later treatment of Jews and Christians under Islam.

In 630 Muhammad returned to Mecca at the head of a large army, and he soon welded together most communities, settled or nomadic, in western Arabia into an even larger umma. They initially called themselves "believers" (*mu'minun* in Arabic), but by the end of the seventh century called themselves Muslims, a word meaning "those who comply with God's will." The religion itself came to be called Islam, which means "submission to God." The Ka'ba was rededicated as a Muslim holy place, and Mecca became the most holy city in Islam.

By the time Muhammad died in 632, the crescent of Islam, the Muslim symbol, prevailed throughout the Arabian peninsula. During the next century one rich province of the old Roman Empire after another came under Muslim domination — first Syria, then Egypt, and then all of North Africa (Map 8.1). Long and bitter wars (572–591, 606–630) between the Byzantine and Persian Empires left both so weak and exhausted that they easily fell to Muslim attack.

## The Teachings and Expansion of Islam

Muhammad's religion eventually attracted great numbers of people, partly because of the straightforward nature of its doctrines. The strictly monotheistic theology outlined in the Qur'an has only a few central tenets: Allah, the Arabic word for God, is all-powerful and all-knowing. Muhammad, Allah's prophet, preached his word and carried his message. Muhammad described himself as the successor both of the Jewish patriarch Abraham and of Christ, and he claimed that his teachings replaced theirs. He invited and won converts from Judaism and Christianity. Because Allah is all-powerful, believers must submit themselves to him. All Muslims have the obligation of the *jihad* (literally, "self-exertion") to strive or struggle to lead a virtuous life and to spread God's rule and law. In some cases striving is an individual struggle against sin; in others it is social and communal and could involve armed conflict, though this is not an essential part of jihad (jee-HAHD). The Islamic belief of "striving in the path of God" is closely related to the central feature of Muslim doctrine, the coming Day of Judgment. Muslims believe with conviction that the Day of Judgment will come; consequently, all of a Muslim's thoughts and actions should be oriented toward the Last Judgment and the rewards of Heaven.

To merit the rewards of Heaven, a person must follow the strict code of moral behavior that Muhammad prescribed. The Muslim must recite a profession of faith in God and in Muhammad as God's prophet: "There is no god but God and Muhammad is his prophet." The believer must pray five times a day, fast

■ **Qur'an** The sacred book of Islam.

and pray during the sacred month of Ramadan, and contribute alms to the poor and needy. If possible, the believer must make a pilgrimage to Mecca once during his or her lifetime. According to the Muslim *shari'a* (shuh-REE-uh), or sacred law, these five practices — the profession of faith, prayer, fasting, giving alms to the poor, and pilgrimage to Mecca — constitute the **Five Pillars of Islam**.

The Qur'an forbids alcoholic beverages and gambling, as well as a number of foods, such as pork, a dietary regulation adopted from the Mosaic law of the Hebrews. It condemns business usury — that is, lending money at interest rates or taking advantage of market demand for products by charging high prices for them.

Polygyny, the practice of men having more than one wife, was common in Arabian society before Muhammad, though for economic reasons the custom was limited to the well-to-do. The Qur'an limited the number of wives a man could have to four. The Qur'an sets forth a strict sexual morality and condemns immoral behavior on the part of men as well as women. It also sets out rules for inheritance that give widows a set share of the inheritance, and sons twice as much as daughters.

Though sons received a greater share of inheritance, in general with respect to matters of property, Muslim women of the early Middle Ages had more rights than Western women. For example, a Muslim woman retained complete jurisdiction over one-third of her property when she married and could dispose of it in any way she wished. Women in most European countries and the United States did not gain these rights until the nineteenth century.

## Sunni and Shi'a Divisions

Despite the clarity and unifying force of Muslim doctrine, divisions developed within the Islamic faith within decades of Muhammad's death. Neither the Qur'an nor the hadith gave clear guidance about how successors to Muhammad were to be chosen, but, according to tradition, in 632 a group of Muhammad's closest followers chose Abu Bakr (uh-BOO BAH-kuhr), a close friend of the Prophet and a member of a clan affiliated with the Prophet's clan, as **caliph** (KAY-luhf), a word meaning "successor" and used from that point on for the chief Muslim ruler. He was succeeded by two other caliphs, but these provoked opposition that coalesced around Ali, Muhammad's cousin and son-in-law. Ali was chosen as the fourth caliph in 656, but he was assassinated only five years later by backers of the initial line of caliphs. Ali's supporters began to assert that the Prophet had

**MAP 8.1 The Spread of Islam, 622–900** The rapid expansion of Islam in a relatively short span of time testifies to the Arabs' superior fighting skills, religious zeal, and economic organization as well as to their enemies' weakness.

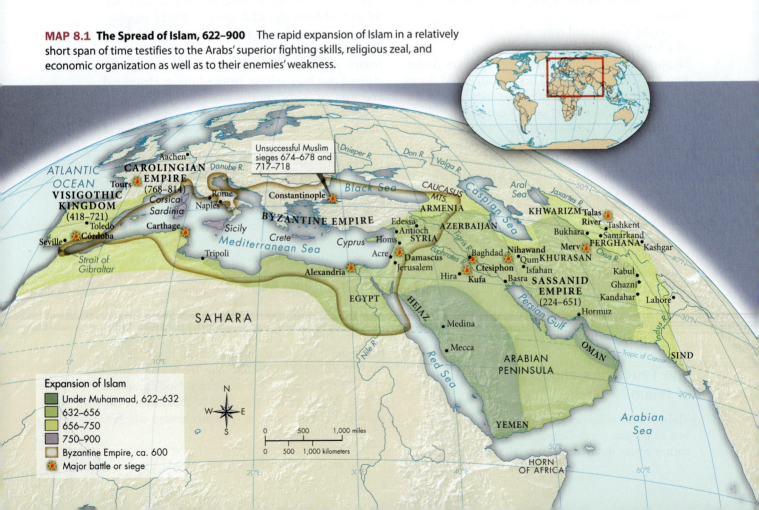

**Dome of the Rock, Jerusalem**    Completed in 691 and revered by Muslims as the site where Muhammad ascended to Heaven, the Dome of the Rock is the third-holiest place in Islam, after Mecca and Medina. Influenced by Byzantine and Persian architecture, it also has distinctly Islamic features, such as Qur'anic inscriptions. (Jeremy Woodhouse/Getty Images)

designated Ali as *imam*, or leader, and that he should rightly have been the first caliph; thus, any caliph who was not a descendant of Ali was a usurper. These supporters of Ali — termed Shi'ites (SHEE-ights) or Shi'a (SHEE-ah) from Arabic terms meaning "supporters" or "partisans" of Ali — saw Ali and subsequent imams as the divinely inspired leaders of the whole community. The larger body of Muslims who accepted the first elections — termed Sunnis, a word derived from *Sunna*, the practices of the community derived from Muhammad's example — saw the caliphs as proper political leaders. Since Islam did not have an organized priesthood, the caliphs had an additional function of safeguarding and enforcing the religious law (shari'a) with the advice of scholars (*ulama*), particularly the jurists, judges, and scholastics who were knowledgeable about the Qur'an and hadith. Over the centuries enmity between Sunni and Shi'a Muslims has sometimes erupted into violence, and discord still exists today.

After the assassination of Ali, the caliphate passed to members of the Umayyad (oo-MIGH-uhd) clan, who asserted control and brought stability to the growing Muslim empire. They established their capital at Damascus in Syria, and the Muslim faith continued to expand eastward to India and westward across North Africa. That expansion was facilitated everywhere by three main factors: military strength, trade connections, and tolerance toward non-Muslims.

## Life in Muslim Spain

In Europe, Muslim political and cultural influence was felt most strongly in the Iberian Peninsula. In 711 a Muslim force crossed the Strait of Gibraltar and easily defeated the weak Visigothic kingdom. (See "Viewpoints: The Muslim Conquest of Spain," page 206.) A few Christian princes supported by the Frankish rulers held out in northern mountain fortresses, but by 720 the Muslims controlled most of Spain. A member of the Umayyad Dynasty, Abd al-Rahman (r. 756–788), established a kingdom in Spain with its capital at Córdoba (KAWR-doh-buh).

Throughout the Islamic world, Muslims used the term **al-Andalus** to describe the part of the Iberian Peninsula under Muslim control. The name probably derives from the Arabic for "land of the Vandals," the

■ **Five Pillars of Islam**   The five practices Muslims must fulfill according to the shari'a, or sacred law, including the profession of faith, prayer, fasting, giving alms to the poor, and pilgrimage to Mecca.

■ **caliph**   The chief Muslim ruler, regarded as a successor to the Prophet Muhammad.

■ **al-Andalus**   The part of the Iberian Peninsula under Muslim control in the eighth century, encompassing most of modern-day Spain.

There are no contemporary descriptions from either Muslim or Christian authors of the Muslim conquest of the Iberian Peninsula that began in 711. One of the few existing documents is a treaty from 713, written in Arabic, between 'Abd al-'Aziz, the son of the conquering Muslim governor and general Musa ibn Nusair, and Tudmir, the Visigothic Christian ruler of the city of Murcia in southern Spain. Treaties such as this, and military aspects of the conquest, were also described in the earliest surviving account, an anonymous Latin chronicle written by a Christian living in Muslim Spain in 754.

### Treaty of Tudmir, from 713

In the name of God, the merciful and the compassionate.

This is a document [granted] by 'Abd al-'Aziz ibn Musa ibn Nusair to Tudmir, son of Ghabdush, establishing a treaty of peace and the promise and protection of God and his Prophet (may God bless him and grant him peace). We ['Abd al-'Aziz] will not set special conditions for him or for any among his men, nor harass him, nor remove him from power. His followers will not be killed or taken prisoner, nor will they be separated from their women and children. They will not be coerced in matters of religion, their churches will not be burned, nor will sacred objects be taken from the realm, [so long as] he [Tudmir] remains sincere and fulfills the [following] conditions that we have set for him. He has reached a settlement concerning seven towns: Orihuela, Valentilla, Alicante, Mula, Bigastro, Ello, and Lorca. He will not give shelter to fugitives, nor to our enemies, nor encourage any protected person to fear us, nor conceal news of our enemies. He and [each of] his men shall [also] pay one dinar every year, together with four measures of wheat, four measures of barley, four liquid measures of concentrated fruit juice, four liquid measures of vinegar, four of honey, and four of olive oil. Slaves must each pay half of this amount.

### Christian Chronicle of Events in 711, Written in 754

In Justinian's time [711], . . . Musa . . . entered the long plundered and godlessly invaded Spain to destroy it. After forcing his way to Toledo, the royal city, he imposed on the adjacent regions an evil and fraudulent peace. He decapitated on a scaffold those noble lords who had remained, arresting them in their flight from Toledo with the help of Oppa, King Egica's son [a Visigothic Christian prince]. With Oppa's support, he killed them all with the sword. Thus he devastated not only [the former Roman province of] Hispania Ulterior, but [the former Roman province of] Hispania Citerior up to and beyond the ancient and once flourishing city of Zaragoza, now, by the judgment of God, openly exposed to the sword, famine, and captivity. He ruined beautiful cities, burning them with fire; condemned lords and powerful men to the cross; and butchered youths and infants with the sword. While he terrorized everyone in this way, some of the cities that remained sued for peace under duress and, after persuading and mocking them with a certain craftiness, the Saracens [Muslims] granted their requests without delay.

### QUESTIONS FOR ANALYSIS

1. What conditions and guarantees are set for Christians living under Muslim rule in the treaty between Musa and Tudmir?
2. How does the author of the chronicle view Musa and treaties such as his?
3. What evidence do these documents provide for coexistence between Christians and Muslims in Spain and for hostility between the two groups?

Source: Olivia Remie Constable, ed., *Medieval Iberia: Readings from Christian, Muslim, and Jewish Sources,* pp. 30–31, 37–38. Copyright © 2012 University of Pennsylvania Press. Reprinted with permission of the University of Pennsylvania Press.

Germanic people who swept across Spain in the fifth century. In the eighth century al-Andalus included the entire peninsula from Gibraltar in the south to the Cantabrian Mountains in the north (see Map 8.1). Today we often use the word *Andalusia* (an-duh-LOO-zhuh) to refer especially to southern Spain, but eighth-century Christians throughout Europe called the peninsula "Moorish Spain" because the Muslims who invaded and conquered it were Moors — Berbers from northwest Africa.

The ethnic term *Moorish* can be misleading, however, because the peninsula was home to sizable numbers of Jews and Christians as well as Muslim Moors and Muslims of other backgrounds. In business transactions and in much of daily life, all peoples used the Arabic language. With Muslims, Christians, and Jews trading with and learning from one another and occasionally intermarrying, Moorish Spain and Norman Sicily (see "Italy" in Chapter 9) were the only distinctly pluralistic societies in medieval Europe.

Some scholars believe that the eighth and ninth centuries in Andalusia were an era of remarkable interfaith harmony. Jews in Muslim Spain were generally treated well, and Córdoba became a center of Jewish as well as Muslim learning. Many Christians adopted Arabic patterns of speech and dress, gave up eating pork, and developed an appreciation for Arabic music and poetry. Records describe Muslim and Christian youths joining in celebrations and merrymaking. From the sophisticated centers of Muslim culture in Baghdad, Damascus, and Cairo, al-Andalus seemed a provincial backwater, a frontier outpost with little significance in the wider context of Islamic civilization. On the other hand, "northern barbarians," as Muslims called the European peoples, acknowledged the splendor of Spanish culture. The Saxon nun and writer Hroswitha of Gandersheim (roz-WEETH-uh of GAHN-duhr-sheym) called the city of Córdoba "the ornament of the world." By 950 the city had a population of about a half million, making it Europe's largest and most prosperous city. Many residents lived in large houses and easily purchased the silks and brocades made by the city's thousands of weavers. The streets were well paved and well lit—a sharp contrast to the dark and muddy streets of other cities in Europe—and there was an abundance of freshwater for drinking and bathing. The largest library contained four hundred thousand volumes, a vast collection, particularly when compared with the largest library in northern Europe at the Benedictine abbey of St. Gall in Switzerland, which had only six hundred books.

In Spain, as elsewhere in the Arab world, Muslims had an enormous impact on agricultural development. They began the cultivation of rice, sugarcane, citrus fruits, dates, figs, eggplants, carrots, and, after the eleventh century, cotton. These crops, together with new methods of field irrigation, provided the population with food products unknown in the rest of Europe. Muslims also brought technological innovations westward, including new kinds of sails and navigational instruments, as well as paper.

## Muslim-Christian Relations

What did early Muslims think of Jesus? Jesus is mentioned many times in the Qur'an, which affirms that he was born of Mary the Virgin. He is described as a righteous prophet chosen by God who performed miracles and continued the work of Abraham and Moses, and he was a sign of the coming Day of Judgment. But Muslims held that Jesus was an apostle only, not God. The Christian doctrine of the Trinity—that there is one God in three persons (Father, Son, and Holy Spirit)—posed a powerful obstacle to Muslim-Christian understanding because of Islam's emphasis on the absolute oneness of God. Muslims esteemed the Judeo-Christian Scriptures

**Muslim Garden in Spain** Tranquil gardens such as this one built by Muslim rulers in Granada represented paradise in Islamic culture, perhaps because of the religion's desert origins. Muslim architectural styles shaped those of Christian Spain and were later taken to the New World by Spanish conquerors. (PHAS/Universal Images Group/Getty Images)

as part of God's revelation, although they believed that the Qur'an superseded them.

Muslims call Jews and Christians *dhimmis*, or "protected people," because they were "people of the book," that is, the Hebrew Scriptures. Christians and Jews in the areas Muslims conquered were allowed to continue practicing their faith, although they did have to pay a special tax. This toleration was sometimes accompanied by suspicion, however. In Spain, Muslim teachers increasingly feared that close contact with Christians and Jews would lead to Muslim contamination and threaten the Islamic faith. Thus, beginning in the late tenth century, Muslim regulations began to officially prescribe what Christians, Jews, and Muslims could do. A Christian or Jew, however much

**Qur'an Written on Paper**    This thirteenth-century Qur'an, written on paper, was produced in southern Spain, with colorful ornamental letters and gold leaf. Paper was invented in China and brought west by Muslims; by about 1100 there were paper mills in Muslim Spain, and from there papermaking spread into Christian Europe. (Pictures from History/Bridgeman Images)

## Cross-Cultural Influences in Science and Medicine

Despite growing suspicions on both sides, the Islamic world profoundly shaped Christian European culture in Spain and elsewhere. Toledo, for example, became an important center of learning through which Arabic intellectual achievements entered and influenced western Europe. Muslim knowledge of science and mathematics, derived from the Chinese, Greeks, and Hindus, was highly sophisticated. The Muslim mathematician al-Khwarizmi (al-KHWAHR-uhz-mee) (d. 830) wrote the important treatise *Algebra*, the first work in which the word *algebra* is used mathematically. Al-Khwarizmi adopted the Hindu system of numbers (1, 2, 3, 4), used it in his *Algebra*, and applied mathematics to problems of physics and astronomy. (Since our system of numbers is actually Indian in origin, the term *Arabic numerals*, coined about 1847, is a misnomer.) Muslims also instructed Westerners in the use of the zero, which permitted the execution of complicated problems of multiplication and long division. Scholars in Baghdad translated Euclid's *Elements*, the basic text for plane and solid geometry.

Muslim scholars also translated and codified the scientific and philosophical learning of Greek and Persian antiquity. In the ninth and tenth centuries that knowledge was brought to Spain, where between 1150 and 1250 it was translated into Latin. Europeans' knowledge of Aristotle (see "The Flowering of Philosophy" in Chapter 3) changed the entire direction of European philosophy and theology, as European Christian thinkers used ideas drawn from Aristotle as well as Christian texts in their writings (see "Theology and Philosophy" in Chapter 10).

Muslim medical knowledge far surpassed that of the West. By the ninth century Muslim physicians had translated most of the treatises of the ancient Greek physician Hippocrates and produced a number of important works of their own. Muslim science reached its peak in the physician, philologist, philosopher, poet, and scientist ibn-Sina of Bukhara (980–1037), known in the West as Avicenna (ah-vuh-SEH-nuh). His *Canon of Medicine* codified all Greco-Arabic medical thought, described the contagious nature of tuberculosis and the spreading of diseases, and listed 760 pharmaceutical drugs.

Unfortunately, many of these treatises came to the West as translations from Greek to Arabic and then to Latin and inevitably lost a great deal in translation. Nevertheless, in the ninth and tenth centuries Arabic knowledge and experience in anatomy and pharmaceutical prescriptions much enriched Western knowledge.

assimilated, remained an **infidel**. An infidel was an unbeliever, and the word carried a pejorative or disparaging connotation.

By about 950 Caliph Abd al-Rahman III (912–961) of the Umayyad Dynasty of Córdoba ruled most of the Iberian Peninsula. Christian Spain consisted of the tiny kingdoms of Castile, León, Catalonia, Aragon, Navarre, and Portugal. Civil wars among al-Rahman's descendants weakened the caliphate, and the small northern Christian kingdoms began to expand southward, sometimes working together. When Christian forces conquered Muslim territory, Christian rulers regarded their Muslim and Jewish subjects as infidels and enacted restrictive measures similar to those imposed on Christians in Muslim lands. Christian bishops worried that even a knowledge of Islam would lead to ignorance of essential Christian doctrines, and interfaith contacts declined. Christians' perception of Islam as a menace would help inspire the Crusades of the eleventh through thirteenth centuries (see "Background and Motives of the Crusades" in Chapter 9).

# How did the Franks build and govern a European empire?

Over two centuries before the Muslim conquest of Spain, the Frankish king Clovis converted to Roman Christianity and established a large kingdom in what had been Roman Gaul (see Chapter 7). Though at that time the Frankish kingdom was simply one barbarian kingdom among many, it grew to become the most important state in Europe, expanding to become an empire. Frankish rulers after Clovis, especially Charles the Great (r. 768–814), generally known by the French version of his name, Charlemagne (SHAHR-luh-mayne), used a variety of tactics to enhance their authority and create a stable system.

## The Merovingians

Clovis established the Merovingian dynasty in about 481 (see "Germanic Kingdoms and the End of the Roman Empire" in Chapter 7), and under him the Frankish kingdom included much of what is now France and a large section of southwestern Germany. Following Frankish traditions in which property was divided among male heirs, at Clovis's death the kingdom was divided among his four sons. Historians have long described Merovingian Gaul in the sixth and seventh centuries as wracked by civil wars, chronic violence, and political instability as Clovis's descendants fought among themselves. So brutal and destructive were these wars and so violent the conditions of daily life that the term *Dark Ages* was at one time used to designate the entire Merovingian period, although more recently historians have noted that the Merovingians also created new political institutions, so the era was not uniformly bleak.

Merovingian rulers also developed diverse sources of income. These included revenues from the royal estates and the "gifts" of subject peoples, such as plunder and tribute paid by peoples east of the Rhine River. New lands that might be conquered and confiscated served to replace lands donated as monastic or religious endowments. All free landowners paid a land tax, although some landowners gradually gained immunity from doing so. Fines imposed for criminal offenses and tolls and customs duties levied on roads and waterways also yielded income.

The Franks also based some aspects of their government on Roman principles. For example, the basis of the administrative system in the Frankish kingdom was the **civitas** (SIH-vih-tahs) — Latin for a city and surrounding territory — similar to the provinces of the Roman Empire. A **comites** (KOH-meh-tehs) — a senior official or royal companion, later called a count — presided over the civitas, as had governors

**Gold Coin of King Clovis II**   A small solid gold coin showing the Merovingian Frankish king Clovis II (633–657), wearing a pearl necklace and headdress, with a Christian cross on the reverse. Clovis inherited the throne as a child, as did his own sons, a common pattern among Merovingian kings. Frankish rulers adopted the minting of this kind of gold coin, called a tremissis, from the Romans, one of many continuities between Roman and Frankish culture. (Tallandier/Bridgeman Images)

in Rome. He collected royal revenue, heard lawsuits, enforced justice, and raised troops. Many comites were not conquerors from outside, but came from families that had been administrators in Roman Gaul and were usually native to the regions they administered and knew their areas well. Frankish royal administration involved another official, the *dux* (dooks) or duke. He was a military leader, commanding troops in the territory of several civitas, and thus responsible for all defensive and offensive strategies. Clovis and his descendants also issued capitularies — Roman-style administrative and legislative orders — in an attempt to maintain order in Merovingian society.

Within the royal household, Merovingian politics provided women with opportunities, and some queens not only influenced but occasionally also dominated events. Because the finances of the kingdom were merged with those of the royal family, queens often had control of the royal treasury just as more ordinary

■ **infidel**  A disparaging term used for a person who does not believe in a particular religion.

■ **civitas**  The city and surrounding territory that served as a basis of the administrative system in the Frankish kingdoms, based on Roman models.

■ **comites**  A senior official or royal companion, later called a count, who presided over the civitas.

women controlled household expenditures. The status of a princess or queen also rested on her diplomatic importance, with her marriage sealing or her divorce breaking an alliance with a foreign kingdom or powerful noble family; on her personal relationship with her husband and her ability to give him sons and heirs; and on her role as the mother and guardian of princes who had not reached legal adulthood.

Queen Brunhilda (543?–613), for example, married first one Frankish king and at his death another. When her second husband died, Brunhilda overcame the objections of the nobles and became regent, ruling on behalf of her son until he came of age. Later she governed as regent for her grandsons and, when she was nearly seventy, for her great-grandson. Stories of her ruthlessness spread during her lifetime and were later much embellished by Frankish historians uncomfortable with such a powerful woman. The evil Brunhilda, they alleged, killed ten Frankish kings in pursuit of her political goals, and was finally executed by being torn apart by horses while cheering crowds looked on. How much of this actually happened is impossible to say, but Brunhilda's legend became a model for the wicked queen in European folklore.

Merovingian rulers and their successors traveled constantly to check up on local administrators and peoples. Merovingian kings also relied on the comites and bishops to gather and send local information to them. The court or household of Merovingian kings included scribes who kept records, legal officials who advised the king on matters of law, and treasury agents responsible for aspects of royal finance. These officials could all read and write Latin. Over them all presided the mayor of the palace, the most important secular figure after the king, who governed the palace and the kingdom in the king's absence. Mayors were usually from one of the great aristocratic families, which increasingly through intermarriage blended Frankish and Roman elites. These families possessed landed wealth — villas over which they exercised lordship, dispensing local customary, not royal, law — and they often had rich and lavish lifestyles.

## The Rise of the Carolingians

From this aristocracy, one family gradually emerged to replace the Merovingian dynasty. The rise of the Carolingians — whose name comes from the Latin *Carolus*, or Charles, the name of several important members of the family — rests on several factors. First, the Carolingian Pippin I (d. 640) acquired the powerful position of mayor of the palace and passed the title on to his heirs. As mayors of the palace and heads of the Frankish bureaucracy, Pippin I and his descendants were entrusted with extraordinary amounts of power and privilege by the Merovingian

kings. Although the mayor of the palace was technically employed by the ruling family, the Carolingians would use their influential position to win support for themselves and eventually subvert Merovingian authority. Second, a series of advantageous marriage alliances brought the family estates and influence in different parts of the Frankish world, and provided the Carolingians with landed wealth and treasure with which to reward their allies and followers. Third, military victories over supporters of the Merovingians gave the Carolingians a reputation for strength and ensured their dominance. Pippin I's great-grandson, Charles Martel (r. 714–741), waged war successfully against the Saxons, Frisians, Alamanni, and Bavarians, which further enhanced the family's prestige. In 732 Charles Martel defeated a Muslim force near Poitiers (pwah-tee-AY) in central France. While Muslims saw the battle as nothing more than a minor skirmish, Charles Martel and later Carolingians used it to enhance their reputation, portraying themselves as defenders of Christendom against the Muslims.

The Battle of Poitiers helped the Carolingians acquire the support of the church, perhaps their most important asset. Charles Martel and his son Pippin III (r. 751–768) further strengthened their ties to the church by supporting the work of Christian missionaries. The most important of these missionaries was the Englishman Boniface (BAH-nuh-fays) (680–754), who had close ties to the Roman pope. Boniface ordered the oak of Thor, a tree sacred to many pagans, cut down and used the wood to build a church. When the god Thor did not respond by killing him with his lightning bolts, Boniface won many converts. As missionaries preached, baptized, and established churches, they included the Christian duty to obey secular authorities as part of their message, thus extending to Frankish rulers the church's support of secular power that had begun with Constantine (see "The Acceptance of Christianity" in Chapter 7).

As mayor of the palace, Charles Martel had exercised the power of king of the Franks. His son Pippin III aspired to the title as well as the powers it entailed. Pippin's diplomats were able to convince an embattled Pope Zacharias to rule in his favor against the Merovingians in exchange for military support against the Lombards, who were threatening the papacy. Zacharias invoked his apostolic authority as pope, deposed the Merovingian ruler Chilperic in 752, and declared that Pippin should be king. An assembly of Frankish magnates elected Pippin king, and Boniface anointed him. When in 754 Lombard expansion again threatened the papacy, Pope Stephen II journeyed to the Frankish kingdom seeking help. On this occasion, he personally anointed Pippin with the sacred oils and gave him the title "Patrician of the Romans," thus linking him symbolically with the ruling patrician class of ancient Rome. Pippin promised restitution of the papal lands and later made a gift of estates in central Italy. An important alliance had been struck between the papacy and the Frankish monarchs. When Pippin died, his son Charles, generally known as Charlemagne, succeeded him.

## The Warrior-Ruler Charlemagne

Charlemagne's adviser and friend Alcuin (ca. 735–804; see "The Carolingian Renaissance") wrote that "a king should be strong against his enemies, humble to Christians, feared by pagans, loved by the poor and judicious in counsel and maintaining justice."[1] Charlemagne worked to realize that ideal in all its aspects. Through brutal military expeditions that brought wealth — lands, booty, slaves, and tribute — and by peaceful travel, personal appearances, and the sheer force of his personality, Charlemagne sought to awe newly conquered peoples and rebellious domestic enemies.

If an ideal king was "strong against his enemies" and "feared by pagans," Charlemagne more than met the standard, as his reign was characterized by constant warfare. He subdued all of the north of modern France, but his greatest successes were in today's Germany, where he fought battles he justified as spreading Christianity to pagan peoples. In the course of a bloody thirty-year war against the Saxons, he added most of the northwestern German peoples to the Frankish kingdom. In his biography of the ruler, Charlemagne's royal secretary Einhard reported that Charlemagne ordered more than four thousand Saxons killed on one day and deported thousands more. Those who surrendered were forced to become Christian, often in mass baptisms. He established bishoprics in areas he had conquered, so church officials and church institutions became important means of imposing Frankish rule.

Charlemagne also achieved spectacular results in the south, incorporating Lombardy in today's northern Italy into the Frankish kingdom. He ended Bavarian independence and defeated the nomadic Avars, opening eastern Germany for later settlement by Franks. He successfully fought the Byzantine Empire for Venetia, Istria, and Dalmatia and temporarily annexed those areas to his kingdom. Charlemagne's only defeat came at the hands of the Basques of northwestern Spain. By around 805 the Frankish kingdom included all of northwestern Europe except Scandinavia and Britain (Map 8.2). Not since the Roman emperors of the third century C.E. had any ruler controlled so much of the Western world. Other than brief periods under Napoleon and Hitler, Europe would never again see as large a unified state as it had under Charlemagne. For that reason, Charlemagne

**MAP 8.2 Charlemagne's Conquests, ca. 768–814**
Though Charlemagne's hold on much of his territory was relatively weak, the size of his empire was not equaled again until the nineteenth-century conquests of Napoleon.

is today an important symbol of European unity; the European Union named one of its central buildings in Brussels the Charlemagne Building, and the Charlemagne Prize and Charlemagne Youth Prize are awarded for contributions to the process of European integration.

## Carolingian Government and Society

Charlemagne's empire was not a state as people today understand that term; it was a collection of peoples and clans. For administrative purposes, Charlemagne divided his entire kingdom into counties based closely on the old Merovingian civitas. Each of the approximately six hundred counties was governed by a count (or in his absence by a viscount), who published royal orders, held courts and resolved legal cases, collected taxes and tolls, raised troops for the army, and supervised maintenance of roads and bridges. Counts were originally sent out from the royal court; later a person native to the region was appointed. As a link between local authorities and the central government, Charlemagne appointed officials called *missi dominici* (mih-see doh-MEH-nee-chee), "agents of the lord king," who checked up on the counts and held courts to handle judicial and financial issues.

Considering the size of Charlemagne's empire, the counts and royal agents were few and far between, and the authority of the central government was weak. Society was held together by alliances among powerful families, along with dependent relationships cemented by oaths promising faith and loyalty.

Family alliances were often cemented by sexual relations, including those of Charlemagne himself. Charlemagne had a total of four or five legal wives, most from other Frankish tribes, and at least six concubines. (See "Evaluating Visual Evidence: Charlemagne and His Second Wife Hildegard," page 213.) Charlemagne's personal desires certainly shaped his complicated relationships — even after the age of sixty-five he continued to sire children — but the security and continuation of his dynasty and the need for diplomatic alliances were also important motives. Of his eighteen children, Charlemagne married the sons who reached adulthood to the daughters of kings and high nobles, and their descendants established most of the ruling dynasties of Europe. He prevented his daughters from marrying to avoid side branches of the family developing, though two had long-term relationships with courtiers, and their children became abbots or abbesses of major monasteries or married into noble houses. Several of Charlemagne's children born out of wedlock headed monasteries or convents as well, thus connecting his family with the church as well as the secular hierarchy. Throughout the Middle Ages, the children of kings and high nobles born out of wedlock were legally disadvantaged, but many had illustrious careers or made good marriages themselves, as there was relatively little stigma.

In terms of social changes, the Carolingian period witnessed moderate population growth. The highest aristocrats and church officials lived well, with fine clothing and at least a few rooms heated by firewood. Male nobles hunted and managed their estates, while female nobles generally oversaw the education of their children and sometimes inherited and controlled land on their own. Craftsmen and craftswomen on manorial estates manufactured textiles, weapons, glass, and pottery, primarily for local consumption. Sometimes abbeys and manors served as markets; goods were shipped away to towns and fairs for sale; and a good deal of interregional commerce existed. In the towns, artisans and merchants produced and traded luxury goods for noble and clerical patrons. When compared with earlier Roman cities or with Muslim cities of the time, such as Córdoba and Baghdad, however, Carolingian cities were small. Even in Charlemagne's main political center at Aachen, most buildings were made of wood and earth, streets were narrow and muddy, and beggars were a common sight.

The modest economic expansion benefited townspeople and nobles, but it did not significantly alter the lives of most people, who continued to live in a vast rural world dotted with isolated estates and small villages. Here life was precarious. Crops could easily be wiped out by hail, cold, or rain, and transporting food from other areas was impossible. People's diets centered on grain, which was baked into bread, brewed into beer, and especially cooked into gruel. To this were added seasonal vegetables such as peas, cabbage, and onions, and tiny amounts of animal protein, mostly cheese. Clothing and household goods were just as simple, and houses were drafty, smoky, and often shared with animals. Lice, fleas, and other vermin spread disease, and the poor diet led to frequent stomach disorders. Work varied by the season, but at all times of the year it was physically demanding and yielded relatively little. What little there was had to be shared with landowners, who demanded their taxes and rents in the form of crops, animals, or labor.

## The Imperial Coronation of Charlemagne

In autumn of the year 800, Charlemagne paid a momentous visit to Rome. Einhard gives this account of what happened:

His last journey there [to Rome] was due to another factor, namely that the Romans, having inflicted many injuries on Pope Leo — plucking out his eyes and tearing out his tongue, he had been compelled to beg the assistance of the king. Accordingly, coming to Rome in order that he might set in order those things which had exceedingly disturbed the condition of the Church, he remained there the whole winter. It was at the time that he accepted the name of Emperor and Augustus. At first he was so much opposed to this that he insisted that although that day was a great [Christian] feast, he would not have entered the Church if he had known beforehand the pope's intention. But he bore very patiently the jealousy of the Roman Emperors [that is, the Byzantine rulers] who were indignant when he received these titles. He overcame their arrogant haughtiness with magnanimity, . . . by sending frequent ambassadors to them and in his letters addressing them as brothers.[2]

# Charlemagne and His Second Wife Hildegard

This illumination from a ninth-century manuscript portrays Charlemagne with the woman who was his second or third wife, Hildegard of the Vinzgau (ca. 754–783). She had nine children during her twelve years of marriage, including a set of twins (one of whom was Louis the Pious, Charlemagne's successor), and she died from complications of childbirth. She accompanied Charlemagne on many of his military campaigns and used her position as his wife to gain offices and land for her relatives. She gave extensive financial and political support to the Benedictine Abbey of Kempten in what is today southern Germany. Marriage was an important tool of diplomacy for Charlemagne, and he had a succession of wives, along with concubines during and between his marriages. Whether Hildegard was wife two or three depends on whether Himiltrude, the mother of Charlemagne's first-born son, Pepin the Hunchback, was his wife or his concubine; the sources are unclear. He did briefly marry the daughter of the king of the Lombards (her name is disputed) before he married Hildegard. A few months after Hildegard's death he married again, to Fastrada, the daughter of an East Frankish count who was helping him fight the Saxons, and when she died he married Luitgard, the daughter of another count.

(Abbey Library, St. Paul im Lavanttal, Austria/Erich Lessing/Art Resource, NY)

### EVALUATE THE EVIDENCE

1. What does Charlemagne appear to be doing? How would you characterize his wife's reaction?
2. Why do you think the artist (whose identity is unknown) portrayed them like this?
3. How does this depiction of a Frankish queen match what you have read about Frankish queens? On what accomplishments did a queen's status rest?

For centuries scholars have debated the reasons for the imperial coronation of Charlemagne. Did Charlemagne plan the ceremony in Saint Peter's on Christmas Day, or did he merely accept the title of emperor? What did he have to gain from it? If, as Einhard implies, the coronation displeased Charlemagne, was that because it put the pope in the superior position of conferring power on the emperor? What were Pope Leo's motives in arranging the coronation?

Though definitive answers will probably never be found, several things seem certain. First, after the coronation Charlemagne considered himself an emperor ruling a Christian people. Through his motto, *Renovatio romani imperi* (Revival of the Roman Empire), Charlemagne was consciously perpetuating old Roman imperial notions while at the same time identifying with the new Rome of the Christian Church. In this sense, Charlemagne might be considered a precursor of the eventual Holy Roman emperor, although that term didn't come into use for two more centuries. Second, Leo's ideas about gender and rule undoubtedly influenced his decision to crown Charlemagne. In 800 the ruler of the Byzantine Empire was the empress Irene, the first woman to rule Byzantium in her own name, but Leo did not regard her authority as legitimate because she was female. He thus claimed to be placing Charlemagne on a vacant throne. Third, both parties gained: the Carolingian family received official recognition from the leading spiritual power in Europe, and the papacy gained a military protector.

Not surprisingly, the Byzantines regarded the papal acts as rebellious and Charlemagne as a usurper. The imperial coronation thus marks a decisive break between Rome and Constantinople. From Baghdad, however, Harun al-Rashid (r. 786–809), caliph of the Abbasid Empire, congratulated the Frankish ruler with the gift of an elephant. It was named Abu'l Abbas after the founder of the Abbasid Dynasty and may have served as a symbol of the diplomatic link Harun al-Rashid hoped to forge with the Franks against Byzantium. Having plodded its way to Charlemagne's court at Aachen, the elephant survived for nine years, and its death was considered important enough to be mentioned in the Frankish *Royal Annals*, the official chronological record of events, for the year 810. Like everyone else at Aachen, the elephant lived in a city that was far less sophisticated, healthy, and beautiful than the Baghdad of Harun al-Rashid.

The coronation of Charlemagne, whether planned by the Carolingian court or by the papacy, was to have a profound effect on the course of German history and on the later history of Europe. In the centuries that followed, German rulers were eager to gain the imperial title and to associate themselves with the legends of Charlemagne and ancient Rome. Ecclesiastical authorities, on the other hand, continually cited the event as proof that the dignity of the imperial crown could be granted only by the pope.

## What were the significant intellectual and cultural developments in Charlemagne's era?

As he built an empire through conquest and strategic alliances, Charlemagne also set in motion a cultural revival that had long-lasting consequences.

The stimulus he gave to scholarship and learning may, in fact, be his most enduring legacy, although at the time most people continued to live in a world where knowledge was transmitted orally.

### The Carolingian Renaissance

**Carolingian Minuscule** In the Carolingian period books played a large role in the spread of Christianity and in the promotion of learning. The development of the clearer script known as Carolingian minuscule shown here made books more legible and copying more efficient because more words could fit on the page. (Bibliothèque Nationale, Paris, France/ akg-images)

In Roman Gaul through the fifth century, the culture of members of the elite rested on an education that stressed grammar, Greco-Roman works of literature and history, and the legal and medical treatises of the Roman world. Beginning in the seventh and eighth centuries, a new cultural tradition common to Gaul, Italy, the British Isles, and to some extent Spain emerged. This culture was based primarily on Christian sources. Scholars have called the new Christian and ecclesiastical culture of the period from about 760 to 840, and the educational foundation on which it was based, the "Carolingian Renaissance" because Charlemagne was its major patron.

Charlemagne directed that every monastery in his kingdom should cultivate learning and educate the monks and secular clergy so that they would have a better understanding of the Christian writings. He also urged the establishment of cathedral and monastic schools where boys might learn to read and to pray properly. Thus the main purpose of this rebirth of learning was to promote an understanding of the Scriptures and of Christian writers and to instruct people to pray and praise God in the correct manner.

Women shared with men the work of evangelization and the new Christian learning. Rulers, noblemen, and noblewomen founded monasteries for nuns, each governed by an abbess. The abbess oversaw all aspects of life in the monastery. She handled the business affairs, supervised the copying of manuscripts, and directed the daily round of prayer and worship. Women's monasteries housed women who were unmarried, and also often widows, children being taught to read and recite prayers and chants, elderly people seeking a safe place to live, and travelers needing hospitality. Some female houses were, in fact, double monasteries in which the abbess governed two adjoining establishments, one for women and one for men. Monks provided protection from attack and did the heavy work on the land in double monasteries, but nuns handled everything else.

In monasteries and cathedral schools, monks, nuns, and scribes copied books and manuscripts and built up libraries. They developed the beautifully clear handwriting known as "Carolingian minuscule," with both uppercase and lowercase letters, from which modern Roman type is derived. In this era before printed books, works could survive only if they were copied. Almost all of the works of Roman authors that we are now able to read, both Christian and secular, were preserved by the efforts of Carolingian scribes. Some scholars went beyond copying to develop their own ideas, and by the middle years of the ninth century there was a great outpouring of more sophisticated original works.

The most important scholar at Charlemagne's court was Alcuin (al-KYOO-ihn), who came from Northumbria, one of the kingdoms in England. Alcuin was the leader of a palace school at Aachen, where Charlemagne assembled learned men from all over Europe. From 781 until his death, he was the emperor's chief adviser on religious and educational matters. Alcuin's letters to Charlemagne set forth political theories on the authority, power, and responsibilities of a Christian ruler.

Through monastic and cathedral schools, basic literacy in Latin was established among some of the clergy and even among some of the nobility, a change from Merovingian times. By the tenth century the patterns of thought and the lifestyles of educated western Europeans were those of Rome and Latin Christianity. Most people, however, continued to live in an oral world. They spoke local languages, which did not have a written form. Christian services continued to be conducted in Latin, but not all village priests were able to attend a school, and many simply learned the service by rote. Some Latin words and phrases gradually penetrated the various vernacular languages, but the Carolingian Renaissance did not trickle down to ordinary people.

This division between a learned culture of Latin that built on the knowledge of the ancient world and a vernacular culture of local traditions can also be seen in medicine. The foundation of a medical school at Salerno in southern Italy in the ninth century gave a tremendous impetus to medical study, and the school attracted students from all over the Mediterranean and Europe, including Christians, Jews, and Muslims. Despite the advances at Salerno, however, physicians were few in the early Middle Ages, and only the rich could afford them. Local folk medicine practiced by nonprofessionals provided help for commoners, with treatments made from herbs, bark, and other natural ingredients. Infants and children were especially susceptible to a range of illnesses, and about half of the children born died before age five. Although a few people lived into their seventies, most did not, and a forty-year-old was considered old.

## Northumbrian Learning and Writing

Charlemagne's court at Aachen was not the only center of learning in early medieval Christian Europe. Another was the Anglo-Saxon kingdom of Northumbria, situated at the northernmost tip of the old Roman world in what is today northern England. Northumbrian monasteries produced scores of books: missals (used for the celebration of the Mass); psalters (SAL-tuhrs), which contained the 150 psalms and other prayers used by the monks in their devotions; commentaries on the Scriptures; illuminated manuscripts; law codes; and collections of letters and sermons. (See "Individuals in Society: The Venerable Bede," page 216.) The finest product of Northumbrian art is probably the Gospel book produced at Lindisfarne monastery around 700. The book was produced by a single scribe working steadily over a period of several years, with the expenses involved in the production of such a book—for vellum, coloring, and gold leaf—probably supplied by the monastery's aristocratic patrons.

As in Charlemagne's empire, women were important participants in Northumbrian Christian culture. Perhaps the most important abbess of the early medieval period anywhere in Europe was Saint Hilda (d. 680). A noblewoman of considerable learning and administrative ability, she ruled the double monastery of Whitby on the Northumbrian coast, advised kings and princes, and encouraged scholars and poets. Hilda played a key role in the adoption of Roman practices by Anglo-Saxon churches (see "Missionaries' Actions" in Chapter 7).

At about the time the monks at Lindisfarne were producing their Gospel book, another author was probably at work on a nonreligious epic poem, *Beowulf* (BAY-uh-woolf). The poem tells the story of the hero Beowulf's progress from valiant warrior to wise ruler. (See "Evaluating Written Evidence: The Death of Beowulf," page 217.) In contrast to most writings of this era, which were in Latin, *Beowulf* was written in the vernacular Anglo-Saxon. The identity of its author (or authors) is unknown, and it survives only

France. There the Vikings established the province of "Northmanland," or Normandy as it was later known, intermarrying with the local population and creating a distinctive Norman culture. From there they sailed around Spain and into the Mediterranean, eventually seizing Sicily from the Muslim Arabs in 1060–1090, while other Normans crossed the English Channel, defeating Anglo-Saxon forces in 1066. Between 850 and 1000 Viking control of northern Europe reached its zenith. Norwegian Vikings moved farther west than any Europeans had before, establishing permanent settlements on Iceland and short-lived settlements in Greenland and Newfoundland in what is now Canada.

The Vikings made positive contributions to the areas they settled. They carried their unrivaled knowledge of shipbuilding and seamanship everywhere. The northeastern and central parts of England where the Vikings settled became known as the *Danelaw* because Danish, not English, laws and customs prevailed there. Scholars believe that some legal institutions, such as the ancestor of the modern grand jury, originated in the Danelaw. Exports from Ireland included iron tools and weapons manufactured there by Viking metal-smiths.

## Slavs and Vikings in Eastern Europe

Vikings also brought change in eastern Europe, which was largely populated by Slavs. In antiquity the Slavs lived in central Europe, farming with iron

technology, building fortified towns, and worshipping a variety of deities. With the start of the mass migrations of the late Roman Empire, the Slavs moved in different directions and split into what historians later identified as three groups: West, South, and East Slavs.

The group labeled the West Slavs included the Poles, Czechs, Slovaks, and Wends. The South Slavs, comprising peoples who became the Serbs, Croats, Slovenes, Macedonians, and Bosnians, migrated southward into the Balkans. In the seventh century Slavic peoples of the west and south created the state of Moravia along the banks of the Danube River. By the tenth century Moravia's residents were Roman Christian, along with most of the other West and South Slavs. The pattern of conversion was similar to that of the Germanic tribes: first the ruler was baptized, and then missionaries preached, built churches, and spread Christian teachings among the common people. The ruler of Poland was able to convince the pope to establish an independent archbishopric there in 1000, the beginning of a long-lasting connection between Poland and the Roman Church. In the Balkans the Serbs accepted Orthodox Christianity, while the Croats became Roman Christian, a division with a long-standing impact. This religious division was one of the factors in the civil war that split the large country of Yugoslavia into a number of smaller states in the late twentieth century.

Between the fifth and ninth centuries the eastern Slavs moved into present-day European Russia

**Oseberg Ship** This well-preserved and elaborately decorated Viking ship, discovered in a large burial mound in southern Norway, could be powered by sail or oars. Boatbuilders recently constructed a full-scale replica using traditional building methods and materials, and sailed it on the open ocean in 2014, reaching a speed of ten knots. The burial mound contained the skeletons of two older women, one wearing a dress made of fine wool and silk, along with a cart, several sleighs, horses, dogs, and many artifacts, suggesting that this was the grave of a powerful and prominent woman, though her identity is unknown. (Werner Forman Archive/Bridgeman Images)

and Ukraine. This enormous area consisted of an immense virgin forest to the north, where most of the eastern Slavs settled, and an endless prairie grassland to the south. In the tenth century Ibrahim Ibn Jakob, a learned Jew from the Muslim caliphate in Córdoba in Spain, traveled in Slavic areas. He found the Slavs to be "violent and inclined to aggression," but far cleaner than Christians in other parts of Europe in which he had traveled, "who wash only once or twice a year." Such filthy habits were unacceptable to someone raised in Muslim Spain, but the Slavs had an ingenious way of both getting clean and staying healthy: "They have no bathhouses as such, but they do make use of wooden huts [for bathing]. They build a stone stove, on which, when it is heated, they pour water. . . . They hold a bunch of grass in their hands, and waft the steam around. Then their pores open, and all excess matter escapes from their bodies."[3]

In the ninth century the Vikings appeared in the lands of the eastern Slavs. Called "Varangians" in the old Russian chronicles, the Vikings were interested primarily in gaining wealth through plunder and trade, and the opportunities were good. Moving up and down the rivers, they soon linked Scandinavia and northern Europe to the Black Sea and to the Byzantine Empire's capital at Constantinople. They raided and looted the cities along the Caspian Sea several times in the tenth century, taking booty and slaves, which they then sold elsewhere; thus raiding turned into trading, and the Scandinavians later established settlements, intermarried, and assimilated with Slavic peoples.

To increase and protect their international commerce and growing wealth, the Vikings declared themselves the rulers of the eastern Slavs. According to tradition, the semi-legendary chieftain Ruirik founded a princely dynasty about 860. In any event, the Varangian ruler Oleg (r. 878–912) established his residence at Kiev in modern-day Ukraine. He and his successors ruled over a loosely united confederation of Slavic territories known as Rus, with its capital at Kiev, until 1054. (The word *Russia* comes from *Rus*.)

Oleg and his clansmen quickly became assimilated into the Slavic population, taking local wives and emerging as the noble class. Missionaries of the

**Kievan Rus, ca. 1050**

Byzantine Empire converted the Vikings and local Slavs to Eastern Orthodox Christianity, accelerating the unification of the two groups. Thus the rapidly Slavified Vikings left two important legacies for the future: in about 900 they created a loose unification of Slavic territories, **Kievan Rus**, under a single ruling prince and dynasty, and they imposed a basic religious unity by accepting Orthodox Christianity, as opposed to Roman Catholicism, for themselves and the eastern Slavs.

Even at its height under Great Prince Iaroslav (YAHR-uh-slahv) the Wise (r. 1019–1054), the unity of Kievan Rus was extremely tenuous. Trade, not government, was the main concern of the rulers. Moreover, the Slavified Vikings failed to find a way to peacefully transfer power from one generation to the next. In early Rus there were apparently no fixed rules, and much strife accompanied each succession. Possibly to avoid such chaos, Great Prince Iaroslav, before his death in 1054, divided Kievan Rus among his five sons, who in turn divided their properties when they died. Between 1054 and 1237, Kievan Rus disintegrated into more and more competing units, each ruled by a prince claiming to be a descendant of Ruirik. The princes divided their land like private property because they thought of it as private property. A prince owned a certain number of farms or landed estates and had them worked directly by his people, mainly slaves, called *kholops* in Russian. Outside of these estates, which constituted the princely domain, the prince exercised only limited authority in his principality.

Excluding the clergy, two kinds of people lived on these estates: the noble boyars and the commoner peasants. The **boyars** were descendants of the original Viking warriors, and they also held their lands as free and clear private property. The boyars normally fought in princely armies, and the customary law declared that they could serve any prince they wished. Ordinary peasants could also move at will if they thought that opportunities would be greater elsewhere. In short, fragmented princely power, private property, and personal freedom all went hand in hand.

---

■ **Kievan Rus** A confederation of Slavic territories, with its capital at Kiev, ruled by descendants of the Vikings.

■ **boyars** High-ranking nobles in Russia who were descendants of Viking warriors and held their lands as free and clear private property.

## Magyars and Muslims

Groups of central European steppe peoples known as Magyars also raided villages in the late ninth century, taking plunder and captives, and forcing leaders to pay tribute in an effort to prevent further looting and destruction. Moving westward, small bands of Magyars on horseback reached as far as Spain and the Atlantic coast. They subdued northern Italy, compelled Bavaria and Saxony to pay tribute, and even penetrated into the Rhineland and Burgundy (see Map 8.3). Because of their skill with horses and their Eastern origins, the Magyars were often identified with the earlier Huns by those they conquered, though they are probably unrelated ethnically. This identification, however, may be the origin of the word *Hungarian*.

Magyar forces were defeated by a combined army of Frankish and other Germanic troops at the Battle of Lechfeld near Augsburg in southern Germany in 955, and the Magyars settled in the area that is now Hungary in eastern Europe. Much as Clovis had centuries earlier, the Magyar ruler Géza (GEE-zuh) (r. 970–997), who had been a pagan, became a Roman Christian. This gave him the support of the papacy and offered prospects for alliances with other Roman Christian rulers against the Byzantine Empire, Hungary's southern neighbor. Géza's son Stephen I (r. 997–1038) was officially crowned the king of Hungary by a papal representative on Christmas Day of 1000. He supported the building of churches and monasteries, increased royal power, and encouraged the use of Latin and the Roman alphabet. Hungary's alliance with the papacy shaped the later history of eastern Europe just as Charlemagne's alliance with the papacy shaped western European history. The Hungarians adopted settled agriculture, wrote law codes, and built towns, and Hungary became an important crossroads of trade for German and Muslim merchants.

The ninth century also saw Muslim invasions into Europe from the south. In many ways these were a continuation of the earlier conquests in the Iberian Peninsula, but now they focused on Sicily and mainland Italy. Muslims sacked Rome in 846 and captured towns along the Adriatic coast almost all the way to Venice. In the tenth century Frankish, papal, and Byzantine forces were able to retake much territory, though the Muslims continued to hold Sicily. Under their rule, agricultural innovations from elsewhere in the Muslim world led to new crops such as cotton and sugar, and fortified cities became centers of Muslim learning. Disputes among the Muslim rulers on the island led one faction to ask the Normans for assistance, and between 1060 and 1090 the Normans gradually conquered all of Sicily.

What was the impact of these invasions? From the perspective of those living in what had been Charlemagne's empire, Viking, Magyar, and Muslim attacks contributed to increasing disorder and violence. Italian, French, and English sources often describe this period as one of terror and chaos: "Save us, O God, from the fury of the Northmen." People in other parts of Europe might have had a different opinion, however. In Muslim Spain scholars worked in thriving cities, and new crops such as rice enhanced ordinary people's lives. In eastern Europe, states such as Moravia and Hungary became strong kingdoms. A Viking point of view might be the most positive, for by 1100 descendants of the Vikings not only ruled their homelands in Denmark, Norway, and Sweden, but also ruled Normandy, England, Sicily, Iceland, and Kievan Rus, with an outpost in Greenland and occasional voyages to North America.

---

# How and why did Europe become politically and economically decentralized in this period?

The large-scale division of Charlemagne's empire into three parts in the ninth century led to a decentralization of power at the local level. Civil wars weakened the power and prestige of kings, who could do little about domestic violence. The great invasions, especially those of the Vikings, also weakened royal authority. The western Frankish kings were unable to halt the invaders, and the local aristocracy had to assume responsibility for defense. Thus, in the ninth and tenth centuries great aristocratic families increased their authority in the regions of their vested interests. They lived in private castles for defense, and they governed virtually independent territories in which distant and weak kings could not interfere. Common people turned for protection to the strongest power, the local counts, whom they considered their rightful rulers, and free peasants sank to the level of serfs.

## Decentralization and the Origins of "Feudalism"

The political power of the Carolingian rulers had long rested on the cooperation of the dominant social class, the Frankish aristocracy. Charlemagne and his predecessors relied on the nobles to help wage wars of expansion and suppress rebellions, and in return these families were given a share of the lands and riches confiscated by the rulers. The most powerful nobles were those able to gain the allegiance of warriors, often symbolized in an oath-swearing ceremony in which a warrior (knight) swore his loyalty as a **vassal**—from a Celtic term meaning "servant"—to the more powerful individual, who became his lord. In return for the vassal's loyalty, aid, and military assistance, the lord promised him protection and material support. This support might be a place in the lord's household, but was more likely a piece of land called a *feudum* or **fief** (feef). In the Roman Empire soldiers had been paid for their services with money, but in the cash-poor early Middle Ages their reward was instead a piece of land. Most legal scholars and historians have seen these personal ties of loyalty cemented by grants of land rather than allegiance to an abstract state as a political and social system they term **feudalism**. They have traced its spread from Frankish areas to other parts of Europe.

In the last several decades, increasing numbers of medieval historians have found the idea of a "feudal system" problematic. They note that the word *feudalism* was a later invention, and that vassalage ceremonies, military obligations, and the ownership rights attached to fiefs differed widely from place to place and changed considerably in form and pattern over time. Thus, to these historians, "feudalism" is so varied that it doesn't really have a clear meaning, and it would be better not to use the term at all. The problem is that no one has come up with a better term for the loose arrangements of personal and property ties that developed among elites in the ninth century.

Whether one chooses to use the word *feudalism* or not, these relationships provided some degree of cohesiveness in a society that lacked an adequate government bureaucracy or method of taxation. In fact, because vassals owed administrative as well as military service to their lords, vassalage actually functioned as a way to organize political authority. Vassals were expected to serve as advisers to their lord, and also to pay him fees for important family events, such as the marriage of the vassal's children.

Along with granting land to knights, lords gave land to the clergy for spiritual services or promises of allegiance. In addition, the church held its own lands, and bishops, archbishops, and abbots and abbesses of monasteries sometimes granted fiefs to their own knightly vassals. Thus the "lord" in a feudal relationship was sometimes an institution. Women other than abbesses were generally not granted fiefs, but in most parts of Europe daughters could inherit them if their fathers had no sons. Occasionally, women did go through ceremonies swearing homage and fealty and swore to send fighters when the lord demanded them. More commonly, women acted as surrogates when their husbands were away, defending the territory from attack and carrying out administrative duties.

## Manorialism, Serfdom, and the Slave Trade

In feudal relationships, the "lord" was the individual or institution that had authority over a vassal, but the word *lord* was also used to describe the person or institution that had economic and political authority over peasants who lived in villages and farmed the land. Thus a vassal in one relationship was a slightly different type of lord in another. Most European people in the early Middle Ages were peasants who lived in family groups in villages or small towns and made their living predominantly by raising crops and animals. The village and the land surrounding it were called a manor, from the Latin word for "dwelling" or "homestead." Some fiefs might include only one manor, while great lords or kings might have hundreds of manors under their direct control. Residents of manors worked for the lord in exchange for protection, a system that was later referred to as **manorialism**. Free peasants surrendered themselves and their lands to the lord's jurisdiction. The land was given back, but the peasants became tied to it by various kinds of payments and services. Thus, like vassalage, manorialism involved an exchange. Because the economic power of the warring class rested on landed estates worked

- **vassal** A warrior who swore loyalty and service to a noble in exchange for land, protection, and support.

- **fief** A piece of land granted by a feudal lord to a vassal in return for service and loyalty.

- **feudalism** A term devised by later scholars to describe the political system in which a vassal was generally given a piece of land in return for his loyalty.

- **manorialism** A system in which peasant residents of manors, or farming villages, provided work and goods for their lord in exchange for protection.

**Selling a Goose, ca. 1023**    In this illustration from an eleventh-century manuscript copy of the Carolingian bishop and scholar Rabanus Maurus's (ca. 780–856) encyclopedic *De universo*, a man sells another a goose. Despite the rise of serfdom, small-scale trade continued on many manors, often by barter, though here one of the men appears to be holding a coin. (Gianni Dagli Orti/ Shutterstock)

by peasants, feudalism and manorialism were linked, but they were not the same system.

Local custom determined precisely what services villagers would provide to their lord, but certain practices became common throughout Europe. The peasant was obliged to give the lord a percentage of the annual harvest, usually in produce, sometimes in cash. The peasant paid a fee to marry someone from outside the lord's estate. To inherit property, the peasant paid a fine, often the best beast the person owned. Above all, the peasant became part of the lord's permanent labor force. With vast stretches of uncultivated virgin land and a tiny labor population, manorial lords encouraged population growth and immigration. The most profitable form of capital was not land but laborers.

In entering into a relationship with a manorial lord, free farmers lost status. Their position became servile, and they became **serfs**. That is, they were bound to the land and could not leave it without the lord's permission. Serfdom was not the same as slavery in that lords did not own the person of the serf, but serfs were subject to the jurisdiction of the lord's court in any dispute over property and in any case of suspected criminal behavior.

The transition from freedom to serfdom was slow. In the late eighth century there were still many free peasants. And within the legal category of serfdom there were many economic levels, ranging from the highly prosperous to the desperately poor. Nevertheless, a social and legal revolution was taking place. By the year 800 perhaps 60 percent of the population of western Europe — completely free a century before — had been reduced to serfdom. The ninth-century Viking assaults on Europe created extremely unstable conditions and individual insecurity, increasing the need for protection, accelerating the transition to serfdom, and leading to additional loss of personal freedom.

Though serfdom was not slavery, the Carolingian trade in actual slaves was extensive, generally involving persons captured in war or raids. Merchants in early medieval towns used slaves to pay the suppliers of the luxury goods their noble and clerical customers desired, most of which came into Europe from the East. The Muslim conquest of Spain produced thousands of prisoner-slaves, as did Charlemagne's long wars and the Viking raids. When Frankish conquests declined in the tenth century, German and Viking merchants obtained people on the empire's eastern border who spoke Slavic languages, the origin of our word *slave*. Slaves sold across the Mediterranean fetched three or four times the amounts brought within the Carolingian Empire, so most slaves were sold to Muslims. Christian moralists sometimes complained about the sale of Christians to non-Christians, but they did not object to slavery itself.

## NOTES

1. Quoted in R. McKitterick, *The Frankish Kingdoms Under the Carolingians, 751–987* (New York: Longman, 1983), p. 77.
2. Quoted in B. D. Hill, ed., *Church and State in the Middle Ages* (New York: John Wiley & Sons, 1970), pp. 46–47.
3. From Charles Melville and Ahmad Ubaydli, eds. and trans., *Christians and Moors in Spain*, vol. 3 (New York: Oxbow Books, 1992), p. 54.

■ **serfs** Peasants bound to the land by a relationship with a manorial lord.

# LOOKING BACK LOOKING AHEAD

The culture that emerged in Europe in the early Middle Ages has justifiably been called the first "European" civilization. While it was by no means "civilized" by modern standards, it had definite characteristics that were shared across a wide region. Other than in Muslim Spain and the pagan areas of northern and eastern Europe, almost all people were baptized Christians. Everywhere — including Muslim and pagan areas — most people lived in small villages, supporting themselves and paying their obligations to their superiors by raising crops and animals. These villages were on pieces of land increasingly granted to knights in exchange for loyalty and service to a noble lord. The educated elite was infused with Latin ideas and models, for Latin was the common language — written as well as spoken — of educated people in most of Europe.

In the several centuries after 1000, these characteristics — Christianity, village-based agriculture, vassalage, and Latin culture — would not disappear. Historians conventionally term the era from 1000 to about 1300 the "High Middle Ages," but this era built on a foundation that had already been established. The soaring Gothic cathedrals that were the most glorious architectural feature of the High Middle Ages were often constructed on the footings of early medieval churches, and their walls were built of stones that had once been part of Carolingian walls and castles. Similarly, political structures grew out of the institutions established in the Carolingian period, and later literary and cultural flowerings followed the model of the Carolingian Renaissance in looking to the classical past. Less positive developments also had their roots in the early Middle Ages, including hostilities between Christians and Muslims that would motivate the Crusades, and the continued expansion of serfdom and other forms of unfree labor.

## Make Connections

Think about the larger developments and continuities within and across chapters.

1. In both Christianity and Islam, political leaders played an important role in the expansion of the faith into new territory. How would you compare the actions of Constantine and Clovis (both in Chapter 7) with those of the Muslim caliphs and Charlemagne (in this chapter) in promoting, extending, and establishing their chosen religion?

2. Charlemagne considered himself to be the reviver of the Roman Empire. Thinking about Roman and Carolingian government and society, do you think this is an accurate self-description? Why or why not?

3. How were the ninth-century migrations and invasions of the Vikings, Magyars, and Muslims similar to the earlier barbarian migrations discussed in Chapter 7? How were they different?

## 8    REVIEW & EXPLORE

### Identify Key Terms

Identify and explain the significance of each item below.

| | |
|---|---|
| Qur'an (p. 202) | Kievan Rus (p. 223) |
| Five Pillars of Islam (p. 204) | boyars (p. 223) |
| caliph (p. 204) | vassal (p. 225) |
| al-Andalus (p. 205) | fief (p. 225) |
| infidel (p. 208) | feudalism (p. 225) |
| civitas (p. 209) | manorialism (p. 225) |
| comites (p. 209) | serfs (p. 226) |
| Treaty of Verdun (p. 218) | |

### Review the Main Ideas

Answer the section heading questions from the chapter.

1. What were the origins of Islam, and what impact did it have on Europe as it spread? (p. 202)

2. How did the Franks build and govern a European empire? (p. 209)

3. What were the significant intellectual and cultural developments in Charlemagne's era? (p. 214)

4. How did the ninth-century invasions and migrations shape Europe? (p. 218)

5. How and why did Europe become politically and economically decentralized in this period? (p. 224)

### Suggested Resources

#### BOOKS

- Barbero, Allesandro. *Charlemagne: Father of a Continent.* 2004. A wonderful biography of Charlemagne and study of the times in which he lived that argues for the complexity of his legacy.

- Barford, P. M. *The Early Slavs: Culture and Society in Early Medieval Eastern Europe.* 2001. An excellent survey of developments in much of eastern Europe.

- Bitel, Lisa. *Women in Early Medieval Europe, 400–1100.* 2002. Uses literary works and archaeological evidence as well as more traditional sources to trace all aspects of women's lives: social, intellectual, political, and economic.

- Donner, Fred M., *Muhammad and the Believers: At the Origins of Islam.* 2010. Examines the relationship between Jews, Christians, and Muslims in the early history of Islam.

- Esposito, John L. *Islam: The Straight Path*, updated ed. 2004. An informed and balanced work on Islam based on the best modern scholarship and original sources.

- Heather, Peter. *Empires and Barbarians: The Fall of Rome and the Birth of Europe.* 2010. Evaluates the dynamics of migration and the social, economic, and ethnic interactions that created Europe.

- James, Edward. *The Origins of France: From Clovis to the Capetians, 500–1000*, 2d ed. 2006. A solid introductory survey of early French history with an emphasis on family relationships.

- McKitterick, Rosamond. *Charlemagne: The Formation of a European Identity.* 2008. Analyzes Charlemagne's understanding of his role and methods of rule.

- Reynolds, Susan. *Fiefs and Vassals: The Medieval Evidence Reconsidered.* 1996. A comprehensive challenge to traditional conceptions of feudalism, the fief, and vassalage that has led to a rethinking of medieval political relationships.

- Riche, Pierre. *Daily Life in the World of Charlemagne.* Trans. JoAnn McNamara. 1988. A detailed study of many facets of Carolingian society.

- Verhulst, Adriaan. *The Carolingian Economy.* 2002. A brief survey, designed for students, of all aspects of the Carolingian economy, including agrarian production, crafts, and commerce.

- Watt, W. Montgomery, and Pierre Cachea. *A History of Islamic Spain.* 2007. A succinct analysis of Islam's influence on Spain.

- Wickham, Chris. *Framing the Early Middle Ages: Europe and the Mediterranean, 400–800.* 2007. A massive, yet accessible, survey of economic and social changes in many regions, with great attention to ordinary people.

- Winroth, Anders. *The Age of the Vikings.* 2014. Insightful look at all aspects of Viking society: raiding, trade, religion, art, poetry, and life at home in early medieval Scandinavia.

## MEDIA

- *Beowulf and Grendel* (Sturla Gunnarsson, 2005). A feature-film version of the *Beowulf* story with some new plot elements; loaded with violence and shot in the bleak landscape of Iceland.

- *Cities of Light: The Rise and Fall of Islamic Spain* (PBS, 2007). A documentary focusing on the culture of pluralism in tenth-century Muslim Spain, especially in the city of Córdoba, and its collapse because of internal and external forces. With an accompanying website at **www.islamicspain.tv**.

- *The Dark Ages* (History Channel, 2007). A blood-and-gore-filled documentary of the violence and instability of the early Middle Ages that also looks at Charlemagne and others as heroic creators of new institutions.

- *Internet Medieval Sourcebook.* The definitive online location for primary sources from the Middle Ages. Most of the texts are in English and are organized chronologically and thematically. **www.fordham .edu/halsall/sbook.html**

- *The Labyrinth: Resources for Medieval Studies.* Run by Georgetown University, this website provides free access to electronic resources in medieval studies, which are organized thematically. **labyrinth .georgetown.edu**

- *The Vikings* (*Nova*, 2000). A two-hour special that presents the Vikings as merchants, shipbuilders, artisans, and colonizers, and that re-creates Viking voyages in the Atlantic and eastern Europe using replicas of their ships.

# 9

# State and Church in the High Middle Ages

## 1000–1300

**The concept of the state** had been one of Rome's great legacies to Western civilization, but for almost five hundred years after the disintegration of the Roman Empire in the West, the state did not exist. Political authority was decentralized, with power spread among many lords, bishops, abbots, and other types of local rulers. The deeply fragmented political units that covered the early medieval European continent did not have the characteristics or provide the services of a modern state.

Beginning in the last half of the tenth century, the invasions and migrations that had contributed to European fragmentation gradually ended, and domestic disorder slowly subsided. Rulers began to develop new institutions of law and government that enabled them to assert their power over lesser lords and the general population. Although nobles remained the dominant class, centralized states slowly crystallized, first in western Europe, and then in eastern and northern Europe. At the same time, energetic popes built their power within the Western Christian Church and tried to assert their superiority over kings and emperors. Monks, nuns, and friars played significant roles in medieval society, both as individuals and as members of institutions. A papal call to retake the holy city of Jerusalem led to nearly two centuries of warfare between Christians and Muslims. Christian warriors, clergy, and settlers moved out from western and central Europe in all directions, so that through conquest and colonization border regions were gradually incorporated into a more uniform Christian realm. ■

TRAhVNT:CARRVM
CVM VINO:ETARM IS:

## CHAPTER PREVIEW

**Hauling Supplies for Battle**
In this detail from the *Bayeux tapestry*, men pull a cart loaded with wine, helmets, and spears to the ships with which Duke William of Normandy crossed the English Channel in his invasion of England in 1066. Medieval chronicles, songs, and stories focus on the heroic glories of battle, but logistics and supply were just as important to a medieval army as they are today. Now on display in Bayeux, France, the Bayeux tapestry is actually not a tapestry, but an embroidery panel measuring 231 feet by 19 inches that records the entire conquest. (Musée de la Tapisserie, Bayeux, France/Bridgeman Images)

# How did monarchs try to centralize political power?

Beginning in the eleventh century, rulers in some parts of Europe began to manipulate existing institutions to build up their power, becoming kings over growing and slowly centralizing states. As rulers expanded their territories and extended their authority, they developed larger bureaucracies, armies, judicial systems, and other institutions to maintain control and ensure order. Because these institutions cost money, rulers also initiated systems for generating revenue and handling financial matters. Some rulers were more successful than others, and the solutions they found to these problems laid the foundations for modern national states.

## England

Throughout the ninth century the Vikings had made a concerted effort to conquer and rule all of Anglo-Saxon England. In 878 Alfred, king of the West Saxons (or Wessex), one of several kingdoms in England, defeated the Vikings, inaugurating a period of recovery and stability in England. Alfred and his immediate successors built a system of local defenses and slowly extended royal rule beyond Wessex to other Anglo-Saxon peoples until one law, royal law, took precedence over local custom. England was divided into local units called shires, or counties, each under the jurisdiction of a shire-reeve (a word that soon evolved into *sheriff*) appointed by the king. Sheriffs were unpaid officials from well-off families responsible for collecting taxes, catching and trying criminals, and raising infantry when the king required it.

The Viking invasions of England resumed, however, and the island eventually came under Viking rule. The Viking Canute (r. 1016–1035) made England the center of his empire while promoting a policy of assimilation and reconciliation between Anglo-Saxons and Vikings. When Canute died, his son Harthacnut struggled to maintain this empire, and at his sudden death in 1042 it was broken up, with separate rulers in Denmark, Norway, and England, though all were related by blood or marriage to one another, as was common for medieval rulers. England went to Edward the Confessor (r. 1042–1066), who was in the Wessex dynasty and was also Harthacnut's half brother; they had the same mother, Emma of Normandy, who played an important political role in the reigns of both her sons. Succession troubles continued when Edward died childless, and there were three claimants to the throne of England—the Anglo-Saxon noble Harold Godwinson (ca. 1022–1066), who had been crowned by English nobles; the Norwegian king Harald III

(r. 1045–1066), the grandson of Canute; and Duke William of Normandy, the illegitimate son of Edward's cousin.

In 1066 the forces of Harold Godwinson crushed Harald's invading army in northern England, then quickly marched south when they heard that William had invaded England with his Norman vassals. Harold was decisively defeated by William at the Battle of Hastings—an event now known as the Norman Conquest. In both England and Normandy, William the Conqueror limited the power of the nobles and church officials, and built a unified monarchy. In England he retained the office of sheriffs, but named Normans to the posts. To determine how much wealth there was in his new kingdom and who held what land, he sent royal officials to every part of the country, and in every village local men were put under oath to answer the questions of these officials. In the words of a contemporary chronicler:

> So very narrowly did he have it investigated, that there was no single hide [a hide was a measure of land large enough to support one family], nor yard of land, nor indeed . . . one ox nor one cow nor one pig was there left out, and not put down in his record: and all these records were brought to him afterwards.[1]

The resulting record, called the **Domesday Book** (DOOMZ-day) from the Anglo-Saxon word *doom*, meaning "judgment," helped William and his descendants tax land appropriately. The book still survives and is an invaluable source of social and economic information about medieval England. It also helped William and future English kings regard their country as one unit.

William's son Henry I (r. 1100–1135) established a bureau of finance called the Exchequer that became the first institution of the government bureaucracy of England. In addition to various taxes and annual gifts, Henry's income came from money paid to the Crown for settling disputes and as penalties for crimes, as well as money due to him in his private position as landowner and lord. Officials of the Exchequer began to keep careful records of all of this.

In 1128 Henry's daughter Matilda was married to Geoffrey of Anjou, a count of a large province in what is now France; their son became Henry II of England and inaugurated the Angevin (AN-juh-vuhn; from Anjou, his father's county) dynasty. Henry II inherited the French provinces of Anjou, Normandy,

# TIMELINE

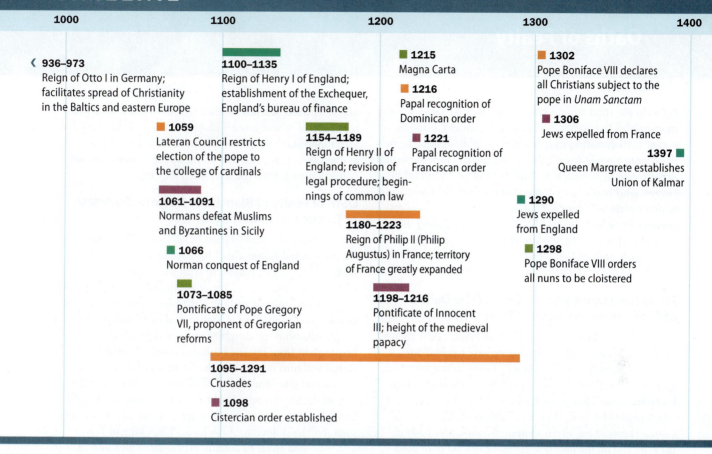

**1000**     **1100**     **1200**     **1300**     **1400**

**936–973**
Reign of Otto I in Germany; facilitates spread of Christianity in the Baltics and eastern Europe

**1100–1135**
Reign of Henry I of England; establishment of the Exchequer, England's bureau of finance

**1215**
Magna Carta

**1302**
Pope Boniface VIII declares all Christians subject to the pope in *Unam Sanctam*

**1059**
Lateran Council restricts election of the pope to the college of cardinals

**1154–1189**
Reign of Henry II of England; revision of legal procedure; beginnings of common law

**1216**
Papal recognition of Dominican order

**1306**
Jews expelled from France

**1061–1091**
Normans defeat Muslims and Byzantines in Sicily

**1221**
Papal recognition of Franciscan order

**1397**
Queen Margrete establishes Union of Kalmar

**1066**
Norman conquest of England

**1180–1223**
Reign of Philip II (Philip Augustus) in France; territory of France greatly expanded

**1290**
Jews expelled from England

**1073–1085**
Pontificate of Pope Gregory VII, proponent of Gregorian reforms

**1298**
Pope Boniface VIII orders all nuns to be cloistered

**1198–1216**
Pontificate of Innocent III; height of the medieval papacy

**1095–1291**
Crusades

**1098**
Cistercian order established

---

Maine, and Touraine in northwestern France, and in 1152 he married Eleanor of Aquitaine, heir to Aquitaine, Poitou (pwah-TOO), and Gascony in southwestern France. As a result, Henry claimed nearly half of today's France, and the histories of England and France became closely intertwined, leading to disputes and conflicts down to the fifteenth century.

## France

French kings overcame the Angevin threat to expand and increasingly unify their realm. Following the death of the last Carolingian ruler in 987, an assembly of nobles selected Hugh Capet (kah-PAY) as his successor. Soon after his own coronation, Hugh crowned his oldest surviving son Robert as king to ensure the succession and prevent disputes after his death. This broke with the earlier practices of elective kingship or dividing a kingdom among one's sons, establishing instead the principle of **primogeniture** (prigh-muh-JEH-nuh-choor), in which the king's eldest son received the Crown as his rightful inheritance. Primogeniture became the standard pattern of succession in medieval western Europe, and also became an increasingly common pattern of inheritance for noble titles

as well as land and other forms of wealth among all social classes.

The Capetian (kuh-PEE-shuhn) kings were weak, but they laid the foundation for later political stability. This stability came slowly. In the early twelfth century France still consisted of a number of virtually independent provinces, and the king of France maintained clear jurisdiction over a relatively small area in the center of France, the Île-de-France. Over time medieval French kings worked to increase the royal domain and extend their authority over the provinces.

The work of unifying France began under the Capetian king Philip II (r. 1180–1223), also known as Philip Augustus. He took Normandy by force from King John of England in 1204, gained other northern provinces as well, and was able to secure oaths of fealty from nobles in provinces not under his direct rule. (See "Viewpoints: Oaths of Fealty," page 234.) In the thirteenth century Philip Augustus's descendants acquired important holdings in the south. By the end of the thirteenth century most of the provinces of modern France had been added to the royal domain

---

■ **Domesday Book** A general inquiry about the wealth of his lands ordered by William of Normandy.

■ **primogeniture** An inheritance system in which the oldest son inherits all land and noble titles.

# VIEWPOINTS

## Oaths of Fealty

Rulers in the High Middle Ages often required oaths of fealty from nobles in conquered or allied provinces, building on earlier oath-swearing that linked lords and vassals. The first document below, from 1198, is Philip II of France's formal acceptance of the oath of fealty of Count Theobald III of Troyes, who had just become ruling count in Champagne, which bordered France. Theobald died three years later, leaving his wife, Blanche of Navarre, with a young daughter and pregnant with another child. The second document is Blanche's oath of fealty to Philip. She ruled as regent for twenty-one years, surviving a war of succession.

### Philip II of France's Acceptance of the Oath of Fealty from Theobald of Troyes, 1198

Philip, by the grace of God king of France. Be it known to all men, present and future, that we have received our beloved nephew, Theobald, count of Troyes, as our liege man, against every creature, living or dead, for all the lands which his father, count Henry, our uncle, held from our father, and which count Henry, the brother of Theobald, held from us. Count Theobald has sworn to us on the most holy body of the Lord and on the holy gospel that he will aid us in good faith, as his liege lord, against every creature, living or dead; at his command the following persons have sworn to us that they approve of this and will support and aid him in keeping this oath: Guy of Dampierre, Gualcher of Chatillon, Geoffroy, marshal of Champagne, etc. [vassals of the count of Champagne]. . . . We have sworn with our own hand that we will aid count Theobald against every creature, living or dead; at our command the following men have sworn that they approve of this and will support and aid us in keeping this oath: Pierre, count of Nevers, Drogo of Mello, William of Galande, etc. [vassals of the king]. . . . We have also agreed that our beloved uncle, William, archbishop of Rheims, and the bishops of Chalons and Meaux, may place those of our lands that are in their dioceses under interdict [a ban of all Christian ceremonies], as often as we fail in our duty to count Theobald, unless we make amends within a month from the time when they learn of it; and count Theobald has agreed that the same archbishop and bishops may place his lands under an interdict as often as he fails in his duty to us, unless he makes amends within a month from the time when they learn of it.

### Oath of Fealty of Blanche of Navarre, Countess of Troyes and Champagne, 1201

I, Blanche, countess palatine of Troyes. Be it known to all, present and future, that I have voluntarily sworn to my lord, Philip, king of France, to keep the agreements contained in this charter. . . . I have voluntarily sworn that I will never take a husband without the advice, consent, and wish of my lord, Philip, king of France, and that I will place under his guardianship my daughter and any child of whom I may be pregnant from my late husband, count Theobald. In addition, I will turn over to him the fortresses of Bray and Montereau, and give him control of all the men who dwell there and all the knights who hold fiefs of the castles, so that if I break my promise to keep these agreements, all the aforesaid men shall hold directly of my lord, Philip, king of France; and they shall swear to aid him even against men and against every other man or woman. . . . I will do liege homage to my lord, Philip, king of France, and I will keep faith with him against all creatures, living or dead.

### QUESTIONS FOR ANALYSIS

1. Philip is a male ruler accepting an oath of fealty, Blanche a female noble making one. How does this shape what is required of them in these oaths?
2. How are others incorporated into these promises? What does this suggest about links among nobles and between state and church?

Source: Oliver J. Thatcher and Edgar Holmes McNeal, eds., *A Source Book for Medieval History* (New York: Scribners, 1905), pp. 369–370, 371–372.

---

through diplomacy, marriage, war, and inheritance (Map 9.1).

In addition to expanding the royal territory, Philip Augustus devised a method of governing the provinces and providing for communication between the central government in Paris and local communities. Each province retained its own institutions and laws, but royal agents were sent from Paris into the provinces as the king's official representatives with authority to act for him. These agents were never natives of the provinces to which they were assigned, and they could not own land there. This policy reflected the fundamental principle of French administration that officials should gain their power from their connection to the monarchy, not from their own wealth or local alliances. Philip Augustus and his successors were slower and less effective, however, than were English kings at setting up an efficient bureau of finance.

## Central Europe

In central Europe the German king Otto I (r. 936–973) defeated many other lords to build his power from his original base in Saxony. Some of our knowledge of Otto derives from *The Deeds of Otto*, a history of his reign in heroic verse written by a nun, Hroswitha of Gandersheim (ca. 935–ca. 1003). Hroswitha viewed Otto's victories as part of God's plan: "As often as he set out for war, there was not a people, though haughty because of its strength, that could harm or conquer him, supported as he was by the consolation of the heavenly King."[2]

Otto garnered financial support from church leaders and also asserted the right to control ecclesiastical appointments. Before receiving religious consecration and being invested with the staff and ring symbolic of their offices, bishops and abbots had to perform feudal homage for the lands that accompanied the church office. This practice, later known as "lay investiture," created a grave crisis between the church and the monarchy in the eleventh century (see "Emperor Versus Pope").

In 955 Otto I inflicted a crushing defeat on the Magyars in the Battle of Lechfeld (see "Magyars and Muslims" in Chapter 8), which made Otto a great hero to the Germans. In 962 he used this victory to have himself crowned emperor by the pope in Aachen, which had been the capital of the Carolingian Empire. He chose this site to symbolize his intention to continue the tradition of Charlemagne and to demonstrate papal support for his rule. Though it was not exactly clear what Otto was the emperor of, by the eleventh century people were increasingly using the term **Holy Roman Empire** to refer to a loose confederation of principalities, duchies, cities, bishoprics, and other types of regional governments stretching from Denmark to Rome and from Burgundy to Poland (Map 9.2).

In this large area of central Europe and northern Italy, the Holy Roman emperors shared power with princes, dukes, archbishops, counts, bishops, abbots, and cities. The office of emperor remained an elected one, though the electors numbered seven—four secular rulers of large territories within the empire and three archbishops.

None of Otto's successors were as forceful as he had been, and by the first half of the twelfth century civil wars wracked the empire. The electors decided the only alternative to continued chaos was the selection of a strong ruler. They chose Frederick Barbarossa of the house of Hohenstaufen (HOH-uhn-shtow-fuhn) (r. 1152–1190). Like William the Conqueror in England and Philip in France, Frederick required vassals to take an oath of allegiance to him as emperor and appointed officials to exercise full imperial authority over local communities.

Between 1154 and 1188 Frederick made six military expeditions into Italy in an effort to assert his imperial

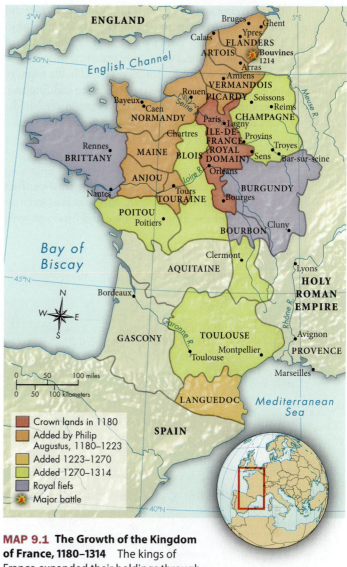

**MAP 9.1  The Growth of the Kingdom of France, 1180–1314**   The kings of France expanded their holdings through warfare, diplomacy, and strategic marriages, annexing lands that had belonged to independent nobles and taking over territory from the Angevin kings who also ruled England. The province of Toulouse in the south became part of France as a result of the crusade against the Albigensians (see "Criticism and Heresy").

rights over the increasingly wealthy towns of northern Italy. While he initially made significant conquests, the Italian cities formed leagues to oppose him, and also allied with the papacy. In 1176 Frederick suffered a crushing defeat at Legnano, where the league armies took massive amounts of booty and many prisoners (see Map 9.2). This battle marked the first time a cavalry of armed knights was decisively defeated by an army largely made of infantrymen from the cities. Frederick was forced to recognize

■ **Holy Roman Empire**  The loose confederation of principalities, duchies, cities, bishoprics, and other types of regional governments stretching from Denmark to Rome and from Burgundy to Poland.

the municipal autonomy of the northern Italian cities and the pope's sovereignty in central Italy. His campaigns in Italy took him away from the parts of the empire north of the Alps, and regional rulers there reasserted their authority toward the end of Frederick's reign and in the reigns of his successors. Thus, in contrast to France and England, Germany did not become a unified state in the Middle Ages, and would not until the nineteenth century.

## Italy

The emperor and the pope also came into conflict over Sicily and southern Italy, disputes that eventually involved the kings of France and Spain as well.

**MAP 9.2  The Holy Roman Empire and the Kingdom of Sicily, ca. 1200**  Frederick Barbarossa greatly expanded the size of the Holy Roman Empire, but it remained a loose collection of various types of government. The Christian kingdom of Sicily was created when Norman knights overthrew the Muslim rulers, but was later ruled by Frederick II, who was also the Holy Roman emperor.

Between 1061 and 1091 a bold Norman knight, Roger de Hauteville, with papal support and a small band of mercenaries, defeated the Muslims and Byzantines who controlled the island of Sicily. Roger then faced the problem of governing Sicily's heterogeneous population of native Sicilians, Italians, Greeks, Jews, Arabs, and Normans. Roger distributed scattered lands to his followers so no vassal would have a centralized power base. He took an inquest of royal property and forbade his followers to engage in war with one another. To these Norman practices, Roger fused Arab and Greek institutions, such as the bureau for record keeping and administration that had been established by the previous Muslim rulers.

In 1137 Roger's son and heir, Count Roger II, took the city of Naples and much of the surrounding territory in southern Italy. The entire area came to be known as the kingdom of Sicily (or sometimes the Kingdom of the Two Sicilies). Roger II's grandson Frederick II (r. 1212–1250) was also the grandson of Frederick Barbarossa of Germany. He was crowned king of the Germans at Aachen (1216) and Holy Roman emperor at Rome (1220), but he concentrated all his attention on the southern parts of the empire. Frederick had grown up in multicultural Sicily, knew six languages, wrote poetry, and supported scientists, scholars, and artists, whatever their religion or background. In 1224 he founded the University of Naples to train officials for his growing bureaucracy, sending them out to govern the towns of the kingdom. He tried to administer justice fairly to all his subjects, declaring, "We cannot in the least permit Jews and Saracens [Muslims] to be defrauded of the power of our protection and to be deprived of all other help, just because the difference of their religious practices makes them hateful to Christians," implying a degree of toleration exceedingly rare at the time.[3]

Because of his broad interests and abilities, Frederick's contemporaries called him the "Wonder of the World." But ruling Sicily required constant attention, and Frederick was often gone, on campaigns in mainland Italy or on the Crusades—holy wars sponsored by the papacy for the recovery of Jerusalem from the Muslims. He did not oversee his officials or the royal bureaucracy well, and shortly after he died, the kingdom fell to pieces. The pope, worried about

**MAP 9.3 The Reconquista, ca. 750–1492** The Christian conquest of Muslim Spain was followed by ecclesiastical reorganization, with the establishment of dioceses, monasteries, and the Latin liturgy, which gradually tied the peninsula to the heartland of Christian Europe and to the Roman papacy.

being encircled by imperial power, called in a French prince to rule the kingdom of Sicily. Like Germany, Italy would remain divided until the nineteenth century.

## The Iberian Peninsula

From the eleventh to the thirteenth centuries, power in the Iberian Peninsula shifted from Muslim to Christian rulers. Castile, in the north-central part of the peninsula, became the strongest of the growing Christian kingdoms, and Aragon, in the northeast, the second most powerful. Alfonso VIII (1158–1214) of Castile, aided by the kings of Aragon, Navarre, and Portugal, won a crushing victory over the Muslims in 1212, accelerating the Christian push southward. Over the next several centuries, successive popes gave Christian warriors in the Iberian Peninsula the same spiritual benefits that they gave those who traveled to Jerusalem, such as granting them forgiveness for their sins, transforming this advance into a crusade. Christian troops captured the great Muslim cities of Córdoba in 1236 and Seville in 1248. With this, Christians controlled nearly the entire Iberian Peninsula, save for the small state of Granada (Map 9.3). The chief mosques in Muslim cities became cathedrals, and Christian rulers recruited immigrants from western and southern Europe. The cities quickly became overwhelmingly Christian,

**Emperor Frederick II Granting Privileges** A young and handsome Frederick II, with a laurel wreath symbolizing his position as emperor, signs a grant of privileges for a merchant of the Italian city of Asti in this thirteenth-century manuscript. Frederick wears the flamboyant and fashionable clothing of a high noble — long-toed shoes, slit sleeves, and a cape of ermine tails — while the merchant seeking his favor is dressed in more sober and less expensive garb. (Miniature from the *Codex of Astensis*, Archivio Municipale, Asti, Italy/Scala/Art Resource, NY)

and gradually rural areas did as well. Fourteenth-century clerical writers would call the movement to expel the Muslims the **reconquista** (reconquest), a

sacred and patriotic crusade to wrest the country from "alien" Muslim hands. This idea became part of Spanish political culture and of the national psychology.

# How did the administration of law evolve in this period?

Throughout Europe in 1000, the law was a hodge-podge of local customs and provincial practices. Over the course of the High Middle Ages, national rulers tried to blend these elements into a uniform system of rules acceptable and applicable to all their peoples, though their success at doing so varied.

## Local Laws and Royal Courts

In France, the effort to create a royal judicial system was launched by Louis IX (r. 1226–1270). Each French province, even after being made part of the kingdom of France, had retained its unique laws and procedures, but Louis IX published laws for the entire kingdom and sent royal judges to hear complaints of injustice. He established the Parlement of Paris, a kind

**Child and Mother Plead Before the King**   In this fourteenth-century manuscript of Justinian's code of civil law, made in France, a mother and her child stand before the king to plead their case. He holds a sword, a symbol of both power and justice. Ordinary people did appear before royal courts, though they often sent legal representatives. (Gianni Dagli Orti/Shutterstock)

of supreme court that heard appeals from local administrators and regional courts, and also registered (or announced) royal laws. By the very act of appealing the decisions of local courts to the Parlement of Paris, French people in far-flung provinces were recognizing the superiority of royal justice.

In the Holy Roman Empire, justice was administered at multiple levels. The manorial or seigneurial court, presided over by the local lay or ecclesiastical lord, dealt with such matters as damage to crops and fields, trespass, boundary disputes, and debt. Dukes, counts, bishops, and abbots possessed authority over larger regions, and they dispensed justice in serious criminal cases there. The Holy Roman emperors established a court of appeal similar to that of the French kings, but in their disunited empire it had little power.

England also had a variety of local laws with procedures and penalties that varied from one part of the country to another. Henry I occasionally sent out circuit judges, royal officials who traveled a given circuit or district, to hear civil and criminal cases. Henry II (r. 1154–1189) made this way of extending royal justice an annual practice. Every year royal judges left London and set up court in the counties. These courts regularized procedures in civil cases, gradually developing the idea of a **common law**, one that applied throughout the whole country. Over the next two or three centuries common law became a reality as well as a legal theory. Common law relied on precedent: a decision in an important case served as an authority for deciding similar cases. Thus written codes of law played a less important role in England than they did elsewhere. (This practice has continued to today; in contrast to the United States and most other countries, the United Kingdom does not have a written constitution.)

Henry also improved procedure in criminal justice. In 1166 he instructed the sheriffs to summon local juries to conduct inquests and draw up lists of known or suspected criminals, to be presented to the royal judges when they arrived in the community. This accusing jury is the ancestor of the modern grand jury. Gradually, in the course of the thirteenth century, the king's judges adopted the practice of calling on twelve people (other than the accusing jury) to consider the question of innocence or guilt; this was the forerunner of the trial jury.

One aspect of Henry II's judicial reforms encountered stiff resistance from an unexpected source. In 1164 Henry insisted that everyone, including clerics, be subject to the royal courts. The archbishop of Canterbury Thomas Becket, who was Henry's friend and former chief adviser, vigorously protested that church law required clerics to be subject to church courts.

The disagreement between king and archbishop dragged on for years. Late in December 1170, in a fit of rage, Henry expressed the wish that Becket be destroyed. Four knights took the king at his word. They rode to Canterbury Cathedral and, as the archbishop was leaving evening services, murdered him, slashing off the crown of his head and scattering his brains on the floor of the cathedral. The assassination of an archbishop turned public opinion in England and throughout western Europe against the king, and Henry had to back down. He did public penance for the murder and gave up his attempts to bring clerics under the authority of the royal courts. Miracles were recorded at Becket's tomb; Becket was made a saint; and in a short time Canterbury Cathedral became a major pilgrimage and tourist site.

## The Magna Carta

In the later years of Henry's reign, his sons, spurred on by their mother, Eleanor of Aquitaine, fought against their father and one another for power and land. Richard I, known as the Lion-Hearted (r. 1189–1199), won this civil war and acceded to the throne on Henry's death. Soon after, however, he departed on one of the Crusades. Richard was captured on his way back from the Crusades and held by the Holy Roman emperor for a very high ransom, paid primarily through loans and high taxes on the English people. He was freed but died several years later as the result of a wound on yet another military campaign.

John (r. 1199–1216) inherited his father's and brother's heavy debts, and his efforts to squeeze money out of his subjects created an atmosphere of resentment. In July 1214 John's cavalry suffered a severe defeat at the hands of Philip Augustus of France, strengthening the opposition to John back in England. A rebellion begun by northern barons eventually grew to involve many key members of the English nobility. After lengthy negotiations, John met the barons in 1215 at Runnymede and was forced to approve the charter of rights later called **Magna Carta**.

The charter was simply meant to assert traditional rights enjoyed by certain groups, including the barons, the clergy, and the merchants of London, and thus state limits on the king's power. In time, however, it came to signify the broader principle that everyone, including the king and the government, must obey the law. The Magna Carta also contains the germ of the idea of "due process of law," meaning that a person has the right to be heard and defended in court and is entitled to the protection of the law. Because later generations referred to Magna Carta as a written statement of English liberties, it gradually came to have an almost sacred symbolic importance.

## Law in Everyday Life

Statements of legal principles such as the Magna Carta were not how most people experienced the law in medieval Europe. Instead they were involved in or witnessed something judged to be a crime, and then experienced or watched the determination of guilt and the punishment. Judges determined guilt or innocence in a number of ways. In some cases, particularly those in which there was little clear evidence, they ordered a trial by ordeal. An accused person could be tried by fire or water. In the latter case, the accused was tied hand and foot and dropped in a lake or river. People believed that water was a pure substance and would reject anything foul or unclean. Thus a person who sank was considered innocent; a person who floated was found guilty. Trial by ordeal was a ritual that appealed to the supernatural for judgment. Trials by ordeal are fascinating to modern audiences, but they were relatively rare, and their use declined over the High Middle Ages as judges and courts increasingly favored more rational procedures. Judges heard testimony, sought witnesses, and read written evidence if it was available.

A London case in 1277 provides a good example of how law worked. Around Easter, a man was sent to clean a house that had been abandoned, "but when he came to a dark and narrow place where coals were usually kept, he there found [a] headless body; upon seeing which, he sent word to the chamberlain and sheriffs." These officials went to the house and interviewed the neighbors. The men who lived nearby said that the headless body belonged to Symon de Winten, a tavern owner, whom they had seen quarreling with his servant Roger in early December. That night Roger "seized a knife, and with it cut the throat of Symon quite through, so that the head was entirely severed from the body." He had stuffed the

---

■ **reconquista** The Christian term for the conquest of Muslim territories in the Iberian Peninsula by Christian forces.

■ **common law** A body of English law established by King Henry II's court that in the next two or three centuries became common to the entire country.

■ **Magna Carta** A peace treaty intended to redress the grievances that particular groups had against King John; it was later viewed as the source of English rights and liberty more generally.

body in the coal room, stolen clothes and a silver cup, and disappeared.[4] The surviving records don't indicate whether Roger was ever caught, but they do indicate that the sheriffs took something as "surety" from the neighbors who testified, that is, cash or goods as a pledge that their testimony was true. Taking sureties from witnesses was a common practice, which may be why the neighbors had not come forward on their own even though they seemed to have detailed knowledge of the murder. People were supposed to report crimes, and they could be fined for not doing so, but it is clear from this case that such

community involvement in crime fighting did not always happen.

Had Roger been caught and found guilty, his punishment would have been as public as the investigation. Murder was a capital crime, as were a number of other violent acts, and executions took place outdoors on a scaffold. Hanging was the most common method of execution, although nobles might be beheaded because hanging was seen as demeaning. Minor crimes were punished by fines, corporal punishments such as whipping, or banishment from the area.

# What were the political and social roles of nobles?

The expansion of centralized royal power and law involved limiting the power of the nobility, but rulers also worked through nobles, who retained their privileged status and cultural importance. In fact, despite political, scientific, and industrial revolutions, the nobility continued to hold real political and social power in Europe into the nineteenth century.

## Origins and Status of the Nobility

In the early Middle Ages noble status was generally limited to a very few families who either were descended from officials at the Carolingian court or were leading families among Germanic tribes. Beginning in the eleventh century, knights in the service of higher nobles or kings began to claim noble status. Although nobles were only a small fraction of the total population, the noble class grew larger and more diverse, ranging from poor knights who held tiny pieces of land (or sometimes none at all) to dukes and counts with vast territories.

Originally, most knights focused solely on military skills, but around 1200 there emerged a different ideal of knighthood, usually termed **chivalry** (shih-vuhl-ree). Chivalry was a code of conduct in which fighting to defend the Christian faith and protecting one's countrymen were declared to have a sacred purpose. (See "Evaluating Visual Evidence: Saint Maurice, Ideal Knight," page 241.) Other qualities gradually became part of chivalry: bravery, generosity, honor, graciousness, mercy, and eventually gallantry toward women, which came to be called "courtly love." The chivalric ideal created a new standard of masculinity for nobles, in which

loyalty and honor remained the most important qualities, but graceful dancing and intelligent conversation were not considered unmanly.

## Training, Marriage, and Inheritance

At about the age of seven, a boy of the noble class who was not intended for the church was placed in the household of one of his father's friends or relatives. There he became a servant to the lord and received formal training in arms, learning to ride, wield a sword, hurl a lance, and shoot with a bow and arrow. Increasingly, noble youths learned to read and write some Latin. Formal training was concluded around the age of twenty-one, often with the ceremony of knighthood.

The ceremony of knighthood did not necessarily mean attainment of adulthood, power, and responsibility. Sons were completely dependent on their fathers for support. A young man remained a youth until he was in a financial position to marry — that is, until his father died. Increasingly, families adopted primogeniture, with property passing to the oldest son. Younger sons might be forced into the clergy or simply forbidden to marry.

Once knighted, the young man traveled for two to three years, visiting other noble households, engaging in local warfare, and perhaps going on a crusade. He hunted, meddled in local conflicts, and did the tournament circuit. The tournament, in which a number of men competed from horseback (in contrast to the joust, which involved only two competitors), gave the young knight experience in pitched battle and a way to show off his masculinity before an audience. Since the horses and equipment of the vanquished were forfeited to the victors, the knight could also gain a profit. Everywhere they went, young knights stirred up trouble, for chivalric ideals of honorable valor and

■ **chivalry** Code of conduct in which fighting to defend the Christian faith and protecting one's countrymen were declared to have a sacred purpose.

# Saint Maurice, Ideal Knight

Young noble men and women learned about ideals of behavior through stories, songs, and visual images of real and mythical individuals, as well as through training. One of these was the third-century Saint Maurice, who according to accounts of the lives of the saints was a soldier in the Roman army from Thebes in Egypt and was executed on the orders of the pagan Roman emperor Maximian for refusing to attack fellow Christians who were revolting against Rome. He first emerges in the Carolingian period, and later he was held up as a model knight and declared a patron of the Holy Roman Empire and protector of the imperial army in wars against the pagan Slavs. His image was used on coins, and his cult was promoted by the archbishops of Magdeburg, who moved his relics, including a head acquired in Jerusalem, to their cathedral. This statue, made around 1250, is the first surviving portrayal of Maurice as a black man, which became common in Germany until the late sixteenth century. He has been the patron saint of several military orders, including the Order of Saint Maurice of the National Infantry Association in the United States, and so his role as a model soldier lives on.

(Markus Hilbich/akg-images)

## EVALUATE THE EVIDENCE

1. Saint Maurice is portrayed in the dress of a thirteenth-century knight, not a third-century Roman soldier. How might this have enhanced his appeal as an ideal?
2. This statue stands next to the tomb of the Holy Roman emperor Otto I (r. 936–973) in Magdeburg Cathedral. Why might the archbishops have chosen to place it there, and what might this placement have conveyed to those who worshipped in the cathedral?
3. Images of Saint Maurice as black man largely ended in the mid-sixteenth century, at a point when the Atlantic slave trade was expanding. What does this suggest about attitudes toward race in Europe?

gallant masculinity rarely served as a check on actual behavior.

While noble girls were also trained in preparation for their future tasks, that training was quite different. They were often taught to read the local language and perhaps some Latin and to write and do enough arithmetic to keep household accounts. They also learned music, dancing, and embroidery and how to ride and hunt, both common noble pursuits. Much of this took place in the girl's own home, but, like boys, noble girls were often sent to the homes of relatives or higher nobles to act as servants or ladies in waiting or to learn how to run a household.

Parents often wanted to settle daughters' futures as soon as possible. Men tended to prefer young brides who would have more years to produce children. Therefore, aristocratic girls in the High Middle Ages were married at around the age of sixteen, often to much older men. In the early Middle Ages the custom was for the groom to present a dowry to the bride and her family, but by the late twelfth century the process was reversed because men were in greater demand. Thereafter, the sizes of dowries

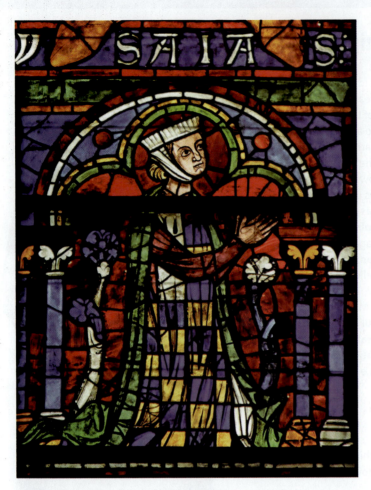

**Female Donor in Chartres Cathedral Windows**   Nobles and other wealthy people who paid for stained-glass windows often had their portraits included. In the south transept of Chartres Cathedral at the foot of the prophet Isaiah is the portrait of Alix of Thouars, hereditary duchess of Brittany. The windows were made in 1221–1230, right after Alix's death in childbirth, and were donated by her husband, who is also shown in one of the windows; the remaining windows show their son and daughter, though as young adults rather than as the small children they would have been at the time the windows were made. (Chartres Cathedral, Chartres, France/Bridgeman Images)

offered by brides and their families rose higher and higher.

## Power and Responsibility

A male member of the nobility became fully adult when he came into the possession of property. He then acquired authority over lands and people, protecting them from attack, maintaining order, and settling disputes. With this authority went responsibility. In the words of Honorius of Autun:

> Soldiers: You are the arm of the Church, because you should defend it against its enemies. Your duty is to aid the oppressed, to restrain yourself from rapine and fornication, to repress those who impugn the Church with evil acts, and to resist those who are rebels against priests. Performing such a service, you will obtain the most splendid of benefices from the greatest of Kings.[5]

Nobles rarely lived up to this ideal, however, and there are countless examples of nobles stealing church lands instead of defending them, tyrannizing the oppressed rather than aiding them, and regularly engaging in "rapine and fornication" rather than resisting them.

Women played a large and important role in the functioning of the estate. They were responsible for the practical management of the household's "inner economy" — cooking, brewing, spinning, weaving, caring for yard animals. When the lord was away for long periods, the women frequently managed the herds, barns, granaries, and outlying fields as well. Often the responsibilities of the estate fell to them permanently, as the number of men slain in medieval warfare ran high.

Throughout the High Middle Ages, fighting remained the dominant feature of the noble lifestyle. The church's preaching and condemnations reduced but did not stop violence, and the military values of the nobles' social class encouraged petty warfare and disorder. The nobility thus represented a constant source of trouble for the monarchy.

**Harlech Castle**   King Edward I of England built Harlech Castle in the 1280s on a cliff overlooking the sea on the west coast of Wales as part of his campaign to conquer Wales and destroy the power of the Welsh nobility. It housed a garrison of men, along with the families and servants of some of them, who lived in the inner halls and towers. Harlech had strategic as well as symbolic importance, and was besieged in several revolts by the Welsh against the English — during the Wars of the Roses between noble factions (see "England" in Chapter 12), and again during the English Civil War (see "Religious Divides and Civil War" in Chapter 15). (DEA/G. Wright/Getty Images)

# How did the papacy reform the church, and what were the reactions to these efforts?

Kings and emperors were not the only rulers consolidating their power in the High Middle Ages; popes did so as well, through a series of measures that made the church more independent of secular control. The popes' efforts were sometimes challenged by medieval kings and emperors, and the wealth of the church came under sharp criticism.

## The Gregorian Reforms

During the ninth and tenth centuries the local church had come under the control of kings and feudal lords, who chose priests and bishops in their territories, granting them land and expecting loyalty and service in return. Church offices from village priest to pope were sources of income as well as positions of authority. Officeholders had the right to collect taxes and fees and often the profits from the land under their control. Church offices were thus sometimes sold outright — a practice called **simony** (SIGH-muh-nee). Not surprisingly, clergy at all levels who had bought their positions

or had been granted them for political reasons provided little spiritual guidance, and their personal lives were rarely models of high moral standards. Although the Roman Church officially required men to be unmarried in order to be ordained, there were many married priests and others simply living with women. Popes were chosen by wealthy Roman families from among their members, and after gaining the papal office, they paid more attention to their families' political fortunes than to the health of the church.

Serious efforts to change all this began under Pope Leo IX (pontificate 1049–1054). Leo ordered clergy in Rome to dismiss their wives and invalidated the ordination of church officials who had purchased their offices. Pope Leo and several of his successors believed that secular or lay control over the church was largely responsible for its lack of moral leadership, so in a radical shift they proclaimed the church independent of secular rulers. The Lateran Council of 1059 decreed

■ **simony**  The buying and selling of church offices, a policy that was officially prohibited but often practiced.

that the authority and power to elect the pope rested solely in the **college of cardinals**, a special group of priests from the major churches in and around Rome. The college retains that power today, though the membership has grown and become international.

Leo's successor Pope Gregory VII (pontificate 1073–1085) was even more vigorous in his championing of reform and expansion of papal power; for that reason, the eleventh-century movement is frequently called the "Gregorian reform movement." He denounced clerical marriage and simony in harsh language and ordered **excommunication** (being cut off from the sacraments and all Christian worship) for those who disagreed. He believed that the pope, as the successor of Saint Peter, was the vicar of God on earth and that papal orders were thus the orders of God. Gregory was particularly opposed to lay investiture—the selection and appointment of church officials by secular authority. In February 1075 he held a council at Rome that decreed that clerics who accepted investiture from laymen were to be deposed and laymen who invested clerics were to be excommunicated.

In the late eleventh century and throughout the twelfth and thirteenth, the papacy pressed Gregory's campaign for reform of the church. The popes held a series of councils, known as the Lateran Councils, that ratified decisions ending lay investiture, ordered bishops to live less extravagantly, and ordered married priests to give up their wives and children or face dismissal. Most church officials apparently obeyed, though we have little information on what happened to the families. In other reforms, marriage was defined as a sacrament—a ceremony that provided visible evidence of God's grace—and divorce was forbidden.

Gregory's reforms had a profound effect on nuns and other women in religious orders. The movement built a strict hierarchical church structure with bishops and priests higher in status than nuns, who could not be ordained. The double monasteries of the early Middle Ages were placed under the authority of male abbots. Church councils forbade monks and nuns to sing church services together and ordered priests to limit their visits to convents. The reformers' emphasis on clerical celibacy and chastity led them to portray women as impure and lustful. Thus, in 1298 in the papal decree *Periculoso*, Pope Boniface VIII ordered all nuns to be strictly cloistered, that is, to remain permanently inside the walls of the convent, and for visits with people from outside the house, including family

members, to be limited. *Periculoso* was not enforced everywhere, but it did mean that convents became more cut off from medieval society than monasteries were.

## Emperor Versus Pope

Gregory thought that the threat of excommunication would compel rulers to abide by his move against lay investiture. Immediately, however, Henry IV in the Holy Roman Empire, William the Conqueror in England, and Philip I in France protested, as the reform would deprive them not only of church income but also of the right to choose which monks and clerics would help them administer their kingdoms. The strongest reaction came from the Holy Roman Empire. Within the empire, religious and secular leaders took sides to pursue their own advantage. In January 1076 many of the German bishops who had been invested by Henry withdrew their allegiance from the pope. Gregory promptly suspended them and excommunicated Henry. The pope told German nobles they no longer owed allegiance to Henry, which obviously delighted them. When powerful nobles invited the pope to come to Germany to settle their dispute with Henry, Gregory traveled to the north. Christmas of 1076 thus witnessed an ironic situation in Germany: the clergy supported the emperor while the great nobility favored the pope.

Henry managed to outwit the pope temporarily. In January 1077 he approached the castle where the pope was staying. According to a letter later sent by Gregory to his German noble allies, Henry stood for three days in the snow, imploring the pope to lift the excommunication. Henry's pleas for forgiveness won him public sympathy, and the pope readmitted the emperor to the Christian community. When the sentence of excommunication was lifted, however, Henry regained the emperorship and authority over his rebellious subjects, but continued his moves against papal power. In 1080 Gregory again excommunicated and deposed the emperor. In return, when Gregory died in 1085, Henry invaded Italy and captured Rome. But Henry won no lasting victory. Gregory's successors encouraged Henry's sons to revolt against their father.

Finally, in 1122 at a conference held at Worms, the issue was settled by compromise. Bishops were to be chosen by the clergy. But since lay rulers were permitted to be present at ecclesiastical elections and to accept or refuse homage from the new prelates, they still possessed an effective veto over ecclesiastical appointments. Papal power was enhanced, but neither side won a clear victory.

The long controversy over lay investiture had tremendous social and political consequences in Germany. The lengthy struggle between papacy and emperor allowed emerging noble dynasties to enhance

■ **college of cardinals** A special group of high clergy with the authority and power to elect the pope and the responsibility to govern the church when the office of the pope is vacant.

■ **excommunication** A penalty used by the Christian Church that meant being cut off from the sacraments and all Christian worship.

■ **canon law** Church law, which had its own courts and procedures.

their position. To control their lands, the great lords built castles, symbolizing their increased power and growing independence. When the papal-imperial conflict ended in 1122, the nobility held the balance of power in Germany, and later German kings, such as Frederick Barbarossa, would fail in their efforts to strengthen the monarchy. For these reasons, division and local independence characterized the Holy Roman Empire in the High Middle Ages.

## Criticism and Heresy

The Gregorian reform movement contributed to dissatisfaction with the church among townspeople as well as monarchs. Papal moves against simony, for example, led to widespread concern about the role of money in the church just as papal tax collectors were becoming more efficient and sophisticated. Papal efforts to improve the sexual morality of the clergy led some laypersons to assume they could, and indeed should, remove priests for any type of immorality.

Criticism of the church emerged in many places but found its largest audience in the cities, where the contrast between wealth and poverty could be seen more acutely. In northern Italian towns, the monk Arnold of Brescia (BREH-shah) (ca. 1090–1155), a vigorous advocate of strict clerical poverty, denounced clerical wealth. In France, Peter Waldo (ca. 1140–ca. 1218), a rich merchant of the city of Lyons, gave his money to the poor and preached that only prayers, not sacraments, were needed for salvation. The Waldensians (wawl-DEHN-shuhnz) — as Peter's followers were called — bitterly attacked the sacraments and church hierarchy, and they carried these ideas across Europe. In the towns and cities of southern France, the Albigensians (al-buh-JEHN-see-uhns), also known as the Cathars, used the teachings of Jesus about the evils of material goods to call for the church to give up its property. They asserted that the material world was created not by the good God of the New Testament, but by a different evil God of the Old Testament. People who rejected worldly things, not wealthy bishops or the papacy, should be the religious leaders.

Critical of the clergy and spiritually unfulfilled, townspeople joined the Waldensians and the Albigensians. The papacy denounced supporters of both movements as heretics and began extensive campaigns to wipe them out. In 1208 Pope Innocent III proclaimed a crusade against the Albigensians, and the French monarchy and northern French knights willingly joined in, eager to gain the lands and wealth of southern French cities. After years of fighting, the leaders agreed to terms of peace, which left the French monarchy the primary beneficiary. Later popes sent inquisitors with the power to seek out and eliminate the remaining heretics.

## The Popes and Church Law

Pope Urban II laid the foundations for the papal monarchy by reorganizing the papal *curia* (the central government of the Roman Church) and recognizing the college of cardinals as a definite consultative body. The papal curia had its greatest impact as a court of law. As the highest ecclesiastical tribunal, it formulated church law, termed **canon law**. The church developed a system of courts separate from those of secular rulers that handled disputes over church property and ecclesiastical elections and especially questions of marriage and annulment. Most of the popes in the twelfth and thirteenth centuries were canon lawyers who expanded the authority of church courts.

The most famous of the lawyer-popes was Innocent III (pontificate 1198–1216), who became the most powerful pope in history. During his pontificate the church in Rome declared itself to be supreme, united, and "catholic" (worldwide), responsible for the earthly well-being as well as the eternal salvation of Christians everywhere. Innocent pushed the kings of Europe to do his will, compelling King Philip Augustus of France to take back his wife, Ingeborg of Denmark, and King John of England to accept as archbishop of Canterbury a man John did not want.

Innocent called the Fourth Lateran Council in 1215, which affirmed the idea that ordained priests had the power to transform bread and wine during church ceremonies into the body and blood of Christ (a change termed transubstantiation). According to papal doctrine, priests now had the power to mediate for everyone with God, setting the spiritual hierarchy of the church above the secular hierarchies of kings and other rulers. The council affirmed that Christians should confess their sins to a priest at least once a year, and that marriage was a sacrament, and thus indissoluble. It also ordered Jews and Muslims to wear special clothing that set them apart from Christians.

By the early thirteenth century papal efforts at reform begun more than a century earlier had attained phenomenal success, and the popes ruled a powerful, centralized institution. At the end of the century, however, the papacy again came into a violent dispute with secular rulers. Pope Boniface VIII (pontificate 1294–1303), arguing from precedent, insisted that King Edward I of England and Philip IV of France obtain his consent for taxes they had imposed on the clergy. Edward immediately denied the clergy the protection of the law, and Philip halted the shipment of all ecclesiastical revenue to Rome. Boniface had to back down.

The battle for power between the papacy and the French monarchy became a bitter war of propaganda, with Philip at one point calling the pope a heretic. Finally, in 1302, in a formal written statement known as a papal bull, Boniface insisted that all

**Bishop Ending a Marriage**
In this thirteenth-century illumination from a legal manual, a bishop ends a marriage. Marriage was first declared a sacrament by officials in the Catholic Church in the late eleventh century as part of the condemnation of the Cathars, and confirmed as such at the Fourth Lateran Council. Because of this, divorce was prohibited, although marriages could be annulled — that is, declared never to have been valid in the first place — for a variety of reasons, and annulments did occur, particularly for members of the nobility. (Bibliothèque Sainte-Genevieve, Paris, France/Archives Charmet/Bridgeman Images)

Christians — including kings — were subject to the pope in all things. (See "Evaluating Written Evidence: Pope Boniface VIII, *Unam Sanctam,*" page 247.) In retaliation, French mercenary troops assaulted and arrested the aged pope at Anagni in Italy. Although Boniface was soon freed, he died shortly afterward. The confrontation at Anagni foreshadowed further difficulties in the Christian Church in the fourteenth century.

## What roles did monks, nuns, and friars play in medieval society?

While the reforming popes transformed the Christian Church into an institution free of lay control at the highest level, leaders of monasteries and convents asserted their independence from secular control on the local level as well. Monks, nuns, and friars played significant roles in medieval society, both as individuals and as members of institutions. Medieval people believed that monks and nuns performed an important social service when they prayed, for their prayers and chants secured God's blessing for society. The friars worked in the cities, teaching and preaching Christian doctrine, but also investigating heretics.

### Monastic Revival

In the early Middle Ages many religious houses followed the Benedictine *Rule*, while others developed their own patterns (see "Monastery Life" in Chapter 7). In the High Middle Ages this diversity became more formalized, and **religious orders**, groups of

monastic houses following a particular rule, were established. Historians term the foundation, strengthening, and reform of religious orders in the High Middle Ages the "monastic revival."

In the period of political disorder that followed the disintegration of the Carolingian Empire, many religious houses fell under the control and domination of local lords. Powerful laymen appointed themselves or their relatives as abbots, took the lands and goods of monasteries, and seized monastic revenues. Accordingly, the level of spiritual observance and intellectual activity in monasteries and convents declined. The local lords also compelled abbots from time to time to provide contingents of soldiers, an obligation stemming from the abbots' judicial authority over knights and peasants on monastic lands.

The first sign of reform came in 909, when William the Pious, duke of Aquitaine, established the abbey of Cluny in Burgundy. Duke William declared that the monastery was to be free from any feudal

# Pope Boniface VIII, *Unam Sanctam*

In late 1302, after several years of bitter conflict with King Philip IV of France over control and taxation of the clergy in France, Pope Boniface VIII issued a papal bull declaring the official church position on the proper relationships between church and state. Throughout, the pope uses the "royal we," that is, the plural "we" instead of "I" when talking about himself.

We are obliged by the faith to believe and hold—and we do firmly believe and sincerely confess—that there is one Holy Catholic and Apostolic Church, and that outside this Church there is neither salvation nor remission of sins. . . . In which Church there is "one Lord, one faith, one baptism." . . . Of this one and only Church there is one body and one head—not two heads, like a monster—namely Christ, and Christ's vicar is Peter, and Peter's successor, for the Lord said to Peter himself, "Feed my sheep." "My sheep" He said in general, not these or those sheep; wherefore He is understood to have committed them all to him. . . .

And we learn from the words of the Gospel that in this Church and in her power are two swords, the spiritual and the temporal. . . . Truly he who denies that the temporal sword is in the power of Peter, misunderstands the words of the Lord, "Put up thy sword into the sheath." Both are in the power of the Church, the spiritual sword and the material. But the latter is to be used for the Church, the former by her; the former by the priest, the latter by kings and captains but at the will and by the permission of the priest. The one sword, then, should be under the other, and temporal authority subject to spiritual. . . .

If, therefore, the earthly power err, it shall be judged by the spiritual power; and if a lesser power err, it shall be judged by a greater. But if the supreme power [the papacy] err, it can only be judged by God, not by man. . . . For this authority, although given to a man and exercised by a man, is not human, but rather divine, given at God's mouth to Peter and established on a rock for him and his successors in Him whom he confessed, the Lord saying to Peter himself, "Whatsoever thou shalt bind," etc. Whoever therefore resists this power thus ordained of God, resists the ordinance of God. . . . Furthermore, we declare, state, define, and pronounce that it is altogether necessary to salvation for every human creature to be subject to the Roman pontiff.

## EVALUATE THE EVIDENCE

1. According to Pope Boniface, what is the proper relationship between the authority of the pope and the authority of earthly rulers? What is the basis for that relationship?
2. How might the earlier conflicts between popes and secular rulers traced in this chapter have influenced Boniface's declaration?

Source: Henry Bettenson, ed., *Documents of the Christian Church* (Oxford: Oxford University Press, 1963), pp. 115–116. Copyright Oxford University Press 1963, 1999, 2011. Reproduced with permission of Oxford University Press through PLSclear.

---

responsibilities to him or any other lord, its members subordinate only to the pope. The monastery at Cluny, which initially held high standards of religious behavior, came to exert vast religious influence. In the eleventh century Cluny was fortunate in having a series of highly able abbots who ruled for a long time. In a disorderly world, Cluny gradually came to represent stability. Therefore, laypersons placed lands under its custody and monastic priories under its jurisdiction (a priory is a religious house, with generally fewer residents than an abbey, governed by a prior or prioress). In this way, hundreds of religious houses, primarily in France and Spain, came under Cluny's authority.

Deeply impressed laypeople showered gifts on monasteries with good reputations, such as Cluny and its many daughter houses. But as the monasteries became richer, the lifestyle of the monks grew increasingly luxurious. Monastic observance and spiritual fervor declined. Soon fresh demands for reform were heard, resulting in the founding of new religious orders in the late eleventh and early twelfth centuries.

The Cistercians (sihs-TUHR-shuhnz) best represent the new reforming spirit because of their phenomenal expansion and great economic, political, and spiritual influence. In 1098 a group of monks left the rich abbey of Molesmes in Burgundy and founded a new house in the swampy forest of Cîteaux (see TOH). The early Cistercians (the word is derived from *Cîteaux*) determined to keep their services simple and their lives austere, returning to work in the fields and other sorts of manual labor. As with Cluny, their high ideals made them a model, and 525 Cistercian monasteries were founded in the course of the twelfth century all over Europe. The Cistercians'

■ **religious orders** Groups of monastic houses following a particular rule.

influence on European society was profound, for they used new agricultural methods and technology and spread them throughout Europe. Their improvements in farming and animal raising brought wealth, however, and wealth brought power. By the later twelfth century, as with Cluny earlier, economic prosperity and political power had begun to compromise the original Cistercian ideals.

## Life in Convents and Monasteries

Medieval monasteries were religious institutions whose organization and structure fulfilled the social needs of the nobility. The monasteries provided noble boys with education and opportunities for ecclesiastical careers. Beginning in the thirteenth century an increasing number of boys and men from professional and merchant families became monks, seeking to take advantage of the opportunities monasteries offered.

Throughout the Middle Ages social class also defined the kinds of religious life open to women. Kings and nobles usually established convents for their daughters, sisters, aunts, or aging mothers, and other women of their class. Like monks, many nuns came into the convent as children, and very often sisters, cousins, aunts, and nieces could all be found in the same place. Thus, though nuns were to some degree cut off from their families by being cloistered, family relationships were maintained within the convent.

The office of abbess or prioress was the most powerful position a woman could hold in medieval society. (See "Individuals in Society: Hildegard of Bingen," page 249.) Abbesses were part of the political structure in the same way that bishops and abbots were, with manors under their financial and legal control. They appointed tax collectors, bailiffs, judges, and often priests in their lands. Some abbesses in the Holy Roman Empire even had the right to name bishops and send representatives to imperial assemblies. Abbesses also opened and supported hospitals, orphanages, and schools and hired builders, sculptors,

and painters to construct and decorate residences and churches.

Monasteries for men were headed by an abbot or a prior, who was generally a member of a noble family, often a younger son in a family with several sons. The main body of monks, known as "choir monks" because one of their primary activities was reciting prayers and services while sitting in the part of the church called the choir, were largely of noble or middle-class background, and they did not till the land themselves. Men from peasant families sometimes became choir monks, but more often they served as lay brothers, doing the manual labor essential to running the monastery. The novice master or novice mistress was responsible for the training of recruits.

The pattern of life within individual monasteries varied widely from house to house and from region to region. One central activity, however, was performed everywhere. Daily life centered on the liturgy or Divine Office, psalms and other prayers prescribed by Saint Benedict that monks and nuns prayed seven times a day and once during the night. Prayers were offered for peace, rain, good harvests, the civil authorities, and the monks' families and benefactors. Everything connected with prayer was understood as praise of God, so abbeys spent a large percentage of their income on splendid objects to enhance the service, including sacred vessels of embossed silver or gold, altar cloths of the finest silks or velvets, embroideries, and beautiful reliquaries to house the relics of the patron saint.

**Monastery and Convent Life**   Life in monasteries and convents involved physical labor as well as spiritual activities. In this twelfth-century French manuscript, a monk and a lay brother chop down a tree. Such work was a common part of monastic life because monasteries, especially those of the Cistercians, were often built in heavily forested wilderness areas. (Bibliothèque Municipale, Dijon, France/Bridgeman Images)

# INDIVIDUALS IN SOCIETY
## Hildegard of Bingen

The tenth child of a lesser noble family, Hildegard (1098–1179) was given as a child to an abbey in the Rhineland when she was eight years old; there she learned Latin and received a good education. She spent most of her life in various women's religious communities, two of which she founded herself. When she was a child, she began having mystical visions, often of light in the sky, but told few people about them. In middle age, however, her visions became more dramatic: "And it came to pass . . . when I was 42 years and 7 months old, that the heavens were opened and a blinding light of exceptional brilliance flowed through my entire brain. And so it kindled my whole heart and breast like a flame, not burning but warming . . . and suddenly I understood of the meaning of expositions of the books."* She wanted the church to approve of her visions and wrote first to Bernard of Clairvaux, who answered her briefly and dismissively, and then to Pope Eugenius, who encouraged her to write them down. Her first work was *Scivias* (Know the Ways of the Lord), a record of her mystical visions that incorporates vast theological learning.

Possessed of leadership and administrative talents, Hildegard left her abbey in 1147 to found the convent of Rupertsberg near Bingen. There she produced *Physica* (On the Physical Elements) and *Causa et Curae* (Causes and Cures), scientific works on the curative properties of natural elements, as well as poems, a mystery play, and several more works of mysticism. She carried on a huge correspondence with scholars, prelates, and ordinary people. When she was over fifty, she left her community to preach to audiences of clergy and laity, and she was the only woman of her time whose opinions on religious matters were considered authoritative by the church.

Hildegard's visions have been explored by theologians and also by neurologists, who judge that they may have originated in migraine headaches, as she reports many of the same phenomena that migraine sufferers do: auras of light around objects, areas of blindness, feelings of intense doubt and intense euphoria. The interpretations that she develops come from her theological insight and learning, however, not illness. That same insight also emerges in her music, for which she is best known today. Eighty of her compositions survive—a huge number for a medieval composer—most of them written to be sung by the nuns in her convent, so they have strong lines for female voices. Many of her songs and chants have been recorded and are available on CD, as downloads, and on several websites.

Inspired by heavenly fire, Hildegard begins to dictate her visions to her scribe. The original of this elaborately illustrated twelfth-century copy of Scivias disappeared from Hildegard's convent during World War II, but fortunately a facsimile copy had already been made. (Private Collection/ Bridgeman Images)

### QUESTIONS FOR ANALYSIS

1. Why do you think Hildegard sought church approval for her visions after keeping them secret for so many years?
2. In what ways is Hildegard's life representative of nuns' lives in the High Middle Ages? In what ways were her accomplishments extraordinary?

*From *Scivias*, trans. Mother Columba Hart and Jane Bishop, *The Classics of Western Spirituality* (New York/Mahwah: Paulist Press, 1990), p. 65.

---

In some abbeys monks and nuns spent much of their time copying books and manuscripts and then illuminating them, decorating them with human and animal figures or elaborate designs, often painted in bright colors or gold. A few monasteries and convents became centers of learning where talented residents wrote their own works as well as copying those of others.

Monks and nuns also performed a variety of social services in an age when there was no state and no conception

**Saint Dominic Rescuing Shipwrecked Fishermen from Drowning**    In this detail from an altarpiece in the convent of St. Clare de Vic in present-day northeastern Spain, painted by the Catalan artist Lluís Borrassà in 1415, Saint Dominic miraculously saves fishermen from drowning. Accounts of miracles were an important part of devotion to saints, and often the subject of religious artwork in the Middle Ages. The altarpiece of which this is a part, made for a convent of Poor Clares, shows Saint Francis of Assisi in the center, surrounded by other male and female saints, including Saint Clare, whose followers founded the convent for which it was made. (Museo Episcopal, Vich, Osona, Catalonia, Spain/Bridgeman Images)

of social welfare as a public responsibility. Monasteries often ran schools that gave primary education to young boys; convents did the same for girls. Monasteries served as hotels and resting places for travelers, and frequently operated hospitals and leprosariums, which provided care and attention to the sick, the aged, and the afflicted.

## The Friars

Monks and nuns carried out their spiritual and social services largely within the walls of their institutions, but in the thirteenth century new types of religious orders were founded whose members lived out in the world. Members of these new groups were **friars**, not monks. They thought that more contact with ordinary Christians, not less, was a better spiritual path. Friars stressed apostolic poverty, a life based on the teaching of

the Gospels in which they would own no property and depend on Christian people for their material needs. Hence they were called mendicants, from the Latin word for begging. The friars' service to the towns and the poor, their ideal of poverty, and their compassion for the human condition made them popular.

One order of friars was started by Domingo de Gúzman (1170?–1221), born in Castile. Domingo (later called Dominic), a well-educated priest, accompanied his bishop in 1206 on an unsuccessful mission to win the Albigensians in southern France back to orthodox teaching. Determined to succeed through ardent preaching, he subsequently returned to France with a few followers. In 1216 the group—officially known as the Preaching Friars, though often called Dominicans—won papal recognition as a new religious order.

Francesco di Bernardone (1181–1226), son of a wealthy Italian cloth merchant of Assisi, had a religious conversion and decided to live and preach the Gospel in absolute poverty. Francis of Assisi, as he came to be known, emphasized not withdrawal from the world, but joyful devotion. In contrast to the Albigensians, who saw the material world as evil, Francis saw all creation as God-given and good. He was widely reported to perform miracles involving animals and birds, and wrote hymns to natural objects.

The simplicity, humility, and joyful devotion with which Francis carried out his mission soon attracted others. Although he resisted pressure to establish an order, his followers became so numerous that he was obliged to develop some formal structure. In 1221 the papacy approved the Rule of the Little Brothers of Saint Francis, generally called the Franciscans (frahn-SIHS-kuhnz).

Friars worked among the poor, but also addressed the spiritual and intellectual needs of the middle classes and the wealthy. The Dominicans preferred that their friars be university graduates in order to better preach to a sophisticated urban society. Dominicans soon held professorial chairs at leading universities, and the Franciscans followed suit.

Beginning in 1231 the papacy also used friars to investigate heretics, sometimes under the auspices of a new ecclesiastical court, the Inquisition, in which accused people were subjected to lengthy interrogations and torture could be used to extract confessions. It is ironic that groups whose teachings were similar in so many ways to those of heretics were charged with rooting them out. That irony deepened in the case of the Spiritual Franciscans, a group that broke away from the main body of Franciscans to follow Francis's original ideals of absolute poverty. When they denied the pope's right to countermand that ideal, he ordered them tried as heretics.

Women sought to develop similar orders devoted to active service out in the world. Clare of Assisi (1193–1253) became a follower of Francis, who established a place for her to live in a church in Assisi. She

■ **friars**  Men belonging to certain religious orders who lived not in monasteries but out in the world.

was joined by other women, and they attempted to establish a rule that would follow Francis's ideals of absolute poverty and allow them to serve the poor. This rule was accepted by the papacy only after many decades, and then only because she agreed that the order, the Poor Clares, would be cloistered.

In the growing cities of Europe, especially in the Netherlands, groups of laywomen seeking to live religious lives came together as what later came to be known as Beguines (bay-GEENS). They lived communally in small houses called *beguinages*, combining lives of prayer with service to the needy. Beguine spirituality emphasized direct personal communication with God, sometimes through mystical experiences, rather than through the intercession of a saint or official church rituals. Initially some church officials gave guarded approval of the movement, but the church grew increasingly uncomfortable with women who were neither married nor cloistered nuns. By the fourteenth century Beguines were declared heretical, and much of their property was confiscated.

# What were the causes, course, and consequences of the Crusades and the broader expansion of Christianity?

The Crusades of the eleventh and twelfth centuries were the most obvious manifestation of the papal claim to the leadership of Christian society. The **Crusades** were wars sponsored by the papacy for the recovery of the holy city of Jerusalem from the Muslims. The enormous popular response to papal calls for crusading reveals the influence of the reformed papacy and the depth of religious fervor among many different types of people. The Crusades also reflected the church's new understanding of the noble warrior class, for whom war against the church's enemies was understood as a religious duty. The word *crusade* was not actually used at the time and did not appear in English until the late sixteenth century. It means literally "taking the cross," from the cross that soldiers sewed on their garments as a Christian symbol. At the time people going off to fight simply said they were taking "the way of the cross" or "the road to Jerusalem."

## Background and Motives of the Crusades

The medieval church's attitude toward violence was contradictory. On the one hand, church councils threatened excommunication for anyone who attacked peasants, clerics, or merchants or destroyed crops and unfortified places, a movement termed the Peace of God. Councils also tried to limit the number of days on which fighting was permitted, prohibiting it on Sundays, on special feast days, and in the seasons of Lent and Advent. On the other hand, popes supported armed conflict against kings and emperors if this worked to their advantage, thus encouraging warfare among Christians. After a serious theological disagreement in 1054 split the Orthodox Church of Byzantium and the Roman Church of the West, the pope also contemplated invading the Byzantine Empire, an idea that subsequent popes considered as well.

Although conflicts in which Christians fought Christians were troubling to many thinkers, war against non-Christians was another matter. By the ninth century popes and other church officials encouraged war in defense of Christianity, promising spiritual benefits to those who died fighting. By the eleventh century these benefits were extended to all those who simply joined a campaign: their sins would be remitted without having to do penance, that is, without having to confess to a priest and carry out some action to make up for the sins. Around this time, Christian thinkers were developing the concept of purgatory, a place where those on their way to Heaven stayed for a while to do any penance they had not completed while alive. (Those on their way to Hell went straight there.) Engaging in holy war could shorten one's time in purgatory, or, as many people understood the promise, allow one to head straight to paradise. Popes signified this by providing **indulgences**, grants with the pope's name on them that lessened earthly penance and postmortem purgatory. Popes promised these spiritual benefits, and also provided financial support, for Christian armies in the reconquista in Spain and the Norman campaign against the Muslims in Sicily. Preachers communicated these ideas widely and told stories about warrior-saints who slew hundreds of enemies.

Religious devotion had long been expressed through pilgrimages to holy places, and these were increasingly described in military terms, as battles against the hardships along the way. Pilgrims to Jerusalem were often armed, so the line between pilgrimage and holy war on this particular route was increasingly blurred. In the midst of these developments came a change in possession of Jerusalem. The Arab Muslims who had ruled Jerusalem and the surrounding territory for centuries had generally

---

■ **Crusades** Wars sponsored by the papacy for the recovery of Jerusalem and surrounding territories from the Muslims in the late eleventh to the late thirteenth centuries.

■ **indulgences** Grants by the pope that lessened or eliminated the penance that sinners had to pay on earth and in purgatory before ascending to Heaven.

**Persecution of Jews**    This marginal illustration from the *Rochester Chronicle*, a fourteenth-century copy made by a monk in the English city Rochester of an earlier Latin chronicle, shows a man beating Jews with a club. The Jews are wearing badges in the form of two white tablets on their clothes, first ordered by royal mandate in 1218, "so that in this way Jews may be clearly distinguished from Christians." Both royal restrictions and local violence continued, so that by the time this illustration was made, Jews had been expelled from England. They would not be allowed to return until 1657. (Cotton Nero D. III, f.183v, from "Chronica Roffense," 14th century/British Library, London, UK/© British Library Board. All Rights Reserved/Bridgeman Images)

The Crusades proved to be a disaster for Jewish-Christian relations. In many parts of Europe, Jews lent money to peasants, townspeople, and nobles, and indebtedness bred resentment. Inspired by the ideology of holy war and resentment of Jewish economic activities, Christian armies on their way to Jerusalem on the First Crusade joined with local people to attack Jewish families and sometimes entire Jewish communities. In the German cities along the Rhine River, for example, an army of Crusaders under the leadership of a German noble forced Jews to convert through mass baptisms and killed those who resisted; more than eight hundred Jews were killed in Worms and more than a thousand in Mainz. Later Crusades brought similar violence, enhanced by rumors that Jews engaged in the ritual murder of Christians to use their blood in religious rites. As a result of growing hostility, legal restrictions on Jews gradually increased throughout Europe. In 1290 King Edward I of England expelled the Jews from England and confiscated their property and goods; it would be four centuries before they would be allowed back in. King Philip IV of France followed Edward's example in 1306.

The long-term cultural legacy of the Crusades may have been more powerful than their short-term impact. The ideal of a sacred mission to conquer or convert Muslim peoples entered some Europeans' consciousness, and was later used in other situations. When Christopher Columbus sailed west in 1492, he hoped to reach

India in part to establish a Christian base from which a new crusade against Islam could be launched. Muslims later looked back on the Crusades as expansionist and imperialist, the beginning of a long trajectory of Western attempts to limit or destroy Islam.

## The Expansion of Christianity

The Crusades were not the only example of Christian expansion in the High Middle Ages. As we saw earlier, Christian kingdoms were established in the Iberian Peninsula through the reconquista. This gradual Christian advance was replicated in northern and eastern Europe in the centuries after 1000. People and ideas moved from western France and western Germany into Ireland, Scandinavia, the Baltic lands, and eastern Europe, with significant consequences for those territories. Wars of expansion, the establishment of new Christian bishoprics, and the vast migration of colonists, together with the papal emphasis on a unified Christian world, brought about the gradual Christianization of a larger area. By 1350 Roman Catholic Europe was double the size it had been in 950.

Ireland had been Christian since the days of Saint Patrick (see "Missionaries' Actions" in Chapter 7), but in the twelfth century Norman knights crossed from England, defeated Irish lords, and established bishoprics with defined territorial dioceses. Latin Christian influences also entered the Scandinavian and Baltic regions primarily through the erection of dioceses. Otto I established the first Scandinavian dioceses in Denmark. In Norway Christianity spread in coastal

■ **Christendom**    The term used by early medieval writers to refer to the realm of Christianity.

areas beginning in the tenth century, and King Olaf II (r. 1015–1028) brought in clergy and bishops from England and Germany to establish the church more firmly. From Norway Christianity spread to Iceland; from Denmark it spread to Sweden and Finland. In all of these areas, Christian missionaries preached, baptized, and built churches. Royal power advanced institutional Christianity, and traditional Norse religions practiced by the Vikings were outlawed.

In 1397 Queen Margrete I (1353–1412) united the crowns of Denmark, Sweden-Finland, and Norway in the Union of Kalmar. She continued royal support of bishops and worked toward creating a stronger state by checking the power of the nobility and creating a stronger financial base for the monarchy.

In eastern Europe, the German emperor Otto I planted a string of dioceses along his northern and eastern frontiers, hoping to pacify the newly conquered Slavs. German nobles built castles and ruthlessly crushed revolts by Slavic peoples, sometimes using the language of crusade to describe their actions. A military order of German knights founded in Palestine, the Teutonic (too-TAH-nihk) Knights, moved their operations to eastern Europe and waged wars against the pagan Prussians in the Baltic region, again terming these "crusades." After 1230, from a base in Poland, they established a new Christian territory, Prussia, and gradually the entire eastern shore of the Baltic came under their hegemony.

The church also moved into central Europe, first in Bohemia in the tenth century and from there into Poland and Hungary in the eleventh. In the twelfth and thirteenth centuries, thousands of settlers poured into eastern Europe. These immigrants were German in descent, name, language, and law. Larger towns such as Kraków and Riga engaged in long-distance trade and gradually grew into large urban centers.

## Christendom

Through the actions of the Roman emperors Constantine and Theodosius (see Chapter 7), Christianity became in some ways a state as well as a religion. Early medieval writers began to use the word **Christendom** to refer to this Christian realm. When the pope called for holy war against the Muslims, for example, he spoke not only of the retaking of Jerusalem, but also of the defense of Christendom. When missionaries, officials, and soldiers took Christianity into the Iberian Peninsula, Scandinavia, or the Baltic region, they understood their actions as aimed at the expansion of Christendom.

From the point of view of popes such as Gregory VII and Innocent III, Christendom was a unified hierarchy with the papacy at the top. They pushed for uniformity of religious worship and campaigned continually for use of the same religious service, the Roman liturgy in Latin, in all countries and places. They forbade vernacular Christian rituals or those that differed in their pattern of worship. As we have seen in this chapter, however, not everyone had the same view. Kings and emperors may have accepted the Roman liturgy in their lands, but they had their own ideas of the way power should operate in Christendom, even if this brought them into conflict with the papacy. They remained loyal to Christendom as a concept, but they had a profoundly different idea about how it should be structured and who could best defend it. The battles in the High Middle Ages between popes and kings and between Christians and Muslims were signs of how deeply religion had replaced tribal, political, and ethnic structures as the essence of Western culture.

## NOTES

1. D. C. Douglas and G. E. Greenaway, eds., *English Historical Documents*, vol. 2 (London: Eyre & Spottiswoode, 1961), p. 853.
2. *Hrosvithae Liber Tertius, a Text with Translation*, ed. and trans. Mary Bernardine Bergman (Covington, Ky.: The Sisters of Saint Benedict, 1943), p. 45.
3. J. Johns, *Arabic Administration in Norman Sicily: The Royal Diwān* (New York: Cambridge University Press, 2002), p. 293.
4. H. T. Riley, ed., *Memorials of London* (London: Longmans Green, 1868).
5. Honorius of Autun, "Elucidarium sive Dialogus," vol. 172, col. 1148.

# LOOKING BACK  LOOKING AHEAD

The High Middle Ages were a time when kings, emperors, and popes expanded their powers and created financial and legal bureaucracies to support those powers. With political expansion and stability came better communication of information, more uniform legal systems, and early financial institutions. Nobles remained the dominant social group, but as monarchs developed new institutions, their kingdoms began to function more like modern states than disorganized territories. Popes made the church more independent of lay control, established the papal curia and a separate system of canon law, approved new religious orders that provided spiritual and social services, and developed new ways of raising revenue. They supported the expansion of Christianity in southern, northern, and eastern Europe and proclaimed a series of Crusades against Muslims to extend still further the boundaries of a Christendom under their control.

Many of the systems of the High Middle Ages expanded in later centuries and are still in existence today: the financial department of the British government remains the Exchequer; the legal systems of Britain and many former British colonies (including the United States) are based on common law; the pope is still elected by the college of cardinals and assisted by the papal curia; the Roman Catholic, Eastern Orthodox, and Anglican Churches still operate law courts that make rulings based on canon law. These systems also contained the seeds of future problems, however, for wealthier nations could sustain longer wars, independent popes could more easily abuse their power, and leaders who espoused crusading ideology could justify the enslavement or extermination of whole peoples.

Despite the long-lived impact of the growth of centralized political and ecclesiastical power—for good or ill—most people who lived during the high medieval period did not have direct experience of centralized institutions. Kings and popes sent tax collectors, judges, and sometimes soldiers, but they themselves remained far away. For most people, what went on closer to home in their families and local communities was far more important.

## Make Connections

Think about the larger developments and continuities within and across chapters.

1. What similarities and differences do you see between the institutions and laws established by medieval rulers and those of Roman and Byzantine emperors (Chapters 6 and 7)?

2. What factors over the centuries enabled the Christian Church to become the most powerful and wealthy institution in Europe, and what problems did this create?

3. How would you compare the privileges and roles of medieval nobles with those of earlier hereditary elites, such as those of ancient Mesopotamia and Egypt (Chapter 1) or the patricians of republican Rome (Chapter 5)?

## 9   REVIEW & EXPLORE

### Identify Key Terms

Identify and explain the significance of each item below.

*Domesday Book* (p. 232)

primogeniture (p. 233)

Holy Roman Empire (p. 235)

reconquista (p. 238)

common law (p. 238)

Magna Carta (p. 239)

chivalry (p. 240)

simony (p. 243)

college of cardinals (p. 244)

excommunication (p. 244)

canon law (p. 245)

religious orders (p. 246)

friars (p. 250)

Crusades (p. 251)

indulgences (p. 251)

Christendom (p. 257)

### Review the Main Ideas

Answer the section heading questions from the chapter.

1. How did monarchs try to centralize political power? (p. 232)

2. How did the administration of law evolve in this period? (p. 238)

3. What were the political and social roles of nobles? (p. 240)

4. How did the papacy reform the church, and what were the reactions to these efforts? (p. 243)

5. What roles did monks, nuns, and friars play in medieval society? (p. 246)

6. What were the causes, course, and consequences of the Crusades and the broader expansion of Christianity? (p. 251)

## Suggested Resources

### BOOKS

- Bartlett, Robert. *England Under the Norman and Angevin Kings, 1075–1225*. 2000. An excellent synthesis of social, cultural, and political history in highly readable prose.
- Deane, Jennifer Kolpacoff. *A History of Medieval Heresy and Inquisition*. 2011. A concise history of the increasingly bitter encounters between dissent and the institutional church.
- Edgington, Susan B., and Sarah Lambert, eds. *Gendering the Crusades*. 2002. Articles that look at the roles of men and women.
- Kaeuper, Richard W. *Chivalry and Violence in Medieval Europe*. 2006. Examines the role chivalry played in promoting violent disorder.
- Karras, Ruth M. *From Boys to Men: Formations of Masculinity in Late Medieval Europe*. 2002. Explores the way boys of different social groups were trained in what it meant to be a man; designed for students.
- Lawrence, C. H. *Medieval Monasticism: Forms of Religious Life in Western Europe in the Middle Ages*, 4th ed. 2015. Provides a solid introduction to monastic life as it was practiced.

- Madden, Thomas. *The New Concise History of the Crusades*. 2005. A highly readable brief survey by the preeminent American scholar of the Crusades.
- Moore, R. I. *The Formation of a Persecuting Society*, 2d ed. 2007. Sets the Inquisition and medieval heresy within a broad cultural, social, and political context.
- Newman, Barbara. *Voice of the Living Light: Hildegard of Bingen and Her World*. 1998. A book designed for general readers that places the medieval mystic within her social, intellectual, and political contexts.
- O'Callaghan, Joseph. *Reconquest and Crusade in Medieval Spain*. 2004. A broad survey that situates the Spanish reconquista within the context of crusading efforts.
- Rubin, Miri. *Gentile Tales: The Narrative Assault on Late Medieval Jews*. 2004. Explores the way that stories that were spread about Jews contributed to violence against them.
- Starkey, David. *Magna Carta: The Medieval Roots of Modern Politics*. 2015. A lively account for general readers of the document and its impact.
- Tyerman, Christopher. *Fighting for Christendom: Holy War and the Crusades*. 2005. Assesses the impact of the Crusades on modern times.

### MEDIA

- *Battle Castle* (Parallax, 2012). A six-part interactive documentary, first shown on Canadian television, with an accompanying website and computer game, that examines sieges and battles involving six formidable castles in Syria, France, Spain, Wales, Poland, and England. Reflects high production values and excellent scholarship.
- *Becket* (Peter Glenville, 1964). Richard Burton stars as Thomas Becket and Peter O'Toole as King Henry II of England in a widely acclaimed film that focuses on the conflict between the two and the growth of royal power.
- *Braveheart* (Mel Gibson, 1995). Loosely based on the story of the thirteenth-century Scottish nobleman William Wallace, this historical epic regularly shows up on lists of best medieval films (for its battle scenes) and worst medieval films (for its historical inaccuracy).
- *De Re Militari*. The official website of the Society for the Study of Medieval Military History, with primary sources, articles, dissertations, and other resources for the study of military actions, technology, and topics from the fall of Rome to the early seventeenth century. **deremilitari.org/**

- *The Lion in Winter* (Anthony Harvey, 1968) (Andrey Konchalovskiy, 2003). Two award-winning film versions of the same play, centering on the intense and hostile relationships among Henry II, his wife Eleanor of Aquitaine, and their sons. The 1968 version stars Katharine Hepburn and Peter O'Toole, and the 2003 version stars Glenn Close and Patrick Stewart.
- *Medievalists.net*. This medieval-oriented blog provides news, articles, videos, reviews, and general information about the Middle Ages and medieval society. **www.medievalists.net**
- *Monastic Matrix*. A database website designed to make available all existing data about nuns and other women in religious communities in Christian Europe between 400 and 1600. Organized thematically and very easy to use. **monasticmatrix.osu.edu/**
- *Vision: From the Life of Hildegard von Bingen* (Margarethe von Trotta, 2010). A German film, with English subtitles, that focuses on the famed twelfth-century Benedictine nun, mystic, composer, and philosopher. Shot on location in the convent of Bingen and the surrounding countryside.

# 10

# *Life* in Villages and Cities of the High Middle Ages

## 1000–1300

**Kings, emperors, nobles, and their officials** created political and legal institutions that structured many aspects of life in the High Middle Ages, but ordinary people typically worked and lived without paying much attention to the political developments that took place at faraway centers of power. Similarly, the conflicts between popes and secular leaders were dramatic, but for most people religion was primarily a matter of joining with neighbors and family members in rituals to express beliefs, thanks, and hopes.

While the routines of medieval life followed familiar rhythms for centuries, this does not mean that life in the High Middle Ages was unchanging. Agricultural improvements such as better plows and water mills increased the amount and quality of food, and the population grew. Relative security and the increasing food supply allowed for the growth and development of towns and a revival of long-distance trade. Some urban merchants and bankers became as wealthy as great nobles. Trade brought in new ideas as well as merchandise, and cities developed into intellectual and cultural centers. The university, a new type of educational institution, came into being, providing advanced training in theology, medicine, and law. Traditions and values were spread orally and in written form through poems, stories, and songs. Gothic cathedrals, where people saw beautiful stained-glass windows and listened to complex music, were physical manifestations of medieval people's deep faith and pride in their own community. ■

... IAM CRISTI · VI TI ...

## CHAPTER PREVIEW

- What was village life like in medieval Europe?

- How did religion shape everyday life in the High Middle Ages?

- What led to Europe's economic growth and reurbanization?

- What was life like in medieval cities?

- How did universities serve the needs of medieval society?

- How did literature and architecture express medieval values?

**Mosaic of a Woman Feeding Chickens**
In this detail from a magnificent gold mosaic in the ceiling of the Basilica of Saint Clement in Rome, made in the twelfth century, a woman feeds her chickens. Scenes from everyday life often feature in the margins of paintings, mosaics, and books, and provide information about the lives of ordinary people that is unavailable elsewhere. (Basilica of St. Clement, Rome, Italy/De Agostini Picture Library/G. Dagli Orti/ Bridgeman Images)

# What was village life like in medieval Europe?

The vast majority of people in medieval Europe were peasants who lived in small villages and rarely traveled very far, but since villagers did not perform what were considered "noble" deeds, the aristocratic monks and clerics who wrote the records that serve as historical sources did not spend time or precious writing materials on the peasantry. When common people were mentioned, it was usually with contempt or in terms of the services and obligations they owed. Today's scholars are far more interested than were their medieval predecessors in the lives of ordinary people, however, and are using archaeological, artistic, and material sources to fill in details that are rarely mentioned in written documents.

## Slavery, Serfdom, and Upward Mobility

There were many levels of peasants, ranging from outright slaves to free but poor peasants to very rich farmers. The number of slaves who worked the land declined steadily in the High Middle Ages, and most rural people in western Europe during this period were serfs rather than slaves, though the distinction between slave and serf was not always clear. Both lacked freedom, and both were subject to the will of one person, the manorial lord. Serfs remained bound to the land when their lords died, but unlike slaves they could not be bought and sold outright.

Most serfs worked small plots of land; in addition, all serfs were required to provide a certain number of days of labor a week—more in planting and harvest seasons—on a lord's land. Serfs were also often obliged to pay fees on common occurrences, such as marriage or the inheritance of land from one generation to the next. Serfdom was a hereditary condition. As money became more widely available and widely used, however, some serfs bought their freedom. Some gained it when manorial lords organized groups of villagers to cut down forests or fill in swamps and marshes to make more land available for farming. A serf could clear a patch of fen or forestland, make it productive, and, through prudent saving, buy more land and eventually purchase freedom. Serfs who migrated longer distances, such as German peasants who moved eastward into Slavic lands, were often granted a reduction in labor services as a reward. Thus both internal and external frontier lands in the High Middle Ages provided some opportunities for upward mobility.

## The Manor

Most peasants, free and serf, lived in family groups in small villages. One or more villages and the land surrounding them made up a manor controlled by a noble lord or a church official such as a bishop, abbot, or abbess. Most villages had a church. In some the

**Harvesting Hay**   A peasant with his socks rolled down to stay cool mows hay with a long scythe, while in the background a mill along a stream stands ready to grind grain or carry out other tasks. This illustration comes from a book of hours made in France in the early fifteenth century, probably for the duke of Bedford. Books of hours were devotional books with psalms, prayers, and calendars of church holidays, sometimes lavishly decorated. They often included cycles of months that linked seasonal rural activities to signs of the zodiac; here Cancer the crab shows that this is June. (Add Ms 18850 f.6r Book of Hours [The Bedford Hours] ca. 1410–30/British Library, London, UK/ © British Library Board. All Rights Reserved/ Bridgeman Images)

# TIMELINE

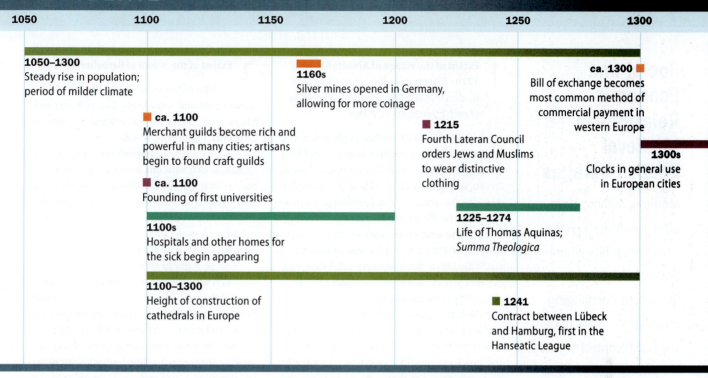

| | 1050 | 1100 | 1150 | 1200 | 1250 | 1300 |
|---|---|---|---|---|---|---|

**1050–1300**
Steady rise in population; period of milder climate

**1160s**
Silver mines opened in Germany, allowing for more coinage

**ca. 1300**
Bill of exchange becomes most common method of commercial payment in western Europe

**ca. 1100**
Merchant guilds become rich and powerful in many cities; artisans begin to found craft guilds

**1215**
Fourth Lateran Council orders Jews and Muslims to wear distinctive clothing

**1300s**
Clocks in general use in European cities

**ca. 1100**
Founding of first universities

**1100s**
Hospitals and other homes for the sick begin appearing

**1225–1274**
Life of Thomas Aquinas; *Summa Theologica*

**1100–1300**
Height of construction of cathedrals in Europe

**1241**
Contract between Lübeck and Hamburg, first in the Hanseatic League

---

lord's large residence was right next to the small peasant houses, while in others the lord lived in a castle or manor house separate from the village. Manors varied greatly in size; some contained a number of villages, and some were very small.

The arable land of the manor was divided between the lord and the peasantry, with the lord's portion known as the demesne (dih-MAYN), or home farm. The manor usually also held pasture or meadowland for the grazing of livestock, and often had some forestland as well. Forests were valuable resources, providing wood, ash, and resin for a variety of purposes, and were also used for feeding domestic animals on nuts, roots, and wild berries.

Lords generally appointed officials, such as bailiffs, to oversee the legal and business operations of their manors, collect taxes and fees, and handle disputes. Villages in many parts of Europe also developed institutions of self-government to handle issues such as crop rotation, and villagers themselves chose additional officials such as constables, jurors, and ale-tasters. Women had no official voice in running the village, but they did buy, sell, and hold land independently, especially as widows who headed households. In areas of Europe where men left seasonally or more permanently in search of work elsewhere, women played a larger decision-making role, though they generally did not hold official positions. (See "Thinking Like a Historian: Social and Economic Relations in Medieval English Villages," page 264.)

Manors did not represent the only form of medieval rural economy. In parts of Germany and the Netherlands and in much of southern France, free independent farmers owned land outright, free of rents and service obligations. In Scandinavia the climate was so harsh and the soil was so poor that people tended to live on widely scattered farms rather than in villages, growing what crops they could. They also fished and cut timber, for their own use and to trade.

## Work

The peasants' work was typically divided according to gender. Men cleared new land, plowed, and cared for large animals; women cared for small animals, spun yarn, and prepared food. Both sexes planted and harvested.

Once children were able to walk, they helped their parents in the hundreds of chores that had to be done. Small children collected eggs if the family had chickens or gathered twigs and sticks for firewood. As they grew older, children had more responsible tasks, such as weeding the family's vegetable garden, milking the cows, and helping with the planting or harvesting.

In many parts of Europe, medieval farmers employed the **open-field system**, a pattern that differs sharply from modern farming practices. In the open-field system, the arable land of a manor was divided into two or three fields without hedges or fences to mark the individual holdings of the lord, serfs, and free men. The village as a whole decided what would be planted in each field, rotating the

> ■ **open-field system** System in which the arable land of a manor was divided into two or three fields without hedges or fences to mark individual holdings.

## Social and Economic Relations in Medieval English Villages

Medieval villages have often been portrayed as squalid hamlets where downtrodden peasants lived in an unchanging equality of misery under the harsh control of a lord. Do sources about actual rural life support this view of village social and economic relations, do they refute it, or do they make it more complex?

### 1 Extent of the village of Alwalton, 1279. Extents were surveys taken by land-holders that listed the land and obligations of each household in a village.

The abbot of Peterborough holds the manor at Alwalton and village from the lord king directly. . . . Hugh Miller holds 1 virgate [about 25–30 acres] of land in villeinage by paying thence to the abbot 3 s. 1 d. [3 shillings, 1 denarius, or pence; there were 12 pence per shilling]. Likewise the same Hugh works through the year except 1 week at Christmas, 1 week at Easter, and 1 at Whitsuntide that is in each week 3 days, each day with 1 man, and in autumn each day with 2 men, performing the said works at the will of the said abbot as in plowing and other work. Likewise he gives 1 bushel of wheat for seed and 18 sheaves of oats for foddercorn. Likewise he gives 3 hens and 1 cock yearly and 5 eggs at Easter. Likewise he does carrying to Peterborough and to Jakele and nowhere else, at the will of the said abbot. Likewise if he sells a brood mare in his courtyard for 6 s. or more, he shall give to the said abbot 4 d., and if for less he shall give nothing. He gives also merchet [a payment when his daughters marry] and heriot [a payment when a family member dies] and is taxed at the feast of St. Michael, at the will of the said abbot. There are also 17 other villeins . . . paying and doing in all things, each for himself, to the said abbot yearly just as the said Hugh Miller. . . .

Henry, son of the miller, holds a cottage with a croft which contains 1 rood [¼ acre, a square about 100 feet on a side], paying thence yearly to the said abbot 2 s. Likewise he works for 3 days in carrying hay and in other works at the will of the abbot, each day with 1 man and in autumn 1 day in cutting grain with 1 man. . . . Likewise William Drake holds a cottage with a croft which contains half a rood [⅛ acre], paying to the abbot 6 d.; and he works just as the said Henry. There are also 18 other crofters . . . doing all things just as the said Henry.

### 2 Extent of the manor of Bernehorne, 1307.

John of Cayworth holds a house and 30 acres of land and owes yearly 2 s., at Easter and Michaelmas; and he owes a cock and two hens at Christmas, of the value of 4 d.

And he ought to harrow for 2 days at the Lenten sowing with one man and his own horse and his own harrow; the value of the work being 4 d.; and he is to receive from the lord on each day 3 meals, of the value of 5 d., and then his food will be at a loss of 1 d. Thus his harrowing is of no value to the service of the lord.

And he ought to carry the manure of the lord for 2 days with one cart, with his own 2 oxen, the value of the work being 8 d.; and he is to receive from the lord each day 3 meals of the price as above. And thus the service is worth 3 d. clear.

And he shall find one man for 2 days of mowing the meadow of the lord, who can mow, by estimation 1 acre and a half, the value of the mowing of an acre being 6 d.: the sum is therefore 9 d. and he is to receive each day 3 meals of the value given above; and thus that mowing is worth 4 d. clear. . . .

And he ought to carry the hay of the lord with a cart and 3 animals of his own . . . and in autumn carry beans and oats for 2 days with a cart . . . and carry wood from the woods of the lord as far as the manor house for two days in summer. . . . And he ought to find 1 man for 2 days to cut heath [for fuel] . . . and carry the heath that he has cut . . . and carry to Battle [a nearby town] twice in the summer season, each time a half a load of grain.

### ANALYZING THE EVIDENCE

1. What types of obligations did peasants owe their lord? What types of obligations did they have to each other? How were these enforced?
2. What concerns of the villagers themselves emerge in the bylaws in Source 4? What do these concerns suggest about village society?
3. Are all villagers equal? What social and economic differences do you see among them?
4. What evidence do you see of growing commercialization, such as money, wage labor, market exchange, and considerations of market value?

**3** **Cart being pulled and pushed up a hill.** This marginal illustration comes from the Luttrell Psalter, an illuminated manuscript commissioned by Sir Geoffrey Luttrell (1276–1345), the lord of a manor in Lincolnshire, and made by scribes and artists whose identity is unknown.

(Add 42130 f.173v Psalm 97: Harvest cart manhandled uphill, from the "Luttrell Psalter," ca. 1325–35/British Library, London, UK/© British Library Board. All Rights Reserved/Bridgeman Images)

**4** **Village bylaws, Great Horwood, 1306 and 1319.** Villagers themselves set rules regarding activities that they saw as problems. ("Gleaning" was picking up small bits of grain that had fallen from the stalks, an activity reserved for the elderly, small children, and ill or handicapped people.)

No one shall accept any outsider as a gleaner in autumn nor any man or woman to glean who is able to earn a penny a day for reaping if he finds someone who wishes to hire him.

Nor shall anyone pay in the field with whole sheaves, only handfuls of grain.

Nor shall anyone reap or cart except by day.

Nor shall anyone allow his calves or foals to go into the common fields of grain.

Nor shall anyone gather straw in the fields unless it be each from his own land. . . .

And if anyone is found guilty he shall pay the lord 4 d.

**5** **Court records from the village of Broughton, 1286.** Several times a year villagers gathered for court proceedings during which the legal and financial affairs of both the lord and village were handled; this is a small part of the records from one day in one village.

John Nuncium le Mung [was fined] 12 d. because he did not send to the first day of service for the lord as many men as he had at his own work. . . .

William de Broughton is compelled to answer at the next court for the damage done by his two horses in the lord's peas.

Richard de Broughton [is compelled to answer] because he did not come to work for the lord in ditching. . . .

Alice Robynes is compelled to pay 6 d. for her geese damaging the lord's grain. . . .

Thomas Prat acknowledges that he is in debt to Agnes Gylot for goods to the value of 6 d. Therefore he shall make satisfaction to her for the aforesaid 6 d.

The chief pledges [male villagers responsible to know what was going on] say that the bailiff of the lord abbot made two pits in the town, to its nuisance. Therefore the bailiff is ordered to put them right. . . . And they say that Hugh Knyt harbored a strange woman who is not profitable to the town. Fined 6 d. . . . And they say that Robert Strypling pastured the grass of the neighbors by night. Fined 12 d. . . . And they say that the wife of Thomas le Hund was a gleaner against the common statute of the town. Fined 12 d. . . . And they say that Reginald Gylbert overused the pasture with twenty sheep. Fined 12 d. And they say that William Kepline paid with sheaves in the field in autumn contrary to the common statute of the town. Fined 12 d.

## PUTTING IT ALL TOGETHER

Using the sources above, along with what you have learned in class and in this chapter and Chapters 8 and 9, write a short essay that analyzes social and economic relations in an English village in the High Middle Ages. To what extent is the traditional view of village life as uniformly oppressive warranted? If you believe that the traditional view is not accurate, what would be a better description?

Sources: (1, 2) *Translations and Reprints from the Original Sources of European History*, vol. 3, no. 5 (Philadelphia: University of Pennsylvania Department of History, 1897), pp. 4–7, 10–11; (4, 5) Warren O. Ault, *Open Field Farming in Medieval England: A Study of Village By-Laws* (London: George Allen and Unwin, 1972), pp. 86, 89, 155–159.

crops according to tradition and need. Some fields would be planted with crops such as wheat, rye, peas, or barley for human consumption, some with oats or other crops for both animals and humans, and some left unworked or fallow to allow the soil to rejuvenate. In addition, legume crops such as peas and beans helped the soil rebuild nutrients and also increased the villagers' protein consumption. In most areas with open-field agriculture, the holdings farmed by any one family did not consist of a whole field but consisted, instead, of strips in many fields. Families worked their own land and the lord's, but also cooperated with other families if they needed help, particularly during harvest time. This meant that all shared in any disaster as well as in any large harvest.

Meteorologists think that a slow but steady retreat of polar ice occurred between the ninth and eleventh centuries, and Europe experienced a significant warming trend from 1050 to 1300. The mild winters and dry summers that resulted helped increase agricultural output throughout Europe, particularly in the north.

The tenth and eleventh centuries also witnessed a number of agricultural improvements, especially in the development of mechanisms that replaced or aided human labor. Mills driven by wind and water power dramatically reduced the time and labor required to grind grain, crush seeds for oil, and carry out other tasks. This change had a significant impact on women's productivity, for grinding was women's work. When water- and wind-driven mills were introduced into an area, women were freed from the task of grinding grain and could turn to other tasks, such as raising animals, working in gardens or vineyards, and raising and preparing flax to make linen. They could also devote more time to spinning yarn, which was the bottleneck in cloth production, as each weaver needed at least six spinners. Thus the spread of wind and water power indirectly contributed to an increase in cloth production in medieval Europe.

Another change, which came in the early twelfth century, was a significant increase in the production of iron. Much of this was used for weapons and armor, but it also filled a growing demand in agriculture. Iron was first used for plowshares (the part of the plow that cuts a deep furrow), and then for pitchforks, harrows (dragged tools that raked soil), spades, and axes. Peasants needed money to buy iron implements from village blacksmiths, and they increasingly also needed money to pay their obligations to their lords. To get the cash they needed, they sold whatever surplus they produced in nearby towns, transporting it there in wagons with iron parts.

In central and northern Europe, peasants made increasing use of heavy wheeled iron plows pulled by teams of oxen to break up the rich, clay-filled soil common there, and agricultural productivity increased. Further technological improvements, including padded horse collars and iron horseshoes, allowed horses to be used for plowing as well as oxen. The use of horses spread in the twelfth century because their greater speed brought greater efficiency to farming and reduced the amount of human labor involved. Horses were also used to haul goods to markets, where peasants sold any excess vegetables, grain, and animals.

By modern standards, medieval agricultural yields were very low, but there was striking improvement between the fifth and the thirteenth centuries. Increased output had a profound impact on society, improving Europeans' health, commerce, industry, and general lifestyle. More food meant that fewer people suffered from hunger and malnourishment and that devastating famines were rarer. Higher yields brought more food for animals as well as people, and the amount of meat that people ate increased slightly. A better diet had an enormous impact on women's lives in particular. More food meant increased body fat, which increased fertility, and more meat—which provided iron—meant that women were less anemic and less subject to disease. Some researchers believe that it was during the High Middle Ages that Western women began to outlive men. Improved opportunities also encouraged people to marry somewhat earlier, which meant larger families and further population growth. Demographers estimate that in an era before birth control, every three years earlier that a woman married meant she bore one more child, though not all of them reached adulthood.

## Home Life

In western and central Europe, villages were generally made up of small houses for individual families. Households consisted of a married couple, their children (including stepchildren), and perhaps one or two other relatives. Some homes contained only an unmarried person, a widow, or several unmarried people living together. In southern and eastern Europe, extended families were more likely to live in the same household.

The size and quality of peasants' houses varied according to their relative prosperity, which usually depended on the amount of land held. Poorer peasants lived in windowless one-room cottages. Prosperous peasants added rooms; some wealthy peasants in the early fourteenth century had two-story houses with separate bedrooms for parents and children. For most people, however, living space—especially living space close enough to a fire to feel some warmth in cold weather—was cramped, dark, smoky, and smelly, with animals and people both sharing tight quarters, sometimes with each other.

The mainstay of the diet for peasants—and for all other classes—was bread. It was a hard, black substance made of barley, millet, and oats, rarely of expensive wheat, which they were more likely to use to pay their taxes and fees to the lord than for their own bread. Most households did not have ovens, which were expensive to build and posed a fire danger; their bread was baked in communal ovens or purchased from households that specialized in bread-baking. The main meal was often bread and a thick soup of vegetables and grains eaten around noon. Peasants ate vegetables not because they appreciated their importance for good health but because there was usually little else available. Animals were too valuable to be used for food on a regular basis, but weaker animals were often slaughtered in the fall so that they did not need to be fed through the winter. Their meat was salted for preservation and eaten on great feast days such as Christmas and Easter.

The diet of people with access to a river, lake, or stream would be supplemented with fish, which could be eaten fresh or preserved by salting. People living close to the sea gathered shellfish. Many places had severe laws against hunting and trapping in the forests. Deer, wild boars, and other game were reserved for the king and nobles. These laws were flagrantly violated, however, and rabbits and wild game often found their way to peasants' tables.

Medieval households were not self-sufficient but bought cloth, metal, leather goods, and even some food in village markets. They also bought ale, the universal drink of the common people in northern Europe. Women dominated in the production of ale. Ale provided needed calories and was safer to drink than the water from many rivers and streams, and it also provided some relief from the difficult, monotonous labor that filled people's lives. Medieval men and women often drank heavily, and brawls and violent fights were frequent at taverns.

The steady rise in population between the mid-eleventh and fourteenth centuries was primarily the result of warmer climate, increased food supply, and a reduction of violence with growing political stability, rather than dramatic changes in health care. Most treatment of illness was handled by home remedies. Treatments were often mixtures of herbal remedies, sayings, specific foods, prayers, amulets, and ritual healing activities. People suffering from wounds, skin diseases, or broken bones sometimes turned to barber-surgeons. For internal ailments, people consulted apothecaries, who suggested and mixed compounds taken internally or applied as a salve or ointment.

Beginning in the twelfth century in England, France, and Italy, the clergy, noble men and women, and newly rich merchants also established small hospitals and other institutions to care for the sick or for those who could not take care of themselves. Such institutions might be staffed by members of religious orders or by laymen and laywomen who were paid for their work.

## Childbirth and Childhood

The most dangerous period of life for any person, peasant or noble, was infancy and early childhood. In normal years perhaps as many as one-third of all children died before age five from illness, malnutrition, and accidents, and this death rate climbed to more than half in years with plagues, droughts, or famines. However, once people reached adulthood, many lived well into their fifties and sixties.

Childbirth was dangerous for mothers as well as infants. Village women helped one another through childbirth, and women who were more capable acquired midwifery skills. In larger towns and cities, such women gradually developed into professional midwives who were paid for their services and who trained younger women as apprentices. For most women, however, childbirth was handled by female friends and family.

**A Mother Carrying Her Infant**   In this marginal illustration in a fourteenth-century French book of poetry, a mother carries her tightly swaddled infant in a cradle, while she crosses what appears to be a stream. The manuscript illuminator chose to portray parental caring rather than parental coldness, which suggests that love for one's children was viewed as a praiseworthy quality. (Marginalia from *Les voeux du paon*, by Jacques de Longuyon, Northern France or Flanders, possibly Tournai, ca. 1350. MS. G.24, f. 34/The Pierpont Morgan Library, New York, NY, USA/ Art Resource, NY)

Historians used to paint a grim picture of medieval childhood. Childhood, they argued, was not recognized as a distinct stage in life until at least the late eighteenth century, and because so many children died young, they received little parental attention by parents wary about coming to love them too much. These views were derived largely from advice about raising children provided by priests and educators who advocated strict discipline and warned against coddling, from portraits of children that showed them dressed as little adults, and from the fact that parents sometimes abandoned infants, or gave them to monasteries as religious acts, donating them to the service of God in the same way they might donate money.

This view has been made less bleak more recently by scholars using sources that reveal how children were actually treated. They have discovered that many parents showed great affection for their children and experienced deep grief when they died young. Parents left children to monasteries not because they were indifferent, but because they hoped thereby to ensure them a better material and spiritual future. Parents made toys for children: balls, dolls, rattles, boats, hobbyhorses, tops, and many other playthings. They tried to protect their children with religious amulets and pilgrimages to special shrines and sang them lullabies. Even practices that to us may seem cruel, such as tight swaddling, were motivated by a concern for the child's safety and health at a time when most households had open fires, domestic animals wandered freely, and mothers and older siblings engaged in labor-intensive work that prevented them from continually watching a toddler.

## How did religion shape everyday life in the High Middle Ages?

Apart from the land, the weather, and local legal and social conditions, religion had the greatest impact on the daily lives of ordinary people in the High Middle Ages. Religious practices varied widely from country to country and even from province to province. But nowhere was religion a one-hour-a-week affair. Most people in medieval Europe were Christian, but there were small Jewish communities scattered in many parts of Europe, and Muslims lived in the Iberian Peninsula, Sicily, and other Mediterranean islands.

### Christian Life in Medieval Villages

For Christians the village church was the center of community life — social, political, and economic, as well as religious — with the parish priest in charge of a host of activities. Although church law placed the priest under the bishop's authority, the manorial lord appointed the priest. Rural priests were peasants and often worked in the fields with the people during the week. On Sundays and holy days, they put on a robe and celebrated Mass, or the Eucharist, the ceremony in which the priest consecrated bread and wine and distributed it to believers, in a re-enactment of Jesus's Last Supper. They recited the Mass in Latin, a language that few commoners, sometimes including the priest himself, could understand. At least once a year villagers were expected to take part in the ceremony and eat the consecrated bread. This usually happened at Easter, after they had confessed their sins to the priest and been assigned a penance.

In everyday life people engaged in rituals and used language heavy with religious symbolism. Before planting, the village priest customarily went out and sprinkled the fields with water, symbolizing refreshment and life. Everyone participated in village processions to honor the saints and ask their protection. The entire calendar was filled with reference to events in the life of Jesus and his disciples, such as Christmas (celebrating Jesus's birth), Easter (celebrating Jesus's resurrection after death), and Pentecost (commemorating the descent of the Holy Spirit on the disciples). Scriptural references and proverbs dotted everyone's language. The English *good-bye*, the French *adieu*, and the Spanish *adios* all derive from words meaning "God be with you." The signs and symbols of Christianity were visible everywhere, but so, people believed, was the Devil, who lured them to evil deeds. In some medieval images and literature, the Devil is portrayed as black, an identification that shaped Western racial attitudes.

### Saints and Sacraments

Along with days marking events in the life of Jesus, the Christian calendar was filled with saints' days. Veneration of the saints had been an important tool of Christian conversion since late antiquity (see "The Process of Conversion" in Chapter 7), and the cult of the saints was a central feature of popular culture in the Middle Ages. In return for the saint's healing and support, peasants offered the saint prayers, loyalty, and gifts. In the later Middle Ages popular hagiographies (ha-gee-AH-gruh-fees) — biographies of saints based on myths, legends, and popular stories — attributed specialized functions to the saints. Every occupation had a patron saint, as did cities and even realms.

The Virgin Mary, Christ's mother, was the most important saint. In the eleventh century theologians began to emphasize Mary's spiritual motherhood of all Christians. Special Masses commemorated her, churches were built in her honor, and hymns and prayers to her multiplied. Villagers listened intently to sermons telling stories about her life and miracles. One favorite story told of a minstrel and acrobat inspired to perform tumbling feats in Mary's honor:

[He performed] until from head to heel sweat stood upon him, drop by drop, as blood falls from meat turning on a hearth. . . . [Then] there came down from the heavens a Dame so glorious, that certainly no man had seen one so precious, nor so richly crowned. . . . Then the sweet and courteous Queen herself took a white napkin in her hand, and with it gently fanned her minstrel before the altar. . . . She blesses her minstrel with the sign of God.[1]

People reasoned that if Mary would even bless tumbling (a disreputable form of popular entertainment) as long as it was done with a reverent heart, she would certainly bless their lives of hard work and pious devotion even more.

Along with the veneration of saints, sacraments were an important part of religious practice. Twelfth-century theologians expanded on Saint Augustine's understanding of sacraments (see "Saint Augustine on Human Nature, Will, and Sin" in Chapter 7) and created an entire sacramental system. In 1215 the Fourth Lateran Council formally accepted seven sacraments (baptism, penance, the Eucharist, confirmation, marriage, priestly ordination, anointment of the dying). Medieval Christians believed that these seven sacraments brought God's grace, the divine assistance or help needed to lead a good Christian life and to merit salvation. Most sacraments had to be dispensed by a priest, although spouses officially administered the sacrament of marriage to each other, and laypeople could baptize a dying infant or anoint a dying person if no priest could be found. In this way, the sacramental system enhanced the authority of priests over people's lives, but did not replace strong personal devotion to the saints.

## Muslims and Jews

The centrality of Christian ceremonies to daily life for most Europeans meant that those who did not participate were clearly marked as outsiders. Many Muslims left Spain as the Christian "reconquest" proceeded and left Sicily when this became a Christian realm (see "Italy" and "The Iberian Peninsula" in Chapter 9), but others converted. In more isolated villages, people simply continued their Muslim rituals and practices, though they might hide this from the local priest or visiting officials.

Islam was geographically limited in medieval Europe, but by the late tenth century Jews could be found in many areas, often brought in from other areas as clients of rulers to help with finance. Jewish communities could be found in Italian and French cities and in the cities along the Rhine. Jewish dietary laws require meat to be handled in a specific way, so Jews had their own butchers; there were Jewish artisans in

**Statue of Saint Anne, the Virgin Mary, and the Christ Child**
Nearly every church had at least one image of the Virgin Mary, the most important figure of Christian devotion in medieval Europe. In this thirteenth-century wooden sculpture, she is shown holding the infant Jesus, and is herself sitting on the lap of her mother, Anne. Statues such as this reinforced people's sense that the heavenly family was much like theirs, with grandparents who sometimes played important roles. (Museo Nazionale del Bargello, Florence, Italy/Scala/Art Resource, NY)

many other trades as well. Jews held weekly religious services on Saturday, the Sabbath, and celebrated their own annual cycle of holidays. Each of these holidays involved special prayers, services, and often foods, and many of them commemorated events from Jewish history, including various times when Jews had been rescued from captivity.

Jews could supply other Jews with goods and services, but rulers and city leaders increasingly restricted their trade with Christians to banking and money-lending. This enhanced Christian resentment, as did the ideology of holy war that accompanied the Crusades (see "Background and Motives of the Crusades" in Chapter 9). Violence against Jews and restrictions on their activities increased further in much of Europe. Jews were expelled from England and later from France. However, Jews continued to live in the independent cities of the Holy Roman Empire and Italy, and some migrated eastward into new towns that were being established in Slavic areas.

**Wedding Door of the Cathedral in Strasbourg** Medieval cathedrals, such as this one from the thirteenth century, sometimes had a side door depicting a biblical story of ten young women who went to meet a bridegroom. Five of them wisely took extra oil for their lamps, while five foolishly did not (Matthew 25:1–13). In the story, which is a parable about being prepared for the end of the world, the foolish maidens were out of oil when the bridegroom arrived and missed the wedding feast. The "maidens' door" became a popular site for weddings, which were held right in front of it. (Paul M. R. Maeyaert/akg-images)

## Rituals of Marriage and Birth

Increasing suspicion and hostility marked relations between religious groups throughout the Middle Ages, but there were also important similarities in the ways Christians, Jews, and Muslims understood and experienced their religions. In all three traditions, every major life transition was marked by a ceremony that included religious elements.

Christian weddings might be held in the village church or at the church door, though among well-to-do families the ceremony took place in the house of the bride or bridegroom. A priest's blessing was often sought, though it was not essential to the marriage. Muslim weddings were also finalized by a contract between the bride and groom and were often overseen by a wedding official. Jewish weddings were guided by statements in Talmudic law that weddings were complete when the bride had entered the *chuppah*, which medieval Jewish authorities interpreted to mean a room in the groom's house.

In all three faiths, the wedding ceremony was followed by a wedding party that often included secular rituals. Some rituals symbolized the proper hierarchical relations between the spouses — such as placing the husband's shoe on the bedstead over the couple, symbolizing his authority — or were meant to ensure the couple's fertility — such as untying all the knots in the household, for it was believed that people possessing magical powers could tie knots to inhibit a man's reproductive power. All this came together in what was often the final event of a wedding: the religious official blessed the couple in their marriage bed, often with family and friends standing around or banging on pans, yelling, or otherwise making as much noise as possible to make fun of the couple's first sexual encounter. (Tying cans on the back of the car in which a couple leaves the wedding is a modern remnant of such rituals.)

Friends and family members had generally been part of the discussions, negotiations, and activities leading up to the marriage; marriage united two families and was far too important to leave up to two people alone. Among serfs, the manorial lord's permission was often required, with a special fee required to obtain it. (This permission did not, as often alleged, give the lord the right to deflower the bride. Though lords certainly forced sex on female serfs, there is no evidence in any legal sources that lords had the "right of first night," the *jus primae noctis*.) The involvement of family and friends in choosing one's spouse might lead to conflict, but more often the wishes of the couple and their parents, kin, and community were quite similar: all hoped for marriages that provided economic security, honorable standing, and a good number of healthy children. The best marriages offered companionship, emotional support, and even love, but these were understood to grow out of the marriage, not necessarily precede it. Breaking up a marriage meant breaking up the basic production and consumption unit, a very serious matter. The Christian Church forbade divorce, and even among non-Christians marital dissolution by any means other than the death of one spouse was rare.

Most brides hoped to be pregnant soon after the wedding. Christian women hoping for children said special prayers to the Virgin Mary or her mother, Anne. Some wore amulets of amber, bone, or mistletoe, thought to increase fertility. Others repeated charms and verses they had learned from other women, or, in desperate cases, went on pilgrimages to make special supplications. Muslim and Jewish women wore small cases with sacred verses or asked for blessings from religious leaders. Women continued these prayers and rituals throughout pregnancy and childbirth, often combining religious traditions with folk beliefs.

Judaism, Christianity, and Islam all required women to remain separate from the community for a short time after childbirth and often had special ceremonies welcoming them back once this period was over. These rituals often included prayers, such as this one from the Christian ritual of thanksgiving and purification, called churching, which a woman celebrated six weeks after giving birth: "Almighty and everlasting God, who has freed this woman from the danger of bearing a child, consider her to be strengthened from every pollution of the flesh so that with a clean heart and pure mind she may deserve to enter into the bosom of our mother, the church, and make her devoted to Your service."[2]

Religious ceremonies also welcomed children into the community. Among Christian families, infants were baptized soon after they were born to ensure that they could enter Heaven. Midwives who delivered children who looked especially weak and sickly often baptized them in an emergency service. In normal baptisms, the women who had assisted the mother in the birth often carried the baby to church, where godparents vowed their support. Godparents were often close friends or relatives, but parents might also choose prominent villagers or even the local lord in the hope that he might later look favorably on the child and provide for him or her in some way.

Within Judaism, a boy was circumcised by a religious official and given his name in a ceremony on his eighth day of life. This *brit milah*, or "covenant of circumcision," was viewed as a reminder of the Covenant between God and Abraham described in Hebrew Scripture. Muslims also circumcised boys in a special ritual, though the timing varied from a few days after birth to adolescence.

## Death and the Afterlife

Death was similarly marked by religious ceremonies, and among Europeans of all faiths death did not sever family obligations and connections. Christians called for a priest to perform the sacrament of extreme unction, with holy water, holy oil, a crucifix, and a censer with incense, when they thought the hour of death was near.

Once the person had died, the body was washed and dressed in special clothing—or a sack of plain cloth—and buried within a day or two. Family and friends joined in a funeral procession. The wealthy were sometimes buried inside the church—in the walls, under the floor, or under the building itself in a crypt—but most people were buried in the churchyard or a cemetery close by. At the graveside, the priest asked for God's grace for the soul of the deceased and also asked that soul to "rest in peace." This final request was made not only for the benefit of the dead, but also for that of the living as the souls of the dead were widely believed to return to earth. Priests were hired to say memorial Masses on anniversaries of family deaths, especially one week, one month, and one year afterward.

During the High Middle Ages, learned theologians increasingly emphasized the idea of purgatory, the place where souls on their way to Heaven went after death to make amends for their earthly sins. Memorial Masses, prayers, and donations made in their names could shorten their time in purgatory. So could indulgences, those papal grants that relieved a person from earthly penance. Indulgences were initially granted for performing meritorious acts, such as going on a pilgrimage or crusade, but later on they could be obtained by paying a small fee (see "Background and Motives of the Crusades" in Chapter 9). With this development, their spiritual benefits became transferable, so indulgences could be purchased to shorten the stay in purgatory of one's deceased relatives, as well as to lessen one's own penance or time in purgatory.

The living also had obligations to the dead among Muslims and Jews. In both groups deceased people were buried quickly, and special prayers were said by mourners and family members. Muslims fasted on behalf of the dead and maintained a brief period of official mourning. The Qur'an promises an eternal paradise with flowing rivers to "those who believe and do good deeds" (Qur'an, 4:57) and a Hell of eternal torment to those who do not.

Jews observed specified periods of mourning during which the normal activities of daily life were curtailed. Every day for eleven months after a death and every year after that on the anniversary of the death, a son of the deceased was to recite Kaddish, a special prayer of praise and glorification of God. Judaism emphasized life on earth more than an afterlife, so beliefs about what happens to the soul after death were more varied; the very righteous might go directly to a place of spiritual reward, but most souls went first to a place of punishment and purification generally referred to as *Gehinnom*. After a period that did not exceed twelve

months, the soul ascended to the world to come. Those who were completely wicked during their lifetimes might simply go out of existence or continue in an eternal state of remorse.

# What led to Europe's economic growth and reurbanization?

Most people continued to live in villages in the High Middle Ages, but the rise of towns and the growth of a new business and commercial class were a central part of Europe's recovery after the disorders of the tenth century. As towns gained legal and political rights, merchant and craft guilds grew more powerful, and towns became centers of production as well as commerce.

## The Rise of Towns

Medieval towns began in many different ways. Some were fortifications erected as a response to ninth-century invasions; the peasants from the surrounding countryside moved within the walls when their area was attacked. Other towns grew up around great cathedrals (see "Churches and Cathedrals" at the end of this chapter) and monasteries whose schools drew students from distant areas. Many other towns grew from the sites of Roman army camps or cities, which had shrunk in the early Middle Ages but never entirely disappeared. Still others arose where a trade route crossed a river or a natural harbor allowed ships to moor easily.

Regardless of their origins, medieval towns had a few common characteristics. Each town had a marketplace,

and most had a mint for the coining of money. The town also had a court to settle disputes. In addition, medieval towns were enclosed by walls. The terms *burgher* (BUHR-guhr) and *bourgeois* derive from the Old English and Old German words *burg, burgh, borg,* and *borough* for "a walled or fortified place." Thus a burgher or bourgeois originally was a person who lived or worked inside the walls. Townspeople supported themselves primarily by exchanging goods and services with one another, becoming artisans, shopkeepers, and merchants. They bought their food from the surrounding countryside, and purchased goods from far away brought by traveling merchants.

No matter where people congregated, they settled on someone's land and had to secure permission to live there from the king, count, abbot, or bishop. Aristocratic nobles and churchmen were sometimes hostile to the towns set up on their land, but they soon realized that these could be a source of profits and benefits.

The growing towns of medieval Europe slowly gained legal and political rights, including the rights to hold municipal courts, select the mayor and other municipal officials, and tax residents and visitors. Lords were often reluctant to grant towns self-government,

**Walled Town of Carcassone**   The walls of Carcassone, a hilltop town in southern France, were built over many centuries from the Roman period into the Middle Ages, and restored in the nineteenth century. Linking more than fifty towers, the walls defended the city in a number of sieges. The vineyards in the foreground may have been there in the Middle Ages as well, as southern France was already an important wine-growing area. (Patrick Frilet/Shutterstock)

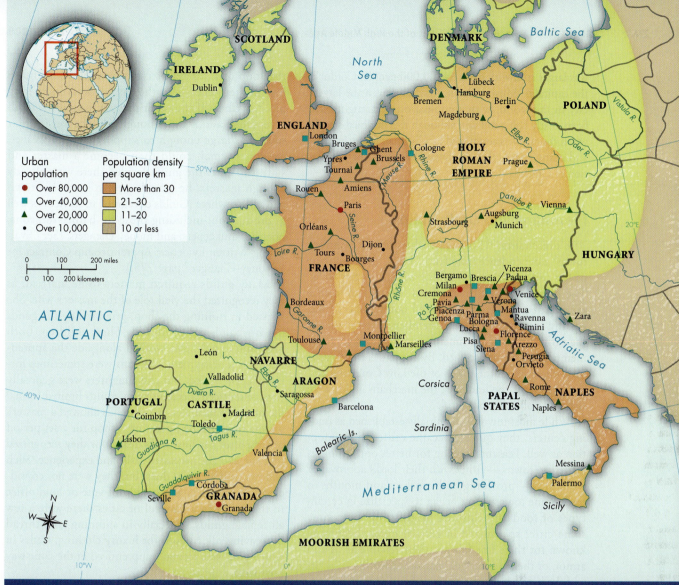

## MAPPING THE PAST

### MAP 10.1 European Population Density, ca. 1300

The development of towns and the reinvigoration of trade were directly related in medieval Europe. Using this map, Maps 10.2 and 10.3, and the information in this chapter, answer the following questions.

**ANALYZING THE MAP** What were the four largest cities in Europe? What part of Europe had the highest density of towns?

**CONNECTIONS** What role did textile and other sorts of manufacturing play in the growth of towns? How was the development of towns related to that of universities, monastery schools, and cathedral schools?

fearing loss of authority and revenue if they gave the residents full independence. When burghers bargained for a town's political independence, however, they offered sizable amounts of ready cash and sometimes promised payments for years to come. Consequently, lords ultimately agreed to self-government.

In addition to working for the independence of the towns, townspeople tried to acquire liberties for themselves. In the Middle Ages the word *liberties* meant special privileges. The most important privilege a medieval townsperson could gain was personal freedom. It

gradually developed that an individual who fled his or her manor and lived in a town for a year and a day was free of servile obligations and status. Thus the growth of towns contributed to a slow decline of serfdom in western Europe, although this took centuries.

Towns developed throughout much of Europe, but the concentration of the textile industry led to the growth of many towns in the Low Countries (present-day Holland, Belgium, and French Flanders). In 1300 Paris was the largest city in western Christian Europe, with a population of about 200,000 (Map 10.1), and Constantinople was larger still, with perhaps 300,000 people. Córdoba, the capital of Muslim Spain, may have been the largest city in the world, with a population that might have been nearly half a million, although this declined steeply when the city was conquered by Christian forces in 1236 and many people fled southward, swelling the population of Granada.

## Merchant and Craft Guilds

The merchants, who were influential in winning towns' independence from feudal lords, also used their power and wealth to control life within the city walls. The merchants of a town joined together to form a **merchant guild** that prohibited nonmembers from trading in the town. Guild members often made up the earliest town government, serving as mayors and members of the city council. By the late eleventh century, especially in the towns of the Low Countries and northern Italy, the leaders of the merchant guilds were rich and politically powerful.

While most towns were initially established as trading centers, they quickly became centers of production as well. Peasants looking for better opportunities moved to towns—either with their lord's approval or without it—providing both workers and mouths to feed. Some townspeople began to specialize in certain types of food and clothing production. Over time some cities specialized in certain items, becoming known for their fine fabrics, their reliable arms and armor, or their elegant gold and silver work.

Like merchants, producers recognized that organizing would bring benefits, and beginning in the twelfth century in many cities they formed **craft guilds** that regulated most aspects of production. Guilds set quality standards for their particular product and regulated the size of workshops and the conduct of members. In most cities individual guilds, such as those of shoemakers or blacksmiths, achieved a monopoly in the production of one particular product, forbidding nonmembers to work. The craft guild then chose some of its members to act as inspectors and set up a court to hear disputes between members, though the city court remained the final arbiter.

Each guild set the pattern by which members were trained and the length of the training period. A boy who wanted to become a weaver, for instance, or whose parents wanted him to, spent four to seven years as an apprentice, often bound by a contract. When the apprenticeship was finished, a young artisan spent several years as a journeyman, working in

the shop of a master artisan. He then could make his "masterpiece"—in the case of weavers, a long piece of cloth. If the other masters judged the cloth acceptable, and if they thought the market in their town was large enough to support another weaver, the journeyman could then become a master and start a shop. If the guild decided there were already enough masters, he would need to leave that town and try elsewhere. Guilds developed in services as well as production, including those for barber-surgeons, notaries, innkeepers, and money-changers. (See "Evaluating Written Evidence: Apprenticeship Contract for a Money-Changer," page 275.)

Many guilds required masters to be married, as they recognized the vital role of the master's wife. She assisted in running the shop, often selling the goods her husband had produced. Their children, both male and female, also worked alongside the apprentices and journeymen. The sons were sometimes formally apprenticed, but the daughters were generally not apprenticed, because many guilds limited formal membership to males. Most guilds allowed a master's widow to continue operating a shop for a set period of time after her husband's death, for they recognized that she had the necessary skills and experience. Such widows paid all guild dues, but they were not considered full members and could not vote or hold office in the guild. In a handful of cities there were a few all-female guilds, especially in spinning gold thread or weaving silk ribbons for luxury clothing, trades in which girls were formally apprenticed in the same way boys were.

Both craft and merchant guilds were not only economic organizations, but also systems of social support. They took care of elderly masters who could no longer work, and they often supported masters' widows and orphans. They maintained an altar at a city church and provided for the funerals of members and baptisms of their children. Guild members marched together in city parades and reinforced their feelings of solidarity with one another by special ceremonies and distinctive dress. Merchant guilds in some parts of Europe, such as the German cities of Hamburg, Lübeck, and Bremen, had special buildings for celebrations and ceremonies.

## The Revival of Long-Distance Trade

The growth of towns went hand in hand with a revival of trade as artisans and craftsmen manufactured goods for both local and foreign consumption (Map 10.2). Most trade centered in towns and was controlled by professional traders. Long-distance trade was risky and required large investments of capital. Thus, merchants would often pool their resources to finance an

■ **merchant guild** A band of merchants in a town that prohibited nonmembers from trading in that town.

■ **craft guild** A band of producers in a town that regulated most aspects of production of a good in that town.

# Apprenticeship Contract for a Money-Changer

Most medieval cities minted their own money, as did rulers, abbots, and some nobles, so in every city there were money-changers who exchanged money from outside the city for that used in the city itself. They needed to know the value of a huge array of currencies in silver and gold, and keep track of those in which base metals such as tin and lead might have been mixed in, as these were worth less. Money-changing became a guild in many cities, and young men learned through apprenticeship, sealed by a contract, as this one from the Mediterranean port of Marseilles in 1248.

May twelfth, in the year of the Incarnation of Our Lord 1248. I, John of St. Maximin, lawyer, place with you John Cordier, money-changer, my son William Deodat, as an apprentice, so that you may teach and instruct him in the art of money-changing, for two complete and continuous years from this date. I promise by this agreement that I will take care that my son will serve his apprenticeship with you and that he will be faithful and honest in all his dealings for the whole of the said period, and that he will not depart from you nor take anything away from you. And if it should happen, which God forbid, that the said William should cause you any loss I promise to reimburse you by this agreement, believing in your unsupported word, etc. Also I promise to give by this agreement for the expenses of the said William food, that is bread and wine and meat,

fourteen *heminae* [a liquid and dry measure] of good grain and fifty solidi of the money now current in Marseilles, at your request, and to provide the said William with clothing and necessaries, pledging all my goods, etc.; renouncing the benefit of all laws, etc. To this I, the said John Cordier, receive the said William as a pupil and promise you, the said John St. Maximin, to teach your son well and faithfully the business of money-changing, etc., pledging all my goods, etc.; renouncing the benefit of all laws, etc. Witnesses, etc.

## EVALUATE THE EVIDENCE

1. What does John of St. Maximin promise to give John Cordier for training his son William, and what does he promise about William's conduct? What does John Cordier promise in return?
2. What is John of St. Maximin's occupation, and what does this suggest about the profession of money-changer in medieval cities?
3. Like modern contracts, medieval contracts were often formulaic, drawn up by notaries, who used standardized language. What evidence do you see for such standardization in this source, and what does this suggest about apprenticeship contracts?

Source: Roy C. Cave and Herbert H. Coulson, eds., *A Source Book for Medieval Economic History* (New York: Biblio and Tannen, 1965), p. 145.

expedition to a distant place. When the ship or caravan returned and the cargo was sold, these investors would share the profits. If disaster struck the caravan, an investor's loss was limited to the amount of that individual's investment.

In the late eleventh century the Italian cities, especially Venice, led the West in trade in general and completely dominated trade with the East. Venetian ships carried salt from the city's own lagoon, pepper and other spices from India and North Africa, silks and carpets from Central Asia, and slaves from many places. In northern Europe, the towns of Bruges, Ghent, and Ypres (EE-pruh) in Flanders built a vast cloth industry, becoming leaders in both the manufacture and trade of textiles. With easy access to high-quality English wool, Flemish clothmakers could produce high-quality cloth, the most important manufactured product handled by merchants and one of the few European products for which there was a market in the East.

From the late eleventh through the thirteenth centuries, Europe enjoyed a steadily expanding volume

of international trade. Trade surged markedly with demand for sugar from the Mediterranean islands to replace honey; spices from Asia to season a bland diet; and fine wines from the Rhineland, Burgundy, and Bordeaux to make life more pleasant. Other consumer goods included luxury woolens from Flanders and Tuscany, furs from Ireland and Russia, brocades and tapestries from Flanders, and silks from Constantinople and even China. As the trade volume expanded, the use of cash became more widespread. Beginning in the 1160s the opening of new silver mines in Germany, Bohemia, northern Italy, northern France, and western England led to the minting and circulation of vast quantities of silver coins.

Increased trade also led to a higher standard of living. Contact with Eastern civilizations introduced Europeans to eating utensils, and table manners improved. Nobles learned to eat with forks and knives instead of tearing the meat from a roast with their hands. They began to use napkins instead of wiping their greasy fingers on their clothes or on the dogs lying under the table.

## Business Procedures

The economic surge of the High Middle Ages led merchants to invent new business procedures. Beginning in Italy, merchants formalized their agreements with new types of contracts, including temporary contracts for land and sea trading ventures and permanent partnerships termed *compagnie* (kahm-pah-NYEE; literally "bread together," that is, sharing bread; the root of the word *company*). Many of these agreements were initially between brothers or other relatives and in-laws, but they quickly grew to include people who were not family members. In addition, they began to involve individuals—including a few women—who invested only their money, leaving the actual running of the business to the active partners. Commercial correspondence, unnecessary when one businessperson

oversaw everything and made direct bargains with buyers and sellers, proliferated. Accounting and record keeping became more sophisticated, and credit facilitated business expansion.

The ventures of the German Hanseatic League illustrate these new business procedures. The **Hanseatic League** (often called simply the Hansa) was a mercantile association of towns. It originated in agreements between merchants for mutual security and exclusive trading rights, and it gradually developed into agreements among towns themselves, the first of which was one between Hamburg and Lübeck in 1241. At its height, the league included perhaps two hundred cities from Holland to Poland. From the fourteenth to the sixteenth centuries the Hanseatic League controlled the trade of northern Europe. In

**MAP 10.2  Trade and Manufacturing in Thirteenth-Century Europe**  Note the overland and ocean lines of trade and the sources of silver, iron, copper, lead, paper, wool, carpets and rugs, and slaves.

cities such as Bruges and London, Hansa merchants secured special trading concessions, exempting them from all tolls and allowing them to trade at local fairs.

The dramatic increase in trade ran into two serious difficulties in medieval Europe. One was the problem of minting money. Despite investment in mining operations to increase the production of metals, the amount of gold, silver, and copper available for coins was not adequate for the increased flow of commerce. Merchants developed paper bills of exchange, in which coins or goods in one location were exchanged for a sealed letter (much like a modern deposit statement), which could be used in place of metal coinage elsewhere. This made the long, slow, and very dangerous shipment of coins unnecessary, and facilitated the expansion of credit and commerce. By about 1300 the bill of exchange was the normal method of making commercial payments among the cities of western Europe, and it proved to be a decisive factor in their later economic development. The second problem was a moral and theological one. Church doctrine frowned on lending money at interest, termed *usury* (YOO-zhuh-ree). This doctrine was developed in the early Middle Ages when loans were mainly for consumption, for instance, to tide a farmer over until the next harvest. Theologians reasoned that it was wrong for a Christian to take advantage of the bad luck or need of another Christian. This restriction on Christians' charging interest is one reason why Jews were frequently the moneylenders in early medieval society; it was one of the few occupations not forbidden them. As money-lending became more important to commercial ventures, the church relaxed its position. It declared that some interest was legitimate as a payment for the risk the investor was taking, and that only interest above a certain level would be considered usury. (Even today, governments generally set limits on the rate businesses may charge for loaning money.) The church itself then got into the money-lending business, opening pawnshops in cities.

The stigma attached to lending money was in many ways attached to all the activities of a merchant. Medieval people were uneasy about a person making a profit merely from the investment of money rather than labor, skill, and time. Merchants themselves shared these ideas to some degree, so they gave generous donations to the church and to charities, and took pains not to flaunt their wealth through flashy dress and homes.

- Principal Hanseatic town
▲ Hanseatic trading partner

**The Hanseatic League, 1300–1400**

## The Commercial Revolution

Changes in business procedures, combined with the growth in trade, led to a transformation of the European economy often called the **commercial revolution** by historians, who see it as the beginning of the modern capitalist economy. In using this label, historians point not only to increases in the sheer volume of trade and in the complexity and sophistication of business procedures, but also to the development of a new "capitalist spirit" in which making a profit is regarded as a good thing in itself, regardless of the uses to which that profit is put. Because capitalism in the Middle Ages primarily involved trade rather than production, it is referred to as mercantile capitalism.

Part of this capitalist spirit was a new attitude toward time. Country people needed only approximate times — dawn, noon, sunset — for their work. Monasteries needed more precise times to call monks together for the recitation of the Divine Office. In the early Middle Ages monks used a combination of hourglasses, sundials, and water-clocks to determine the time, and then rang bells by hand. In about 1280 new types of mechanical mechanisms seem to have been devised in which weights replaced falling water and bells were rung automatically. Records begin to use the word *clock* (from the Latin word for bell) for these machines, which sometimes indicated the movement of astronomical bodies as well as the hours. The merchants who ran city councils quickly saw clocks as useful, as these devices allowed the opening and closing of markets and shops to be set to certain hours, and beginning about 1300, they ordered the construction of large public clocks. Through regulations that specified times and bells that marked the day, city people began to develop a mentality that conceived of the universe in quantitative terms. Beautiful and elaborate mechanical clocks were also symbols of a city's prosperity.

The commercial revolution created a great deal of new wealth, which did not escape the attention of kings and other rulers. Wealth could be taxed, and through taxation kings could create strong and centralized states. The commercial revolution also

■ **Hanseatic League**  A mercantile association of towns begun in northern Europe that allowed for mutual protection and trading rights.

■ **commercial revolution**  The transformation of the European economy as a result of changes in business procedures and growth in trade.

**Astronomical Clock in Prague** The central part of this clock, an astronomical dial representing the sun and moon in the sky and the ring of the zodiac, was installed on the town hall of Prague in 1410, and the other parts were added later in the century. It has been renovated several times, including in 2018, so that it still functions. Beautiful and elaborate mechanical clocks, usually installed on the cathedral or town church, were in general use in Italy by the 1320s, in Germany by the 1330s, in England by the 1370s, and in France by the 1380s. (François Pugnet/Getty Images)

provided the opportunity for thousands of serfs to improve their social position. The slow but steady transformation of European society from almost completely rural and isolated to urban and relatively more sophisticated constituted the greatest effect of the commercial revolution that began in the eleventh century.

Even so, merchants and business people did not run medieval communities other than in central and northern Italy and in the county of Flanders. Kings and nobles maintained ultimate control over most European cities. Most towns remained small, and urban residents never amounted to more than 10 percent of the total European population. The commercial changes of the eleventh through thirteenth centuries did, however, lay the economic foundations for the development of urban life and culture.

# What was life like in medieval cities?

In their backgrounds and abilities, townspeople represented diversity and change. Their occupations and their preoccupations were different from those of nobles and peasants. Cities were crowded and polluted, though people flocked into them because they offered the possibility of economic advancement, social mobility, and improvement in legal status. Some urban residents grew spectacularly rich, but the numbers of poor swelled as well.

## City Life

Walls surrounded almost all medieval towns and cities, and constant repair of these walls was usually the town's greatest expense. Gates pierced the walls, and visitors waited at the gates to gain entrance to the town. Most streets in a medieval town were marketplaces as much as passages for transit. Poor people selling soap,

candles, wooden dishes, and similar cheap products stood next to farmers from the surrounding countryside selling eggs, chickens, or vegetables. Because there was no way to preserve food easily, people — usually female family members or servants — had to shop every day, and the market was where they met their neighbors, exchanged information, and talked over recent events, as well as purchased needed supplies.

Some selling took place not in the open air but in the craftsman's home. The family lived above the business on the second or third floor. As the business and the family expanded, additional stories were added. Second and third stories jutted out over the ground floor and thus over the street. Because the streets were narrow to begin with, houses lacked fresh air and light. Fire was a constant danger; because houses were built so close to one another, fires spread rapidly.

Most medieval cities developed with little planning. As the population increased, space became increasingly limited. Air and water pollution presented serious problems. Horses and oxen, the chief means of transportation and power, dropped tons of dung on the streets every year. It was universal practice in the early towns to dump household waste, both animal and human, into the road in front of one's house. The stench must have been abominable. In 1298 the citizens of the town of Boutham in Yorkshire, England, received the following order:

> To the bailiffs of the abbot of St. Mary's York, at Boutham. Whereas it is sufficiently evident that the pavement of the said town of Boutham is so very greatly broken up . . . , and in addition the air is so corrupted and infected by the pigsties situated in the king's highways and in the lanes of that town and by the swine feeding and frequently wandering about . . . and by dung and dunghills and many other foul things placed in the streets and lanes, that great repugnance overtakes the king's ministers staying in that town and also others there dwelling and passing through . . . : the king, being unwilling longer to tolerate such great and unbearable defects there, orders the bailiffs to cause the pavement to be suitably repaired . . . before All Saints next, and to cause the pigsties, aforesaid streets and lanes to be cleansed from all dung . . . and to cause them to be kept thus cleansed hereafter.[3]

People of all sorts, from beggars to wealthy merchants, regularly rubbed shoulders in the narrow streets and alleys of crowded medieval cities. This interaction did not mean that people were unaware of social differences, however, for clothing clearly indicated social standing and sometimes occupation. Friars wore black, white, or gray woolen clothing that marked them as members of a particular religious order. Military men and servants who lived in noble households dressed in the nobles' distinctive colors known as livery (LIH-vuh-ree). Wealthier urban residents wore bright colors, imported silk or fine woolen fabrics, and fancy headgear, while poorer ones wore darker clothing made of rough linen or linen and wool blends. In university towns, students wore clothing and headgear that marked their status. University graduates—lawyers, physicians, and professors—often wore dark robes, trimmed with fur if they could afford it.

In the later Middle Ages many cities attempted to make clothing distinctions a matter of law as well as of habit. City councils passed **sumptuary laws** that regulated the value of clothing and jewelry that people of different social groups could wear; only members of high social groups could wear velvet, satin, pearls, or fur, for example, or wear clothing embroidered with gold thread or dyed in colors that were especially expensive to produce, such as the purple dye that came from mollusk shells. Along with enforcing social differences, sumptuary laws also attempted to impose moral standards by prohibiting plunging necklines on women or doublets (fitted buttoned jackets) that were too short on men. Their limits on imported fabrics or other materials also served to protect local industries.

Some of these laws called for marking certain individuals as members of groups not fully acceptable in urban society. Many cities ordered prostitutes to wear red or yellow bands on their clothes that were supposed to represent the flames of Hell, and the Fourth Lateran Council required Jews and Muslims to dress in ways that distinguished them from their Christian neighbors. (Many Jewish communities also developed their own sumptuary laws prohibiting extravagant or ostentatious dress.) Sumptuary laws were frequently broken and were difficult to enforce, but they provide evidence of the many material goods available to urban dwellers as well as the concern of city leaders about the social mobility and extravagance they saw all around them.

## Servants and the Poor

Many urban houses were larger than the tiny village dwellings, so families took in domestic servants. A less wealthy household employed one woman who assisted in all aspects of running the household; a wealthier one employed a large staff of male and female servants with specific duties. In Italian cities, household servants included slaves, usually young women brought in from areas outside of Western Christianity, such as the Balkans.

Along with live-in servants, many households hired outside workers to do specific tasks. These workers laundered clothing and household linens, cared for children or invalids, repaired houses and walls, and carried messages or packages around the city or the surrounding countryside. Urban workers had to buy all their food, so they felt any increase in the price of ale or bread immediately. Their wages were generally low, and children from such families sought work at very young ages.

---

■ **sumptuary laws** Laws that regulated the value and style of clothing and jewelry that various social groups could wear as well as the amount they could spend on celebrations.

**Notre Dame Cathedral, Paris**   This view offers a fine example of the twin towers (left), the spire and great rose window over the south portal (center), and the flying buttresses that support the walls and the vaults. Like hundreds of other churches in medieval Europe, it was dedicated to the Virgin Mary. With a spire rising more than 300 feet, Notre Dame was the tallest building in Europe. In April 2019, a massive fire destroyed the spire and most of the lead-covered wooden roof, though the stone-vaulted ceiling prevented the fire from reaching the interior. Firefighters were able to save the façade, towers, walls, buttresses, stained-glass windows, and much of the artwork. French president Emmanuel Macron pledged to rebuild the cathedral and launched an international fund-raising campaign. (David R. Frazier/Science Source)

Stained glass beautifully reflects the creative energy of the High Middle Ages. It is both an integral part of Gothic architecture and a distinct form of visual art. From large sheets of colored glass made by glassblowers, artisans cut small pieces, linked them together with narrow strips of lead, and set them in an iron frame prepared to fit the window opening. Windows showed scenes from the Old and New Testaments and the lives of the saints, designed to teach people doctrines of the Christian faith. They also showed scenes from the lives of the artisans and merchants who paid for them.

Once at least part of a cathedral had been built, the building began to be used for religious services. Town residents gathered for Masses, baptisms, funerals, and saint's day services, and also used it for guild meetings and other secular purposes. Services became increasingly complex to fit with their new surroundings, with music, incense, candles, statuary, tapestry wall hangings, and the building itself all contributing to making services in a Gothic cathedral a rich experience.

The frenzy to create the most magnificent Gothic cathedrals eventually came to an end. Begun in 1247, the cathedral in Beauvais reached a height of 157 feet in the interior, exceeding all others. Unfortunately, the weight imposed on the vaults was too great, and the building collapsed in 1284. The collapse was viewed as an aberration, for countless other cathedrals were in various stages of completion at the same time, and none of them fell. In hindsight, however, it can be viewed as a harbinger. Very few cathedrals not yet completed at the time of its collapse were ever finished, and even fewer were started. In the fourteenth century the church itself splintered, and the cities that had so proudly built cathedrals were decimated by famine and disease.

**NOTES**

1. Thirteenth-century sermon story, in David Herlihy, ed., *Medieval Culture and Society* (New York: Harper and Row, 1968), pp. 295, 298.

2. Translated and quoted in Susan C. Karant-Nunn, *The Reformation of Ritual: An Interpretation of Early Modern Germany* (London: Routledge, 1997), p. 77.

3. H. Rothwell, ed., *English Historical Documents*, vol. 3 (London: Eyre & Spottiswoode, 1975), p. 854.

4. www.classical.net/music/comp.lst/works/orff-cb/carmlyr.php#track14. This verse is from one of the songs known as the Carmina Burana, which are widely available as recordings, downloadable files, and even cell phone ring tones.

# LOOKING BACK  LOOKING AHEAD

The High Middle Ages represent one of the most creative periods in the history of Western society. Institutions that are important parts of the modern world, including universities, jury trials, and investment banks, were all developed in this era. Advances were made in the mechanization of labor, business procedures, architectural design, and education. Through the activities of merchants, Europeans again saw products from Africa and Asia in city marketplaces, as they had in Roman times, and wealthier urban residents bought them. Individuals and groups such as craft guilds provided money for building and decorating magnificent Gothic cathedrals, where people heard increasingly complex music and watched plays that celebrated both the lives of the saints and their own daily struggles.

Toward the end of the thirteenth century, however, there were increasing signs of impending problems. The ships and caravans bringing exotic goods also brought new pests. The new vernacular literature created a stronger sense of national identity, which increased hostility toward others. The numbers of poor continued to grow, and efforts to aid their suffering were never enough. As the century ended, villagers and city residents alike continued to gather for worship, but they also wondered whether God was punishing them.

## Make Connections

Think about the larger developments and continuities within and across chapters.

1. How was life in a medieval city different from life in a Hellenistic city (Chapter 4), or life in Rome during the time of Augustus (Chapter 6)? In what ways was it similar? What problems did these cities confront that are still issues for cities today?

2. Historians have begun to turn their attention to the history of children and childhood. How were children's lives in the societies you have examined shaped by larger social structures and cultural forces? What commonalities do you see in children's lives across time?

3. Chapter 4 and this chapter both examine ways in which religion and philosophy shaped life for ordinary people and for the educated elite. How would you compare Hellenistic religious practices with those of medieval Europe? How would you compare the ideas of Hellenistic philosophers such as Epicurus or Zeno with those of Scholastic philosophers such as Thomas Aquinas?

# 10    REVIEW & EXPLORE

## Identify Key Terms

Identify and explain the significance of each item below.

open-field system (p. 263)

merchant guild (p. 274)

craft guild (p. 274)

Hanseatic League (p. 276)

commercial revolution (p. 277)

sumptuary laws (p. 279)

Scholastics (p. 282)

vernacular literature (p. 285)

troubadours (p. 285)

cathedral (p. 287)

Romanesque (p. 287)

Gothic (p. 287)

## Review the Main Ideas

Answer the section heading questions from the chapter.

1. What was village life like in medieval Europe? (p. 262)

2. How did religion shape everyday life in the High Middle Ages? (p. 268)

3. What led to Europe's economic growth and reurbanization? (p. 272)

4. What was life like in medieval cities? (p. 278)

5. How did universities serve the needs of medieval society? (p. 280)

6. How did literature and architecture express medieval values? (p. 285)

## Suggested Resources

### BOOKS

- Bennett, Judith M. *A Medieval Life: Cecelia Penifader of Brigstock, c. 1297–1344.* 1998. An excellent brief introduction to all aspects of village life from the perspective of one woman; designed for students.

- Coldstream, Nicola. *Medieval Architecture.* 2002. A beautifully illustrated discussion of all types of buildings and how they reflect the material and spiritual concerns of the people who built and used them.

- Epstein, Steven A. *An Economic and Social History of Later Medieval Europe, 1000–1500.* 2009. Examines European social and economic history in its cultural setting.

- Gaunt, Simon, and Sarah Kay, eds. *The Troubadours: An Introduction.* 1999. A collection of essays that trace the development of troubadour song and the reception of troubadour poetry.

- Gies, Frances, and Joseph Gies. *Life in a Medieval City.* 2016. A newly reissued classic account of life in medieval cities, using Troyes in 1250 as its example.

- Glick, Leonard B. *Abraham's Heirs: Jews and Christians in Medieval Europe.* 1999. Provides information on many aspects of Jewish life and Jewish-Christian relations.

- Janin, Hunt. *The University in Medieval Life, 1179–1499.* 2008. An overview of medieval universities, designed for general readers.

- Mews, Constant. *Abelard and Heloise.* 2005. Examines the lives and ideas of these two thinkers in the context of their times.

- Moore, R. I. *The First European Revolution: 970–1215.* 2000. A bold assessment of the long-term significance of the changes discussed in this chapter.

◆ Shahar, Shulamit. *The Fourth Estate: A History of Women in the Middle Ages*, 2d ed. 2003. Provides information on the lives of women, including nuns, peasants, noblewomen, and townswomen.

◆ Shinners, John. *Medieval Popular Religion, 1000–1500*, 2d ed. 2006. A wide variety of sources that provide evidence about the beliefs and practices of ordinary Christians.

◆ Spufford, Peter. *Power and Profit: The Merchant in Medieval Europe.* 2003. A comprehensive history of medieval commerce, designed for general readers.

## MEDIA

◆ *Epistolae: Medieval Women's Letters.* A collection of letters to and from women in the Middle Ages, from the fourth to the thirteenth centuries, on a range of topics including religion, diplomacy, family, and politics. Includes both the original Latin and English translations and, where available, information about the writer and the historical context of the letter. **epistolae.ccnmtl.columbia.edu/**

◆ *Index of Medieval Medical Images.* Provides access to a huge variety of images related to medicine in the Middle Ages. Most easily used through the "browse" function, the site includes topics ranging from "abortion" to "zodiac." **digital.library.ucla.edu /immi/**

◆ *Inside the Medieval Mind* (BBC, 2008). Professor Robert Bartlett of St. Andrew's University in Scotland examines the ways in which medieval people understood the world, including knowledge systems, religious beliefs, and ideas about sexuality.

◆ *Monty Python and the Holy Grail* (Terry Gilliam and Terry Jones, 1975). A spoof of the King Arthur legend and a send-up of popular views of many aspects of the Middle Ages (chivalry, dirt, disease, witchcraft). The basis for Eric Idle's 2005 Tony Award–winning musical *Spamalot*, and the source of countless pop culture references.

◆ *Sorceress* (Suzanne Schiffman, 1987). Written by a medieval historian and shot in both French and English, this wonderful film is based on an actual text by a thirteenth-century Dominican friar investigating the cult of Saint Guinefort, the holy greyhound, near Lyons in France. The film addresses issues relating to healing, popular religion, and the role of women.

◆ *TEAMS Middle English Texts.* Run by the Consortium for Teaching the Middle Ages (TEAMS), this website provides a well-organized portal into the world of medieval English literature through more than 350 poems, prose narratives, sermons, books of advice, and other works. Each text has an introduction giving the cultural context. **www.lib.rochester.edu/camelot /teams/tmsmenu.htm**

◆ *Terry Jones' Medieval Lives* (BBC, 2004). Award-winning eight-part documentary series that focuses on the real experiences of certain kinds of medieval people often portrayed stereotypically, including the peasant, the damsel, the minstrel, the knight, and the outlaw.

# 11

# The Later Middle Ages

## 1300–1450

**During the later Middle Ages** the last book of the New Testament, the book of Revelation, inspired thousands of sermons and hundreds of religious tracts. The book of Revelation deals with visions of the end of the world, with disease, war, famine, and death—often called the "Four Horsemen of the Apocalypse"—triumphing everywhere. It is no wonder this part of the Bible was so popular in this period, for between 1300 and 1450 Europeans experienced a frightful series of shocks. The climate turned colder and wetter, leading to poor harvests and famine. People weakened by hunger were more susceptible to disease, and in the middle of the fourteenth century a new disease, probably the bubonic plague, spread throughout Europe. With no effective treatment, the plague killed millions of people. War devastated the countryside, especially in France, leading to widespread discontent and peasant revolts. Workers in cities also revolted against dismal working conditions, and violent crime and ethnic tensions increased as well. Massive deaths and preoccupation with death make the fourteenth century one of the most wrenching periods of Western civilization. Yet, in spite of the pessimism and crises, important institutions and cultural forms, including representative assemblies and national literatures, emerged. Even institutions that experienced severe crisis, such as the Christian Church, saw new types of vitality. ■

# CHAPTER PREVIEW

- How did climate change shape the late Middle Ages?

- How did the plague affect European society?

- What were the causes, course, and consequences of the Hundred Years' War?

- Why did the church come under increasing criticism?

- What explains the social unrest of the late Middle Ages?

**Noble Violence in the Late Middle Ages**
In this French manuscript illumination from 1465, armored knights kill peasants while they work in the fields or take refuge in a castle. Aristocratic violence was a common feature of late medieval life, although nobles would generally not have bothered to put on their armor to harass villagers. (From *Cas des Nobles Hommes et Femmes* by Giovanni Boccaccio, 1465/Musée Condé, Chantilly, France/Bridgeman Images)

# How did climate change shape the late Middle Ages?

Toward the end of the thirteenth century the expanding European economy began to slow down, and in the first half of the fourteenth century Europe experienced ongoing climate change that led to lower levels of food production, which had dramatic and disastrous ripple effects.

## Climate Change and Famine

The period from about 1000 to about 1300 saw a warmer-than-usual climate in Europe, which underlay all the changes and vitality of the High Middle Ages. Around 1300, however, the climate changed for the worse, becoming colder and wetter. Historical geographers refer to the period from 1300 to about 1800 as a "little ice age," which they can trace through both natural and human records.

Evidence from nature emerges through the study of Alpine and polar glaciers, tree rings, and pollen left in bogs. Human-produced sources include written reports of rivers freezing and crops never ripening, as well as archaeological evidence such as the collapsed houses and emptied villages of Greenland, where ice floes cut off contact with the rest of the world and the harshening climate meant that the few hardy crops grown in earlier times could no longer survive. The Viking colony on Greenland died out completely, though Inuit people who relied on hunting sea mammals continued to live in the far north, as they had before the arrival of Viking colonists.

Across Europe, an unusual number of storms brought torrential rains, ruining the wheat, oat, and hay crops on which people and animals almost

**Death from Famine** In this fifteenth-century painting, dead bodies lie in the middle of a path, while a funeral procession at the right includes a man with an adult's coffin and a woman with the coffin of an infant under her arm. People did not simply allow the dead to lie in the street in medieval Europe, though during famines and epidemics it was sometimes difficult to maintain normal burial procedures. (From *Chroniques d'Angleterre*, by Jean de Wavrin, ca. 1470–1480/British Library, London, UK/© British Library Board. All Rights Reserved/Bridgeman Images)

# TIMELINE

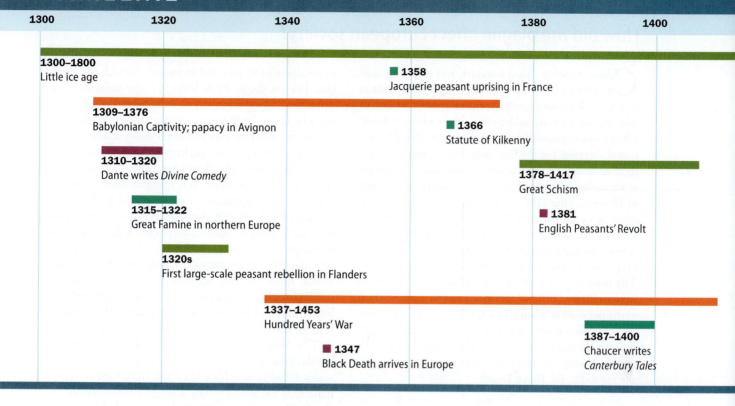

| | | | | | |
|---|---|---|---|---|---|
| 1300 | 1320 | 1340 | 1360 | 1380 | 1400 |

**1300–1800**
Little ice age

**1358**
Jacquerie peasant uprising in France

**1309–1376**
Babylonian Captivity; papacy in Avignon

**1366**
Statute of Kilkenny

**1310–1320**
Dante writes *Divine Comedy*

**1378–1417**
Great Schism

**1315–1322**
Great Famine in northern Europe

**1381**
English Peasants' Revolt

**1320s**
First large-scale peasant rebellion in Flanders

**1337–1453**
Hundred Years' War

**1347**
Black Death arrives in Europe

**1387–1400**
Chaucer writes
*Canterbury Tales*

everywhere depended. Long-distance transportation of food was expensive and difficult, so most urban areas depended on areas no more than a day's journey away for grain, produce, and meat. Poor harvests led to scarcity and starvation, and almost all of northern Europe suffered a **Great Famine** in the years 1315 to 1322. Rulers attempted to find solutions and provide famine relief, but government responses to these crises were ineffectual.

Even in non-famine years, the cost of grain, livestock, and dairy products rose sharply, in part because diseases hit cattle and sheep. Increasing prices meant that fewer people could afford to buy food. Reduced caloric intake meant increased susceptibility to disease, especially for infants, children, and the elderly. Workers on reduced diets had less energy, which meant lower productivity, lower output, and higher grain prices.

## Social Consequences

The changing climate and resulting agrarian crisis of the fourteenth century had grave social consequences. Poor harvests and famine led to the abandonment of homesteads. In parts of the Low Countries and in the Scottish-English borderlands, entire villages were deserted, and many people became vagabonds, wandering in search of food and work. In Flanders and eastern England, some peasants were forced to mortgage, sublease, or sell their holdings to richer farmers in order to buy food. Throughout the affected areas, young men and women sought work in the towns, delaying marriage.

As the subsistence crisis deepened, starving people focused their anger on the rich, speculators, and the Jews, who were often portrayed as creditors fleecing the poor through pawnbroking. (As explained in Chapter 10, Jews often became moneylenders because Christian authorities restricted their ownership of land and opportunities to engage in other trades.) Rumors spread of a plot by Jews and their alleged agents, the lepers, to kill Christians by poisoning wells. Based on "evidence" collected by torture, many lepers and Jews were killed, beaten, or heavily fined.

Meanwhile, the international character of trade and commerce meant that a disaster in one country had serious implications elsewhere. For example, the infection that attacked English sheep in 1318 caused a sharp decline in wool exports in the following years. Without wool, Flemish weavers could not work, and thousands were laid off. Without woolen cloth, the businesses of Flemish, Hanseatic, and Italian merchants suffered. Unemployment encouraged people to turn to crime.

**Great Famine** A terrible famine in 1315–1322 that hit much of Europe after a period of climate change.

# How did the plague affect European society?

Colder weather, failed harvests, and resulting malnourishment left Europe's population susceptible to disease, and unfortunately for the continent, a virulent one appeared in the mid-fourteenth century. Around 1300 improvements in ship design had allowed year-round shipping for the first time. European merchants took advantage of these advances, and ships continually at sea carried all types of cargo. They also carried vermin of all types, especially insects and rats, both of which often harbored pathogens. Just as modern air travel has allowed diseases such as AIDS and the H1N1 virus to spread quickly over very long distances, medieval shipping allowed the diseases of the time to do the same. The most frightful of these diseases first emerged in western Europe in 1347 and killed as much as one-third of the population when it first reached an area. Contemporaries called it the "great plague" or "great pestilence," though by the nineteenth century this fourteenth-century epidemic became known by the name we generally use today, the **Black Death**.

## Pathology

The Black Death was one of several types of plague caused by the bacterium *Yersinia pestis*. The disease normally afflicts rats and is passed through the fleas that live on them. Fleas living on the infected rats drink their blood and then pass the bacteria that cause the plague on to the next rat they bite. Usually the disease is limited to rats and other rodents, but at certain points in history—perhaps when most rats have been killed off—the fleas have jumped from their rodent hosts to humans and other animals. One of these instances appears to have occurred in the Eastern Roman Empire in the sixth century, when what became known as Justinian's plague killed millions of people (see "Byzantine Learning and Science" in Chapter 7). Another was in China and India in the 1890s, when millions again died. Doctors and epidemiologists closely studied this outbreak, identified the bacterium, and learned about the exact cycle of infection for the first time.

The fourteenth-century outbreak showed many similarities to the nineteenth-century one, but also some differences, which led a few historians to speculate that the Black Death was not *Yersinia pestis*. In the 2010s, however, microbiologists studying human tooth pulp in mass graves associated with the Black Death in several parts of Europe found the presence of the DNA of *Yersinia pestis*. Those studying a grave in

**Burial of Plague Victims** In this manuscript illumination from the Flemish city of Tournai in 1349, men and women bury the dead in plain wooden coffins. The death rate overwhelmed the ability of people to carry out normal funeral ceremonies, and in some places the dead were simply dumped in mass graves, with no coffins at all. (Black Death at Tournai, 1349/Gilles Le Muisit [1272–1352]/Bibliothèque Royale de Belgique, Brussels, Belgium/Bridgeman Images)

London were able to sequence the bacterium's whole genome, showing that it differed little from the *Y. pestis* that is still in the world today. The causes of the very high mortality rate of the fourteenth-century outbreak may have included a high level of direct person-to-person infection through coughing and sneezing (what epidemiologists term *pneumonic plague*), as well as other factors that we don't yet fully understand. Research into the plague is a thriving interdisciplinary field of study, with new findings coming every year from various outbreaks around the world that occurred in different eras of the past or are happening today.

There is no dispute about the plague's dreadful effects on the body. Whether it gets into the body from a cough or a flea bite, *Yersinia pestis* enters the lymph system, creating the classic symptom of the bubonic plague, a growth the size of a nut or an apple in the lymph nodes of the armpit, groin, or neck. This was the boil, or *bubo*, that gave the disease its name and caused agonizing pain. If the bubo was lanced and the pus thoroughly drained, the victim had a chance of recovery. If the boil was not lanced, however—and in the fourteenth century, it rarely was—the next stage was the appearance of black spots or blotches caused by bleeding under the skin as *Yersinia pestis* moved into the bloodstream. Finally, the victim began to cough violently and spit blood. This stage, indicating the presence of millions of bacilli in the bloodstream, signaled the end, and death followed in two or three days. The coughing also released those pathogens into the air, infecting others when they were breathed in and beginning the deadly cycle again on new victims.

## Spread of the Disease

The newest genetic research on the plague finds that it originated in western China and then spread throughout multiple radiations into Europe, Africa, and elsewhere in Asia. Several new strains developed in the thirteenth or early fourteenth century, which spread from western China along the trade routes of the Mongol Empire, for caravans carrying silk, spices, and gold across Central Asia were accompanied by rats and other vermin. Rats and humans carried the disease onto ships, especially in the ports of the Black Sea. One Italian chronicler told of a more dramatic means of spreading the disease as well: Mongol armies besieging the city of Kaffa on the shores of the Black Sea catapulted plague-infected corpses over the walls to infect those inside, a type of early biological warfare. The chronicler was not an eyewitness, but modern epidemiologists find his account plausible, though the plague most likely spread from many Black Sea ports, not just Kaffa.

In October 1347 Genoese ships brought the plague from the Black Sea to Messina, from which it spread across Sicily and then to Italy and over the Alps to Germany. Frightened French authorities chased a galley bearing plague victims away from the port of Marseilles, but not before plague had infected the city, from which it spread to southern France and Spain. In June 1348 two ships entered the Bristol Channel and introduced it into England, and from there it traveled northeast into Scandinavia. The plague seems to have entered Poland through the Baltic seaports and spread eastward from there (Map 11.1).

Medieval urban conditions were ideal for the spread of disease. Narrow streets were filled with refuse, human excrement, and dead animals. Houses whose upper stories projected over the lower ones blocked light and air. In addition, people were already weakened by famine, standards of personal hygiene remained frightfully low, and the urban populace was crowded together. Fleas and body lice were universal afflictions: everyone from peasants to archbishops had them. One more bite did not cause much alarm, and the association between rats, fleas, and the plague was unknown.

Mortality rates can be only educated guesses because population figures for the period before and after the arrival of the plague do not exist for most countries and cities. Densely populated Italian cities endured incredible losses. Florence lost between one-half and two-thirds of its population when the plague visited in 1348. Of a total English population of perhaps 4.2 million, probably 1.4 million died in the Black Death, but the number may actually have been higher. Archaeologists studying the amounts of pottery shards left at various sites in eastern England conclude that the pottery-using population—which would have included all social classes—in the period after the Black Death was 45 percent lower than it had been before. Islamic parts of Europe were not spared, nor was the rest of the Muslim world. The most widely accepted estimate for western Europe and the Mediterranean is that the plague killed about one-third of the population in the first wave of infection. (Some areas, including such cities as Milan, Liège, and Nuremberg, were largely spared, primarily because city authorities closed the gates to all outsiders when plague was in the area and enough food had been stored to sustain the city until the danger had passed.)

Nor did central and eastern Europe escape the ravages of the disease. One chronicler records that, in the summer and autumn of 1349, between five hundred and six hundred died every day in Vienna. As the plague took its toll on the Holy Roman Empire, waves of emigrants fled to Poland, Bohemia, and Hungary,

■ **Black Death** Plague that first struck Europe in 1347 and killed perhaps one-third of the population.

## MAP 11.1 The Course of the Black Death in Fourteenth-Century Europe

The bubonic plague spread across Europe after beginning in the mid-1340s, with the first cases of disease reported in Black Sea ports.

**ANALYZING THE MAP**  When did the plague reach Paris? How much time passed before it spread to the rest of northern France and southern Germany? Which cities and regions were spared?

**CONNECTIONS**  How did the expansion of trade contribute to the spread of the Black Death?

---

taking the plague with them. In the Byzantine Empire the plague ravaged the population. The youngest son of Emperor John VI Kantakouzenos died just as his father took over the throne in 1347. "So incurable was the evil," wrote John later in his history of the Byzantine Empire, "that neither any regularity of life, nor any bodily strength could resist it. Strong and weak bodies were all similarly carried away, and those best cared for died in the same manner as the poor."[1]

Across Europe, there was a second wave of the plague in 1359–1363, and then it recurred intermittently for centuries, though never with the same virulence because by then Europeans had some resistance. Improved standards of hygiene and strictly enforced quarantine measures also lessened the plague's toll, but

only in 1721 did it make its last appearance in Europe, in the French port of Marseilles. And only in 1947, six centuries after the arrival of the plague in Europe, did the American microbiologist Selman Waksman discover an effective treatment, streptomycin. Plague continues to infect rodent and human populations sporadically today.

## Care of the Sick

Fourteenth-century medical literature indicates that physicians tried many different methods to prevent and treat the plague, basing treatments on their understanding of how the body worked, as do doctors in any era. People understood that plague and other diseases could be transmitted person to person, and they observed that crowded cities had high death rates, especially when the weather was warm and moist. We now understand that warm, moist conditions make it easier for germs to grow and spread, but fourteenth-century people thought in terms of "poisons" in the air or "corrupted air" coming from swamps, unburied animals, or the positions of the stars. These poisons caused the fluids in the body to become unbalanced, which led to illness, an idea that had been the core of Western ideas about the primary cause of disease since the ancient Greeks. Certain symptoms of the plague, such as boils that oozed and blood-filled coughing, were believed to be the body's natural reaction to too much fluid. Doctors thus recommended preventive measures that would block the poisoned air from entering the body, such as burning incense or holding strong-smelling herbs or other substances, like rosemary, juniper, or sulfur, in front of the nose. Other treatments focused on ridding the air and the body of these poisons and on rebalancing bodily fluids through vomiting, sweating, or letting blood, which was also thought to rid the body of poisons.

In their fear and dread, people tried anything they thought might help. Perhaps loud sounds like ringing church bells or firing the newly invented cannon would clean poisoned air. Medicines made from plants that were bumpy or that oozed liquid might work, keeping the more dangerous swelling and oozing of the plague away. Magical letter and number combinations, called cryptograms, were especially popular in Muslim areas. They were often the first letters of words in prayers or religious sayings, and they gave people a sense of order when faced with the randomness with which the plague seemed to strike.

To avoid contagion, wealthier people often fled cities for the countryside, though sometimes this simply spread the plague faster. (See "Viewpoints: Italian and English Views of the Plague," page 300.) Some cities tried shutting their gates to prevent infected people and animals from coming in, which worked in a few cities. They also walled up houses in which there was plague, trying to isolate those who were sick from those who were still healthy. Though some members of the clergy took flight, many cared for the sick and buried the dead, which meant they had a high mortality rate.

## Economic, Religious, and Cultural Effects

Economic historians and demographers dispute the impact of the plague on the economy in the late fourteenth century, and this clearly was different in different parts of Europe. Some places never recovered their economic standing, while in others, those people who survived may have had a higher standard of living. By the mid-1300s the population of Europe had grown somewhat beyond what could easily be supported by available agricultural technology, particularly in the worsening climate of the little ice age. The dramatic drop in population allowed less fertile land to be abandoned, making yields per acre somewhat better. People also turned to less labor-intensive types of agriculture, such as raising sheep or wine grapes, which in the long run proved to be a better use of the land.

The Black Death did bring on a general European inflation. High mortality produced a fall in production, shortages of goods, and a general rise in prices. The price of wheat in most of Europe increased, as did the costs of meat, sausage, and cheese. This inflation continued to the end of the fourteenth century. But labor shortages resulting from the high mortality caused by the plague meant that workers could demand better wages. The greater demand for labor also meant greater mobility for peasants in rural areas and for artisans in towns and cities.

The plague also had effects on religious practices. Not surprisingly, some people sought release from the devastation through wild living, but more became more deeply pious. Rather than seeing the plague as a medical issue, they interpreted it as the result of an evil within themselves. God must be punishing them for terrible sins, they thought, so the best remedies were religious ones: asking for forgiveness, praying, trusting in God, making donations to churches, and trying to live better lives. In Muslim areas, religious leaders urged virtuous living in the face of death: give to the poor, reconcile with your enemies, free your slaves, and say a proper good-bye to your friends and family.

Believing that the Black Death was God's punishment for humanity's wickedness, some Christians turned to the severest forms of asceticism and frenzied religious fervor, joining groups of **flagellants** (FLA-juh-luhnts), who whipped and scourged themselves as penance for their own and society's sins. Groups of flagellants traveled from town to town, often growing into unruly mobs. Officials, worried that they would provoke violence and riots, ordered groups to disband or forbade them to enter cities.

Along with seeing the plague as a call to reform their own behavior, however, people also searched for scapegoats, and savage cruelty sometimes resulted. As in the decades before the plague, many people believed that the Jews had poisoned the wells of Christian communities and thereby infected the drinking water. Others thought that killing Jews would prevent the plague from spreading to their town, a belief encouraged by flagellant groups. These charges led to the murder of thousands of Jews across Europe, especially in the cities

■ **flagellants** People who believed that the plague was God's punishment for sin and sought to do penance by flagellating (whipping) themselves.

Eyewitness commentators on the plague include the Italian writer Giovanni Boccaccio (1313–1375), who portrayed the course of the disease in Florence in the preface to his book of tales, *The Decameron*, and the English monastic chronicler Henry Knighton (d. 1396), who described the effects of the plague on English towns and villages in his four-volume chronicle of English history.

### Giovanni Boccaccio

〰 Against this pestilence no human wisdom or foresight was of any avail. . . . Men and women in great numbers abandoned their city, their houses, their farms, their relatives, and their possessions and sought other places, going at least as far away as the Florentine countryside — as if the wrath of God could not pursue them with this pestilence wherever they went but would only strike those it found within the walls of the city! . . . Almost no one cared for his neighbor, and relatives hardly ever visited one another — they stayed far apart. This disaster had struck such fear into the hearts of men and women that brother abandoned brother, uncle abandoned nephew, sister left brother, and very often wife abandoned husband, and — even worse, almost unbelievable — fathers and mothers neglected to tend and care for their children as if they were not their own. . . . So many corpses would arrive in front of a church every day and at every hour that the amount of holy ground for burials was certainly insufficient for the ancient custom of giving each body its individual place; when all the graves were full, huge trenches were dug in all the cemeteries of the churches and into them the new arrivals were dumped by the hundreds; and they were packed in there with dirt, one on top of another, like a ship's cargo, until the trench was filled. . . . Oh how many great palaces, beautiful homes and noble dwellings, once filled with families, gentlemen, and ladies, were now emptied, down to the last servant!

### Henry Knighton

〰 Then that most grievous pestilence penetrated the coastal regions [of England] by way of Southampton, and came to Bristol, and people died as if the whole strength of the city were seized by sudden death. For there were few who lay in their beds more than three days or two and half days; then that savage death snatched them about the second day.

In Leicester, in the little parish of St. Leonard, more than three hundred and eighty died; in the parish of Holy Cross, more than four hundred. . . . And so in each parish, they died in great numbers. . . . At the same time, there was so great a lack of priests everywhere that many churches had no divine services. . . . One could hardly hire a chaplain to minister to the church for less than ten marks, whereas before the pestilence, when there were plenty of priests, one could hire a chaplain for five or four marks. . . . Meanwhile, the king ordered that in every county of the kingdom, reapers and other labourers should not receive more than they were accustomed to receive, under the penalty provided in the statute, and he renewed the statute at this time. The labourers, however, were so arrogant and hostile that they did not heed the king's command, but if anyone wished to hire them, he had to pay them what they wanted, and either lose his fruits and crops or satisfy the arrogant and greedy desire of the labourers as they wished. . . . Similarly, those who received day-work from their tenants throughout the year, as is usual from serfs, had to release them and to remit such service. They either had to excuse them entirely or had to fix them in a laxer manner at a small rent, lest very great and irreparable damage be done to the buildings and the land everywhere remain uncultivated.

### QUESTIONS FOR ANALYSIS

1. How did the residents of Florence respond to the plague, as described by Boccaccio?
2. What were some of the effects of the plague in England, as described by Knighton?
3. How might the fact that Boccaccio was writing in an urban setting and Knighton was writing from a rural monastery that owned a large amount of land have shaped their perspectives?

Sources: Giovanni Boccaccio, *The Decameron*, trans. Mark Musa and Peter Bondanella (New York: W. W. Norton, 1982), pp. 7, 9, 12; Henry Knighton, *Chronicon Henrici Knighton*, in *The Portable Medieval Reader*, ed. James Bruce Ross and Mary Martin McLaughlin, copyright © 1949 by Viking Penguin, inc.; copyright renewed © 1976 by James Bruce Ross and Mary Martin McLaughlin. Used by permission of Viking Books, an imprint of Penguin Publishing Group, a division of Penguin Random House LLC. All rights reserved.

of France and Germany. In Strasbourg, for example, several hundred Jews were publicly burned alive. Their houses were looted, their property was confiscated, and the remaining Jews were expelled from the city.

The literature and art of the late Middle Ages reveal a people gripped by morbid concern with death. One highly popular literary and artistic motif, the Dance of Death, depicted a dancing skeleton leading away living people, often in order of their rank. (See "Evaluating Visual Evidence: Dance of Death," page 301.)

The years of the Black Death witnessed the foundation of new colleges at old universities and of

# Dance of Death

In this allegorical fresco from the Holy Trinity Church in the village of Hrastovlje, Slovenia, skeletons lead people of all social classes in a procession. One of them carries a scythe for reaping grain, long a symbol of death cutting off human life. In the late fifteenth century the Croatian artist John of Kastav painted the entire church in frescoes, which were discovered in 1949 under layers of plaster. The Dance of Death became a common theme in late medieval painting, especially on the walls of cemeteries, churches, and chapels, and in engravings and woodcuts. Designed as *memento mori* (in Latin: "Remember that you have to die"), symbolic reminders of mortality, they encouraged viewers to think about the fleetingness of human life.

(The Dance of Death [fresco]/Kastav, Janez [fl. ca. 1490]/Church of the Holy Trinity, Hrastovlje, Slovenia/Bridgeman Images)

## EVALUATE THE EVIDENCE

1. Based on their clothing and the objects they are carrying, who are the people shown in the fresco? What does this suggest about the artist's message about death?
2. Paintings such as this clearly provide evidence of the preoccupation with death in this era, but does this work highlight other social issues as well? Is so, what are they?

entirely new universities. The foundation charters give the shortage of priests and the decay of learning as the reasons for their establishment. Whereas older universities such as those at Bologna and Paris had international student bodies, these new institutions established in the wake of the Black Death had more national or local constituencies. Thus the international character of medieval culture weakened, paving the way for schism (SKIH-zuhm) in the Catholic Church even before the Reformation.

As is often true with devastating events, the plague highlighted central qualities of medieval society: deep religious feeling, suspicion of those who were different, and a view of the world shaped largely by oral tradition, with a bit of classical knowledge mixed in among the educated elite.

**Isabella of France and Her Son Edward Invade England**    Isabella, the sister of Charles IV of France and the wife of Edward II of England, and her son Edward are welcomed by clergy into the city of Oxford in 1326, in this illustration for the chronicles of the counts of Flanders, made in 1477. Isabella and Edward, who was only fourteen at the time, had just invaded England with a small army to overthrow her husband. Isabella ruled as regent for her son for three years before he assumed personal rule by force. She lived another twenty-eight years in high style as a wealthy woman, watching her son lead successful military ventures in France in the first decades of the Hundred Years' War. (By kind permission of Lord Leicester and the Trustees of Holkham Estate, Norfolk/Bridgeman Images)

## What were the causes, course, and consequences of the Hundred Years' War?

A long international war that began a decade or so before the plague struck and lasted well into the next century added further misery to a disease-ravaged population. England and France had engaged in sporadic military hostilities from the time of the Norman Conquest in 1066, and in the middle of the fourteenth century these became more intense. From 1337 to 1453 the two countries intermittently fought one another in what was the longest war in European history, ultimately dubbed the **Hundred Years' War**, though it actually lasted 116 years.

### Causes

The Hundred Years' War had a number of causes, including disagreements over rights to land, a dispute over the succession to the French throne, and economic conflicts. Many of these revolved around the duchy of Aquitaine, a province in southern France

that became part of the holdings of the English crown when Eleanor of Aquitaine married King Henry II of England in 1152 (see "England" in Chapter 9; a duchy is a territory ruled by a duke). In 1259 Henry III of England had signed the Treaty of Paris with Louis IX of France, affirming English claims to Aquitaine in return for becoming a vassal of the French crown. French policy in the fourteenth century was strongly expansionist, however, and the French kings resolved to absorb the duchy into the kingdom of France. Aquitaine therefore became a disputed territory.

The immediate political cause of the war was a disagreement over who would inherit the French throne after Charles IV of France, the last surviving son of Philip the Fair, died childless in 1328. With him ended the male line of the Capetian dynasty of France. Charles IV had a sister, Isabella, married to Edward II, the king of England, and just two years earlier she and her lover Roger Mortimer had invaded England with a small army to overthrow her husband and end the influence of his male favorite, Hugh le Despenser. They captured and imprisoned both men, executed Despenser, deposed the king (and may have ordered his murder), and put her teenage son Edward III on the throne. Seeking to keep Isabella and Edward from the French throne, an assembly of French high nobles proclaimed that "no woman nor her son could succeed to the [French] monarchy." French lawyers defended the position with the claim that the exclusion of women from ruling or passing down the right to rule was part of Salic law, a sixth-century law code of the Franks (see "Customary and Written Law" in Chapter 7), and that Salic law itself was part of the fundamental law of France. They used this invented tradition to argue that Edward should be barred from the French throne. (The ban on female succession became part of French legal tradition until the end of the monarchy in 1789.) The nobles passed the crown to Philip VI of Valois (r. 1328–1350), a nephew of Philip the Fair.

In 1329 Edward III formally recognized his status as a vassal to Philip VI for Aquitaine, as required by the 1259 Treaty of Paris. Eight years later, in 1337, Philip, eager to exercise full French jurisdiction there, confiscated the duchy. Edward III interpreted this action as a gross violation of the treaty and as a cause for war. Moreover, Edward argued, as the eldest directly surviving male descendant of Philip the Fair, he deserved the title of king of France. To increase their independent power, many French nobles abandoned Philip VI, using the excuse that they accepted Edward's claims to the throne. One reason the war lasted so long was that it became a French civil war, with some French nobles, especially the dukes of Burgundy, supporting English monarchs in order to thwart the centralizing goals of the French kings. On the other side, Scotland—resisting English efforts of assimilation—often allied with France; the French supported Scottish raids in northern England, and Scottish troops joined with French armies on the continent.

The governments of both England and France manipulated public opinion to support the war. Kings in both countries instructed the clergy to deliver sermons filled with patriotic sentiment. Royal propaganda on both sides fostered a kind of early nationalism, and both sides developed a deep hatred of the other.

Economic factors involving the wool trade and the control of Flemish towns were linked to these political issues. The wool trade between England and Flanders served as the cornerstone of both countries' economies; they were closely interdependent. Flanders technically belonged to the French crown, and the Flemish aristocracy was highly sympathetic to that monarchy.

| THE HUNDRED YEARS' WAR | |
|---|---|
| 1337 | Philip VI of France confiscates Aquitaine; war begins |
| 1346 | English longbowmen defeat French knights at Crécy |
| 1356 | English defeat French at Poitiers |
| 1370s–1380s | French recover some territory |
| 1415 | English defeat the French at Agincourt |
| 1429 | French victory at Orléans; Charles VII crowned king |
| 1431 | Joan of Arc declared a heretic and burned at the stake |
| 1440s | French reconquer Normandy and Aquitaine |
| 1453 | War ends |
| 1456 | Joan cleared of charges of heresy and declared a martyr |

But the wealth of Flemish merchants and cloth manufacturers depended on English wool, and Flemish burghers strongly supported the claims of Edward III. The disruption of commerce with England threatened their prosperity.

The war also presented opportunities for wealth and advancement. Poor and idle knights were promised regular wages. Criminals who enlisted were granted pardons. The great nobles expected to be rewarded with estates. Royal exhortations to the troops before battles repeatedly stressed that, if victorious, the men might keep whatever they seized.

## English Successes

The war began with a series of French sea raids on English coastal towns in 1337, but the French fleet was almost completely destroyed when it attempted to land soldiers on English soil, and from that point on the war was fought almost entirely in France and the Low Countries (Map 11.2). It consisted mainly of a series of random sieges and cavalry raids, fought in fits and starts, with treaties along the way to halt hostilities.

During the war's early stages, England was highly successful. At Crécy in northern France in 1346, English longbowmen scored a great victory over French knights and crossbowmen. Although the aim

■ **Hundred Years' War** A war between England and France from 1337 to 1453, with political and economic causes and consequences.

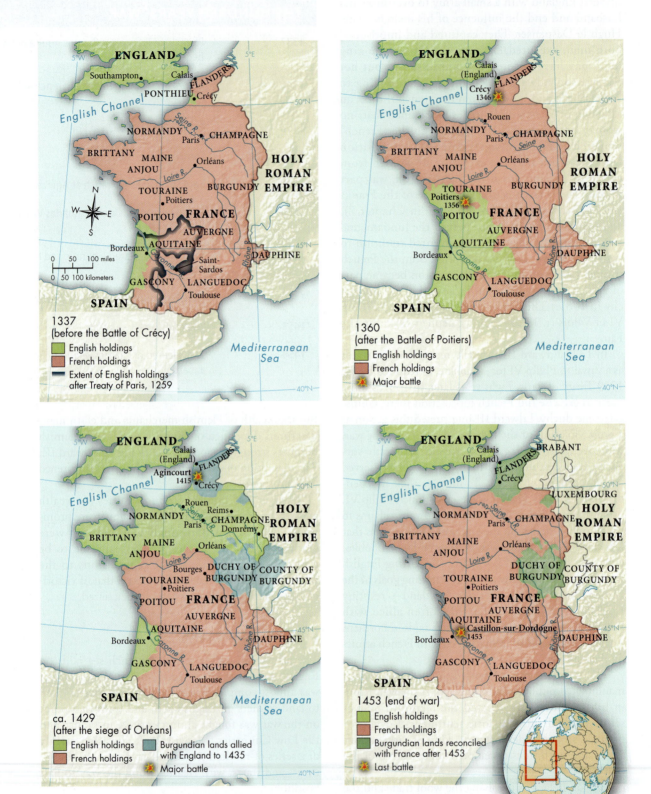

**MAP 11.2 The Hundred Years' War, 1337–1453** These maps show the change in the land held by the English and French crowns over the course of the Hundred Years' War. Which year marked the greatest extent of English holdings in France?

of longbowmen was not very accurate, the weapon allowed for rapid reloading, and an English archer could send off three arrows to the French crossbowman's one. The result was a blinding shower of arrows that unhorsed the French knights and caused mass confusion. The roar of English cannon — probably the first use of artillery in the Western world — created further panic. Edward's son, Edward the Black Prince, used the same tactics ten years later to smash the French at Poitiers, where he captured the French king and held him for ransom. Edward was not able to take all of France, but the English held Aquitaine and other provinces, and allied themselves with many of France's nobles. After a brief peace, the French fought back and recovered some territory during the 1370s and 1380s, and then a treaty again halted hostilities as both sides concentrated on conflicts over power at home.

War began again in 1415 when the able English soldier-king Henry V (r. 1413–1422) invaded France. At Agincourt (AH-jihn-kort), Henry's army defeated a much larger French force, again primarily through the skill of English longbowmen. Henry followed up his triumph at Agincourt with the reconquest of Normandy, and by 1419 the English had advanced to the walls of Paris (see Map 11.2). Henry married the daughter of the French king, and a treaty made Henry and any sons the couple would have heir to the French throne. It appeared as if Henry would indeed rule

both England and France, but he died unexpectedly in 1422, leaving an infant son as heir. The English continued their victories, however, and besieged the city of Orléans (or-lay-AHN), the only major city in northern France not under their control. But the French cause was not lost.

## Joan of Arc and France's Victory

The ultimate French success rests heavily on the actions of Joan, an obscure French peasant girl whose vision and military leadership revived French fortunes and led to victory. (Over the centuries, she acquired the name "of Arc" — *d'Arc* in French — based on her father's name; she never used this name for herself, but called herself "the maiden" — *la Pucelle* in French.) Born in 1412 to well-to-do peasants in the village of Domrémy in Champagne, Joan grew up in a religious household. During adolescence she began to hear voices, which she later said belonged to Saint Michael, Saint Catherine, and Saint Margaret. In 1428 these voices spoke to her with great urgency, telling her that the dauphin (DOH-fehn), the uncrowned King Charles VII, had to be crowned and the English expelled from France. Joan traveled to the French court wearing male clothing. She had an audience with Charles, who had her questioned about her angelic visions and examined to make sure she was the virgin she said she was. She secured his support to travel with the French army to Orléans dressed as a knight — with borrowed armor and

**Battle of Poitiers, 1356** This fifteenth-century manuscript highlights the role of English longbowmen in defeating French armies. Though the scene is fanciful, the artist accurately depicts a standard tactic, shooting unarmored horses rather than the heavily armored knights, who were killed or captured when they fell from horseback. Commentators at the time and military historians since judge this tactic to have been especially important in the English victory. (From *Froissart's Chronicle*, by Jean Froissart/Bibliothèque Nationale, Paris, France/Bridgeman Images)

sword. There she dictated a letter to the English ordering them to surrender:

> King of England . . . , do right in the King of Heaven's sight. Surrender to The Maid sent hither by God the King of Heaven, the keys of all the good towns you have taken and laid waste in France. She comes in God's name to establish the Blood Royal, ready to make peace if you agree to abandon France and repay what you have taken. And you, archers, comrades in arms, gentles and others, who are before the town of Orléans, retire in God's name to your own country.[2]

Such words coming from a teenage girl—even one inspired by God—were laughable given the recent course of the conflict, but Joan was amazingly successful. She inspired and led French attacks, forcing the English to retreat from Orléans. The king made Joan co-commander of the entire army, and she led it to a string of victories; other cities simply surrendered without a fight and returned their allegiance to France. In July 1429, two months after the end of the siege of Orléans, Charles VII was crowned king at Reims.

Joan and the French army continued their fight against the English and their Burgundian allies. In 1430 the Burgundians captured Joan. Charles refused to ransom her, and she was sold to the English. A church court headed by a pro-English bishop tried her for heresy, and though nothing she had done was heretical by church doctrine, she was found guilty and burned at the stake in the marketplace at Rouen. (See "Evaluating Written Evidence: The Trial of Joan of Arc," page 307.)

The French army continued its victories without her. Sensing a shift in the balance of power, the Burgundians switched their allegiance to the French, who reconquered Normandy and, finally, ejected the English from Aquitaine in the 1440s. As the war dragged on, loss of life mounted, and money appeared to be flowing into a bottomless pit, demands for an end increased in England. Parliamentary opposition to additional war grants stiffened, fewer soldiers were sent, and more territory passed into French hands. At the war's end in 1453, only the town of Calais (KA-lay) remained in English hands.

What of Joan? A new trial in 1456—requested by Charles VII, who either had second thoughts about his abandonment of Joan or did not wish to be associated with a condemned heretic—was held by the pope. It cleared her of all charges and declared her a martyr. She became a political symbol of France from that

point on, and sometimes also a symbol of the Catholic Church in opposition to the government of France. In 1920, for example, she was canonized as a saint shortly after the French government declared separation of church and state in France. Similarly, Joan has been (and continues to be) a symbol of deep religious piety to some, of conservative nationalism to others, and of gender-bending cross-dressing to others. Beneath the pious and popular legends is a teenage girl who saved the French monarchy, the embodiment of France.

## Aftermath

In France thousands of soldiers and civilians had been slaughtered and hundreds of thousands of acres of rich farmland ruined, leaving the rural economy of many areas a shambles. These losses exacerbated the dreadful losses caused by the plague. The war had disrupted trade and the great trade fairs, resulting in the drastic reduction of French participation in international commerce. Defeat in battle and heavy taxation contributed to widespread dissatisfaction and aggravated peasant grievances.

The war had wreaked havoc in England as well, even though only the southern coastal ports saw actual battle. England spent the huge sum of over £5 million on the war effort, and despite the money raised by some victories, the net result was an enormous financial loss. The government attempted to finance the war by raising taxes on the wool crop, which priced wool out of the export market.

In both England and France, men of all social classes had volunteered to serve in the war in the hope of acquiring booty and becoming rich, and some were successful in the early years of the war. As time went on, however, most fortunes seem to have been squandered as fast as they were made. In addition, the social order was disrupted because the knights who ordinarily served as sheriffs, coroners, jurymen, and justices of the peace were abroad.

The war stimulated technological experimentation, especially with artillery. Cannon revolutionized warfare, making the stone castle no longer impregnable. Because only central governments, not private nobles, could afford cannon, their use strengthened the military power of national states.

The long war also had a profound impact on the political and cultural lives of the two countries. Most notably, it stimulated the development of the English Parliament. Between 1250 and 1450 **representative assemblies** flourished in many European countries. In the English Parliament, German *diets*, and Spanish *cortes*, deliberative practices developed that laid the foundations for the representative institutions of modern democratic nations. While representative assemblies declined in most countries after the fifteenth

■ **representative assemblies** Deliberative meetings of lords and wealthy urban residents that flourished in many European countries between 1250 and 1450.

# The Trial of Joan of Arc

Joan's interrogation was organized and led by Bishop Pierre Cauchon, one of many French clergy who supported the English. In a number of sessions that took place over several months, she was repeatedly asked about her voices, her decision to wear men's clothing, and other issues. This extract is from the fourth session, on Tuesday, February 27, 1431; Joan is here referred to with the French spelling of her name, Jeanne.

In their presence Jeanne was required by my lord the Bishop of Beauvais to swear and take the oath concerning what touched her trial. To which she answered that she would willingly swear as to what touched her trial, but not as to everything she knew. . . .

Asked whether she had heard her voice since Saturday, she answered: "Yes, indeed, many times." . . . Asked what it said to her when she was back in her room, she replied: "That I should answer you boldly." . . . Questioned as to whether it were the voice of an angel, or of a saint, or directly from God, she answered that the voices were those of Saint Catherine and of Saint Margaret. And their heads are crowned with beautiful crowns, most richly and preciously. And [she said] for [telling you] this I have leave from our Lord. . . .

Asked if the voice ordered her to wear a man's dress, she answered that the dress is but a small matter; and that she had not taken it by the advice of any living man; and that she did not take this dress nor do anything at all save by the command of Our Lord and the angels.

Questioned as to whether it seemed to her that this command to take male dress was a lawful one, she answered that everything she had done was at Our Lord's command, and if He had ordered Jeanne to take a different dress, she would have done so, since it would have been at God's command. . . .

Asked if she had her sword when she was taken prisoner, she said no, but that she had one which was taken from a Burgundian. . . . Asked whether, when she was before the city of Orleans, she had a standard, and of what colour it was, she replied that it had a field sown with fleurs-de-lis, and showed a world with an angel on either side, white in colour, of linen or *boucassin* [a type of fabric], and she thought that the names JESUS MARIA were written on it; and it had a silk fringe. . . . Asked which she preferred, her sword or her standard, she replied that she was forty times fonder of her standard than she was of her sword. . . . She said moreover that she herself bore her standard during an attack, in order to avoid killing anyone. And she added that she had never killed anyone at all. . . .

She also said that during the attack on the fort at the bridge she was wounded in the neck by an arrow, but she was greatly comforted by Saint Catherine, and was well again in a fortnight. . . . Asked whether she knew beforehand that she would be wounded, she said that she well knew it, and had informed her king of it; but that notwithstanding she would not give up her work.

## EVALUATE THE EVIDENCE

1. How does Joan explain the way that she chose to answer the interrogators' questions, and her decisions about clothing and actions in battle?
2. Thinking about the structures of power and authority in fifteenth-century France, how do you believe the interrogators would have regarded Joan's answers?

Source: *The Trial of Joan of Arc*, translated with an introduction by W. S. Scott (Westport, Conn.: Associated Booksellers, 1956), 76, 77, 79–80, 82, 83. © 1956, The Folio Society. Reprinted by permission.

---

century, the English Parliament endured. Edward III's constant need for money to pay for the war compelled him to summon not only the great barons and bishops, but knights of the shires and citizens from the towns as well. Parliament met in thirty-seven of the fifty years of Edward's reign.

The frequency of the meetings is significant. Representative assemblies were becoming a habit in England. Knights and wealthy urban residents—or the "Commons," as they came to be called—recognized their mutual interests and began to meet apart from the great lords. The Commons gradually realized that

they held the country's purse strings, and a parliamentary statute of 1341 required parliamentary approval of most new taxes. By signing the law, Edward III acknowledged that the king of England could not tax without Parliament's consent. In France, by contrast, there was no single national assembly, and regional or provincial assemblies never gained much power over taxation.

In both countries, the war promoted the growth of nationalism—the feeling of unity and identity that binds together a people. After victories, each country experienced a surge of pride in its military strength. Just as English patriotism ran strong after Crécy and Poitiers, so French national confidence rose after Orléans. French national feeling demanded the expulsion of the enemy not merely from Normandy and Aquitaine but from all French soil. Perhaps no one expressed this national consciousness better than Joan when she exulted that the enemy had been "driven out of *France*."

## Why did the church come under increasing criticism?

In times of crisis or disaster, people of all faiths have sought the consolation of religion. In the fourteenth century, however, the official Christian Church offered little solace. Many priests and friars helped the sick and the hungry, but others paid more attention to worldly matters, and the leaders of the church added to the sorrow and misery of the times. In response to this lack of leadership, members of the clergy challenged the power of the pope, and laypeople challenged the authority of the church itself. Women and men increasingly relied on direct approaches to God, often through mystical encounters, rather than on the institutional church.

### The Babylonian Captivity and Great Schism

Conflicts between the secular rulers of Europe and the popes were common throughout the High Middle Ages, and in the early fourteenth century the dispute between King Philip the Fair of France and Pope Boniface VIII became particularly bitter (see "The Popes and Church Law" in Chapter 9). After Boniface's death, Philip pressured the new pope, Clement V, to settle permanently in Avignon in southeastern France, so that he, Philip, could control the church and its policies. The popes lived in Avignon from 1309 to 1376, a period in church history often called the **Babylonian Captivity** (referring to the seventy years the ancient Hebrews were held captive in Mesopotamian Babylon).

The Babylonian Captivity badly damaged papal prestige. The leadership of the church was cut off from its historic roots and the source of its ancient authority, the city of Rome. The seven popes at Avignon concentrated on bureaucratic and financial matters to the exclusion of spiritual objectives, and the general atmosphere was one of luxury and extravagance, which was also the case at many bishops' courts. Raimon de Cornet, a troubadour poet from southern France who was himself a priest, was only one among many criticizing the church. He wrote:

> I see the pope his sacred trust betray,
> For while the rich his grace can gain alway,
> His favors from the poor are aye withholden.
> He strives to gather wealth as best he may,
> Forcing Christ's people blindly to obey,
> So that he may repose in garments golden.
>
> . . .
>
> Our bishops, too, are plunged in similar sin,
> For pitilessly they flay the very skin
> From all their priests who chance to have fat livings.
> For gold their seal official you can win
> To any writ, no matter what's therein.
> Sure God alone can make them stop their thievings.[3]

In 1377 Pope Gregory XI brought the papal court back to Rome but died shortly afterward. Roman citizens pressured the cardinals to elect an Italian, and they chose a distinguished administrator, the archbishop of Bari, Bartolomeo Prignano, who took the name Urban VI.

Urban VI (pontificate 1378–1389) had excellent intentions for church reform, but he went about it in a tactless manner. He attacked clerical luxury, denouncing individual cardinals and bishops by name, and even threatened to excommunicate some of them. The cardinals slipped away from Rome and met at Anagni. They declared Urban's election invalid because it had come about under threats from the Roman mob, and excommunicated the pope. The cardinals then elected Cardinal Robert of Geneva, the cousin of King Charles V of France, as pope. Cardinal Robert took the name Clement VII. There were thus two popes in 1378 — Urban at Rome and Clement VII (pontificate 1378–1394) at Avignon. So began the **Great Schism**, which divided Western Christendom until 1417.

The powers of Europe aligned themselves with Urban or Clement along strictly political lines. France naturally recognized the French pope, Clement. England, France's long-time enemy, recognized the Italian pope, Urban. Scotland, an ally of France, supported Clement. Aragon, Castile, and Portugal hesitated before deciding for Clement as well. The German emperor, hostile to France, recognized Urban. At first

Allegiance to Rome
Allegiance to Avignon
Official allegiance to Rome but with shifting local allegiances

**The Great Schism, 1378–1417**

the Italian city-states recognized Urban; later they opted for Clement. The schism weakened the religious faith of many Christians and brought church leadership into serious disrepute.

## Critiques, Divisions, and Councils

Criticism of the church during the Avignon papacy and the Great Schism often came from the ranks of highly learned clergy and lay professionals. One of these was William of Occam (1289?–1347?), a Franciscan friar and philosopher who saw the papal court at Avignon during the Babylonian Captivity. Occam argued vigorously against the papacy and also wrote philosophical works in which he questioned the connection between reason and faith that had been developed by Thomas Aquinas (see "Theology and Philosophy" in Chapter 10). All governments should have limited powers and be accountable to those they govern, according to Occam, and church and state should be separate.

The Italian lawyer and university official Marsiglio of Padua (ca. 1275–1342) agreed with Occam. In his *Defensor Pacis* (The Defender of the Peace), Marsiglio argued against the medieval idea of a society governed by both church and state, with church supreme. Instead, Marsiglio claimed, the state was the great unifying power in society, and the church should be subordinate to it. Church leadership should rest in a general council that is made up of laymen as well as priests and that is superior to the pope. Marsiglio was excommunicated for these radical ideas, and his work was condemned as heresy—as was Occam's—but in the later part of the fourteenth century many thinkers agreed with these two critics of the papacy. They believed that reform of the church could best be achieved through periodic assemblies, or councils, representing all the Christian people. Those who argued this position were called **conciliarists**.

The English scholar and theologian John Wyclif (WIH-klihf) (ca. 1330–1384) went further than the conciliarists in his argument against medieval church structure. He wrote that the Scriptures alone should be the standard of Christian belief and practice and that papal claims of secular power had no foundation in the Scriptures. He urged that the church be stripped of its property. He also wanted Christians to read the Bible for themselves and produced the first complete translation of the Bible into English. Wyclif's followers, dubbed Lollards, from a Dutch word for "mumble," by those who ridiculed them, spread his ideas and made many copies of his Bible. Lollard teaching allowed women to preach, and women played a significant role

**The Hussite Revolution, 1415–1436**

in the movement. Lollards were persecuted in the fifteenth century; some were executed, some recanted, and others continued to meet secretly in houses, barns, and fields to read and discuss the Bible and other religious texts in English.

Bohemian students returning from study at the University of Oxford around 1400 brought Wyclif's ideas with them to Prague, the capital of what was then Bohemia and is now the Czech Republic. There another university theologian, Jan Hus (ca. 1372–1415), built on these ideas. He also denied papal authority, called for translations of the Bible into the local Czech language, and declared indulgences—papal offers of remission of penance—useless. Hus gained many followers, who linked his theological ideas with their opposition to the church's wealth and power and with a growing sense of Czech nationalism in opposition to the pope's international power. Hus's followers were successful at defeating the combined armies of the pope and the emperor many times. In the 1430s the emperor finally agreed to recognize the Hussite Church in Bohemia, which survived into the Reformation and then merged with other Protestant churches.

The ongoing schism threatened the church, and in response to continued calls throughout Europe for a council, the cardinals of Rome and Avignon summoned a council at Pisa in 1409. That gathering of prelates and theologians deposed both popes and selected another. Neither the Avignon pope nor the Roman pope would resign, however, and the appalling result was the creation of a threefold schism.

Finally, under pressure from the German emperor Sigismund, a great council met at the imperial city of Constance (1414–1418). It had three objectives: to wipe out heresy, to end the schism, and to reform the church. Members included cardinals, bishops, abbots, and professors of theology and canon law from across Europe. The council moved first on the first point: despite being granted a safe-conduct to go to Constance by the emperor, Jan Hus was tried, condemned, and burned at the stake as a heretic in 1415. The council also eventually healed the schism. It deposed both

■ **Babylonian Captivity** The period from 1309 to 1376 when the popes resided in Avignon rather than in Rome. The phrase refers to the seventy years when the Hebrews were held captive in Babylon.

■ **Great Schism** The division, or split, in church leadership from 1378 to 1417 when there were two, then three, popes.

■ **conciliarists** People who believed that the authority in the Roman Church should rest in a general council composed of clergy, theologians, and laypeople, rather than in the pope alone.

**The Arrest and Execution of Jan Hus** In this woodcut from Ulrich of Richental's chronicle of the Council of Constance, Hus is arrested by bishops, led away by soldiers while wearing a hat of shame with the word *arch-heretic* on it, and burned at the stake. The final panel shows executioners shoveling his ashes and burned bones into the Rhine. Ulrich of Richental was a merchant in Constance and an eyewitness to Hus's execution and many of the other events of the council. He wrote his chronicle in German shortly after the council ended and paid for it to be illustrated. The original is lost, but many copies were made later in the fifteenth century, and the volume was printed in 1483 with many woodcuts, including this one. Hus became an important symbol of Czech independence, and in 1990 the Czech Republic declared July 6, the date of his execution in 1415, a national holiday. (From "History of the Council of Constance"/Bibliothèque Polonaise, Paris, France/Archives Charmet/Bridgeman Images)

the Roman pope and the successor of the pope chosen at Pisa, and it isolated the Avignon pope. A conclave elected a new leader, the Roman cardinal Colonna, who took the name Martin V (pontificate 1417–1431).

Martin proceeded to dissolve the council. Nothing was done about reform, the third objective of the council. In the later part of the fifteenth century the papacy concentrated on Italian problems to the exclusion of universal Christian interests. But the schism and the conciliar movement had exposed the crying need for ecclesiastical reform, thus laying the foundation for the great reform efforts of the sixteenth century.

## Lay Piety and Mysticism

The failings of the Avignon papacy followed by the scandal of the Great Schism did much to weaken the spiritual mystique of the clergy in the popular mind.

Laypeople had already begun to develop their own forms of piety somewhat separate from the authority of priests and bishops, and these forms of piety became more prominent in the fourteenth century.

In the thirteenth century lay Christian men and women had formed **confraternities**, voluntary lay groups organized by occupation, devotional preference, neighborhood, or charitable activity. Some confraternities specialized in praying for souls in purgatory, or held collections to raise money to clean and repair church buildings and to supply churches with candles and other liturgical objects. Like craft guilds, most confraternities were groups of men, but separate women's confraternities were formed in some towns, often to oversee the production of vestments, altar cloths, and other items made of fabric. All confraternities carried out special devotional practices such as prayers or processions, often without the leadership of a priest. Famine, plague, war, and other crises led

■ **confraternities** Voluntary lay groups organized by occupation, devotional preference, neighborhood, or charitable activity.

# INDIVIDUALS IN SOCIETY

## Meister Eckhart

Mysticism — the direct experience of the divine — is an aspect of many world religions and has been part of Christianity throughout its history. During the late Middle Ages, however, the pursuit of mystical union became an important part of the piety of many laypeople, especially in the Rhineland area of Germany. In this they were guided by the sermons of the churchman generally known as Meister Eckhart. Born into a German noble family, Eckhart (1260–1329?) joined the Dominican order and studied theology at Paris and Cologne, attaining the academic title of *master* (*Meister* in German). The leaders of the Dominican order appointed him to a series of administrative and teaching positions, and he wrote learned treatises in Latin that reflected his Scholastic training and deep understanding of classical philosophy.

He also began to preach in German, attracting many listeners through his beautiful language and mystical insights. God, he said, was "an oversoaring being and an overbeing nothingness," whose essence was beyond the ability of humans to express: "if the soul is to know God, it must know Him outside time and place, since God is neither in this or that, but One and above them." Only through "unknowing," emptying oneself, could one come to experience the divine. Yet God was also present in individual human souls, and to a degree in every creature, all of which God had called into being before the beginning of time. Within each human soul there was what Eckhart called a "little spark," an innermost essence that allows the soul — with God's grace and Christ's redemptive action — to come to God. "Our salvation depends upon our knowing and recognizing the Chief Good which is God Himself," preached Eckhart; "the Eye with which I see God is the same Eye with which God sees me." "I have a capacity in my soul for taking in God entirely," he went on, a capacity that was shared by all humans, not only members of the clergy or those with special spiritual gifts. Although Eckhart did not reject church sacraments or the hierarchy, he frequently stressed that union with God was best accomplished through quiet detachment and simple prayer rather than pilgrimages, extensive fasts, or other activities: "If the only prayer you said in your whole life was 'thank you,' that would suffice."*

Eckhart's unusual teachings led to charges of heresy in 1327, which he denied. The pope — who was at this point in Avignon — presided over a trial condemning him, but Eckhart appears to have died during the course of the proceedings or shortly thereafter. His writings were ordered destroyed, but his followers preserved many and spread his teachings.

A sixteenth-century woodcut of Meister Eckhart teaching.
(Visual Connection Archive)

In the last few decades, Meister Eckhart's ideas have been explored and utilized by philosophers and mystics in Buddhism, Hinduism, and neo-paganism, as well as by Christians. His writings sell widely for their spiritual insights, and quotations from them — including the one above about thank-you prayers — can be found on coffee mugs, tote bags, and T-shirts.

### QUESTIONS FOR ANALYSIS

1. Why might Meister Eckhart's preaching have been viewed as threatening by the leaders of the church?
2. Given the situation of the church in the late Middle Ages, why might mysticism have been attractive to pious Christians?

*Meister Eckhart's Sermons, trans. Claud Field (London: n.p., 1909).

to an expansion of confraternities in larger cities and many villages.

In Holland beginning in the late fourteenth century, a group of pious laypeople called the Brethren and Sisters of the Common Life lived in stark simplicity while daily carrying out the Gospel teaching of feeding the hungry, clothing the naked, and visiting the sick. They sought to both ease social problems and make religion a personal inner experience. The spirituality of the Brethren and Sisters of the Common Life found its finest expression in the classic *The Imitation of Christ* by the Dutch monk Thomas à Kempis (1380?–1471), which gained wide appeal among laypeople. It urges Christians to take Christ as their model, seek perfection in a simple way of life, and look to the Scriptures for guidance in living a spiritual life. In the mid-fifteenth century the movement had founded houses in the Netherlands, in central Germany, and in the Rhineland.

For some individuals, both laypeople and clerics, religious devotion included mystical experiences. (See

"Individuals in Society: Meister Eckhart," page 311.) Bridget of Sweden (1303–1373) was a noblewoman who journeyed to Rome after her husband's death. She began to see visions and gave advice based on these visions to both laypeople and church officials. At the end of her life Bridget made a pilgrimage to Jerusalem, where she saw visions of the Virgin Mary, who described to her exactly how she was standing "with [her] knees bent" when she gave birth to Jesus, and how she "showed to the shepherds the nature and male sex of the child."[4] Bridget's visions provide evidence of the ways in which laypeople used their own experiences to enhance their religious understanding; her own experiences of childbirth shaped the way she viewed the birth of Jesus, and she related to the Virgin Mary in part as one mother to another.

The confraternities and mystics were generally not considered heretical unless they began to challenge the authority of the papacy the way Wyclif, Hus, and some conciliarists did. However, the movement of lay piety did alter many people's perceptions of their own spiritual power.

## What explains the social unrest of the late Middle Ages?

At the beginning of the fourteenth century famine and disease profoundly affected the lives of European peoples. As the century wore on, decades of slaughter and destruction, punctuated by the decimating visits of the Black Death, added further woes. In many parts of France and the Low Countries, fields lay in ruin or untilled for lack of labor. In England, as taxes increased, criticisms of government policy and mismanagement multiplied. Crime and new forms of business organization aggravated economic troubles, and throughout Europe the frustrations of the common people erupted into widespread revolts.

### Peasant Revolts

Nobles and clergy lived on the food produced by peasant labor, thinking little of adding taxes to the burden of peasant life. While peasants had endured centuries of exploitation, the difficult conditions of the fourteenth and fifteenth centuries spurred a wave of peasant revolts across Europe. Peasants were sometimes joined by those low on the urban social ladder, resulting in a wider revolution of poor against rich. (See "Thinking Like a Historian: Popular Revolts in the Late Middle Ages," page 314.)

The first large-scale rebellion was in the Flanders region of present-day Belgium in the 1320s

(Map 11.3). In order to satisfy peace agreements, Flemish peasants were forced to pay taxes to the French. Monasteries also pressed peasants for additional money above their customary tithes. In retaliation, peasants burned and pillaged castles and aristocratic country houses. A French army crushed the peasant forces, however, and savage repression and the confiscation of peasant property followed in the 1330s.

In the following decades, revolts broke out in many other places. In 1358, when French taxation for the Hundred Years' War fell heavily on the poor, the frustrations of the French peasantry exploded in a massive uprising called the **Jacquerie** (zhah-kuh-REE), after a mythical agricultural laborer, Jacques Bonhomme (Good Fellow). Peasants blamed the nobility for oppressive taxes, for the criminal banditry of the countryside, for losses on the battlefield, and for the general misery. Artisans and small merchants in cities and parish priests joined the peasants. Rebels committed terrible destruction, killing nobles and burning castles, and for several weeks the nobles were on the defensive. Then the upper class united to repress the revolt with merciless ferocity. That forcible suppression of social rebellion, without any effort to alleviate its underlying causes, served to drive protest underground.

■ **Jacquerie** A massive uprising by French peasants in 1358 protesting heavy taxation.

**MAP 11.3 Fourteenth-Century Revolts** In the later Middle Ages peasant and urban uprisings were endemic, as common as factory strikes in the industrial world. The threat of insurrection served to check unlimited exploitation.

In England the Black Death drastically cut the labor supply, and as a result peasants demanded higher wages and fewer manorial obligations. Their lords countered in 1351 with the Statute of Laborers, a law issued by the king that froze wages and bound workers to their manors. This attempt to freeze wages could not be enforced, but a huge gap remained between peasants and their lords, and the peasants sought release for their economic frustrations in revolt. Other factors combined with these economic grievances to fuel the rebellion. The south of England, where the revolt broke out, had been subjected to destructive French raids during the Hundred Years' War. The English government did little to protect the region, and villagers grew increasingly frightened and insecure. Moreover, decades of aristocratic violence against the weak peasantry had bred hostility and bitterness. Social and religious agitation by the popular preacher John Ball fanned the embers of discontent.

The English revolt was ignited by the reimposition of a tax on all adult males to pay for the war with France. Despite widespread opposition to the tax, the royal council ordered sheriffs to collect unpaid taxes by force in 1381. This led to a major uprising later termed the **English Peasants' Revolt**, which involved thousands of people, including artisans and the poor in cities as well as rural residents. Many nobles, including the archbishop of Canterbury, who had ordered the collection of the tax, were murdered. The center of the revolt lay in the highly populated and economically advanced south and east, but sections of the north also witnessed rebellions (see Map 11.3).

The boy-king Richard II (r. 1377–1399) met the leaders of the revolt, agreed to charters ensuring peasants' freedom, tricked them with false promises, and then crushed the uprising with terrible ferocity. In the aftermath of the revolt, the nobility tried to restore the labor obligations of serfdom, but they were not successful, and the conversion to money rents continued.

■ **English Peasants' Revolt** Revolt by English peasants in 1381 in response to changing economic conditions.

## Popular Revolts in the Late Middle Ages

Famine, plague, and war led to population decline and economic problems in the fourteenth century, which fueled both resentment and fear.

How did such crises, and the response of those in power to these crises, spur calls for reform and revolts among peasants and workers?

**1** **The Statute of Laborers, 1351.** After the English population declined by one-third because of the Black Death, rural and urban workers demanded higher wages and better working conditions, which led the English Parliament and King Edward III to pass the following law.

Because a great part of the people and especially of the workmen and servants has now died in that pestilence, some, seeing the straights of the masters and the scarcity of servants, are not willing to serve unless they receive excessive wages, and others, rather than through labour to gain their living, prefer to beg in idleness: We, considering the grave inconveniences which might come from the lack especially of ploughmen and such labourers . . . have seen fit to ordain: that every man and woman of our kingdom of England, of whatever condition, whether bond or free, who is able bodied and below the age of sixty years, . . . shall be bound to serve him who has seen fit so to seek after him; and he shall take only the wages . . . or salary which, in the places where he sought to serve, were accustomed to be paid in the twentieth year of our reign of England [1346], . . . and if any man or woman, being thus sought after in service, will not do this, the fact being proven by two faithful men before the sheriffs or the bailiffs of our lord the king, or the constables of the town where this happens . . . shall be taken and sent to the next jail, and there he shall remain in strict custody until he shall find surety for serving in the aforesaid form. . . .

Likewise saddlers, skinners, white-tawers, cordwainers, tailors, smiths, carpenters, masons, tilers, shipwrights, carters and all other artisans and labourers shall not take for their labour and handiwork more than what, in the places where they happen to labour, was customarily paid to such persons in [1346]; and if any man take more, he shall be committed to the nearest jail in the manner aforesaid.

**2** **John Ball preaches to the peasants.** Beginning in the 1360s, the priest John Ball traveled around England delivering radical sermons, such as this one, reported in a fourteenth-century chronicle by Jean Froissart. In the aftermath of the 1381 English Peasants' Revolt, Ball was arrested, imprisoned, and executed; his body was drawn and quartered; and his head was stuck on a pike on London Bridge.

John Ball was accustomed to assemble a crowd around him in the marketplace and preach to them. On such occasions he would say: "My good friends, matters cannot go on well in England until all things shall be in common; where there shall be neither vassals nor lords; when the lords shall be no more masters than ourselves. How ill they behave to us! For what reasons do they thus hold us in bondage? Are we not all descended from the same parents, Adam and Eve? When Adam delved and Eve span, who was then the gentleman? What reason can they give, why they should be more masters than ourselves? They are clothed in velvet and rich stuffs, ornamented with ermine and other furs, while we are forced to wear poor clothing. They have wines, spices, and fine bread, while we have only rye and the refuse of straw, and when we drink it must be water. They have handsome seats and manors, while we must brave the wind and rain in our labors in the field; and it is by our labor they have wherewith to support their pomp. We are called slaves, and if we do not perform our service we are beaten, and we have no sovereign to whom we can complain or who would be willing to hear us. Let us go to the King and remonstrate with him; he is young, and from him we may obtain a favorable answer, and if not we must ourselves seek to amend our condition."

### ANALYZING THE EVIDENCE

1. In Source 1, what does the law require laborers to do, and what penalties does it provide if they do not do so? How did laws such as this contribute to growing social tensions?
2. What do John Ball in Source 2 and the peasants mentioned in Source 3 view as wrong in English society, and what do they want done about it?
3. In Sources 4 and 5, what do the wool workers in Florence want? How do the authors of these sources differ in their opinions about these demands?
4. What was the response of those in power to the demands of peasants and workers?

**3** **English peasants meet with the king.** In 1381 peasants angered by taxes imposed to pay for the war with France seized the city of London and forced the young king Richard II to meet with them, as reported in this contemporary chronicle by Henry Knighton, an Augustinian priest.

The King advanced to the assigned place, while many of the wicked mob kept following him. . . . They complained that they had been seriously oppressed by many hardships and that their condition of servitude was unbearable, and that they neither could nor would endure it longer. The King, for the sake of peace, and on account of the violence of the times, yielding to their petition, granted to them a charter with the great seal, to the effect that all men in the kingdom of England should be free and of free condition, and should remain both for themselves and their heirs free from all kinds of servitude and villeinage forever. . . . [But] the charter was rejected and decided to be null and void by the King and the great men of the kingdom in the Parliament held at Westminster [later] in the same year.

**4** **Judicial inquiry of a labor organizer in Florence, 1345.** The rulers of Florence investigated the actions of a man seeking to organize a guild of carders and combers, the lowest-paid workers in the cloth industry; he was arrested and executed by hanging.

This is the inquisition which the lord captain and his judge . . . have conducted . . . against Ciuto Brandini, of the parish of S. Piero Maggiore, a man of low condition and evil reputation. . . . Together with many others who were seduced by him, he planned to organize an association . . . of carders, combers, and other laborers in the woolen cloth industry, in the largest number possible. In order that they might have the means to congregate and to elect consuls and leaders of their association . . . he organized meetings on several occasions and on various days of many persons of lowly condition. . . . Moving from bad to worse, he sought . . . to accomplish similar and even worse things, seeking always [to incite] noxious disorders, to the harm, opprobrium, danger, and destruction of the citizens of Florence, their persons and property, and of the stable regime of that city.

**5** **Chronicle of the Ciompi Revolt, 1378.** An anonymous chronicle describes the 1378 revolt of the ciompi, the lowest-paid workers in the wool trade in Florence, against the Lana guild of wool merchants, which controlled all aspects of cloth production and dominated the city government. The changes described lasted four years, until an army organized by the wool merchants overthrew the new government.

When the *popolo* [common people, that is, the *ciompi*] and the guildsmen had seized the palace, they sent a message . . . that they wished to make certain demands by means of petitions, which were just and reasonable. . . . They said that, for the peace and repose of the city, they wanted certain things which they had decided among themselves. . . . The first chapter [of the petition] stated that the Lana guild would no longer have a [police] official of the guild. Another was that the combers, carders, trimmers, washers, and other cloth workers would have their own [guild]. . . . Moreover, all penalties involving a loss of a limb would be cancelled, and those who were condemned would pay a money fine instead. . . . Furthermore, for two years none of the poor people could be prosecuted for debts of 50 florins or less.

The *popolo* entered the palace and the podestà [the highest official in Florence] departed, without any harm being done to him. . . . Then the banners of the other guilds were unfurled from the windows . . . and also the standard of justice [the city's official banner]. Those inside the palace threw out and burned . . . every document that they found . . . and they entered all the rooms and they found many ropes which [the authorities] had bought to hang the poor people. . . . Several young men climbed the bell tower and rang the bells to signal the victory which they had won in seizing the palace, in God's honor. . . . Then [the *popolo*] decided to call priors who would be good comrades . . . and these priors called together the colleges and consuls of the guilds. . . . And this was done to give a part to more people, and so that each would be content, and each would have a share of the offices, and so that all of the citizens would be united. Thus poor men would have their due, for they have always borne the expenses [of government] and only the rich have profited. . . . And they deliberated to expand the lower guilds, and where there had been fourteen, there would now be seventeen, and thus they would be stronger, and this was done. . . . So all together, the lower guilds increased by some thirteen thousand men.

## PUTTING IT ALL TOGETHER

Using the sources above, along with what you have learned in class and in this chapter and Chapters 9 and 10, write a short essay that analyzes popular revolts in the late Middle Ages. How did population decline and economic crisis, and the response of those in power to these challenges, spur calls for reform and revolts among peasants and workers? Why do you think the response to these revolts by those in power was so brutal?

Sources: (1) Ernest F. Henderson, trans. and ed., *Select Historical Documents of the Middle Ages* (London: George Bell and Sons, 1892), pp. 165–167; (2) Sir John Froissart, *The Chronicles of England, France, Spain, etc.* (London: Everyman's Library, 1911), pp. 207–208; (3) Edward P. Cheyney, *Readings in English History Drawn from the Original Sources* (Boston: Ginn, 1935), p. 263; (4, 5) Gene Brucker, ed., *The Society of Renaissance Florence: A Documentary Study* (New York: Harper Torchbooks, 1971), pp. 235, 237–239. Used by permission of the author.

Though selling sex for money was legal in the Middle Ages, the position of women who did so was always marginal. In the late fifteenth century cities began to limit brothel residents' freedom of movement and choice of clothing, requiring them to wear distinctive head coverings or bands on their clothing so that they would not be mistaken for "honorable" women. Cities also began to impose harsher penalties on women who did not live in the designated house or section of town. A few women who sold sex did earn enough to donate money to charity or buy property, but most were very poor.

Along with buying sex, young men also took it by force. Unmarried women often found it difficult to avoid sexual contact. Many worked as domestic servants, where their employers or employers' sons or male relatives could easily coerce them, or they worked in proximity to men. Notions of female honor kept upper-class women secluded in their homes, particularly in southern and eastern Europe, but there was little attempt anywhere to protect female servants or day laborers from the risk of seduction or rape. Rape was a capital crime in many parts of Europe, but the actual sentences handed out were more likely to be fines and brief imprisonment, with the severity of the sentence dependent on the social status of the victim and the perpetrator.

According to laws regarding rape in most parts of Europe, the victim had to prove that she had cried out and had attempted to repel the attacker, and she had to bring the charge within a short period of time after the attack had happened. Women bringing rape charges were often more interested in getting their own honorable reputations back than in punishing the perpetrators. For this reason, they sometimes asked the judge to force their rapists to marry them.

Same-sex relations—what in the late nineteenth century would be termed "homosexuality"—were another feature of medieval urban life (and of village life, though there are very few sources relating to sexual relations of any type in the rural context). Same-sex relations were of relatively little concern to church or state authorities in the early Middle Ages, but this attitude changed beginning in the late twelfth century. By 1300 most areas had defined such actions as "crimes against nature," with authorities seeing them as particularly reprehensible because they thought they did not occur anywhere else in creation. Same-sex relations, usually termed "sodomy," became a capital crime in most of Europe, with adult offenders threatened with execution by fire. The Italian cities of Venice, Florence, and Lucca created special courts to deal with sodomy, which saw thousands of investigations.

How prevalent were same-sex relations? This is difficult to answer, even in modern society, but the city of Florence provides a provocative case study. In 1432 Florence set up a special board of adult men, the Office of the Night, in an attempt to end sodomy. Between 1432 and the abolition of the board in 1502, about seventeen thousand men came to its attention, which, even over a seventy-year period, represents a great number in a population of about forty thousand. The men came from all classes of society, but almost all cases involved an adult man and an adolescent boy; they ranged from sex exchanged for money or gifts to long-term affectionate relationships. Like the ancient Romans, late medieval Florentines believed in a generational model in which different roles were appropriate to different stages in life. In a socially and sexually hierarchical world, the boy in the passive role was identified as subordinate, dependent, and mercenary, words usually applied to women. Florentines, however, never described the dominant partner in feminine terms, for he had not compromised his masculine identity or violated a gender ideal; in fact, the adult partner might be married or have female sexual partners as well as male. Only if an adult male assumed the passive role was his masculinity jeopardized.

Thus in Florence, and no doubt elsewhere in Europe, sodomy was not a marginal practice, which may account for the fact that, despite harsh laws and special courts, actual executions for sodomy were rare. Same-sex relations often developed within the context of all-male environments, such as the army, the craft shop, and the artistic workshop, and were part of the collective male experience. Homoerotic relationships played important roles in defining stages of life, expressing distinctions of status, and shaping masculine gender identity. Same-sex relations involving women almost never came to the attention of legal authorities, so it is difficult to find out how common they were. However, female-female desire was expressed in songs, plays, and stories, as was male-male desire, offering evidence of the way people understood same-sex relations.

## Fur-Collar Crime

The fourteenth and fifteenth centuries witnessed a great deal of what we might term "fur-collar crime," a medieval version of today's white-collar crime in which those higher up the social scale prey on those who are less well-off. The Hundred Years' War had provided employment and opportunity for thousands of idle and fortune-seeking knights. But during periods of truce and after the war finally ended, many nobles once again had little to do. Inflation hurt them. Although many were living on fixed incomes, their chivalric code demanded lavish generosity and an aristocratic lifestyle. Many nobles thus turned to crime as a way of raising money.

This "fur-collar crime" involved both violence and fraud. Groups of noble bandits roamed the English countryside, stealing from both rich and poor. Operating like modern urban racketeers, knightly gangs demanded that peasants pay protection money or else have their hovels burned and their fields destroyed. They seized wealthy travelers and held them for ransom. Corrupt landowners, including some churchmen, pushed peasants to pay higher taxes and extra fees. When accused of wrongdoing, fur-collar criminals intimidated witnesses, threatened jurors, and used their influence to persuade judges to support them—or used cash to bribe them outright.

Aristocratic violence led to revolt, and it also shaped popular culture. The ballads of Robin Hood, a collection of folk legends from late medieval England, describe the adventures of the outlaw hero and his merry men as they avenge the common people against fur-collar criminals—grasping landlords, wicked sheriffs, and mercenary churchmen. Robin Hood was a popular figure because he symbolized the deep resentment of aristocratic corruption and abuse; he represented the struggle against tyranny and oppression.

## Ethnic Tensions and Restrictions

Large numbers of people in the twelfth and thirteenth centuries migrated from one part of Europe to another in search of land, food, and work: the English into Scotland and Ireland; Germans, French, and Flemings into Poland, Bohemia, and Hungary; Christians into Muslim Spain. Everywhere in Europe, towns recruited people from the countryside as well (see "The Rise of Towns" in Chapter 10). In frontier regions, townspeople were usually long-distance immigrants and, in eastern Europe, Ireland, and Scotland, ethnically different from the surrounding rural population. In eastern Europe, German was the language of the towns; in Irish towns, French, the tongue of Norman or English settlers, predominated. As a result of this colonization and movement to towns, peoples of different ethnic backgrounds lived side by side.

In the early periods of conquest and colonization, and in all regions with extensive migrations, a legal dualism existed: native peoples remained subject to their traditional laws; newcomers brought and were subject to the laws of the countries from which they came. The great exception to this broad pattern of legal pluralism was Ireland. From the start, the English practiced an extreme form of discrimination toward the native Irish. The English distinguished between the free and the unfree, and the entire Irish population, simply by the fact of Irish birth, was unfree. When English legal structures were established

beginning in 1210, the Irish were denied access to the common-law courts. In civil (property) disputes, an English defendant did not need to respond to an Irish plaintiff; no Irish person could make a will. In criminal procedures, the murder of an Irishman was not considered a felony.

The later Middle Ages witnessed a movement away from legal pluralism or dualism and toward legal homogeneity and an emphasis on blood descent. The dominant ethnic group in an area tried to bar others from positions of church leadership and guild membership. Marriage laws were instituted that attempted to maintain ethnic purity by prohibiting intermarriage, and some church leaders actively promoted ethnic discrimination. As Germans moved eastward, for example, German bishops refused to appoint non-Germans to any church office, while Czech bishops closed monasteries to Germans.

The most extensive attempt to prevent intermarriage and protect ethnic purity is embodied in the **Statute of Kilkenny** (1366), a law the ruling English imposed on Ireland, which states that "there were to be no marriages between those of immigrant and native stock; that the English inhabitants of Ireland must employ the English language and bear English names; that they must ride in the English way [that is, with saddles] and have English apparel; that no Irishmen were to be granted ecclesiastical benefices or admitted to monasteries in the English parts of Ireland."[5]

Late medieval chroniclers used words such as *gens* (race or clan) and *natio* (NAH-tee-oh; species, stock, or kind) to refer to different groups. They held that peoples differed according to language, traditions, customs, and laws. None of these were unchangeable, however, and commentators increasingly also described ethnic differences in terms of "blood," which made ethnicity heritable. As national consciousness grew with the Hundred Years' War, for example, people began to speak of "French blood" and "English blood." Religious beliefs came to be conceptualized in terms of blood as well, with people regarded as having Jewish blood, Muslim blood, or Christian blood. The most dramatic expression of this was in Spain, where "purity of blood"—having no Muslim or Jewish ancestors—became an obsession. Blood also came to be used as a way to talk about social differences, especially for nobles. Just as the Irish and English were prohibited from marrying each other, those of "noble blood" were prohibited from marrying commoners in many parts of Europe. As Europeans increasingly came into contact with people from Africa and Asia,

■ **Statute of Kilkenny** Law issued in 1366 that discriminated against the Irish, forbidding marriage between the English and the Irish, requiring the use of the English language, and denying the Irish access to ecclesiastical offices.

and particularly as they developed colonial empires, these notions of blood also became a way of conceptualizing racial categories.

## Literacy and Vernacular Literature

The development of ethnic identities had many negative consequences, but a more positive effect was the increasing use of the vernacular, that is, the local language that people actually spoke, rather than Latin (see "Vernacular Literature and Drama" in Chapter 10). Two masterpieces of European culture, Dante's *Divine Comedy* (1310–1320) and Chaucer's *Canterbury Tales* (1387–1400), illustrate a sophisticated use of the rhythms and rhymes of the vernacular.

The *Divine Comedy* of Dante Alighieri (DAHN-tay ah-luh-GYEHR-ee) (1265–1321) is an epic poem of one hundred cantos (verses), each of whose three equal parts describes one of the realms of the next world: Hell, Purgatory, and Paradise. The Roman poet Virgil, representing reason, leads Dante through Hell, where Dante observes the torments of the damned and denounces the disorders of his own time. Passing up into Purgatory, Virgil shows the poet how souls are purified of their disordered inclinations. From Purgatory, Beatrice, a woman Dante once loved and who serves as the symbol of divine revelation in the poem, leads him to Paradise.

The *Divine Comedy* portrays contemporary and historical figures, comments on secular and ecclesiastical affairs, and draws on the Scholastic philosophy of uniting faith and reason. Within the framework of a symbolic pilgrimage, the *Divine Comedy* embodies the psychological tensions of the age. A profoundly Christian poem, it also contains bitter criticism of some church authorities. In its symmetrical structure and use of figures from the ancient world such as Virgil, the poem perpetuates the classical tradition, but as the first major work of literature in the Italian vernacular, it is distinctly modern.

Geoffrey Chaucer (1342–1400) was an official in the administrations of the English kings Edward III and Richard II and wrote poetry as an avocation. His *Canterbury Tales* is a collection of stories in lengthy rhymed narrative. On a pilgrimage to the shrine of Saint Thomas Becket at Canterbury (see "Local Laws and Royal Courts" in Chapter 9), thirty people of various social backgrounds tell tales. In depicting the interests and behavior of all types of people, Chaucer presents a rich panorama of English social life in the fourteenth century. Like the *Divine Comedy*, the *Canterbury Tales* reflects the cultural tensions of the times. Ostensibly Christian, many

**Chaucer's Wife of Bath**  Chaucer's *Canterbury Tales* were filled with memorable characters, including the often-married Wife of Bath, shown here in a fifteenth-century manuscript. In the prologue that details her life, she denies the value of virginity and criticizes her young and handsome fifth husband for reading a book about "wicked wives." "By God, if women had but written stories . . . ," she comments, "They would have written of men more wickedness / Than all the race of Adam could redress." (Private Collection/Bridgeman Images)

of the pilgrims are also materialistic, sensual, and worldly, suggesting the ambivalence of the broader society's concern for the next world and frank enjoyment of this one.

Beginning in the fourteenth century, a variety of evidence attests to the increasing literacy of laypeople. Wills and inventories reveal that many people, not just nobles, possessed books — mainly devotional texts, but also romances, manuals on manners and etiquette, histories, and sometimes legal and philosophical texts. In England the number of schools in the diocese of York quadrupled between 1350 and 1500. Information from Flemish and German towns is similar: children were sent to schools and were taught the fundamentals of reading, writing, and arithmetic. Laymen increasingly served as managers or stewards of estates and as clerks to guilds and town governments; such positions obviously required the ability to keep administrative and financial records.

The penetration of laymen into the higher positions of governmental administration, long the preserve of clerics, also illustrates rising lay literacy. With growing frequency, the upper classes sent their daughters to convent schools, where, in addition to instruction in singing, religion, needlework, deportment, and household management, they gained the rudiments of reading and sometimes writing.

The spread of literacy represents a response to the needs of an increasingly complex society. Trade, commerce, and expanding government bureaucracies required an increasing number of literate people. Late medieval culture remained a decidedly oral culture. But by the fifteenth century the evolution toward a more literate culture was already perceptible, and craftsmen would develop the new technology of the printing press in response to the increased demand for reading materials.

## NOTES

1. Christos S. Bartsocas, "Two Fourteenth Century Descriptions of the 'Black Death,'" *Journal of the History of Medicine* (October 1966): 395.
2. W. P. Barrett, trans., *The Trial of Jeanne d'Arc* (London: George Routledge, 1931), pp. 165–166.
3. James Harvey Robinson, *Readings in European History*, vol. 1 (Boston: Ginn and Company, 1904), pp. 375–376.
4. Quoted in Katharina M. Wilson, ed., *Medieval Women Writers* (Athens: University of Georgia Press, 1984), p. 245.
5. Quoted in R. Bartlett, *The Making of Europe: Conquest, Colonization and Cultural Change, 950–1350* (Princeton, N.J.: Princeton University Press, 1993), p. 239.

# LOOKING BACK  LOOKING AHEAD

The fourteenth and early fifteenth centuries were certainly times of crisis in western Europe, meriting the label *calamitous* given to them by one popular historian. Famine, disease, and war decimated the European population, and traditional institutions, including secular governments and the church, did little or nothing or, in some cases, made things worse. Trading connections that had been reinvigorated in the High Middle Ages spread the most deadly epidemic ever experienced through western Asia, North Africa, and almost all of Europe. No wonder survivors experienced a sort of shell shock and a fascination with death.

The plague did not destroy the prosperity of the medieval population, however, and it may in fact have indirectly improved the European economy. Wealthy merchants had plenty of money to spend on luxuries and talent. In the century after the plague, Italian artists began to create new styles of painting, writers to pen new literary forms, educators to found new types of schools, and philosophers to develop new ideas about the purpose of human life. These cultural changes eventually spread to the rest of Europe, following many of the same paths that the plague had traveled.

## Make Connections

Think about the larger developments and continuities within and across chapters.

1. The Black Death has often been compared with later pandemics, including the global spread of HIV/AIDS, which began in the 1980s. It is easy to note the differences between these two, but what similarities do you see in the course of the two diseases and their social and cultural consequences?

2. Beginning with Chapter 7, every chapter in this book has discussed the development of the papacy and relations between popes and secular rulers. How were the problems facing the papacy in the fourteenth century the outgrowth of long-term issues? Why had attempts to solve these issues not been successful?

**3.** In Chapter 3 you learned about the Bronze Age Collapse, and in Chapter 7 about the end of the Roman Empire in the West, both of which have also been seen as "calamitous." What similarities and differences do you see in these earlier times of turmoil and those of the late Middle Ages?

# 11  REVIEW & EXPLORE

## Identify Key Terms

Identify and explain the significance of each item below.

Great Famine (p. 295)

Black Death (p. 296)

flagellants (p. 299)

Hundred Years' War (p. 302)

representative assemblies (p. 306)

Babylonian Captivity (p. 308)

Great Schism (p. 308)

conciliarists (p. 309)

confraternities (p. 310)

Jacquerie (p. 312)

English Peasants' Revolt (p. 313)

Statute of Kilkenny (p. 319)

## Review the Main Ideas

Answer the section heading questions from the chapter.

**1.** How did climate change shape the late Middle Ages? (p. 294)

**2.** How did the plague affect European society? (p. 296)

**3.** What were the causes, course, and consequences of the Hundred Years' War? (p. 302)

**4.** Why did the church come under increasing criticism? (p. 308)

**5.** What explains the social unrest of the late Middle Ages? (p. 312)

## Suggested Resources

### BOOKS

- Allmand, Christopher. *The Hundred Years War: England and France at War, ca. 1300–1450*, rev. ed. 2005. Designed for students; examines the war from political, military, social, and economic perspectives, and compares the way England and France reacted to the conflict.
- Cohn, Samuel K. *Lust for Liberty: The Politics of Social Revolt in Medieval Europe*. 2006. Analyzes a number of revolts from across Europe in terms of the aims of their leaders and participants.
- Dunn, Alastair. *The Peasants' Revolt: England's Failed Revolution of 1381*. 2004. Offers new interpretations of the causes and consequences of the English Peasants' Revolt.

- Dyer, Christopher. *Standards of Living in the Later Middle Ages*. 1989. Examines economic realities and social conditions more generally.
- Green, Monica. *Pandemic Disease in the Medieval World: Rethinking the Black Death*. 2015. Collection of essays by historians and scientists that contains the newest research on the plague and its impact.
- Harrington, Joel. *Dangerous Mystic: Meister Eckhart's Path to the God Within*. 2018. An illuminating biography and study of Eckhart's spiritual ideas.
- Jordan, William Chester. *The Great Famine: Northern Europe in the Early Fourteenth Century*. 1996. Discusses catastrophic weather, soil exhaustion, and

other factors that led to the Great Famine and the impact of the famine on community life.

- Karras, Ruth M. *Sexuality in Medieval Europe: Doing unto Others*. 3d ed. 2017. A brief overview designed for undergraduates that incorporates the newest scholarship.

- McGinn, Bernard. *The Varieties of Vernacular Mysticism, 1350–1550*. 2012. A comprehensive survey that demonstrates how this period gave rise to mystical writers who remain influential even today.

- Swanson, R. N. *Religion and Devotion in Europe, c. 1215–c. 1515*. 2004. Explores many aspects of spirituality.

- Tanner, Norman. *The Church in the Later Middle Ages*. 2008. A concise survey of institutional and intellectual issues and developments.

- Tuchman, Barbara. *A Distant Mirror: The Calamitous Fourteenth Century*. 1978. Written for a general audience, it remains a vivid description of this tumultuous time.

## MEDIA

- *Henry V* (Kenneth Branagh, 1989). A widely acclaimed film adaptation of Shakespeare's play about the English king and the Battle of Agincourt, with nearly every well-known English actor.

- *The Hundred Years' War* (BBC, 2012). This three-part series examines the military, political, and cultural aspects of the Hundred Years' War.

- *Michael Wood's Story of England* (BBC, 2010). This series focuses on the village of Kibworth in central England, for which extensive archives survive that give insight into daily life. Episode 3 examines the Great Famine and the Black Death, and episode 4 the Hundred Years' War and economic change.

- *The Name of the Rose* (Jean-Jacques Annaud, 1986). Based on the novel by Umberto Eco about a fourteenth-century monk (played by Sean Connery), this feature film is both a murder mystery and a commentary on issues facing the church.

- *The Plague* (History Channel, 2005). A documentary examining the path and impact of the plague in Europe, with firsthand accounts taken from diaries and journals.

- *The Reckoning* (Paul McGuigan, 2003). The story of a troupe of actors who perform a morality play for the villagers of a fourteenth-century English town, combined with a murder mystery about the death of a child.

# 12

# European Society in the Age of the Renaissance

## 1350–1550

**While the Hundred Years' War gripped northern Europe,** a new culture emerged in southern Europe. The fourteenth century witnessed remarkable changes in Italian intellectual, artistic, and cultural life. Artists and writers thought that they were living in a new golden age, but not until the sixteenth century was this change given the label we use today—the *Renaissance*, derived from the French word for "rebirth." That word was first used by art historian Giorgio Vasari (1511–1574) to describe the art of "rare men of genius" such as his contemporary Michelangelo. Through their works, Vasari judged, the glory of the classical past had been reborn after centuries of darkness. Over time, the word's meaning was broadened to include many aspects of life during that period. The new attitude had a slow diffusion out of Italy, so that the Renaissance "happened" at different times in different parts of Europe. The Renaissance was a movement, not a time period.

Later scholars increasingly saw the cultural and political changes of the Renaissance, along with the religious changes of the Reformation (see Chapter 13) and the European voyages of exploration (see Chapter 14), as ushering in the "modern" world. Some historians view the Renaissance as a bridge between the medieval and modern eras because it corresponded chronologically with the late medieval period and because there were many continuities with that period along with the changes that suggested aspects of the modern world. Others have questioned whether the word *Renaissance* should be used at all to describe an era in which many social groups saw decline rather than improvement. The debates remind us that these labels—*medieval*, *Renaissance*, *modern*—are intellectual constructs devised after the fact, and all contain value judgments. ■

## CHAPTER PREVIEW

- How did political and economic developments in Italy shape the Renaissance?

- What new ideas were associated with the Renaissance?

- How did art reflect new Renaissance ideals?

- What were the key social hierarchies in Renaissance Europe?

- How did nation-states develop in this period?

**Birth in the Renaissance**

In this detail from a fresco of the birth of the Virgin Mary in the Church of San Michele al Pozzo Bianco in Bergamo, Italian painter Lorenzo Lotto depicts a birth scene that would have been common among upper-class urban residents in Renaissance Italy. The birth occurs at home, with lots of women bustling about, including servants, dressed simply, and female relatives, in fancier clothing. A professional midwife sits by the side of the bed, and the mother looks quite content, a sign that this has been a successful and fairly easy childbirth, which was not always the case. (Nativity of the Virgin, lunette from the Lotto Chapel, 1525 [fresco]/ Lorenzo Lotto [ca. 1480–1556]/Church of San Michele al Pozzo Bianco, Bergamo, Italy/photo © Mauro Ranzani/Bridgeman Images)

# How did political and economic developments in Italy shape the Renaissance?

The magnificent art and new ways of thinking in the **Renaissance** rested on economic and political developments in the city-states of northern Italy. Economic growth laid the material basis for the Italian Renaissance, and ambitious merchants gained political power to match their economic power. They then used their money and power to buy luxuries and hire talent in a system of **patronage**, through which cities, groups, and individuals commissioned writers and artists to produce specific works. Political leaders in Italian cities admired the traditions and power of ancient Rome, and this esteem shaped their commissions. Thus economics, politics, and culture were interconnected.

## Trade and Prosperity

Northern Italian cities led the way in the great commercial revival of the eleventh century (see "What led to Europe's economic growth and reurbanization?" in Chapter 10). By the middle of the twelfth century Venice, supported by a huge merchant marine, had grown enormously rich through overseas trade, as had Genoa and Milan, which had their own sizable fleets. These cities made important strides in shipbuilding that allowed their ships to sail all year long at accelerated speeds and to carry more and more merchandise.

Another commercial leader, and the city where the Renaissance began, was Florence, situated on fertile soil along the Arno River. Its favorable location on the main road northward from Rome made Florence a commercial hub, and the city grew wealthy buying and selling all types of goods throughout Europe and the Mediterranean — grain, cloth, wool, weapons, armor, spices, glass, and wine.

Florentine merchants also loaned and invested money, and toward the end of the thirteenth century they acquired control of papal banking. Florentine mercantile families began to dominate European banking on both sides of the Alps, setting up offices in major European and North African cities. The profits from loans, investments, and money exchanges that poured back to Florence were pumped into urban industries such as clothmaking, and by the early fourteenth century the city had about eighty thousand people, about twice the population of London at that time. Profits contributed to the city's economic vitality and allowed banking families to control the city's politics and culture.

By the first quarter of the fourteenth century, the economic foundations of Florence were so strong that even severe crises could not destroy the city. In 1344 King Edward III of England repudiated his huge debts to Florentine bankers, forcing some of them into bankruptcy. Soon after, Florence suffered frightfully from the Black Death, losing at least half its population, and serious labor unrest shook the political establishment (see "How did the plague affect European society?" in Chapter 11). Nevertheless, the basic Florentine economic structure remained stable, and the city grew again.

In Florence, Venice, and other thriving Italian cities, wealth allowed many people greater material pleasures, a more comfortable life, imported luxuries, and leisure time to appreciate and patronize the arts. Merchants and bankers commissioned public and private buildings from architects and hired sculptors and painters to decorate their homes and churches. Despite the massive loss of life in the plague, the rich, social-climbing residents of Venice, Florence, Genoa, and Rome came to see life more as an opportunity to be enjoyed than as a painful pilgrimage to the City of God.

## Communes and Republics of Northern Italy

The northern Italian cities were **communes**, sworn associations of free men led by members of merchant guilds. Like merchants elsewhere, merchants in Italy began in the twelfth century to seek political and economic independence from the nobles who owned the land (see "The Rise of Towns" in Chapter 10). In contrast to nobles elsewhere who maintained their social distinction from merchants, those in Italy frequently moved into the cities, marrying the daughters of rich commercial families and starting their own businesses, often with money they had gained through the dowries provided by their wives. This merger of the northern

- **Renaissance** A French word meaning "rebirth," used to describe the rebirth of the culture of classical antiquity in Italy during the fourteenth to sixteenth centuries.

- **patronage** Financial support of writers and artists by cities, groups, and individuals, often to produce specific works or works in specific styles.

- **communes** Sworn associations of free men in Italian cities led by merchant guilds.

- **popolo** Disenfranchised common people in Italian cities who resented their exclusion from power.

- **signori** Government by one-man rule in Italian cities such as Milan; also refers to these rulers.

- **courts** Magnificent households and palaces where signori and other rulers lived, conducted business, and supported the arts.

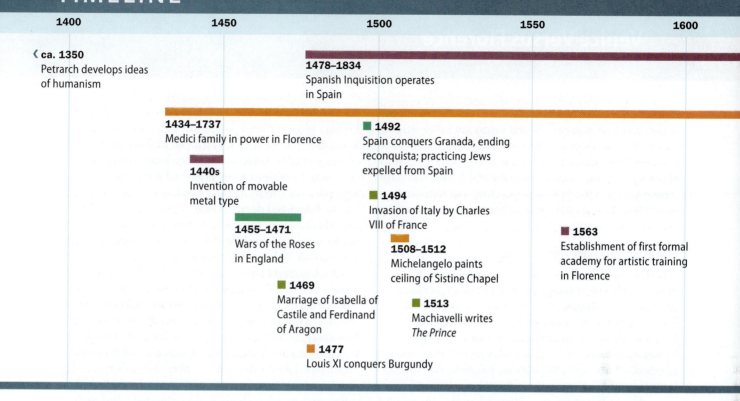

‹ **ca. 1350**
Petrarch develops ideas
of humanism

**1478–1834**
Spanish Inquisition operates
in Spain

**1434–1737**
Medici family in power in Florence

**1440s**
Invention of movable
metal type

**1455–1471**
Wars of the Roses
in England

**1469**
Marriage of Isabella of
Castile and Ferdinand
of Aragon

**1477**
Louis XI conquers Burgundy

**1492**
Spain conquers Granada, ending
reconquista; practicing Jews
expelled from Spain

**1494**
Invasion of Italy by Charles
VIII of France

**1508–1512**
Michelangelo paints
ceiling of Sistine Chapel

**1513**
Machiavelli writes
*The Prince*

**1563**
Establishment of first formal
academy for artistic training
in Florence

Italian nobility and the commercial elite created a powerful oligarchy, a small group that ruled the city and surrounding countryside. Yet because of rivalries among competing powerful families within this oligarchy, Italian communes were often politically unstable.

Unrest from below exacerbated the instability. Merchant elites made citizenship in the communes dependent on a property qualification, years of residence within the city, and social connections. Only a tiny percentage of the male population possessed these qualifications and thus could hold political office. The common people, called the **popolo**, were disenfranchised and heavily taxed, and they bitterly resented their exclusion from power. Throughout most of the thirteenth century, in city after city, the popolo used armed force to take over the city governments. Republican government—in which political power theoretically resides in the people and is exercised by their chosen representatives—was sometimes established in numerous Italian cities. These victories of the popolo proved temporary, however, because they could not establish civil order within their cities. Merchant oligarchies reasserted their power and sometimes brought in powerful military leaders to establish order. These military leaders, called *condottieri* (kahn-duh-TYER-ee; singular *condottiero*), had their own mercenary armies and sometimes took over political power once they had supplanted the existing government.

Many cities in Italy became **signori** (seen-YOHR-ee), in which one man—whether condottiero, merchant, or noble—ruled and handed down the right to rule to his son. Some signori (the word is plural in Italian and is used for both persons and forms of government) kept the institutions of communal government in place, but these had no actual power. As a practical matter, there wasn't much difference between oligarchic regimes and signori.

In the fifteenth and sixteenth centuries the signori in many cities and the most powerful merchant oligarchs in others transformed their households into **courts**. Courtly culture afforded signori and oligarchs the opportunity to display and assert their wealth and power. They built magnificent palaces in the centers of cities and required all political business to be done there. Ceremonies connected with family births, baptisms, marriages, and funerals offered occasions for magnificent pageantry and elaborate ritual. Cities welcomed rulers who were visiting with magnificent entrance parades that often included fireworks, colorful banners, mock naval battles, decorated wagons filled with people in costume, and temporary triumphal arches modeled on those of ancient Rome. Rulers of nation-states later copied and adapted all these aspects of Italian courts.

## City-States and the Balance of Power

Renaissance Italians had a passionate attachment to their individual city-states: they were politically loyal and felt centered on the city. This intensity of local feeling perpetuated the dozens of small states and hindered the development of one unified state. (See "Viewpoints: Venice Versus Florence," page 328.)

Praise of one's own city, a form of written work that developed in ancient Rome, was revived and expanded in Renaissance Italy. In the first selection below, written in 1493, the Venetian patrician Marin Sanudo (1466–1536) praises Venice in a work of praise, which was a common genre at the time, and in the second selection the Florentine merchant and historian Benedetto Dei (DAY-ee) (1418–1492) praises his own city in a letter to an acquaintance from Venice.

### Marin Sanudo on Venice, 1493

The city of Venice is a free city, a common home to all men, and it has never been subjugated by anyone, as have all other cities. . . . Moreover it was founded not by shepherds as Rome was, but by rich and powerful people, such as have ever been since that time, with their faith in Christ, an obstacle to barbarians and attackers. . . . For it takes pride of place before all others, if I may say so, in prudence, fortitude, magnificence, benignity and clemency; everyone throughout the world testifies to this. . . . It is, then, a very big and beautiful city, excelling over all others, with houses and piazze [public squares] founded upon salt water, and it has a Grand Canal. . . . On either side are houses of patricians and others; they are very beautiful, costing from 20,000 ducats downwards. . . . The Venetians, just as they were merchants in the beginning, continue to trade every year; they send galleys to Flanders, the Barbary Coast, Beirut, Alexandria, the Greek Lands, and Auiges-Mortes [a city in southern France]. . . . Here, on the Canal, there are embankments where on one side there are barges for timber, and on the other side wine; they are rented as though they were shops. There is a very large butchery, which is full every day of good meat, and there is another one at St. Mark's. The Fishmarket overlooks the Grand Canal; here are the most beautiful fish, high in price and of good quality. . . . And in the city nothing grows, yet whatever you want can be found in abundance. And this is because of the great turnover in merchandise; everything comes here, especially things to eat, from every city and every part of the world, and money is made very quickly. This is because everyone is well-off for money.

### Benedetto Dei on Florence, 1472

Florence is more beautiful and five hundred forty years older than your Venice. We spring from triply noble blood. We are one-third Roman, one-third Frankish, and one-third Fiesolan [three different groups that were all viewed as honorable]. . . . We have round about us thirty thousand estates, owned by noblemen and merchants, citizens and craftsmen, yielding us yearly bread and meat, wine and oil, vegetables and cheese, hay and wood, to the value of nine hundred thousand ducats in cash, as you Venetians, Genoese, and Rhodians who come to buy them know well enough. We have two trades greater than any four of yours in Venice put together—the trades of wool and silk. . . .

Our beautiful Florence contains within the city in this present year two hundred seventy shops belonging to the wool merchants' guild. . . . It contains also eighty-three rich and splendid warehouses of the silk merchants' guild, and furnishes gold and silver stuffs, velvet, brocade, damask, taffeta, and satin to Rome, Naples, Catalonia, and the whole of Spain, especially Seville, and to Turkey and Barbary. . . . The number of banks amounts to thirty-three; the shops of the cabinetmakers, whose business is carving and inlaid work, to eighty-four; and the workshops of the stonecutters and marble workers in the city and its immediate neighborhood, to fifty-four. There are forty-four goldsmiths' and jewelers' shops, thirty goldbeaters, silver wire-drawers, and a wax-figure maker. . . . Sixty-six is the number of the apothecaries' and grocer shops; seventy that of the butchers, besides eight large shops in which are sold fowls of all kinds, as well as game and also the native wine called Trebbiano, from San Giovanni in the upper Arno Valley; it would awaken the dead in its praise.

### QUESTIONS FOR ANALYSIS

1. What qualities do the two men choose to highlight in praising their hometowns?
2. How do these praises of Florence and Venice represent new values that emerged in the Renaissance?

Sources: David Chambers, Brian Pullan, and Jennifer Fletcher, eds., *Venice: A Documentary History, 1450–1630* (Oxford: Basil Blackwell, 1992), pp. 4–5, 11, 13. Reprinted by permission of The Renaissance Society of America; Gertrude R. B. Richards, ed., *Florentine Merchants in the Age of the Medici* (Cambridge, Mass.: Harvard University Press, 1932). Copyright © 1932 by the President and Fellows of Harvard College. Reprinted by permission.

In the fifteenth century five powers dominated the Italian peninsula: Venice, Milan, Florence, the Papal States, and the kingdom of Naples (Map 12.1). The major Italian powers controlled the smaller city-states, such as Siena, Mantua, Ferrara, and Modena, and competed furiously among themselves for territory. While the states of northern Europe were moving toward centralization and consolidation, the world of Italian politics resembled a jungle where the powerful dominated the weak. Venice, with its enormous trade empire, was a republic in name, but an oligarchy of merchant-aristocrats actually ran the city. Milan was also called a

**MAP 12.1 The Italian City-States, ca. 1494** In the fifteenth century the Italian city-states represented great wealth and cultural sophistication, though the many political divisions throughout the peninsula invited foreign intervention.

republic, but the condottieri-turned-signori of the Sforza (SFORT-sah) family ruled harshly and dominated Milan. Likewise, in Florence the form of government was republican, with authority vested in several councils of state, but the city was effectively ruled by the great Medici (MEH-duh-chee) banking family for three centuries, beginning in 1434. Though not public officials, Cosimo (1389–1464), his son Piero, and his grandson Lorenzo (1449–1492), called Lorenzo the Magnificent by his contemporaries, ruled from behind the scenes from 1434 to 1492. The Medici were then in and out of power for several decades, and in 1569 Florence became no longer a republic but the hereditary Grand Duchy of Tuscany, with the Medici as the Grand Dukes until 1737. The Medici family produced three popes, and most other

Renaissance popes were also members of powerful Italian families, selected for their political skills, not their piety. Along with the Italians was one Spaniard, Pope Alexander VI (pontificate 1492–1503), who was the most ruthless; aided militarily and politically by his illegitimate son Cesare Borgia, he reasserted papal authority in the papal lands. South of the Papal States, the kingdom of Naples was under the control of the king of Aragon.

In one significant respect, however, the Italian city-states anticipated future relations among competing European states after 1500. Whenever one Italian state appeared to gain a predominant position within the peninsula, other states combined against it to establish a balance of power. In the formation of these alliances, Renaissance Italians invented the machinery

**Savonarola Preaching** With vigorous gestures, Savonarola preaches to a crowd of Florentines, the women separated from the men and surrounded by a curtain, reflecting Savonarola's views of the moral changes needed in Florence. This woodcut appeared in a printed version of his sermons published in 1496, when he was at the height of his power. (World History Archive/Alamy)

of modern diplomacy: permanent embassies with resident ambassadors in capitals where political relations and commercial ties needed continual monitoring.

At the end of the fifteenth century Venice, Florence, Milan, and the papacy possessed great wealth and represented high cultural achievement. Wealthy and divided, however, they were also an inviting target for invasion. When Florence and Naples entered into an agreement to acquire Milanese territories, Milan called on France for support, and the French king Charles VIII (r. 1483–1498) invaded Italy in 1494.

Prior to this invasion, the Dominican friar Girolamo Savonarola (1452–1498) had preached to large crowds in Florence a number of fiery sermons predicting that God would punish Italy for its moral vice and corrupt leadership. Florentines interpreted the French invasion as the fulfillment of this prophecy and expelled the Medici dynasty. Savonarola became the political and religious leader of a new Florentine republic and promised Florentines even greater glory in the future if they would reform their ways. He reorganized the government; convinced it to pass laws against same-sex relations, adultery, and drunkenness; and organized groups of young men to patrol the streets looking for immoral

dress and behavior. He held religious processions and what became known as "bonfires of the vanities," huge fires on the main square of Florence in which fancy clothing, cosmetics, pagan books, musical instruments, paintings, and poetry that celebrated human beauty were gathered together and burned.

For a time Savonarola was wildly popular, but eventually people tired of his moral denunciations, and he was excommunicated by the pope, tortured, and burned at the very spot where he had overseen the bonfires. The Medici returned as the rulers of Florence.

The French invasion inaugurated a new period in Italian and European power politics. Italy became the focus of international ambitions and the battleground of foreign armies, particularly those of the Holy Roman Empire and France in a series of conflicts called the Habsburg-Valois wars (named for the German and French dynasties). The Italian cities suffered severely from continual warfare, especially in the frightful sack of Rome in 1527 by imperial forces under the emperor Charles V. Thus the failure of the city-states to consolidate, or at least to establish a common foreign policy, led to centuries of subjection by outside invaders. Italy was not to achieve unification until 1870.

## What new ideas were associated with the Renaissance?

The Renaissance was characterized by a self-conscious conviction among educated Italians that they were living in a new era. Somewhat ironically, this idea rested on a deep interest in ancient Latin and Greek literature and philosophy. Through reflecting on the classics, Renaissance thinkers developed new notions of human nature, new plans for education, and new concepts of political rule. The advent of the printing press with movable type would greatly accelerate the spread of these ideas throughout Europe.

### Humanism

Giorgio Vasari was the first to use the word *Renaissance* in print, but he was not the first to feel that something was being reborn. Two centuries earlier the Florentine poet and scholar Francesco Petrarch (1304–1374) spent long hours searching for classical Latin manuscripts in dusty monastery libraries and wandering around the many ruins of the Roman Empire remaining in Italy. He became obsessed with the classical past and felt that the writers and artists of ancient Rome had reached a level of perfection in their work that had not since been duplicated. Petrarch believed that the recovery of classical texts and their use as models would bring about a new golden age of intellectual achievement, an idea that many others came to share.

Petrarch clearly thought he was witnessing the dawning of a new era in which writers and artists would recapture the glory of the Roman Republic. Around 1350 he proposed a new kind of education to help them do this, in which young men would study the works of ancient Roman authors, using them as models of how to write clearly, argue effectively, and speak persuasively. The study of Latin classics became known as the *studia humanitates* (STOO-dee-uh oo-mahn-ee-TAH-tayz), usually translated as "liberal studies" or the "liberal arts." People who advocated it were known as *humanists* and their program as **humanism**. Humanism was the main intellectual component of the Renaissance. Like all programs of study, it contained an implicit philosophy: that human nature and human achievements, evident in the classics, were worthy of contemplation.

Many humanists saw Julius Caesar's transformation of Rome from a republic into an empire as a betrayal of the great society, marking the beginning of a long period of decay that the barbarian migrations then accelerated. In his history of Florence written in 1436, the humanist historian and Florentine city official Leonardo Bruni (1374–1444) closely linked the decline of the Latin language to the decline of the Roman Republic: "After the liberty of the Roman people had been lost through the rule of the emperors . . . the flourishing condition of studies and of letters perished, together with the welfare of the city of Rome."[1] In this same book, Bruni was also very clear that by the time of his writing, the period of decay had ended and a new era had begun. He was the first to divide history into three eras—ancient, medieval, and modern—though it was another humanist historian who actually invented the term *Middle Ages*.

In the fifteenth century Florentine humanists became increasingly interested in Greek philosophy as well as Roman literature, especially in the ideas of Plato. Under the patronage of the Medici, the scholar Marsilio Ficino (1433–1499) began to lecture to an informal group of Florence's cultural elite; his lectures became known as the Platonic Academy, but they were not really a school. Ficino regarded Plato as a divinely inspired precursor to Christ. He translated Plato's dialogues into Latin and wrote commentaries attempting to synthesize Christian and Platonic teachings. Plato's emphasis on the spiritual and eternal over the material and transient fit well with Christian teachings about the immortality of the soul. The Platonic idea that the highest form of love was spiritual desire for pure, perfect beauty uncorrupted by bodily desires could easily be interpreted as the Christian desire for the perfection of God.

For Ficino and his most gifted student, Giovanni Pico della Mirandola (1463–1494), both Christian and classical texts taught that the universe was a hierarchy of beings from God down through spiritual beings to material beings, with humanity, right in the middle, as the crucial link that possessed both material and spiritual natures. Pico developed his ideas in a series of nine hundred theses, or points of argumentation, and offered to defend them against anyone who wanted to come to Rome. The pope declared some of the ideas heretical and arrested Pico, though he was freed through the influence of Lorenzo de' Medici. At Lorenzo's death, Pico became a follower of Savonarola, renounced his former ideas and writings, and died of arsenic poisoning, perhaps at the hands of the recently ousted Medici family.

Along with Greek and Roman writings, Renaissance thinkers were also interested in individual excellence. Families, religious brotherhoods, neighborhoods, workers' organizations, and other groups continued to have meaning in people's lives, but Renaissance thinkers increasingly viewed these groups as springboards to far greater individual achievement. They were especially interested in individuals who had risen above their background to become brilliant, powerful, or unique. (See "Individuals in Society: Leonardo da Vinci," page 332.) Such individuals had the admirable quality of **virtù** (vihr-TOO), which is not virtue in the sense of moral goodness, but instead the ability to shape the world around according to one's will. Bruni and other historians included biographies of individuals with virtù in their histories of cities and nations, describing ways in which these people had affected the course of history. Through the quality of their works and their influence on others, artists could also exhibit virtù, an idea that Vasari captures in the title of his major work, *The Lives of the Most Excellent Painters, Sculptors, and Architects*. His subjects had achieved not simply excellence but the pinnacle of excellence.

The last artist included in Vasari's book is Vasari himself, for Renaissance thinkers did not exclude themselves when they searched for models of talent and achievement. Vasari begins his discussion of his own works modestly, saying that these might "not lay claim to excellence and perfection" when compared with those of other artists, but he then goes on for more than thirty pages, clearly feeling he has achieved some level of excellence.

Leon Battista Alberti (1404–1472) had similar views of his own achievements. He had much to be proud of: he wrote novels, plays, legal treatises, a study of the family, and the first scientific analysis of perspective; he designed churches, palaces, and fortifications

---

■ **humanism** A program of study designed by Italians that emphasized the critical study of Latin and Greek literature with the goal of understanding human nature.

■ **virtù** The quality of being able to shape the world according to one's own will.

# INDIVIDUALS IN SOCIETY

## Leonardo da Vinci

What makes a genius? A deep curiosity about an extensive variety of subjects? A divine spark that emerges in talents that far exceed the norm? Or is it just "one percent inspiration and ninety-nine percent perspiration," as Thomas Edison said? However it is defined, Leonardo da Vinci counts as a genius. In fact, Leonardo was one of the individuals whom the Renaissance label *genius* was designed to describe: a special kind of human being with exceptional creative powers. Leonardo (who, despite the title of a popular novel and film, is always called by his first name) was born in Vinci, near Florence, the illegitimate son of Caterina, a local peasant girl, and Ser Piero da Vinci, a notary public. When Ser Piero's marriage to Donna Albrussia produced no children, he and his wife took in Leonardo, whose mother had married another man. Ser Piero secured Leonardo an apprenticeship with the painter and sculptor Andrea del Verrocchio in Florence. In 1472, when Leonardo was just twenty years old, he was already listed as a master in Florence's "Company of Artists."

Leonardo's most famous portrait, *Mona Lisa*, shows a woman with an enigmatic smile that Giorgio Vasari described as "so pleasing that it seemed divine rather than human." The portrait, probably of the young wife of a rich Florentine merchant (her exact identity is hotly debated), may be the best-known painting in the history of art. One of its competitors for that designation would be another work of Leonardo, *The Last Supper*, which has been called "the most revered painting in the world."

Leonardo's reputation as a genius does not rest on his paintings, however, which are actually few in number, but rather on the breadth of his abilities and interests. He is considered by many the first "Renaissance man," a phrase still used for a multi-talented individual. Hoping to reproduce what the eye can see, he drew everything he saw around him, including executed criminals hanging on gallows as well as the beauties of nature. Trying to understand how the human body worked, Leonardo studied live and dead bodies, doing autopsies and dissections to investigate muscles and circulation. He carefully analyzed the effects of light, and he experimented with perspective.

Leonardo used his drawings not only as the basis for his paintings but also as a tool of scientific investigation. He drew

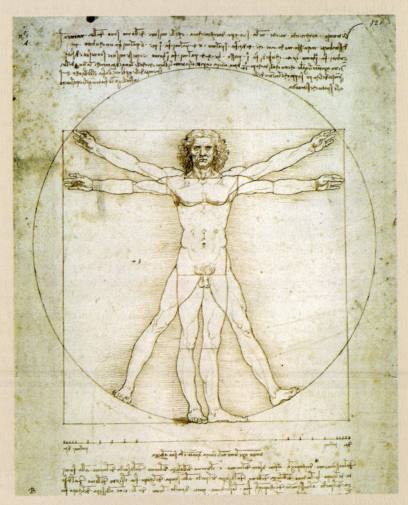

*Vitruvian Man,* a drawing by Leonardo showing correlations between the ideal human proportions and the geometric shapes of the circle and square, is based on the ideas of the ancient Roman architect Vitruvius, whose works Leonardo read. (Galleria dell'Accademia, Venice, Italy/ Bridgeman Images)

plans for hundreds of inventions, many of which would become reality centuries later, such as the helicopter, tank, machine gun, and parachute. He was hired by one of the powerful new rulers in Italy, Duke Ludovico Sforza of Milan, to design weapons, fortresses, and water systems, as well as to produce works of art. When Sforza was overthrown, Leonardo left Milan and spent the last years of his life painting, drawing, and designing for the pope and the French king.

Leonardo experimented with new materials for painting and sculpture, not all of which worked. The experimental method he used to paint *The Last Supper* caused the picture to deteriorate rapidly, and it began to flake off the wall as soon as it was finished. Leonardo regarded it as never quite completed, for he could not find a model for the face of Christ who would evoke the spiritual depth he felt the figure deserved. His gigantic equestrian statue in honor of Ludovico's father, Duke Francesco Sforza, was never made, and the clay model collapsed. He planned to write books on many subjects but never finished any of them, leaving only notebooks. Leonardo once said that "a painter is not admirable unless he is universal." The patrons who supported him — and he was supported very well — perhaps wished that his inspirations would have been a bit less universal in scope, or at least accompanied by more perspiration.

## QUESTIONS FOR ANALYSIS

1. In what ways do the notions of a "genius" and of a "Renaissance man" both support and contradict each other? Which better fits Leonardo?
2. Has the idea of artistic genius changed since the Renaissance? How?

Sources: Giorgio Vasari, *Lives of the Artists*, vol. 1, trans. G. Bull (London: Penguin Books, 1965); S. B. Nuland, *Leonardo da Vinci* (New York: Lipper/Viking, 2000).

effective against cannon; he invented codes for sending messages secretly and a machine that could cipher and decipher them. In his autobiography — written late in his life, and in the third person, so that he calls himself "he" instead of "I" — Alberti described his personal qualities and accomplishments:

> Assiduous in the science and skill of dealing with arms and horses and musical instruments, as well as in the pursuit of letters and the fine arts, he was devoted to the knowledge of the most strange and difficult things. . . . He played ball, hurled the javelin, ran, leaped, wrestled. . . . He learned music without teachers . . . and then turned to physics and the mathematical arts. . . . Ambition was alien to him. . . . When his favorite dog died he wrote a funeral oration for him.[2]

His achievements in many fields did make Alberti a "Renaissance man," as we use the term, though it may be hard to believe his assertion that "ambition was alien to him."

Biographies and autobiographies presented individuals that humanist authors thought were worthy models, but sometimes people needed more direct instruction. The ancient Greek philosopher Plato, whom humanists greatly admired, taught that the best way to learn something was to think about its perfect, ideal form. If you wanted to learn about justice, for example, you should imagine what ideal justice would be, rather than look at actual examples of justice in the world around you, for these would never be perfect. Following Plato's ideas, Renaissance authors speculated about perfect examples of many things. Alberti wrote about the ideal country house, which was to be useful, convenient, and elegant. The English humanist Thomas More described a perfect society, which he called Utopia (see "Evaluating Written Evidence: Thomas More, *Utopia*," page 339).

## Education

Humanists thought that their recommended course of study in the classics would provide essential skills for future politicians, diplomats, lawyers, military leaders, and businessmen, as well as writers and artists. It would provide a much broader and more practical type of training than that offered at universities, which at the time focused on theology and philosophy or on theoretical training for lawyers and physicians. Humanists poured out treatises, often in the form of letters, on the structure and goals of education and the training of rulers and leaders. (See "Thinking Like a Historian: Humanist Learning," page 334.)

Humanists put their ideas into practice. Beginning in the early fifteenth century, they opened schools and academies in Italian cities and courts in which

## Humanist Learning

Renaissance humanists wrote often and forcefully about education, and learning was also a subject of artistic works shaped by humanist ideas. What did humanists see as the best course of study and the purpose of education, and how were these different for men and women?

**1** **Peter Paul Vergerius, letter to Ubertinus of Padua, 1392.** The Venetian scholar and church official Vergerius (1370–1445) advises the son of the ruler of Padua about the proper education for men.

〜 We call those studies liberal which are worthy of a free man; those studies by which we attain and practise virtue and wisdom; that education which calls forth, trains and develops those highest gifts of body and of mind which ennoble men, and which are rightly judged to rank next in dignity to virtue only. . . . Amongst these I accord the first place to History, on grounds both of its attractiveness and of its utility, qualities which appeal equally to the scholar and to the statesman. Next in importance ranks Moral Philosophy, which indeed is, in a peculiar sense, a "Liberal Art," in that its purpose is to teach men the secret of true freedom. History, then, gives us the concrete examples of the precepts inculcated by philosophy. The one shews what men should do, the other what men have said and done in the past, and what practical lessons we may draw therefrom for the present day. I would indicate as the third main branch of study, Eloquence, which indeed holds a place of distinction amongst the refined Arts. By philosophy we learn the essential truth of things, which by eloquence we so exhibit in orderly adornment as to bring conviction to differing minds. And history provides the light of experience—a cumulative wisdom fit to supplement the force of reason and the persuasion of eloquence. For we allow that soundness of judgment, wisdom of speech, integrity of conduct are the marks of a truly liberal temper.

**2** **Leonardo Bruni, letter to Lady Baptista Malatesta, ca. 1405.** The Florentine humanist and city official Leonardo Bruni advises the daughter of the duke of Urbino about the proper education for women.

〜 There are certain subjects in which, whilst a modest proficiency is on all accounts to be desired, a minute knowledge and excessive devotion seem to be a vain display. For instance, subtleties of Arithmetic and Geometry are not worthy to absorb a cultivated mind, and the same must be said of Astrology. You will be surprised to find me suggesting (though with much more hesitation) that the great and complex art of Rhetoric should be placed in the same category. My chief reason is the obvious one, that I have in view the cultivation most fitting to a woman. To her neither the intricacies of debate nor the oratorical artifices of action and delivery are of the least practical use, if indeed they are not positively unbecoming. Rhetoric in all its forms—public discussion, forensic argument, logical fence, and the like—lies absolutely outside the province of woman. What Disciplines then are properly open to her? In the first place she has before her, as a subject peculiarly her own, the whole field of religion and morals. The literature of the Church will thus claim her earnest study. . . . Moreover, the cultivated Christian lady has no need in the study of this weighty subject to confine herself to ecclesiastical writers. Morals, indeed, have been treated of by the noblest intellects of Greece and Rome. [Then] I place History: a subject which must not on any account be neglected by one who aspires to true cultivation. For it is our duty to understand the origins of our own history and its development; and the achievements of Peoples and of Kings.

### ANALYZING THE EVIDENCE

1. According to these sources, what should people learn? Why should they learn?
2. Renaissance humanism has sometimes been viewed as opposed to religion, especially to the teachings of the Catholic Church at the time. Do these sources support this idea?
3. How are the programs of study recommended for men and women similar? How and why are they different?
4. How does the gender of the author shape his or her ideas about the human capacity for reason and learning?

**3** **Luca della Robbia, *Grammar*, 1437–1439.** In this hexagonal panel made for the bell tower of the cathedral of Florence, Luca della Robbia conveys ideas about the course and goals of learning with the open classical door in the background.

(Museo Opera del Duomo, Florence, Italy/De Agostini/Getty Images)

**4** **Giovanni Pico della Mirandola, "Oration on the Dignity of Man," 1486.** Pico, the brilliant son of an Italian count and protégé of Lorenzo de' Medici, wrote an impassioned summary of human capacities for learning that ends with this selection.

〜 Oh unsurpassed generosity of God the Father, Oh wondrous and unsurpassable felicity of man, to whom it is granted to have what he chooses, to be what he wills to be! The brutes, from the moment of their birth, bring with them, as Lucilius [a classical Roman author] says, "from their mother's womb" all that they will ever possess. The highest spiritual beings were, from the very moment of creation, or soon thereafter, fixed in the mode of being which would be theirs through measureless eternities. But upon man, at the moment of his creation, God bestowed seeds pregnant with all possibilities, the germs of every form of life. Whichever of these a man shall cultivate, the same will mature and bear fruit in him. If vegetative, he will become a plant; if sensual, he will become brutish; if rational, he will reveal himself a heavenly being; if intellectual, he will be an angel and the son of God. And if, dissatisfied with the lot of all creatures, he should recollect himself into the center of his own unity, he will there become one spirit with God, in the solitary darkness of the Father, Who is set above all things, himself transcend all creatures. Who then will not look with awe upon this our chameleon, or who, at least, will look with greater admiration on any other being?

**5** **Cassandra Fedele, "Oration on Learning," 1487.** The Venetian Cassandra Fedele (1465–1558), the best-known female scholar of her time, gave an oration in Latin at the University of Padua in honor of her (male) cousin's graduation.

〜 I shall speak very briefly on the study of the liberal arts, which for humans is useful and honorable, pleasurable and enlightening since everyone, not only philosophers but also the most ignorant man, knows and admits that it is by reason that man is separated from beasts. For what is it that so greatly helps both the learned and the ignorant? What so enlarges and enlightens men's minds the way that an education in and knowledge of literature and the liberal arts do? . . . But erudite men who are filled with the knowledge of divine and human things turn all their thoughts and considerations toward reason as though toward a target, and free their minds from all pain, though plagued by many anxieties. These men are scarcely subjected to fortune's innumerable arrows and they prepare themselves to live well and in happiness. They follow reason as their leader in all things; nor do they consider themselves only, but they are also accustomed to assisting others with their energy and advice in matters public and private. . . . The study of literature refines men's minds, forms and makes bright the power of reason, and washes away all stains from the mind, or at any rate, greatly cleanses it. . . . States, however, and their princes who foster and cultivate these studies become more humane, more gracious, and more noble. . . . But enough on the utility of literature since it produces not only an outcome that is rich, precious, and sublime, but also provides one with advantages that are extremely pleasurable, fruitful, and lasting—benefits that I myself have enjoyed. And when I meditate on the idea of marching forth in life with the lowly and execrable weapons of the little woman—the needle and the distaff [the rod onto which yarn is wound after spinning]—even if the study of literature offers women no rewards or honors, I believe women must nonetheless pursue and embrace such studies alone for the pleasure and enjoyment they contain.

## PUTTING IT ALL TOGETHER

Using the sources above, along with what you have learned in class and in this chapter, write a short essay that analyzes humanist learning. What were the goals and purposes of humanist education, and how were these different for men and women? How did these differences reflect Renaissance society more generally?

Sources: (1, 2) W. H. Woodward, ed. and trans., *Vittorino da Feltre and Other Humanist Educators* (London: Cambridge University Press, 1897), pp. 102, 106–107, 126–127; (4) ebooks, University of Adelaide, https://ebooks.adelaide.edu.au/p/pico_della_mirandola/giovanni/dignity/; (5) Cassandra Fedele, *Letters and Orations*, ed. and trans. Diana Robin. Copyright © 2000 by The University of Chicago Press. All rights reserved. Used with permission of the publisher.

pupils began with Latin grammar and rhetoric, went on to study Roman history and political philosophy, and then learned Greek in order to study Greek literature and philosophy. Gradually, humanist education became the basis for intermediate and advanced education for well-to-do urban boys and men. Humanist schools were established in Florence, Venice, and other Italian cities, and by the early sixteenth century across the Alps in Germany, France, and England.

Humanists disagreed about education for women. Many saw the value of exposing women to classical models of moral behavior and reasoning, but they also wondered whether a program of study that emphasized eloquence and action was proper for women, whose sphere was generally understood to be private and domestic. In his book on the family, Alberti stressed that a wife's role should be restricted to the orderliness of the household, food preparation and the serving of meals, the education of children, and the supervision of servants. (Alberti never married, so he never put his ideas into practice in his own household.) Women themselves were bolder in their claims about the value of the new learning. Although humanist academies were not open to women, a few women did become educated in the classics, and they wrote and published poetry, fiction, and essays in Latin and vernacular languages.

No book on education had broader influence than Baldassare Castiglione's *The Courtier* (1528). This treatise sought to train, discipline, and fashion the young man into the courtly ideal, the gentleman. According to Castiglione (kahs-teel-YOH-nay), himself a courtier serving several different rulers, the educated man should have a broad background in many academic subjects and should train his spiritual and physical faculties as well as his intellect. Castiglione envisioned a man who could compose a sonnet, wrestle, sing a song while accompanying himself on an instrument, ride expertly, solve difficult mathematical problems, and, above all, speak and write eloquently. Castiglione also discussed the perfect court lady, who, like the courtier, was to be well educated and able to paint, dance, and play a musical instrument. Physical beauty, delicacy, affability, and modesty were also important qualities for court ladies.

In the sixteenth and seventeenth centuries *The Courtier* was translated into most European languages and widely read. It influenced the social mores and patterns of conduct of elite groups in Renaissance and early modern Europe and became a how-to manual for people seeking to improve themselves and rise in the social hierarchy. Echoes of its ideal for women have perhaps had an even longer life.

## Political Thought

Ideal courtiers should preferably serve an ideal ruler, and biographies written by humanists often described rulers who were just, wise, pious, dignified, learned, brave, kind, and distinguished. In return for such flattering portraits of living rulers or their ancestors, authors sometimes received positions at court, or at least substantial payments. Particularly in Italian cities, however, which often were divided by political factions, taken over by homegrown or regional despots, and attacked by foreign armies, such ideal rulers were hard to find. Humanists thus looked to the classical past for their models. Some, such as Bruni, argued that republicanism was the best form of government. Others used the model of Plato's philosopher-king in the *Republic* to argue that rule by an enlightened individual might be best. Both sides agreed that educated men should be active in the political affairs of their city, a position historians have since termed "civic humanism."

***Portrait of Baldassare Castiglione*** In this portrait by Raphael, the most sought-after portrait painter of the Renaissance, Castiglione is shown dressed exactly as he advised courtiers to dress, in elegant but subdued clothing that would enhance the splendor of the court but never outshine the ruler. (By Raphael [Raffaello Sanzio of Urbino] [1483–1520]/Art Media/Print Collector/Getty Images)

The most famous (or infamous) civic humanist, and ultimately the best-known political theorist of this era, was Niccolò Machiavelli (1469–1527). After the ouster of the Medici with the French invasion of 1494, Machiavelli was secretary to one of the governing bodies in the city of Florence; he was responsible for diplomatic missions and organizing a citizen army. Almost two decades later, power struggles in Florence between rival factions brought the Medici family back to power, and Machiavelli was arrested, tortured, and imprisoned on suspicion of plotting against them. He was released but had no government position, and he spent the rest of his life writing — political theory, poetry, prose works, plays, and a multivolume history of Florence — and making fruitless attempts to regain employment.

The first work Machiavelli finished — though not the first to be published — is his most famous: *The Prince* (1513), which uses the examples of classical and contemporary rulers to argue that the function of a ruler (or any government) is to preserve order and security. Weakness only leads to disorder, which might end in civil war or conquest by an outsider, situations clearly detrimental to any people's well-being. To preserve the state, a ruler should use whatever means he needs — brutality, lying, manipulation — but should not do anything that would make the populace turn against him; stealing or cruel actions done for a ruler's own pleasure would lead to resentment and destroy the popular support needed for a strong, stable realm. "It is much safer for the prince to be feared than loved," Machiavelli advised, "but he ought to avoid making himself hated."[3]

Like the good humanist he was, Machiavelli knew that effective rulers exhibited the quality of virtù. He presented examples from the classical past of just the type of ruler he was describing, but also wrote about contemporary leaders. Cesare Borgia (1475?–1507), Machiavelli's primary example, was the son of Rodrigo Borgia, a Spanish nobleman who later became Pope Alexander VI. Cesare Borgia combined his father's power and his own ruthlessness to build up a state of his own in central Italy. He made good use of new military equipment and tactics, hiring Leonardo da Vinci (1452–1519) as a military engineer, and murdered his political enemies, including the second husband of his sister, Lucrezia. Despite Borgia's efforts, his state fell apart after his father's death, which Machiavelli ascribed not to weakness, but to the operations of fate (*fortuna*, for-TOO-nah, in Italian), whose power even the best-prepared and most merciless ruler could not fully escape, though he should try. Fortuna was personified and portrayed as a goddess in ancient Rome and Renaissance Italy, and Machiavelli's last words about fortune are expressed in gendered terms: "It is better to be impetuous than cautious, for fortune is a

woman, and if one wishes to keep her down, it is necessary to beat her and knock her down."[4]

*The Prince* is often seen as the first modern guide to politics, though Machiavelli was denounced for writing it, and people later came to use the word *Machiavellian* to mean cunning and ruthless. Medieval political philosophers had debated the proper relation between church and state, but they regarded the standards by which all governments were to be judged as emanating from moral principles established by God. Machiavelli argued that governments should instead be judged by how well they provided security, order, and safety to their populace. A ruler's moral code in maintaining these was not the same as a private individual's, for a leader could — indeed, should — use any means necessary. Machiavelli put a new spin on the Renaissance search for perfection, arguing that ideals needed to be measured in the cold light of the real world. This more pragmatic view of the purposes of government, along with Machiavelli's discussion of the role of force and cruelty, was unacceptable to many.

Even today, when Machiavelli's more secular view of the purposes of government is widely shared, scholars debate whether Machiavelli actually meant what he wrote. Most regard him as realistic or even cynical, but some suggest that he was being ironic or satirical, showing princely government in the worst possible light to contrast it with republicanism, which he favored, and also wrote about at length in the *Discourses on Livy*. He dedicated *The Prince* to the new Medici ruler of Florence, however, so any criticism was deeply buried within what was, in that era of patronage, essentially a job application.

## Christian Humanism

In the last quarter of the fifteenth century, students from the Low Countries, France, Germany, and England flocked to Italy, absorbed the "new learning," and carried it back to their own countries. Northern humanists shared the ideas of Ficino and Pico about the wisdom of ancient texts, but they went beyond Italian efforts to synthesize the Christian and classical traditions to see humanist learning as a way to bring about reform of the church and deepen people's spiritual lives. These **Christian humanists**, as they were later called, thought that the best elements of classical and Christian cultures should be combined. For example, the classical ideals of calmness, stoical patience, and broadmindedness should be joined in human conduct with the Christian virtues of love, faith, and hope.

The English humanist Thomas More (1478–1535) began life as a lawyer, studied the classics, and entered

**■ Christian humanists** Northern humanists who interpreted Italian ideas about and attitudes toward classical antiquity and humanism in terms of their own religious traditions.

government service. Despite his official duties, he had time to write, and he became most famous for his controversial dialogue *Utopia* (1516), a word More invented from the Greek words for "nowhere." *Utopia* describes a community on an island somewhere beyond Europe where all children receive a good education, primarily in the Greco-Roman classics, and adults divide their days between manual labor or business pursuits and intellectual activities. The problems that plagued More's fellow citizens, such as poverty and hunger, have been solved by a beneficent government. There is religious toleration, and order and reason prevail. Because Utopian institutions are perfect, however, dissent and disagreement are not acceptable. (See "Evaluating Written Evidence: Thomas More, *Utopia*," page 339.)

More's purposes in writing *Utopia* have been debated just as much as have Machiavelli's in penning *The Prince*. Some view it as a revolutionary critique of More's own hierarchical and violent society, some as a call for an even firmer hierarchy, and others as part of the humanist tradition of satire. It was widely read by learned Europeans in the Latin in which More wrote it, and later in vernacular translations, and its title quickly became the standard word for any imaginary society.

Better known by contemporaries than Thomas More was the Dutch humanist Desiderius Erasmus (dehz-ih-DARE-ee-us ih-RAZ-muhs) (1466?–1536) of Rotterdam. Erasmus's long list of publications includes *The Education of a Christian Prince* (1504), a book combining idealistic and practical suggestions for the formation of a ruler's character through the careful study of the Bible and classical authors; *The*

*Praise of Folly* (1509), a witty satire poking fun at political, social, and especially religious institutions; and, most important, a new Latin translation of the New Testament alongside the first printed edition of the Greek text (1516). In the preface to the New Testament, Erasmus expressed his ideas about Bible translations: "I wish that even the weakest woman should read the Gospel — should read the epistles of Paul. And I wish these were translated into all languages, so that they might be read and understood, not only by Scots and Irishmen, but also by Turks and Saracens."[5]

Two fundamental themes run through all of Erasmus's work. First, education in the Bible and the classics is the means to reform, the key to moral and intellectual improvement. Erasmus called for a renaissance of the ideals of the early church to accompany the renaissance in classical education that was already going on, and criticized the church of his day for having strayed from these ideals. Second, renewal should be based on what he termed "the philosophy of Christ," an emphasis on inner spirituality and personal morality rather than Scholastic theology or outward observances such as pilgrimages or the veneration of relics. His ideas, and Christian humanism in general, were important roots of the Protestant Reformation, although Erasmus himself denied this and never became a follower of Luther (see "Martin Luther" in Chapter 13).

## The Printed Word

The fourteenth-century humanist Petrarch and the sixteenth-century humanist Erasmus had similar ideas on many topics, but the immediate impact of their

**Printer's Shop** This engraving from a late-sixteenth-century book captures the many tasks and mix of individuals in a print shop. On the far left three compositors assemble pieces of type into a framework, while in the left foreground another checks a frame and a proofreader, wearing glasses, checks printed proof. At the back a woman, perhaps the printer's wife, inks type, while in front of her the printer pulls a lever to operate the press. In the front a young apprentice hangs sheets to dry, and the well-dressed man at the right may be the patron or official who ordered the print job. (INTERFOTO/Alamy)

# Thomas More, *Utopia*

Published in 1516, *Utopia* is written as a dialogue between Thomas More and Raphael Hythloday, a character More invented who has, in More's telling, recently returned from the newly discovered land of Utopia somewhere in the New World. More and Hythloday first discuss the problems in Europe, and then Hythloday describes how these have been solved in Utopia, ending with a long discussion of the Utopians' ban on private property.

❧

Well, that's the most accurate account I can give you of the Utopian Republic. To my mind, it's not only the best country in the world, but the only one that has the right to call itself a republic. Elsewhere, people are always talking about the public interest, but all they really care about is private property. In Utopia, where there's no private property, people take their duty to the public seriously. And both attitudes are perfectly reasonable. In other "republics" practically everyone knows that, if he doesn't look out for himself, he'll starve to death, however prosperous his country may be. He's therefore compelled to give his own interests priority over those of the public; that is, of other people. But in Utopia, where everything's under public ownership, no one has any fear of going short, as long as the public storehouses are full. Everyone gets a fair share, so there are never any poor men or beggars. Nobody owns anything, but everyone is rich—for what greater wealth can there be than cheerfulness, peace of mind, and freedom from anxiety? Instead of being worried about his food supply, upset by the plaintive demands of his wife, afraid of poverty for his son, and baffled by the problem of finding a dowry for his daughter, the Utopian can feel absolutely sure that he, his wife, his children, his grandchildren, his great-grandchildren, and as long a line of descendants as the proudest peer could wish to look forward to, will always have enough to eat and enough to make them happy. There's also the further point that those who are too old to work are just as well provided for as those who are still working.

Now, will anyone venture to compare these fair arrangements in Utopia with the so-called justice of other countries?—in which I'm damned if I can see the slightest trace of justice or fairness. For what sort of justice do you call this? People like aristocrats, goldsmiths, or money-lenders, who either do no work at all, or do work that's really not essential, are rewarded for their laziness or their unnecessary activities by a splendid life of luxury. But labourers, coachmen, carpenters, and farmhands, who never stop working like cart-horses, at jobs so essential that, if they did stop working, they'd bring any country to a standstill within twelve months—what happens to them? They get so little to eat, and have such a wretched time, that they'd be almost better off if they were cart-horses. Then at least, they wouldn't work quite such long hours, their food wouldn't be very much worse, they'd enjoy it more, and they'd have no fears for the future. As it is, they're not only ground down by unrewarding toil in the present, but also worried to death by the prospect of a poverty-stricken old age.

## EVALUATE THE EVIDENCE

1. How does the Utopians' economic system compare with that of Europe, in Hythloday's opinion?
2. Hythloday's comments about wealth have been seen by some scholars as More's criticism of his own society, and by others as proof that More wrote this as a satire, describing a place that could never be. Which view seems most persuasive to you?

Source: Thomas More, *Utopia*, trans. Paul Turner (London: Penguin Books, 1965), pp. 128–129. Reproduced by permission of Penguin Books Ltd.

ideas was very different because of one thing: the invention of the printing press with movable metal type. The ideas of Petrarch were spread slowly from person to person by hand copying. The ideas of Erasmus were spread quickly through print, allowing hundreds or thousands of identical copies to be made in a short time.

Printing with movable metal type developed in Germany in the 1440s as a combination of existing technologies. Several metalsmiths, most prominently Johann Gutenberg, recognized that the metal stamps used to mark signs on jewelry could be covered with ink and used to mark symbols onto a surface in the same way that other craftsmen were using carved wood stamps to print books. (This woodblock printing technique originated in China and Korea centuries earlier.) Gutenberg and his assistants made metal stamps—later called *type*—for every letter of the alphabet and built racks that held the type in rows. This type could be rearranged for every page and so used over and over.

The printing revolution was also made possible by the ready availability of paper, which was also produced using techniques that had originated in China, though, unlike the printing press, this technology had been brought into Europe through Muslim Spain rather than developing independently.

By the fifteenth century the increase in urban literacy, the development of primary schools, and the opening of

**Printing centers with date of establishment**
◆ 15th century
▲ 16th century
— Political boundaries in 1490

Gutenberg establishes first printing press, 1448

**MAPPING THE PAST**

## MAP 12.2 The Growth of Printing in Europe, 1448–1554

The speed with which artisans spread printing technology across Europe provides strong evidence for the growing demand for reading material. Presses in the Ottoman Empire were first established by Jewish immigrants who printed works in Hebrew, Greek, and Spanish.

**ANALYZING THE MAP** What part of Europe had the greatest number of printing presses by 1554? What explains this?

**CONNECTIONS** Printing was developed in response to a market for reading materials. Use Maps 10.2 and 10.3 (pages 276 and 281) to help explain why printing spread the way it did.

more universities had created an expanding market for reading materials. When Gutenberg developed movable type printing as a faster way to copy, professional copyists writing by hand and block-book makers, along with monks and nuns, were already churning out reading materials on paper as fast as they could for the growing number of people who could read.

Gutenberg was not the only one to recognize the huge market for books, and his invention was quickly copied. Other craftsmen made their own type, built their own presses, and bought their own paper, setting

themselves up in business (Map 12.2). Historians estimate that, within a half century of the publication of Gutenberg's Bible in 1456, somewhere between 8 million and 20 million books were printed in Europe. Whatever the actual figure, the number is far greater than the number of books produced in all of Western history up to that point.

The effects of the invention of movable-type printing were not felt overnight. Nevertheless, movable type radically transformed both the private and the public lives of Europeans by the dawn of the sixteenth century. Print shops became gathering places for people interested in new ideas. Though printers were trained through apprenticeships just as blacksmiths or butchers were, they had connections to the world of politics, art, and scholarship that other craftsmen did not.

Printing gave hundreds or even thousands of people identical books, allowing them to more easily discuss the ideas that the books contained with one another in person or through letters. Printed materials reached an invisible public, allowing silent individuals to join causes and groups of individuals widely separated by geography to form a common identity; this new group consciousness could compete with and transcend older, localized loyalties.

Government and church leaders both used and worried about printing. They printed laws, declarations of war, battle accounts, and propaganda, and they also attempted to censor books and authors whose ideas they thought challenged their authority or were incorrect. Officials developed lists of prohibited books and authors, enforcing their prohibitions by confiscating books, arresting printers and booksellers, or destroying the presses of printers who disobeyed. None of this was very effective, and books were printed secretly, with fake title pages, authors, and places of publication, and smuggled all over Europe.

Printing also stimulated the literacy of laypeople and eventually came to have a deep effect on their private lives. Although most of the earliest books and pamphlets dealt with religious subjects, printers produced anything that would sell. They printed professional reference sets for lawyers, doctors, and students, and historical romances, biographies, and how-to manuals for the general public. They discovered that illustrations increased a book's sales, so they published books on a wide range of topics — from history to pornography — full of woodcuts and engravings. Single-page broadsides and fly sheets allowed great public events and "wonders" such as comets and two-headed calves to be experienced vicariously by a stay-at-home readership. Since books and other printed materials were read aloud to illiterate listeners, print also bridged the gap between the written and oral cultures.

# How did art reflect new Renaissance ideals?

No feature of the Renaissance evokes greater admiration than its artistic masterpieces. The 1400s (*quattrocento*) and 1500s (*cinquecento*) bore witness to dazzling creativity in painting, architecture, and sculpture. In all the arts, the city of Florence led the way. But Florence was not the only artistic center, for Rome and Venice also became important, and northern Europeans perfected their own styles.

## Patronage and Power

In early Renaissance Italy, powerful urban groups often flaunted their wealth by commissioning works of art. In the late fifteenth century, wealthy individuals and rulers, rather than corporate groups, sponsored works of art. Patrician merchants and bankers, popes, and princes spent vast sums on the arts to glorify themselves and their families. Writing in about 1470, Florentine ruler Lorenzo de' Medici declared that his family had spent hundreds of thousands of gold florins for artistic and architectural commissions, but commented, "I think it casts a brilliant light on our estate [public reputation] and it seems to me that the monies were well spent and I am very pleased with this."[6]

Patrons varied in their level of involvement as a work progressed; some simply ordered a specific subject or scene, while others oversaw the work of the artist or architect very closely, suggesting themes and styles and demanding changes while the work was in progress. For example, Pope Julius II (pontificate 1503–1513), who commissioned Michelangelo to paint the ceiling of the Vatican's Sistine Chapel in 1508, demanded that the artist work as fast as he could and frequently visited him at his work with suggestions and criticisms. Michelangelo, a Florentine who had spent his young adulthood at the court of Lorenzo de' Medici, complained in person and by letter about the pope's meddling, but his reputation did not match the power of the pope, and he kept working until the chapel was finished in 1512.

In addition to power, art reveals changing patterns of consumption among the wealthy elite in European society. In the rural world of the Middle Ages, society had been organized for war, and men of wealth spent their money on military gear. As Italian nobles settled in towns, they adjusted to an urban culture (see "What led to Europe's economic growth and reurbanization?" in Chapter 10). Rather than employing knights for warfare, cities hired mercenaries. Accordingly, expenditures on military hardware by nobles declined. For the noble recently arrived from the countryside or the rich merchant of the city, a grand urban palace represented the greatest outlay of cash. Wealthy individuals and families ordered gold dishes, embroidered

**Plate Showing the Abduction of Helen of Troy** Filled with well-muscled men, curvaceous women, and exotic landscapes, this colorful plate with a gold rim depicts a well-known scene from Greek mythology, the abduction of Helen, which sparked the Trojan War. Such tin-glazed pottery, known as maiolica and made in many places in Italy beginning in the late fifteenth century, was sold throughout Europe to wealthy consumers, who favored designs with family crests or legendary or historical scenes, known as istoriato ("painted with stories"). (Museo Nazionale del Bargello, Florence, Italy/Bridgeman Images)

tablecloths, wall tapestries, paintings on canvas (an innovation), and sculptural decorations to adorn these homes. Expanded trade brought in silks, pearls, gemstones, feathers, dyes, and furs, which tailors, goldsmiths, seamstresses, furriers, and hatmakers turned into magnificent clothing and jewelry. Men and women wore clothing that displayed many layers of expensive fabrics, with golden rings, earrings, pins, and necklaces to provide additional glamour.

## Changing Artistic Styles

Both the content and style of Renaissance art often differed from those of the Middle Ages. Religious topics remained popular among both patrons and artists, but frequently the patron had himself and his family portrayed in the scene. As the fifteenth century advanced and humanist ideas spread more widely, classical themes and motifs figured increasingly in painting and sculpture, with the facial features of the gods sometimes modeled on living people.

The individual portrait emerged as a distinct artistic genre in this movement. Rather than reflecting a spiritual ideal, as medieval painting and sculpture tended to do, Renaissance portraits showed human ideals, often portrayed in the more realistic style increasingly favored by both artists and patrons. The Florentine painter Giotto (JAH-toh) (1276–1337) led the way in the use of realism; his treatment of

the human body and face replaced the formal stiffness and artificiality that had long characterized representation of the human body. Piero della Francesca (frahn-CHAY-skah) (1420–1492) and Andrea Mantegna (mahn-TEHN-yuh) (1430/31–1506) pioneered perspective, the linear representation of distance and space on a flat surface, which enhanced the realism of paintings and differentiated them from the flatter and more stylized images of medieval art. The sculptor Donatello (1386–1466) revived the classical figure, with its balance and self-awareness. In architecture, Filippo Brunelleschi (1377–1446) looked to the classical past for inspiration, designing a hospital for orphans and foundlings in which all proportions — of the windows, height, floor plan, and covered walkway with a series of rounded arches — were carefully thought out to achieve a sense of balance and harmony.

Art produced in northern Europe tended to be more religious in orientation than that produced in Italy. Some Flemish painters, notably Rogier van der Weyden (1399/1400–1464) and Jan van Eyck (1366–1441), were considered the artistic equals of Italian painters and were much admired in Italy. Van Eyck was one of the earliest artists to use oil-based paints successfully, and his religious scenes and portraits all show great realism and remarkable attention to human personality. Albrecht Dürer (1471–1528), from the German city of Nuremberg, studied with artists in Italy and produced woodcuts, engravings, and etchings that rendered the human form and the natural world in amazing detail.

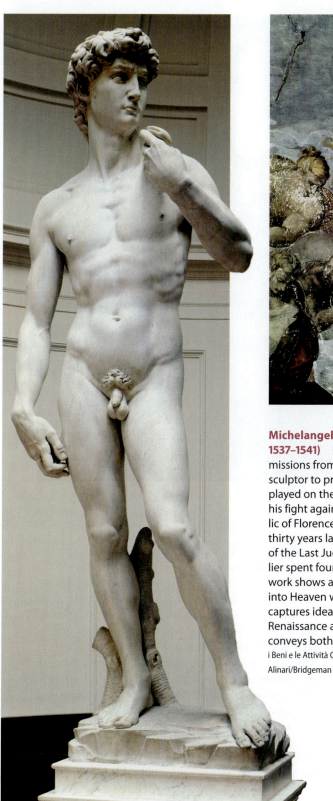

**Michelangelo's *David* (1501–1504) and the *Last Judgment* (detail, 1537–1541)**   Like all Renaissance artists, Michelangelo worked largely on commissions from patrons. Officials of the city of Florence contracted the young sculptor to produce a statue of the Old Testament hero David (left) to be displayed on the city's main square. Michelangelo portrayed David anticipating his fight against the giant Goliath, and the statue came to symbolize the republic of Florence standing up to its larger and more powerful enemies. More than thirty years later, Michelangelo was commissioned by the pope to paint a scene of the Last Judgment on the altar wall of the Sistine Chapel, where he had earlier spent four years covering the ceiling with magnificent frescoes. The massive work shows a powerful Christ standing in judgment, with souls ascending into Heaven while others are dragged by demons into Hell (above). The David captures ideals of human perfection and has come to be an iconic symbol of Renaissance artistic brilliance, while the dramatic and violent Last Judgment conveys both terror and divine power. (sculpture: Accademia, Florence, Italy/Ministero per i Beni e le Attività Culturali/Scala/Art Resource, NY; painting: Vatican Museums and Galleries, Vatican State/Alinari/Bridgeman Images)

Fascinated with the theoretical and practical problems of perspective, he designed mechanical devices that could assist artists in solving these problems. Like many Renaissance artists, Dürer was open to new ideas, no matter what their source. Late in his life he saw the first pieces of Aztec art shipped back to Europe from the New World and commented in his diary about how amazing they were.

In the early sixteenth century, the center of the new art shifted from Florence to Rome, where wealthy cardinals and popes wanted visual expression of the church's and their own families' power and piety.

**The Madonna of Chancellor Rolin, ca. 1435**  This exquisitely detailed oil painting by Jan van Eyck, commissioned by Nicolas Rolin, the chancellor of the duchy of Burgundy, shows the Virgin Mary presenting the infant Jesus to Rolin, whose portrait in a brocade fur-lined robe takes up the entire left side. The foreground is an Italian-style loggia with an inlaid floor, while the background shows Rolin's hometown of Autun, where he was a major landowner and where the painting was displayed in his parish church. Renaissance paintings from southern and northern Europe often show their patrons together with biblical figures and highlight exactly the qualities the patron wanted: wealth, learning, piety, and power. ("La Vierge au Chancelier Rolin," ca. 1435, panel by Jan van Eyck [ca. 1390–1441]/Musée du Louvre, Paris, France/Bridgeman Images)

Renaissance popes expended enormous enthusiasm and huge sums of money to beautify the city. Pope Julius II tore down the old Saint Peter's Basilica and began work on the present structure in 1506. Michelangelo went to Rome from Florence in about 1500 and began the series of statues, paintings, and architectural projects from which he gained an international reputation: the *Pietà*, *Moses*, the redesigning of the plaza and surrounding palaces on the Capitoline Hill in central Rome, and, most famously, the dome for Saint Peter's and the ceiling and altar wall of the nearby Sistine Chapel.

Raphael Sanzio (1483–1520), another Florentine, got the commission for frescoes in the papal apartments, and in his relatively short life he painted hundreds of portraits and devotional images, becoming the most sought-after artist in Europe. Raphael also oversaw a large workshop with many collaborators and apprentices—who assisted on the less difficult sections of some paintings—and wrote treatises on his philosophy of art in which he emphasized the importance of imitating nature and developing an orderly sequence of design and proportion.

Venice became another artistic center in the sixteenth century. Titian (TIH-shuhn) (1490–1576) produced portraits, religious subjects, and mythological scenes; he developed techniques of painting in oil without doing elaborate drawings first, which speeded up the process and pleased patrons eager to display their acquisitions. Titian and other sixteenth-century painters developed an artistic style known in English as "mannerism" (from *maniera* or "style" in Italian) in which artists sometimes distorted figures, exaggerated musculature, and heightened color to express emotion and drama more intently. (Paintings by Titian can be found on pages 348 and 414; this is also the style in which Michelangelo painted the *Last Judgment* in the Sistine Chapel, shown on page 343.)

## The Renaissance Artist

Some patrons rewarded certain artists very well, and some artists gained great public acclaim as, in Vasari's words, "rare men of genius." This adulation of the artist has led many historians to view the Renaissance

**Villa Capra**   Architecture as well as literature and art aimed to re-create classical styles. The Venetian architect Andrea Palladio modeled this country villa, constructed for a papal official in 1566, on the Pantheon of ancient Rome (see "The Nerva-Antonine Dynasty" in Chapter 6). Surrounded by statues of classical deities, it is completely symmetrical, capturing humanist ideals of perfection and balance. This villa and other buildings that Palladio designed influenced later buildings all over the world, including the U.S. Capitol in Washington, D.C., and countless state capitol buildings. (age-fotostock/Superstock)

as the beginning of the concept of the artist as having a special talent. In the Middle Ages people believed that only God created, albeit through individuals; the medieval conception recognized no particular value in artistic originality. Renaissance artists and humanists came to think that a work of art was the deliberate creation of a unique personality who transcended traditions, rules, and theories. A genius had a peculiar gift that ordinary laws should not inhibit. (See "Individuals in Society: Leonardo da Vinci," page 332.)

However, it is important not to overemphasize the Renaissance notion of genius. As certain artists became popular and well known, they could assert their own artistic styles and pay less attention to the wishes of patrons, but even major artists like Raphael generally worked according to the patron's specific guidelines. Whether in Italy or northern Europe, most Renaissance artists trained in the workshops of older artists; Botticelli, Raphael, Titian, and at times even Michelangelo were known for their large, well-run, and prolific workshops. Though they might be men of genius, artists were still expected to be well trained in proper artistic techniques and stylistic conventions; the notion that artistic genius could show up in the work of an untrained artist did not emerge until the twentieth century. Beginning artists

spent years mastering their craft by copying drawings and paintings; learning how to prepare paint and other artistic materials; and, by the sixteenth century, reading books about design and composition. Younger artists gathered together in the evenings for further drawing practice; by the later sixteenth century some of these informal groups had turned into more formal artistic "academies," the first of which was begun in 1563 in Florence by Vasari under the patronage of the Medici.

As Vasari's phrase indicates, the notion of artistic genius that developed in the Renaissance was gendered. All the most famous and most prolific Renaissance artists were male. The types of art in which more women were active, such as textiles, needlework, and painting on porcelain, were regarded not as "major arts," but only as "minor" or "decorative" arts. (The division between "major" and "minor" arts begun in the Renaissance continues to influence the way museums and collections are organized today.) Like painting, embroidery changed in the Renaissance to become more naturalistic, more visually complex, and more classical in its subject matter. Embroiderers were not trained to view their work as products of individual genius, however, so they rarely included their names on the works, and there is no way to discover their identities.

There are no female architects whose names are known and only one female sculptor, though several women did become well known as painters in their day. Stylistically, their works are different from one another, but their careers show many similarities. Most female painters were the daughters of painters or of minor noblemen with ties to artistic circles. Many were eldest daughters or came from families in which there were no sons, so their fathers took unusual interest in their careers. Many women painters began their careers before they were twenty and either produced far fewer paintings after they married or stopped painting entirely. Women were not allowed to study the male nude, a study that was viewed as essential if one wanted to paint large history or biblical paintings with many figures. Women also could not learn the technique of fresco, in which colors are applied directly to wet plaster walls, because such work had to be done in public, which was judged inappropriate for women. Joining a group of male artists for informal practice was also seen as improper, so women had no access to the newly established artistic academies. Like universities, humanist academies, and most craft guild shops, artistic workshops were male-only settings in which men of different ages came together for training and created bonds of friendship, influence, patronage, and sometimes intimacy.

Women were not alone in being excluded from the institutions of Renaissance culture. Though a few rare men of genius such as Leonardo and Michelangelo emerged from artisanal backgrounds, most scholars and artists came from families with at least some money. The ideas of the highly educated humanists did not influence the lives of most people in cities and did not affect life in the villages at all. For rural people and for less well-off town residents, work and play continued much as they had in the High Middle Ages: religious festivals and family celebrations provided people's main amusements, and learning came from one's parents, not through formal schooling.

**Botticelli, *Primavera* (Spring), ca. 1482**    Framed by a grove of orange trees, Venus, goddess of love, is flanked on the right by Flora, goddess of flowers and fertility, and on the left by the Three Graces, goddesses of banquets, dance, and social occasions. Above, Venus's son Cupid, the god of love, shoots darts of desire, while at the far right the wind-god Zephyrus chases the nymph Chloris. The entire scene rests on classical mythology, though some art historians claim that Venus is an allegory for the Virgin Mary. Botticelli captured the ideal for female beauty in the Renaissance: slender, with pale skin, a high forehead, red-blond hair, and sloping shoulders. (Galleria degli Uffizi, Florence, Italy/Bridgeman Images)

***The Chess Game*, 1555**   In this oil painting, the Italian artist Sofonisba Anguissola (1532–1625) shows her three younger sisters playing chess, a game that was growing in popularity in the sixteenth century. Each sister looks at the one immediately older than herself, with the girl on the left looking out at her sister, the artist. Anguissola's father, a minor nobleman, recognized his daughter's talent and arranged for her to study with several painters. She became a court painter at the Spanish royal court, where she painted many portraits. Returning to Italy, she continued to be active, painting her last portrait when she was over eighty. (Museum Narodowe, Poznan, Poland/Bridgeman Images)

# What were the key social hierarchies in Renaissance Europe?

The division between educated and uneducated people was only one of many social hierarchies evident in the Renaissance. Every society has social hierarchies; in ancient Rome, for example, there were patricians and plebeians (see "The Roman State" in Chapter 5). Such hierarchies are to some degree descriptions of social reality, but they are also idealizations — that is, they describe how people imagined their society to be, without all the messy reality of social-climbing plebeians or groups that did not fit the standard categories. Social hierarchies in the Renaissance were built on those of the Middle Ages that divided nobles from commoners, but new concepts were also developed that contributed to modern social hierarchies, such as those of race, class, and gender.

## Race and Slavery

Renaissance people did not use the word *race* the way we do, but often used *race*, *people*, and *nation* interchangeably for ethnic, national, religious, or other groups — the French race, the Jewish nation, the Irish people, "the race of learned gentlemen," and so on. They did make distinctions based on skin color that provide some of the background for later conceptualizations of race, but these distinctions were interwoven with other characteristics when people thought about human differences.

Since the time of the Roman Republic, a small number of black Africans had lived in western Europe. They had come, along with white slaves, as the spoils of war. Even after the collapse of the Roman Empire, Muslim and Christian merchants continued to import them. The evidence of medieval art attests to the continued presence of Africans in Europe throughout the Middle Ages and to Europeans' awareness of them.

Beginning in the fifteenth century sizable numbers of black slaves entered Europe. Portuguese sailors brought perhaps a thousand Africans a year to the markets of Seville, Barcelona, Marseilles, and Genoa. In the late fifteenth century this flow increased, with thousands of people taken from the west coast of Africa. Most of them ended up in Spain and Portugal. By the mid-sixteenth century blacks, both slave and free, constituted about 10 percent of the population of the Portuguese cities of Lisbon and Évora and roughly 3 percent of the Portuguese population overall. Cities such as Lisbon also had significant numbers of people of mixed African and European descent, as African slaves intermingled with the people they lived among and sometimes intermarried.

Although blacks were concentrated in the Iberian Peninsula, some Africans must have lived in northern Europe as well. In the 1580s, for example, Queen Elizabeth I of England complained that there were too many "blacka-moores" competing with needy English people for places as domestic servants. Black servants were much sought after; the medieval interest in curiosities, the exotic, and the marvelous continued in the Renaissance. Italian aristocrats had their portraits painted with their black page boys to indicate their wealth (as in the painting on page 348). Blacks were so greatly in demand at the Renaissance courts of northern Italy, in fact, that the Venetians defied papal threats of excommunication to secure them. In 1491 Isabella d'Este, the duchess of Mantua and a major patron of the arts, instructed her agent to secure a black girl between four and eight years old, "shapely and as black as possible." She hoped the girl would become "the

*Laura de Dianti,* 1523    The Venetian artist Titian portrays a young Italian woman with a gorgeous blue dress and an elaborate pearl and feather headdress, accompanied by a young black page with a gold earring. Both the African page and the headdress connect the portrait's subject with the exotic, though slaves from Africa and the Ottoman Empire were actually common in wealthy Venetian households. (Private Collection/© Human Bios International AG)

best buffoon in the world," and noted, "[W]e shall make her very happy and shall have great fun with her."[7] The girl would join musicians, acrobats, and dancers at Isabella's court as a source of entertainment, her status similar to that of the dwarves who could be found at many Renaissance courts.

Africans were not simply amusements at court. In Portugal, Spain, and Italy slaves supplemented the labor force in virtually all occupations—as servants, agricultural laborers, craftsmen, and seamen on ships going to Lisbon and Africa. Agriculture in Europe did not involve large plantations, so large-scale agricultural slavery did not develop there as it would in the late fifteenth century in the New World.

Until the voyages down the African coast in the late fifteenth century, Europeans had little concrete knowledge of Africans and their cultures. They saw Africa as a remote place, the home of people isolated by heresy and Islam from superior European civilization. Europeans thought that Africans' contact, even as slaves, with Christian Europeans could only "improve" them. The expanding slave trade reinforced negative preconceptions about the inferiority of black Africans.

## Wealth and the Nobility

The word *class*—as in working class, middle class, and upper class—was not used in the Renaissance to describe social divisions, but by the thirteenth century, and even more so by the fifteenth, the idea of a hierarchy based on wealth was emerging. This was particularly true in cities, where wealthy merchants who oversaw vast trading empires lived in splendor that rivaled the richest nobles. As we saw earlier, in many cities these merchants had gained political power to match their economic might, becoming merchant oligarchs who ruled through city councils. This hierarchy of wealth was more fluid than the older divisions into noble and commoner, allowing individuals and families to rise—and fall—within one generation.

The development of a hierarchy of wealth did not mean an end to the prominence of nobles, however, and even poorer nobility still had higher status than wealthy commoners. Thus wealthy Italian merchants enthusiastically bought noble titles and country villas in the fifteenth century, and wealthy English or Spanish merchants eagerly married their daughters and sons into often-impoverished noble families. The nobility maintained its status in most parts of Europe not by maintaining rigid boundaries, but by taking in and integrating the new social elite of wealth.

Along with being tied to hierarchies of wealth and family standing, social status was linked to considerations of honor. Among the nobility, for example, certain weapons and battle tactics were favored because they were viewed as more honorable. Among urban dwellers, certain occupations, such as city executioner or manager of the municipal brothel, might be well paid but were understood to be dishonorable and so of low status. In cities, sumptuary laws reflected both wealth and honor (see "City Life" in Chapter 10); merchants were specifically allowed fur and jewels, while prostitutes were ordered to wear yellow bands that would remind potential customers of the flames of Hell.

## Gender Roles

Renaissance people would not have understood the word *gender* to refer to categories of people, but they would have easily grasped the concept. Toward the end of the fourteenth century, learned men (and a few women) began what was termed the **debate about women** (*querelle des femmes*), a debate about women's character and nature that would last for centuries. Misogynist (muh-SAH-juh-nihst) critiques of women from both clerical and secular authors denounced females as devious, domineering, and demanding. In answer, several authors compiled long lists of famous and praiseworthy women exemplary for their loyalty, bravery, and morality. Christine de Pizan (1364?–1430), an Italian woman who became the first woman in Europe to make her living as a writer, was among the writers who were interested not only in defending women, but also in exploring the reasons behind women's secondary status—that is, why the great philosophers, statesmen, and poets had generally been men. In this they were anticipating discussions about the "social construction of gender" by six hundred years.

With the development of the printing press, popular interest in the debate about women grew, and works were translated, reprinted, and shared around Europe. Prints that juxtaposed female virtues and vices were also very popular, with the virtuous women depicted as those of the classical or biblical past and the vice-ridden dressed in contemporary clothes. The favorite metaphor for the virtuous wife was either the snail or the tortoise, both animals that never leave their "houses" and are totally silent, although such images were never as widespread as those depicting wives beating their husbands or hiding their lovers from them.

Beginning in the sixteenth century, the debate about women also became a debate about female rulers, sparked primarily by dynastic accidents in many countries, including Spain, England, Scotland, and France, that led to women's ruling in their own right or serving as advisers to child-kings. The questions were vigorously and at times viciously argued. They directly concerned the social construction of gender: Could a woman's being born into a royal family and educated to rule allow her to overcome the limitations of her sex? Should it? Or stated another way: which was (or should be) the stronger determinant of character and social role, gender or rank? Despite a prevailing sentiment that women were not as fit to rule as men, there were no successful rebellions against female rulers simply because they were women, but in part this was because female rulers, especially Queen Elizabeth I of England, emphasized qualities regarded as masculine—physical bravery, stamina, wisdom, duty—whenever they appeared in public.

Ideas about women's and men's proper roles determined the actions of ordinary men and women even more forcefully. The dominant notion of the "true" man was that of the married head of household, so men whose social status and age would have normally conferred political power but who remained unmarried did not participate in politics at the same level as their married brothers. Unmarried men in Venice, for example, could not be part of the ruling council.

Women were also understood as either "married or to be married," even if the actual marriage patterns in Europe left many women (and men) unmarried until quite late in life (see "Sex in the City" in Chapter 11). This meant that women's work was not viewed as financially supporting a family—even if it did—and was valued less than men's. If they worked for wages, and many women did, women earned about half to two-thirds of what men did, even for the same work. Regulations for vineyard workers in the early sixteenth century, for example, specified:

**Fashionable Young Men**   Two young men, side figures in *The Adoration of the Magi*, by Luca Signorelli (1445–1523), wear multicolored garments that were a favorite of young well-to-do urban men, topping their ensembles with matching hats on carefully combed long hair. The padded shoulders, large sleeves, and tight hose emphasized and accentuated the male form, as did the short doublet and split hose that revealed a brightly colored codpiece. (Galleria degli Uffizi, Florence, Italy/Scala/Art Resource, NY)

Men who work in the vineyards, doing work that is skilled, are to be paid 16 pence per day; in addition, they are to receive soup and wine in the morning, at midday beer, vegetables and meat, and in the evening soup, vegetables and wine. Young boys are to be paid 10 pence per day. Women who work as haymakers are to be given 6 pence a day. If the employer wants to have them doing other work, he may make an agreement with them to pay them 7 or 8 pence. He may also give them soup and vegetables to eat in the morning—but no wine—milk and bread at midday, but nothing in the evening.[8]

■ **debate about women** Debate among writers and thinkers in the Renaissance about women's qualities and proper role in society.

The maintenance of appropriate power relationships between men and women, with men dominant and women subordinate, served as a symbol of the proper functioning of society as a whole. Disorder in the proper gender hierarchy was linked with social upheaval and was viewed as threatening. Of all the ways in which Renaissance society was hierarchically arranged—social rank, age, level of education, race, occupation—gender was regarded as the most "natural" and therefore the most important to defend.

## How did nation-states develop in this period?

The High Middle Ages had witnessed the origins of many of the basic institutions of the modern state. Sheriffs, inquests, juries, circuit judges, professional bureaucracies, and representative assemblies all trace their origins to the twelfth and thirteenth centuries. The linchpin for the development of states, however, was strong monarchy, and during the period of the Hundred Years' War no ruler in western Europe was able to provide effective leadership. The resurgent power of feudal nobilities weakened the centralizing work begun earlier.

Beginning in the fifteenth century, however, rulers utilized aggressive methods to rebuild their governments. First in the regional states of Italy, then in the expanding monarchies of France, England, and Spain, rulers began the work of reducing violence, curbing unruly nobles, and establishing domestic order. They attempted to secure their borders and enhanced the methods of raising revenue.

### France

The Black Death and the Hundred Years' War left France drastically depopulated, commercially ruined, and agriculturally weak. Nonetheless, the ruler whom Joan of Arc had seen crowned at Reims, Charles VII (r. 1422–1461), revived the monarchy and France. Charles reconciled the Burgundians and Armagnacs (ahr-muhn-YAKZ), who had been waging civil war for thirty years. By 1453 French armies had expelled the English from French soil except in Calais. Charles reorganized the royal council, giving increased influence to lawyers and bankers, and strengthened royal finances through taxes on certain products and on land, which remained the Crown's chief sources of income until the Revolution of 1789.

**The Expansion of France, 1475–1500**

Crown lands, ca. 1475
Territory added by 1483
Territory added by 1498
Independent fiefs
Boundary of France, ca. 1500

By establishing regular companies of cavalry and archers — recruited, paid, and inspected by the state—Charles created the first permanent royal army anywhere in Europe. His son Louis XI (r. 1461–1483) improved upon Charles's army and used it to control the nobles' separate militias and to curb urban independence. The army was also employed in 1477 when Louis conquered Burgundy upon the death of its ruler Charles the Bold. Three years later, the extinction of the house of Anjou with the death of its last legitimate male heir brought Louis the counties of Anjou, Bar, Maine, and Provence.

Two further developments strengthened the French monarchy. The marriage of Louis XII (r. 1498–1515) and Anne of Brittany added the large western duchy of Brittany to the state. Then King Francis I and Pope Leo X reached a mutually satisfactory agreement about church and state powers in 1516. The new treaty, the Concordat of Bologna, approved the pope's right to receive the first year's income of newly named bishops and abbots in France. In return, Leo X recognized the French ruler's right to select French bishops and abbots. French kings thereafter effectively controlled the appointment and thus the policies of church officials in the kingdom.

### England

English society also suffered severely from the disorders of the fifteenth century. The aristocracy dominated the government of Henry IV (r. 1399–1413) and indulged in disruptive violence at the local level, fighting each other, seizing wealthy travelers for ransom, and plundering merchant caravans (see "Fur-Collar Crime" in Chapter 11). Population continued to decline. Between 1455 and 1471 adherents of the ducal houses of York and Lancaster contended for control of the Crown in a civil war, commonly called the Wars of the Roses because the symbol of the Yorkists was a white rose and that of the Lancastrians a red one. The chronic disorder hurt trade, agriculture, and domestic industry. Under the pious but mentally disturbed Henry VI (r. 1422–1461), the authority of the monarchy sank lower than it had been in centuries.

The Yorkist Edward IV (r. 1461–1483) began establishing domestic tranquility. He succeeded in defeating the Lancastrian forces and after 1471 began to reconstruct the monarchy. Edward, his brother Richard III (r. 1483–1485), and Henry VII (r. 1485–1509) of the

Welsh house of Tudor worked to restore royal prestige, to crush the power of the nobility, and to establish order and law at the local level. All three rulers used methods that Machiavelli himself would have praised—ruthlessness, efficiency, and secrecy.

Edward IV and subsequently the Tudors, except Henry VIII, conducted foreign policy on the basis of diplomacy, avoiding expensive wars. Thus the English monarchy did not have to depend on Parliament for money, and the Crown undercut that source of aristocratic influence.

Henry VII did summon several meetings of Parliament in the early years of his reign, primarily to confirm laws, but the center of royal authority was the royal council, which governed at the national level. Henry VII revealed his distrust of the nobility through his appointments to the council: though not completely excluded, very few great lords were among the king's closest advisers. Instead he chose men from among the smaller landowners and urban residents trained in law. The council conducted negotiations with foreign governments and secured international recognition of the Tudor dynasty through the marriage in 1501 of Henry VII's eldest son, Arthur, to Catherine of Aragon, the daughter of Ferdinand and Isabella of Spain. The council dealt with real or potential aristocratic threats through a judicial offshoot, the Court of Star Chamber, so called because of the stars painted on the ceiling of the room. The court applied methods that were sometimes terrifying: accused persons were not entitled to see evidence against them, sessions were secret, juries were not called, and torture could be applied to extract confessions. These procedures ran directly counter to English common-law precedents, but they effectively reduced aristocratic troublemaking. When Henry VII died in 1509, he left a country at peace both domestically and internationally, a substantially augmented treasury, an expanding wool trade, and a crown with its dignity and role much enhanced.

## Spain

While England and France laid the foundations of unified nation-states during the Middle Ages, Spain remained a conglomerate of independent kingdoms. By the middle of the fifteenth century, the kingdoms of Castile and Aragon dominated the weaker Navarre, Portugal, and Granada; and the Iberian Peninsula, with the exception of Granada, had been won for Christianity (Map 12.3). But even the wedding in 1469 of the dynamic and aggressive Isabella of Castile (r. 1474–1504) and the crafty and persistent Ferdinand of Aragon (r. 1479–1516) did not bring about administrative unity, as each state maintained its own cortes (parliament), laws, courts, and systems of coinage and taxation until about 1700. But the two rulers pursued a common foreign policy, and under their heirs Spain became a more unified realm.

Ferdinand and Isabella were able to exert their authority in ways similar to the rulers of France and England.

They curbed aristocratic power by excluding high nobles from the royal council, which had full executive, judicial, and legislative powers under the monarchy, instead appointing lesser landowners. The council and various government boards recruited men trained in Roman law, which exalted the power of the Crown. (See "Evaluating Visual Evidence: A Gold Coin of Ferdinand and Isabella," page 353.) They also secured from the Spanish Borgia pope Alexander VI—Cesare Borgia's father—the right to appoint bishops in Spain and in the Hispanic territories in America, enabling them to establish the equivalent of a national church. With the revenues from ecclesiastical estates, they were able to expand their territories to include the remaining land held by Arabs in southern Spain. The victorious entry of Ferdinand and Isabella into Granada on January 6, 1492, signaled the conclusion of the reconquista (see Map 9.3, page 237). Granada was incorporated into the Spanish kingdom, and after Isabella's death Ferdinand conquered Navarre in the north.

There still remained a sizable and, in the view of the majority of the Spanish people, potentially dangerous minority, the Jews. When the kings of France and England had expelled the Jews from their kingdoms (see "Consequences of the Crusades" in Chapter 9), many had sought refuge in Spain. During the long centuries of the reconquista, Christian kings had recognized Jewish rights and privileges; in fact, Jewish industry, intelligence, and money had supported royal power. While Christians borrowed from Jewish moneylenders and while all who could afford them sought Jewish physicians, a strong undercurrent of resentment of Jewish influence and wealth festered.

In the fourteenth century anti-Semitism in Spain was aggravated by fiery anti-Jewish preaching, by economic dislocation, and by the search for a scapegoat during the Black Death. Anti-Semitic pogroms swept the towns of Spain, and perhaps 40 percent of the Jewish population was killed or forced to convert. Those converted were called *conversos* or **New Christians**. Conversos were often well educated and held prominent positions in government, the church, medicine, law, and business. Numbering perhaps 200,000 in a total Spanish population of about 7.5 million, New Christians and Jews in fifteenth-century Spain exercised influence disproportionate to their numbers.

Such successes bred resentment. Aristocratic grandees resented the conversos' financial independence, the poor hated the converso tax collectors, and churchmen doubted the sincerity of their conversions. Queen Isabella shared these suspicions, and she and Ferdinand had received permission from Pope Sixtus IV in 1478 to establish their own Inquisition to "search out and punish converts from Judaism who had transgressed against

■ **New Christians** A term for Jews and Muslims in the Iberian Peninsula who accepted Christianity; in many cases they included Christians whose families had converted centuries earlier.

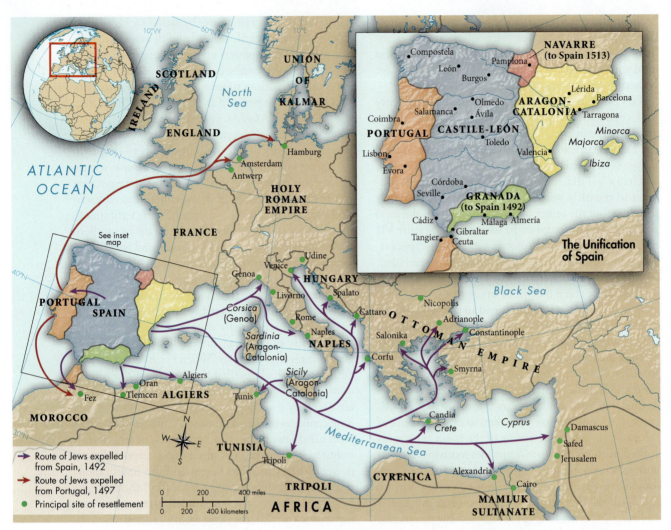

**MAP 12.3 The Unification of Spain and the Expulsion of the Jews, Fifteenth Century**  The marriage of Ferdinand of Aragon and Isabella of Castile in 1469 brought most of the Iberian Peninsula under one monarchy, although different parts of Spain retained distinct cultures, languages, and legal systems. In 1492 Ferdinand and Isabella conquered Granada, where most people were Muslim, and expelled the Jews from all of Spain. Spanish Jews resettled in cities of Europe and the Mediterranean that allowed them in, including Muslim states such as the Ottoman Empire. Muslims were also expelled from Spain over the course of the sixteenth and early seventeenth centuries.

Christianity by secretly adhering to Jewish beliefs and performing rites of the Jews."[9] Investigations and trials began immediately, as officials of the Inquisition looked for conversos who showed any sign of incomplete conversion, such as not eating pork.

Recent scholarship has carefully analyzed documents of the Inquisition. Most conversos identified themselves as sincere Christians; many came from families that had received baptism generations before. In response to conversos' statements, officials of the Inquisition developed a new type of anti-Semitism. A person's status as a Jew, they argued, could not be changed by religious conversion, but was in the person's blood and was heritable, so Jews could never be true Christians. In what were known as "purity of blood" laws, having pure Christian blood became a requirement for noble status. Ideas about Jews developed in Spain were important components in

European concepts of race, and discussions of "Jewish blood" later expanded into notions of the "Jewish race."

In 1492, shortly after the conquest of Granada, Isabella and Ferdinand issued an edict expelling all practicing Jews from Spain. Of the community of perhaps 200,000 Jews, 150,000 fled. Many Muslims in Granada were forcibly baptized and became another type of New Christian investigated by the Inquisition. Absolute religious orthodoxy and purity of blood served as the theoretical foundation of the Spanish national state.

The Spanish national state rested on marital politics as well as military victories and religious courts. Following their own example, the royal couple made astute marriages for their children with every country that could assist them against France, their most powerful neighbor. In 1496 Ferdinand and Isabella married their second daughter, Joanna, heiress to Castile,

## A Gold Coin of Ferdinand and Isabella

Minting coins provided a way for Renaissance monarchs to enhance their economies and also to show royal might and communicate other messages. This large gold coin, known as the "double excelente," was issued by the Seville mint in 1475, one year after Isabella had become queen in her own right of Castile and Ferdinand had become king because he was her husband. (Ferdinand would become king of Aragon in 1479 when his father died.) The eagle on the reverse holds both their coats of arms.

### EVALUATE THE EVIDENCE

1. What symbols of power are shown with the monarchs on the coin? How does the coin convey the fact that their marriage was the union of two rulers?
2. Rulers sometimes stipulated that all major transactions within their realms be carried out with certain coins, much the same way governments today allow only the national currency. What was their aim in doing this, and why might such policies have been hard to enforce?

(photos: Seville Mint, 1475/Fitzwilliam Museum, University of Cambridge, UK/Bridgeman Images)

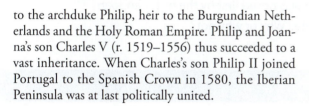

to the archduke Philip, heir to the Burgundian Netherlands and the Holy Roman Empire. Philip and Joanna's son Charles V (r. 1519–1556) thus succeeded to a vast inheritance. When Charles's son Philip II joined Portugal to the Spanish Crown in 1580, the Iberian Peninsula was at last politically united.

### NOTES

1. From *The Portable Renaissance Reader*, p. 27, by James B. Ross and Mary Martin McLaughlin, editors. Copyright 1953, 1968, renewed © 1981 by Penguin Random House LLC. Used by permission of Viking Books, an imprint of Penguin Publishing Group, a division of Penguin Random House LLC.
2. *The Portable Renaissance Reader*, pp. 480–481, 482, 492. Copyright 1953, 1968, renewed © 1981 by Penguin Random House LLC. Used by permission of Viking Books, an imprint of Penguin Publishing Group, a division of Penguin Random House LLC.
3. Niccolò Machiavelli, *The Prince*, trans. Leo Paul S. de Alvarez (Prospect Heights, Ill.: Waveland Press, 1980), p. 101.
4. Machiavelli, *The Prince*, p. 149.
5. Quoted in F. Seebohm, *The Oxford Reformers* (London: J. M. Dent & Sons, 1867), p. 256.
6. Quoted in Lauro Martines, *Power and Imagination: City-States in Renaissance Italy* (New York: Vintage Books, 1980), p. 253.
7. Quoted in J. Devisse and M. Mollat, *The Image of the Black in Western Art*, vol. 2, trans. W. G. Ryan (New York: William Morrow, 1979), pt. 2, pp. 187–188.
8. Stuttgart, Württembergische Hauptstaatsarchiv, Generalreskripta, A38, Bü. 2, 1550; trans. Merry Wiesner-Hanks.
9. Quoted in Benzion Netanyahu, *The Origins of the Inquisition in Fifteenth Century Spain* (New York: Random House, 1995), p. 921.

## LOOKING BACK  LOOKING AHEAD

The art historian Giorgio Vasari, who first called this era the Renaissance, thought that his contemporaries had both revived the classical past and gone beyond it. Vasari's judgment was echoed for centuries as historians sharply contrasted the art, architecture, educational ideas, social structures, and attitude toward life of the Renaissance with those of the Middle Ages: in this view, whereas the Middle Ages were corporate and religious, the Renaissance was individualistic and secular. More recently, historians and other scholars have stressed continuity as well as change. Families, kin networks, guilds, and other corporate groups remained important in the Renaissance, and religious belief remained firm. This re-evaluation changes our view of the relationship between the Middle Ages and the Renaissance.

It may also change our view of the relationship between the Renaissance and the dramatic changes in religion that occurred in Europe in the sixteenth century. Those religious changes, the Reformation, used to be viewed as a rejection of the values of the Renaissance and a return to the intense concern with religion of the Middle Ages. This idea of the Reformation as a sort of counter-Renaissance may be true to some degree, but there are powerful continuities as well. Both movements looked back to a time that people regarded as purer and better than their own, and both offered opportunities for strong individuals to shape their world in unexpected ways.

## Make Connections

Think about the larger developments and continuities within and across chapters.

1. The word *Renaissance*, invented to describe the cultural flowering in Italy that began in the fifteenth century, has often been used for other periods of advances in learning and the arts, such as the "Carolingian Renaissance" that you read about in Chapter 8. Can you think of other, more recent "Renaissances"? How else is the word used today?

2. Many artists in the Renaissance consciously modeled their works on those of ancient Greece (Chapters 3 and 4) and Rome (Chapters 5 and 6). Comparing the art and architecture shown in those chapters with those in this chapter, what similarities do you see? Are there aspects of classical art and architecture that were *not* emulated in the Renaissance? Why do you think this might be?

3. The Renaissance was clearly a period of cultural change for educated men. Given what you have read about women's lives and ideas about women in this and earlier chapters, did women have a Renaissance? (This question was posed first by the historian Joan Kelly in 1977 and remains a topic of great debate.) Why or why not?

## 12  REVIEW & EXPLORE

### Identify Key Terms

Identify and explain the significance of each item below.

Renaissance (p. 326)

patronage (p. 326)

communes (p. 326)

popolo (p. 327)

signori (p. 327)

courts (p. 327)

humanism (p. 331)

virtù (p. 331)

Christian humanists (p. 337)

debate about women (p. 348)

New Christians (p. 351)

### Review the Main Ideas

Answer the section heading questions from the chapter.

1. How did political and economic developments in Italy shape the Renaissance? (p. 326)

2. What new ideas were associated with the Renaissance? (p. 330)

3. How did art reflect new Renaissance ideals? (p. 341)

4. What were the key social hierarchies in Renaissance Europe? (p. 347)

5. How did nation-states develop in this period? (p. 350)

## Suggested Resources

### BOOKS

- Earle, T. F., and K. J. P. Lowe, eds. *Black Africans in Renaissance Europe*. 2005. Includes essays discussing many aspects of ideas about race and the experience of Africans in Europe.

- Eisenstein, Elizabeth. *The Printing Press as an Agent of Change: Communications and Cultural Transformations in Early Modern Europe*. 1979. The definitive study of the impact of printing.

- Ertman, Thomas. *The Birth of Leviathan: Building States and Regimes in Medieval and Early Modern Europe*. 1997. A good introduction to the creation of nation-states.

- Hartt, Frederick, and David Wilkins. *History of Italian Renaissance Art*, 7th ed. 2010. A comprehensive survey of painting, sculpture, and architecture in Italy.

- Jardine, Lisa. *Worldly Goods: A New History of the Renaissance*. 1998. Discusses changing notions of social status, artistic patronage, and consumer goods.

- Johnson, Geraldine. *Renaissance Art: A Very Short Introduction*. 2005. An excellent brief survey that includes male and female artists, and sets the art in its cultural and historical context.

- King, Ross. *Machiavelli: Philosopher of Power*. 2006. A brief biography that explores Machiavelli's thought in its social and political context.

- Man, John. *Gutenberg Revolution: The Story of a Genius and an Invention That Changed the World*. 2002. Presents a rather idealized view of Gutenberg, but has good discussions of his milieu and excellent illustrations.

- Najemy, John M. *A History of Florence, 1200–1575*. 2008. A comprehensive survey of cultural, political, and social developments, based on the newest research.

- Nauert, Charles. *Humanism and the Culture of Renaissance Europe*, 2d ed. 2006. A thorough introduction to humanism throughout Europe.

- Rummel, Erica. *Desiderius Erasmus*. 2006. An excellent short introduction to Erasmus as a scholar and Christian thinker.

- Waley, Daniel, and Trevor Dean. *The Italian City-Republics*, 4th ed. 2009. Analyzes the rise of independent city-states in northern Italy, including discussion of the artistic and social lives of their inhabitants.

- Wiesner-Hanks, Merry E. *Women and Gender in Early Modern Europe*, 4th ed. 2019. Discusses all aspects of women's lives and ideas about gender.

### MEDIA

- *The Agony and the Ecstasy* (Carol Reed, 1965). A classic film highlighting the conflict between Michelangelo and Pope Julius II over the painting of the Sistine Chapel, with Charlton Heston as the artist and Rex Harrison as the pope.

- *The Borgias* (Showtime, 2011). A fictionalized docudrama of the rise of the Borgia family to power in the church and in Italy, with Jeremy Irons as Pope Alexander VI.

- *Dangerous Beauty* (Marshall Herskovitz, 1998). A biographical drama about the life of Veronica Franco, a well-educated courtesan in sixteenth-century Venice, based on the biography of Franco written by Margaret Rosenthal.

- *Heilbrunn Timeline of Art History*. An online chronological, geographical, and thematic exploration of the history of art from around the world, run by the Metropolitan Museum of Art. It includes numerous special topics sections on nearly every aspect of

Renaissance art, and also on book production, musical instruments, clothing, household furnishings, and political and economic developments. **www .metmuseum.org/toah/**

- *Leonardo da Vinci* (BBC, 2004). A three-part documentary telling the life story of Leonardo as an artist, inventor, and engineer. Features tests of his designs for the parachute, tank, diving suit, and glider, and an investigation of the *Mona Lisa*.

- *Medici Archive Project*. An online database for researching the nearly 3 million letters held by the archives on the Medici Grand Dukes of Tuscany, who ruled Florence from 1537 to 1743. Includes topical "document highlights" in English and Italian, accompanied by illustrations. **www.medici.org/**

- *The Medici: Godfathers of the Renaissance* (PBS, 2004). A four-part documentary examining the power and patronage of the Medici family, shot on location, with extensive coverage of art and architecture.

# 13

# Reformations and Religious Wars

## 1500–1600

**Calls for reform of the Christian Church** began very early in its history. Throughout the centuries, many Christians believed that the early Christian Church represented a golden age, akin to the golden age of the classical past celebrated by Renaissance humanists. When Christianity became the official religion of the Roman Empire in the fourth century, many believers thought that the church had abandoned its original mission, and they called for a return to a church that was not linked to the state. Throughout the Middle Ages, individuals and groups argued that the church had become too wealthy and powerful and urged monasteries, convents, bishoprics, and the papacy to give up their property and focus on service to the poor. Some asserted that basic teachings of the church were not truly Christian and that changes were needed in theology as well as in institutional structures and practices. The Christian humanists of the late fifteenth and early sixteenth centuries such as Erasmus urged reform, primarily through educational and social change. What was new in the sixteenth century was the breadth of acceptance and the ultimate impact of the calls for reform. This acceptance was due not only to religious issues and problems within the church, but also to political and social factors. In 1500 there was one Christian Church in western Europe to which all Christians at least nominally belonged. One hundred years later there were many, a situation that continues today. ■

## CHAPTER PREVIEW

- What were the central ideas of the reformers, and why were they appealing to different social groups?

- How did the political situation in Germany shape the course of the Reformation?

- How did Protestant ideas and institutions spread beyond German-speaking lands?

- What reforms did the Catholic Church make, and how did it respond to Protestant reform movements?

- What were the causes and consequences of religious violence, including riots, wars, and witch-hunts?

**Religious Violence in the Reformation**

This 1590 painting shows Catholic military forces, including friars in their robes, parading through one of the many towns affected by the French religious wars that followed the Reformation. ("Procession of the Holy League" by François Bunel, 1590/Musée des Beaux-Arts, Valenciennes, France/Bridgeman Images)

# What were the central ideas of the reformers, and why were they appealing to different social groups?

In early-sixteenth-century Europe a wide range of people had grievances with the church. Educated laypeople such as Christian humanists and urban residents, villagers and artisans, and church officials themselves called for reform. This widespread dissatisfaction helps explain why the ideas of Martin Luther, an obscure professor from a new and not very prestigious German university, found a ready audience. Within a decade of his first publishing his ideas (using the new technology of the printing press), much of central Europe and Scandinavia had broken with the Catholic Church, and even more radical concepts of the Christian message were being developed and linked to calls for social change.

## The Christian Church in the Early Sixteenth Century

If external religious observances are an indication of conviction, Europeans in the early sixteenth century were deeply pious. People participated in processions, made pilgrimages to the great shrines, and devoted an enormous amount of their time and income to religious causes and organizations. Despite—or perhaps because of—the depth of their piety, many people were also highly critical of the Roman Catholic Church and its clergy. The papal conflict with the German emperor Frederick II in the thirteenth century, followed by the Babylonian Captivity and the Great Schism, badly damaged the prestige of church leaders, and the fifteenth-century popes' concentration on artistic patronage and building up family power did not help matters. Papal tax collection methods were attacked orally and in print. Some criticized the papacy itself as an institution, and even the great wealth and powerful courts of the entire church hierarchy. Some groups and individuals argued that certain doctrines taught by the church, such as the veneration of saints and the centrality of the sacraments, were incorrect. They suggested measures to reform institutions, improve clerical education and behavior, and alter basic doctrines. Occasionally these reform efforts had some success, and in at least one area, Bohemia (the modern-day Czech Republic), they led to the formation of a church independent of Rome a century before Luther (see "Critiques, Divisions, and Councils" in Chapter 11).

In the early sixteenth century court records, bishops' visitations of parishes, and popular songs and printed images show widespread **anticlericalism**, or opposition to the clergy. The critics concentrated primarily on three problems: clerical immorality, clerical ignorance, and clerical pluralism (the practice of holding more than one church office at a time), with the related problem of absenteeism. Many priests, monks, and nuns lived pious lives of devotion, learning, and service and had strong support from the laypeople in their areas, but everyone also knew (and repeated) stories about lecherous monks, lustful nuns, and greedy priests.

In regard to absenteeism and pluralism, many clerics held several benefices, or offices, simultaneously, but they seldom visited the benefices, let alone performed the spiritual responsibilities those offices entailed. Instead, they collected revenues from all of them and hired a poor priest, paying him just a fraction of the income to fulfill the spiritual duties of a particular local church. Many Italian officials in the papal curia, the pope's court in Rome, held benefices in England, Spain, and Germany. Revenues from those countries paid the Italian clerics' salaries, provoking not only charges of absenteeism but also nationalistic resentment aimed at the upper levels of the church hierarchy, which was increasingly viewed as foreign. This was particularly the case in Germany, where the lack of a strong central government to negotiate with the papacy meant that church demands for revenue were especially high.

There was also local resentment of clerical privileges and immunities. Priests, monks, and nuns were exempt from civic responsibilities, such as defending the city and paying taxes. Yet religious orders frequently held large amounts of urban property, in some cities as much as one-third. City governments were increasingly determined to integrate the clergy into civic life by reducing their privileges and giving them public responsibilities. Urban leaders wanted some say in who would be appointed to high church offices, rather than having this decided far away in Rome. This brought city leaders into opposition with bishops and the papacy, which for centuries had stressed the independence of the church from lay control and the distinction between members of the clergy and laypeople.

## Martin Luther

By itself, widespread criticism of the church did not lead to the dramatic changes of the sixteenth century. Instead, the personal religious struggle of a

■ **anticlericalism** Opposition to the clergy.

■ **indulgence** A document issued by the Catholic Church lessening penance or time in purgatory, widely believed to bring forgiveness of all sins.

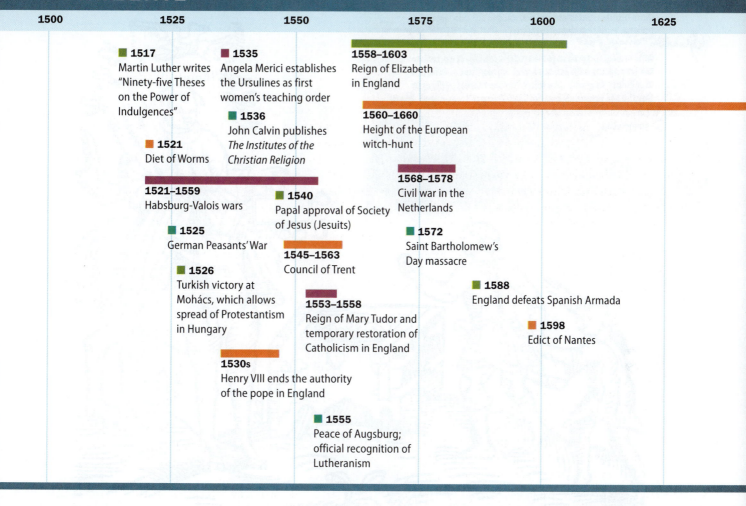

| | | | | | |
|---|---|---|---|---|---|
| 1500 | 1525 | 1550 | 1575 | 1600 | 1625 |

**1517**
Martin Luther writes "Ninety-five Theses on the Power of Indulgences"

**1535**
Angela Merici establishes the Ursulines as first women's teaching order

**1558–1603**
Reign of Elizabeth in England

**1536**
John Calvin publishes *The Institutes of the Christian Religion*

**1560–1660**
Height of the European witch-hunt

**1521**
Diet of Worms

**1521–1559**
Habsburg-Valois wars

**1540**
Papal approval of Society of Jesus (Jesuits)

**1568–1578**
Civil war in the Netherlands

**1525**
German Peasants' War

**1545–1563**
Council of Trent

**1572**
Saint Bartholomew's Day massacre

**1526**
Turkish victory at Mohács, which allows spread of Protestantism in Hungary

**1553–1558**
Reign of Mary Tudor and temporary restoration of Catholicism in England

**1588**
England defeats Spanish Armada

**1598**
Edict of Nantes

**1530s**
Henry VIII ends the authority of the pope in England

**1555**
Peace of Augsburg; official recognition of Lutheranism

German university professor and priest, Martin Luther (1483–1546), propelled the wave of movements we now call the Reformation. Luther's education was intended to prepare him for a legal career. Instead, however, a sense of religious calling led him to join the Augustinian friars, a religious order whose members often preached to, taught, and assisted the poor. (Religious orders were groups whose members took vows and followed a particular set of rules.) Luther was ordained a priest in 1507 and after additional study earned a doctorate of theology. From 1512 until his death in 1546, he served as professor of the Scriptures at the new University of Wittenberg.

Martin Luther was a very conscientious friar, but he was plagued with anxieties about sin and his ability to meet God's demands. Through his study of Saint Paul's letters in the New Testament, he gradually arrived at a new understanding of Christian doctrine. His understanding is often summarized as "faith alone, grace alone, Scripture alone." He believed that salvation and justification come through faith. Faith is a free gift of God's grace, not the result of human effort. God's word is revealed only in the Scriptures, not in the traditions of the church.

At the same time that Luther was engaged in scholarly reflections and professorial lecturing, Pope Leo X authorized the sale of a special Saint Peter's indulgence to finance his building plans in Rome. The archbishop who controlled the area in which Wittenberg was located, Albert of Mainz, was an enthusiastic promoter of this indulgence sale, from which he received a share of the profits.

What exactly was an **indulgence**? According to Catholic theology, individuals who sin could be reconciled to God by confessing their sins to a priest and by doing an assigned penance, such as praying or fasting. But beginning in the twelfth century learned theologians increasingly emphasized the idea of purgatory, a place where souls on their way to Heaven went to make further amends for their earthly sins. Both earthly penance and time in purgatory could be shortened by drawing on what was termed the "treasury of merits," which was a collection of all the virtuous acts that Christ, the apostles, and the saints had done during their lives. People thought of it as a sort of strongbox, like those in which merchants carried coins. An indulgence was a piece of parchment (later, paper), signed by the pope or another church official,

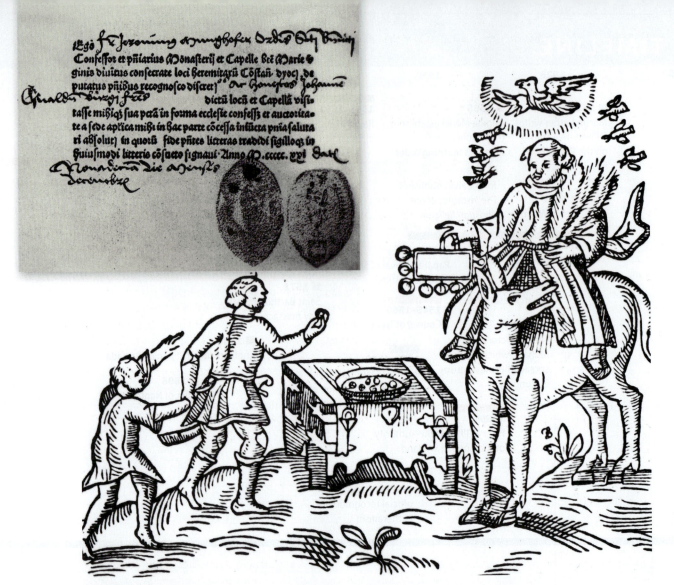

**Selling Indulgences**   A German single-page pamphlet shows a monk offering an indulgence, with the official seals of the pope attached, as people run to put their money in the box in exchange for his promise of heavenly bliss, symbolized by the dove above his head. Indulgences were sold widely in Germany and became the first Catholic practice that Luther criticized openly. This pamphlet also attacks the sale of indulgences, calling this practice devilish and deceitful, a point of view expressed in the woodcut by the peddler's riding on a donkey, an animal that had long been used as a symbol of ignorance. Indulgences were often printed fill-in-the-blank forms. This indulgence (upper left), purchased in 1521, has space for the indulgence seller's name at the top, the buyer's name in the middle, and the date at the bottom. (pamphlet: ullstein bild/Getty Images; indulgence: bpk, Bildagentur/Art Resource, NY)

that substituted a virtuous act from the treasury of merits for penance or time in purgatory.

Archbishop Albert's indulgence sale, run by a Dominican friar named Johann Tetzel who mounted an advertising blitz, promised that the purchase of indulgences would bring full forgiveness for one's own sins or release from purgatory for a loved one. One of the slogans—"As soon as coin in coffer rings, the soul from purgatory springs"—brought phenomenal success, and people traveled from miles around to buy indulgences.

Luther was severely troubled that many people believed they had no further need for repentance once they had purchased indulgences. In 1517 he wrote a letter to Archbishop Albert on the subject and enclosed in Latin his "Ninety-five Theses on the Power of Indulgences." His argument was that indulgences undermined the seriousness of the sacrament of penance, competed with the preaching of the Gospel, and downplayed the importance of charity in Christian life. After Luther's death, biographies reported that the theses were also nailed to the door of the church at Wittenberg Castle on October 31, 1517. Such an act would have been very strange—they were in Latin and written for those learned in theology, not for ordinary churchgoers—but it has become a standard part of Luther lore.

Whether the theses were posted or not, they were quickly printed, first in Latin and then in German translation. Luther was ordered to come to Rome, although because of the political situation in the empire, he was able instead to engage in formal scholarly debate with a representative of the church, Johann Eck, at Leipzig in 1519. He refused to take back his ideas and continued to develop his calls for reform, publicizing them in a series of pamphlets in which he moved further and further away from Catholic theology. Both popes and church councils could err, he wrote, and secular leaders should reform the church if the pope and clerical hierarchy did not. There was no distinction between clergy and laypeople, and requiring clergy to be celibate was a fruitless attempt to control a natural human drive. Luther clearly understood the power of the new medium of print, so he authorized the publication of his works.

The papacy responded with a letter condemning some of Luther's propositions, ordering that his books be burned, and giving him two months to recant or be excommunicated. Luther retaliated by publicly burning the letter. By 1521, when the excommunication was supposed to become final, Luther's theological issues had become interwoven with public controversies about the church's wealth, power, and basic structure. In this highly charged atmosphere, the twenty-one-year-old emperor Charles V held his first diet (assembly of representatives of the nobility, clergy, and cities of the Holy Roman Empire) in the German city of Worms and summoned Luther to appear. Luther refused to give in to demands that he take back his ideas. "Unless I am convinced by the evidence of Scripture or by plain reason," he said, "I cannot and will not recant anything, for it is neither safe nor right to go against conscience."[1] His appearance at the Diet of Worms in 1521 created an even broader audience for reform ideas, and throughout central Europe other individuals began to preach and publish against the existing doctrines and practices of the church, drawing on the long tradition of calls for change as well as on Luther's teachings.

## Protestant Thought

The most important early reformer other than Luther was the Swiss humanist, priest, and admirer of Erasmus, Ulrich Zwingli (ZWIHNG-lee) (1484–1531). Zwingli was convinced that Christian life rested on the Scriptures, which were the pure words of God and the sole basis of religious truth. He went on to attack indulgences, the Mass, the institution of monasticism, and clerical celibacy. In his gradual reform of the church in Zurich, which began in 1519, he had the strong support of the city authorities, who had long resented the privileges of the clergy.

The followers of Luther, Zwingli, and others who called for a break with Rome came to be called Protestants. The word **Protestant** derives from the protest drawn up by a small group of reforming German princes at the Diet of Speyer in 1529. The princes "protested" the decisions of the Catholic majority, and the word gradually became a general term applied to all non-Catholic western European Christians.

Luther, Zwingli, and other early Protestants agreed on many things. First, how is a person to be saved? Traditional Catholic teaching held that salvation is achieved by both faith and good works. Protestants held that salvation comes by faith alone, irrespective of good works or the sacraments. God, not people, initiates salvation. (See "Evaluating Written Evidence: Martin Luther, *On Christian Liberty*," page 362.) Second, where does religious authority reside? Christian doctrine had long maintained that authority rests both in the Bible and in the traditional teaching of the church. For Protestants, authority rested in the Bible alone. For a doctrine or issue to be valid, it had to have a scriptural basis. Because of this, most Protestants rejected Catholic teachings about the sacraments — the rituals that the church had defined as imparting God's benefits on the believer (see "Saints and Sacraments" in Chapter 10) — holding that only baptism and the Eucharist have scriptural support.

Third, what is the church? Protestants held that the church is a spiritual priesthood of all believers, an invisible fellowship not fixed in any place or person, which differed markedly from the Roman Catholic practice of a hierarchical clerical institution headed by the pope in Rome. Fourth, what is the highest form of Christian life? The medieval church had stressed the superiority of the monastic and religious life over the secular. Protestants disagreed and argued that every person should serve God in his or her individual calling.

Protestants did not agree on everything, and one important area of dispute was the ritual of the Eucharist (also called communion, the Lord's Supper, and, in Catholicism, the Mass). Catholicism holds the dogma of transubstantiation: by the consecrating words of the priest during the Mass, the bread and wine become the actual body and blood of Christ. Luther also believed that Christ was really present in the consecrated bread and wine, but held that this is the result of God's mystery, not the actions of a priest. Zwingli understood the Eucharist as a memorial in which Christ was present in spirit among the faithful, but not in the bread and wine. The Colloquy of Marburg, summoned in 1529 to unite Protestants, failed to resolve these differences, though Protestants reached agreement on almost everything else.

■ **Protestant** The name originally given to followers of Luther, which came to mean all non-Catholic Western Christian groups.

# Martin Luther, *On Christian Liberty*

The idea of liberty has a religious as well as political dimension, and the reformer Martin Luther formulated a classic interpretation of liberty in his treatise *On Christian Liberty* (sometimes translated as *On the Freedom of a Christian*), arguably his finest piece. Written in Latin for the pope but translated immediately into German and published widely, it contains the main themes of Luther's theology: the importance of faith, the relationship between Christian faith and good works, the dual nature of human beings, and the fundamental importance of the Scriptures.

A Christian man is the most free lord of all, and subject to none; a Christian man is the most dutiful servant of all, and subject to everyone. Although these statements appear contradictory, yet, when they are found to agree together, they will do excellently for my purpose. They are both the statements of Paul himself, who says, "Though I be free from all men, yet have I made myself a servant unto all" (I Corinthians 9:19) and "Owe no man anything but to love one another" (Romans 13:8). Now love is by its own nature dutiful and obedient to the beloved object. Thus even Christ, though Lord of all things, was yet made of a woman; made under the law; at once free and a servant; at once in the form of God and in the form of a servant.

Let us examine the subject on a deeper and less simple principle. Man is composed of a twofold nature, a spiritual and a bodily. As regards the spiritual nature, which they name the soul, he is called the spiritual, inward, new man; as regards the bodily nature, which they name the flesh, he is called the fleshly, outward, old man. . . .

We first approach the subject of the inward man, that we may see by what means a man becomes justified, free, and a true Christian; that is, a spiritual, new, and inward man. It is certain that absolutely none among outward things, under whatever name they may be reckoned, has any influence in producing Christian righteousness or liberty, nor, on the other hand, unrighteousness or slavery. This can be shown by an easy argument. What can it profit to the soul that the body should be in good condition, free, and full of life, that it should eat, drink, and act according to its pleasure, when even the most impious slaves of every kind of vice are prosperous in these matters? Again, what harm can ill health, bondage, hunger, thirst, or any other outward evil, do to the soul, when even the most pious of men, and the freest in the purity of their conscience, are harassed by these things? Neither of these states of things has to do with the liberty or the slavery of the soul. . . .

One thing, and one alone, is necessary for life, justification, and Christian liberty; and that is the most Holy Word of God, the Gospel of Christ, as He says, "I am the resurrection and the life; he that believeth in me shall not die eternally" (John 9:25), and also, "If the Son shall make you free, ye shall be free indeed" (John 8:36), and "Man shall not live by bread alone, but by every word that proceedeth out of the mouth of God" (Matthew 4:4).

Let us therefore hold it for certain and firmly established that the soul can do without everything except the Word of God, without which none at all of its wants is provided for. But, having the Word, it is rich and wants for nothing, since that is the Word of life, of truth, of light, of peace, of justification, of salvation, of joy, of liberty, of wisdom, of virtue, of grace, of glory, and of every good thing. . . .

But you will ask, "What is this Word, and by what means is it to be used, since there are so many words of God?" I answer, "The Apostle Paul (Romans 1) explains what it is, namely the Gospel of God, concerning His Son, incarnate, suffering, risen, and glorified through the Spirit, the Sanctifier." To preach Christ is to feed the soul, to justify it, to set it free, and to save it, if it believes the preaching. For faith alone, and the efficacious use of the Word of God, bring salvation. "If thou shalt confess with thy mouth the Lord Jesus, and shalt believe in thine heart that God hath raised Him from the dead, thou shalt be saved" (Romans 9:9); . . . and "The just shall live by faith" (Romans 1:17). . . .

And since it [faith] alone justifies, it is evident that by no outward work or labour can the inward man be at all justified, made free, and saved; and that no works whatever have any relation to him. . . . Therefore the first care of every Christian ought to be to lay aside all reliance on works, and strengthen his faith alone more and more, and by it grow in knowledge, not of works, but of Christ Jesus, who has suffered and risen again for him, as Peter teaches (I Peter 5).

## EVALUATE THE EVIDENCE

1. What did Luther mean by liberty?
2. Why, for Luther, were the Scriptures basic to Christian life?
3. For Luther, how were Christians made free?

Source: *Luther's Primary Works*, ed. H. Wace and C. A. Buchheim (London: Hodder and Stoughton, 1896), pp. 256–259.

## The Appeal of Protestant Ideas

Pulpits and printing presses spread the Protestant message all over Germany, and by the middle of the sixteenth century people of all social classes had rejected Catholic teachings and had become Protestant. What was the immense appeal of Luther's religious ideas and those of other Protestants?

Educated people and many humanists were much attracted by Luther's teachings. He advocated a simpler personal religion based on faith, a return to the spirit of the early church, the centrality of the Scriptures in the liturgy and in Christian life, and the abolition of elaborate ceremonies — precisely the reforms the Christian humanists had been calling for. The Protestant insistence that everyone should read and reflect on the Scriptures attracted literate and thoughtful city residents. This included many priests and monks who left the Catholic Church to become clergy in the new Protestant churches. In addition, townspeople who envied the church's wealth and resented paying for it were attracted by the notion that the clergy should also pay taxes and should not have special legal privileges.

Scholars in many disciplines have attributed Luther's fame and success to the invention of the printing press, which rapidly reproduced and made known his ideas. Many printed works included woodcuts and other illustrations, so that even those who could not read could grasp the main ideas. (See "Evaluating Visual Evidence: Lucas Cranach's *The True Church and the False Church*, ca. 1546," page 364.) Equally important was Luther's incredible skill with language, as seen in his two catechisms (compendiums of basic religious knowledge) and in hymns that he wrote for congregations to sing. Luther's linguistic skill, together with his translation of the New Testament into German in 1523, led to the acceptance of his dialect of German as the standard written version of the German language.

Both Luther and Zwingli recognized that for reforms to be permanent, political authorities as well as concerned individuals and religious leaders would

**The Four Apostles**   Albrecht Dürer, the most prominent artist north of the Alps, painted these panels of the four apostles (John, Peter, Paul, and Mark) in 1526 and gave them to the city of Nuremberg, where he lived and worked. Like many cities in Germany, Nuremberg had become officially Protestant, and paintings such as this that emphasized biblical figures and books rather than saints and miracles were appealing to city leaders. Whether Dürer himself had officially left the Catholic Church is not clear, but his letters indicate that he had Protestant sympathies, and he had contacts with many Christian humanists and reformers. (Alte Pinakothek, Munich, Germany/Bridgeman Images)

# Lucas Cranach's *The True Church and the False Church*, ca. 1546

Both Protestants and Catholics used art for propaganda purposes. Lucas Cranach the Elder (1472–1553) produced a huge number of altarpieces, portraits, mythological scenes, and engravings; he was one of Martin Luther's closest friends and created a style of art that reflected Protestant ideas and themes. His son Lucas Cranach the Younger (1515–1586) continued his father's legacy, often copying his most popular paintings and producing other works as well. In *The True Church and the False Church*, Lucas Cranach the Younger shows Luther standing in a pulpit, preaching the word of God from an open Bible. At the right, a flaming open mouth symbolizing the jaws of Hell engulfs the pope, cardinals, and friars, one kind of "false church." At the left, Cranach shows a crucified Christ emerging out of the "lamb of God" on the altar as people are receiving communion. This image of the "true church" represents the Lutheran understanding of the Lord's Supper, in which Christ is really present in the bread and wine. This contrasts with the view of other Protestants such as Zwingli, who saw the ceremony as a symbol or memorial, and which Cranach viewed as another kind of "false church."

(akg/Newscom)

## EVALUATE THE EVIDENCE

1. What does Cranach's woodcut convey about Catholic teachings? What does it suggest about Protestants who had a different interpretation than Luther's about the Lord's Supper?
2. Cranach's woodcut could be easily reproduced through the technology of the printing press. How would this have enhanced its impact?

have to accept them. Zwingli worked closely with the city council of Zurich, and city councils themselves took the lead in other cities and towns of Switzerland and south Germany. They appointed pastors who they knew had accepted Protestant ideas, required them to swear an oath of loyalty to the council, and oversaw their preaching and teaching.

Luther lived in a territory ruled by a noble — the elector of Saxony — and he also worked closely with political authorities, viewing them as fully justified in asserting control over the church in their territories. Indeed, he demanded that German rulers reform the papacy and its institutions, and he instructed all Christians to obey their secular rulers, whom he saw as divinely ordained to maintain order. Individuals may have been convinced of the truth of Protestant teachings by hearing sermons, listening to hymns, or reading pamphlets, but a territory became Protestant when its ruler, whether a noble or a city council, brought in a reformer or two to re-educate the territory's clergy, sponsored public sermons, and confiscated church property. This happened in many of the states of the Holy Roman Empire during the 1520s.

## The Radical Reformation and the German Peasants' War

While Luther and Zwingli worked with political authorities, some individuals and groups rejected the idea that church and state needed to be united. Beginning in the 1520s groups in Switzerland, Germany, and the Netherlands sought instead to create a voluntary community of believers separate from the state, as they understood it to have existed in New Testament times. In terms of theology and spiritual practices, these individuals and groups varied widely, though they are generally termed "radicals" for their insistence on a more extensive break with prevailing ideas. Some adopted the baptism of adult believers, for which they were called by their enemies "Anabaptists," which means "rebaptizers." (Early Christians had practiced adult baptism, but infant baptism became the norm, which meant that adults undergoing baptism were repeating the ritual.) Some groups attempted communal ownership of property, living very simply and rejecting anything they thought unbiblical. Some reacted harshly to members who deviated, but others argued for complete religious toleration and individualism.

The radicals' unwillingness to accept a state church marked them as societal outcasts and invited hatred and persecution, for both Protestant and Catholic authorities saw a state church as key to maintaining order. Anabaptists and other radicals were banished or cruelly executed by burning, beating, or drowning. (See "Individuals in Society: Anna Jansz of Rotterdam," page 366.) Their community spirit and heroism in the face of martyrdom, however, contributed to the survival of radical ideas. The opposition to the "establishment of religion" (state churches) in the U.S. Constitution is, in part, an outgrowth of the ideas of the radicals of the sixteenth century.

Radical reformers sometimes called for social as well as religious change, a message that resonated with the increasingly struggling German peasantry. In the early sixteenth century the economic condition of the peasantry varied from place to place but was generally worse than it had been in the fifteenth century and was deteriorating. Crop failures in 1523 and 1524 aggravated an explosive situation. Nobles had aggrieved peasants by seizing village common lands, by imposing new rents and requiring additional services, and by taking the peasants' best horses or cows whenever a head of household died. The peasants made demands that they believed conformed to the Scriptures, and they cited radical thinkers as well as Luther as proof that they did.

Initially Luther sided with the peasants, blasting the lords for robbing their subjects. But when rebellion broke out, peasants who expected Luther's support were soon disillusioned. Freedom for Luther meant independence from the authority of the Roman Church; it did not mean opposition to legally established secular powers. He maintained that the Scriptures had nothing to do with earthly justice or material gain, a position that Zwingli supported. Firmly convinced that rebellion would hasten the end of civilized society, Luther wrote the tract *Against the Murderous, Thieving Hordes of the Peasants*: "Let everyone who can smite, slay, and stab [the peasants], secretly and openly, remembering that nothing can be more poisonous, hurtful or devilish than a rebel."[2] The nobility ferociously crushed the revolt. Historians estimate that more than seventy-five thousand peasants were killed in 1525.

The German Peasants' War of 1525 greatly strengthened the authority of lay rulers. Not surprisingly, the Reformation lost much of its popular appeal after 1525, though peasants and urban rebels sometimes found a place for their social and religious ideas in radical groups. Peasants' economic conditions did moderately improve, however. For example, in many parts of Germany, enclosed fields, meadows, and forests were returned to common use.

## Marriage, Sexuality, and the Role of Women

Luther and Zwingli both believed that a priest's or nun's vows of celibacy went against human nature and God's commandments, and that marriage brought spiritual advantages and so was the ideal state for nearly all human beings. Luther married a former nun, Katharina von Bora (1499–1532), and Zwingli married a Zurich widow, Anna Reinhart (1491–1538). Both women quickly had several children. Most other Protestant reformers also married, and their wives had to create a new and respectable role for themselves—pastor's wife—to overcome being viewed as simply a new type of priest's concubine. They were living demonstrations of their husband's convictions about the superiority of marriage

# INDIVIDUALS IN SOCIETY

## Anna Jansz of Rotterdam

Anna Jansz (1509–1539) was born into a well-to-do family in the small city of Briel in the Netherlands. She married, and when she was in her early twenties she and her husband came to accept Anabaptism after listening to a traveling preacher. They were baptized in 1534 and became part of a group who believed that God would soon come to bring judgment on the wicked and deliver his true followers. Jansz wrote a hymn conveying these apocalyptic beliefs and foretelling vengeance on those who persecuted Anabaptists: "I hear the Trumpet sounding, From far off I hear her blast! . . . O murderous seed, what will you do? Offspring of Cain, you put to death The lambs of the Lord, without just cause—It will be doubly repaid to you! Death now comes riding on horseback, We have seen your fate! The sword is passing over the land, With which you will be killed and slain, And you will not escape from Hell!"

An etching of Anna Jansz on the way to her execution, from a 1685 Anabaptist martyrology. (Used by permission of the Mennonite Historical Library, Goshen College, Indiana)

Jansz and her husband traveled to England, where she had a child, but in November 1538 she and her infant son, Isaiah, returned to the Netherlands, along with another woman. As the story was later told, the two women were recognized as Anabaptists by another traveler because of songs they were singing, perhaps her "Trumpet Song" among them. They were arrested and interrogated in the city of Rotterdam, and sentenced to death by drowning. The day she was executed—January 24, 1539—Anna Jansz wrote a long testament to her son, providing him with spiritual advice: "My son, hear the instruction of your mother, and open your ears to hear the words of my mouth. Watch, today I am travelling the path of the Prophets, Apostles, and Martyrs, and drink from the cup from which they have all tasted. . . . But if you hear of the existence of a poor, lowly, cast-out little company, that has been despised and rejected by the World, go join it. . . . Honor the Lord through the works of your hands. Let the light of Scripture shine in you. Love your Neighbor; with an effusive, passionate heart deal your bread to the hungry."

Anabaptists later compiled accounts of trials and executions, along with letters and other records, into martyrologies designed to inspire deeper faith. One of the most widely read of these describes Jansz on her way to the execution. She offered a certain amount of money to anyone who would care for her son; a poor baker with six children agreed, and she passed the child to him. The martyrology reports that the baker later became quite wealthy, and that her son, Isaiah, became mayor of the city of Rotterdam. As such, he would have easily been able to read the court records of his mother's trial.

Anna Jansz was one of thousands of people executed for their religious beliefs in sixteenth-century Europe. A few of these were high-profile individuals such as Thomas More, the Catholic former chancellor of England executed by King Henry VIII, but most were quite ordinary people. Many were women. Women's and men's experiences of martyrdom were similar in many ways, but women also confronted additional challenges. Some were pregnant while in prison—execution was delayed until the baby was born—or, like Jansz, had infants with them. They faced procedures of questioning, torture, and execution that brought dishonor as well as pain. Eventually many Anabaptists, as well as others whose religion put them in opposition to their rulers, migrated to parts of Europe that were more tolerant. By the seventeenth century the Netherlands had become one of the most tolerant places in Europe, and Rotterdam was no longer the site of executions for religious reasons.

### QUESTIONS FOR ANALYSIS

1. How did religion, gender, and social class all shape Jansz's experiences and the writings that she left behind?
2. Why might Jansz's hymn and her Anabaptist beliefs have seemed threatening to those who did not share her beliefs?

Source: Quotations from *Elisabeth's Manly Courage: Testimonials and Songs of Martyred Anabaptist Women in the Low Countries*, ed. and trans. Hermina Joldersma and Louis Peter Grijp (Milwaukee: Marquette University Press, 2001).

**Martin Luther and Katharina von Bora**    Lucas Cranach the Elder painted this double marriage portrait to celebrate Luther's wedding in 1525 to Katharina von Bora, a former nun. The artist was one of the witnesses at the wedding and, in fact, had presented Luther's marriage proposal to Katharina. Using a go-between for proposals was very common, as was having a double wedding portrait painted. This particular couple quickly became a model of the ideal marriage, and many churches wanted their portraits. More than sixty similar paintings, with slight variations, were produced by Cranach's workshop and hung in churches and wealthy homes. (Galleria degli Uffizi, Florence, Italy/Alinari/Bridgeman Images)

to celibacy, and they were expected to be models of wifely obedience and Christian charity.

Though they denied that marriage was a sacrament, Protestant reformers stressed that it had been ordained by God when he presented Eve to Adam, served as a "remedy" for the unavoidable sin of lust, provided a site for the pious rearing of the next generation of God-fearing Christians, and offered husbands and wives companionship and consolation. A proper marriage was one that reflected both the spiritual equality of men and women and the proper social hierarchy of husbandly authority and wifely obedience.

Protestants did not break with medieval Scholastic theologians in their idea that women were to be subject to men. Women were advised to be cheerful rather than grudging in their obedience, for in doing so they demonstrated their willingness to follow God's plan. Men were urged to treat their wives kindly and considerately, but also to enforce their authority, through physical coercion if necessary. European marriage manuals used the metaphor of breaking a horse for teaching a wife obedience, though laws did set limits on the husband's power to do so.

Most Protestants came to allow divorce and remarriage for marriages that were irretrievably broken. Protestant allowance of divorce differed markedly from Catholic doctrine, which viewed marriage as a sacramental union that, if validly entered into, could not be dissolved (Catholic canon law allowed only separation with no remarriage). Although permitting divorce was a dramatic legal change, it did not have a dramatic impact on newly Protestant areas. Because marriage was the cornerstone of society socially and economically, divorce was a desperate last resort. In many Protestant jurisdictions the annual divorce rate hovered around 0.02 to 0.06 per thousand people. (By contrast, in 2016 the U.S. divorce rate was 3.2 per thousand people.)

As Protestants believed marriage was the only proper remedy for lust, they uniformly condemned prostitution. The licensed brothels that were a common feature of late medieval urban life (see "Sex in the City" in Chapter 11) were closed in Protestant cities, and harsh punishments were set for prostitution. Many Catholic cities soon closed their brothels as well, although Italian cities favored stricter regulations rather than closure. Selling sex was couched in moral rather than economic terms, as simply one type of "whoredom," a term that also included premarital sex, adultery, and other unacceptable sexual activities. *Whore* was also a term that reformers used for their theological opponents; Protestants compared the pope to the biblical whore of Babylon, a symbol of the end of the world, while Catholics called Luther's wife a whore because she had first been married to Christ as a nun before her marriage to Luther. Closing brothels did not end the exchange of sex for money, of course, but simply reshaped it. Smaller illegal brothels were established, or women selling sex moved to areas right outside city walls.

The Protestant Reformation raised the status of marriage in people's minds, but its impact on women was more mixed. Many nuns were in convents not out of a strong sense of religious calling, but because their parents placed them there. Convents nevertheless provided women of the upper classes with an opportunity to use their literary, artistic, medical, or administrative talents if they could not or would not marry. The Reformation generally brought the closing of monasteries and convents, and marriage became virtually the only occupation for upper-class Protestant women. Women in some convents recognized this and fought the Reformation, or argued that they could still be pious Protestants within convent walls. Most nuns left, however, and we do not know what happened to them. The Protestant emphasis on marriage made unmarried women (and men) suspect, for they did not belong to the type of household regarded as the cornerstone of a proper, godly society.

A few women took Luther's idea about the priesthood of all believers to heart and wrote religious works. Argula von Grumbach, a German noblewoman, supported Protestant ideas in print, asserting, "I am not unfamiliar with Paul's words that women should be silent in church but when I see that no man will or can speak, I am driven by the word of God when he said, he who confesses me on earth, him will I confess, and he who denies me, him will I deny."[3] No sixteenth-century Protestants allowed women to be members of the clergy, however, though monarchs such as Elizabeth I of England and female territorial rulers of the states of the Holy Roman Empire did determine religious policies just as male rulers did.

# How did the political situation in Germany shape the course of the Reformation?

Although criticism of the church was widespread in Europe in the early sixteenth century, reform movements could be more easily squelched by the strong central governments that had evolved in Spain and France. England, too, had a strong monarchy, but the king broke from the Catholic Church for other reasons (see "Henry VIII and the Reformation in England" later in this chapter). The Holy Roman Empire, in contrast, included hundreds of largely independent states. Against this background of decentralization and strong local power, Martin Luther had launched a movement to reform the church. Two years after he published the "Ninety-five Theses," the electors of the Holy Roman Empire chose as emperor a nineteen-year-old Habsburg prince who ruled as Charles V (r. 1519–1556). The course of the Reformation was shaped by this election and by the political relationships surrounding it.

## The Rise of the Habsburg Dynasty

War and diplomacy were important ways that states increased their power in sixteenth-century Europe, but so was marriage. Royal and noble sons and daughters were important tools of state policy. The benefits of an advantageous marriage stretched across generations, a process that can be seen most dramatically with the Habsburgs. The Holy Roman emperor Frederick III, a Habsburg who was the ruler of most of Austria, acquired only a small amount of territory—but a great deal of money—with his marriage to Princess Eleonore of Portugal in 1452. He arranged for his son Maximilian to marry Europe's most prominent heiress, Mary of Burgundy, in 1477; she inherited the Netherlands, Luxembourg, and the County of Burgundy in what is now eastern France. Through this union with the rich and powerful duchy of Burgundy, the Austrian house of Habsburg, already the strongest ruling family in the empire, became an international power. The marriage of Maximilian and Mary angered the French, however, who considered Burgundy French territory, and inaugurated centuries of conflict between the Austrian house of Habsburg and the kings of France.

Maximilian learned the lesson of marital politics well, marrying his son and daughter to the children of Ferdinand and Isabella, the rulers of Spain, much of southern Italy, and eventually the Spanish New World empire. His grandson Charles V fell heir to a vast and incredibly diverse collection of states and peoples, each governed in a different manner and held together only by the person of the emperor (Map 13.1). Charles, raised in the Netherlands but spending much of his later life in Spain, remained a Catholic and was convinced that it was his duty to maintain the political and religious unity of Western Christendom.

## Religious Wars in Switzerland and Germany

In the sixteenth century the practice of religion remained a public matter. The ruler determined the official form of religious practice in his (or occasionally her) jurisdiction. Almost everyone believed that the presence of a faith different from that of the majority represented a political threat to the security of the state, and few believed in religious liberty.

Luther's ideas appealed to German rulers for a variety of reasons. Though Germany was not a nation, people did have an understanding of being German because of their language and traditions. Luther frequently used the phrase "we Germans" in his attacks on the papacy. Luther's appeal to national feeling influenced many rulers otherwise confused by or indifferent to the complexities of the religious matters of the time. Some German rulers were sincerely attracted to Lutheran ideas, but material considerations swayed many others to embrace the new faith. The rejection of Roman Catholicism and adoption of Protestantism would mean the legal confiscation of lush farmlands, rich monasteries, and wealthy shrines. Thus many political authorities in the empire became Protestant in part to extend their financial and political power and to enhance their independence from the emperor.

**MAP 13.1** **The Global Empire of Charles V, ca. 1556**    Charles V exercised theoretical jurisdiction over more European territory than anyone since Charlemagne. He also claimed authority over large parts of North and South America (see Map 14.2 on page 399), though actual Spanish control was weak in much of the area.

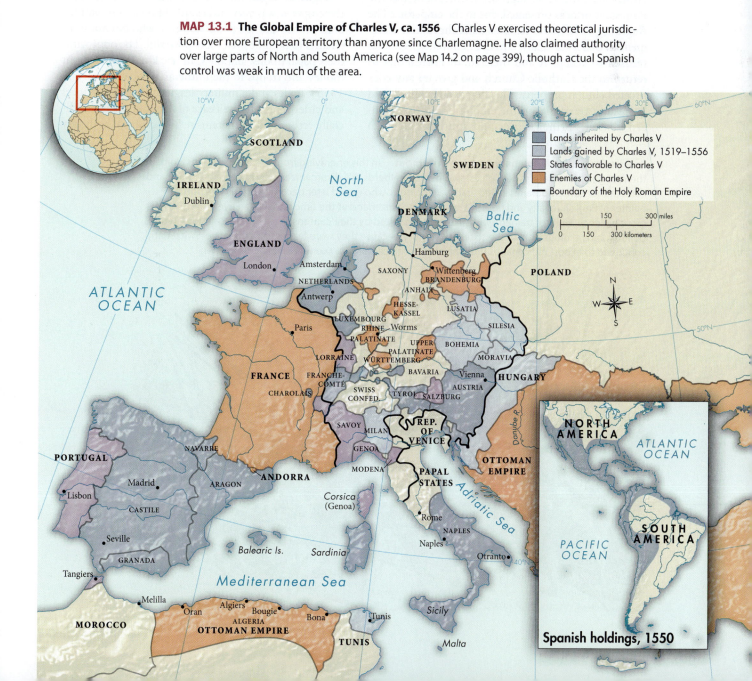

Charles V was a vigorous defender of Catholicism, so it is not surprising that the Reformation led to religious wars. The first battleground was Switzerland, which was officially part of the Holy Roman Empire, though it was really a loose confederation of thirteen largely autonomous territories called cantons. Some cantons remained Catholic, and some became Protestant, and in the late 1520s the two sides went to war. Zwingli was killed on the battlefield in 1531, and both sides quickly decided that a treaty was preferable to further fighting. The treaty basically allowed each canton to determine its own religion and ordered each side to give up its foreign alliances, a policy of neutrality that has been characteristic of modern Switzerland.

Trying to halt the spread of religious division, Charles V called an Imperial Diet in 1530, to meet at Augsburg. The Lutherans developed a statement of faith, later called the Augsburg Confession, and the Protestant princes presented this to the emperor. (The Augsburg Confession remains an authoritative statement of belief for many Lutheran churches.) Charles refused to accept it and ordered all Protestants to return to the Catholic Church and give up any confiscated church property. This demand backfired, and Protestant territories in the empire—mostly northern German principalities and southern German cities—formed a military alliance. The emperor could not respond militarily, as he was in the midst of a series of wars with the French: the Habsburg-Valois wars (1521–1559). The Ottoman Turks had also taken much of Hungary and in 1529 were besieging Vienna.

The 1530s and early 1540s saw complicated political maneuvering among many of the powers of Europe. Various attempts were made to heal the religious split with a church council, but stubbornness on both sides made it increasingly clear that this would not be possible and that war was inevitable. Charles V realized that he was fighting not only for religious unity, but also for a more unified state, against territorial rulers who wanted to maintain their independence. He was thus defending both church and empire.

Fighting began in Germany in 1546, and initially the emperor was very successful. This success alarmed both France and the pope, however, who did not want Charles to become even more powerful. The pope withdrew papal troops, and the Catholic king of France sent money and troops to the Lutheran princes. Finally, in 1555 Charles and a military league of German princes and cities agreed to the Peace of Augsburg, which officially recognized Lutheranism. The political authority

**Swiss and German Mercenary Soldiers in Combat**   In this engraving from the 1520s by Hans Holbein the Younger, foot soldiers wield pikes, swords, and halberds in a disorganized way in fierce hand-to-hand combat that contemporaries called "bad war." Holbein, who would later become famous as a portrait painter of English royalty and nobles, was living in Switzerland at the time and was an eyewitness to religious violence. Units of trained Swiss pikemen, organized by their cantons, were hired by all sides in the political and religious wars of the sixteenth century because they were fearless and effective. Switzerland continued to export mercenaries until the nineteenth century. (De Agostini Picture Library/Getty Images)

in each territory within the Holy Roman Empire was permitted to decide whether the territory would be Catholic or Lutheran. Most of northern and central Germany became Lutheran, while the south remained Roman Catholic. There was no freedom of religion within the territories, however. Princes or town councils established state churches to which all subjects of the area had to belong, and those who disagreed had to convert or leave. Religious refugees became a common feature on the roads of the empire, and eventually in other parts of Europe as well.

The Peace of Augsburg ended religious war in Germany for many decades. His hope of uniting his empire under a single church dashed, Charles V abdicated in 1556 and moved to a monastery, transferring power over his holdings in Spain and the Netherlands to his son Philip and his imperial power to his brother Ferdinand.

# How did Protestant ideas and institutions spread beyond German-speaking lands?

States within the Holy Roman Empire were the earliest territories to accept the Protestant Reformation, but by the later 1520s and 1530s religious change came to Denmark-Norway, Sweden, England, France, and eastern Europe. In most of these areas, a second generation of reformers, the most important of whom was John Calvin, built on Lutheran and Zwinglian ideas to develop their own theology and plans for institutional change.

## Scandinavia

The first area outside the empire to officially accept the Reformation was the kingdom of Denmark-Norway under King Christian III (r. 1536–1559). Danish scholars studied at the University of Wittenberg, and Lutheran ideas spread into Denmark very quickly. In the 1530s the king officially broke with the Catholic Church, and most clergy followed. The process went smoothly in Denmark, but in northern Norway and Iceland (which Christian also ruled) there were violent reactions, and Lutheranism was only gradually imposed on a largely unwilling populace.

In Sweden, Gustavus Vasa (r. 1523–1560), who came to the throne during a civil war with Denmark, also took over control of church personnel and income. Protestant ideas spread, though the Swedish Church did not officially accept Lutheran theology until later in the century.

## Henry VIII and the Reformation in England

As on the continent, the Reformation in England had economic and political as well as religious causes. The impetus for England's break with Rome was the desire of King Henry VIII (r. 1509–1547) for a new wife, though his own motives also included political, social, and economic elements.

Henry VIII was married to Catherine of Aragon, the daughter of Ferdinand and Isabella and widow of Henry's older brother, Arthur. Marriage to a brother's widow went against canon law, and Henry had been required to obtain a special papal dispensation to marry Catherine. The marriage had produced only one living heir, a daughter, Mary. By 1527 Henry decided that God was showing his displeasure with the marriage by denying him a son, and he appealed to the pope to have the marriage annulled. He was also in love with a court lady in waiting, Anne Boleyn, and assumed that she would give him the son he wanted. Normally an annulment would not have been a problem, but the troops of Emperor Charles V were in Rome at that point, and Pope Clement VII was essentially their prisoner. Charles V was the nephew of Catherine of Aragon and thus was vigorously opposed to an annulment.

With Rome thwarting his matrimonial plans, Henry decided to remove the English Church from papal jurisdiction. In a series of measures during the 1530s, Henry used Parliament to end the authority of the pope and make himself the supreme head of the church in England. Some opposed the king and were beheaded, among them Thomas More, the king's chancellor and author of *Utopia* (see "Christian Humanism" in Chapter 12). When Anne Boleyn failed twice to produce a male child, Henry VIII charged her with adulterous incest and in 1536 had her beheaded. His third wife, Jane Seymour, gave Henry the desired son, Edward, but she died a few days after childbirth. Henry went on to three more wives.

Theologically, Henry was conservative, and the English Church retained such traditional Catholic practices and doctrines as confession, clerical celibacy, and transubstantiation. Under the influence of his chief minister, Thomas Cromwell, and the man he had appointed archbishop of Canterbury, Thomas Cranmer, he did agree to place an English Bible in every church. He also decided to dissolve the English monasteries, primarily because he wanted their wealth. Working through Parliament, between 1535 and 1539 the king ended nine hundred years of

**Allegory of the Tudor Dynasty**    The unknown creator of this work intended to glorify the virtues of the Protestant succession; the painting has no historical reality. Henry VIII (seated) hands the sword of justice to his Protestant son Edward VI. The Catholic queen Mary and her husband, Philip of Spain (left), are followed by Mars, god of war, signifying violence and civil disorder. At right the figures of Peace and Plenty accompany the Protestant Elizabeth I, symbolizing England's happy fate under her rule. (Yale Center for British Art, Paul Mellon Collection, USA/Bridgeman Images)

English monastic life, dispersing the monks and nuns and confiscating their lands. Hundreds of properties went first into the royal treasury and then were sold to the middle and upper classes, which tied them to both the Tudor dynasty and the new Protestant Church.

The nationalization of the church and the dissolution of the monasteries led to important changes in government administration. Vast tracts of formerly monastic land came temporarily under the Crown's jurisdiction, and new bureaucratic machinery had to be developed to manage those properties. Cromwell reformed and centralized the king's household, the council, the secretariats, and the Exchequer. New departments of state were set up. Surplus funds from all departments went into a liquid fund to be applied to areas where there were deficits. This balancing resulted in greater efficiency and economy, and Henry VIII's reign saw the growth of the modern centralized bureaucratic state.

Did the religious changes under Henry VIII have broad popular support? Historians disagree about this.

Some English people had been dissatisfied with the existing Christian Church before Henry's measures, and Protestant literature circulated. Traditional Catholicism exerted an enormously strong and vigorous hold over the imagination and loyalty of the people, however. Most clergy and officials accepted Henry's moves, but all did not quietly acquiesce. In 1536 popular opposition in the north to the religious changes led to the Pilgrimage of Grace, a massive rebellion that proved the most serious uprising in Tudor history. The "pilgrims" accepted a truce, but their leaders were arrested, tried, and executed. Recent scholarship points out that people rarely "converted" from Catholicism to Protestantism overnight. People responded to an action of the Crown that was played out in their own neighborhood—the closing of a monastery, the ending of Masses for the dead—with a combination of resistance, acceptance, and collaboration. Some enthusiastically changed to Protestant forms of prayer, for example, while others recited Protestant prayers in church while keeping pictures of the Catholic saints at home.

Loyalty to the Catholic Church was particularly strong in Ireland. Ireland had been claimed by English

■ **Spanish Armada**    The fleet sent by Philip II of Spain in 1588 against England as a religious crusade against Protestantism. Weather and the English fleet defeated it.

kings since the twelfth century, but in reality the English had firm control of only the area around Dublin, known as the Pale. In 1536, on orders from London, the Irish Parliament, which represented only the English landlords and the people of the Pale, approved the English laws severing the church from Rome. The Church of Ireland was established on the English pattern, and the (English) ruling class adopted the new reformed faith. Most of the Irish people remained Roman Catholic, thus adding religious antagonism to the ethnic hostility that had been a feature of English policy toward Ireland for centuries (see "Ethnic Tensions and Restrictions" in Chapter 11). The Roman Church was essentially driven underground, and the Catholic clergy acted as national as well as religious leaders.

## Upholding Protestantism in England

In the short reign of Henry's sickly son, Edward VI (r. 1547–1553), Protestant ideas exerted a significant influence on the religious life of the country. Archbishop Thomas Cranmer simplified the liturgy, invited Protestant theologians to England, and prepared the first *Book of Common Prayer* (1549), a book of services and prayers, which was later approved by Parliament.

The equally brief reign of Mary Tudor (r. 1553–1558) witnessed a sharp move back to Catholicism. The devoutly Catholic daughter of Catherine of Aragon, Mary rescinded the Reformation legislation of her father's reign and restored Roman Catholicism. Mary's marriage to her cousin Philip II of Spain (r. 1556–1598), son of the emperor Charles V, proved highly unpopular in England, and her execution of several hundred Protestants further alienated her subjects. During her reign, about a thousand Protestants fled to the continent. Mary's death raised to the throne her half-sister Elizabeth, Henry's daughter with Anne Boleyn, who had been raised a Protestant. Elizabeth's reign from 1558 to 1603 inaugurated the beginnings of religious stability.

At the start of Elizabeth's reign, sharp religious differences existed in England. On the one hand, Catholics wanted a Roman Catholic ruler. On the other hand, a vocal number of returning exiles wanted all Catholic elements in the Church of

**The Route of the Spanish Armada, 1588**

England eliminated. The latter, because they wanted to "purify" the church, were called "Puritans."

Shrewdly, Elizabeth chose a middle course between Catholic and Puritan extremes. Working through Parliament, she ordered church and government officials to swear that she was supreme in matters of religion as well as politics, required her subjects to attend services in the Church of England or risk a fine, and called for frequent preaching of Protestant ideas. She did not interfere with people's privately held beliefs, however. As she put it, she did not "want to make windows into men's souls." The Anglican Church, as the Church of England was called, moved in a moderately Protestant direction. Services were conducted in English, monasteries were not re-established, and clergymen were allowed to marry. But the church remained hierarchical, with archbishops and bishops, and services continued to be elaborate, with the clergy in distinctive robes, in contrast to the simpler services favored by many continental Protestants and English Puritans.

Toward the end of the sixteenth century Elizabeth's reign was threatened by European powers attempting to re-establish Catholicism. Philip II of Spain had hoped that his marriage to Mary Tudor would reunite England with Catholic Europe, but Mary's death ended those plans. Another Mary — Mary, Queen of Scots (r. 1560–1567) — provided a new opportunity. Mary was Elizabeth's cousin, but she was Catholic. Mary was next in line to the English throne, and Elizabeth imprisoned her because she worried — quite rightly — that Mary would become the center of Catholic plots to overthrow her. In 1587 Mary became implicated in a plot to assassinate Elizabeth, a conspiracy that had Philip II's full backing. When the English executed Mary, the Catholic pope urged Philip to retaliate.

Philip prepared a vast fleet to sail from Lisbon to Flanders, where a large army of Spanish troops was stationed because of religious wars in the Netherlands (see "The Netherlands Under Charles V" later in this chapter). The Spanish ships were to escort barges carrying some of the troops across the English Channel to attack England. On May 9, 1588, the **Spanish Armada,** composed of more than 130 vessels, sailed from Lisbon harbor. It met an

English fleet in the Channel before it reached Flanders. A combination of storms and squalls, spoiled food and rank water, inadequate Spanish ammunition, and, to a lesser extent, English fire ships that caused the Spanish to scatter gave England the victory. On the journey home many Spanish ships went down in the rough seas around Ireland; perhaps sixty-five ships managed to reach home ports.

The battle in the English Channel has frequently been described as one of the decisive battles in world history. In fact, it had mixed consequences. Spain soon rebuilt its navy, and after 1588 the quality of the Spanish fleet improved. The war between England and Spain dragged on for years. Yet the defeat of the Spanish Armada prevented Philip II from reimposing Catholicism on England by force. In England the victory contributed to a David and Goliath legend that enhanced English national sentiment.

## Calvinism

In 1509, while Luther was preparing for a doctorate at Wittenberg, John Calvin (1509–1564) was born in Noyon in northwestern France. As a young man he studied law, which had a decisive impact on his mind and later his thought. In 1533 he experienced a religious crisis, as a result of which he converted to Protestantism.

Calvin believed that God had specifically selected him to reform the church. Accordingly, he accepted an invitation to assist in the reformation of the city of Geneva. There, beginning in 1541, Calvin worked assiduously to establish a well-disciplined Christian society in which church and state acted together.

To understand Calvin's Geneva, it is necessary to understand Calvin's ideas. These he embodied in *The Institutes of the Christian Religion*, published first in 1536 and in its final form in 1559. The cornerstone of Calvin's theology was his belief in the absolute sovereignty and omnipotence of God and the total weakness of humanity. Before the infinite power of God, he asserted, men and women are as insignificant as grains of sand.

Calvin did not ascribe free will to human beings because that would detract from the sovereignty of God. Men and women cannot actively work to achieve salvation; rather, God in his infinite wisdom decided at the beginning of time who would be saved and who damned. This viewpoint constitutes the theological principle called **predestination**. Calvin explained his view:

> Predestination we call the eternal decree of God, by which he has determined in himself, what he would have become of every individual. . . . For they are not all created with a similar destiny; but eternal life is foreordained for some, and eternal damnation for others. . . . To those whom he devotes to condemnation, the gate of life is closed by a just and irreprehensible, but incomprehensible, judgment. How exceedingly presumptuous it is only to inquire into the causes of the Divine will; which is in fact, and is justly entitled to be, the cause of everything that exists. . . . For the will of God is the highest justice; so that what he wills must be considered just, for this very reason, because he wills it.[4]

Many people consider the doctrine of predestination, which dates back to Saint Augustine and Saint Paul, to be a pessimistic view of the nature of God. But "this terrible decree," as even Calvin called it, did not lead to pessimism or fatalism. Instead, many Calvinists came to believe that although one's own actions could do nothing to change one's fate, hard work, thrift, and proper moral conduct could serve as signs that one was among the "elect" chosen for salvation.

Calvin transformed Geneva into a community based on his religious principles. The most powerful organization in the city became the Consistory, a group of laymen and pastors charged with investigating and disciplining deviations from proper doctrine and conduct. (See "Thinking Like a Historian: Social Discipline in the Reformation," page 376.)

Serious crimes and heresy were handled by the civil authorities, which, with the Consistory's approval, sometimes used torture to extract confessions. Between 1542 and 1546 alone seventy-six persons were banished from Geneva, and fifty-eight were executed for heresy, adultery, blasphemy, and witchcraft (see "The Great European Witch-Hunt" at the end of this chapter).

Geneva became the model of a Christian community for many Protestant reformers. Religious refugees from France, England, Spain, Scotland, and Italy visited Calvin's Geneva, and many of the most prominent exiles from Mary Tudor's England stayed. Subsequently, the church of Calvin—often termed "Reformed"—served as the model for the Presbyterian Church in Scotland, the Huguenot Church in France (see "French Religious Wars" later in this chapter), and the Puritan churches in England and New England.

Calvinism became the compelling force in international Protestantism in the sixteenth and seventeenth centuries. Calvinists believed that any occupation could be a God-given "calling," and should be carried out with diligence and dedication. This doctrine encouraged an aggressive, vigorous activism in both work and religious life. Consistories, boards of elders and ministers, were established in Calvinist congregations, with regional elected bodies usually called presbyteries having authority over some issues. Church services became simpler but longer, with a focus on the sermon, and art and ornamentation were removed from churches, with the pulpit rather than an elaborate altar in the middle of the church. (See "Viewpoints: Catholic and Calvinist Churches," page 378.)

Calvinism spread on the continent of Europe, and also found a ready audience in Scotland. There, as elsewhere, political authority was the decisive influence in reform. King James V and his daughter Mary, Queen of Scots, staunch Catholics and close allies of Catholic France, opposed reform, but the Scottish nobles supported it. One man, John Knox (1505?–1572), dominated the reform movement, which led to the establishment of a state church. Knox was determined to structure the Scottish Church after the model of Geneva, where he had studied and worked with Calvin. In 1560 Knox persuaded the Scottish Parliament, which was dominated by reform-minded barons, to end papal authority and rule by bishops, substituting governance by presbyteries. The Presbyterian Church of Scotland was strictly Calvinist in doctrine, and, as with Calvinists everywhere, adopted a simple and dignified service of worship, with great emphasis on preaching.

## The Reformation in Eastern Europe

While political and economic issues determined the course of the Reformation in western and northern Europe, ethnic factors often proved decisive in eastern Europe, where people of diverse backgrounds had settled in the later Middle Ages. In Bohemia in the fifteenth century, a Czech majority was ruled by Germans. Most Czechs had adopted the ideas of Jan Hus, and the emperor had been forced to recognize a separate Hussite Church (see "Critiques, Divisions, and Councils" in Chapter 11). Yet Lutheranism appealed to Germans in Bohemia in the 1520s and 1530s, and the nobility embraced Lutheranism in opposition to the Catholic Habsburgs. The forces of the Catholic Reformation (see "Papal Reform and the Council of Trent" later in the chapter) promoted a Catholic spiritual

revival in Bohemia, and some areas reconverted. This complicated situation would be one of the causes of the Thirty Years' War in the early seventeenth century.

By 1500 Poland and the Grand Duchy of Lithuania were jointly governed by king, senate, and diet (parliament), but the two territories retained separate officials, judicial systems, armies, and forms of citizenship. The population of Poland-Lithuania was also very diverse; Germans, Italians, Tartars, and Jews lived among Poles and Lithuanians. Such peoples had come as merchants, invited by medieval rulers because of their wealth or to make agricultural improvements. Each group spoke its native language, though all educated people spoke Latin. Luther's ideas took root in Germanized towns but were opposed by King Sigismund I (r. 1506–1548) as well as by ordinary Poles, who held strong anti-German feeling. The Reformed tradition of John Calvin, with its stress on the power of church elders, appealed to the Polish nobility, however. The fact that Calvinism originated in France, not in Germany, also made it more attractive than Lutheranism. But doctrinal differences among Calvinists, Lutherans, and other groups prevented united opposition to Catholicism, and a Catholic Counter-Reformation gained momentum. By 1650, due largely to the efforts of the Jesuits (see "New and Reformed Religious Orders" in this chapter), Poland was again staunchly Roman Catholic.

Hungary's experience with the Reformation was even more complex. Lutheranism was spread by Hungarian students who had studied at Wittenberg, and sympathy for it developed at the royal court of King Louis II in Buda. But concern about "the German heresy" by the Catholic hierarchy and among the high nobles found expression in a decree of the Hungarian Diet in 1523 that Lutherans and those who favored them should be executed and their property confiscated.

Before such measures could be acted on, a military event on August 26, 1526, had profound consequences for both the Hungarian state and the Protestant Reformation there. On the plain of Mohács in southern Hungary, the Ottoman sultan Suleiman the Magnificent inflicted a crushing defeat on the Hungarians, killing King Louis II, many of the nobles, and more than sixteen thousand ordinary soldiers. The Hungarian kingdom was then divided into three parts: the Ottoman Turks absorbed the great plains, including the capital, Buda; the Habsburgs ruled the north and west; and Ottoman-supported Janos Zapolya held eastern Hungary and Transylvania.

■ ***The Institutes of the Christian Religion*** Calvin's formulation of Christian doctrine, which became a systematic theology for Protestantism.

■ **predestination** The teaching that God has determined the salvation or damnation of individuals based on his will and purpose, not on their merit or works.

## Social Discipline in the Reformation

Both Protestant and Catholic leaders thought it important that people understand the basics of their particular version of Christianity, and they also wanted people to lead proper, godly lives. How and why did religious and secular authorities try to shape people's behavior?

### 1 Ordinances in Calvin's Geneva, 1547.

**Blasphemy:** Whoever shall have blasphemed, swearing by the body or by the blood of our Lord, or in similar manner, he shall be made to kiss the earth for the first offence; for the second to pay 5 sous, and for the third 6 sous, and for the last offence be put in the pillory [a wooden frame set up in a public place, in which a person's head and hands could be locked] for one hour.

**Drunkenness:** No one shall invite another to drink under penalty of 3 sous. Taverns shall be closed during the sermon, under penalty that the tavern-keeper shall pay 3 sous, and whoever may be found therein shall pay the same amount. If anyone be found intoxicated he shall pay for the first offence 3 sous and shall be remanded to the consistory; for the second offence he shall be held to pay the sum of 6 sous, and for the third 10 sous and be put in prison.

**Songs and Dances:** If anyone sing immoral, dissolute or outrageous songs, or dance the *virollet* or other dance, he shall be put in prison for three days and then sent to the consistory.

**Usury:** No one shall take upon interest or profit [on a loan] more than five percent, upon penalty of confiscation of the principal and of being condemned to make restitution as the case may demand.

**Games:** No one shall play at any dissolute game or at any game whatsoever it may be, neither for gold nor silver nor for any excessive stake, upon penalty of 5 sous and forfeiture of the stake played for.

### 2 Ordinances of the (Lutheran) city of Malmø, Denmark, 1540.

No one should be sitting and drinking alcohol during the sermon on Sundays or other holy days, nor should anyone wander around in the street or in the chapel behind the choir during the sermon. Nor should any [wine] cellar be opened on aforesaid days before the noonday sermon is over, unless it is done for the sake of strangers and travelers who arrive and want to leave at once. Whoever breaks this rule will be punished accordingly.

All single men and unemployed manservants should at once appear at the City Hall and swear an oath to the Mayors and the Council acting on behalf of His Royal Majesty and the city of Malmø [that they will try to find a position as a servant or journeyman] or they should at once be expelled from the city. Similarly, all girls who are self-supporting should enter into service again or be expelled from the city.

### 3 School ordinance from the (Lutheran) duchy of Württemberg, 1559.

Each pastor shall make in his sermons serious admonitions to parishioners that they must be diligent in sending their children to school. And let him stress the great benefit bound to come from this, schools being necessary not only for learning the liberal arts, but also the fear of God, virtue, and discipline. Where the young are neglected and kept out of school, permanent harm, both eternal and temporal, must result, as children grow up without fear and knowledge of God, like dumb beasts of the field, learning nothing about what is needed for their salvation, nor what is useful to them and their neighbors in worldly life. And the pastor shall inform them, furthermore, that school-mastering is a troublesome office and laborious, thankless work for which teachers should be honored and respected, and their hard-earned pay given to them willingly and without grudge. . . . In addition, all parents are obliged on the danger

## ANALYZING THE EVIDENCE

1. Given the actions prohibited or required in the ordinances, how would you describe ideal Christian behavior, in the eyes of religious and political authorities?
2. What would an ideal Christian household look and sound like? An ideal community?
3. Are there differences between Protestant and Catholic visions of ideal households and communities, and if so, how do these distinctions relate to differences in theology or institutional structures?
4. Judging by the two visitation reports in Sources 5 and 6, did measures like those in Sources 1–3 work? What other sources would allow you to better assess this?

of losing their souls to teach the catechism to their children and domestic servants. Ask them also what they remember from last Sunday's sermon, and, if they remember nothing, admonish them to pay closer attention. And if kind words don't help, take the stick to them or give them nothing to eat and drink for supper until they have repeated something from the sermon.

**4** **Decrees of the Council of Trent, 1563.** Like Protestant authorities, the Roman Catholic Council of Trent (see "Papal Reform and the Council of Trent") also issued decrees about teaching and behavior.

〜 That the faithful may approach the sacraments with greater reverence and devotion of mind, the holy Council commands all bishops that not only when they themselves are about to administer them to the people, they shall first, in a manner adapted to the mental ability of those who receive them, explain their efficacy and use, but also that they shall see to it that the same is done piously and prudently by every parish priest, and in the vernacular tongue. . . . In like manner shall they explain on all festivals and solemnities during the solemnization of the Mass or the celebration of divine office, in the vernacular tongue, the divine commands and the maxims of salvation, and leaving aside useless questions, let them strive to engraft these things on the hearts of all and instruct them in the law of the Lord. . . .

When therefore anyone has publicly and in the sight of many committed a crime by which there is no doubt that others have been offended and scandalized, it is proper that a penance commensurate with his guilt be publicly imposed on him, so that those whom he by his example has led to evil morals, he may bring back to an upright life by the evidence of his correction.

**5** **Visitation report from (Catholic) Ourense, Spain, 1566.** Visitations were inspection tours by religious and secular officials in which they traveled from village to village, trying to assess how well ordinances were actually being followed.

〜 His majesty is informed that on past visits Gregorio Gomez and Alonso Galente, inhabitants of Dacon, Juan de Mondian and Juan Bernáldez, inhabitants of Toscana, and Gabriel de Dacon, all tavern owners, were admonished not to open the taverns nor sell wine, bread or meat to the parishioners on Sundays and holidays before High Mass. They have not wanted to comply, opening the taverns and selling wine and meat so that the parishioners quit coming to Mass in order to be there playing and drinking. Being compassionate with them he fines each one of them three reales [a very small amount] for the fabric of the church for this first time, except Alonso Galente, who is fined only one and a half reales on account of his poverty. Henceforth, they will be fined one ducat for each time that they open during the Mass.

**6** **Visitation report from (Lutheran) Nassau-Wiesbaden, Germany, 1594.**

〜 First, gruesome cursing and blaspheming, as for instance "by God," "by God's Holy Cross," "by God's Passion, death, flesh, blood, heart, hand, etc.," "A Thousand Sacraments," "thunder and hail," "earth." Also dreadful swearing by various fears, epidemics, and injuries. These oaths are very common among young and old, women as well as men. People cannot carry on a friendly chat, or even address their children, without the use of these words. And none of them considers it a sin to swear.

Everyone is very lax about going to church, both young and old. Many have not been seen by their pastor in a year or more. . . . Those who come to service are usually drunk. As soon as they sit down they lean their heads on their arms and sleep through the whole sermon, except that sometimes they fall off the benches, making a great clatter, or women drop their babies on the floor. . . . At times the wailing of babies is so loud the preacher cannot make himself heard in the church. And the moment that the sermon ends, everyone runs out. No one stays for the hymn, prayer, or blessing. They behave as if they were at a dance, not a divine service. . . . On Sunday afternoons, hardly ten or fifteen of the 150 householders come to catechism practice, nor do they oblige their children and servants to attend. Instead they loaf at home, or sit about gossiping.

## PUTTING IT ALL TOGETHER

Using the sources above, along with what you have learned in class and in this chapter, write a short essay that analyzes social discipline in the Reformation. How and why did religious and secular authorities try to shape people's behavior and instill morality and piety? Were they successful?

Sources: (1) Merrick Whitcomb, ed., *Translations and Reprints from the Original Sources of European History*, vol. 3 (Philadelphia: University of Pennsylvania, 1897), no. 3, pp. 10–11; (2) *Malmø standsbog 1549–1559* (Copenhagen: Selskabet for Udgivelse af Kilder til dansk Historie, 1952), p. 35. Trans. Grethe Jacobsen and Pernille Arenfeldt; (3) Gerald Strauss, *Luther's House of Learning: Indoctrination of the Young in the German Reformation* (Baltimore: Johns Hopkins University Press, 1978), pp. 45–46; (4) H. J. Schroeder, *Canons and Decrees of the Council of Trent* (St. Louis: B. Herder, 1941), pp. 197–198; (5) *Libro de Visitas,* Santa Maria Amarante, Archivo Histórico Diocesano de Ourense, 24.1.13, fols. 9–10, 1566. Trans. Allyson Poska; (6) Strauss, *Luther's House of Learning,* pp. 283–284.

**Old Church, Delft (built thirteenth century)** (By Hendrik Cornelisz van Vliet, [ca. 1611–1675]/Johnny van Haeften Gallery, London, UK/Bridgeman Images)

**Church of St. Ignatius, Rome (built 1626–1650)** (Adam Eastland/ Alamy)

Protestant and Catholic ideas were expressed orally and in writing, and also in the churches in which services were held. The church on the left is a painting made by Hendrik Cornelisz van Vliet (ca. 1611–1675) of the Old Church in Delft in the Netherlands, where the painter himself would be buried. Built originally in the thirteenth century, the church was the scene of iconoclasm in the 1560s that removed or destroyed much of the artwork. It was then renovated to fit with the Calvinist principles of the Dutch Reformed Church, with the pulpit for the preacher in the middle of the church. The Catholic church on the right is the Church of St. Ignatius at Campius Martius in Rome, built between 1626 and 1650 and dedicated to the founder of the Jesuits. The interior was designed by Orazio Grazzi (1583–1684), himself a Jesuit, in the powerful new style later labeled "baroque," with elaborate Corinthian pillars, colored marble, many stucco figures, paintings on the walls and ceiling, and a gilded high altar.

### QUESTIONS FOR ANALYSIS

1. Imagine yourself a worshipper or visitor to each of these churches. How would you describe their interiors and the mood they convey?
2. How do these interiors reflect and express Calvinist and Catholic ideas?

The Turks were indifferent to the religious conflicts of Christians, whom they regarded as infidels. Christians of all types paid extra taxes to the sultan, but kept their faith. Many Magyar (Hungarian) nobles accepted Lutheranism; Lutheran schools and parishes headed by men educated at Wittenberg multiplied; and peasants welcomed the new faith. The majority of Hungarian people were Protestant until the late seventeenth century, when Hungarian nobles recognized Habsburg (Catholic) rule and Ottoman Turkish withdrawal in 1699 led to Catholic restoration.

# What reforms did the Catholic Church make, and how did it respond to Protestant reform movements?

Between 1517 and 1547 Protestantism made remarkable advances. Nevertheless, the Roman Catholic Church made a significant comeback. After about 1540 no new large areas of Europe, other than the Netherlands, accepted Protestant beliefs (Map 13.2). Many historians see the developments within the Catholic Church after the Protestant Reformation as two interrelated movements: one a drive for internal reform linked to earlier reform efforts, the other a Counter-Reformation that opposed Protestants intellectually, politically, militarily, and institutionally. In both movements, the papacy, new religious orders, and the Council of Trent that met from 1545 to 1563 were important agents.

## Papal Reform and the Council of Trent

Renaissance popes and their advisers were not blind to the need for church reforms, but they resisted calls for a general council representing the entire church, and feared that any transformation would mean a loss of power, revenue, and prestige. This changed beginning with Pope Paul III (pontificate 1534–1549), when the papal court became the center of the reform movement rather than its chief opponent. The lives of the pope and his reform-minded cardinals, abbots, and bishops were models of decorum and piety, in contrast to Renaissance popes, who concentrated on building churches and enhancing the power of their own families. Paul III and his successors supported improvements in education for the clergy, the end of simony (the selling of church offices), and stricter control of clerical life.

In 1542 Pope Paul III established the Supreme Sacred Congregation of the Roman and Universal Inquisition, often called the **Holy Office**, with jurisdiction over the Roman Inquisition, a powerful instrument of the Catholic Reformation. The Roman Inquisition was a committee of six cardinals with judicial authority over all Catholics and the power to arrest, imprison, and execute suspected heretics. The Holy Office published the *Index of Prohibited Books*, a catalogue of forbidden reading that included works by Christian humanists such as Erasmus as well as by Protestants. Within the Papal States the Inquisition effectively destroyed heresy, but outside the papal territories its influence was slight.

Pope Paul III also called a general council that met intermittently from 1545 to 1563 at Trent, an imperial city close to Italy. The council was called to reform the Catholic Church and to secure reconciliation with the Protestants, though the latter proved impossible. Nonetheless, the decrees of the Council of Trent laid a solid basis for the spiritual renewal of the Catholic Church. They gave equal validity to the Scriptures and to tradition as sources of religious truth and authority. They also reaffirmed the seven sacraments and the traditional Catholic teaching on transubstantiation. They tackled the disciplinary matters that had disillusioned the faithful, including absenteeism, pluralism, priests having sex with local women or keeping concubines, and the selling of church offices. Bishops were given greater authority and ordered to establish a seminary in their diocese for the education and training of the clergy. Seminary professors were to determine whether candidates for ordination had vocations, or genuine callings to the priesthood. This was a novel idea, since from the time of the early church, parents had determined their sons' (and daughters') religious careers. For the first time, great emphasis was laid on preaching and instructing the laity, especially the uneducated. (See "Thinking Like a Historian: Social Discipline in the Reformation," page 376.)

One decision had especially important social consequences for laypeople. The Council of Trent stipulated that for a marriage to be valid, the marriage vows had to be made publicly before a priest and witnesses. Trent thereby ended the widespread practice of private marriages in Catholic countries, curtailing the number of denials and conflicts that inevitably resulted from marriages that took place in secret.

Although it did not achieve all of its goals, the Council of Trent composed decrees that laid a solid basis for the spiritual renewal of the church. The

■ **Holy Office** The official Roman Catholic agency founded in 1542 to combat international doctrinal heresy.

**Predominant religion in 1555**

- Lutheran
- Calvinist (Reformed)
- Church of England
- Roman Catholic
- Eastern Orthodox
- Muslim
- → Spread of Calvinism, from 1541
- ▲ Huguenot center
- — Ottoman Empire, 1566

Penetration of Calvinism to England after 1558

Wittenberg
Martin Luther writes
Ninety-five Theses
1517

Worms
Edict of Worms
1521

Nantes
Edict of Nantes
1598

Trent
Council of Trent
1545–1563

Augsburg
Peace of Augsburg
1555

Geneva
Calvin assists in
Reformation beginning
in 1541

**MAPPING THE PAST**

## MAP 13.2  Religious Divisions in Europe, ca. 1555

The Reformations shattered the religious unity of Western Christendom. The situation was even more complicated than a map of this scale can show. Many cities within the Holy Roman Empire, for example, accepted a different faith than the surrounding countryside; Augsburg, Basel, and Strasbourg were all Protestant, though surrounded by territory ruled by Catholic nobles.

**ANALYZING THE MAP**  Which countries were the most religiously diverse in Europe? Which were the least diverse?

**CONNECTIONS**  Where was the first arena of religious conflict in sixteenth-century Europe, and why did it develop there and not elsewhere? To what degree can nonreligious factors be used as an explanation for the religious divisions in sixteenth-century Europe?

**Pasquale Cati, *The Council of Trent* (1588)**    Cati's imagined depiction of the Council of Trent, painted for a church in Rome twenty-five years after the council ended, shows the representatives seated in rows, with the cardinals in front. Cati includes allegorical female figures in the foreground, and at their center the Church Triumphant, wearing the papal tiara and the splendid white robe of doctrinal clarity and trampling a figure representing the enemies of Catholicism. (Fresco by Pasquale Cati [1550–1620]/Santa Maria in Trastevere, Rome, Italy/Bridgeman Images)

doctrinal and disciplinary legislation of Trent served as the basis for Roman Catholic faith, organization, and practice through the middle of the twentieth century.

## New and Reformed Religious Orders

Just as seminaries provided education, so did religious orders, which aimed at raising the moral and intellectual level of the clergy and people. The monasteries and convents of many existing religious orders were reformed so that they followed more rigorous standards. In Spain, for example, the Carmelite nun Teresa of Ávila (1515–1582) traveled around the country reforming her Carmelite order to bring it back to stricter standards of asceticism and poverty, a task she understood God had set for her in mystical visions, which she described in her own writings. Some officials in the church criticized her as a "restless gadabout, a disobedient and obstinate woman" who had gone against Saint Paul's commands that women were not to teach. At one point she was even investigated by the Spanish Inquisition in an effort to make sure her inspiration came from God and not the Devil. The process was dropped, however, and she founded many new convents, which she saw as answers to the Protestant takeover of Catholic churches elsewhere in Europe. "We shall fight for Him [God]," she wrote, "even though we are very cloistered."[5]

New religious orders were founded, some of which focused on education. The Ursuline order of nuns, for example, founded in 1535 by Angela Merici (1474–1540), focused on the education of women. The Ursulines concentrated on teaching young girls, with the goal of re-Christianizing society by training future wives and mothers. After receiving papal approval in 1565, the Ursulines rapidly spread to France and the New World.

The most significant new order was the Society of Jesus, or **Jesuits**. Founded by Ignatius Loyola (1491–1556), the Jesuits played a powerful international role in strengthening Catholicism in Europe and spreading the faith around the world. While recuperating from a severe battle wound in his legs, Loyola studied books about Christ and the saints and decided to give up his military career and become a soldier of Christ. During a year spent in seclusion, prayer, and asceticism, he gained insights that went into his great classic, *Spiritual Exercises* (1548). This

■ **Jesuits**  Members of the Society of Jesus, founded by Ignatius Loyola, whose goal was the spread of the Roman Catholic faith.

work, intended for study during a four-week period of retreat, set out a training program of structured meditation designed to develop spiritual discipline and allow one to meld one's will with that of God. Loyola introduces his program:

> By the term "Spiritual Exercises" is meant every method of examination of conscience, of meditation, of contemplation, of vocal and mental prayer, and of other spiritual activities. For just as taking a walk, journeying on foot, and running are bodily exercises, so we call Spiritual Exercises every way of preparing and disposing the soul to rid itself of all inordinate attachments, and, after their removal, of seeking and finding the will of God in the disposition of our life for the salvation of our soul.[6]

Just like today's physical trainers, Loyola provides daily exercises that build in intensity over the four weeks of the program, as well as charts on which the exerciser can track his progress.

Loyola was a man of considerable personal magnetism. After study at universities in Salamanca and Paris, he gathered a group of six companions and in 1540 secured papal approval of the new Society of Jesus. The first Jesuits, recruited primarily from wealthy merchant and professional families, saw their mission as improving people's spiritual condition rather than altering doctrine. Their goal was not to reform the church, but "to help souls."

The Society of Jesus developed into a highly centralized, tightly knit organization. In addition to the traditional vows of poverty, chastity, and obedience, professed members vowed special obedience to the pope. Flexibility and the willingness to respond to the needs of time and circumstance formed the Jesuit tradition, which proved attractive to many young men. The Jesuits achieved phenomenal success for the papacy and the reformed Catholic Church, carrying Christianity to India and Japan before 1550 and to Brazil, North America, and the Congo in the seventeenth century. Within Europe the Jesuits brought southern Germany and much of eastern Europe back to Catholicism. Jesuit schools adopted the modern humanist curricula and methods, educating the sons of the nobility as well as the poor. As confessors and spiritual directors to kings, Jesuits exerted great political influence.

Revitalization of the Catholic Church was not simply a matter of the church hierarchy and new religious orders, but also of devotional life at the local level. Confraternities of laypeople were established or expanded in many parishes, which held processions and feasts, handed out charity, and supported the church financially. The papacy, the Jesuits, and other patrons built and renovated churches and chapels, often filling them with objects and paintings, as they thought dramatic art would glorify the reformed and reinvigorated Catholic Church, appealing to the senses and proclaiming the power of the church to all who looked at paintings or sculpture or worshipped in churches. (See "Viewpoints: Catholic and Calvinist Churches," page 378.)

# What were the causes and consequences of religious violence, including riots, wars, and witch-hunts?

In 1559, France and Spain signed the Treaty of Cateau-Cambrésis (CAH-toh kam-BRAY-sees), which ended the long conflict known as the Habsburg-Valois wars. Spain was the victor. France, exhausted by the struggle, had to acknowledge Spanish dominance in Italy, where much of the fighting had taken place. However, true peace was elusive, and over the next century religious differences led to riots, civil wars, and international conflicts. Especially in France and the Netherlands, Protestants and Catholics used violent actions as well as preaching and teaching against each other, for each side regarded the other as a poison in the community that would provoke the wrath of God. Catholics continued to believe that Calvinists and Lutherans could be reconverted; Protestants persisted in thinking that the Roman Church should be destroyed. Catholics and Protestants alike feared people of other faiths, whom they often saw

as agents of Satan. Even more, they feared those who were explicitly identified with Satan: witches living in their midst. This era was the time of the most virulent witch persecutions in European history, as both Protestants and Catholics tried to make their cities and states more godly.

## French Religious Wars

The costs of the Habsburg-Valois wars, waged intermittently through the first half of the sixteenth century, forced the French to increase taxes and borrow heavily. King Francis I (r. 1515–1547) also tried two new devices to raise revenue: the sale of public offices and a treaty with the papacy. The former proved to be only a temporary source of money: once a man bought an office, he and his heirs were exempt from taxation. But the latter, known as the Concordat of Bologna

**Spanish Soldiers Killing Protestants in Haarlem** In this engraving by the Calvinist artist Franz Hogenberg, Spanish soldiers accompanied by priests kill residents of the Dutch city of Haarlem by hanging or beheading, and then dump their bodies in the river. Haarlem had withstood a seven-month siege by Spanish troops in 1572–1573, and after the starving city surrendered, the garrison of troops and forty citizens judged guilty of sedition were executed. Images such as this were part of the propaganda battle that accompanied the wars of religion, but in many cases there were actual atrocities, on both sides. (Private Collection/Bridgeman Images)

(see "France" in Chapter 12), gave the French Crown the right to appoint all French bishops and abbots and require them to pay taxes to the Crown. Because French rulers possessed control over the personnel of the church and had a vested financial interest in Catholicism, they had no need to revolt against Rome.

Significant numbers of those ruled, however, were attracted to the Reformed religion of Calvinism. Initially, Calvinism drew converts from among reform-minded members of the Catholic clergy, industrious city dwellers, and artisan groups. Most French Calvinists, called **Huguenots**, lived in major cities, such as Paris, Lyons, and Rouen. By the time King Henry II (r. 1547–1559) died in 1559—accidentally shot in the face at a tournament celebrating the Treaty of Cateau-Cambrésis—perhaps one-tenth of the population had become Calvinist.

Strong religious fervor combined with a weak French monarchy led to civil violence. Both Calvinists and Catholics believed that the other's books, services, and ministers polluted the community, and preachers incited violence. The three weak sons of Henry II who occupied the throne could not provide the necessary leadership, and they were often dominated by their mother, Catherine de' Medici. The French nobility took advantage of this monarchical weakness. Just as German princes in the Holy Roman Empire had adopted Lutheranism as a means of opposition to Emperor Charles V, so French nobles frequently adopted Protestantism as a religious cloak for their independence. Armed clashes between the forces of Catholic royalist lords and Calvinist antimonarchical lords occurred in many parts of France, beginning a series of religious wars that lasted for decades.

Calvinist teachings called the power of sacred images into question, and mobs in many cities took down and smashed statues, stained-glass windows, and paintings, viewing this as a way to purify the church. Though it was often inspired by fiery Protestant sermons, this iconoclasm, or destruction of religious images, is an example of ordinary men and women carrying out the Reformation themselves. Catholic mobs responded by defending images, and crowds on both sides killed their opponents, often in gruesome ways.

A savage Catholic attack on Calvinists in Paris on Saint Bartholomew's Day, August 24, 1572, followed the usual pattern. This happened a few days after the marriage ceremony of the king's sister Margaret of Valois to the Protestant Henry of Navarre, which was intended to help reconcile Catholics and Huguenots. Instead, Huguenot leaders who had come to Paris to attend the wedding were massacred by the king's soldiers. Other Protestants were slaughtered by mobs and their houses looted. Traditionally Catherine de' Medici was blamed for instigating this violence, but more recently historians have pointed to other members of the royal family and to Catholic fears of a Protestant takeover. The massacre spread to the provinces, where thousands of Protestants were killed by Catholic mobs who thought they were doing God's and the king's will. The Saint Bartholomew's Day massacre led to a renewal of the wars of religion, which dragged on for decades.

What ultimately saved France was a small group of moderates of both faiths, called **politiques**, who

■ **Huguenots** French Calvinists.

■ **politiques** Catholic and Protestant moderates who held that only a strong monarchy could save France from total collapse.

believed that only the restoration of a strong monarchy could reverse the trend toward collapse. The politiques also favored accepting the Huguenots as an officially recognized and organized group. The death of Catherine de' Medici, followed by the assassination of King Henry III, paved the way for the accession of Henry of Navarre (the unfortunate bridegroom of the Saint Bartholomew's Day massacre), a politique who became Henry IV (r. 1589–1610).

Henry's willingness to sacrifice religious principles to political necessity saved France. He converted to Catholicism but also issued the **Edict of Nantes** in 1598, which granted liberty of conscience and liberty of public worship to Huguenots in 150 fortified towns. The reign of Henry IV and the Edict of Nantes prepared the way for French absolutism in the seventeenth century by helping restore internal peace in France.

## The Netherlands Under Charles V

In the Netherlands, what began as a movement for the reformation of the church developed into a struggle for independence. Emperor Charles V had inherited the seventeen provinces that compose present-day Belgium and the Netherlands. In the Low Countries, as elsewhere, corruption in the Roman Church and the critical spirit of the Renaissance provoked pressure for reform, and Lutheran ideas took root. Charles V had grown up in the Netherlands, however, and he was able to limit the impact of Protestant ideas. But Charles V abdicated in 1556 and transferred power over the Netherlands to his son Philip II, who had grown up in Spain.

Protestant ideas spread, and by the 1560s Protestants in the Netherlands were primarily Calvinists. Calvinism's intellectual seriousness, moral gravity, and emphasis on any form of labor well done appealed to urban merchants, financiers, and artisans. Whereas Lutherans taught respect for the powers that be, Calvinists tended to encourage opposition to political authorities who were judged to be ungodly. Thus when Spanish authorities attempted to suppress Calvinist worship and raised taxes in the 1560s, rioting ensued. Calvinists sacked thirty

United Provinces
Spanish Netherlands
Treaty line, 1609

North Sea
Amsterdam
Utrecht
Bruges
Ghent
Antwerp
Brussels
HOLY ROMAN EMPIRE
FRANCE

**The Netherlands, 1609**

Catholic churches in Antwerp, destroying the religious images in them in a wave of iconoclasm. From Antwerp the destruction spread. Philip II sent twenty thousand Spanish troops under the duke of Alva to pacify the Low Countries. Alva interpreted "pacification" to mean ruthless extermination of religious and political dissidents. To Calvinists, all this was clear indication that Spanish rule was ungodly and should be overthrown.

Between 1568 and 1578 civil war raged in the Netherlands between Catholics and Protestants and between the seventeen provinces and Spain. Eventually the ten southern provinces, the Spanish Netherlands (the future Belgium), came under the control of the Spanish Habsburg forces. The seven northern provinces, led by Holland, formed the **Union of Utrecht** and in 1581 declared their independence from Spain. The north was Protestant; the south remained Catholic. Philip did not accept this, and war continued. England was even drawn into the conflict, supplying money and troops to the northern United Provinces. (Spain launched an unsuccessful invasion of England in response; see "Upholding Protestantism in England" in this chapter.) Hostilities ended in 1609 when Spain agreed to a truce that recognized the independence of the United Provinces.

## The Great European Witch-Hunt

The relationship between the Reformation and the upsurge in trials for witchcraft that occurred at roughly the same time is complex. Increasing persecution for witchcraft actually began before the Reformation in the 1480s, but it became especially common about 1560, and the mania continued until roughly 1660. Both Protestants and Catholics tried and executed witches, with church officials and secular authorities acting together.

The heightened sense of God's and the Devil's power in the Reformation era was an important factor in the witch-hunts, but so was a change in the idea of what a witch was. In the later Middle Ages, many educated Christian theologians, canon lawyers, and officials added a demonological component to the common notion of witches as people who use magic. For them, the essence of witchcraft was making a pact with the Devil. Witches were no longer simply people who used magical power to get what they wanted, but rather people used by the Devil to do what he wanted. Witches were thought to engage in wild sexual orgies with the Devil, fly through the night to meetings called sabbats that parodied Christian services, and steal communion wafers and unbaptized babies to use in their rituals. Some demonological theorists also claimed that witches were organized in an international conspiracy to overthrow Christianity.

Witchcraft was thus spiritualized, and witches became the ultimate heretics, enemies of God.

Scholars estimate that during the sixteenth and seventeenth centuries between 100,000 and 200,000 people were officially tried for witchcraft and between 40,000 and 60,000 were executed. Though the gender balance varied widely in different parts of Europe, between 75 and 85 percent of those tried and executed were women. Ideas about women and the roles women actually played in society were thus important factors shaping the witch-hunts. Some demonologists expressed virulent misogyny, or hatred of women, and particularly emphasized women's powerful sexual desire, which could be satisfied only by a demonic lover. Most people viewed women as weaker than men and so more likely to give in to an offer by the Devil. In both classical and Christian traditions, women were associated with nature, disorder, and the body, all of which were linked with the demonic. Women's actual lack of power in society and gender norms about the use of violence meant that they were more likely to use scolding and cursing to get what they wanted instead of taking people to court or beating them up. Curses were generally expressed (as they often are today) in religious terms; "go to Hell" was calling on the powers of Satan.

Legal changes also played a role in causing, or at least allowing for, massive witch trials. One of these was a change from an accusatorial legal procedure to an inquisitorial procedure. In the former, a suspect knew the accusers and the charges they had brought, and an accuser could in turn be liable for trial if the charges were not proven. In the latter, legal authorities themselves brought the case. This change made people much more willing to accuse others, for they never had to take personal responsibility for the accusation or face the accused person's relatives. Inquisitorial procedure involved intense questioning of the suspect, often with torture.

The use of inquisitorial procedure did not always lead to witch-hunts. The most famous inquisitions in early modern Europe, those in Spain, Portugal, and Italy, were in fact very lenient in their treatment of people accused of witchcraft. The Inquisition in Spain executed only a handful of witches, the Portuguese Inquisition only one, and the Roman Inquisition none, though in each of these there were hundreds of cases. Inquisitors believed in the power of the Devil and were no less misogynist than other judges, but they doubted very much whether the people accused of witchcraft had actually made pacts with the Devil that gave them special powers. They viewed such people not as diabolical Devil worshippers but as superstitious and ignorant peasants who should be educated rather than executed. Thus most people brought up before the Inquisition for witchcraft were sent home with a warning and a penance.

Most witch trials began with a single accusation in a village or town. Individuals accused someone they knew of using magic to spoil food, make children ill, kill animals, raise a hailstorm, or do other types of harm. Tensions within families, households, and neighborhoods often played a role in these accusations. Women number very prominently among accusers and witnesses as well as among those accused of witchcraft because the actions witches were initially charged with, such as harming children or curdling milk, were generally part of women's sphere. A woman also gained economic and social security by conforming to the standard of the good wife and mother and by confronting women who deviated from it.

Once a charge was made, the suspect was brought in for questioning. One German witch pamphlet from 1587 described a typical case:

> Walpurga Hausmännin . . . upon kindly questioning and also torture . . . confessed . . . that the Evil One indulged in fornication with her . . . and made her many promises to help her in her poverty and need. . . . She promised herself body and soul to him and disowned God in heaven. . . . She destroyed a number of cattle, pigs, and geese . . . and dug up [the bodies] of one or two innocent children. With her devil-paramour and other playfellows she has eaten these and used their hair and their little bones for witchcraft.

Confession was generally followed by execution. In this case, Hausmännin was "dispatched from life to death by burning at the stake . . . her body first to be torn five times with red-hot irons."[7]

Detailed records of witch trials survive for many parts of Europe. They have been used by historians to study many aspects of witchcraft, but they cannot directly answer what seems to us an important question: did people really practice witchcraft and think they were witches? They certainly confessed to evil deeds and demonic practices, sometimes without torture, but where would we draw the line between reality and fantasy? Clearly people were not riding through the air on pitchforks, but did they think they did? Did they actually invoke the Devil when they were angry

■ **Edict of Nantes**  A document issued by Henry IV of France in 1598, granting liberty of conscience and of public worship to Calvinists, which helped restore peace in France.

■ **Union of Utrecht**  The alliance of seven northern provinces (led by Holland) that declared its independence from Spain and formed the United Provinces of the Netherlands.

**Witch Pamphlet**   This printed pamphlet presents the confession of "Mother Waterhouse," a woman convicted of witchcraft in England in 1566, who describes her "many abominable deeds" and "execrable sorcery" committed over fifteen years, and asks for forgiveness right before her execution. Enterprising printers often produced cheap, short pamphlets during witch trials, knowing they would sell, sometimes based on the actual trial proceedings and sometimes just made up. They both reflected and helped create stereotypes about what witches were and did.
(Private Collection/Bridgeman Images)

at a neighbor, or was this simply in the minds of their accusers? Trial records cannot tell us, and historians have answered these questions very differently, often using insights from psychoanalysis or the study of more recent victims of torture in their explanations.

After the initial suspect had been questioned, and particularly if he or she had been tortured, the people who had been implicated were brought in for questioning. This might lead to a small hunt, involving from five to ten suspects, and it sometimes grew into a much larger hunt, which historians have called a "witch panic." Panics were most common in the part of Europe that saw the most witch accusations

in general: the Holy Roman Empire, Switzerland, and parts of France. Most of this area consisted of very small governmental units that were jealous of each other and, after the Reformation, were divided by religion. The rulers of these small territories often felt more threatened than did the monarchs of western Europe, and they saw persecuting witches as a way to demonstrate their piety and concern for order. Moreover, witch panics often occurred after some type of climatic disaster, such as an unusually cold and wet summer, and they came in waves.

In large-scale panics a wider variety of suspects were taken in—wealthier people, children, a greater proportion of men. Mass panics tended to end when it became clear to legal authorities, or to the community itself, that the people being questioned or executed were not what they understood witches to be, or that the scope of accusations was beyond belief.

As the seventeenth century ushered in new ideas about science and reason, many began to question whether witches could make pacts with the Devil or engage in the wild activities attributed to them. Doubts about whether secret denunciations were valid or whether torture would ever yield truthful confessions gradually spread among the same types of religious and legal authorities who had so vigorously persecuted witches. Prosecutions for witchcraft became less common and were gradually outlawed. The last official execution for witchcraft in England was in 1682, though the last one in the Holy Roman Empire was not until 1775.

## NOTES

1. Quoted in E. H. Harbison, *The Age of Reformation* (Ithaca, N.Y.: Cornell University Press, 1963), p. 52.
2. Quoted in S. E. Ozment, *The Age of Reform, 1250–1550: An Intellectual and Religious History of Late Medieval and Reformation Europe* (New Haven, Conn.: Yale University Press, 1980), p. 284.
3. Ludwig Rabus, *Historien der heyligen Außerwolten Gottes Zeugen, Bekennern und Martyrern* (n.p., 1557), fol. 41. Trans. Merry Wiesner-Hanks.
4. J. Allen, trans., *John Calvin: The Institutes of the Christian Religion* (Philadelphia: Westminster Press, 1930), bk. 3, chap. 21, para. 5, 7.
5. Teresa of Avila, *The Way of Perfection,* translated and quoted in Jodi Bilinkoff, *The Avila of St. Teresa: Religious Reform in a Sixteenth-Century City* (Ithaca: Cornell University Press, 1989), p. 136.
6. *The Spiritual Exercises of St. Ignatius of Loyola,* trans. Louis J. Puhl, S.J. (Chicago: Loyola University, 1951), p. 1.
7. From *The Fugger News-Letters,* ed. Victor von Klarwell, trans. P. de Chary (London: John Lane, The Bodley Head Ltd., 1924), quoted in James Bruce Ross and Mary Martin McLaughlin, *The Portable Renaissance Reader* (New York: Penguin, 1968), pp. 258, 260, 262.

# LOOKING BACK  LOOKING AHEAD

The Renaissance and the Reformation are often seen as two of the key elements in the creation of the "modern" world. The radical changes brought by the Reformation contained many aspects of continuity, however. Sixteenth-century reformers looked back to the early Christian Church for their inspiration, and many of their reforming ideas had been advocated for centuries. Most Protestant reformers worked with political leaders to make religious changes, just as early church officials had worked with Emperor Constantine and his successors as Christianity became the official religion of the Roman Empire in the fourth century. The spread of Christianity and the spread of Protestantism were accomplished not only by preaching, persuasion, and teaching, but also by force and violence. The Catholic Reformation was carried out by activist popes, a church council, and new religious orders, as earlier reforms of the church had been.

Just as they linked with earlier developments, the events of the Reformation were also closely connected with what is often seen as the third element in the "modern" world: European exploration and colonization. Only a week after Martin Luther stood in front of Charles V at the Diet of Worms declaring his independence in matters of religion, Ferdinand Magellan, a Portuguese sea captain with Spanish ships, was killed in a group of islands off the coast of Southeast Asia. Charles V had provided the backing for Magellan's voyage, the first to circumnavigate the globe. Magellan viewed the spread of Christianity as one of the purposes of his trip, and later in the sixteenth century institutions created as part of the Catholic Reformation, including the Jesuit order and the Inquisition, would operate in European colonies overseas as well as in Europe itself. The islands where Magellan was killed were later named the Philippines, in honor of Charles's son Philip, who sent the ill-fated Spanish Armada against England. Philip's opponent Queen Elizabeth was similarly honored when English explorers named a huge chunk of territory in North America "Virginia" as a tribute to their "Virgin Queen." The desire for wealth and power was an important motivation in the European voyages and colonial ventures, but so was religious zeal.

## Make Connections

Think about the larger developments and continuities within and across chapters.

1. Martin Luther is always on every list of the one hundred most influential people of all time. Should he be? Why or why not? Who else from this chapter should be on such a list, and why?

2. How did Protestant ideas about gender, marriage, and the role of women break with those developed earlier in the history of the Christian Church (Chapters 6, 7, 9)? What continuities do you see? What factors account for the pattern that you have found?

3. In what ways was the Catholic Reformation of the sixteenth century similar to earlier efforts to reform the church, including the Gregorian reforms of the twelfth century (Chapter 9) and late medieval reform efforts (Chapter 11)? In what ways was it different?

# 13   REVIEW & EXPLORE

## Identify Key Terms

Identify and explain the significance of each item below.

anticlericalism (p. 358)

indulgence (p. 359)

Protestant (p. 361)

Spanish Armada (p. 373)

*The Institutes of the Christian Religion* (p. 374)

predestination (p. 374)

Holy Office (p. 379)

Jesuits (p. 381)

Huguenots (p. 383)

politiques (p. 383)

Edict of Nantes (p. 384)

Union of Utrecht (p. 384)

## Review the Main Ideas

Answer the section heading questions from the chapter.

1. What were the central ideas of the reformers, and why were they appealing to different social groups? (p. 358)

2. How did the political situation in Germany shape the course of the Reformation? (p. 368)

3. How did Protestant ideas and institutions spread beyond German-speaking lands? (p. 371)

4. What reforms did the Catholic Church make, and how did it respond to Protestant reform movements? (p. 379)

5. What were the causes and consequences of religious violence, including riots, wars, and witch-hunts? (p. 382)

## Suggested Resources

### BOOKS

- Brady, Thomas A. *German Histories in the Age of Reformations, 1400–1650.* 2009. Examines the broad political context of the Holy Roman Empire and the ways in which this shaped both the Reformation and subsequent German history.

- Cameron, Euan. *The European Reformation,* 2d ed. 2012. A thorough analysis of the Protestant and Catholic Reformations throughout Europe.

- Gordon, Bruce. *John Calvin.* 2009. Situates Calvin's theology and life within the context of his relationships and the historical events of his time.

- Hendrix, Scott. *Luther.* 2009. A brief introduction to Luther's thought; part of the Abingdon Pillars of Theology series.

- Holt, Mack P. *The French Wars of Religion, 1562–1629,* 2d ed. 2005. A thorough survey designed for students.

- Hsia, R. Po-Chia. *The World of Catholic Renewal, 1540–1770,* 2d ed. 2005. Situates the Catholic Reformation in a global context and provides coverage of colonial Catholicism.

- Levack, Brian. *The Witch-Hunt in Early Modern Europe,* 4th ed. 2015. A good introduction to the witch-hunts, with helpful bibliographies of the vast literature on witchcraft.

- Levi, Anthony. *Renaissance and Reformation: The Intellectual Genesis.* 2002. Surveys the ideas of major Reformation figures against the background of important political issues.

- Matheson, Peter, ed. *Reformation Christianity.* 2004. This volume in the People's History of Christianity series explores social issues and popular religion.
- O'Malley, John W. *Trent and All That: Renaming Catholicism in the Early Modern Era.* 2000. Provides an excellent historiographical review of the literature,

and explains why and how early modern Catholicism influenced early modern European history.
- Shagan, Ethan. *Popular Politics and the English Reformation.* 2003. Analyzes the process of the Reformation in local areas.

## MEDIA

- *H. Henry Meeter Center for Calvin Studies.* Resources, including audio and video recordings, on John Calvin and Calvinism, collected by the Meeter Center at Calvin College in Michigan. **www.calvin.edu/meete**
- *A Man for All Seasons* (Fred Zinnemann, 1966). A classic Academy Award–winning film on Thomas More's confrontation with Henry VIII over the king's efforts to obtain a divorce; portrays More as a heroic figure who followed his principles.
- *Martin Luther: The Idea That Changed the World* (PBS, 2017). A well-received documentary produced for the 500th anniversary of the Reformation.
- *Project Wittenberg.* Concordia Theological Seminary's website devoted to the life and works of Martin Luther, with the largest online collection of Luther's writings in English, and many of his works in the original German or Latin. **iclnet.org/pub/resources/text /wittenberg/wittenberg-home.html**
- *The Protestant Revolution* (BBC, 2007). A four-part documentary series that examines the religious roots

and the scientific, cultural, social, economic, and political impact of Protestantism, viewing these as wide ranging and global in scope.
- *The Tudors* (Showtime, 2007–2010). A four-season historical fiction extravaganza centering on Henry VIII and his wives, full of sex and intrigue. Great fun, but not-so-great history.
- *Witchcraze* (BBC, 2003). A docudrama examining the Scottish witch trials of 1590–1591, when thirty women and one man were arrested, tortured, and eventually hanged or burned at the stake; based on original documents from the period, including court records.
- *Wolf Hall* (BBC, 2015). A miniseries based on the award-winning historical novels by Hilary Mantel that focuses on Thomas Cromwell, Henry VIII's chief minister. Praised for its acting and staging, but criticized for its harsh treatment of Thomas More.

# 14

# European Exploration and Conquest

## 1450–1650

**In 1450 Europeans were relatively marginal players** in a centuries-old trading system that linked Africa, Asia, and Europe. In this vibrant cosmopolitan Afro-Eurasian trading world centered on the Indian Ocean, Arab, Persian, Turkish, Indian, African, Chinese, and European merchants and adventurers competed for trade in spices, silks, and other goods.

A century later, by 1550, the Portuguese search for better access to African gold and Asian trade goods had led to a new overseas empire and Spanish explorers had accidentally discovered the Western Hemisphere. Through violent conquest, the Iberian powers established large-scale colonies in the Americas, and northern European powers sought to establish colonies of their own. The era of European expansion had begun, creating new political systems and forms of economic exchange as well as cultural assimilation, conversion, and resistance. The Age of Discovery (1450–1650), as the time of these encounters is known, laid the foundations for the modern world. ■

# CHAPTER PREVIEW

- **What was the Afro-Eurasian trading world before Columbus?**

- **How and why did Europeans undertake ambitious voyages of expansion?**

- **What was the impact of European conquest on the New World?**

- **How did Europe and the world change after Columbus?**

- **How did expansion change European attitudes and beliefs?**

**Life in the Age of Discovery**
The arrival of the Portuguese in Japan in 1543 inspired a series of artworks depicting the *namban-jin,* or southern barbarians, as the Japanese called them. This detail from an early-seventeenth-century painted screen shows a Portuguese merchant with three South Asian slaves unloading trade goods from a merchant ship. (Museu Nacional de Soares dos Reis, Porto, Portugal/Bridgeman Images)

# What was the Afro-Eurasian trading world before Columbus?

Columbus did not sail west on a whim. To understand his and other Europeans' voyages of exploration, we must first understand late medieval trade networks. Historians now recognize that a type of world economy, known as the Afro-Eurasian trade world, linked the products, people, and ideas of Africa, Europe, and Asia during the Middle Ages. The West was not the dominant player before Columbus, and the voyages derived from a desire to gain direct access to the goods of overseas trade. European monarchs and explorers also wished to spread Christianity. Their projects for exploration and conquest received support from the papacy in Rome.

## The Trade World of the Indian Ocean

Covering 20 percent of the earth's total ocean area, the Indian Ocean is the globe's third-largest waterway (after the Atlantic and Pacific). Moderate and predictable, monsoon winds blow from the northwest or northeast between November and January and from the south and southwest between April and August. These wind patterns enabled cross-oceanic travel and shaped its rhythms, creating a vibrant trade world in which goods, people, and ideas circulated among China, India, the Middle East, Southeast Asia, and Africa (Map 14.1). From the seventh through the fourteenth centuries, the volume and integration of Indian Ocean trade steadily increased, favored by two parallel movements: political unification and economic growth in China and the spread of Islam through much of the Indian Ocean world.

Merchants congregated in a series of cosmopolitan port cities strung around the Indian Ocean. Most of these cities had some form of autonomous self-government, and no one state or region dominated. Ethnic, religious, and family ties encouraged trust among traders and limited violence.

Located at the northeastern edge of the Indian Ocean trade world, China exercised a powerful economic and cultural influence. In addition to safeguarding the famous Silk Road overland trade routes through Central Asia and the Middle East, the Mongols also increased connections with Indian Ocean trade. The Venetian trader Marco Polo's tales of his travels from 1271 to 1295, including his encounter with the Great Khan, fueled Western fantasies about the exotic Orient. Polo vividly recounted the splendors of the khan's court and the city of Hangzhou, which he described as "the finest and noblest in the world" in which "the number and wealth of the merchants, and the amount of goods that passed through their hands, was so enormous that no man could form a just estimate thereof."[1]

After the Mongols fell to the Ming Dynasty in 1368, China entered a new period of economic expansion, population growth, and urbanization. China's huge cities hungered for luxury products of the Indian Ocean world, and its artisans produced goods highly prized in export markets, especially porcelain and silk. The Ming emperor dispatched Admiral Zheng He (JEHNG HUH) on a remarkable series of naval expeditions that traveled the oceanic web as far west as Egypt. From 1405 to 1433 each of his seven expeditions involved hundreds of ships and tens of thousands of men. In one voyage alone, Zheng He sailed more than 12,000 miles.[2] Although the ships brought back many wonders, such as giraffes and zebras, the purpose of the voyages was primarily diplomatic, to enhance China's prestige and seek tribute-paying alliances. After the deaths of Zheng He and the emperor, the voyages ceased, but Chinese overseas traders continued vigorous activity in the South China Sea and throughout the Indian Ocean.

India was the central hinge of Indian Ocean trade. Muslim Arab and Persian merchants who circumnavigated India on their way to trade in the South China Sea established trading posts along the southern coasts of east and west India. Cities such as Calicut and Quilon became thriving commercial centers. India was also an important contributor of goods to the world trading system. Most of the world's pepper was grown in India, and Indian cotton and silk textiles, mainly from the Gujarat region, were also highly prized.

Southeast Asia maintained an active trade with China across the South China Sea and with ports on the Coromandel Coast of southeast India. In the fifteenth century the strategically located port of Malacca became a great commercial entrepôt (AHN-truh-poh), a trading post to which goods were shipped for storage while awaiting redistribution. To Malacca came porcelains, silks, and camphor (used in the manufacture of many medications) from China; pepper, cloves, nutmeg, and raw materials such as sandalwood from the Moluccas; and textiles, copper weapons, incense, and dyes from India.

## The Trading States of Africa

By 1450 Africa had a few large empires along with hundreds of smaller states. After the Mongol invasion of Baghdad in 1258, the Mamluk rulers of Egypt proclaimed a new Abbasid caliphate. Until its defeat by the Ottomans in 1517, the Mamluk empire was one of the most powerful on the continent. Its capital, Cairo, was a center of Islamic learning and religious authority as well as being a major hub for goods

# TIMELINE

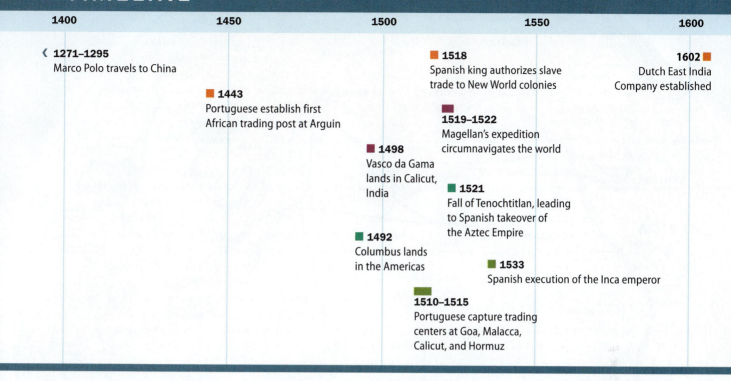

**1400**   **1450**   **1500**   **1550**   **1600**

**1271–1295**
Marco Polo travels to China

**1443**
Portuguese establish first
African trading post at Arguin

**1518**
Spanish king authorizes slave
trade to New World colonies

**1602**
Dutch East India
Company established

**1519–1522**
Magellan's expedition
circumnavigates the world

**1498**
Vasco da Gama
lands in Calicut,
India

**1521**
Fall of Tenochtitlan, leading
to Spanish takeover of
the Aztec Empire

**1492**
Columbus lands
in the Americas

**1533**
Spanish execution of the Inca emperor

**1510–1515**
Portuguese capture trading
centers at Goa, Malacca,
Calicut, and Hormuz

---

moving between the Indian Ocean trade world and the Mediterranean.

On the east coast of Africa, Swahili-speaking city-states engaged directly in the Indian Ocean trade, exchanging ivory, rhinoceros horn, tortoise shells, and slaves for textiles, spices, cowrie shells, porcelain, and other goods. Cities such as Kilwa, Malindi, Mogadishu, and Mombasa, dominated by Muslim merchants, were known for their prosperity and culture.

In the fifteenth century most of the gold that reached Europe came from the western part of the Sudan region in West Africa and from the Akan (AH-kahn) peoples living near present-day Ghana. Transported across the Sahara by Arab and African traders on camels, the gold was sold in the ports of North Africa. Other trading routes led to the Egyptian cities of Alexandria and Cairo, where the Venetians held commercial privileges.

Inland nations that sat astride the north-south caravan routes grew wealthy from this trade. In the mid-thirteenth century the kingdom of Mali emerged as an important player on the overland trade route, gaining prestige from its ruler Mansa Musa's fabulous pilgrimage to Mecca in 1324/25. Desire to gain direct access to African gold motivated the initial Portuguese voyages into northern and western Africa.

Gold was one important object of trade; slaves were another. Slavery was practiced in Africa, as it was virtually everywhere else in the world, long before the arrival of Europeans. Arab and East African merchants took West African slaves to the Mediterranean to be sold in European, Egyptian, and Middle Eastern markets and also brought eastern Europeans — a major element of European slavery — to West Africa as slaves. In addition, Indian and Arab merchants traded slaves in the coastal regions of East Africa.

## The Middle East

From its capital in Baghdad, the Abbasid caliphate (750–1258) controlled an enormous region from Spain to the western borders of China, including the Red Sea and the Persian Gulf, the two major waterways linking the Indian Ocean trade world to the West. The political stability enshrined by the caliphate, along with the shared language, legal system, and culture of Islam, served to foster economic prosperity and commercial activity. During this period, Muslim Arab traders, who had spread through eastern Africa and western India in the early Middle Ages, reached even further across the trade routes of the Indian Ocean to obtain spices, porcelain, and other goods for the bustling cities of the caliphate.

After the Abbasids fell to Mongol invasions, two great rival Muslim empires, the Persian Safavids (sah-FAH-vidz) and the Turkish Ottomans, dominated the region and competed for control of east-west trade. Like Arabs, Persian merchants could be found in trading communities in India and throughout the Afro-Eurasian trade world. Persia was also a major producer and exporter of silk cloth.

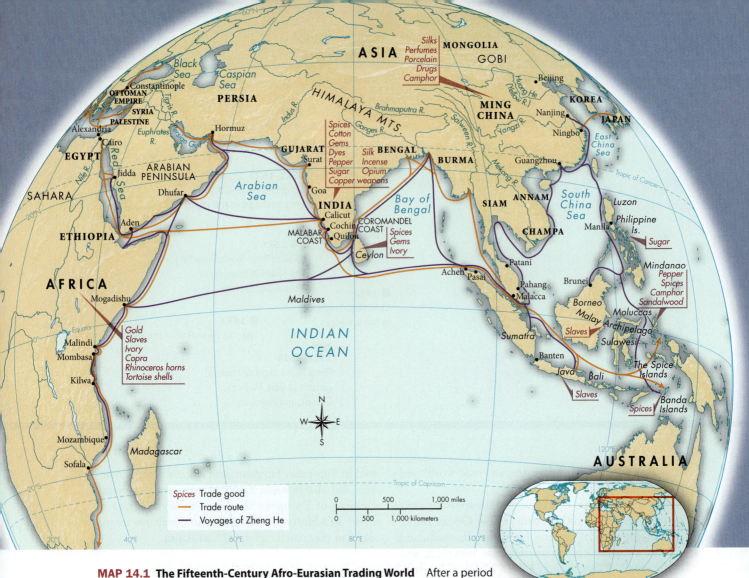

**MAP 14.1  The Fifteenth-Century Afro-Eurasian Trading World** After a period of decline following the Black Death and the Mongol invasions, trade revived in the fifteenth century. Muslim merchants dominated trade, linking ports in East Africa and the Red Sea with those in India and the Malay Archipelago. Chinese admiral Zheng He's voyages (1405–1433) followed the most important Indian Ocean trade routes.

Under Sultan Mohammed II (r. 1451–1481), the Ottomans captured Europe's largest city, Constantinople, in May 1453. The city became the capital of the Ottoman Empire. By the mid-sixteenth century the Ottomans had established control over the maritime trade in the eastern Mediterranean and their power extended into Europe as far west as Vienna. The extension of Ottoman control provided impetus for European traders to seek direct access to Eastern trade goods.

## Genoese and Venetian Middlemen

In the late Middle Ages, the Italian city-states of Venice and Genoa controlled the European luxury trade with the East. In 1304 Venice established formal relations with the sultan of Mamluk Egypt, opening operations in Cairo, a major outlet for Asian trade goods brought through the Red Sea. Venetian merchants purchased goods such as spices, silks, and carpets in Cairo for re-export throughout Europe. Venetians funded these purchases through trade in European woolen cloth and metal goods, as well as through shipping and trade in firearms and slaves.

Venice's ancient rival was Genoa. In the wake of the Crusades, Genoa dominated the northern route to Asia through the Black Sea. Expansion in the thirteenth and fourteenth centuries took the Genoese as far as Persia and the Far East. In 1291 they sponsored an expedition into the Atlantic in search of India. The ships were lost, and their exact destination and motivations remain unknown. This voyage reveals the long roots of Genoese interest in Atlantic exploration.

In the fifteenth century, with Venice claiming victory in the spice trade, the Genoese shifted their focus from trade to finance and from the Black Sea to the western Mediterranean. When Spanish and Portuguese voyages began to explore the western Atlantic,

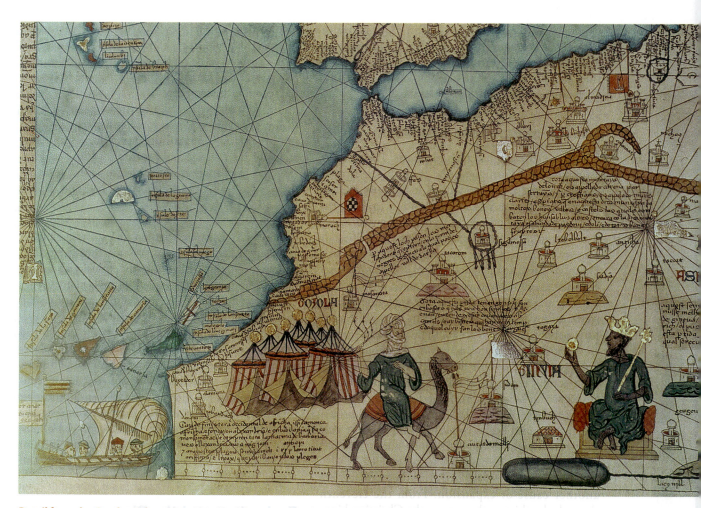

**Detail from the *Catalan Atlas*, 1375**   This detail from a medieval map depicts Mansa Musa (lower right), who ruled the powerful West African empire of Mali from 1312 to 1337. Musa's golden crown and scepter, and the gold ingot he holds in his hand, represent the empire's wealth. The map also depicts Catalan sailors heading from the Balearic Islands out to the Atlantic Ocean. (From *The Catalan Atlas*, 1375, by Abraham Cresques/Bibliothèque Nationale, Paris, France/Getty Images)

Genoese merchants, navigators, and financiers provided their skills and capital to the Iberian monarchs, whose own subjects had less commercial experience. Genoese merchants would eventually help finance Spanish colonization of the New World.

A major element of Italian trade was slavery. Merchants purchased slaves, many of whom were fellow Christians, in the Balkans. The men were sold to Egypt for the sultan's army or sent to work as agricultural laborers in the Mediterranean. Young girls, who constituted the majority of the trade, were sold in western Mediterranean ports as servants and concubines. After the loss of the Black Sea — and thus the source of slaves — to the Ottomans, the Genoese sought new supplies of slaves in the West, taking the Guanches (indigenous peoples from the Canary Islands), Muslim prisoners, Jewish refugees from Spain, and by the early 1500s both sub-Saharan and Berber Africans. With the growth of Spanish colonies in the New World in the sixteenth century, Genoese and Venetian merchants would become important players in the transatlantic slave trade.

## How and why did Europeans undertake ambitious voyages of expansion?

As we have seen, Europe was by no means isolated before the voyages of exploration and the "discovery" of the New World. Italian merchants traded actively in North Africa for gold and in eastern Mediterranean depots for Indian Ocean luxury goods, but trade through intermediaries was slow and expensive. In the first decades of the fifteenth century, new players entered the scene with novel technology, eager

# Columbus Describes His First Voyage

On his return voyage to Spain in February 1493, Christopher Columbus composed a letter intended for wide circulation and had copies of it sent ahead to Queen Isabella and King Ferdinand. Because the letter sums up Columbus's understanding of his achievements, it is considered the most important document of his first voyage. Remember that his knowledge of Asia rested heavily on Marco Polo's *Travels*, published around 1298.

❧

I write to inform you how in thirty-three days I crossed from the Canary Islands to the Indies, with the fleet which our most illustrious sovereigns gave me. I found very many islands with large populations and took possession of them all for their Highnesses; this I did by proclamation and unfurled the royal standard. No opposition was offered.

I named the first island that I found "San Salvador," in honour of our Lord and Saviour who has granted me this miracle. . . . When I reached Cuba, I followed its north coast westwards, and found it so extensive that I thought this must be the mainland, the province of Cathay. . . .* From there I saw another island eighteen leagues eastwards which I then named "Hispaniola." . . .†

Hispaniola is a wonder. The mountains and hills, the plains and meadow lands are both fertile and beautiful. They are most suitable for planting crops and for raising cattle of all kinds, and there are good sites for building towns and villages. The harbours are incredibly fine and there are many great rivers with broad channels and the majority contain gold.‡

The inhabitants of this island, and all the rest that I discovered or heard of, go naked, as their mothers bore them, men and women alike. A few of the women, however, cover a single place with a leaf of a plant or piece of cotton which they weave for the purpose. They have no iron or steel or arms and are not capable of using them, not because they are not strong and well built but because they are amazingly timid. All the weapons they have are canes cut at seeding time, at the end of which they fix a sharpened stick, but they have not the courage to make use of these, for very often when I have sent two or three men to a village to have conversation with them a great number of them have come out. But as soon as they saw my men all fled immediately, a father not even waiting for his son. And this is not because we have harmed any of them; on the contrary, wherever I have gone and been able to have conversation with them, I have given them some of the various things I had, a cloth and other articles, and received nothing in exchange. But they have still remained incurably timid.

True, when they have been reassured and lost their fear, they are so ingenuous and so liberal with all their possessions that no one who has not seen them would believe it. If one asks for anything they have they never say no. On the contrary, they offer a share to anyone with demonstrations of heartfelt affection, and they are immediately content with any small thing, valuable or valueless, that is given them. I forbade the men to give them bits of broken crockery, fragments of glass or tags of laces, though if they could get them they fancied them the finest jewels in the world. . . .

I hoped to win them to the love and service of their Highnesses and of the whole Spanish nation and to persuade them to collect and give us of the things which they possessed in abundance and which we needed. They have no religion and are not idolaters; but all believe that power and goodness dwell in the sky and they are firmly convinced that I have come from the sky with these ships and people. In this belief they gave me a good reception everywhere, once they had overcome their fear; and this is not because they are stupid—far from it, they are men of great intelligence, for they navigate all those seas, and give a marvellously good

* Cathay is the old name for China. In the logbook and later in this letter, Columbus accepts the native story that Cuba is an island that can be circumnavigated in something more than twenty-one days, yet he insists here and during the second voyage that it is part of the Asiatic mainland.

† Hispaniola is the second-largest island of the West Indies. Haiti occupies the western third of the island, the Dominican Republic the rest.

‡ This did not prove to be true.

Christopher Columbus, a native of Genoa, was an experienced seaman and navigator, with close ties to the world of Portuguese seafaring. He had worked as a mapmaker in Lisbon and spent time on Madeira, where his wife's father led the Portuguese colony. He was familiar with *portolans*—written descriptions of the courses along which ships sailed—and the use of the compass for dead reckoning. (He carried an astrolabe on his first voyage, but did not use it for navigation.) Columbus was also a deeply religious man. He had witnessed the Spanish conquest of Granada and shared fully in the religious and nationalistic fervor surrounding that event. Like the Spanish rulers and most Europeans of his age, Columbus understood Christianity as a missionary religion that should be carried to all places of the earth.

Given Portugal's leading role in Atlantic exploration and his personal connections, Columbus first appealed to the Portuguese rulers for support for a voyage to find a westward passage to the Indies in 1483.

account of every thing—but because they have never before seen men clothed or ships like these. . . .

In all these islands the men are seemingly content with one woman, but their chief or king is allowed more than twenty. The women appear to work more than the men and I have not been able to find out if they have private property. As far as I could see whatever a man had was shared among all the rest and this particularly applies to food. . . . In another island, which I am told is larger than Hispaniola, the people have no hair. Here there is a vast quantity of gold, and from here and the other islands I bring Indians as evidence.

In conclusion, to speak only of the results of this very hasty voyage, their Highnesses can see that I will give them as much gold as they require, if they will render me some very slight assistance; also I will give them all the spices and cotton they want. . . . I will also bring them as much aloes as they ask and as many slaves, who will be taken from the idolaters.§

## EVALUATE THE EVIDENCE

1. What was Columbus's view of the Native Americans he met, and what does he want the Spanish rulers to know about them?
2. How trustworthy do you think Columbus's account of the wealth of the Caribbean islands in gold, cotton, and spices is, and the Native Americans' eagerness to share their possessions with the Spanish? Why would he exaggerate these elements of his voyage?
3. What impression does Columbus seem to want to convey of his treatment of the people he encountered? What does this convey about Europeans' attitudes to the peoples they encountered in the New World?

Source: *The Four Voyages of Christopher Columbus*, pp. 115–123, ed. and trans. J. M. Cohen (Penguin Books, 1992). Copyright © J. M. Cohen 1969, 1992. Reproduced by permission of Penguin Books Ltd.

§ This contradicts his earlier statement that the natives were not "idolaters"; elsewhere in the letter he comments that the inhabitants of the Caribbean could be easily enslaved.

When they refused, he turned, unsuccessfully, to Ferdinand and Isabella in 1486 and then finally won the backing of the Spanish monarchy in 1492. Buoyed by the success of the reconquista and eager to earn profits from trade, the Spanish crown named Columbus viceroy over any territory he might discover and promised him one-tenth of the material rewards of the journey.

Columbus and his small fleet left Spain on August 3, 1492. Inspired by the stories of Mandeville and Marco Polo, Columbus dreamed of reaching the court

**Columbus's First Voyage to the New World, 1492–1493**

of the Great Khan (not realizing that the Ming Dynasty had overthrown the Mongols in 1368). Based on Ptolemy's *Geography* and other texts, he expected to pass the islands of Japan and then land on the east coast of China.

On October 12, 1492, he landed in the Bahamas, which he christened San Salvador and claimed for the Spanish crown. In a letter submitted to Ferdinand and Isabella on his return to Spain, Columbus described the natives as handsome, peaceful, and primitive people whose body painting reminded him of that of the Canary Islands natives. Believing he was somewhere off the east coast of Japan, in what he considered the Indies, he called them "Indians," a name later applied to all inhabitants of the Americas. Columbus concluded that they would make good slaves and could easily be converted to Christianity. (See "Evaluating Written Evidence: Columbus Describes His First Voyage," left.)

Scholars have identified the inhabitants of the islands as the Taino people, who inhabited Hispaniola (modern-day Haiti and Dominican Republic) and other islands in the Caribbean. From San Salvador, Columbus sailed southwest, landing on Cuba on October 28. Deciding that he must be on the mainland near the coastal city of Quinsay (now Hangzhou), described by Marco Polo, he sent a small embassy inland with letters from Ferdinand and Isabella and instructions to locate the grand city. Although they found no large settlement or any evidence of a great kingdom, the sight of Taino people wearing gold ornaments on Hispaniola suggested that gold was available in the region. In January, confident that its source would soon be found, Columbus headed back to Spain to report on his discovery.[4]

On his second voyage in 1493, Columbus brought with him settlers for the new Spanish territories, along with agricultural seed and livestock. Columbus and his followers forcibly took control of the island of Hispaniola and enslaved its indigenous people. Columbus himself, however, had limited skills in governing. Revolt soon broke out against him and his brother on Hispaniola. A royal expedition sent to investigate his leadership returned the brothers to Spain in chains, and a royal governor assumed control of the colony.

Columbus was very much a man of his times. To the end of his life in 1506, he incorrectly believed that he had found small islands off the coast of Asia. He could not know that the scale of his discoveries would revolutionize world power and set in motion a new era of trade, conquest, and empire.

## Spain "Discovers" the Pacific

The Florentine navigator Amerigo Vespucci (veh-SPOO-chee) (1454–1512) was one of the first to begin to perceive what Columbus had not. Writing about his discoveries on the coast of modern-day Venezuela, Vespucci stated: "Those new regions which we found and explored with the fleet . . . we may rightly call a New World." This letter, titled *Mundus Novus* (The New World), was the first document to describe America as a continent separate from Asia. In recognition of Amerigo's bold claim, a German mapmaker named the new continent for him in 1507.

As soon as Columbus returned from his first voyage, Isabella and Ferdinand sought to establish their claims to the new territories and forestall potential opposition from Portugal, which had previously dominated Atlantic exploration. Spanish-born Pope Alexander VI, to whom they appealed for support, proposed drawing an imaginary line down the Atlantic, giving Spain possession of all lands discovered to the west and Portugal everything to the east. The pope enjoined both powers to carry the Christian faith to these newly discovered lands and their peoples. The **Treaty of Tordesillas** (tor-duh-SEE-yuhs) negotiated between Spain and Portugal in 1494 retained the pope's idea, but moved the line further west as a concession to the Portuguese. This arbitrary division worked in Portugal's favor when in 1500 an expedition led by Pedro Álvares Cabral, en route to India, landed on the coast of Brazil, which Cabral claimed as Portuguese territory. (Because the line was also imagined to extend around the globe, it meant that the Philippine Islands would eventually end up in Spanish control.)

The search for profits determined the direction of Spanish exploration. Because its revenue from Hispaniola and other Caribbean islands was insignificant compared to the enormous riches that the Portuguese were reaping in Asia, Spain renewed the search for a western passage to Asia. In 1519 Charles I of Spain (who was also Holy Roman emperor Charles V) sent the Portuguese mariner Ferdinand Magellan (1480–1521) to find a sea route to the spices of Southeast Asia. Magellan sailed southwest across the Atlantic to Brazil, and after a long search along the coast he located the treacherous straits that now bear his name (see Map 14.2). The new ocean he sailed into after a rough passage through the straits seemed so calm that Magellan dubbed it the Pacific, from the Latin word for peaceful. His fleet sailed north up the west coast of South America and then headed west into the immense expanse of the Pacific in 1520 toward the Malay Archipelago, which includes modern-day Indonesia and other island nations.

Magellan's first impressions of the Pacific were terribly mistaken. Terrible storms, disease, starvation, and violence devastated the expedition. Magellan himself died in a skirmish in the Malay Archipelago, and only one of the five ships that began the expedition made it back to Spain. The ship returned home in 1522 with only 18 of the approximately 270 men who originally set out, having traveled from the east by way of the Indian Ocean, the Cape of Good Hope, and the Atlantic. The voyage—the first to circumnavigate the globe—had taken close to three years.

Despite the losses, this voyage revolutionized Europeans' understanding of the world by demonstrating the vastness of the Pacific. The earth was clearly much larger than Ptolemy's map had shown. Although the voyage made a small profit in spices, it also demonstrated that the westward passage to the Indies was too long and dangerous for commercial purposes. Spain's rulers soon abandoned the attempt to oust Portugal from the Eastern spice trade and concentrated on exploiting its New World territories.

## Early Exploration by Northern European Powers

Shortly following Columbus's voyages, northern European nations entered the competition for a northwest passage to the Indies. In 1497 John Cabot, a Venetian merchant living in London, obtained support from English king Henry VII for such a voyage. Following a northern route that he believed would provide shorter passage to Asia, Cabot and his crew landed on Newfoundland. In subsequent years, Cabot made two additional voyages to explore the northeast coast of Canada. These forays did not reveal a passage to the Indies, and Cabot made no attempt to establish settlements in the coastal areas he explored.

News of the riches of Mexico and Peru later inspired the English to renew their efforts to find a westward passage, this time in the extreme north. Between 1576 and 1578 Martin Frobisher made three voyages in and around the Canadian bay that now bears his name. Frobisher brought a quantity of ore back to England with him, hoping he had found a new source of gold or silver, but it proved to be worthless.

The French crown also sponsored efforts to find a westward passage to Asia. Between 1534 and 1541 Frenchman Jacques Cartier made several voyages and explored the St. Lawrence River of Canada. His exploration of the St. Lawrence was halted at the great rapids west of the present-day island of Montreal; he named the rapids "La Chine" in the optimistic belief that China lay just beyond. When this hope proved vain, the French turned to a new source of profit within Canada itself: trade in beavers and other furs. As had the Portuguese in Asia, French traders bartered with local people, who maintained autonomous control of their trade goods.

French fishermen also competed with Portuguese and Spanish, and later English, ships for the teeming schools of cod they found in the Atlantic waters around Newfoundland, one of the richest fish stocks in the world. Fishing vessels salted the catch on board and brought it back to Europe, where a thriving market for fish was created by the Catholic prohibition on eating meat on Fridays and during Lent.

# What was the impact of European conquest on the New World?

Before Columbus's arrival, the Americas were inhabited by thousands of groups of indigenous peoples with different languages and cultures. These groups ranged from hunter-gatherer tribes organized into tribal confederations to settled agriculturalists to large-scale empires containing bustling cities and towns. The best estimate is that the peoples of the Americas numbered between 35 and 50 million in 1492. Their lives were radically transformed by the arrival of Europeans.

The growing European presence in the New World transformed its land and its peoples forever. While Iberian powers conquered enormous territories in Central and South America, incorporating pre-existing peoples and empires, the northern European powers came later to colonization and established scattered settlements hugging the North American Atlantic coastline.

## Conquest of the Aztec Empire

The first two decades after Columbus's arrival in the New World saw Spanish settlement of Hispaniola, Cuba, Puerto Rico, and other Caribbean islands. Based on rumors of a wealthy mainland civilization, the Spanish governor in Cuba sponsored expeditions to the Yucatán coast of the Gulf of Mexico, including one in 1519 under the command of Hernán Cortés (1485–1547), a minor Spanish nobleman who had spent fifteen years in the Caribbean as an imperial administrator. Alarmed by Cortés's ambition, the governor decided to withdraw his support, but Cortés quickly set sail before being removed from command. Cortés, accompanied by several hundred fellow conquistadors as well as Taino and African slaves, landed on the Mexican coast on April 21, 1519. His camp soon received visits by delegations from the Aztec emperor bearing gifts and news of their great emperor.

The **Aztec Empire** was formed in the early fifteenth century through an alliance of the Mexica people of Tenochtitlan (tay-nawch-teet-LAHN) with other city-states in the Valley of Mexico. Over the next decades, the empire expanded rapidly through conquest. At the time of the Spanish arrival, emperor Moctezuma II (r. 1502–1520) ruled an empire of several million inhabitants from the capital at Tenochtitlan, now Mexico City. The Aztec Empire had a highly developed culture with advanced mathematics, astronomy, and engineering, as well as oral poetry and written record keeping. Aztec society was highly hierarchical. A hereditary nobility dominated the army, the priesthood, and the state bureaucracy, and lived from tribute collected from conquered states and its own people. The Aztec state practiced constant warfare against neighboring peoples to secure captives for religious sacrifices and laborers for agricultural and building projects.

After arriving on the mainland, Cortés took steps to establish authority independent of Cuba and the Spanish governor. He formally declared the establishment of a new town called Vera Cruz, naming his leading followers as town councilors and himself as military commander. He then sent letters to the Spanish crown requesting authorization to conquer and govern new lands.

The brutal nature of the Aztec Empire provided an opening for Cortés to obtain local assistance, a necessity for conquistadors throughout the Americas given their small numbers and ignorance of local conditions. Within weeks of his arrival, Cortés acquired translators who provided vital information on the empire and its weaknesses (see "Thinking Like a Historian: Who Was Doña Marina?" page 404). In September 1519, after initial hostilities in which many Spaniards died, Cortés formed an alliance with Tlaxcala (tlah-SKAH-lah), an independent city-state that had successfully resisted incorporation into the Aztec Empire.

In October a combined Spanish-Tlaxcalan force marched to the city of Cholula, which had recently switched loyalties from Tlaxcala to the Aztec Empire and massacred many thousands of inhabitants,

---

■ **Treaty of Tordesillas** A 1494 treaty that settled competing claims to newly discovered Atlantic territories by giving Spain everything to the west of an imaginary line drawn down the Atlantic and giving Portugal everything to the east.

■ **Aztec Empire** A large and complex Native American civilization in modern Mexico and Central America that possessed advanced mathematical, astronomical, and engineering technology.

## Who Was Doña Marina?

In April 1519 Doña Marina was among twenty women given to the Spanish as slaves. Fluent in Nahuatl (NAH-wah-tuhl) and Yucatec Maya (spoken by a Spanish priest accompanying Cortés), she acted as an interpreter and diplomatic guide for the Spanish. She had a close relationship with Cortés and bore his son, Don Martín Cortés, in 1522. Although no writings by Doña Marina survive, she figures prominently in both Spanish and indigenous sources on the conquest.

**1 Cortés's letter to Charles V, 1522.** This letter to Charles V contains one of only two written references to Doña Marina found in Cortés's correspondence with the emperor. He describes her as his "interpreter."

During the three days I remained in that city they fed us worse each day, and the lords and principal persons of the city came only rarely to see and speak with me. And being somewhat disturbed by this, my interpreter, who is an Indian woman from Putunchan, which is the great river of which I spoke to Your Majesty in the first letter, was told by another Indian woman and a native of this city that very close by many of Mutezuma's men were gathered, and that the people of the city had sent away their women and children and all their belongings, and were about to fall on us and kill us all; and that if she wished to escape she should go with her and she would shelter her. All this she told to Gerónimo de Aguilar, an interpreter whom I acquired in Yucatán, of whom I have also written to Your Highness; and he informed me.

**2 Díaz's account of the conquest of the Aztecs.** Bernal Díaz del Castillo participated in the conquest of the Aztecs alongside Cortés. His historical account of the conquest, written much later in life, provides the lengthiest descriptions of Doña Marina.

Early the next morning many Caciques and chiefs of Tabasco and the neighbouring towns arrived and paid great respect to us all, and they brought a present of gold, . . . and some other things of little value. . . . This present, however, was worth nothing in comparison with the twenty women that were given us, among them one very excellent woman called Doña Marina, for so she was named when she became a Christian.

. . . Cortés allotted one of the women to each of his captains and Doña Marina, as she was good looking and intelligent and without embarrassment, he gave to Alonzo Hernández Puertocarrero. When Puertocarrero went to Spain, Doña Marina lived with Cortés, and bore him a son named Don Martin Cortés.

. . . Her father and mother were chiefs and Caciques of a town called Paynala. . . . Her father died while she was still a little child, and her mother married another Cacique, a young man, and bore him a son. It seems that the father and mother had a great affection for this son and it was agreed between them that he should succeed to their honours when their days were done. So that there should be no impediment to this, they gave the little girl, Doña Marina, to some Indians from Xicalango, and this they did by night so as to escape observation, and they then spread the report that she had died, and as it happened at this time that a child of one of their Indian slaves died they gave out that it was their daughter and the heiress who was dead.

The Indians of Xicalango gave the child to the people of Tabasco and the Tabasco people gave her to Cortés.

. . . As Doña Marina proved herself such an excellent woman and good interpreter throughout the wars in New Spain, Tlaxcala and Mexico (as I shall show later on) Cortés always took her with him, and during that expedition she was married to a gentleman named Juan Jaramillo at the town of Orizaba.

Doña Marina was a person of the greatest importance and was obeyed without question by the Indians throughout New Spain.

### ANALYZING THE EVIDENCE

1. How would you compare the attitudes toward Doña Marina displayed in Cortés's letter to the Spanish crown (Source 1) and Díaz's account of the conquest (Source 2)? Why would Cortés downplay his reliance on Doña Marina in correspondence with the Spanish emperor?
2. What skills and experience enabled Doña Marina to act as an intermediary between the Spanish and the Aztecs? Based on the evidence, what role did she play in interactions between the Spanish and the Aztecs?
3. According to Díaz (Source 2), how did Doña Marina feel about her relationship with Cortés and the Spanish? How do you interpret this passage? Is there any evidence in the other sources that supports or undermines the sentiments he attributed to her?
4. Based on the evidence of these sources, what role did indigenous women play in relations between Spanish and Aztec men? How exceptional was Doña Marina?

**3** **Doña Marina translating for Hernán Cortés during his meeting with Moctezuma.** This image was created by Tlaxcalan artists approximately six decades after the conquest of Mexico and represents one indigenous perspective on the events.

Marina . . . said that God had been very gracious to her in freeing her from the worship of idols and making her a Christian, and letting her bear a son to her lord and master Cortés and in marrying her to such a gentleman as Juan Jaramillo, who was now her husband. That she would rather serve her husband and Cortés than anything else in the world, and would not exchange her place to be Cacica of all the provinces in New Spain.

Doña Marina knew the language of Coatzacoalcos, which is that common to Mexico, and she knew the language of Tabasco, as did also Jerónimo de Aguilar, who spoke the language of Yucatan and Tabasco, which is one and the same. So that these two could understand one another clearly, and Aguilar translated into Castilian for Cortés.

This was the great beginning of our conquests and thus, thanks be to God, things prospered with us. I have made a point of explaining this matter, because without the help of Doña Marina we could not have understood the language of New Spain and Mexico.

**4** **The *Florentine Codex*.** In the decades following the conquest, a Franciscan monk, Bernardino de Sahagún, worked with indigenous partners to compile a history of Aztec society. Known today as the *Florentine Codex,* it contains images and text written in both Nahuatl and Spanish. The following excerpt describes the entry of the victorious Spanish into Tenochtitlan.

Next they went to Motecuhzoma's storehouse, in the place called Totocalco, where his personal treasures were kept. The Spaniards grinned like little beasts and patted each other with delight.

When they entered the hall of treasures, it was as if they had arrived in Paradise. They searched everywhere and coveted everything; they were slaves to their own greed. . . .

They seized these treasures as they were their own, as if this plunder were merely a stroke of good luck. And when they had taken all the gold, they heaped up everything else in the middle of the patio.

La Malinche [Doña Marina] called all the nobles together. She climbed up to the palace roof and cried: "Mexicanos, come forward! The Spaniards need your help! Bring them food and pure water. They are tired and hungry; they are almost fainting from exhaustion! Why do you not come forward? Are you angry with them?"

The Mexicas were too frightened to approach. They were crushed by terror and would not risk coming forward. They shied away as if the Spaniards were wild beasts, as if the hour were midnight on the blackest night of the year. Yet they did not abandon the Spaniards to hunger and thirst. They brought them whatever they needed, but shook with fear as they did so. They delivered the supplies to the Spaniards with trembling hands, then turned and hurried away.

## PUTTING IT ALL TOGETHER

Using the sources above, along with what you have learned in class and in this chapter, imagine the events and experiences described in these sources from Doña Marina's point of view. Reflect on the various aspects of Doña Marina described in the sources—betrayed daughter, slave, concubine, mother, wife, interpreter, and commander—and write an essay that uses her experience to explore the interaction among Spanish, Aztec, and other indigenous groups during the conquest period.

Sources: (1) Hernán Cortés to Emperor Carlos V, 1522, in *Hernán Cortés: Letters from Mexico,* trans. and ed. Anthony Pagden (New Haven: Yale University Press, 1986), pp. 72–74; (2) Bernal Díaz del Castillo, *The Discovery and Conquest of Mexico, 1517–1521,* trans. A. P. Maudslay (New York: Noonday Press, 1965), pp. 62–63, 64, 66–67; (4) Miguel León-Portilla, ed., *The Broken Spears: The Aztec Account of the Conquest of Mexico,* pp. 68–69. Copyright © 1962, 1990 by Miguel León-Portilla. Expanded and Updated Edition © 1992 by Miguel León-Portilla. Reprinted by permission of Beacon Press, Boston.

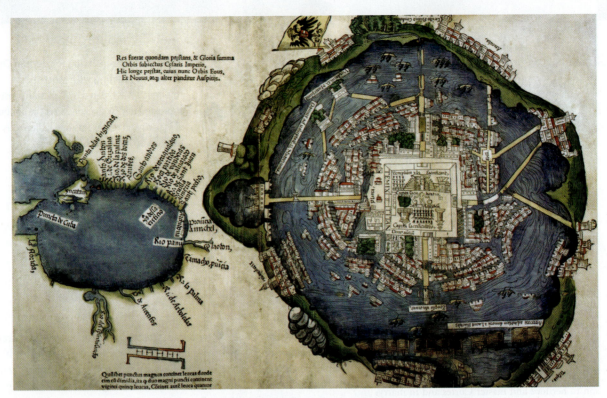

**The Mexica Capital of Tenochtitlan** This woodcut map was published in 1524 along with Cortés's letters describing the conquest of the Aztec Empire. As it shows, Tenochtitlan occupied an island and was laid out in concentric circles. The administrative and religious buildings were at the heart of the city, which was surrounded by residential quarters. Cortés himself marveled at the city in his letters: "The city is as large as Seville or Cordoba. . . . There are bridges, very large, strong, and well constructed, so that, over many, ten horsemen can ride abreast. . . . The city has many squares where markets are held. . . . There is one square . . . where there are daily more than sixty thousand souls, buying and selling. In the service and manners of its people, their fashion of living was almost the same as in Spain, with just as much harmony and order." (Newberry Library, Chicago, Illinois, USA/Bridgeman Images)

including women and children. Impressed by this display of ruthless power, the other native kingdoms joined Cortés's alliance against Aztec rule. In November 1519, these combined forces marched on Tenochtitlan.

Historians have long debated Moctezuma's response to the arrival of the Spanish. Despite the fact that Cortés was allied with enemies of the empire, Moctezuma refrained from attacking the Spaniards and instead welcomed Cortés and approximately 250 Spanish followers into Tenochtitlan. Cortés later claimed that at this meeting the emperor, inspired by prophecies of the Spaniards' arrival, agreed to become a vassal of the Spanish king. Although impossible for historians to verify, Cortés and later Spanish colonists used this claim to legitimate violence against any who resisted their rule.

After spending more than seven months in the city, in an ambiguous

**Invasion of Tenochtitlan, 1519–1521**

position that combined the status of honored guests, occupiers, and detainees, the Spanish seized Moctezuma as a hostage. During the ensuing attacks and counterattacks, Moctezuma was killed. The city's population rose up against the Spaniards, who fled with heavy losses. In May 1521 the Spanish-Tlaxcalan alliance assaulted Tenochtitlan a second time with an army of approximately one thousand Spanish and seventy-five thousand native warriors.[5]

The fall of the Aztec capital in late summer 1521 was hard-won and greatly facilitated by the effects of smallpox, which had devastated the besieged population of the city. After establishing a new capital in the ruins of Tenochtitlan, Cortés and other conquistadors began the systematic conquest of Mexico. Major campaigns continued in Mesoamerica for at least two decades against ongoing resistance.

## The Fall of the Incas

More surprising than the defeat of the Aztecs was the fall of the remote **Inca Empire**. Living in a settlement located more than 9,800 feet above sea level, the Incas were isolated from North American indigenous cultures and knew nothing of the Aztec Empire or its collapse. In 1438 the hereditary ruler of the Incas had himself crowned emperor and embarked on a successful campaign of conquest. At its greatest extent, the empire extended to the frontier of present-day Ecuador and Colombia in the north and to present-day Chile in the south, an area containing some 16 million people and 350,000 square miles.

Ruled from the capital city of Cuzco, the empire was divided into four major regions containing eighty provinces and twice as many districts. Officials at each level used an extensive network of roads to transmit information and orders back and forth through the empire. While the Aztecs used a system of glyphs for writing, the Incas had devised a complex system of colored and knotted cords, called *khipus*, for administrative bookkeeping. The empire also benefited from the use of llamas as pack animals (by contrast, no beasts of burden existed in Mesoamerica). The Incas integrated regions they conquered by spreading their religion and imposing their language, Quechua, as the official language of the empire.

By the time of the Spanish invasion, however, the Inca Empire had been weakened by a civil war over succession and an epidemic of disease, possibly smallpox, which may have spread through trade with groups in contact with Europeans. Francisco Pizarro (ca. 1475–1541), a conquistador of modest Spanish origins, landed on the northern coast of Peru on May 13, 1532, the very day the Inca leader Atahualpa (ah-tuh-WAHL-puh) won control of the empire after five years of fighting. As Pizarro advanced across the steep Andes toward Cuzco, the capital of the Inca Empire, Atahualpa was also heading there for his coronation.

Like Moctezuma in Mexico, Atahualpa was aware of the Spaniards' movements. He sent envoys to invite the Spanish to meet him in the provincial town of Cajamarca. His plan was to lure the Spanish into a trap, seize their horses and ablest men for his army, and execute the rest. With an army of some forty thousand men stationed nearby, Atahualpa felt he had little to fear. Instead, the Spaniards ambushed and captured him, collected an enormous ransom in gold, and then executed him in 1533 on trumped-up charges. The Spanish then marched on to Cuzco, profiting once again from internal conflicts to form alliances with local peoples. When Cuzco fell in 1533, the Spanish plundered the empire's wealth in gold and silver.

As with the Aztec Empire, the fall of the imperial capital did not end hostilities. Warfare between Spanish and Inca forces continued to the 1570s. During this period, civil war broke out among Spanish settlers vying for power.

For centuries students have wondered how it was possible for several hundred Spanish conquistadors to defeat powerful empires commanding large armies, vast wealth, and millions of inhabitants. This question is based on a mistaken understanding of the conquest as the rapid work of Spaniards acting alone, ideas that were spread in the aftermath by the conquistadors themselves. Instead, the defeat of the Aztec and Inca Empires was a long process enabled by divisions within the empires that produced political weakness and many skilled and motivated native allies who fought alongside the Spanish. Spanish steel swords, guns, horses, and dogs produced military advantages, but these tools of war were limited in number and effectiveness. Very few of the conquistadors were experienced soldiers. Perhaps the most important factor was the devastating impact of contagious diseases among the indigenous population, which swept through the Aztec and Inca Empires at the time of the conquest.

## Portuguese Brazil

Unlike Mesoamerica or the Andes, the territory of Brazil contained no urban empires, but instead roughly 2.5 million nomadic and settled people divided into small tribes and many different language groups. In 1500 the Portuguese crown named Pedro Álvares Cabral commander of a fleet headed for the spice trade of the Indies. En route the fleet sailed far to the west, accidentally landing on the coast of Brazil, which Cabral claimed for Portugal under the terms of the Treaty of Tordesillas. The Portuguese soon undertook a profitable trade with local people in brazilwood, a valued source of red dye.

Portuguese settlers began arriving in the 1530s, with numbers rising after 1550. In the early years of settlement, the Portuguese brought sugarcane production to Brazil. They initially used enslaved indigenous laborers on sugar plantations, but the rapid decline in the indigenous population soon led to the use of forcibly transported Africans. In Brazil the Portuguese thus created a new form of colonization in the Americas: large plantations worked by enslaved people. This model would spread throughout the Caribbean along with sugar production in the seventeenth century.

## Colonial Empires of England and France

For almost a century after the fall of the Aztec capital of Tenochtitlan, the Spanish and Portuguese dominated European overseas trade and colonization. In the

---

■ **Inca Empire** The vast and sophisticated Peruvian empire centered at the capital city of Cuzco that was at its peak from 1438 until 1533.

early seventeenth century, however, northern European powers began to challenge the Iberian monopoly. They eventually succeeded in creating multisited overseas empires, consisting of settler colonies in North America, slave plantations in the Caribbean, and scattered trading posts in West Africa and Asia. Competition among European states for colonies was encouraged by mercantilist economic doctrine, which dictated that foreign trade was a zero-sum game in which one country's gains necessarily entailed another's losses.

Unlike the Iberian powers, whose royal governments financed exploration and directly ruled the colonies, England, France, and the Netherlands conducted the initial phase of colonization via chartered

**The Chief of the Powhatan Tribe**   In the first years of the seventeenth century, Native American leader Wahunsenacawh, known as Chief Powhatan of the Powhatan people, ruled some thirty tribal groups in the Chesapeake Bay region. After initially assisting the Jamestown colony, in 1609 Chief Powhatan began to resent English demands and became hostile to them. After his daughter Pocahontas married an English settler (after having been captured and converted to Christianity), peaceful relations returned. This image, which shows the ruler in a traditional Powhatan wooden house, is a detail from a map of the Chesapeake Bay based on an original by John Smith, who spent several weeks as a captive of Powhatan. (Detail from the "Nova Virginiae Tabula," 1647/Bibliothèque des Arts Decoratifs, Paris, France/Archives Charmet/Bridgeman Images)

companies endowed with government monopolies over settlement and trade in a given area. These corporate bodies were granted extensive powers over faraway colonies, including exclusive rights to conduct trade, wage war, raise taxes, and administer justice.

The colony of Virginia, founded at Jamestown in 1607, initially struggled to grow sufficient food and faced hostility from the Powhatan Confederacy, a military alliance composed of around thirty Algonquian-speaking Native American tribes. Eventually it thrived by producing tobacco for a growing European market. Indentured servants obtained free passage to the colony in exchange for several years of work and the promise of greater opportunity for economic and social advancement than in England. In the 1670s English colonists from the Caribbean island of Barbados settled Carolina, where conditions were suitable for large rice plantations. During the late seventeenth century, following the Portuguese model in Brazil, enslaved Africans replaced indentured servants as laborers on tobacco and rice plantations, and a harsh racial divide was imposed.

Settlement on the coast of New England was undertaken for different reasons. There, radical Protestants sought to escape Anglican repression in England and begin new lives. The small and struggling outpost of Plymouth Colony (1620), founded by the Pilgrims who arrived on the *Mayflower*, was followed by Massachusetts Bay Colony (1630), which grew into a prosperous settlement. Because New England lacked the conditions for plantation agriculture, slavery was always a minor element of life there.

French navigator and explorer Samuel de Champlain founded the first permanent French settlement, at Quebec, in 1608. Ville-Marie, later named Montreal, was founded in 1642. Following the waterways of the St. Lawrence, the Great Lakes, and the Mississippi, the French ventured into much of modern-day Canada and at least thirty-five of the fifty states of the United States. French traders forged relations with the Huron Confederacy, a league of four indigenous nations that dominated a large region north of Lake Erie, as a means of gaining access to hunting grounds and trade routes for beaver and other animals. In 1682, French explorer René-Robert Cavelier LaSalle descended the Mississippi to the Gulf of Mexico, opening the way for French occupation of Louisiana.

Spanish expansion shared many similarities with that of other European powers, including the use of violence against indigenous populations and efforts toward Christian conversion, but there were important differences. Whereas the Spanish conquered indigenous empires, forcing large population groups to render tribute and enter state labor systems, English settlements merely hugged the Atlantic coastline and did not seek to incorporate the indigenous population. The English disinterest in full-scale conquest did not prevent conflict with native groups over land and resources, however. At Jamestown, for example, English expansion undermined prior cooperation with the Powhatan Confederacy; disease and warfare with the English led to drastic population losses among the Powhatans.

In the first decades of the seventeenth century, English and French naval captains also defied Spain's hold over the Caribbean Sea (see Map 14.2). The English seized control of Bermuda (1612), Barbados (1627), and a succession of other islands. The French took Cayenne (1604), St. Christophe (1625), Martinique and Guadeloupe (1635), and, finally, Saint-Domingue (1697) on the western half of Spanish-occupied Hispaniola. These islands acquired new importance after 1640, when the Portuguese brought sugar plantations to Brazil. Sugar and slaves quickly followed in the West Indies (see "Sugar and Slavery"), making the Caribbean plantations the most lucrative of all colonial possessions.

Northern European expansion also occurred in West Africa. In the seventeenth century France and England—along with Denmark and other northern European powers—established fortified trading posts in West Africa as bases for purchasing enslaved people and in India and the Indian Ocean as bases for purchasing spices and other luxury goods. Thus, by the end of the seventeenth century, a handful of European powers possessed overseas empires that truly spanned the globe.

## Colonial Administration

In 1482, King John II of Portugal established a royal trading house in Lisbon to handle gold and other goods (including enslaved people) being extracted from Africa. After Portuguese trade expanded into the Indian Ocean spice trade, it was named the *Casa da India* (House of the Indies). Through the Casa, the Crown exercised a monopoly over the export of European goods and the import and distribution of spices and precious metals. It charged taxes on all other incoming goods. The Casa also established a viceroy in the Indian city of Goa to administer Portuguese trading posts and naval forces in Africa and Asia.

To secure the vast expanse of Brazil, in the 1530s the Portuguese implemented the system of captaincies, hereditary grants of land given to nobles and loyal officials who were to bear the costs of settling and administering their territories. The failure of this system led the Crown to bring the captaincies under state control by appointing royal governors to act as administrators. The captaincy of Bahia was the site of the capital, Salvador, home to the governor general and other royal officials.

Spain adopted a similar system for overseas trade. In 1503 the Spanish granted the port of Seville a monopoly over all traffic to the New World and established the *Casa de la Contratación* (House of Trade) to oversee economic matters. In 1524 Spain created the Royal and Supreme Council of the Indies, with authority over all colonial affairs, subject to approval by the king.

By the end of the sixteenth century the Spanish had successfully overcome most indigenous groups and expanded their territory throughout modern-day Mexico, the southwestern United States, and Central and South America (with the exception of Portuguese Brazil). In Mesoamerica and the Andes, the Spanish had taken over the cities and tribute systems of the Aztecs and the Incas, leaving in place well-established cities and towns, but redirecting tribute payments toward the Crown. Through laws and regulations, the Spanish crown strove to maintain two separate populations, a "Spanish Republic" and an "Indian Republic," with distinct rights and duties for each group.

The Spanish crown divided its New World possessions initially into two **viceroyalties**, or administrative divisions: New Spain, created in 1535, with its capital at Mexico City, and Peru, created in 1542, with its capital at Lima. In the eighteenth century two additional viceroyalties were added: New Granada, with Bogotá as its administrative center; and La Plata, with Buenos Aires as its capital (see Map 14.2).

Within each territory the viceroy, or imperial governor, exercised broad military and civil authority as the direct representative of Spain. The viceroy presided over the *audiencia* (ow-dee-EHN-see-ah), a board of twelve to fifteen judges that served as his advisory council and the highest judicial body. As in Spain, settlement in the Americas was centered on cities and towns. In each city, the municipal council, or *cabildo*, exercised local authority. Women were denied participation in public life, a familiar pattern from both European and precolonial indigenous society.

By the end of the seventeenth century the French crown had followed the Iberian example and imposed direct rule over its North American colonies. The king appointed military governors to rule alongside intendants, royal officials possessed of broad administrative and financial authority within their intendancies. In the mid-eighteenth century reform-minded Spanish king Charles III (r. 1759–1788) adopted the intendant system for the Spanish colonies.

England's colonies followed a distinctive path. Drawing on English traditions of representative government, its colonists established their own proudly autonomous assemblies to regulate local affairs. Wealthy merchants and landowners dominated the assemblies, yet common men had more say in politics than was the case in England.

---

■ **viceroyalties** The name for the four administrative units of Spanish possessions in the Americas: New Spain, Peru, New Granada, and La Plata.

# How did Europe and the world change after Columbus?

The New and Old Worlds were brought into contact and forever changed by the European voyages of discovery and their aftermath. For the first time, a global economy emerged in the sixteenth and seventeenth centuries, and it forged new links among far-flung peoples, cultures, and societies. The ancient civilizations of Europe, Africa, the Americas, and Asia confronted each other in new and rapidly evolving ways. Those confrontations led to conquest, voluntary and forced migration, devastating population losses, and brutal exploitation. The exchange of goods and people between Europe and the New World brought highly destructive diseases to the Americas, but it also gave both the New and Old Worlds new crops that eventually altered consumption patterns across the globe.

## Economic Exploitation of the Indigenous Population

From the first decades of settlement, the Spanish made use of the **encomienda system**, by which the Crown granted the conquerors the right to employ groups of Native Americans as laborers or to demand tribute from them in exchange for providing food and shelter. The encomiendas were also intended as a means to organize indigenous people for missionary work and Christian conversion. This system was first used in Hispaniola to work goldfields, then in Mexico for agricultural labor, and, when silver was discovered in the 1540s, for silver mining.

A 1512 Spanish law authorizing the use of encomiendas called for indigenous people to be treated fairly, but in practice the system led to terrible abuses, including overwork, beatings, and sexual violence. Spanish missionaries publicized these abuses, leading to debates in Spain about the nature and proper treatment of indigenous people (see "Religious Conversion" ahead in this chapter). King Charles I responded to complaints in 1542 with the New Laws, which set limits on the authority of encomienda holders, including their ability to transmit their privileges to heirs. The New Laws recognized indigenous people who accepted Christianity and Spanish rule as free subjects of the Spanish crown. According to these laws, they had voluntarily accepted to be vassals of the Spanish king and thereby gained personal liberty and the right to form their own communities.

The New Laws provoked a revolt in Peru among encomienda holders, and they were little enforced throughout Spanish territories. For example, although the laws forbade enslavement of indigenous people, the practice did not end completely. To respond to persistent abuses in the encomiendas and a growing shortage of indigenous workers, royal officials established a new government-run system of forced labor, called *repartimiento* in New Spain and *mita* in Peru. Administrators assigned a certain percentage of the inhabitants of native communities to labor for a set period each year in public works, mining, agriculture, and other tasks. Laborers received modest wages in exchange, which they could use to fulfill tribute obligations. In the seventeenth century, as land became a more important source of wealth than labor, elite settlers purchased *haciendas*, large tracts of farmland worked by dependent indigenous laborers and slaves.

Spanish systems for exploiting the labor of indigenous peoples were both a cause of and a response to the disastrous decline in their numbers that began soon after the arrival of Europeans. Some indigenous people died as a direct result of the violence of conquest and the disruption of agriculture and trade caused by warfare, but the most important cause of death was infectious disease. (See "The Columbian Exchange and Population Loss" ahead in this chapter.)

Colonial administrators responded to native population decline by forcibly combining dwindling indigenous communities into new settlements and imposing the rigors of the encomienda and the repartimiento. By the end of the sixteenth century the search for fresh sources of labor had given birth to the new tragedy of the transatlantic slave trade (see "Sugar and Slavery").

## Society in the Colonies

Many factors helped shape life in European colonies, including geographical location, pre-existing indigenous cultures, patterns of settlement, and the policies and cultural values of the different nations that claimed them as empire. Throughout the New World, colonial settlements were hedged by immense borderlands where European power was weak and Europeans and non-Europeans interacted on a more equal basis.

Women played a crucial role in the emergence of colonial societies. The first explorers formed unions with native women, many of whom were enslaved, and relied on them as translators and guides and to form alliances with indigenous powers. As settlement developed, the character of each colony was

■ **encomienda system** A system whereby the Spanish crown granted the conquerors the right to forcibly employ groups of Indians in exchange for providing food, shelter, and Christian teaching.

■ **Columbian Exchange** The exchange of animals, plants, and diseases between the Old and the New Worlds.

influenced by the presence or absence of European women. Where women and children accompanied men, as in the Spanish mainland and British colonies, new settlements took on European languages, religion, and ways of life that have endured, with strong input from local cultures, to this day. Where European women did not accompany men, as on the west coast of Africa and most European outposts in Asia, local populations largely retained their own cultures, to which male Europeans acclimatized themselves.

Most women who crossed the Atlantic were captive Africans, constituting four-fifths of the female newcomers before 1800.[6] Wherever slavery existed, masters profited from their power to coerce sexual relations with enslaved women. One important difference among European colonies was in the status of children born from such unions. In some colonies, mostly those dominated by the Portuguese, Spanish, or French, substantial populations of free people of color descended from the freed children of such unions. In English colonies, masters were less likely to free children they fathered with female slaves. The mixing of indigenous peoples with Europeans and Africans created whole new populations and ethnicities and complex forms of identity (see "New Ideas About Race").

## The Columbian Exchange and Population Loss

The migration of people to the New World led to an exchange of animals, plants, and diseases, a complex process known as the **Columbian exchange**.

Everywhere they settled, the Spanish and Portuguese brought and raised wheat with labor provided by the encomienda system. Grapes and olives brought over from Spain did well in parts of Peru and Chile. Perhaps the most significant introduction to the diet of Native Americans came via the meat and milk of the livestock that the early conquistadors brought with them, including cattle, sheep, and goats. The horse allowed for faster travel and easier transport of heavy loads.

In turn, Europeans returned home with many food crops that became central elements of their diet. Crops originating in the Americas included tomatoes, squash, pumpkins, peppers, and many varieties of beans, as well as tobacco. One of the most important of such crops was maize (corn). By the late seventeenth century maize had become a staple in Spain, Portugal, southern France, and Italy, and in the eighteenth century it became one of the chief foods of southeastern Europe and southern China. Even more valuable was the nutritious white potato, which slowly spread from west to east, contributing everywhere to a rise in population.

While the exchange of foods was a great benefit to both cultures, the introduction of European pathogens to the New World had a disastrous impact on the native population. In Europe, infectious diseases like smallpox, measles, and influenza—originally passed on from domestic animals living among the population—killed many people each year. Given the size of the population and the frequency of outbreaks, in most of Europe these diseases were experienced in childhood, and survivors carried immunity or resistance. Over centuries of dealing with these diseases, the European population had had time to adapt. Prior to contact with Europeans, indigenous peoples of the New World suffered from insect-borne diseases and some infectious ones, but their lack of domestic livestock spared them the host of highly infectious diseases known in the Old World. The arrival of Europeans spread these microbes among a completely unprepared population, and they fell victim in vast numbers.

Overall, the indigenous population declined by as much as 90 percent or more, but with important regional variations. In general, densely populated urban centers were worse hit than rural areas, and tropical, low-lying regions suffered more than cooler, higher-altitude ones. The world after Columbus was thus marked by disease as well as by trade and colonization.

**A Mixed-Race Procession** The Incas used drinking vessels, known as *keros*, for the ritual consumption of maize beer at feasts. This kero from the early colonial period depicts a multiracial procession: an Inca dignitary is preceded by a Spanish trumpet player and an African drummer. This is believed to be one of the earliest visual representations of an African in the Americas. (British Museum, London, UK/Werner Forman/Universal Images Group/Getty Images)

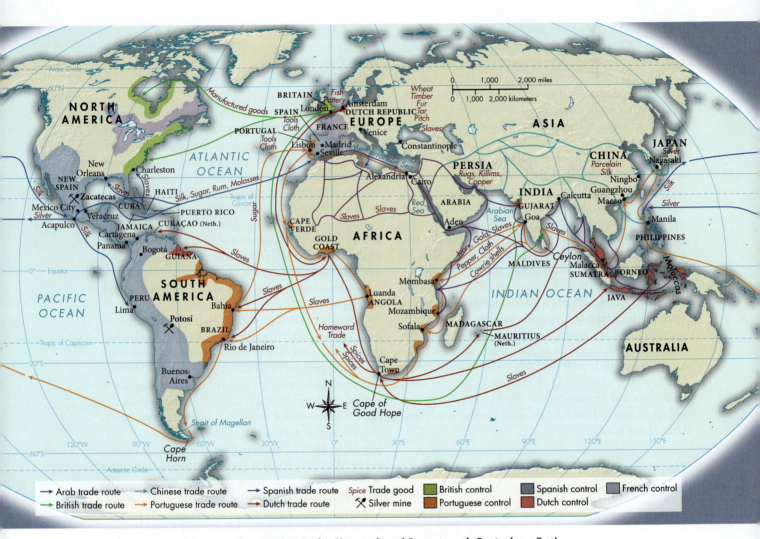

**MAP 14.3** **Seaborne Trading Empires in the Sixteenth and Seventeenth Centuries** By the mid-seventeenth century trade linked all parts of the world except for Australia. Notice that trade in slaves was not confined to the Atlantic but involved almost all parts of the world.

## Sugar and Slavery

Throughout the Middle Ages slavery was deeply entrenched in the Mediterranean. The constant warfare of the reconquista had supplied captive Muslims for domestic slavery in Iberia, but the success of these wars meant that the number of captives had greatly dwindled by the mid-fifteenth century.

As Portuguese explorers began their voyages along the western coast of Africa, one of the first commodities they sought was enslaved human beings. In 1444 the first ship returned to Lisbon with a cargo of enslaved Africans. While the first slaves were simply seized by small raiding parties, Portuguese merchants soon found that it was easier to trade with local leaders, who were accustomed to dealing in captives acquired through warfare with neighboring powers. In 1483 the Portuguese established an alliance with the kingdom of Kongo. The royal family eventually

converted to Christianity, and Portuguese merchants intermarried with Kongolese women, creating a permanent Afro-Portuguese community. From 1490 to 1530 Portuguese traders brought hundreds of enslaved Africans to Lisbon each year (Map 14.3) to work as domestic slaves.

In this stage of European expansion, the history of slavery became intertwined with the history of sugar. Originally sugar was an expensive luxury, but population increases and monetary expansion in the fifteenth century led to increasing demand. Native to the South Pacific, sugar was taken in ancient times to India, where farmers learned to preserve cane juice as granules that could be stored and shipped. From there, sugar crops traveled to China and the Mediterranean, where islands like Crete and Sicily had the warm and humid climate needed for growing sugarcane. When Genoese and other Italians colonized the Canary

**Indians Working in a Spanish Sugar Mill** Belgian engraver Theodor de Bry published many images of the European exploration and settlement of the New World. De Bry never crossed the Atlantic himself, instead drawing on images and stories from those who did. This image depicts the exploitation of indigenous people in a Spanish sugar mill. (ca. 1540 engraving by Theodore de Bry [1528–1598]/Bibliothèque Nationale, Paris, France/Snark/Art Resource, NY)

Islands and the Portuguese settled on the Madeira Islands, which possessed the requisite climate conditions, sugar plantations came to the Atlantic.

Sugar was a difficult and demanding crop to produce for profit. Seed-stems were planted by hand, thousands to the acre. When mature, the cane had to be harvested and processed rapidly to avoid spoiling. Moreover, sugar has a virtually constant growing season, meaning that there was no fallow period when workers could recuperate from the arduous labor. The invention of roller mills to crush the cane more efficiently meant that yields could be significantly augmented, but only if a sufficient labor force was found to supply the mills. Europeans solved the labor problem by forcing first native islanders and then enslaved Africans to provide the backbreaking work.

The transatlantic slave trade began in 1518 when Spanish king Charles I authorized traders to bring enslaved Africans to the Americas. The Portuguese brought the first slaves to Brazil around 1550; by 1600 four thousand were being imported annually. After its founding in 1621, the Dutch West India Company transported thousands of Africans to Brazil and the Caribbean, mostly to work on sugar plantations. In the mid-seventeenth century the English got involved.

Before 1700, when slavers decided it was better business to improve conditions for the slaves, some 20 percent of captives died on the voyage across the Atlantic.[7] The most common cause of death was dysentery induced by poor-quality food and water, crowding, and lack of sanitation. Men were often kept in irons during the passage, while women and girls suffered sexual violence from sailors. On sugar plantations, death rates from the brutal pace of labor were extremely high, leading to demand for a constant stream of new shipments from Africa.

## Spanish Silver and Its Economic Effects

In 1545, at an altitude of fifteen thousand feet, the Spanish discovered an extraordinary source of silver at Potosí (poh-toh-SEE) (in present-day Bolivia) in territory conquered from the Inca Empire. By 1550 Potosí yielded perhaps 60 percent of all the silver mined in the world. From Potosí and the mines at Zacatecas (za-kuh-TAY-kuhhs) and Guanajuato (gwah-nah-HWAH-toh) in Mexico, huge quantities of precious metals poured forth.

Mining became the most important industry in the colonies. Millions of indigenous laborers suffered brutal conditions and death in the silver mines. Demand for new sources of labor for the mines also contributed to the intensification of the African slave trade. Profits for the Spanish crown were immense. The Crown claimed the quinto, one-fifth of all precious metals mined in South America, which represented 25 percent of its total income. Between 1503 and 1650, 35

**Philip II, ca. 1533**    This portrait of Philip II as a young man and crown prince of Spain is by the celebrated artist Titian, court painter to Philip's father, Charles V. After taking the throne, Philip became another great patron of the artist. (Palazzo Pitti, Florence, Italy/Bridgeman Images)

million pounds of silver and over 600,000 pounds of gold entered Seville's port.

Spain's immense profits from silver paid for the tremendous expansion of its empire and for the large armies that defended it. However, the easy flow of money also dampened economic innovation. It exacerbated the rising inflation Spain was already experiencing in the mid-sixteenth century, a period of growing population and stagnant production. Several times between 1557 and 1647, King Philip II and his successors wrote off the state debt, thereby undermining confidence in the government and damaging the economy. Only after 1600, when the population declined, did prices gradually stabilize.

Philip II paid his armies and foreign debts with silver bullion, and thus Spanish inflation was transmitted to the rest of Europe. Between 1560 and 1600 much of Europe experienced large price increases. Because money bought less, people who lived on fixed incomes, such as nobles, were badly hurt. Those who owed fixed sums of money, such as the middle class, prospered because in a time of rising prices, debts lessened in value each year. Food costs rose most sharply, and the poor fared worst of all.

In many ways, though, it was not Spain but China that controlled the world trade in silver. The Chinese demanded silver for their products and for the payment of imperial taxes. China was thus the main buyer of world silver, absorbing half the world's production. The silver market drove world trade, with New Spain and Japan being mainstays on the supply side and China dominating the demand side. The world trade in silver is one of the best examples of the new global economy that emerged in this period.

## The Birth of the Global Economy

With the Europeans' discovery of the Americas and their exploration of the Pacific, the entire world was linked for the first time in history by seaborne trade. The opening of that trade brought into being three commercial empires: the Portuguese, the Spanish, and the Dutch.

The Portuguese were the first worldwide traders. In the sixteenth century they controlled the sea route to India (see Map 14.3). From their fortified bases at Goa on the Arabian Sea and at Malacca on the Malay Peninsula, ships carried goods to the Portuguese settlement at Macao, founded in 1557, in the South China Sea. From Macao Portuguese ships loaded with Chinese silks and porcelains sailed to the Japanese port of Nagasaki and the Philippines, where Chinese goods were exchanged for Spanish silver from New Spain. Throughout Asia the Portuguese traded in slaves, some of whom were brought all the way across the Pacific to Mexico. (See "Individuals in Society: Catarina de San Juan," page 415.) Returning to Portugal, they brought Asian spices that had been purchased with textiles produced in India and with gold and ivory from East Africa. From their colony in Brazil, they shipped sugar produced by enslaved Africans whom they had forcibly transported across the Atlantic.

Coming to empire a few decades later than the Portuguese, the Spanish were determined to claim their place in world trade. The Spanish Empire in the New World was basically a land empire, but across the Pacific the Spaniards built a seaborne empire centered at Manila in the Philippines. Established in 1571, the city of Manila served as a transpacific link between Spanish America and China. In Manila, Spanish traders used silver from American mines to purchase Chinese silk for European markets (see Map 14.3).

In the final years of the sixteenth century the Dutch challenged the Spanish and Portuguese

A long journey led Catarina de San Juan from enslavement in South Asia to adulation as a popular saint in Mexico. Her journey began on the west coast of India around 1610 when Portuguese traders captured a group of children, including the small girl who would become Catarina. Their ship continued around the southern tip of India, across the Bay of Bengal, through the Strait of Malacca, and across the South China Sea. It docked at Manila, a Spanish city in the Philippines, where the girl was sold at a slave auction. In 1619 Catarina boarded a ship that was part of the Manila Galleon, the annual convoy of Spanish ships that crossed the Pacific between Manila and the Mexican port of Acapulco. After a six-month voyage, Catarina arrived in Acapulco; she then walked to Mexico City and continued on to the city of Puebla.

In Puebla, Catarina became the property of a Portuguese merchant and worked as a domestic servant. She was one of thousands of *chinos*, a term for natives of the East Indies who were brought via the Philippines to Spanish America. Many were slaves, transported as part of a transoceanic slave trade that reached from the Indian Ocean to the South China Sea and across the Pacific to the Atlantic world. They constituted a small but significant portion of people forcibly transported by Europeans to the Americas in the late sixteenth and early seventeenth century to replace dwindling numbers of indigenous laborers. Chinos were considered particularly apt for domestic labor, and many wealthy Spanish Americans bought them in Manila.

Before crossing the Pacific, Catarina converted to Catholicism and chose her Christian name. In Puebla her master encouraged Catarina's faith and allowed her to attend Mass every day. He also drafted a will emancipating her after his death, which occurred in 1619. With no money of her own, Catarina became the servant of a local priest. On his advice, Catarina reluctantly gave up her dream of becoming a lay sister and married a fellow chino named Domingo. The marriage was unhappy; Catarina reportedly refused to enter sexual relations with her husband and suffered from his debts, infidelity, and hostility to her faith. She found solace in renewed religious devotion, winning the admiration of priests and neighbors who flocked to her for spiritual comfort and to hear about her ecstatic visions. After fourteen years of marriage, Catarina became a widow and lived out her life in the home of wealthy supporters.

Catarina's funeral in 1688 drew large crowds. Her followers revered her as an unofficial saint, and soon the leaders of Puebla began a campaign to have Catarina beatified (officially recognized by the Catholic Church as a saint). Her former confessors published accounts of her life emphasizing her piety, beauty, and exotic Asian origins and marveling at

**Nineteenth-century painting of Puebla women in traditional clothing.** (De Agostini Picture Library/G. Dagli Orti/Bridgeman Images)

the miraculous preservation of her virginity through the perils of enslavement, long journeys at sea, and marriage. Much of what we know about Catarina derives from these sources and must be viewed as idealized, rather than as strictly historically accurate. The Spanish Inquisition, which oversaw the process of beatification, rejected Catarina's candidacy and, fearing that popular adulation might detract from the authority of the church, forbade the circulation of images of and texts about her. Despite this ban, popular reverence for Catarina de San Juan continued, and continues to this day in Mexico.

### QUESTIONS FOR ANALYSIS

1. Why would the Inquisition react so negatively to popular devotion to Catarina? What dangers did she pose to the Catholic Church in New Spain?
2. What does Catarina's story reveal about the global nature of the Spanish Empire and the slave trade in this period? What does it reveal about divisions within the Catholic Church?

Sources: Tatiana Seijas, *Asian Slaves in Colonial Mexico: From Chinos to Indians* (New York: Cambridge University Press, 2014), pp. 8–26; Ronald J. Morgan, *Spanish American Saints and the Rhetoric of Identity, 1600–1810* (Tucson: University of Arizona Press, 2002), pp. 119–142.

**Goods from the Global Economy** Spices from Southeast Asia were a driving force behind the new global economy and among the most treasured European luxury goods. They were used not only for cooking but also as medicines and health tonics. This fresco (below right) shows a fifteenth-century Italian pharmacist measuring out spices for a customer. After the discovery of the Americas, a wave of new items entered European markets, silver foremost among them. The incredibly rich silver mines at Potosí (modern-day Bolivia) were the source of this eight-reale coin (right) struck at the mine during the reign of Charles II. Such coins were the original "pieces of eight" prized by pirates and adventurers. Soon Asian and American goods were mixed together by enterprising tradesmen. This mid-seventeenth-century Chinese teapot (below left) was made of porcelain with the traditional Chinese design prized in the West, but with a silver handle added to suit European tastes. (teapot: Private Collection/Bridgeman Images; spice shop: Issogne Castle, Val d'Aosta, Italy/Alfredo Dagli Orti/Shutterstock; coin: Hoberman Collection/Hoberman Collection/Superstock)

Empires. During this period the Protestant Dutch were engaged in a long war of independence from their Spanish Catholic overlords. The joining of the Portuguese crown to Spain in 1580 meant that the Dutch had both strategic and commercial reasons to attack Portugal's commercial empire. In 1599 a Dutch fleet returned to Amsterdam carrying 600,000 pounds of pepper and 250,000 pounds of cloves and nutmeg. Those who had invested in the expedition received a 100 percent profit. The voyage led to the establishment in 1602 of the Dutch East India Company, founded with the stated intention of capturing the Asian spice trade from the Portuguese.

In return for assisting Indonesian princes in local conflicts and disputes with the Portuguese, the Dutch won broad commercial concessions and forged military alliances. With Indonesian assistance, they captured the strategically located fort of Malacca in 1641, gaining western access to the Malay Archipelago. Gradually, they acquired political domination over the archipelago itself. The Dutch were willing to use force more ruthlessly than the Portuguese and had superior organizational efficiency. These factors allowed them to expel the Portuguese from Sri Lanka in 1660 and henceforth control the immensely lucrative production and trade of spices. The company also established the colony of Cape Town on the southern tip of Africa as a provisioning point for its Asian fleets.

Not content with challenging the Portuguese in the Indian Ocean, the Dutch also aspired to a role in the Americas. Founded in 1621, during their war with Spain, the Dutch West India Company aggressively sought to open trade with North and South America and capture Spanish territories there. The company captured or destroyed hundreds of Spanish ships, seized the Spanish silver fleet in 1628, and captured portions of Brazil and the Caribbean. The Dutch also successfully interceded in the transatlantic slave trade, establishing a large number of trading stations on the west coast of Africa.

# How did expansion change European attitudes and beliefs?

The age of overseas expansion heightened Europeans' contacts with the rest of the world. Religion was one of the most important arenas of cultural contact, as European missionaries aimed to spread Christianity throughout the territories they acquired, with mixed results. While Christianity was embraced in parts of the New World, it was met largely with suspicion in places such as China and Japan. However, the East-West contacts did lead to exchanges of influential cultural and scientific ideas.

These contacts also gave birth to new ideas about the inherent superiority or inferiority of different races, sparking vociferous debate about the status of Africans and indigenous peoples of the Americas. The essays of Michel de Montaigne epitomized a new spirit of skepticism and cultural relativism, while the plays of William Shakespeare reflected the efforts of one great writer to come to terms with the cultural complexity of his day.

## Religious Conversion

Conversion to Christianity was one of the most important justifications for European expansion. Jesuit missionaries were active in Japan and China in the sixteenth and seventeenth centuries, until authorities banned their teachings. The first missionaries to the New World accompanied Columbus on his second voyage, and more than 2,500 priests and friars of the Franciscan, Dominican, Jesuit, and other Catholic orders crossed the Atlantic in the following century. Later French explorers were also accompanied by missionaries who preached to the Native American tribes with whom the French traded. Protestants also led missionary efforts, but in much smaller numbers than Catholics. Colonial powers built convents, churches, and cathedrals for converted indigenous people and European settlers, and established religious courts to police correct beliefs and morals.

To stamp out old beliefs and encourage sincere conversions, colonial authorities destroyed shrines and objects of religious worship. They harshly persecuted men and women who continued to practice and participate in traditional spiritual rituals. They imposed European Christian norms of family life, especially monogamous marriage. While many resisted these efforts, over time a larger number accepted Christianity. (See "Viewpoints: Aztec and Spanish Views on Christian Conversion in New Spain," page 418.) It is estimated that missionaries had baptized between 4 and 9 million indigenous people in New Spain by the mid-1530s.[8]

**Franciscan Monks Burning Indigenous Temples**   In the late sixteenth century, more than six decades after the fall of Tenochtitlan, Diego Muñoz Camargo, an educated *mestizo*, was chosen to draft a report on the province of Tlaxcala in response to a questionnaire issued by the king of Spain. Camargo produced a history of the Tlaxcala people — one of the first and most important Spanish allies against the Aztecs — starting from the time of conquest. An important theme of the text and its accompanying images was the efforts made by Franciscan missionaries to stamp out polytheistic indigenous religions in favor of Catholicism. This included, as shown here, burning temples, as well as destroying religious texts and punishing lapsed converts. (From "Historia de Tlaxcala" by Diego Munoz Camargo/Glasgow University Library, Scotland/Bridgeman Images)

# VIEWPOINTS

## Aztec and Spanish Views on Christian Conversion in New Spain

In justifying their violent conquest of the Aztec and Inca civilizations, Spanish conquistadors emphasized the need to bring Christianity to heathen peoples. For the conquered, the imposition of Christianity and the repression of their pre-existing religions were often experienced as yet another form of loss. The first document recounts the response of vanquished Aztec leaders of Tenochtitlan to Franciscan missionaries. It was written forty years after the events described by the Spanish missionary and scholar Bernardino de Sahagún based on what he learned from Spanish chroniclers and surviving Aztec leaders. Despite resistance, missionaries eventually succeeded in converting much of the indigenous population to Catholicism. In the second document, an account of the Spanish conquest and its aftermath written in the 1560s by a man who had participated in the conquest, Bernal Díaz del Castillo professes great satisfaction at the Catholic piety of converted indigenous communities and their assimilation into European culture. As you read, ask yourself what motivations Díaz may have had to present such a positive picture.

### Aztec Response to the Franciscans' 1524 Explanation of Mission, 1564

You have told us that we do not know the One who gives us life and being, who is Lord of the heavens and of the earth. You also say that those we worship are not gods. This way of speaking is entirely new to us, and very scandalous. We are frightened by this way of speaking because our forebears who engendered and governed us never said anything like this. On the contrary, they left us this our custom of worshiping our gods, in which they believed and which they worshiped all the time that they lived here on earth. They taught us how to honor them. And they taught us all the ceremonies and sacrifices that we make. They told us that through them [our gods] we live and are, and that we were beholden to them, to be theirs and to serve countless centuries before the sun began to shine and before there was daytime. They said that these gods that we worship give us everything we need for our physical existence: maize, beans, chia seeds, etc. . . .

All of us together feel that it is enough to have lost, enough that the power and royal jurisdiction have been taken from us. As for our gods, we will die before giving up serving and worshiping them.

### Bernal Díaz del Castillo on the Spread of Christianity in New Spain, 1560s

It is a thing to be grateful for to God, and for profound consideration, to see how the natives assist in celebrating a holy Mass. . . . There is another good thing they do [namely] that both men, women and children, who are of the age to learn them, know all the holy prayers in their own languages and are obliged to know them. They have other good customs about their holy Christianity, that when they pass near a sacred altar or Cross they bow their heads with humility, bend their knees, and say the prayer "Our Father," which we Conquistadores have taught them, and they place lighted wax candles before the holy altars and crosses. . . . In addition to what I have said, we taught them to show great reverence and obedience to all the monks and priests. . . . Beside the good customs reported by me they have others both holy and good, for when the day of Corpus Christ comes, or that of Our Lady, or other solemn festivals when among us we form processions, most of the pueblos in the neighbourhood of this city of Guatemala come out in procession with their crosses and lighted wax tapers, and carry on their shoulders, on a litter, the image of the saint who is the patron of the pueblo.

### QUESTIONS FOR ANALYSIS

1. What reasons do the leaders of Tenochtitlan offer for rejecting the teachings of Franciscan missionaries? What importance do they accord their own religious traditions?
2. What evidence does Díaz provide for the conversion of the indigenous people in the city of Guatemala?
3. How and why do you think the attitudes of indigenous peoples might have evolved from those described in the first document to those praised in the second? Why do you think Díaz may have exaggerated the Christian fervor of indigenous people?

Sources: "The Lords and Holy Men of Tenochtitlan Reply to the Franciscans Bernardino de Sahagún, Coloquios y doctrina Cristiana," ed. Miguel León-Portilla, in *Colonial Spanish America: A Documentary History*, ed. Kenneth Mills and William B. Taylor, pp. 20–21. Reproduced with permission of Rowman & Littlefield Publishers; Bernal Díaz, *The True History of the Conquest of New Spain*, in Stuart B. Schwartz, *Victors and Vanquished: Spanish and Nahua Views of the Conquest of Mexico* (Boston: Bedford/St. Martin's, 2000), pp. 218–219.

Rather than a straightforward imposition of Christianity, conversion entailed a complex process of cultural exchange. Catholic friars were among the first Europeans to seek an understanding of native cultures and languages as part of their effort to render Christianity comprehensible to indigenous people. In Mexico they not only learned the Nahuatl language, but also taught it to non-Nahuatl-speaking groups to create a shared language for Christian teaching. In translating Christianity, missionaries, working in partnership with indigenous converts, adapted it to the symbols and ritual objects of pre-existing cultures and beliefs, thereby creating distinctive forms of Catholicism.

## European Debates About Indigenous Peoples

Iberian exploitation of the native population of the Americas began from the moment of Columbus's arrival in 1492. Denunciations of this abuse by Catholic missionaries, however, quickly followed, inspiring vociferous debates both in Europe and in the colonies about the nature of indigenous peoples and how they should be treated. Bartolomé de Las Casas (1474–1566), a Dominican friar and former encomienda holder, was one of the earliest and most outspoken critics of the brutal treatment inflicted on indigenous peoples. He wrote:

> It was upon these gentle lambs [that] . . . the Spanish fell like ravening wolves upon the fold, or like tigers and savage lions who have not eaten meat for days. The pattern established at the outset has remained unchanged to this day, and the Spaniards still do nothing save tear the natives to shreds, murder them and inflict upon them untold misery, suffering and distress, tormenting, harrying and persecuting them mercilessly. . . .⁹

Mounting criticism in Spain led King Charles I to assemble a group of churchmen and lawyers to debate the issue in 1550 in the city of Valladolid. One side, led by Juan Ginés de Sepúlveda, argued that conquest and forcible conversion were both necessary and justified to save indigenous people from the horrors of human sacrifice, cannibalism, and idolatry. He described them as barbarians who belonged to a category of inferior beings identified by the ancient Greek philosopher Aristotle as naturally destined for slavery. Against these arguments, Las Casas and his supporters depicted indigenous people as rational and innocent children, who deserved protection and tutelage from more advanced civilizations. Although Las Casas was more sympathetic to indigenous people, both sides thus agreed on the superiority of European culture.

While the debate did not end exploitation of indigenous people, the Crown did use it to justify limiting the rights of settlers in favor of the Catholic Church and royal authorities and to increase legal protections for their communities. In 1573, Philip II issued detailed laws regulating how new towns should be formed and administered, and how Spanish settlers should interact with indigenous populations. The impact of these laws can still be seen in Mexico's colonial towns, which are laid out as grids around a central plaza.

## New Ideas About Race

European conquest and settlement led to the emergence of new ideas about "race" as a form of biological difference among humans. In medieval Spain and Portugal, sharp distinctions were drawn between, on the one hand, supposedly "pure-blooded" Christians and, on the other hand, Jews and *conversos*, people of Jewish origins who had converted to Christianity. In the fifteenth century, Iberian rulers issued discriminatory laws against conversos as well as against Muslims and their descendants. Feeling that conversion could not erase the taint of heretical belief, they came to see Christian faith as a type of inherited identity that was passed through the blood.

The idea of "purity of blood" changed through experiences in the colonies. There the transatlantic slave trade initiated in the sixteenth century meant that the colonial population comprised people of European, indigenous, and African descent. Spanish colonizers came to believe that the indigenous people of the Americas were free from the taint of unbelief because they had never been exposed to Christianity. Accordingly, the ideology of "purity of blood" they brought from Iberia could more easily incorporate indigenous populations; by contrast, Africans—viewed as having refused the message of Christ that was preached in the Old World—were seen as impure, as much on the grounds of religious difference as physical characteristics. (See "Evaluating Visual Evidence: Depictions of Africans in European Portraiture," page 420.)

Despite later efforts by colonial officials to segregate Europeans, Native Americans, and people of African descent, racial mixing began as soon as the first conquistadors arrived in the Americas. A complex system of racial classification, known as *castas* in Spanish America, emerged to describe different proportions of European, indigenous, and African parentage. Spanish concerns about religious purity were thus transformed in the colonial context into concerns about racial bloodlines, with "pure" Spanish blood occupying the summit of the racial hierarchy and indigenous and African descent ranked in descending order. These concerns put female chastity at the center of anxieties about racial mixing, heightening scrutiny of women's sexual activities.

All European colonies in the New World relied on racial distinctions drawn between Europeans and indigenous people and those of African descent, including later French and English settlements. With its immense slave-based plantation agriculture system, large indigenous population, and relatively low Portuguese immigration, Brazil developed a particularly complex racial and ethnic mosaic.

After 1700 the emergence of new methods of observing and describing nature led to the use of scientific frameworks to define race. Although it originally referred to a nation or an ethnic group, henceforth the term *race* would be used to describe supposedly biologically distinct groups of people, whose physical differences produced differences in culture, character, and intelligence. This occurred at the same time as a shift to defining gender differences as inherent in the biological differences between

# Depictions of Africans in European Portraiture

Starting in the Italian Renaissance, with the emergence of portraiture as a new genre, European elites began to commission images of themselves accompanied by slaves of African descent. Their intentions in doing so were to accentuate their wealth and power. Like imported Persian carpets, spices, and exotic animals, images of enslaved people demonstrated their owners' possession of valuable and exotic foreign goods. The depiction of enslaved Africans in aristocratic portraits began in Portugal and Spain in the mid-1550s and spread to other European nations in the seventeenth century. In this painting by Flemish painter Anthony Van Dyke, Marchesa Elena Grimaldi Cattaneo is shown lavishly dressed and confidently gazing at the viewer.* A young boy of African descent holds a parasol over her head to shield the Marchesa from the sun. In this image, the dark skin of the attendant contrasts with the Marchesa's aristocratic pallor, suggesting that another function of depicting people of African descent was to valorize whiteness as an attribute of European superiority.

## EVALUATE THE EVIDENCE

1. What elements of the painting suggest the Marchesa's elite status within her society and her attendant's servile status? What impression are we meant to have of each of these people?
2. How does the color scheme of the painting help to convey its meaning? How do you explain the different colors used to depict the two people in the painting?

*Marchesa (marquise in English) is a high-ranking noble title.

(By Anthony Van Dyck [1599–1641], 1623 [oil on canvas]/Widener Collection, 1942.9.92/image courtesy National Gallery of Art, Washington)

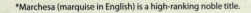

male and female bodies (see "Women and the Enlightenment" in Chapter 16). Science thus served to justify and naturalize existing inequalities between Europeans and non-Europeans and between men and women.

## Michel de Montaigne and Cultural Curiosity

Decades of religious fanaticism and civil war led some Catholics and Protestants to doubt that any one faith contained absolute truth. Added to these doubts was the discovery of peoples in the New World who had radically different ways of life. These shocks helped produce ideas of skepticism and cultural relativism. Skepticism is a school of thought founded on doubt that total certainty or definitive knowledge is ever attainable. Cultural relativism suggests that one culture is not necessarily superior to another, just different. Both notions found expression in the work of Frenchman Michel de Montaigne (duh mahn-TAYN) (1533–1592).

Montaigne developed a new literary genre, the essay, to express his ideas. Intending his works to be accessible, he wrote in French rather than Latin and in an engaging conversational style. His essays were quickly translated into other European languages and became some of the most widely read texts of the early modern period. Montaigne's essay "Of Cannibals" reveals the impact of overseas discoveries on one thoughtful European. In contrast to the prevailing views of his day, he rejected the notion that one culture is superior to another. Speaking of native Brazilians, he wrote: "I find that there is nothing barbarous and savage in this nation [Brazil], . . . except, that everyone gives the title of barbarism to everything that is not according to his usage."[10]

In his own time, few would have agreed with Montaigne's challenge to ideas of European superiority or his even more radical questioning of the superiority of humans over animals. Nevertheless, his popular essays contributed to a basic shift in attitudes. "Wonder," he said, "is the foundation of all philosophy, research is the means of all learning, and ignorance is the end."[11] Montaigne thus inaugurated an era of doubt.

## William Shakespeare and His Influence

In addition to the essay as a literary genre, the period fostered remarkable creativity in other branches of literature, which also reflected the impact of European expansion and changing ideas about race. England—especially in the latter part of Queen Elizabeth I's reign and in the first years of her successor, James I (r. 1603–1625)—witnessed remarkable developments in theater and poetry. The undisputed master of the period was the dramatist William Shakespeare. Born in 1564 to a successful glove manufacturer in Stratford-upon-Avon, his genius lay in the originality of his characterizations, the diversity of his plots, his understanding of human psychology, and his unsurpassed gift for language. Although he wrote sparkling comedies and stirring historical plays, his greatest masterpieces were his later tragedies, including *Hamlet*, *Othello*, and *Macbeth*, which explore an enormous range of human problems and are open to an almost infinite variety of interpretations.

Like Montaigne's essays, Shakespeare's work reveals the impact of the new discoveries and contacts of his day. The title character of *Othello* is described as a "Moor," a term that in Shakespeare's day referred to Muslims of North African origin, including those who had migrated to the Iberian Peninsula. It could also be applied, though, to natives of the Iberian Peninsula who converted to Islam or to non-Muslim Berbers in North Africa. To complicate things even

more, references in the play to Othello as "black" in skin color have led many to believe that Shakespeare intended him to be a sub-Saharan African.

This confusion in the play aptly reflects the important links in this period between racial and religious classifications. In contrast to the prevailing view of Moors as inferior, a view echoed by the Venetian characters in the play, Shakespeare presents Othello as a complex human figure, capable of great courage and nobility, but flawed by jealousy and credulity.

The play also exposes women's suffering at the hands of the patriarchal family. In *Othello*, fathers treat unmarried daughters as property and husbands murder wives they suspect of infidelity. Revealing anxieties about racial purity and miscegenation, several characters assert that Othello's "blackness" has tainted his Venetian wife. The play thus shows how racial ideologies very similar to those developed in the Spanish Empire existed in Elizabethan England.

## NOTES

1. Marco Polo, *The Book of Ser Marco Polo, the Venetian: Concerning the Kingdoms and Marvels of the East*, vol. 2, trans. and ed. Colonel Sir Henry Yule (London: John Murray, 1903), pp. 185–186.
2. Thomas Benjamin, *The Atlantic World: Europeans, Africans, Indians and Their Shared History, 1400–1900* (Cambridge: Cambridge University Press, 2009), p. 56.
3. John Law, "On the Methods of Long Distance Control: Vessels, Navigation, and the Portuguese Route to India," in *Power, Action and Belief: A New Sociology of Knowledge?* ed. John Law, Sociological Review Monograph 32 (London: Routledge & Kegan Paul, 1986), pp. 234–263.
4. Peter Hulme, *Colonial Encounters: Europe and the Native Caribbean, 1492–1797* (London: Methuen, 1986), pp. 22–31.
5. Benjamin, *The Atlantic World*, p. 141.
6. Geoffrey Vaughn Scammell, *The First Imperial Age: European Overseas Expansion, c. 1400–1715* (London: Routledge, 2002), p. 432.
7. Herbert S. Klein, "Profits and the Causes of Mortality," in *The Atlantic Slave Trade*, ed. David Northrup (Lexington, Mass.: D. C. Heath and Co., 1994), p. 116.
8. David Carrasco, *The Oxford Encyclopedia of Mesoamerican Cultures* (Oxford: Oxford University Press, 2001), p. 208.
9. Bartolomé de las Casas, *A Short Account of the Destruction of the Indies*, trans. Nigel Griffin (New York: Penguin, 2004), p. 11.
10. C. Cotton, trans., *The Essays of Michel de Montaigne* (New York: A. L. Burt, 1893), pp. 207, 210.
11. Cotton, *The Essays*, p. 523.

# LOOKING BACK  LOOKING AHEAD

In 1517 Martin Luther issued his "Ninety-five Theses," launching the Protestant Reformation; just five years later, Ferdinand Magellan's expedition sailed around the globe, shattering European notions of terrestrial geography. Within a few short years, old medieval certainties about Heaven and

earth began to collapse. In the ensuing decades, Europeans struggled to come to terms with religious difference at home and the multitudes of new peoples and places they encountered abroad. While some Europeans were fascinated and inspired by this new diversity, much more often the result was hostility and violence. Europeans endured decades of civil war between Protestants and Catholics, and indigenous peoples suffered massive population losses as a result of European warfare, disease, and exploitation. Tragically, both Catholic and Protestant religious leaders condoned the African slave trade that brought suffering and death to millions of people as well as the conquest of Native American land and the subjugation of indigenous people.

Even as the voyages of discovery coincided with the fragmentation of European culture, they also played a role in longer-term processes of state centralization and consolidation. The new monarchies of the Renaissance produced stronger and wealthier governments capable of financing the huge expenses of exploration and colonization. Competition to gain overseas colonies became an integral part of European politics. Spain's investment in conquest proved spectacularly profitable, and yet, as we will see in Chapter 15, the ultimate result was a weakening of its power. Over time the Netherlands, England, and France also reaped tremendous profits from colonial trade, which helped them build modernized, centralized states. The path from medieval Christendom to modern nation-states led through religious warfare and global encounter.

## Make Connections

Think about the larger developments and continuities within and across chapters.

1. Michel de Montaigne argued that people's assessments of what was "barbaric" merely drew on their own habits and customs; based on the earlier sections of this chapter, how widespread was this openness to cultural difference? Was he alone, or did others share this view?

2. To what extent did the European voyages of expansion and conquest inaugurate an era of global history? Is it correct to date the beginning of "globalization" from the late fifteenth century? Why or why not?

## 14   REVIEW & EXPLORE

### Identify Key Terms

Identify and explain the significance of each item below.

conquistadors (p. 396)

caravel (p. 396)

Ptolemy's *Geography* (p. 396)

Treaty of Tordesillas (p. 402)

Aztec Empire (p. 403)

Inca Empire (p. 407)

viceroyalties (p. 409)

encomienda system (p. 410)

Columbian exchange (p. 411)

### Review the Main Ideas

Answer the section heading questions from the chapter.

1. What was the Afro-Eurasian trading world before Columbus? (p. 392)

2. How and why did Europeans undertake ambitious voyages of expansion? (p. 395)

3. What was the impact of European conquest on the New World? (p. 403)

4. How did Europe and the world change after Columbus? (p. 410)

5. How did expansion change European attitudes and beliefs? (p. 417)

## Suggested Resources

### BOOKS

- Brosseder, Claudia. *The Power of Huacas: Change and Resistance in the Andean World of Colonial Peru* (2014). A fascinating study of indigenous religious practitioners in the Andes and their encounter with the colonial Spanish world, which tells the story of religion from the indigenous perspective.

- Crosby, Alfred W. *The Columbian Exchange: Biological and Cultural Consequences of 1492*, 30th anniversary ed. 2003. An innovative and highly influential account of the environmental impact of the trans-atlantic movement of animals, plants, and microbes inaugurated by Columbus.

- Elliott, J. H. *Empires of the Atlantic World: Britain and Spain in America, 1492–1830.* 2006. A masterful comparative account of the British and Spanish Empires in the Americas.

- Fernández-Armesto, Felipe. *Columbus.* 1992. An excellent biography of Christopher Columbus.

- Mann, Charles C. *1491: New Revelations on the Americas Before Columbus*, 2d ed. 2011. A highly readable account of the peoples and societies of the Americas before the arrival of Europeans.

- Martinez, Maria Elena. *Genealogical Fictions: Limpieza de Sangre, Religion and Gender in Colonial Mexico.* 2008. A fascinating study of the relationship between Spanish ideas of religious purity developed during the reconquista and the emergence of racial hierarchies in colonial Mexico.

- Parker, Charles H. *Global Interactions in the Early Modern Age, 1400–1800.* 2010. An examination of the rise of global connections in the early modern period, which situates the European experience in relation to the world's other empires and peoples.

- Pomeranz, Kenneth, and Steven Topik. *The World That Trade Created: Society, Culture, and the World Economy, 1400 to the Present.* 1999. The creation of a world market presented through rich and vivid stories of merchants, miners, slaves, and farmers.

- Restall, Matthew. *Seven Myths of Spanish Conquest.* 2003. A re-examination of common misconceptions about why and how the Spanish conquered native civilizations in the New World.

- Subrahmanyam, Sanjay. *The Portuguese Empire in Asia, 1500–1700: A Political and Economic History*, 2d ed. 2012. A masterful study of the Portuguese overseas empire in Asia that draws on both European and Asian sources.

### MEDIA

- *America Before Columbus* (National Geographic, 2010). Explores the complex societies and cultures of North America before contact with Europeans and the impact of the Columbian exchange.

- *Black Robe* (Bruce Beresford, 1991). A classic film about French Jesuit missionaries among Algonquin and Huron Indians in New France in the seventeenth century.

- *Conquistadors* (PBS, 2000). Traveling in the footsteps of the Spanish conquistadors, the narrator tells their story while following the paths and rivers they used. Includes discussion of the perspectives and participation of native peoples.

- *The Globalization of Food and Plants.* Hosted by the Yale University Center for the Study of Globalization, this website provides information on how various foods and plants—such as spices, coffee, and tomatoes—traveled the world in the Columbian exchange. **yaleglobal.yale .edu/globalization-food-plants**

- *Historic Jamestowne.* Showcasing archaeological work at the Jamestown settlement, the first permanent English settlement in America, this site provides details of the latest digs along with biographical information about settlers, historical background, and resources for teachers and students. **www.historicjamestowne.org**

- *The New World* (Terrence Malick, 2005). Set in 1607 at the founding of the Jamestown settlement, this film retells the story of John Smith and Pocahontas.

- *Plymouth Colony Archive Project.* A site hosted by the anthropology department at the University of Illinois that contains a collection of searchable primary and secondary sources relating to the Plymouth colony, including court records, laws, seventeenth-century journals and memoirs, wills, maps, and biographies of colonists. **www.histarch.uiuc.edu/Plymouth /index.html**

- *Silence* (Martin Scorcese, 2016). Based on a 1966 Japanese novel, the film depicts the travels of two seventeenth-century Jesuits from Portugal to Japan during a time of Japanese persecution of Christians.

# 15

# Absolutism and Constitutionalism

## ca. 1589–1725

**The seventeenth century** was a period of crisis and transformation in Europe. Agricultural and manufacturing slumps led to food shortages and shrinking population rates. Religious and dynastic conflicts led to almost constant war, visiting violence and destruction on ordinary people and reshaping European states. To consolidate their authority and expand their territories, European rulers increased the size of their armies, imposed higher taxes, and implemented bureaucratic forms of government. By the end of the seventeenth century they had largely succeeded in restoring order and securing increased power for the state.

The growth of state power within Europe raised a series of questions for rulers and subjects: Who held supreme power? What made it legitimate? Conflicts over these questions led to rebellions and, in some areas, outright civil war. While absolutism emerged as the solution to these challenges in many European states, a small minority, most notably England and the Dutch Republic, adopted a different path, placing sovereignty in the hands of privileged groups rather than the Crown. ■

# CHAPTER PREVIEW

- **What made the seventeenth century an "age of crisis" and achievement?**

- **Why did France rise and Spain fall during the late seventeenth century?**

- **What explains the rise of absolutism in Prussia and Austria?**

- **What were the distinctive features of Russian and Ottoman absolutism?**

- **Why and how did the constitutional state triumph in the Dutch Republic and England?**

**Life at the French Royal Court**
This painting shows King Louis XIV receiving foreign ambassadors to celebrate a peace treaty. The king grandly occupied the center of his court, which in turn served as the pinnacle for the French people and, at the height of his glory, for all of Europe. (By Charles Le Brun [1619–1690], 1678/ Museum of Fine Arts, Budapest, Hungary/Erich Lessing/Art Resource, NY)

# What made the seventeenth century an "age of crisis" and achievement?

Historians often refer to the seventeenth century as an "age of crisis" because Europe was challenged by population losses, economic decline, and social and political unrest. This was partially due to climate changes that reduced agricultural productivity, but it also resulted from bitter religious divides, war, and increased governmental pressures. Peasants and the urban poor were especially hard hit by the economic problems, and they frequently rioted against high food prices.

The atmosphere of crisis encouraged governments to take emergency measures to restore order, measures that they successfully turned into long-term reforms that strengthened the power of the state. These included a spectacular growth in army size as well as increased taxation, the expansion of government bureaucracies, and the acquisition of land or maritime empires. In the long run, European states proved increasingly able to impose their will on the populace. This period also saw the flourishing of art and music with the drama and emotional intensity of the baroque style.

## The Social Order and Peasant Life

In the seventeenth century, society was organized in hierarchical levels. In much of Europe, the monarch occupied the summit and was celebrated as a semidivine being, chosen by God to embody the state. The clergy generally occupied the second level because of its sacred role in interceding with God and the saints on behalf of its flocks. Next came nobles, whose privileged status derived from their ancient bloodlines and centuries of leadership in battle. Many prosperous mercantile families constituted a second tier of nobles, having bought their way into the nobility through service to the rising monarchies of the fifteenth and sixteenth centuries. Those lower on the social scale, the peasants and artisans who constituted the vast majority of the population, were expected to show deference to their betters. This was the "Great Chain of Being" that linked God to his creation in a series of ranked social groups.

In addition to being rigidly hierarchical, European societies were patriarchal in nature, with men assuming authority over women as a God-given prerogative. The family thus represented a microcosm of the social order. The father ruled his family like a king ruled his domains. Religious and secular law commanded a man's wife, children, servants, and apprentices to defer to his will. Fathers were entitled to use physical violence, imprisonment, and other forceful measures to impose their authority. These powers were balanced by expectations that a good father would provide and care for his dependents.

In the seventeenth century most Europeans lived in the countryside. The hub of the rural world was the small peasant village centered on a church and a manor. In western Europe, a small number of peasants in each village owned enough land to feed themselves and possessed the livestock and plows necessary to work their land. These independent farmers were leaders of the peasant village. They employed the landless poor, rented out livestock and tools, and served as agents for the noble lord. Below them were small landowners and tenant farmers who did not have enough land to be self-sufficient. These families sold their best produce on the market to earn cash for taxes, rent, and food. At the bottom were villagers who worked as dependent laborers and servants. In central and eastern Europe, the vast majority of peasants toiled as serfs for noble landowners and did not own land in their own right, while in the Ottoman Empire (the vast empire comprising modern-day Turkey, southeastern Europe, North Africa, and large portions of the Middle East) all land belonged to the sultan.

## Economic Crisis and Popular Revolts

European rural society lived on the edge of subsistence. Because of crude agricultural technology and low crop yield, peasants were constantly threatened by scarcity and famine. In the seventeenth century a period of colder and wetter climate throughout Europe, dubbed a "little ice age" by historians, meant a shorter farming season with lower yields. A bad harvest created food shortages; a series of bad harvests could lead to famine. Recurrent famines significantly reduced the population of early modern Europe, through reduced fertility and increased susceptibility to disease, as well as outright starvation.

Industry also suffered. The output of woolen textiles, one of the most important European manufactures, declined sharply in the first half of the seventeenth century. Food prices were high, wages stagnated, and unemployment soared. This economic crisis was not universal: it struck various regions at different times and to different degrees. In the middle decades of the century, for example, Spain, France, Germany, and the British Isles all experienced great economic difficulties, but these years were the golden age of the Netherlands because of wealth derived from foreign trade.

The urban poor and peasants were the hardest hit. When the price of bread rose beyond their capacity

# TIMELINE

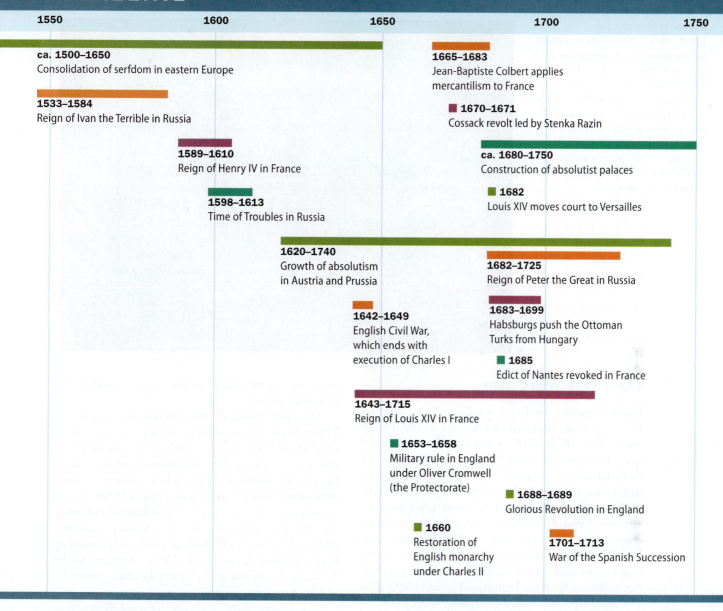

| 1550 | 1600 | 1650 | 1700 | 1750 |
|---|---|---|---|---|

**ca. 1500–1650**
Consolidation of serfdom in eastern Europe

**1533–1584**
Reign of Ivan the Terrible in Russia

**1589–1610**
Reign of Henry IV in France

**1598–1613**
Time of Troubles in Russia

**1620–1740**
Growth of absolutism in Austria and Prussia

**1642–1649**
English Civil War, which ends with execution of Charles I

**1643–1715**
Reign of Louis XIV in France

**1653–1658**
Military rule in England under Oliver Cromwell (the Protectorate)

**1660**
Restoration of English monarchy under Charles II

**1665–1683**
Jean-Baptiste Colbert applies mercantilism to France

**1670–1671**
Cossack revolt led by Stenka Razin

**ca. 1680–1750**
Construction of absolutist palaces

**1682**
Louis XIV moves court to Versailles

**1682–1725**
Reign of Peter the Great in Russia

**1683–1699**
Habsburgs push the Ottoman Turks from Hungary

**1685**
Edict of Nantes revoked in France

**1688–1689**
Glorious Revolution in England

**1701–1713**
War of the Spanish Succession

to pay, they frequently expressed their anger by rioting. Women often led these actions, since their role as mothers gave them some impunity in authorities' eyes. Historians have used the term *moral economy* for this vision of a world in which community needs predominate over competition and profit.

During the middle years of the seventeenth century, harsh conditions transformed neighborhood bread riots into armed uprisings across much of Europe. Popular revolts were common in England, France, and throughout the Spanish Empire, particularly during the 1640s. At the same time that Spanish king Philip IV struggled to put down an uprising in Catalonia, the economic center of the realm, he faced revolt in Portugal and in Spanish-held territories in the northern Netherlands and Sicily. France suffered an uprising in the same period that won enthusiastic support from both nobles and peasants, while the English monarch was tried and executed by his subjects and Russia experienced an explosive rebellion.

Municipal and royal authorities struggled to overcome popular revolt. They feared that stern repressive measures, such as sending in troops to fire on crowds, would create martyrs and further inflame the situation, while full-scale occupation of a city would be very expensive and detract from military efforts elsewhere. The limitations of royal authority gave some leverage to rebels. To quell riots, royal edicts were sometimes suspended, prisoners released, and discussions initiated. By the beginning of the eighteenth century rulers had gained much greater control over their populations as a result of various achievements in state-building (see "State-Building and the Growth of Armies" later in this chapter).

**Peasants Working the Land**  Working the land was harsh toil for seventeenth-century peasants, but strong family and community bonds gave life meaning and made survival possible. The rich and colorful clothing of the peasants shown here reflects an idealized vision of the peasants' material circumstances. ("The Month of March" by the studio of Pieter de Witte [ca. 1548–1628]/photo © Sotheby's/akg-images)

## The Thirty Years' War

Harsh economic conditions were greatly exacerbated by the decades-long conflict known as the Thirty Years' War (1618–1648), a war that drew in almost every European state. The Holy Roman Empire was a confederation of hundreds of principalities, independent cities, duchies, and other polities loosely united under an elected emperor. The uneasy truce between Catholics and Protestants created by the Peace of Augsburg in 1555 (see "Religious Wars in Switzerland and Germany" in Chapter 13) deteriorated as the faiths of various areas shifted. Lutheran princes felt compelled to form the Protestant Union (1608), and Catholics retaliated with the Catholic League (1609). Each alliance was determined that the other should make no religious or territorial advance. Dynastic interests were also involved; the Spanish Habsburgs strongly supported the goals of their Austrian relatives, which was to preserve the unity of the empire and Catholicism within it.

The war began with a conflict in Bohemia (part of the present-day Czech Republic) between the Catholic League and the Protestant Union but soon spread through the Holy Roman Empire, drawing in combatants from across Europe. After a series of initial Catholic victories, the tide of the conflict turned because of the intervention of Sweden, under its king Gustavus Adolphus (r. 1594–1632), and then France, whose prime minister, Cardinal Richelieu (REESH-uh-lyuh),

intervened on the side of the Protestants to undermine Habsburg power.

The 1648 **Peace of Westphalia** that ended the Thirty Years' War marked a turning point in European history. The treaties that established the peace not only ended conflicts fought over religious faith but also recognized the independent authority of more than three hundred German princes (Map 15.1), reconfirming the emperor's severely limited authority. The Augsburg agreement of 1555 became permanent, adding Calvinism to Catholicism and Lutheranism as legally permissible creeds. The United Provinces of the Netherlands, known as the Dutch Republic, won official freedom from Spain.

The Thirty Years' War was the most destructive event in central Europe prior to the world wars of the twentieth century. Perhaps one-third of urban residents and two-fifths of the rural population died, and agriculture and industry withered. Across Europe, states increased taxes to meet the cost of war, further increasing the suffering of a traumatized population.

## State-Building and the Growth of Armies

In the context of warfare, economic crisis, and demographic decline, rulers took urgent measures to restore order and rebuild their states. Traditionally, historians have distinguished between the absolutist governments of France, Spain, central Europe, and Russia and the constitutionalist governments of England and the Dutch Republic. Whereas absolutist monarchs gathered all power under their personal control,

■ **Peace of Westphalia**  The name of a series of treaties that concluded the Thirty Years' War in 1648 and marked the end of large-scale religious violence in Europe.

**MAP 15.1 Europe After the Thirty Years' War** This map shows the political division of Europe after the Peace of Westphalia (1648) ended the war. France expanded its borders to the east and Sweden gained territory on the northern German coastline. The Dutch Republic formally won its independence after a long struggle against Spain, but Spain retained territory in the southern Netherlands and Italy.

Legend:
- Austrian Habsburg lands
- Spanish Habsburg lands
- Other German states
- Swedish lands by 1648
- Ottoman Empire and tributary states
- Boundary of the Holy Roman Empire

English and Dutch rulers were obliged to respect laws passed by representative institutions. More recently, historians have emphasized commonalities among these powers. Despite their political differences, all these states shared common projects of protecting and expanding their frontiers, raising new taxes, consolidating central control, and competing for the new colonies opening up in the New and Old Worlds.

Rulers who wished to increase their authority encountered formidable obstacles, including poor communications, entrenched local power structures, and ethnic and linguistic diversity. Nonetheless, over the course of the seventeenth century both absolutist and constitutional governments achieved new levels of power and national unity. They did so by transforming emergency measures of wartime into permanent structures of government and by subduing privileged groups through the use of force and through economic and social incentives. Increased state authority could be seen in four areas in particular: greater taxation, growth in armed forces, larger and more efficient bureaucracies, and territorial expansion, both within Europe and overseas.

Over time, centralized power added up to something close to sovereignty. A state may be termed sovereign when it possesses a monopoly over the

**Seventeenth-Century Artillery** Mobile light artillery, consisting of bronze or iron cannon mounted on wheeled carriages, played a crucial role in seventeenth-century warfare. In contrast to earlier heavy artillery used in siege operations to breach fortifications, light artillery could be deployed to support troops during battle. This image is from an early seventeenth-century military manual. (Science History Images/Alamy)

instruments of justice and the use of force within clearly defined boundaries. In a sovereign state, no system of courts, such as church tribunals, competes with state courts in the dispensation of justice; and private armies, such as those of feudal lords, present no threat to central authority. While seventeenth-century states did not acquire total sovereignty, they made important strides toward that goal.

The driving force of seventeenth-century state-building was warfare. In medieval times, feudal lords had raised armies only for particular wars or campaigns; now monarchs began to recruit their own forces and maintain permanent standing armies. Instead of serving their own interests, army officers were required to be loyal and obedient to state officials. New techniques for training and deploying soldiers meant a rise in the professional standards of the army.

Along with professionalization came an explosive growth in army size. The French took the lead, with the army growing from roughly 125,000 men in the Thirty Years' War to 340,000 at the end of the seventeenth century.[1] Other European powers were quick to follow the French example. The rise of absolutism in central and eastern Europe led to a vast expansion in the size of armies. England followed a similar, albeit distinctive pattern. Instead of building a land army, the island nation focused on naval forces and eventually built the largest navy in the world.

## Baroque Art and Music

State-building and the growth of armies were not the only achievements of the seventeenth century; the arts flourished as well. Rome and the revitalized Catholic Church of the late sixteenth century spurred the early development of the **baroque style** in art and music. The papacy and the Jesuits encouraged the growth of an intensely emotional, exuberant art. They wanted artists to appeal to the senses and thereby touch the souls and kindle the faith of ordinary churchgoers while proclaiming the power and confidence of the reformed Catholic Church. In addition to this underlying religious emotionalism, the baroque drew its sense of drama, motion, and ceaseless striving from the Catholic Reformation.

Taking definite shape in Italy after 1600, the baroque style in the visual arts developed with exceptional vigor

**Gian Lorenzo Bernini, *The Ecstasy of Saint Teresa of Avila*, 1647–1652** In 1647, Italian sculptor Gian Lorenzo Bernini accepted a commission to build a chapel in honor of the family of a Catholic cardinal and the newly canonized Spanish Carmelite nun and mystic, Teresa of Avila. Bernini's sculpture depicts the saint at the moment of her rapturous union with the divine, symbolized by an angel standing poised to pierce her heart with a golden arrow. In its heightened emotionalism and the drama of its composition, the sculpture is one of the masterpieces of baroque art. (Santa Maria della Vittoria, Rome, Italy /De Agostini Picture Library/G. Nimatallah/Bridgeman Images)

■ **baroque style** A style in art and music lasting from roughly 1600 to 1750 characterized by the use of drama and motion to create heightened emotion, especially prevalent in Catholic countries.

in Catholic countries—in Spain and Latin America, Austria, southern Germany, and Poland. Yet baroque art was more than just "Catholic art" in the seventeenth century and the first half of the eighteenth. It had broad appeal, and Protestants accounted for some of the finest examples of baroque style, especially in music. The baroque style spread partly because its tension and bombast spoke to an agitated age that was experiencing great violence and controversy in politics and religion.

In painting, the baroque reached maturity early with Peter Paul Rubens (1577–1640), the most outstanding and most representative of baroque painters. Studying in his native Flanders and in Italy, where he was influenced by masters of the High Renaissance such as Michelangelo, Rubens developed his own rich,

sensuous, colorful style, which was characterized by animated figures, melodramatic contrasts, and monumental size.

In music, the baroque style reached its culmination almost a century later in the dynamic, soaring lines of the endlessly inventive Johann Sebastian Bach (1685–1750). Organist and choirmaster of several Lutheran churches across Germany, Bach was equally at home writing secular concertos and sublime religious cantatas. Bach's organ music combined the baroque spirit of invention, tension, and emotion in an unforgettable striving toward the infinite. Unlike Rubens, Bach was not fully appreciated in his lifetime, but since the early nineteenth century his reputation has grown steadily.

# Why did France rise and Spain fall during the late seventeenth century?

Kings in absolutist states asserted that, because they were chosen by God, they were responsible to God alone. They claimed exclusive, or absolute, power to make and enforce laws, denying any other institution or group the authority to check their power. In France the founder of the Bourbon monarchy, Henry IV, established foundations upon which his successors Louis XIII and Louis XIV built a stronger, more centralized French state. Louis XIV is often seen as the epitome of an "absolute" monarch, with his endless wars, increased taxes and economic regulation, and glorious palace at Versailles. In truth, his success relied on collaboration with nobles, and thus his example illustrates both the achievements and the compromises of absolutist rule.

As French power rose in the seventeenth century, the glory of Spain faded. Once the fabulous revenue from American silver declined, Spain's economic stagnation could no longer be disguised, and the country faltered under weak leadership.

## The Foundations of French Absolutism

Louis XIV's absolutism had long roots. In 1589, his grandfather Henry IV (r. 1589–1610), the founder of the Bourbon dynasty, acquired a devastated country. Civil wars between Protestants and Catholics had wracked France since 1561. Poor harvests had reduced peasants to starvation, and commercial activity had declined drastically. Henri le Grand (Henry the Great), as the king was called, inaugurated a remarkable recovery by defusing religious tensions and rebuilding France's economy. He issued the Edict of Nantes in 1598, allowing Huguenots (French Protestants) the right to worship in 150 traditionally Protestant towns

throughout France. He sharply lowered taxes and instead charged royal officials an annual fee to guarantee the right to pass their positions down to their heirs. He also improved the infrastructure of the country, building new roads and canals and repairing the ravages of years of civil war. Despite his efforts at peace, Henry was murdered in 1610 by a Catholic zealot.

Cardinal Richelieu (1585–1642) became first minister of the French crown on behalf of Henry's young son, Louis XIII (r. 1610–1643). Richelieu designed his domestic policies to strengthen royal control. He extended the use of intendants, commissioners for each of France's thirty-two districts who were appointed directly by the monarch and whose responsibilities included army recruitment, tax collection, and enforcement of royal law. As the intendants' power increased under Richelieu, so did the power of the centralized French state.

Richelieu also viewed France's Huguenots as potential rebels, and he laid seige to La Rochelle, a Protestant stronghold, to preserve control within France. Richelieu's anti-Protestant measures took second place, however, to his most important policy goal, which was to secure French pre-eminence in European power politics. This meant doing everything within his means to weaken the Habsburgs and prevent them from controlling territories that surrounded France. Consequently, Richelieu supported Habsburg enemies, including the Protestant nation of Sweden, during the Thirty Years' War.

Cardinal Jules Mazarin (1602–1661) succeeded Richelieu as chief minister for the next child-king, the four-year-old Louis XIV, who inherited the throne from his father in 1643. Along with the regent, Queen Mother Anne of Austria, Mazarin continued Richelieu's centralizing policies. However, his struggle to increase royal revenues to meet the costs of the Thirty Years' War led to the uprisings of 1648–1653 known as the **Fronde**. In Paris, magistrates of the Parlement of Paris, the nation's most important law court, were outraged by the Crown's autocratic measures. These so-called robe nobles (named for the robes they wore in court) encouraged violent protest by the common people. As rebellion spread outside Paris and to the sword nobles (the traditional warrior nobility), civil order broke down completely. In 1651, Anne's regency ended with the declaration of Louis as king in his own right. Much of the rebellion died away, and its leaders came to terms with the government.

The French people were desperate for peace and stability after the disorders of the Fronde and were willing to accept a strong monarch who could restore order. Louis pledged to be such a monarch, insisting that only his absolute authority stood between the French people and a renewed descent into chaos.

## Louis XIV and Absolutism

In the reign of Louis XIV (r. 1643–1715), who was known as the "Sun King" in reference to his central role in the divine order, France overcame weakness and division to become the most powerful nation in western Europe. Louis based his authority on the divine right of kings: God had established kings as his rulers on earth, and they were answerable ultimately to him alone. However, Louis also recognized that kings could not simply do as they pleased. They had to obey God's laws and rule for the good of the people.

Louis worked very hard at the business of governing, refusing to delegate power to a first minister. He ruled his realm through several councils of state and insisted on taking a personal role in many of their decisions. Despite increasing financial problems, Louis never called a meeting of the Estates General, the traditional French representative assembly composed of the three estates of clergy, nobility, and commoners. The nobility, therefore, had no means of united expression or action. To further restrict nobles' political power, Louis chose his ministers from capable men of modest origins.

Although personally tolerant, Louis hated division within the realm and insisted that religious unity was essential to his royal dignity and to the security of the state. He thus pursued the policy of Protestant repression launched by Richelieu. In 1685 Louis revoked the Edict of Nantes. The new law ordered the Catholic baptism of Huguenots (French Calvinists), the destruction of Huguenot churches, the closing of schools, and the exile of Huguenot pastors who refused to renounce their faith. Around two hundred thousand Protestants, including some of the king's most highly skilled artisans, fled into exile.

Despite his claims to absolute authority, multiple constraints existed on Louis's power. As a representative of divine power, he was obliged to rule in a manner consistent with virtue and benevolence. (See "Thinking Like a Historian: What Was Absolutism?" on page 434.) He had to uphold the laws issued by his royal predecessors. He also relied on the collaboration of nobles, who maintained tremendous prestige and authority in their ancestral lands. Without their cooperation, it would have been impossible to extend his power throughout France or wage his many foreign wars. Louis's efforts to elicit noble cooperation led him to revolutionize court life at his spectacular palace at Versailles.

## Life at Versailles

Through most of the seventeenth century the French court had no fixed home and instead followed the monarch to his numerous palaces and country residences. In 1682 Louis moved his court and government to the newly renovated palace at Versailles, a former hunting lodge. He then required all great nobles to spend at least part of the year in attendance on him there, so he could keep an eye on their activities. Because Louis controlled the distribution of state power and wealth, nobles had no choice but to obey and compete with each other for his favor at Versailles. The glorious palace, with its sumptuous interiors and extensive formal gardens, was a mirror to the world of French glory and was soon copied by would-be absolutist monarchs across Europe.

Louis further revolutionized court life by establishing an elaborate set of etiquette rituals to mark every moment of his day, from waking up and dressing in the morning to removing his clothing and retiring at night. Courtiers vied for the honor of participating in these ceremonies, with the highest in rank claiming the privilege of handing the king his shirt. These rituals may seem absurd, but they were far from trivial. The king controlled immense resources and privileges; access to him meant favored treatment for government offices, military and religious posts, state pensions, honorary titles, and a host of other benefits. Courtiers sought these rewards for themselves and their family members and followers. A system of patronage—in which a higher-ranked individual protected a lower-ranked one in return for loyalty and services—flowed from the court to the provinces. Through this mechanism Louis gained cooperation from powerful nobles.

Although they could not hold public offices or posts, women played a central role in the patronage system. At court the king's wife, mistresses, and other female relatives recommended individuals for honors,

■ **Fronde** A series of violent uprisings during the early reign of Louis XIV triggered by growing royal control and increased taxation.

***View of the Palace and Gardens of Versailles, 1668***    Located ten miles southwest of Paris, Versailles began as a modest hunting lodge. Louis XIV spent decades enlarging and decorating the structure with the help of architect Louis Le Vau and gardener André Le Nôtre. In 1682, the new palace became the official residence of the Sun King and his court and an inspiration to absolutist palace builders across Europe. (Leemage/Corbis Historical/Getty Images)

advocated policy decisions, and brokered alliances between factions. Noblewomen played a similar role, bringing their family connections to marriage to form powerful social networks.

Louis XIV was also an enthusiastic patron of the arts, commissioning many sculptures and paintings for Versailles as well as performances of dance and music. He also loved the stage, and in the plays of Molière and Racine his court witnessed the finest achievements in the history of French theater. Some of Molière's targets in this period were the aristocratic ladies who wrote many genres of literature and held receptions, called salons, in their Parisian mansions, where they engaged in witty and cultured discussions of poetry, art, theater, and the latest worldly events. Their refined conversational style led Molière and other observers to mock them as "*précieuses*" (PREH-see-ooz; literally "precious"), or affected and pretentious. Despite this mockery, the précieuses represented an important cultural force ruled by elite women.

With Versailles as the center of European politics, French culture grew in international prestige. French became the language of polite society and international diplomacy, gradually replacing Latin as the language of scholarship and learning. Royal courts across Europe spoke French, and the great aristocrats of Russia, Sweden, Germany, and elsewhere were often more fluent in French than in the tongues of their homelands. France inspired a cosmopolitan European culture in the late seventeenth century that looked to Versailles as its center.

## Louis XIV's Wars

In pursuit of dynastic glory, Louis kept France at war for thirty-three of the fifty-four years of his personal rule. Under the leadership of François le Tellier, marquis de Louvois, Louis's secretary of state for war, France acquired a huge professional army that was employed by the French state rather than by private nobles. He standardized uniforms and weapons and devised a rational system of training and promotion. As in so many other matters, the French model influenced the rest of Europe.

## What Was Absolutism?

Historians have long debated the nature of "absolutism" in seventeenth-century Europe. While many historians have emphasized the growth of state power in this period, especially under Louis XIV of France, others have questioned whether such a thing as "absolutism" ever existed. The following documents will allow you to draw your own conclusions about absolutism.

**1** **Jacques-Bénigne Bossuet, political treatise, 1709.** In 1670 Louis XIV appointed Bishop Bossuet tutor to his son and heir, known as the dauphin. In *Politics Drawn from the Very Words of Holy Scripture*, Bossuet argued that royal power was divine and absolute, but not without limits.

∽ It appears from all this that the person of the king is sacred, and that to attack him in any way is sacrilege. God has the kings anointed by his prophets with the holy unction in like manner as he has bishops and altars anointed. But even without the external application in thus being anointed, they are by their very office the representatives of the divine majesty deputed by Providence for the execution of his purposes. Accordingly God calls Cyrus his anointed. "Thus saith the Lord to his anointed, to Cyrus, whose right hand I have holden, to subdue nations before him." Kings should be guarded as holy things, and whosoever neglects to protect them is worthy of death. . . . There is something religious in the respect accorded to a prince. The service of God and the respect for kings are bound together. St. Peter unites these two duties when he says, "Fear God. Honour the king.". . . But kings, although their power comes from on high, as has been said, should not regard themselves as masters of that power to use it at their pleasure; . . . they must employ it with fear and self-restraint, as a thing coming from God and of which God will demand an account.

**2** **Letter of the prince of Condé, royal governor of the province of Burgundy, to Controller General Jean-Baptiste Colbert, June 18, 1662.** In this letter, the king's representative in the province of Burgundy reports on his efforts to compel the leaders of the province to pay taxes levied by the royal government. The Estates of Burgundy comprised representatives of the three orders, or estates, of society: the clergy, the nobility, and the commoners.

∽ Since then the Estates have deliberated every day, persuaded that the extreme misery in this province — caused by the great levies it has suffered, the sterility [of the land] in recent years, and the disorders that have recently occurred — would induce the king to give them some relief. That is why they offered only 500,000 for the free gift. Then, after I had protested this in the appropriate manner, they raised it to 600,000, then 800,000, and finally 900,000 livres. Until then I had stood firm at 1.5 million, but when I saw that they were on the verge of deciding not to give any more . . . I finally came down to the 1.2 million livres contained in my instructions and invited them to deliberate again, declaring that I could not agree to present any other proposition to the king and that I believed that there was no better way to serve their interests than to obey the king blindly. They agreed with good grace and came this morning to offer me a million. They begged me to leave it at that and not to demand more from them for the free gift; and since I told them they would have to do a little better to satisfy the king completely on this occasion, they again exaggerated their poverty and begged me to inform the king of it, but said that, rather than not please him, they preferred to make a new effort, and they would leave it up to me to declare what they had to do. I told them that I believed His Majesty would have the goodness to be satisfied with 1.05 million livres for the free gift, and they agreed. . . . So Monsieur, there is the deed done.

### ANALYZING THE EVIDENCE

1. What elements of royal authority does the portrait of Louis XIV in Source 4 present to viewers? How would you compare this depiction of political power with images from modern-day politicians? How would you explain the differences?
2. What justification do the sources offer for Louis's claim to exercise "absolute" political authority? Based on his own words in Source 3, how do you think Louis would have viewed the constitutional governments of England and the Dutch Republic?
3. Compare and contrast the evidence for Louis's power given in these sources with evidence for limitations on it. What resources would a king have to muster to enlarge his army drastically (Source 5)? What insight do the negotiations over taxation (Source 2) give you into the ways the royal government acquired those resources?

**3** **Louis XIV, *Memoir for the Instruction of the Dauphin*.** In 1670 Louis XIV finished a memoir he had compiled for the education of his son and heir. Presented in the king's voice—although cowritten with several royal aides—the memoir recounts the early years of Louis's reign and explains his approach to absolute rule.

～ For however it be held as a maxim that in every thing a Prince should employ the most mild measures and first, and that it is more to his advantage to govern his subjects by persuasive than coercive means, it is nevertheless certain that whenever he meets with impediments or rebellion, the interest of his crown and the welfare of his people demand that he should cause himself to be indispensably obeyed; for it must be acknowledged there is nothing can so securely establish the happiness and tranquility of a country as the perfect combination of all authority in the single person of the Sovereign. The least division in this respect often produces the greatest calamities; and whether it be detached into the hands of individuals or those of corporate bodies, it always is there in a state of fermentation.

. . . [B]esides the insurrections and the intestine commotions which the ambition of power infallibly produces when it is not repressed, there are still a thousand other evils created by the inactivity of the Sovereign. Those who are nearest his person are the first to observe his weakness, and are also the first who are desirous of profiting by it. Every one of those persons have necessarily others who are subservient to their avaricious views, and to whom they at the same time give the privilege of imitating them. Thus, from the highest to the lowest is a systematic corruption communicated, and it becomes general in all classes.

(Musée du Louvre, Paris, France/Bridgeman Images)

**4** **Hyacinthe Rigaud, portrait of Louis XIV, 1701.** This was one of Louis XIV's favorite portraits of himself. He liked it so much that he had many copies of the portrait made; his successors had their own portraits painted in the same posture with the same clothing and accoutrements.

**5** **Growth of the French Army.**

| Time Period | Size of Army |
|---|---|
| Middle Ages | 10,000 men |
| 1635 (Louis XIII and Richelieu enter Thirty Years' War) | 125,000 men |
| 1670s (Louis XIV wages Dutch War) | 280,000 men |
| 1690s (Louis XIV wages Nine Years' War) | 340,000 men |

## PUTTING IT ALL TOGETHER

Using the sources above, along with what you have learned in class and in this chapter, what was "absolutism"? Write a brief essay explaining what contemporaries thought absolute power entailed and the extent to which Louis XIV achieved such power.

Sources: (1) J. H. Robinson, ed., *Readings in European History*, vol. 2 (Boston: Ginn, 1906), p. 274; (2) William Beik, ed., *Louis XIV and Absolutism: A Brief Study with Documents* (Boston: Bedford/St. Martin's, 2000), pp. 127–128; (3) *Memoirs of Lewis the Fourteenth, Written by Himself, and Addressed to His Son*, vol. 1 (London: Longman, Hurst, Rees and Orme, 1806), pp. 13–14; (5) Based on information from John A. Lynn, *The Wars of Louis XIV, 1667–1714* (London: Routledge, 2013), pp. 5–51.

there was no question in their minds that the Ottomans were outsiders. Even absolutist rulers disdained Ottoman sultans as cruel and tyrannical despots. Despite stereotypes, however, the Ottoman Empire was in many ways more tolerant than its Western counterparts, providing protection and security to other religions while maintaining the Muslim faith. Flexibility and openness to other ideas and practices were sources of strength for the empire.

## Mongol Rule in Russia and the Rise of Moscow

The two-hundred-year period of rule by the Mongol khan (king) set the stage for the rise of absolutist Russia. The Mongols, a group of nomadic tribes from present-day Mongolia, established an empire that, at its height, stretched from Korea to eastern Europe. In the thirteenth century the Mongols had conquered Kievan Rus, the medieval Slavic state that included most of present-day Ukraine, Belarus, and part of northwest Russia. The princes of the Grand Duchy of Moscow, a principality within Kievan Rus, became particularly adept at serving the Mongols. Eventually the Muscovite princes were able to destroy the other princes who were their rivals for power. Ivan III (r. 1462–1505), known as Ivan the Great, successfully

expanded the principality of Moscow eastward toward the Baltic Sea and westward to the Ural Mountains and the Siberian frontier (Map 15.4).

By 1480 Ivan III was strong enough to declare the autonomy of Moscow. To legitimize their new position, Ivan and his successors borrowed elements of Mongol rule. They forced weaker Slavic principalities to render tribute and borrowed Mongol institutions such as the tax system, postal routes, and census. Loyalty from the highest-ranking nobles, or **boyars**, helped the Muscovite princes consolidate their power.

Another source of legitimacy for Moscow was its claim to the political and religious legacy of the Byzantine Empire. After the fall of Constantinople to the Turks in 1453, the princes of Moscow saw themselves as the heirs of both the Byzantine caesars (or emperors) and the empire's Orthodox Christianity. The marriage of Ivan III to the daughter of the last Byzantine emperor further enhanced Moscow's assertion of imperial authority.

## Building the Russian Empire

Developments in Russia took a chaotic turn with the reign of Ivan IV (r. 1533–1584), the famous "Ivan the Terrible," who ascended to the throne at age three. His

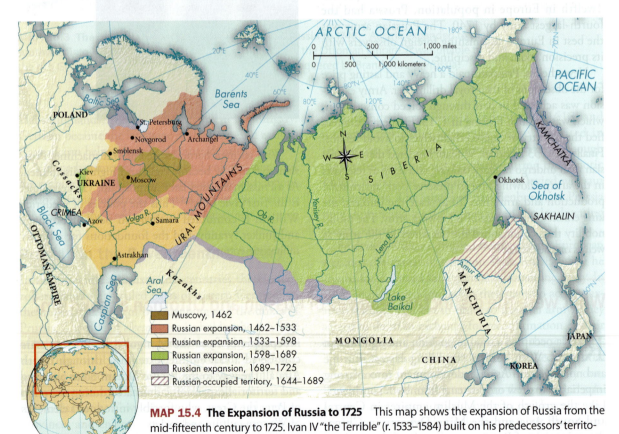

**MAP 15.4  The Expansion of Russia to 1725**    This map shows the expansion of Russia from the mid-fifteenth century to 1725. Ivan IV "the Terrible" (r. 1533–1584) built on his predecessors' territorial gains by defeating remaining Mongol powers in southeastern Russia. During the seventeenth century, the Romanov dynasty extended Russian control across the vast territory of Siberia.

**Peter the Great**    This compelling portrait by Grigory Musikiysky captures the strength and determination of the warrior-tsar in 1723, after more than three decades of personal rule. In his hand Peter holds the scepter, symbol of royal sovereignty, and across his breastplate is draped an ermine fur, a mark of honor. In the background are the battleships of Russia's new Baltic fleet and the famous St. Peter and St. Paul Fortress that Peter built in St. Petersburg. (State Hermitage Museum, St. Petersburg, Russia/Bridgeman Images)

mother died when he was eight, leaving Ivan to suffer insults and neglect from the boyars at court. At age sixteen Ivan pushed aside his advisers and crowned himself tsar.

After the sudden death of his wife, Ivan began a campaign of persecution against those he suspected of opposing him. He executed members of leading boyar families, along with their families, friends, servants, and peasants. To replace them, Ivan created a new service nobility, whose loyalty was guaranteed by their dependence on the state for land and titles.

As landlords demanded more from the serfs who survived the persecutions, growing numbers of peasants fled toward recently conquered territories to the east and south. There they joined free groups and warrior bands known as **Cossacks**. Ivan responded by tying peasants ever more firmly to the land. Simultaneously, so that he could tax them more heavily, he ordered that urban dwellers be bound to their towns and jobs. These restrictions checked the growth of the Russian middle classes and stood in sharp contrast to economic and social developments in western Europe.

Ivan's reign was successful in defeating the remnants of Mongol power and in laying the foundations for the huge, multiethnic Russian Empire. In the 1550s, strengthened by an alliance with Cossack bands, Ivan conquered the Muslim khanates of Kazan and Astrakhan and brought the fertile steppe region around the Volga River under Russian control. In the 1580s Cossacks fighting for the Russian state crossed the Ural Mountains and began the long conquest of Siberia. Because of the size of the new territories and their distance from Moscow, the Russian state did not

initially seek to impose the Orthodox religion and maintained local elites in positions of honor and leadership, buying their loyalty with grants of land.

Following Ivan's death, Russia entered a chaotic period known as the "Time of Troubles" (1598–1613). While Ivan's relatives struggled for power, Cossacks and peasants rebelled against nobles and officials. This social explosion from below brought the nobles together. They crushed the Cossack rebellion and brought Ivan's sixteen-year-old grandnephew, Michael Romanov, to the throne (r. 1613–1645).

Despite the turbulence of the period, the Romanov tsars, like their Western counterparts, made several important achievements in territorial expansion and state-building. After a long war, Russia gained land to the west in Ukraine in 1667. By the end of the century, it had completed the conquest of Siberia (see Map 15.4). This vast territorial expansion brought Russian power to the Sea of Okhotsk in the Pacific Ocean and was only checked by the powerful Qing Dynasty of China. As with the French in Canada, the basis of Russian wealth in Siberia was furs, which the state collected by forced annual tribute payments from local peoples. Profits from furs and other natural resources, especially mining in the eighteenth century, funded expansion of the Russian imperial bureaucracy and the army.

■ **boyars**  The highest-ranking members of the Russian nobility.

■ **Cossacks**  Free groups and outlaw armies originally comprising runaway peasants living on the borders of Russian territory from the fourteenth century onward. By the end of the sixteenth century they had formed an alliance with the Russian state.

# Peter the Great and Foreign Experts

John Deane, an eminent shipbuilder, was one of the many foreign artisans and experts brought to Russia by Peter the Great after the latter's foreign tour of 1697. Several months after his arrival in Russia, Deane sent a glowing account of the tsar's technical prowess to his patron in England, the marquess of Carmarthen, admiral of the English fleet.

At my arrival in Moscow, I fell very ill of the Bloody-Flux, which made me be in Moscow when his Majesty came home: About the latter end of October I was somewhat recovered, his Majesty then carried me down to Voronize* with him. Voronize is about 400 English Miles South-East from Moscow. There the Czar immediately set up a ship of 60 guns, where he is both Foreman and Master-Builder; and not to flatter him, I'll assure your Lordship it will be the best ship among them, and 'tis all from his own Draught; How he fram'd her together and how he made the Mould, and in so short a time as he did is really wonderful: But he is able at this day to put his own notions into practice, and laugh at his Dutch and Italian builders for their ignorance. There are several pieces of workmanship, as in the keel, stem, and post, which are all purely his own invention, and sound good work, and would be approved of by all the shipwrights of England if they saw it. . . .

After some time [I] fell sick again; and at Christmas, when his Majesty came to Moscow, he brought me back again for recovery of my health, where I am at present. . . . The whole place is inhabited by the Dutch; I believe there may be 400 families. Last Sunday and Monday the strangers were invited to the consecration of General La Fort's house, which is the noblest building in Russia, and finely furnisht. There were all the envoys, and as near as I could guess 200 gentlemen, English, French, and Dutch, and about as many ladies; each day were dancing and musick. All the envoys, and all the lords (but three in Moscow) are going to Voronize to see the fleet, I suppose. His majesty went last Sunday to Voronize with Prince Alexander and I am to go down (being something recovered) with the Vice-Admiral about six days hence.

## EVALUATE THE EVIDENCE

1. According to Deane, what evidence did Peter give of his skills in shipbuilding? Based on this document, how would you characterize the relationship between Peter the Great and his foreign experts?
2. What other evidence does Deane provide of the impact of foreigners on life in Russia?

Source: John Deane, *A Letter from Moscow to the Marquess of Carmarthen, Relating to the Czar of Muscovy's Forwardness in His Great Navy, & c. Since His Return Home*, London, 1699.

*Site of the naval shipyard.

---

The growth of state power did nothing to improve the lot of the common people. In 1649 a new law code extended serfdom to all peasants in the realm, giving lords unrestricted rights over their serfs and establishing penalties for harboring runaways. The new code also removed the privileges that non-Russian elites had enjoyed within the empire and required conversion to Russian Orthodoxy. Henceforth, Moscow maintained strict control of trade and administration throughout the empire.

The peace imposed by harsh Russian rule was disrupted in 1670 by a failed rebellion led by the Cossack Stenka Razin, who attracted a great army of urban poor and peasants. The ease with which Moscow crushed the rebellion testifies to the success of the Russian state in unifying and consolidating its empire.

## The Reforms of Peter the Great

Heir to the Romanovs, Peter the Great (r. 1682–1725) embarked on a tremendous campaign to accelerate and complete their efforts at state-building. Peter built on the service obligations of Ivan the Terrible and his successors and continued their tradition of territorial expansion. In particular, he was determined to gain access to the sea for his virtually landlocked state, by extending Russia's borders first to the Black Sea (controlled by the Ottomans) and then to the Baltic Sea (dominated by Sweden).

Peter moved toward the first goal by conquering the Ottoman fort of Azov near the Black Sea in 1696, and quickly built Russia's first navy base. In 1697 the tsar embarked on an eighteen-month tour of western European capitals. Peter was fascinated by foreign technology, and he hoped to forge an anti-Ottoman alliance to strengthen his claims on the Black Sea. Peter failed to secure a military alliance, but he did learn his lessons from the growing power of the Dutch and the English. He also engaged more than a hundred foreign experts to return with him to Russia to help build the navy and improve Russian infrastructure. (See "Evaluating Written Evidence: Peter the Great and Foreign Experts," above.)

To gain access to the Baltic Sea, Peter allied with Denmark and Poland to wage a sudden war of aggression against Sweden. Eighteen-year-old Charles XII of Sweden (1697–1718), however, surprised Peter. He defeated Denmark quickly in 1700 and then turned on Russia. His well-trained professional army attacked and routed unsuspecting Russians besieging the Swedish fortress of Narva on the Baltic coast. It was, for the Russians, a grim beginning to the long and brutal Great Northern War, which lasted from 1700 to 1721.

Peter responded to this defeat with new measures to increase state power, strengthen his military forces, and gain victory. He required all nobles to serve in the army or in the civil administration—for life. Peter also created schools of navigation and mathematics, medicine, engineering, and finance to produce skilled technicians and experts. He established an interlocking military-civilian bureaucracy with fourteen ranks, and he decreed that everyone had to start at the bottom and work toward the top. These measures gradually combined to make the army and government more powerful and efficient.

Peter also greatly increased the service requirements of commoners. In the wake of the Narva disaster, he established a regular standing army of more than two hundred thousand peasant-soldiers, drafted for life and commanded by noble officers. He added an additional hundred thousand men in special regiments of Cossacks and foreign mercenaries. To fund the army, taxes on peasants increased threefold during Peter's reign. Serfs were also arbitrarily assigned to work in the growing number of factories and mines that supplied the military.

In 1709 Peter's new war machine was able to crush the much smaller army of Sweden in Ukraine at Poltava, one of the most significant battles in Russian history. Russia's victory against Sweden was conclusive in 1721, and Estonia and present-day Latvia came under Russian rule for the first time. The cost was high: warfare consumed 80 to 85 percent of all revenues. But Russia became the dominant power in the Baltic and very much a great European power.

After his victory at Poltava, Peter channeled enormous resources into building a new Western-style capital on the Baltic to rival the great cities of Europe. Each summer, 25,000 to 40,000 peasants were sent to provide construction labor in St. Petersburg without pay. Many of these laborers died from hunger, sickness, and accidents. In order to populate his new capital, Peter ordered nobles to build costly palaces in St. Petersburg and to live in them most of the year. He also required merchants and artisans to settle and

**Peter the Great Cutting a Boyar's Beard**
As part of his westernization program, Peter the Great obliged Russian men to shave their long beards, a shock to traditional Orthodox notions of masculinity. Like many of his reforms, these were aimed primarily at the noble boyars; many peasants continued to wear beards in the countryside. (Universal Images Group/Getty Images)

# VIEWPOINTS

## Stuart Claims to Absolutism and the Parliamentary Response

James I (r. 1603–1625), king of England, fervently believed in the divine right of kings, a doctrine he expounded in a speech to Parliament in 1609. The efforts of James I and his son and successor Charles I (r. 1625–1649) to impose absolute rule in England led to conflict with Parliament. In the 1628 Petition of Right, Parliament rebuked Charles I for disregarding the existing laws of the kingdom, which limited royal power.

### James I, Address to Parliament, 1609

Kings are justly called Gods, for that they exercise a manner or resemblance of Divine power upon earth: For if you will consider the Attributes to God, you shall see how they agree in the person of a King. God hath power to create, or destroy, or unmake at his pleasure, to give life, or send death, to judge all, and to be judged nor accountable to none: To raise low things, and to make high things low at his pleasure, and to God are both soul and body due. And the like power have Kings: they make and unmake their subjects: they have power of raising, and casting down: of life, and of death: Judges over all their subjects, and in all causes, and yet accountable to none but God only. They have power to exalt low things, and abase high things, . . . and to cry up, or down [praise or criticize] any of their subjects, as they do their money. And to the King is due both the affection of the soul and the service of the body of his subjects. . . .

. . . So is it sedition in Subjects, to dispute what a King may do in the height of his power: But just Kings will ever be willing to declare what they will do, if they will not incur the curse of God. I will not be content that my power be disputed upon: but I shall ever be willing to make the reason appear of all my doings, and rule my actions according to my Laws.

### Petition of Right, 1628

By . . . the good laws and statutes of this realm, your subjects have inherited this freedom, that they should not be compelled to contribute to any tax, tallage,* aid, or other like charge nor set by common consent, in parliament.

*Tallage was a tax formerly imposed by kings on town citizens.

. . . Yet nevertheless, of late . . . your people have been in divers places assembled, and required to lend certain sums of money unto your Majesty, and many of them, upon their refusal so to do . . . have been therefore imprisoned, confined, and sundry other ways molested and disquieted. . . .

. . . And whereas also, by the statute called, *The Great Charter of the Liberties of England* [i.e., Magna Carta], it is declared and enacted, That no freeman may be taken or imprisoned, or be disseized [dispossessed] of his freehold or liberties, or of his free customs, or be outlawed or exiled, or in any manner destroyed, but by the lawful judgment of his peers, or by the law of the land. . . .

. . . Nevertheless, against the tenor of . . . the good laws and statutes of your realm . . . divers of your subjects have of late been imprisoned without any cause showed. . . .

. . . They do therefore humbly pray your most excellent Majesty; that no man hereafter be compelled to make or yield any gift, loan, benevolence, tax, or such like charge, without common consent, by Act of Parliament: . . . And that no freemen, in any such manner as is before mentioned, be imprisoned or detained. . . .

. . . All which they most humbly pray of your most excellent Majesty as their rights and liberties, according to the laws and statutes of this realm. . . .

### QUESTIONS FOR ANALYSIS

1. In what ways does James I believe royal power resembles divine power? Why does he believe kings possess such extensive powers? Does he see any limits to his powers?

2. What rights and liberties do English subjects believe they possess, and how has Charles violated them? Why do they believe it is Parliament's role to defend these freedoms?

3. Do you see any common ground and possibility for compromise between James's understanding of royal power and the rights of English subjects outlined by Parliament?

Sources: *The Political Works of James I*, ed. Charles Howard McIlwain (Cambridge, Mass.: Harvard University Press, 1918), pp. 307–308, 310. Spellings have been modernized; *Magna Charta, The Bill of Rights; with the Petition of Right, Presented to Charles I* (London: J. Bailey, 1820), pp. 18–20.

James I responded to such ideas by declaring, "No bishop, no king." His son and successor, Charles I, further antagonized religious sentiments by marrying a French Catholic princess and supporting the heavy-handed policies of the archbishop of Canterbury William Laud (1573–1645). Laud attempted to impose two new elements on church organization in Scotland: a new prayer book, modeled on the Anglican *Book*

*of Common Prayer*, and bishoprics. Charles avoided addressing grievances against him by refusing to call Parliament into session from 1629 to 1640. Instead, he financed his government through extraordinary stop-gap levies considered illegal by most English people. However, when Scottish Calvinists revolted against his religious policies, Charles was forced to summon Parliament to obtain funds for an army to put down

**Van Dyck, *Charles I at the Hunt*, ca. 1635**
Anthony Van Dyck was the greatest of Rubens's many students. In 1633 he became court painter to Charles I. This portrait of Charles just dismounted from a horse emphasizes the aristocratic bearing, elegance, and innate authority of the king. Van Dyck's success led to innumerable commissions by members of the court and aristocratic society. He had a profound influence on portraiture in England and beyond; some scholars believe that this portrait influenced Rigaud's 1701 portrayal of Louis XIV (see "Thinking Like a Historian" on page 434). (Musée du Louvre, Paris, France/Bridgeman Images)

the revolt. Angry with his behavior and sympathetic with the Scots' religious beliefs, in 1641 the House of Commons passed the Triennial Act, which compelled the king to summon Parliament every three years. The Commons also impeached Archbishop Laud and then threatened to abolish bishops. King Charles, fearful of a Scottish invasion, reluctantly accepted these measures. The next act in the conflict was precipitated by the outbreak of rebellion in Ireland, where English governors and landlords had long exploited the people. In 1641 the Catholic gentry of Ireland led an uprising in response to a feared invasion by English anti-Catholic forces.

Without an army, Charles I could neither come to terms with the Scots nor respond to the Irish rebellion. After a failed attempt to arrest parliamentary leaders, Charles left London for the north of England and began to raise an army. In response, Parliament formed its own army, the New Model Army, composed of the militia of the city of London and country squires with business connections.

The English Civil War (1642–1649) that erupted pitted the power of the king against that of the Parliament. After three years of fighting, Parliament's army defeated the king's forces at the Battles of Naseby and Langport in the summer of 1645. Charles refused to concede defeat, and both sides waited for a decisive event. This arrived in the form of the army under the leadership of Oliver Cromwell, a member of the House of Commons and a devout Puritan. In 1647 Cromwell's forces captured the king and dismissed anti-Cromwell members of the Parliament. In 1649 the remaining representatives, known as the "Rump Parliament," put

**The English Civil War, 1642–1649**

**Jan Steen,** ***The Merry Family,* 1668** In this painting from the Dutch golden age, a happy family enjoys a bois-terous song while seated around the dining table. Despite its carefree appearance, the painting was intended to teach a moral lesson. The children are shown drinking wine and smoking, bad habits they have learned from their parents. The inscription hanging over the mantelpiece (upper right) spells out the message clearly: "As the Old Sing, so Pipe the Young." (Rijksmuseum, Amsterdam, The Netherlands/Album/Art Resource, NY)

The political success of the Dutch rested on their phenomenal commercial prosperity. The Dutch orig-inally came to dominate European shipping by put-ting profits from their original industry — herring fishing — into shipbuilding. They boasted the lowest shipping rates and largest merchant marine in Europe, which allowed them to undersell foreign competitors. In the seventeenth century global trade and commerce brought the Dutch the highest standard of living in Europe, perhaps in the world. Salaries were high, and all classes of society ate well. A scholar has described the Netherlands as "an island of plenty in a sea of want." Consequently, the Netherlands experienced very few of the food riots that characterized the rest of Europe.[5]

The moral and ethical bases of Dutch commer-cial wealth were thrift, social discipline, and religious toleration. Although there is scattered evidence of anti-Semitism, Jews enjoyed a level of acceptance and assimilation in business and general culture unique in early modern Europe. Anti-Catholic laws existed through the eighteenth century, but they were only partly enforced. In the Dutch Republic, toleration paid off: it attracted a great deal of foreign capital and investment. After Louis XIV revoked the Edict of Nantes, many Huguenots fled France for the Dutch Republic. They brought with them a high level of arti-sanal skill and business experience as well as a loath-ing for state repression that would inspire the political views of the Enlightenment (see "The Early Enlight-enment" in Chapter 16).

## NOTES

1. John A. Lynn, "Recalculating French Army Growth," in *The Mil-itary Revolution Debate: Readings on the Military Transformation of Early Modern Europe,* ed. Clifford J. Rogers (Boulder, Colo.: Westview Press, 1995), p. 125.

2. J. H. Elliott, *Imperial Spain, 1469–1716* (New York: Mentor Books, 1963), pp. 306–308.
3. Quoted in H. Rosenberg, *Bureaucracy, Aristocracy, and Autocracy: The Prussian Experience, 1660–1815* (Boston: Beacon Press, 1966), p. 43.
4. Quoted in Rosenberg, *Bureaucracy, Aristocracy, and Autocracy*, p. 40.
5. S. Schama, *The Embarrassment of Riches: An Interpretation of Dutch Culture in the Golden Age* (New York: Alfred A. Knopf, 1987), pp. 165–170; quotation is on p. 167.

# LOOKING BACK  LOOKING AHEAD

The seventeenth century represented a difficult passage between two centuries of dynamism and growth in Europe. On one side lay the sixteenth century's religious enthusiasm and strife, overseas discoveries, rising populations, and vigorous commerce. On the other side stretched the eighteenth century's renewed population growth, economic development, and cultural flourishing. The first half of the seventeenth century was marked by harsh climate conditions and violent conflict across Europe. Recurring crop failure, famine, and epidemic disease contributed to a stagnant economy and population loss. In the middle decades of the seventeenth century, the very survival of the European monarchies established in the Renaissance appeared in doubt.

With the re-establishment of order in the second half of the century, maintaining stability was of paramount importance to European rulers.

While a few nations placed their trust in constitutionally limited governments, many more were ruled by monarchs proclaiming their absolute and God-given authority. Despite their political differences, most European states emerged from the period of crisis with shared achievements in state power, territorial expansion, and long-distance trade.

The eighteenth century was to see these power politics thrown into question by new Enlightenment aspirations for human society that derived from the inquisitive and self-confident spirit of the Scientific Revolution. These movements are explored in the next chapter. By the end of the eighteenth century demands for real popular sovereignty, colonial self-rule, and slave emancipation challenged the very bases of order so painfully achieved in the seventeenth century.

## Make Connections

Think about the larger developments and continuities within and across chapters.

1. This chapter has argued that, despite their political differences, rulers in absolutist and constitutionalist nations faced similar obstacles in the mid-seventeenth century and achieved many of the same goals. Based on the evidence presented here, do you agree with this argument? Why or why not?

2. Proponents of absolutism in western Europe believed that their form of monarchical rule was fundamentally different from and superior to what they saw as the "despotism" of Russia and the Ottoman Empire. What was the basis of this belief, and how accurate do you think it was?

3. What evidence does this chapter provide for the impact on European states of the discoveries and conquests discussed in Chapter 14?

# 15 REVIEW & EXPLORE

## Identify Key Terms

Identify and explain the significance of each item below.

Peace of Westphalia (p. 428)

baroque style (p. 430)

Fronde (p. 432)

Peace of Utrecht (p. 436)

mercantilism (p. 436)

Junkers (p. 440)

boyars (p. 442)

Cossacks (p. 443)

sultan (p. 447)

janissary corps (p. 447)

millet system (p. 447)

constitutionalism (p. 449)

republicanism (p. 449)

Puritans (p. 449)

Protectorate (p. 452)

Test Act (p. 453)

stadholder (p. 454)

## Review the Main Ideas

Answer the section heading questions from the chapter.

1. What made the seventeenth century an "age of crisis" and achievement? (p. 426)

2. Why did France rise and Spain fall during the late seventeenth century? (p. 431)

3. What explains the rise of absolutism in Prussia and Austria? (p. 438)

4. What were the distinctive features of Russian and Ottoman absolutism? (p. 441)

5. Why and how did the constitutional state triumph in the Dutch Republic and England? (p. 449)

## Suggested Resources

### BOOKS

- Beik, William. *A Social and Cultural History of Early Modern France.* 2009. An overview of early modern French history, by one of the leading authorities on the period.

- Clark, Christopher. *Iron Kingdom: The Rise and Downfall of Prussia, 1600–1947.* 2007. A sweeping survey of Prussian history from the birth of the Prussian state through the horrors of World War II.

- Elliott, John H. *Imperial Spain, 1469–1716,* 2d ed. 2002. An authoritative account of Spain's rise to imperial greatness and its slow decline.

- Gaunt, Peter, ed. *The English Civil War: The Essential Readings.* 2000. A collection showcasing leading historians' interpretations of the civil war.

- Goldgard, Anne. *Tulipmania: Money, Honor, and Knowledge in the Dutch Golden Age.* 2007. A fresh look

at the speculative fever for tulip bulbs in the early-seventeenth-century Dutch Republic.

- Hughes, Lindsey, ed. *Peter the Great and the West: New Perspectives.* 2001. Essays by leading scholars on the reign of Peter the Great and his opening of Russia to the West.

- Ingrao, Charles W. *The Habsburg Monarchy, 1618–1815,* 2d ed. 2000. An excellent synthesis of the political and social development of the Habsburg empire in the early modern period.

- Parker, Geoffrey. *Global Crisis: War, Climate Change and Catastrophe in the Seventeenth Century.* 2013. A sweeping account of the worldwide crisis of the seventeenth century, which the author argues was largely caused by climatic changes known as the "little ice age."

- Pincus, Steven. *1688: The First Modern Revolution.* 2009. Revisionary account of the Glorious Revolution, emphasizing its toll in bloodshed and destruction of property and its global repercussions.
- Roman, Rolf, ed. *Baroque: Architecture, Sculpture, Painting.* 2007. A beautifully illustrated presentation of multiple facets of the baroque across Europe.
- Romaniello, Matthew P. *The Elusive Empire: Kazan and the Creation of Russia, 1552–1671.* 2012. A study of the conquest of Kazan by Ivan the Terrible in 1552 and the Russian Empire built in its aftermath.
- Wilson, Peter H. *The Thirty Years War: Europe's Tragedy.* 2009. An overview of the origins and outcomes of the Thirty Years' War, focusing on political and economic issues in addition to religious conflicts.

## MEDIA

- *Alastriste* (Agustín Díaz Yanes, 2006). Set in the declining years of Spain's imperial glory, this film follows the violent adventures of an army captain who takes the son of a fallen comrade under his care.
- *The Art of Baroque Dance* (Dancetime Publications, 2006). An introduction to baroque dance that incorporates images of the architecture and art of the period alongside dance performances and information on major elements of the style.
- *Charles II: The Power and the Passion* (BBC, 2003). An award-winning television miniseries about the son of executed English king Charles I and the Restoration that brought him to the throne in 1660.
- *Cromwell* (Ken Hughes, 1970). The English Civil War from its origin to Oliver Cromwell's victory, with battle scenes as well as personal stories of Cromwell and other central figures.
- *Girl with a Pearl Earring* (Peter Webber, 2003). The life and career of painter Johannes Vermeer told through the eyes of a fictional servant girl who becomes his assistant and model.
- *The Jesuit Relations.* This site contains the entire English translation of *The Jesuit Relations and Allied Documents*, the reports submitted by Jesuit missionaries in New France to authorities in the home country. **puffin.creighton.edu/jesuit/relations/**
- *Molière* (Laurent Tirard, 2007). A film about the French playwright Molière, a favorite of King Louis XIV, that fancifully incorporates characters and plotlines from some of the writer's most celebrated plays.
- *Rubens: Passion, Faith, Sensuality and the Art of the Baroque* (Kultur Studio, 2011). A documentary introducing viewers to the work of Peter Paul Rubens, one of the greatest artists of the baroque style.
- *Tour of Restoration London.* A website offering information on the places, food, and people of Restoration London, inspired by the novel *Invitation to a Funeral* by Molly Brown (1999). **www.okima.com/**
- *Versailles Palace.* The official website of the palace of Versailles, built by Louis XIV and inhabited by French royalty until the revolution of 1789. **en.chateauversailles.fr/homepage**

# 16

# Toward a New Worldview

## 1540–1789

**In the sixteenth and seventeenth centuries,** new ways of understanding the natural world emerged. Those leading the changes saw themselves as philosophers and referred to their field of study as "natural philosophy." Whereas medieval scholars looked to authoritative texts like the Bible or the classics, early modern natural philosophers performed experiments and relied on increasingly complex mathematical calculations. The resulting conception of the universe and its laws remained in force until Albert Einstein's discoveries at the beginning of the twentieth century. Along with new discoveries in botany, zoology, chemistry, electricity, and other domains, these developments constituted a fundamental shift in the basic framework for understanding the natural world and the methods for examining it, known collectively as the "Scientific Revolution."

In the eighteenth century philosophers extended the use of reason from the study of nature to human society. They sought to bring the light of reason to bear on the darkness of prejudice, long-standing traditions, and general ignorance. Self-proclaimed members of an "Enlightenment" movement, they wished to bring the same progress to human affairs as their predecessors had brought to understanding of the natural world. While the Scientific Revolution ushered in modern science, the Enlightenment created concepts of human rights, equality, progress, universalism, and tolerance that still guide Western societies today. At the same time, some people used their new understanding of nature and reason to proclaim their own superiority, thus rationalizing attitudes now regarded as racist and sexist. These transformations in science and philosophy were encouraged by European overseas expansion, which challenged traditional ways of thinking by introducing an enormous variety of new peoples, plants, and animals. ■

# CHAPTER PREVIEW

- **What revolutionary discoveries were made in the sixteenth and seventeenth centuries?**

- **What intellectual and social changes occurred as a result of the Scientific Revolution?**

- **How did the Enlightenment emerge, and what were major currents of Enlightenment thought?**

- **How did the Enlightenment change social ideas and practices?**

- **What impact did new ways of thinking have on politics?**

**Life During the Scientific Revolution**

This 1768 painting by Joseph Wright captures the popularization of science and experimentation during the Enlightenment. Here, a scientist demonstrates the creation of a vacuum by withdrawing air from a flask, with the suffocating cockatoo serving as shocking proof of the experiment. (*An Experiment on a Bird in the Air Pump*, 1768/National Gallery, London/Bridgeman Images)

# What revolutionary discoveries were made in the sixteenth and seventeenth centuries?

Until the middle of the sixteenth century, Europeans relied on an understanding of motion and matter drawn from the ancient Greek philosopher Aristotle and adapted to Christian theology. The rise of the university, along with the intellectual vitality of the Renaissance and technological advancements, inspired European scholars to seek better explanations. From the work of Nicolaus Copernicus to the work of Isaac Newton, a revolutionary new understanding of the universe had emerged by the end of the seventeenth century. Collectively known as the "Scientific Revolution," the work of these scientists constituted significant milestones in the creation of modern science.

The major figures of the Scientific Revolution (ca. 1540–1700) were for the most part devout Christians who saw their work as heralding the glory of creation and who combined older traditions of magic, astrology, and alchemy with their pathbreaking experimentation. Their discoveries took place in a broader context of international trade, imperial expansion, and cultural exchange. Alongside developments in modern science and natural philosophy, the growth of natural history in this period is now recognized by historians as a major achievement of the Scientific Revolution.

## Contributions from the Muslim World

In 1500 scientific activity flourished in many parts of the world. Between 750 and 950 Muslim, Christian, and Jewish scholars in the expanding Muslim world began translating the legacy of ancient Greek science and natural philosophy into Arabic, especially the works of Aristotle. The interaction of peoples and cultures across the vast Muslim world, facilitated by religious tolerance and the common scholarly language of Arabic, was highly favorable to advances in learning.

In a great period of cultural and intellectual flourishing from 1000 to 1500, Muslim scholars thrived in cultural centers such as Baghdad and Córdoba, the capital of Islamic Spain. They established the world's first institutions of higher learning, called *madrasas*, in Constantinople, Fez (Morocco), and Cairo, which were devoted to Islamic theology and law. In this fertile atmosphere, scholars surpassed the texts they had inherited in areas such as mathematics, physics, astronomy, and medicine. Arab and Persian mathematicians, for example, invented algebra, the concept of the algorithm, and decimal point notation. Arab astronomers built observatories to collect celestial

observations, and an Egyptian scholar, Ibn al-Haytham (d. 1042), revolutionized optics by demonstrating mathematically that light travels in straight lines.

Given the scientific and philosophical knowledge possessed by Arab and Muslim scholars in the tenth and eleventh centuries, one might have expected that modern science would have emerged in the Muslim world first. However, the madrasas excluded study of the natural sciences, and Muslim scholars did not benefit from institutions dedicated to the creation and dissemination of scientific knowledge. This pattern of education was unlike that of the Europeans, who created independent institutions of higher education (universities) and then placed study of the Greek natural sciences at the center of the curriculum.

The growth of trade and the re-establishment of stronger monarchies in the High Middle Ages encouraged the circulation of ideas and the patronage of educational institutions in western Europe. As European scholars became aware of advances in knowledge made in Muslim territories, they traveled to Islamic territories in Iberia, Sicily, and the eastern Mediterranean to gain access to this knowledge. In the twelfth century, these scholars translated many Greek texts — including works of Aristotle, Ptolemy, Galen, and Euclid previously lost to the West — into Latin, along with the commentaries of Arab scholars. With the patronage of kings and religious institutions, groups of scholars created universities in which these translated works, especially those of the ancient Greek philosopher Aristotle, dominated the curriculum.

The intellectual and cultural movement known as the Renaissance provided a crucial foundation for the Scientific Revolution. The quest to restore the glories of the ancient past led to a new period of rediscovery of classical texts, including Ptolemy's *Geography*, which was translated into Latin around 1410. An encyclopedic treatise on botany by Theophrastus was rediscovered in the 1450s moldering on the shelves of the Vatican library. The fall of Constantinople to the Ottomans in 1453 resulted in a great influx of little-known Greek works, as Christian scholars fled to Italy with their precious texts.

In this period, western European universities established new professorships of mathematics, astronomy, and natural philosophy. The prestige of the new fields was low, especially of mathematics, which was reserved for practical problems such as accounting, surveying, and computing planetary tables, but not used to understand the functioning of the physical world itself. Nevertheless, these professorships eventually

■ **natural philosophy** An early modern term for the study of the nature of the universe, its purpose, and how it functioned; it encompassed what we would call "science" today.

# TIMELINE

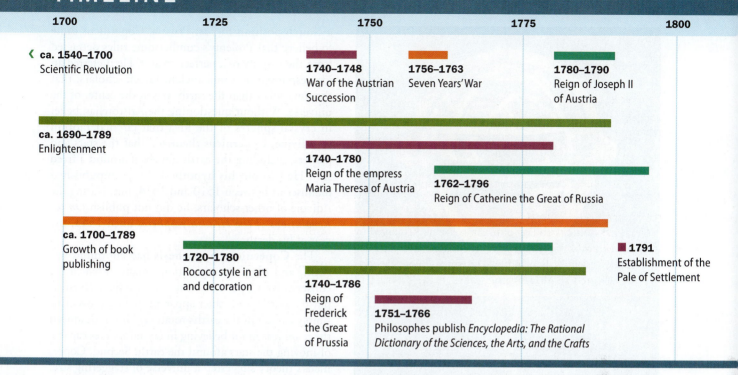

| 1700 | 1725 | 1750 | 1775 | 1800 |
|------|------|------|------|------|

**ca. 1540–1700**
Scientific Revolution

**1740–1748**
War of the Austrian Succession

**1756–1763**
Seven Years' War

**1780–1790**
Reign of Joseph II of Austria

**ca. 1690–1789**
Enlightenment

**1740–1780**
Reign of the empress Maria Theresa of Austria

**1762–1796**
Reign of Catherine the Great of Russia

**ca. 1700–1789**
Growth of book publishing

**1720–1780**
Rococo style in art and decoration

**1791**
Establishment of the Pale of Settlement

**1740–1786**
Reign of Frederick the Great of Prussia

**1751–1766**
Philosophes publish *Encyclopedia: The Rational Dictionary of the Sciences, the Arts, and the Crafts*

---

enabled the union of mathematics with natural philosophy that was to be a hallmark of the Scientific Revolution.

## Scientific Thought to 1500

The term *science* as we use it today came into use only in the nineteenth century. For medieval scholars, philosophy was the path to true knowledge about the world, and its proofs consisted of the authority of ancients (as interpreted by Muslim and Christian theologians) and their techniques of logical argumentation. Questions about the physical nature of the universe and how it functioned belonged to a minor branch of philosophy, called **natural philosophy**. Drawing on scholarship in the Muslim world, natural philosophy was based primarily on the ideas of Aristotle, the great Greek philosopher of the fourth century B.C.E. Medieval theologians such as Thomas Aquinas brought Aristotelian philosophy into harmony with Christian doctrines. According to the Christianized view of Aristotle, a motionless earth stood at the center of the universe and was encompassed by ten separate concentric crystal spheres in which were embedded the moon, the sun, planets, and stars. Beyond the spheres was Heaven, with the throne of God and the souls of the saved. Angels kept the spheres moving in perfect circles.

Aristotle's views also dominated thinking about physics and motion on earth. Aristotle had distinguished between the world of the celestial spheres and that of the earth—the sublunar world. The spheres consisted of a perfect, incorruptible "quintessence," or fifth essence. The sublunar world, however, was made up of four imperfect, changeable elements: air, fire, water, and earth. Aristotle and his followers also believed that a uniform force moved an object at a constant speed and that the object would stop as soon as that force was removed.

Aristotle's cosmology made intellectual sense, but it could not account for the observed motions of the stars and planets and, in particular, provided no explanation for the apparent backward motion of the planets (which we now know occurs as the earth passes the slower-moving outer planets or is passed by the faster-moving inner ones). More than four centuries later the Greek scholar Ptolemy offered a theory for this phenomenon. According to Ptolemy, the planets moved in small circles, called epicycles, each of which moved in turn along a larger circle, or deferent. Ptolemaic astronomy was less elegant than Aristotle's neat nested circles and required complex calculations, but it provided a surprisingly accurate model for predicting planetary motion.

The work of Ptolemy also provided the basic foundation of knowledge about the earth. Rediscovered and translated from Arabic into Latin around 1410, his *Geography* presented crucial advances on medieval cartography by representing a round earth divided into 360 degrees with the major latitude marks. However, Ptolemy's map reflected the limits of ancient knowledge, showing only the continents of Europe, Africa, and Asia, with land covering three-quarters of the world.

463

**Model of the Ptolemaic System**   This seventeenth-century brass model was used to demonstrate the Ptolemaic astronomical system, with the earth at the center and the movement of the sun, stars, and planets around it. (Armillary sphere made by Adam Heroldt [fl. 1648]/Science Museum, London, UK/Bridgeman Images)

These two frameworks reveal the strengths and limitations of European knowledge on the eve of the Scientific Revolution. Overcoming the authority of the ancients to develop a new understanding of the natural world, derived from precise techniques of observation and experimentation, was the Scientific Revolution's monumental achievement. Europeans were not the first to use experimental methods—of which there was a long tradition in the Muslim world and elsewhere—but they were the first to separate scientific knowledge decisively from philosophical and religious beliefs and to accord mathematics a fundamental role in understanding the natural world.

## The Copernican Hypothesis

The first great departure from the medieval system was the work of the Polish cleric Nicolaus Copernicus (1473–1543). Copernicus studied astronomy, medicine, and church law at the famed universities of Bologna, Padua, and Ferrara before taking up

a church position in East Prussia. Copernicus came to believe that Ptolemy's cumbersome rules detracted from the majesty of a perfect creator. He preferred an idea espoused by some ancient Greek scholars: that the sun, rather than the earth, was at the center of the universe. Without questioning the Aristotelian belief in crystal spheres or the idea that circular motion was divine, Copernicus theorized that the stars and planets, including the earth, revolved around a fixed sun. He laid out his hypothesis in an unpublished manuscript between 1510 and 1514, but, fearing the ridicule of other scholars, he did not publish *On the Revolutions of the Heavenly Spheres* until 1543, the year of his death.

The **Copernican hypothesis** had enormous scientific and religious implications, many of which the conservative Copernicus did not anticipate. First, it put the stars at rest, their apparent nightly movement simply a result of the earth's rotation. Thus it destroyed the main reason for believing in crystal spheres capable of moving the stars around the earth. Second, Copernicus's theory suggested a universe of staggering size. If in the course of a year the earth moved around the sun and yet the stars appeared to remain in the same place, then the universe was unthinkably large. Third, by using mathematics, instead of philosophy, to justify his theories, Copernicus challenged the traditional hierarchy of the disciplines. Finally, by characterizing the earth as just another planet, Copernicus destroyed the basic idea of Aristotelian physics—that the earthly sphere was quite different from the heavenly one. Where then were Heaven and the throne of God?

Religious leaders varied in their response to Copernicus's theories. A few Protestant scholars became avid Copernicans, while others accepted some elements of his criticism of Ptolemy but firmly rejected the notion that the earth moved, a doctrine that contradicted the literal reading of some passages of the Bible. Among Catholics, Copernicus's ideas drew little attention prior to 1600. Because the Catholic Church had never insisted on literal interpretations of the Bible, it did not officially declare the Copernican hypothesis false until provoked by the publications of Galileo Galilei in 1616 (see "Science and Religion" later in this chapter).

Other events were almost as influential in creating doubts about traditional astronomy. In 1572 a new star appeared and shone very brightly for almost two years. Actually a distant exploding star, it made an enormous impression on people and seemed to contradict the idea that the heavenly spheres were unchanging and therefore perfect. In 1577 a new comet suddenly moved through the sky, cutting a straight path across the supposedly impenetrable crystal spheres. It was time, as a sixteenth-century scientific writer put it, for "the radical renovation of astronomy."[1]

## Brahe, Kepler, and Galileo: Proving Copernicus Right

One astronomer who partially agreed with the Copernican hypothesis was the Danish astronomer Tycho Brahe (TEE-koh BRAH-hee) (1546–1601). Brahe established himself as Europe's leading astronomer with his detailed observations of the new star that appeared in 1572. Impressed by his work, the king of Denmark provided funds for Brahe to build the most sophisticated observatory of his day. Upon the king's death, Brahe acquired a new patron in the Holy Roman emperor Rudolph II and built a new observatory in Prague.

For twenty years Brahe had observed the stars and planets with the aim of creating new and improved tables of planetary motions. He produced the most exact observations ever carried out with the naked eye, but his limited understanding of mathematics and his sudden death in 1601 prevented him from making much sense out of his mass of data. Part Ptolemaic, part Copernican, he believed that all the planets except the earth revolved around the sun and that the entire group of sun and planets revolved in turn around the earth-moon system.

It was Brahe's assistant, Johannes Kepler (1571–1630), who discovered what his observations revealed about planetary movements. Kepler carefully re-examined his predecessor's notations and came to believe that they could not be explained by Ptolemy's astronomy. Abandoning the notion of the circular paths of epicycles and deferents developed by Ptolemy to explain the retrograde motion of the planets—which even Copernicus had retained in part—Kepler developed three revolutionary laws of planetary motion. First, largely through observations of the planet Mars, he demonstrated that the orbits of the planets around the sun are elliptical rather than circular. Second, he demonstrated that the planets do not move at a uniform speed in their orbits. When a planet is close to the sun it moves more rapidly, and it slows as it moves farther away from the sun. Finally, Kepler's third law stated that the time a planet takes to make its complete orbit is precisely related to its distance from the sun.

Kepler's contribution was monumental. Whereas Copernicus had used mathematics to describe planetary movement, Kepler proved mathematically the precise relations of a sun-centered (solar) system. He thus united for the first time the theoretical cosmology of natural philosophy with mathematics. His work demolished the old system of Aristotle and Ptolemy, and with his third law he came close to formulating the idea of universal gravitation (see the next section). In 1627 he also published the *Rudolphine Tables*, named in honor of Emperor Rudolph and

based on his observations and those of Tycho Brahe. The work consisted of a catalogue of more than one thousand stars as well as tables of the positions of the sun, moon, and planets. They were used by astronomers for many years.

While Kepler was unraveling planetary motion, a Florentine named Galileo Galilei (1564–1642) was challenging Aristotelian ideas about motion on earth. Galileo's fascination with mathematics led to a professorship during which he examined motion and mechanics in a new way. Galileo focused on deficiencies in Aristotle's theories of motion. He measured the movement of a rolling ball across a surface, repeating the action again and again to verify his results. In his famous acceleration experiment, he showed that a uniform force—in this case, gravity—produced a uniform acceleration. He also achieved new insight into the principle of inertia by hypothesizing that an object would continue in motion forever unless stopped by some external force. The **law of inertia** was formulated explicitly after Galileo's death by René Descartes (see "The Methods of Science: Bacon and Descartes" later in this chapter) and Pierre Gassendi. Galileo's work on mechanics proved Aristotelian physics wrong.

On hearing details about the invention of the telescope in Holland, Galileo made one for himself and trained it on the heavens. He quickly discovered that, far from being a perfect crystal sphere, the moon is cratered with mountains and valleys, just like the earth. He then discovered the first four moons of Jupiter, which clearly suggested that Jupiter could not possibly be embedded in an impenetrable crystal sphere as Aristotle and Ptolemy maintained. This discovery provided new evidence for the Copernican theory, in which Galileo already believed. He wrote in 1610 in *The Sidereal Messenger*: "By the aid of a telescope anyone may behold [the Milky Way] in a manner which so distinctly appeals to the senses that all the disputes which have tormented philosophers through so many ages are exploded by the irrefutable evidence of our eyes, and we are freed from wordy disputes upon the subject."[2] (See "Evaluating Written Evidence: Galileo Galilei, *The Sidereal Messenger*, page 466.)

A crucial corner in Western civilization had been turned. No longer should one rely on established authority. A new method of learning and investigating was being developed, one that proved useful in any field of inquiry. A historian investigating documents of the past, for example, is not so different from a Galileo studying stars and rolling balls.

■ **Copernican hypothesis** The idea that the sun, not the earth, is the center of the universe.

■ **law of inertia** A law hypothesized by Galileo that states that motion, not rest, is the natural state of an object, and that an object continues in motion forever unless stopped by some external force.

# Galileo Galilei, *The Sidereal Messenger*

In this passage from *The Sidereal Messenger* (1610), Galileo Galilei recounts his experiments to build a telescope and his observations of the moon. By discovering the irregularity of the moon's surface, Galileo disproved a central tenet of medieval cosmography: that the heavens were composed of perfect, unblemished spheres essentially different from the base matter of earth.

~

About ten months ago a report reached my ears that a Dutchman had constructed a telescope, by the aid of which visible objects, although at a great distance from the eye of the observer, were seen distinctly as if near. . . . A few days after, I received confirmation of the report in a letter written from Paris . . . , which finally determined me to give myself up first to inquire into the principle of the telescope, and then to consider the means by which I might compass [achieve] the invention of a similar instrument, which a little while after I succeeded in doing, through deep study of the theory of refraction; and I prepared a tube, at first of lead, in the ends of which I fitted two glass lenses, both plane on one side, but on the other side one spherically convex, and the other concave. . . . At length, by sparing neither labour nor expense, I succeeded in constructing for myself an instrument so superior that objects seen through it appear magnified nearly a thousand times, and more than thirty times nearer than if viewed by the natural powers of sight alone. . . .

Let me speak first of the surface of the moon, which is turned towards us. For the sake of being understood more easily, I distinguish two parts in it, which I call respectively the brighter and the darker. The brighter part seems to surround and pervade the whole hemisphere, but the darker part, like a sort of cloud, discolours the moon's surface and makes it appear covered with spots. Now these spots . . . are plain to every one, and every age has seen them, wherefore I shall call them *great* or *ancient* spots, to distinguish them from other spots, smaller in size, but so thickly scattered that they sprinkle the whole surface of the moon, but especially the brighter portion of it. These spots have never been observed by any one before me, and from my observations of them, often repeated, I have been led to that opinion which I have expressed, namely, that I feel sure that the surface of the moon is not perfectly smooth, free from inequalities and exactly spherical, as a large school of philosophers considers with regard to the moon and the other heavenly bodies, but that, on the contrary, it is full of inequalities, uneven, full of hollows and protuberances, just like the surface of the earth itself, which is varied everywhere by lofty mountains and deep valleys.

## EVALUATE THE EVIDENCE

1. What did the telescope permit Galileo to see on the moon that was not visible to the naked eye, and how did he interpret his observations?
2. Why were Galileo's observations so important to the destruction of the Ptolemaic universe?

Source: Galileo Galilei, *The Sidereal Messenger* (London: Rivingtons, 1880), pp. 10–11, 14–15.

## Newton's Synthesis

By about 1640 the work of Brahe, Kepler, and Galileo had been largely accepted by the scientific community despite opposition from religious leaders. The old Aristotelian astronomy and physics were in ruins, and several fundamental breakthroughs had been made. But the new findings failed to explain what forces controlled the movement of the planets and objects on earth. That challenge was taken up by English scientist Isaac Newton (1642–1727), a genius who spectacularly united the experimental and theoretical-mathematical sides of modern science.

Newton was born into the lower English gentry, and he enrolled at Cambridge University in 1661. He arrived at some of his most basic ideas about physics in 1666 at age twenty-four but was unable to prove them mathematically. In 1684, after years of studying optics, Newton returned to mechanics for eighteen intensive months. The result was his towering accomplishment, a single explanatory system that could integrate the astronomy of Copernicus, as corrected by Kepler's laws, with the physics of Galileo and his predecessors. Newton did this through a set of mathematical laws that explain motion and mechanics. These laws were published in 1687 in Newton's *Mathematical Principles of Natural Philosophy* (also known as the *Principia Mathematica*). Because of their complexity, it took scientists and engineers two hundred years to work out all their implications.

■ **law of universal gravitation** Newton's law that all objects are attracted to one another and that the force of attraction is proportional to the objects' quantity of matter and inversely proportional to the square of the distance between them.

The key feature of the Newtonian synthesis was the **law of universal gravitation**. According to this law, every body in the universe attracts every other body in the universe in a precise mathematical relationship, whereby the force of attraction is proportional to the quantity of matter of the objects and inversely proportional to the square of the distance between them. The whole universe — from Kepler's elliptical orbits to Galileo's rolling balls — was unified in one majestic system. Newton's synthesis of mathematics with physics and astronomy established him as one of the most important figures in the history of science; it prevailed until Albert Einstein's formulation of the general theory of relativity in 1915. Yet, near the end of his life, he declared: "I do not know what I may appear to the world; but to myself I seem to have been only like a boy, playing on the seashore, and diverting myself, in now and then finding a smoother pebble or a prettier shell than ordinary, whilst the great ocean of truth lay all undiscovered before me."[3]

## Natural History and Empire

At the same time that they made advances in astronomy and physics, Europeans embarked on the pursuit of knowledge about unknown geographical regions and the useful and valuable resources they contained. Because they were the first to acquire a large overseas empire, the Spanish pioneered these efforts. Following the conquest of the Aztec and Inca Empires (see "Conquest of the Aztec Empire" and "The Fall of the Incas" in Chapter 14), they sought to learn about and profit from their New World holdings. The Spanish crown sponsored many scientific expeditions to gather information and specimens, out of which emerged new discoveries that reshaped the fields of botany, zoology, cartography, and metallurgy, among others. These accomplishments have attracted less attention from historians in part because the strict policy of secrecy imposed on scientific discoveries by the Spanish crown limited the documents circulating about them.

**Galileo's Telescopic Observations of the Moon**
Among the many instruments Galileo invented was a telescope that could magnify objects thirty times (other contemporary telescopes could magnify objects only three times). Using this telescope, he obtained the empirical evidence that proved the Copernican system. He sketched many illustrations of his observations, including the six phases of the moon shown here. (telescope: Museo delle Scienze, Florence, Italy/akg-images; moon: Biblioteca Nazionale Centrale, Florence, Italy/Eric Vandeville/Gamma Rapho via Getty Images)

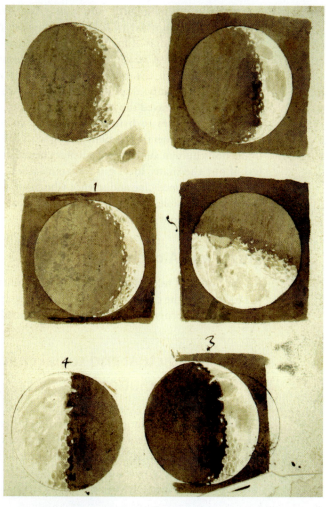

Plants were a particular source of interest because they offered potential for tremendous profits in the form of spices, medicines, dyes, and cash crops. King Philip II of Spain sent his personal physician, Francisco Hernández, to New Spain for seven years in the 1560s. Hernández filled fifteen volumes with illustrations of three thousand plants previously unknown in Europe. He extensively interviewed local healers about the plants' medicinal properties, thereby benefiting from centuries of Mesoamerican botanical knowledge. In the seventeenth century, for example, the Spanish obtained a monopoly on the world's supply of cinchona bark, which comes from a tree native to the high altitudes of the Andes and was the first effective treatment for malaria.

Other countries followed the Spanish example as their global empires expanded, relying on both official expeditions and the private initiative of merchants, missionaries, and settlers. Royal botanical gardens served as living laboratories for cultivating valuable foreign plants. Over time, the stream of new information about plant and animal species overwhelmed existing intellectual frameworks. Carl Linnaeus (1707–1778) of Sweden sent his students on exploratory voyages around the world and, based on their observations and the specimens they collected, devised a formal system of naming and classifying living organisms still used today (with substantial revisions).

New encyclopedias of natural history popularized this knowledge with realistic drawings and descriptions emphasizing the usefulness of animals and plants. Audiences at home eagerly read the accounts of naturalists, who braved the heat, insects, and diseases of tropical jungles to bring home exotic animal, vegetable, and mineral specimens (along with captive indigenous human subjects). Audiences heard much less about the many local guides, translators, and practitioners of medicine and science who made these expeditions possible and who contributed a great deal of knowledge about the natural world.

## Magic and Alchemy

Recent historical research on the Scientific Revolution has focused on the contribution of ideas and practices we no longer recognize as science, such as astrology and alchemy. For most of human history, interest in astronomy was inspired by the belief that the movement of heavenly bodies influenced events on earth. Many of the most celebrated astronomers also worked as astrologers. Used as a diagnostic tool in medicine, astrology formed a regular part of the curriculum of medical schools.

Centuries-old practices of magic and alchemy also remained important traditions for natural philosophers. Early modern practitioners of magic strove to understand and control hidden connections they perceived among different elements of the natural world, such as that between a magnet and iron. The idea that objects possessed hidden or "occult" qualities that allowed them to affect objects at a distance was a particularly important legacy of the magical tradition. Belief in occult qualities—or numerology or cosmic harmony—was not antithetical to belief in God. On the contrary, adherents believed that only a divine creator could infuse the universe with such meaningful mystery.

Johannes Kepler exemplifies the interaction among these different strands of interest. His duties as court mathematician included casting horoscopes for the royal family, and he guided his own life by astrological principles. He also wrote at length on cosmic harmonies and explained elliptical motion through ideas about the beautiful music created by the combined motion of the planets. Kepler's fictional account of travel to the moon, written partly to illustrate the idea of a non-earth-centered universe, caused controversy and may have contributed to the arrest and trial of his mother as a witch in 1620. Kepler also suffered because of his unorthodox brand of Lutheranism, which led to his condemnation by both Lutherans and Catholics.

Another example of the interweaving of ideas and beliefs is Sir Isaac Newton, who was both intensely religious and fascinated by alchemy, whose practitioners believed (among other things) that base metals could be turned into gold. Critics complained that his idea of universal gravitation was merely a restatement of old magical ideas about the innate sympathies between bodies; Newton himself believed that the attraction of gravity resulted from God's actions in the universe.

# What intellectual and social changes occurred as a result of the Scientific Revolution?

The Scientific Revolution was not accomplished by a handful of brilliant individuals working alone. Advancements occurred in many fields—medicine, chemistry, and botany, among others—as scholars developed new methods to seek answers to long-standing problems. They did so in collaboration with skilled craftsmen who invented new instruments and helped conduct experiments. These results circulated in an intellectual community from which women were usually excluded.

## The Methods of Science: Bacon and Descartes

One of the keys to the achievement of a new world-view in the seventeenth century was the development of better ways of obtaining knowledge. Two important thinkers, Francis Bacon (1561–1626) and René Descartes (day-KAHRT) (1596–1650), were influential in describing and advocating for improved scientific methods based, respectively, on empirical observation and on mathematical reasoning.

The English politician and writer Francis Bacon was the greatest early propagandist for the experimental method. Rejecting the Aristotelian and medieval method of using speculative reasoning to build general theories, Bacon called for a new approach to scientific inquiry based on direct observation, free from the preconceptions and prejudices of the past. The researcher who wants to learn more about leaves or rocks, for example, should not speculate about the subject but rather collect a multitude of specimens and then compare and analyze them to derive general principles. This technique of producing knowledge is known as inductive reasoning, which works from specific observations up to broader generalizations and theories. Bacon's work, and his prestige as lord chancellor under James I, led to the widespread adoption of what was called "experimental philosophy" in Britain after his death. In 1660 followers of Bacon created the Royal Society (still in existence), which met weekly to conduct experiments and discuss the latest findings of scholars across Europe.

On the continent, more speculative methods gained support. In 1619, as a twenty-three-year-old soldier serving in the Thirty Years' War, the French philosopher René Descartes experienced a life-changing intellectual vision. Descartes saw that there was a perfect correspondence between geometry and algebra and that geometrical spatial figures could be expressed as algebraic equations and vice versa. A major step forward in the history of mathematics, Descartes's discovery of analytic geometry provided scientists with an important new tool.

Descartes used mathematics to elaborate a new vision of the workings of the cosmos. Accepting Galileo's claim that all elements of the universe are composed of the same matter, Descartes began to investigate the basic nature of matter. Drawing on ancient Greek atomist philosophies, he developed the idea that matter was made up of "corpuscles" (tiny particles) that collided together in an endless series of motions, akin to the workings of a machine. All occurrences in nature could be analyzed as matter in motion, and the total "quantity of motion" in the universe was constant. Descartes's mechanistic view of the universe depended on the idea that space was identical to matter and that empty space—a vacuum—was therefore impossible.

Although Descartes's hypothesis about the vacuum was proved wrong, his notion of a mechanistic universe intelligible through the physics of motion proved inspirational. Decades later, Newton rejected Descartes's idea of a full universe and several of his other ideas, but retained the notion of a mechanistic universe as a key element of his own system.

Descartes's greatest achievement was to develop his initial vision into a whole philosophy of knowledge and science. The Aristotelian cosmos was appealing in part because it corresponded with the evidence of the human senses. When experiments proved that sensory impressions could be wrong, Descartes decided it was necessary to doubt them and everything that could reasonably be doubted, and to then, as in geometry, use deductive reasoning from self-evident truths, which he called "first principles," to ascertain scientific laws.

Descartes's reasoning ultimately reduced all substances to "matter" and "mind"—that is, to the physical and the mental. The devout Descartes believed that God had endowed man with reason for a purpose and that rational speculation could provide a path to the truths of creation. His view of the world as consisting of these two fundamental entities is known as **Cartesian dualism**. Descartes's thought was highly influential in France and the Netherlands, but less so in England, where experimental philosophy won the day.

Both Bacon's inductive experimentalism and Descartes's deductive mathematical reasoning had flaws. Bacon's inability to appreciate the importance of mathematics and his obsession with practical results clearly showed the limitations of antitheoretical empiricism. Likewise, some of Descartes's positions demonstrated the inadequacy of rigid, dogmatic rationalism. For example, he believed that it was possible to deduce the whole science of medicine from first principles. Although insufficient on their own, Bacon's and Descartes's extreme approaches are combined in the modern scientific method, which began to crystallize in the late seventeenth century.

## Medicine, the Body, and Chemistry

The Scientific Revolution, which began with the study of the cosmos, soon transformed the understanding of the microcosm of the human body. For many centuries the ancient Greek physician Galen's explanation of the body carried the same authority as Aristotle's account of the universe. According to Galen, the body contained four humors: blood, phlegm, black bile, and yellow bile. Illness was believed to result from an

■ **Cartesian dualism** Descartes's view that all of reality could ultimately be reduced to mind and matter.

## MAJOR CONTRIBUTORS TO THE SCIENTIFIC REVOLUTION

| | |
|---|---|
| Nicolaus Copernicus (1473–1543) | Wrote *On the Revolutions of the Heavenly Spheres* (1543); theorized that the sun, rather than the earth, was the center of the universe |
| Paracelsus (1493–1541) | Swiss physician and alchemist who pioneered the use of chemicals to address illness |
| Andreas Vesalius (1514–1564) | Wrote *On the Structure of the Human Body* (1543) |
| Tycho Brahe (1546–1601) | Built observatory and recorded data on planetary motions |
| Francis Bacon (1561–1626) | Advocated experimental method, formalizing theory of inductive reasoning known as empiricism |
| Galileo Galilei (1564–1642) | Used telescopic observation to provide evidence for Copernican hypothesis |
| Johannes Kepler (1571–1630) | Used Brahe's data to provide mathematical support for the Copernican hypothesis; his new laws of planetary motion united for the first time natural philosophy and mathematics; completed the *Rudolphine Tables* in 1627 |
| William Harvey (1578–1657) | Discovered the circulation of the blood (1628) |
| René Descartes (1596–1650) | Used deductive reasoning to formulate the theory of Cartesian dualism |
| Robert Boyle (1627–1691) | Formulated Boyle's law (1662) governing the pressure of gases |
| Isaac Newton (1642–1727) | Published *Principia Mathematica* (1687); set forth the law of universal gravitation, synthesizing previous theories of motion and matter |

imbalance of humors, which is why doctors frequently prescribed bloodletting to expel excess blood.

Swiss physician and alchemist Paracelsus (1493–1541) was an early proponent of the experimental method in medicine and pioneered the use of chemicals to address what he saw as chemical, rather than humoral, imbalances. Another experimentalist, Flemish physician Andreas Vesalius (1514–1564), studied anatomy by dissecting human bodies, often those of executed criminals. In 1543, the same year Copernicus published *On the Revolutions*, Vesalius issued his masterpiece, *On the Structure of the Human Body*. Its two hundred precise drawings revolutionized the understanding of human anatomy, disproving Galen, just as Copernicus and his successors had disproved Aristotle and Ptolemy. (See "Evaluating Visual Evidence: Frontispiece to *On the Structure of the Human Body*," page 471.) The experimental approach also led English royal

physician William Harvey (1578–1657) to discover the circulation of blood through the veins and arteries in 1628. Harvey was the first to explain that the heart worked like a pump and to explain the function of its muscles and valves.

Robert Boyle (1627–1691), a key figure in the victory of experimental methods in England, helped create the Royal Society in 1660. Among the first scientists to perform controlled experiments and publish details of them, he helped improve a number of scientific instruments. For example, he built and experimented with an air pump, which he used to investigate the properties of air and create a vacuum, thus disproving Descartes's belief that a vacuum could not exist in nature. Based on these experiments, he formulated a new law in 1662, now known as Boyle's law, that states that the pressure of a gas varies inversely with volume. Boyle also hypothesized that chemical substances were composed of tiny mechanical particles, out of which all other matter was formed.

## Science and Religion

It is sometimes assumed that the relationship between science and religion is fundamentally hostile and that the pursuit of knowledge based on reason and proof is incompatible with faith. Yet during the Scientific Revolution most practitioners were devoutly religious and saw their work as contributing to the celebration of God's glory rather than undermining it. However, the concept of heliocentrism, which displaced the earth from the center of the universe, threatened the understanding of the place of mankind in creation as stated in Genesis. All religions derived from the Old Testament—Catholic, Protestant, Jewish, and Muslim—thus faced difficulties accepting the Copernican system. The leaders of the Catholic Church were initially less hostile than Protestant and Jewish religious leaders, but in the first decades of the sixteenth century the Catholic attitude changed. In 1616, alarmed by research findings by Galileo Galilei and other astronomers that undermined traditional astronomy, the Holy Office placed the works of Copernicus and his supporters on a list of books Catholics were forbidden to read. It also warned Galileo not to espouse heliocentrism or face the consequences.

Out of caution, Galileo silenced his views for several years, until 1623 saw the ascension of Pope Urban VIII,

# Frontispiece to *On the Structure of the Human Body*

During the sixteenth century, anatomists began to perform public dissections on human corpses, often those of executed criminals, with the aim of unveiling the mystery and the complexity of the human body. This was a revolutionary new hands-on approach for physicians, who usually worked from a theoretical, rather than a practical, understanding of the body. To establish their authors' scientific authority and foster readers' interest, books on anatomy in this period began to feature images of their authors engaged in the act of dissection.

One of the pioneers of this new approach was Andreas Vesalius, who occupied the chair of anatomy at the University of Padua in Italy. The frontispiece to his book *On the Structure of the Human Body*, published in 1543, is shown here. The image depicts Vesalius gazing at the viewer while gesturing at the abdomen of a female cadaver he has cut open to reveal the womb. An unruly crowd of onlookers presses around the table to observe the procedure. A plaque hanging above the scene identifies Vesalius as "Andreae Vesalii" of Brussels and provides information about the book. Two barber-surgeons, the craftsmen previously responsible for dissections, sit underneath the table, fighting over surgical instruments. A skeleton is perched on the railing of the seats that overlook the dissection table.

(Universal History Archive/Shutterstock)

## EVALUATE THE EVIDENCE

1. Do you think this is a realistic image of a medical dissection? Why or why not?
2. Why would Vesalius choose to open his book with an image of himself dissecting a corpse? What impression of the author and of the science of anatomy does the frontispiece give?
3. What is the significance of the depiction of a female cadaver with her womb exposed? Overall, what impression of the gendering of scientific knowledge does the image convey?

a man sympathetic to the new science. However, Galileo's 1632 *Dialogue on the Two Chief Systems of the World* went too far. Published in Italian and widely read, it openly lampooned the Aristotelian view and defended Copernicus. In 1633 the papal Inquisition placed Galileo on trial for heresy. Imprisoned and threatened with torture, the aging Galileo recanted, "renouncing and cursing" his Copernican errors.

Thereafter, the Catholic Church became more hostile to science, a change that helped account for the decline of science in Italy (but not in Catholic France, where there was no Inquisition and the papacy held less

sway). At the same time, some Protestant countries, including the Netherlands, Denmark, and England, became quite "pro-science." This was especially true in countries without a strong religious authority capable of imposing religious orthodoxy on scientific questions.

## Science and Society

The rise of modern science had many consequences. First, it created a new social group—the international scientific community. Members of this community were linked together by common interests and values

**Metamorphoses of the Caterpillar and Moth**    Maria Sibylla Merian (1647–1717), the stepdaughter of a Dutch painter, became a celebrated scientific illustrator in her own right. Her finely observed pictures of insects in the South American colony of Suriname introduced many new species. For Merian, science was intimately tied with art: she not only painted but also bred caterpillars and performed experiments on them. Her two-year stay in Suriname, accompanied by a teenage daughter, was a daring feat for a seventeenth-century woman. (From *Metamorphosis Insectorum Surinamensium*, 1705/akg-images)

community became closely tied to the state and its agendas. National academies of science were created under state sponsorship in London in 1660, Paris in 1666, Berlin in 1700, and later across Europe.

It was long believed that the Scientific Revolution had little relationship to practical concerns and the life of the masses until the late-eighteenth-century Industrial Revolution (see Chapter 20). More recently, historians have emphasized the importance of skilled craftsmen in the rise of science, particularly in the development of the experimental method. Many artisans developed a strong interest in emerging scientific ideas, and, in turn, the practice of science in the seventeenth century often relied on artisans' expertise in making instruments and conducting precise experiments.

Some things did not change in the Scientific Revolution. For example, scholars willing to challenge received ideas about the natural universe did not question the seemingly natural inequalities between the sexes. Instead, the emergence of professional science may have worsened them in some ways. When Renaissance courts served as centers of learning, talented noblewomen could find niches in study and research. But the rise of a scientific community raised new barriers for women because the universities and academies that furnished professional credentials refused them entry.

There were, however, a number of noteworthy exceptions. In Italy, universities and academies did offer posts to women. Across Europe, women worked as makers of wax anatomical models and as botanical and zoological illustrators, like Maria Sibylla Merian. They were also very much involved in informal scientific communities, attending salons (see "Women and the Enlightenment" later in this chapter), participating in scientific experiments, and writing learned treatises. Some female intellectuals became full-fledged members of the philosophical dialogue. In England, Margaret Cavendish, Anne Conway, and Mary Astell all contributed to debates about Descartes's mind-body dualism, among other issues. Descartes himself conducted an intellectual correspondence with the princess Elizabeth of Bohemia, of whom he stated: "I attach more weight to her judgment than to those messieurs the Doctors, who take for a rule of truth the opinions of Aristotle rather than the evidence of reason."[4]

as well as by scholarly journals and associations. The personal success of scientists and scholars depended on making new discoveries, and science became competitive. Second, as governments intervened to support and sometimes direct research, the new scientific

## How did the Enlightenment emerge, and what were major currents of Enlightenment thought?

The political, intellectual, and religious developments of the early modern period that gave rise to the Scientific Revolution further contributed to a series of debates about key issues in late-seventeenth- and eighteenth-century Europe and the wider world

that came to be known as the **Enlightenment**. By shattering the unity of Western Christendom, the conflicts of the Reformation brought old religious certainties into question; the strong states that emerged to quell the disorder soon inspired questions about political sovereignty and its limits. Increased movement of peoples, goods, and ideas within and among the continents of Asia, Africa, Europe, and America offered examples of surprisingly different ways of life and patterns of thought. Finally, the tremendous achievements of the Scientific Revolution inspired intellectuals to believe that answers to all the questions being asked could be found through observation and critical thinking. Nothing was to be accepted on faith; everything was to be submitted to **rationalism**, a secular, critical way of thinking. It was believed that through such thinking progress could be made in human society as well as science.

## The Early Enlightenment

Loosely united by certain key ideas, the European Enlightenment (ca. 1690–1789) was a broad intellectual and cultural movement that gained strength gradually and did not reach its maturity until about 1750. Its origins in the late seventeenth century lie in a combination of developments, including political opposition to absolutist rule; religious conflicts between Protestants and Catholics and within Protestantism; European contacts with other cultures; and the attempt to apply principles and practices from the Scientific Revolution to increase knowledge and improve living conditions in human society.

A key crucible for Enlightenment thought was the Dutch Republic, with its traditions of religious tolerance and republican rule. When Louis XIV demanded that all Protestants convert to Catholicism, around two hundred thousand French Protestants, or Huguenots, fled France, many destined for the Dutch Republic. From this haven of tolerance, Huguenots and their supporters began to publish tracts denouncing religious intolerance and suggesting that only a despotic monarch, not a legitimate ruler, would deny religious freedom. Their challenge to authority thus combined religious and political issues.

These dual concerns drove the career of one important early Enlightenment writer, Pierre Bayle (1647–1706), a Huguenot who took refuge in the Dutch Republic. Bayle critically examined the religious beliefs and persecutions of the past in his *Historical and Critical Dictionary* (1697). Demonstrating that human beliefs had been extremely varied and very often mistaken, he concluded that nothing can ever be known beyond all doubt, a view known as skepticism. His influential *Dictionary* was found in more private libraries of eighteenth-century France than any other book.

The Dutch Jewish philosopher Baruch Spinoza (1632–1677) was another key figure in the transition from the Scientific Revolution to the Enlightenment. Deeply inspired by advances in science—in particular

by debates about Descartes's thought—Spinoza sought to apply natural philosophy to thinking about human society. He borrowed Descartes's emphasis on rationalism and his methods of deductive reasoning, but he rejected the French thinker's mind-body dualism. Instead, Spinoza came to espouse monism, the idea that mind and body were united in one substance and that God and nature were merely two names for the same thing. He envisioned a deterministic universe in which good and evil were merely relative values and human actions were shaped by outside circumstances, not free will. Spinoza was excommunicated by the Jewish community of Amsterdam for his controversial religious ideas, but he was heralded by his Enlightenment successors as a model of personal virtue and courageous intellectual autonomy.

The German philosopher and mathematician Gottfried Wilhelm von Leibniz (1646–1716), who had developed calculus independently of Isaac Newton, refuted both Cartesian dualism and Spinoza's monism. Instead, he adopted the idea of an infinite number of substances, or "monads," from which all matter is composed. His *Theodicy* (1710) declared that ours must be "the best of all possible worlds" because it was created by an omnipotent and benevolent God. Leibniz's optimism was later ridiculed by the French philosopher Voltaire in *Candide or Optimism* (1759).

Out of this period of intellectual turmoil came John Locke's *Essay Concerning Human Understanding* (1690), perhaps the most important text of the early Enlightenment. In this work Locke (1632–1704), a physician and member of the Royal Society, set forth a new theory about how human beings learn and form their ideas. Whereas Descartes based his deductive logic on the conviction that certain first principles, or innate ideas, are imbued in humans by God, Locke insisted that all ideas are derived from experience. The human mind at birth is like a blank tablet, or tabula rasa, on which understanding and beliefs are inscribed by experience. Human development is therefore determined by external forces, like education and social institutions, not innate characteristics. Locke's essay contributed to the theory of **sensationalism**, the idea that all human ideas and thoughts are produced as a result of sensory impressions.

Along with Newton's *Principia*, the *Essay Concerning Human Understanding* was one of the great

---

■ **Enlightenment** The influential intellectual and cultural movement of the late seventeenth and eighteenth centuries that introduced a new worldview based on the use of reason, the scientific method, and progress.

■ **rationalism** A secular, critical way of thinking in which nothing was to be accepted on faith and everything was to be submitted to reason.

■ **sensationalism** The idea that all human ideas and thoughts are produced as a result of sensory impressions.

**Philosophes' Dinner Party**  This engraving depicts one of the famous dinners hosted by Voltaire at Ferney, the estate on the French-Swiss border where he spent the last twenty years of his life. A visit to the great philosophe (pictured in the center with arm raised) became a cherished pilgrimage for Enlightenment writers. (Engraving by Jean Huber [1721–1786]/Album/Art Resource, NY)

intellectual inspirations of the Enlightenment. Locke's equally important contribution to political theory, *Two Treatises of Government* (1690), insisted on the sovereignty of the Parliament against the authority of the Crown (see "Constitutional Monarchy" in Chapter 15).

## The Influence of the Philosophes

Divergences among the early thinkers of the Enlightenment show that, while they shared many of the same premises and questions, the answers they found differed widely. The spread of this spirit of inquiry owed a great deal to the work of the **philosophes** (fee-luh-ZAWFZ) (French for "philosopher"), a group of French intellectuals who proudly proclaimed that they were bringing the light of reason to their ignorant fellow humans.

In the mid-eighteenth century France became a hub of Enlightenment thought, for at least three reasons. First, French was the international language of the educated classes, and France was the wealthiest and most populous country in Europe. Second, the rising unpopularity of the French monarchy generated growing discontent and calls for reform among the educated elite. Third, the French philosophes made it their goal to reach a larger audience of elites, many of whom were joined together in a concept inherited from the Renaissance known as the Republic of Letters—an imagined transnational realm in which critical thinkers and writers participated.

To appeal to the public and get around the censors, the philosophes wrote novels and plays, histories and philosophies, and dictionaries and encyclopedias, all filled with satire and double meanings to spread their message. One of the greatest philosophes, the baron de Montesquieu (mahn-tuhs-KYOO) (1689–1755), pioneered this approach in *The Persian Letters*, published in 1721. This work consists of letters written by two fictional Persian travelers, who as outsiders see European customs in unique ways and thereby allow Montesquieu a vantage point for criticizing existing practices and beliefs.

Disturbed by the growth in absolutism under Louis XIV and inspired by the example of the physical sciences, Montesquieu set out to apply the critical method to the problem of government in *The Spirit of Laws* (1748). Arguing that forms of government were shaped by history and geography, Montesquieu identified three main types: monarchies, republics, and despotisms. A great admirer of the English parliamentary system, he argued for a separation of powers, with political power divided among different classes and legal estates holding unequal rights and privileges. Montesquieu was no democrat; he was apprehensive about the uneducated poor and did not question the sovereignty of the French monarchy. But he was concerned that absolutism in France was drifting into tyranny and believed that strengthening the influence of intermediary powers was the best way to prevent it. Decades later, his theory of separation of powers had a great impact on the constitutions of the young United States in 1789 and of France in 1791.

The most famous philosophe was François Marie Arouet, known by the pen name Voltaire (vohl-TAIR) (1694–1778). In his long career, Voltaire wrote more than seventy witty volumes, hobnobbed with royalty, and died a millionaire through shrewd speculations. His early career, however, was turbulent, and he was twice arrested for insulting noblemen. To avoid a prison term, Voltaire moved to England for three years, and there he came to share Montesquieu's enthusiasm for English liberties and institutions.

Returning to France, Voltaire met Gabrielle-Emilie Le Tonnelier de Breteuil, marquise du Châtelet (SHAH-tuh-lay) (1706–1749), a gifted noblewoman. Madame du Châtelet invited Voltaire to live in her country house at Cirey in Lorraine and became his long-time companion, under the eyes of her tolerant husband. Passionate about science, she studied physics and mathematics and published scientific articles and translations, including the first translation of Newton's *Principia* into French, still in use today. Excluded from the Royal Academy of Sciences because she was a woman, Madame du Châtelet had no doubt that women's limited role in science was due to their unequal education. Discussing what she would do if she were a ruler, she wrote, "I would reform an abuse which cuts off, so to speak, half the human race. I would make women participate in all the rights of humankind, and above all in those of the intellect."[5]

While living at Cirey, Voltaire wrote works praising England and popularizing English science. Yet, like almost all of the philosophes, Voltaire was a reformer, not a revolutionary, in politics. He pessimistically concluded that the best one could hope for in the way of government was a good monarch, since human beings "are very rarely worthy to govern themselves." Nor did Voltaire believe in social and economic equality. The only realizable equality, Voltaire thought, was that "by which the citizen only depends on the laws which protect the freedom of the feeble against the ambitions of the strong."[6]

Voltaire's philosophical and religious positions were much more radical. He believed in God, but he rejected Catholicism in favor of **deism**, belief in a distant noninterventionist deity. Drawing on mechanistic philosophy, he envisioned a universe in which God acted like a great clockmaker who built an orderly system and then stepped aside to let it run. Above all, Voltaire and most of the philosophes hated all forms of religious intolerance, which they believed led to fanaticism and cruelty. (See "Thinking Like a Historian: The Enlightenment Debate on Religious Tolerance," page 476.)

The strength of the philosophes lay in their dedication and organization. Their greatest achievement was a group effort — the seventeen-volume *Encyclopedia: The Rational Dictionary of the Sciences, the Arts, and the Crafts*, edited by Denis Diderot (DEE-duh-roh) (1713–1784) and Jean le Rond d'Alembert (dah-luhm-BEHR) (1717–1783). Completed in 1766 despite opposition from the French state and the Catholic Church, the *Encyclopedia* contained

seventy-two thousand articles by leading scientists, writers, skilled workers, and progressive priests. Science and the industrial arts were exalted, religion and immortality questioned. Intolerance, legal injustice, and out-of-date social institutions were openly criticized. The *Encyclopedia* also included many articles describing non-European cultures and societies, and it acknowledged Muslim scholars' contribution to Western science. Summing up the new worldview of the Enlightenment, the *Encyclopedia* was widely read, especially in less expensive reprint editions, and it was extremely influential.

After about 1770 a number of thinkers and writers began to attack the philosophes' faith in reason and progress. The most famous of these was Jean-Jacques Rousseau (1712–1778). The son of a poor Swiss watchmaker, Rousseau made his way into the Parisian Enlightenment through his brilliant intellect. Like other Enlightenment thinkers, he was passionately committed to individual freedom. Unlike them, however, he attacked rationalism and civilization as destroying, rather than liberating, the individual. Warm, spontaneous feeling, Rousseau believed, had to complement and correct cold intellect. Moreover, he asserted, the basic goodness of the individual and the unspoiled child had to be protected from the cruel refinements of civilization. Rousseau's ideals greatly influenced the early Romantic movement, which rebelled against the culture of the Enlightenment in the late eighteenth century.

Rousseau's contribution to political theory in *The Social Contract* (1762) was based on two fundamental concepts: the general will and popular sovereignty. According to Rousseau, the general will is sacred and absolute, reflecting the common interests of all the people, who have displaced the monarch as the holder of sovereign power (and thus exercise popular sovereignty). The general will is not necessarily the will of the majority, however. At times the general will may be the authentic, long-term needs of the people as correctly interpreted by a farsighted minority. Little noticed before the French Revolution, Rousseau's concept of the general will appealed greatly to democrats and nationalists after 1789.

## Enlightenment Movements Across Europe

The Enlightenment was a movement of international dimensions, with thinkers traversing borders in a constant exchange of visits, letters, and printed materials.

■ **philosophes** A group of French intellectuals who proclaimed that they were bringing the light of knowledge to their fellow humans in the Age of Enlightenment.

■ **deism** Belief in a distant, noninterventionist deity; common among Enlightenment thinkers.

## The Enlightenment Debate on Religious Tolerance

Enlightenment philosophers questioned many aspects of European society, including political authority, social inequality, and imperialism. A major focus of their criticism was the dominance of the established church and the persecution of minority faiths. While many philosophers defended religious tolerance, they differed widely in their approaches to the issue.

**1** **Moses Mendelssohn, "Reply to Lavater," 1769.** In 1769 Johann Caspar Lavater, a Swiss clergyman, called on Moses Mendelssohn to either refute proofs of Christianity publicly or submit to baptism. Mendelssohn's reply is both a call for toleration and an affirmation of his religious faith.

It is, of course, the natural obligation of every mortal to diffuse knowledge and virtue among his fellow men, and to do his best to extirpate their prejudices and errors. One might think, in this regard, that it was the duty of every man publicly to oppose the religious opinions that he considers mistaken. But not all prejudices are equally harmful, and hence the prejudices we may think we perceive among our fellow men must not all be treated in the same way. Some are directly contrary to the happiness of the human race. . . . These must be attacked outright by every friend of humanity. . . . Of this kind are all people's errors and prejudices that disturb their own or their fellows' peace and contentment and kill every seed of the true and the good in man before it can germinate. On the one hand, fanaticism, misanthropy, and the spirit of persecution, and on the other, frivolity, luxury, and libertinism.

Sometimes, however, the opinions of my fellow men, which in my belief are errors, belong to the higher theoretical principles which are too remote from practical life to do any direct harm; but, precisely because of their generality, they form the basis on which the nation that upholds them has built its moral and social system, and thus happen to be of great importance to this part of the human race. To oppose such doctrines in public, because we consider them prejudices, is to dig up the ground to see whether it is solid and secure, without providing any other support for the building that stands on it. Anyone who cares more for the good of humanity than for his own fame will be slow to voice his opinion about such prejudices, and will take care not to attack them outright without extreme caution.

**2** **Voltaire, *Treatise on Toleration*, 1763.** Voltaire, the prominent French philosophe, began his *Treatise on Toleration* by recounting the infamous trial of Jean Calas. Although all the evidence pointed toward suicide, the judges concluded that Calas had killed his son to prevent him from converting to Catholicism, and Calas was brutally executed in 1762. For Voltaire, the Calas affair was a battle between fanaticism and reason, extremism and moderation.

Some fanatic in the crowd cried out that Jean Calas had hanged his son Marc Antoine. The cry was soon repeated on all sides; some adding that the deceased was to have abjured Protestantism on the following day, and that the family and young Lavaisse had strangled him out of hatred of the Catholic religion. In a moment all doubt had disappeared. The whole town was persuaded that it is a point of religion with the Protestants for a father and mother to kill their children when they wish to change their faith.

. . . There was not, and could not be, any evidence against the family; but a deluded religion took the place of proof. . . . [The judges] were confounded when the old man, expiring on the wheel, prayed God to witness his innocence, and begged him to pardon his judges.

The daughters were taken from the mother and put in a convent. The mother, almost sprinkled with the blood of her husband, her eldest son dead, the younger banished, deprived of her daughters and all her property, was alone in the world, without bread, without hope, dying of the intolerable misery. Certain persons, having carefully examined the circumstances of this horrible adventure, were so impressed that they urged the widow, who had retired into solitude, to go and demand justice at the feet of the throne. . . . She reached Paris almost at the point of death. She was astonished at her reception, at the help and the tears that were given to her.

At Paris reason dominates fanaticism, however powerful it be; in the provinces fanaticism almost always overcomes reason.

## ANALYZING THE EVIDENCE

1. Based on these sources, what attitudes did eighteenth-century Europeans manifest toward religions other than their own? Were such attitudes always negative?
2. What justifications did Enlightenment philosophers use to argue in favor of religious tolerance? Were these arguments necessarily antireligious?
3. Why did Judaism figure so prominently in debates about religious tolerance in eighteenth-century Europe? In what ways do you think Mendelssohn's experience as a Jew (Source 1) shaped his views on religious tolerance?

**3** **Bernard Picart, "Jewish Meal During the Feast of the Tabernacles," from *Ceremonies and Customs of All the Peoples of the World*, 1724.** Eighteenth-century travel literature provided eager audiences with images and descriptions of religious practices from around the world. This image emphasizes the prosperity and warm family relations of a Jewish family enjoying a holiday meal, echoing the tolerant mind-set of the author.

(Jewish Chronicle/Heritage Images/Getty Images)

**4** **Gotthold Ephraim Lessing, *Nathan the Wise*, 1779.** In this excerpt from *Nathan the Wise*, a play by German writer Gotthold Ephraim Lessing, the sultan Saladin asks a Jewish merchant named Nathan to tell him which is the true religion: Islam, Christianity, or Judaism. Nathan responds with a parable about a man who promised to leave the same opal ring, a guarantor of divine favor, to each of his three beloved sons. He then had two exact replicas of the ring made so that each son would believe he had inherited the precious relic.

NATHAN: Scarce was the father dead,
When each one with his ring appears
Claiming each the headship of the house.
Inspections, quarrelling, and complaints ensue;
But all in vain, the veritable ring
Was not distinguishable —
(*After a pause, during which he expects the Sultan's answer*)
Almost as indistinguishable as to us,
Is now — the true religion.

SALADIN: What? Is that meant as answer to my question?

NATHAN: 'Tis meant but to excuse myself, because
I lack the boldness to discriminate between the rings,
Which the father by express intent had made
So that they might not be distinguished.

SALADIN: The rings! Don't play with me.
I thought the faiths which I have named

Were easily distinguishable,
Even to their raiment, even to meat and drink.

NATHAN: But yet not as regards their proofs:
For do not all rest upon history, written or traditional?
And history can also be accepted
Only on faith and trust. Is it not so?
Now, whose faith and confidence do we least misdoubt?
That of our relatives? Of those whose flesh and blood we are,
Of those who from our childhood
Have lavished on us proofs of love,
Who ne'er deceived us, unless 'twere wholesome for us so?
How can I place less faith in my forefathers
Than you in yours? or the reverse?
Can I desire of you to load your ancestors with lies,
So that you contradict not mine? Or the reverse?
And to the Christian the same applies.
Is that not so?

## PUTTING IT ALL TOGETHER

Using the sources above, along with what you have learned in class and in this chapter, compare and contrast the views on religious toleration presented in the sources. On what would the authors of these works have agreed? How did their arguments in favor of toleration differ? What explanation can you offer for the differences you note?

Sources: (1) Ritchie Robertson, ed., *The German-Jewish Dialogue: An Anthology of Literary Texts, 1749–1993* (New York: Oxford University Press, 1999), pp. 41–42; (2) Voltaire, *A Treatise on Toleration and Other Essays*, trans. Joseph McCabe (Amherst, N.Y.: Prometheus Books, 1994), pp. 147–149, 152–153; (4) Crane Brinton, ed., *The Portable Age of Reason Reader* (New York: Viking Press, 1956), pp. 383–389.

## MAJOR FIGURES OF THE ENLIGHTENMENT

| | |
|---|---|
| Baruch Spinoza (1632–1677) | Early Enlightenment thinker excommunicated from the Jewish religion for his concept of a deterministic universe |
| John Locke (1632–1704) | *Essay Concerning Human Understanding* (1690) |
| Gottfried Wilhelm von Leibniz (1646–1716) | German philosopher and mathematician known for his optimistic view of the universe |
| Pierre Bayle (1647–1706) | *Historical and Critical Dictionary* (1697) |
| Montesquieu (1689–1755) | *The Persian Letters* (1721); *The Spirit of Laws* (1748) |
| Voltaire (1694–1778) | Renowned French philosophe and author of more than seventy works |
| David Hume (1711–1776) | Central figure of the Scottish Enlightenment; *Of Natural Characters* (1748) |
| Jean-Jacques Rousseau (1712–1778) | *The Social Contract* (1762) |
| Denis Diderot (1713–1784) and Jean le Rond d'Alembert (1717–1783) | Editors of *Encyclopedia: The Rational Dictionary of the Sciences, the Arts, and the Crafts* (1751–1766) |
| Adam Smith (1723–1790) | *An Inquiry into the Nature and Causes of the Wealth of Nations* (1776) |
| Immanuel Kant (1724–1804) | *What Is Enlightenment?* (1784); *On the Different Races of Man* (1775) |
| Moses Mendelssohn (1729–1786) | Major philosopher of the Haskalah, or Jewish Enlightenment |
| Cesare Beccaria (1738–1794) | *On Crimes and Punishments* (1764) |

Voltaire alone wrote almost eighteen thousand letters to correspondents in France and across Europe. The Republic of Letters, as this international group of scholars and writers was called, was a truly cosmopolitan set of networks stretching from western Europe to its colonies in the Americas, to Russia and eastern Europe, and along the routes of trade and empire to Africa and Asia.

Within this broad international conversation, scholars have identified numerous regional and national particularities. Outside of France, many strains of Enlightenment—Protestant, Catholic, and Jewish—sought to reconcile reason with faith, rather than emphasizing the errors of religious fanaticism and intolerance. Some scholars point to a distinctive "Catholic Enlightenment" that aimed to renew and reform the church from within, looking to divine grace rather than human will as the source of progress.

The Scottish Enlightenment, which was centered in Edinburgh, was marked by an emphasis on common sense and scientific reasoning. After the Act of Union with England in 1707, Scotland was freed from political crisis to experience a vigorous period of intellectual growth. Advances in philosophy were also stimulated by the creation of the first public educational system in Europe.

A central figure in Edinburgh was David Hume (1711–1776), whose emphasis on civic morality and religious skepticism had a powerful impact at home and abroad. Hume strove to apply Newton's experimental methods to what he called the "science of man." Building on Locke's writings on learning, Hume argued that the human mind is really nothing but a bundle of impressions that originate only in sensory experiences and our habits of mentally joining these experiences together. Therefore, reason cannot tell us anything about questions that cannot be verified by sensory experience (in the form of controlled experiments or mathematics), such as the origin of the universe or the existence of God. Hume further argued, in opposition to Descartes, that reason alone could not supply moral principles and that they derived instead from emotions and desires, such as feelings of approval or shame. Hume's rationalistic inquiry thus ended up undermining the Enlightenment's faith in the power of reason by emphasizing the superiority of the senses and the passions over reason in driving human thought and behavior.

Hume's emphasis on human experience, rather than abstract principle, had a formative influence on another major figure of the Scottish Enlightenment, Adam Smith (1723–1790). Smith argued that social interaction produced feelings of mutual sympathy that led people to behave in ethical ways, despite inherent tendencies toward self-interest. By observing others and witnessing their feelings, individuals imaginatively experienced such feelings and learned to act in ways that would elicit positive sentiments and avoid negative ones. Smith believed that the thriving commercial life of the eighteenth century was likely to produce civic virtue through the values of competition, fair play, and individual autonomy. In *An Inquiry into the Nature and Causes of the Wealth of Nations* (1776), Smith attacked the laws and regulations created by mercantilist governments that, he argued, prevented commerce from reaching its full capacity (see "Adam Smith and Economic Liberalism" in Chapter 17).

Inspired by philosophers of moral sentiments like Hume and Smith, as well as by physiological studies of the role of the nervous system in human perception, the celebration of sensibility became an important element of eighteenth-century culture. *Sensibility* referred to an acute sensitivity of the nerves and brains to outside stimuli, which produced strong emotional and physical reactions. Novels, plays, and other literary genres depicted moral and aesthetic sensibility as a particular characteristic of women and the upper classes. The proper relationship between reason and the emotions (or between *Sense and Sensibility*, as Jane Austen put it in the title of her 1811 novel) became a key question.

After 1760 Enlightenment ideas were hotly debated in the German-speaking states, often in dialogue with Christian theology. Immanuel Kant (1724–1804), a professor in East Prussia, was the greatest German philosopher of his day. Kant posed the question of the age when he published a pamphlet in 1784 titled *What Is Enlightenment?* He answered, "*Sapere Aude* [dare to know]! 'Have the courage to use your own understanding' is therefore the motto of enlightenment." He argued that if intellectuals were granted the freedom to exercise their reason publicly in print, enlightenment would almost surely follow. Kant was no revolutionary; he also insisted that in their private lives individuals must obey all laws, no matter how unreasonable, and should be punished for "impertinent" criticism. Like other Enlightenment figures in central and east-central Europe, Kant thus tried to reconcile absolute monarchical authority and religious faith with a critical public sphere.

Northern Europeans often regarded the Italian states as culturally backward, yet important developments in Enlightenment thought took place in the Italian peninsula. After achieving independence from Habsburg rule (1734), the kingdom of Naples entered a period of intellectual flourishing as reformers struggled to lift the heavy weight of church and noble power. In northern Italy a central figure was Cesare Beccaria (1738–1794), a nobleman educated at Jesuit schools and the University of Pavia. His *On Crimes and Punishments* (1764) was a passionate plea

**Beccaria's *On Crimes and Punishments***    An Italian nobleman, the marquis de Beccaria brought the Enlightenment spirit of rationalism and tolerance to bear on the justice system. In his 1764 work *On Crimes and Punishments*, from which this illustration is taken, he argued for the abolition of torture and capital punishment as being ineffectual deterrents to crime and unethical actions on the part of the state. (Bibliothèque Nationale, Paris, France/Bridgeman Images)

for reform of the penal system that decried the use of torture, arbitrary imprisonment, and capital punishment, and advocated the prevention of crime over the reliance on punishment. The text was quickly translated into French and English and made an impact throughout Europe and its colonies.

## How did the Enlightenment change social ideas and practices?

Europeans' increased interactions with non-European peoples and cultures also helped produce the Enlightenment spirit. Enlightenment thinkers struggled to assess differences between Western and non-Western cultures, often adopting Eurocentric views, but sometimes expressing admiration for other cultures. These same thinkers focused a great deal of attention on other forms of cultural and social difference, developing new ideas about race, gender, and political power. Although new "scientific" ways of thinking often served to justify inequality, the Enlightenment did see a rise in religious tolerance, a particularly crucial issue for Europe's persecuted Jewish population. As literacy rates rose and print

**Portrait of Lady Mary Wortley Montagu**   Lady Mary Wortley Montagu accompanied her husband to the Ottoman Empire after he was named British ambassador to the empire. Her lively letters home, published after her death, question the supposedly inferior social status of Ottoman women compared to that of European women and other European assumptions about Ottoman society and culture. After her return home she publicized Ottoman practices of smallpox inoculation (as yet unknown in the West) and commissioned portraits of herself in Ottoman dress. (By George Knapton [1698–1778]/Private Collection/photo © Christie's Images/Bridgeman Images)

culture flourished, Enlightenment ideas spread in a new "public sphere" composed of coffeeshops, literary salons, lending libraries, and other social institutions.

## Global Contacts

In the wake of the great discoveries of the fifteenth and sixteenth centuries, the rapidly growing travel literature taught Europeans that the peoples of China, India, Africa, and the Americas had very different beliefs and customs. Educated Europeans began to look at truth and morality in relative, rather than absolute, terms. If anything was possible, who could say what was right or wrong?

The powerful and advanced nations of Asia were obvious sources of comparison with the West.

Seventeenth-century Jesuit missionaries brought knowledge to the West about Chinese history and culture. Leibniz corresponded with Jesuits stationed in China, coming to believe that Chinese ethics and political philosophy were superior but that Europeans had equaled China in science and technology; some scholars believe his concept of monads was influenced by Confucian teaching on the harmony between the cosmic order and human society.[7]

During the Enlightenment, European opinion on China was divided. Voltaire and some other philosophes revered China—without ever visiting or seriously studying it—as an ancient culture replete with wisdom and learning, ruled by benevolent absolutist monarchs. They enthusiastically embraced Confucianism as a natural religion in which universal moral truths were uncovered by reason. By contrast, Montesquieu and Diderot criticized China as a despotic land ruled by fear.

Attitudes toward Islam and the Muslim world were similarly mixed. As the Ottoman military threat receded at the end of the seventeenth century, some Enlightenment thinkers assessed Islam favorably. Some deists praised Islam as superior to Christianity and valued Judaism for its rationality, compassion, and tolerance. Others, including Spinoza, saw Islamic culture as superstitious and favorable to despotism. In most cases, writing about Islam and Muslim cultures served primarily as a means to reflect on Western values and practices. Thus Montesquieu's *Persian Letters* used the Persian harem as a symbol of despotic rule that he feared his own country was adopting. Voltaire's play about the life of the Prophet portrayed Muhammad as the epitome of the religious fanaticism the philosophes opposed.

One writer with considerable personal experience in a Muslim country was Lady Mary Wortley Montagu, wife of the English ambassador to the Ottoman Empire. Her letters challenged prevailing ideas by depicting Turkish people as sympathetic and civilized. Montagu also disputed the notion that women were oppressed in Ottoman society.

Apart from debates about Asian and Muslim lands, the "discovery" of the New World and subsequent explorations in the Pacific Ocean also challenged existing norms and values in Europe. One popular idea, among Rousseau and others, was that indigenous peoples of the Americas were living examples of "natural man," who embodied the essential goodness of humanity uncorrupted by decadent society. Others depicted as utopian natural men were the Pacific Island societies explored by Captain James Cook and others from the 1770s on.

## Enlightenment Debates About Race

As scientists developed taxonomies of plant and animal species in response to discoveries in the Americas, they also began to classify humans into hierarchically ordered "races" and to speculate on the origins of such races. In *The System of Nature* (1735), Swedish botanist Carl Linnaeus argued that nature was organized into a God-given hierarchy. The comte de Buffon (komt duh buh-FOHN) argued that humans originated with one species that then developed into distinct races due largely to climatic conditions. Although the notion of a single origin of human beings opened the door to arguments for equality, Buffon and others who espoused this idea maintained that white Europeans represented the human norm, while other groups had degenerated from this norm over time.

Enlightenment thinkers such as David Hume and Immanuel Kant helped popularize ideas about racial difference and inequality. In *Of Natural Characters* (1748), Hume wrote:

> I am apt to suspect the negroes and in general all other species of men (for there are four or five different kinds) to be naturally inferior to the whites. There never was a civilized nation of any other complexion than white, nor even any individual eminent amongst them, no arts, no sciences. . . . Such a uniform and constant difference could not happen, in so many countries and ages if nature had not made an original distinction between these breeds of men.[8]

Kant taught and wrote as much about anthropology and geography as he did about standard philosophical themes such as logic, metaphysics, and moral philosophy. He elaborated his views about race in *On the Different Races of Man* (1775), claiming that there were four human races, each of which had derived from an original race. The closest descendants of the original race, and the most superior, were the white inhabitants of northern Germany. (Scientists now know the human race originated in Africa.)

Using the word *race* to designate biologically distinct groups of humans, akin to distinct animal species, was new. Previously, Europeans had grouped other peoples into "nations" based on their historical, political, and cultural affiliations, rather than on supposedly innate physical differences. Unsurprisingly, when European thinkers drew up a hierarchical classification of human species, their own "race" was placed at the top. Europeans had long believed they were culturally superior to supposedly "barbaric" peoples in Africa and, since 1492, the New World. Now emerging ideas about racial difference taught them they were biologically superior as well. In turn, scientific racism helped legitimate and justify the tremendous growth of slavery that occurred during the eighteenth century.

If one "race" of humans was fundamentally different and inferior, its members could be seen as particularly fit for enslavement and liable to benefit from tutelage by the superior race.

Racist ideas did not go unchallenged. The abbé Raynal's *History of the Two Indies* (1770) fiercely attacked slavery and the abuses of European colonization. *Encyclopedia* editor Denis Diderot adopted Montesquieu's technique of criticizing European attitudes through the voice of outsiders in "Supplement to Bougainville's Voyage," which contains an imaginary dialogue between Tahitian villagers and their European visitors. Scottish philosopher James Beattie (1735–1803) responded directly to claims of white superiority by pointing out that Europeans had started out as savage as nonwhites supposedly were and that many non-European peoples in the Americas, Asia, and Africa had achieved high levels of civilization. Former slaves, like Olaudah Equiano and Ottobah Cugoana, published eloquent memoirs testifying to the horrors of slavery and the innate equality of all humans. These challenges to racism, however, were in the minority. Many other Enlightenment voices supporting racial inequality—Thomas Jefferson among them—may be found.

## Women and the Enlightenment

Dating back to the Renaissance *querelle des dames*, the debate over women's proper role in society and the nature of gender differences continued to fascinate Enlightenment thinkers. Some philosophes championed greater rights and expanded education for women, claiming that the position and treatment of women were the best indicators of a society's level of civilization and decency.[9] In *Persian Letters*, Montesquieu used the oppression of women in the harem, described in letters from the wives of Usbek, one of the Persian voyagers, as a potent symbol of the political tyranny he identified with the Persian Empire. At the end of the book, the rebellion of the harem against the cruel eunuchs Usbek left in charge serves to make Montesquieu's point that despotism must ultimately fail.

In the 1780s the marquis de Condorcet, a celebrated mathematician and contributor to the *Encyclopedia*, went so far as to urge that women should share equal rights with men. This was an extremely rare position. Most philosophes accepted that women were inferior to men intellectually as well as physically. They sought moderate reform at best, particularly in the arena of female education, and had no desire to upend men's traditional dominance over women.

From the first years of the Enlightenment, women writers made crucial contributions both to debates about women's rights and to the broader

Enlightenment conversations. In 1694 Mary Astell published *A Serious Proposal to the Ladies*, which encouraged women to aspire to the life of the mind and proposed the creation of a college for women. Astell also harshly criticized the institution of marriage. Echoing arguments made against the absolute authority of kings during the Glorious Revolution (see "Constitutional Monarchy" in Chapter 15), she argued that husbands should not exercise absolute control over their wives in marriage. Yet Astell, like most female authors of the period, was careful to acknowledge women's God-given duties to be good wives and mothers.

The explosion of printed literature during the eighteenth century (see the next section) brought significant numbers of women writers into print, but they remained a small proportion of published authors. In the second half of the eighteenth century, women produced some 15 percent of published novels, the genre in which they enjoyed the greatest success. They constituted a much tinier proportion of nonfiction authors.[10]

If they remained marginal in the world of publishing, women played a much more active role in the informal dimensions of the Enlightenment: conversation, letter writing, travel, and patronage. A key element of their informal participation was as salon hostesses, or *salonnières* (sah-lahn-ee-EHRZ). **Salons** were weekly meetings held in wealthy households that brought together writers, aristocrats, financiers, and noteworthy foreigners for meals and witty discussions of the latest trends in literature, science, and philosophy. One prominent salonnière was Madame du Deffand, whose weekly Parisian salon included such guests as Montesquieu, d'Alembert, and Benjamin Franklin, then serving as the first U.S. ambassador to France. Invitations to salons were highly coveted; introductions to the rich and powerful could make the career of an ambitious writer, and, in turn, the social elite found amusement and cultural prestige in their ties to up-and-coming artists and men of letters.

Elite women also exercised great influence on artistic taste. Soft pastels, ornate interiors, sentimental portraits, and paintings featuring starry-eyed lovers protected by hovering cupids were all hallmarks of the style they favored. This style, known as **rococo** (ruh-KOH-koh), was popular throughout Europe

**Madame Geoffrin's Salon**   This painting depicts a meeting of the salon of celebrated Parisian hostess Madame Geoffrin, at which an actor reads aloud a new play by the French philosophe Voltaire. The painter, Gabriel Lemonnier, was a regular guest at the salon, and virtually all of the individuals he has depicted here are recognizable members of Parisian salon society, including Enlightenment writers Diderot, d'Alembert, and Rousseau as well as high-ranking nobles, government ministers, and fellow *salonnières*. (Musée National du Chateau de Malmaison, Rueil-Malmaison, France/Bridgeman Images)

**Madame de Pompadour, Mistress to French King Louis XV**    Madame de Pompadour used the wealth at her command to patronize many highly skilled artists and craftsmen. She helped popularize the ornate, lightly colored, and highly decorative rococo style, epitomized by the sumptuous trimmings of her dress. (By François Boucher [1703–1770], [oil on canvas]/© Scottish National Gallery, Edinburgh/Bridgeman Images)

from 1720 to 1780. It was particularly associated with the mistress of Louis XV, Madame de Pompadour, who used her position to commission paintings, furniture, and other luxury objects in the rococo style.

Women's prominent role as society hostesses and patrons of the arts and letters outraged some Enlightenment thinkers. According to Jean-Jacques Rousseau, women and men were radically different by nature and should play diametrically opposed roles in life. Destined by nature to assume the active role in sexual relations, men were naturally suited for the rough-and-tumble of politics and public life. Women's role was to attract male sexual desire in order to marry and create families and then to care for their homes and children in private. For Rousseau, wealthy Parisian women's love for attending social gatherings and pulling the strings of power was unnatural and had a corrupting effect on both politics and society. Some women eagerly accepted Rousseau's idealized view of their domestic role, but others—such as the English writer Mary Wollstonecraft—vigorously rejected his notion of women's limitations. (See "Viewpoints: Rousseau and Wollstonecraft Debate Women's Equality," page 484.)

Rousseau's emphasis on the natural laws governing women echoed a wider shift in ideas about gender during this period, as doctors, scientists, and philosophers increasingly agreed that women's essential characteristics were determined by their sexual organs and reproductive functions. This turn to nature, rather than tradition or biblical scripture, as a means to understand human society had parallels in contemporary views on racial difference. Just as writers like Rousseau used women's allegedly "natural" passivity to argue for their subordinate role in society, so Kant and others used ideas about non-Europeans' "natural" inferiority to defend slavery and colonial domination. The new powers of science and reason were thus marshaled to imbue traditional stereotypes with the force of natural law. Scholars continue to debate the apparent paradox between Enlightenment thinkers' ideals of universalism, progress, and reason and their support for racial and gender inequality.

■ **salon**  Regular social gathering held by talented and rich Parisians in their homes, where philosophes and their followers met to discuss literature, science, and philosophy.

■ **rococo**  A popular style in Europe in the eighteenth century, known for its soft pastels, ornate interiors, sentimental portraits, and starry-eyed lovers protected by hovering cupids.

# VIEWPOINTS

## Rousseau and Wollstonecraft Debate Women's Equality

Enlightenment philosophers fervently debated the essential characteristics of the female sex and the appropriate education and social roles for women. Two of the most vociferous participants in this debate were Jean-Jacques Rousseau and Mary Wollstonecraft. Looking to nature as a guiding principle, Rousseau reasoned that women's role in the process of reproduction meant they were intended to be subordinate to men and to devote themselves to motherhood and home life. Wollstonecraft responded that virtue was a universal human attribute created by God that could not be differentiated by gender. While acknowledging that women were weaker in some ways than men, she insisted that they should strive to honor their God-given human dignity through education and duty, just like men.

### Jean-Jacques Rousseau, *Emile, or on Education*

In the union of the sexes, both pursue one common object, but not in the same manner. From their diversity in this particular, arises the first determinate difference between the moral relations of each. The one should be active and strong, the other passive and weak: it is necessary the one should have both the power and the will, and that the other should make little resistance. . . .

Woman and man are made for each other; but their mutual dependence is not the same. The men depend on the women only on account of their desires; the women on the men both on account of their desires and their necessities: we could subsist better without them than they without us. Their very subsistence and rank in life depend on us, and the estimation in which we hold them, their charms and their merit. By the law of nature itself, both women and children lie at the mercy of the men. . . .

To please, to be useful to us, to make us love and esteem them, to educate us when young, and take care of us when grown up, to advise, to console us, to render our lives easy and agreeable; these are the duties of women at all times, and what they should be taught in their infancy.

### Mary Wollstonecraft, *A Vindication of the Rights of Women*

Rousseau declares that a woman should never, for a moment, feel herself independent, that she should be governed by fear to exercise her *natural* cunning, and made a coquettish slave in order to render her a more alluring object of desire, a *sweeter* companion to man, whenever he chooses to relax himself. . . .

What nonsense! When will a great man arise with sufficient strength of mind to puff away the fumes which pride and sensuality have thus spread over the subject! If women are by nature inferior to men, their virtues must be the same in quality, if not in degree, or virtue is a relative idea; consequently, their conduct should be founded on the same principles, and have the same aim. . . .

. . . [C]ultivate their minds, give them the salutary, sublime curb of principle, and let them attain conscious dignity by feeling themselves only dependent on God. Teach them, in common with man, to submit to necessity instead of giving, to render them more pleasing, a sex to morals. . . . Further, should experience prove that they cannot attain the same degree of strength of mind, perseverance, and fortitude, let their virtues be the same in kind, though they may vainly struggle for the same degree.

### QUESTIONS FOR ANALYSIS

1. How does Rousseau derive his ideas about women's proper relationship to men from his view of "nature"?
2. What does Wollstonecraft mean when she criticizes writers like Rousseau for giving "a sex to morals"? What arguments does she use to oppose such views?
3. Rousseau and Wollstonecraft differed greatly in their ideas on the essential characteristics of men and women, but do you see any areas where they agree?

Sources: Jean-Jacques Rousseau, *Emilius and Sophia: or, a new system of education*, trans. William Kenrick (London: T. Becket and P.A. de Hondt, 1763), vol. 4, pp. 3–4, 18–20; Mary Wollstonecraft, *A Vindication of the Rights of Woman* (London: Johnson, 1792), pp. 47–48, 71.

## Urban Culture and Life in the Public Sphere

Enlightenment ideas did not float on thin air. A series of new institutions and practices encouraged the spread of enlightened ideas. From about 1700 to 1789, the production and consumption of books grew significantly and the types of books people read changed dramatically. For example, the proportion of religious and devotional books published in Paris declined after 1750; history and law held constant; the arts and sciences surged.

Reading more books on many more subjects, the educated public approached reading in a new way. The old style of reading in Europe had been centered on a core of sacred texts read aloud by the father to his assembled family. Now reading involved a broader field of books that constantly changed. Reading became individual and silent, and texts could be questioned.

For those who could not afford to purchase books, lending libraries offered access to the new ideas of the Enlightenment. Coffeehouses, which first appeared in the late seventeenth century, became meccas of philosophical discussion. In addition to these institutions, book clubs, debating societies, Masonic lodges (groups of Freemasons, a secret society based on egalitarian principles that accepted craftsmen and shopkeepers as well as middle-class men and nobles), salons, and newspapers all played roles in the creation of a new **public sphere** that celebrated open debate informed by critical reason. The public sphere was an idealized space where members of society came together as individuals to discuss issues relevant to the society, economics, and politics of the day.

What of the common people? Did they participate in the Enlightenment? Enlightenment philosophes did not direct their message to peasants or urban laborers. They believed that the masses had no time or talent for philosophical speculation and that elevating them would be a long and potentially dangerous process. Deluded by superstitions and driven by violent passions, the people, they thought, were like children in need of firm parental guidance. D'Alembert characteristically made a sharp distinction between "the truly enlightened public" and "the blind and noisy multitude."[11]

Despite these prejudices, the ideas of the philosophes did find an audience among some members of the common people. At a time of rising literacy, book prices were dropping, and many philosophical ideas were popularized in cheap pamphlets and through public reading. Although they were barred from salons and academies, ordinary people were not immune to the new ideas in circulation. Some of them made vital contributions to the debate, like Englishman Thomas Paine, born and apprenticed to a corset-maker, and author of *Common Sense*, a foundational text of the American Revolution.

# What impact did new ways of thinking have on politics?

Enlightenment thinkers' insistence on questioning long-standing traditions and norms inevitably led to issues of power and politics. Most Enlightenment thinkers outside of Britain and the Netherlands, especially in central and eastern Europe, believed that political change could best come from above—from the ruler—rather than from below. Royal absolutism was a fact of life, and the monarchs of Europe's leading states clearly had no intention of giving up their great power. Therefore, the philosophes and their sympathizers realistically concluded that a benevolent absolutism offered the best opportunities for improving society.

Many government officials were interested in philosophical ideas. They were among the best-educated members of society, and their daily involvement in complex affairs of state made them naturally attracted to ideas for improving human society. Encouraged and instructed by these officials, some absolutist rulers tried to reform their governments in accordance with Enlightenment ideals—what historians have called the **enlightened absolutism** of the later eighteenth century. In both Catholic and Protestant lands, rulers typically fused Enlightenment principles with religion, drawing support for their innovations from reform-minded religious thinkers. The most influential of the new-style monarchs were in Prussia, Russia, and Austria, and their example illustrates both the achievements and the great limitations

of enlightened absolutism. France experienced its own brand of enlightened absolutism in the contentious decades prior to the French Revolution.

## Frederick the Great of Prussia

Frederick II (r. 1740–1786) of Prussia, commonly known as Frederick the Great, built masterfully on the work of his father, Frederick William I (see "The Consolidation of Prussian Absolutism" in Chapter 15). Although in his youth he embraced culture and literature rather than the militarism championed by his father, by the time he came to the throne Frederick was determined to use the splendid army he had inherited.

Therefore, when Maria Theresa inherited the Habsburg dominions upon the death of her father, Holy Roman emperor Charles VI, Frederick pounced. He invaded the rich province of Silesia (sigh-LEE-zhuh), which bordered the Prussian territory of Brandenburg, thereby defying solemn Prussian promises to respect the Pragmatic Sanction, a diplomatic

■ **public sphere** An idealized intellectual space that emerged in Europe during the Enlightenment, where the public came together to discuss important issues relating to society, economics, and politics.

■ **enlightened absolutism** Term coined by historians to describe the rule of eighteenth-century monarchs who, without renouncing their own absolute authority, adopted Enlightenment ideals of rationalism, progress, and tolerance.

agreement that had guaranteed Maria Theresa's succession. In 1742, as other powers vied for Habsburg lands in the European War of the Austrian Succession (1740–1748), Maria Theresa was forced to cede almost all of Silesia to Prussia. In one stroke Prussia had doubled its population to 6 million people and now stood as a major European power.

Though successful in 1742, Frederick had to fight against great odds to save Prussia from destruction after competition between Britain and France for colonial empire brought another great conflict in 1756. Maria Theresa, seeking to regain Silesia, formed an alliance with the leaders of France and Russia. The aim of the alliance during the resulting Seven Years' War (1756–1763) was to conquer Prussia and divide up its territory. Despite invasions from all sides, Frederick fought on. In the end he was unexpectedly saved when Peter III came to the Russian throne in 1762 and called off the attack against Frederick, whom he greatly admired.

The terrible struggle of the Seven Years' War tempered Frederick's interest in territorial expansion and brought him to consider how more humane policies for his subjects might also strengthen the state. He tolerantly allowed his subjects to believe as they wished in religious and philosophical matters. He promoted the advancement of knowledge, improving his country's schools and permitting scholars to publish their findings. Moreover, Frederick tried to improve the lives of his subjects more directly. As he wrote to his friend Voltaire in 1770, "[I have to] enlighten mind, cultivate morality, and make the people as happy as it suits human nature, and as the means at my disposal permit."[12]

The legal system and the bureaucracy were Frederick's primary tools. Prussia's laws were simplified, torture was abolished, and judges decided cases quickly and impartially. After the Seven Years' War ended in 1763, Frederick's government energetically promoted the reconstruction of agriculture and industry. Frederick himself set a good example. He worked hard and lived modestly, claiming that he was "only the first servant of the state." Thus Frederick justified monarchy in terms of practical results and said nothing of the divine right of kings.

**The War of the Austrian Succession, 1740–1748**

Frederick's dedication to high-minded government went only so far, however. While he condemned serfdom in the abstract, he accepted it in practice and did not free the serfs on his own estates. He accepted and extended the privileges of the nobility, who remained the backbone of the army and the entire Prussian state.

In reforming Prussia's bureaucracy, Frederick drew on the principles of **cameralism**, the German science of public administration that emerged in the decades following the Thirty Years' War and came to occupy a central place in the university curriculum of the German lands. Cameralism held that monarchy was the best of all forms of government, that all elements of society should be placed at the service of the state, and that, in turn, the state should make use of its resources and authority to improve society. Predating the Enlightenment, cameralist interest in the public good was usually inspired by the needs of war. Cameralism shared with the Enlightenment an emphasis on rationality, progress, and utilitarianism.

## Catherine the Great of Russia

Catherine the Great of Russia (r. 1762–1796) was one of the most remarkable rulers of her age, and the French philosophes adored her. Catherine was a German princess from Anhalt-Zerbst, a small principality sandwiched between Prussia and Saxony. Her father commanded a regiment of the Prussian army, but her mother was related to the Romanovs of Russia, and that proved to be Catherine's opening to power.

Catherine's Romanov connection made her a suitable bride at the age of fifteen for the heir to the Russian throne. It was a mismatch from the beginning, but her *Memoirs* made her ambitions clear: "I did not care about Peter, but I did care about the crown." When her husband, Peter III, came to power during the Seven Years' War, his decision to withdraw Russian troops from the coalition against Prussia alienated the army. Catherine profited from his unpopularity to form a conspiracy to depose her husband. In 1762 Catherine's lover Gregory Orlov and his three brothers, all army officers, murdered Peter, and the German princess became empress of Russia.

Catherine had drunk deeply at the Enlightenment well. Never questioning that absolute monarchy was

**■ cameralism** View that monarchy was the best form of government, that all elements of society should serve the monarch, and that, in turn, the state should use its resources and authority to increase the public good.

**Catherine the Great and Denis Diderot**   Self-proclaimed adherent of Enlightenment ideals, Russian empress Catherine the Great enthusiastically corresponded with philosophes like Voltaire and Denis Diderot. When Diderot put his library on sale to raise much-needed funds, Catherine sent him the money but allowed him to keep his books. Historians have long debated the "enlightened despotism" represented by Catherine and other absolutist rulers. (Catherine: Based on a work by Alexander Roslin [1718–1793], [oil on canvas]/Museum of Art, Serpukhov, Russia/Bridgeman Images; Diderot: Heritage Images/Getty Images)

the best form of government, she set out to rule in an enlightened manner. She had three main goals. First, she worked hard to continue Peter the Great's effort to bring the culture of western Europe to Russia (see "The Reforms of Peter the Great" in Chapter 15). To do so, she imported Western architects, musicians, and intellectuals. She bought masterpieces of Western art and patronized the philosophes. An enthusiastic letter writer, she corresponded extensively with Voltaire and praised him as the "champion of the human race." When the French government banned the *Encyclopedia*, she offered to publish it in St. Petersburg, and she sent money to Diderot when he needed it. With these actions, Catherine won good press in the West for herself and for her country. Moreover, this intellectual ruler, who wrote plays and loved good talk, set the tone for the entire Russian nobility. Peter the Great westernized Russian armies, but it was Catherine who westernized the imagination of the Russian nobility.

Catherine's second goal was domestic reform, and she began her reign with sincere and ambitious projects. In 1767 she appointed a legislative commission to prepare a new law code. This project was never completed, but Catherine did restrict the practice of torture and allowed limited religious toleration. She also tried to improve education and strengthen local government. The philosophes applauded these measures and hoped more would follow.

Such was not the case. In 1773 a Cossack soldier named Emelian Pugachev sparked a gigantic uprising of serfs, very much as Stenka Razin had done a century earlier (see "Building the Russian Empire" in Chapter 15). Proclaiming himself the true tsar, Pugachev issued orders abolishing serfdom, taxes, and army service. Thousands joined his cause, slaughtering landlords and officials over a vast area of southwestern Russia. Pugachev's untrained forces eventually proved no match for Catherine's professional army. Betrayed by his own company, Pugachev was captured and brutally executed.

Pugachev's rebellion put an end to any intentions Catherine had about reforming the system and improving the lot of the peasantry. After 1775 Catherine gave the nobles absolute control of their serfs, and

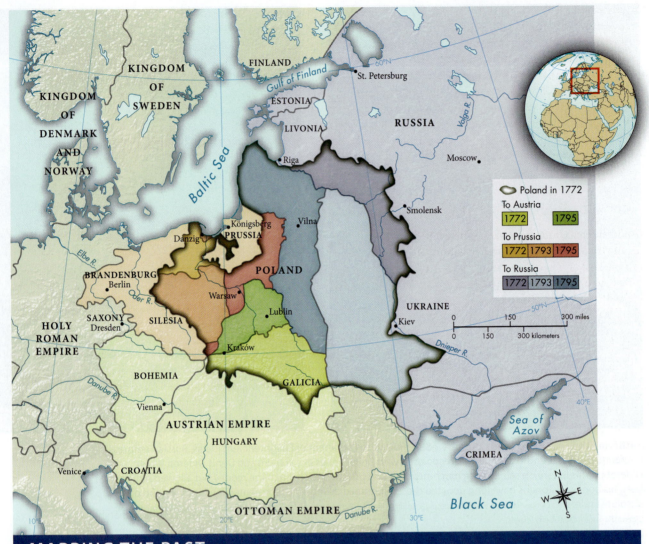

## MAPPING THE PAST

### MAP 16.1 The Partition of Poland, 1772–1795

In 1772 war between Russia and Austria threatened over Russian gains from the Ottoman Empire. To satisfy desires for expansion without fighting, Prussia's Frederick the Great proposed that parts of Poland be divided among Austria, Prussia, and Russia. In 1793 and 1795 the three powers partitioned the remainder, and the republic of Poland ceased to exist.

**ANALYZING THE MAP**  Of the three powers that divided the kingdom of Poland, which gained the most territory? How did the partition affect the geographical boundaries of each state, and what was the significance? What border with the former Poland remained unchanged? Why do you think this was the case?

**CONNECTIONS**  What does it say about European politics at the time that a country could simply cease to exist on the map? Could that happen today?

she extended serfdom into new areas, such as Ukraine. In 1785 she freed nobles from taxes and state service. Under Catherine the Russian nobility attained its most exalted position, and serfdom entered its most oppressive phase.

Catherine's third goal was territorial expansion, and in this respect she was extremely successful. Her

armies subjugated the last descendants of the Mongols and the Crimean Tartars and began the conquest of the Caucasus (KAW-kuh-suhs), the region between the Black Sea and the Caspian Sea. Her greatest coup by far was the partition of Poland (Map 16.1). When, between 1768 and 1772, Catherine's armies scored unprecedented victories against the Ottomans and thereby threatened to disturb the balance of power between Russia and Austria in eastern Europe, Frederick of Prussia obligingly came forward with a deal. He proposed that the Ottomans be let off easily and that Prussia, Austria, and Russia each compensate itself by taking a gigantic slice of the weakly ruled Polish territory. Catherine jumped at the chance. The first partition of Poland took place in 1772. Subsequent partitions in 1793 and 1795 gave away the rest of Polish territory, and the ancient republic of Poland vanished from the map.

## The Austrian Habsburgs

Another female monarch, Maria Theresa (r. 1740–1780) of Austria, set out to reform her nation, although traditional dynastic power politics was a more important motivation for her than were Enlightenment teachings. A devoutly Catholic mother and wife who inherited power from her father, Charles VI, Maria Theresa was a remarkable but old-fashioned absolutist. Her more radical son, Joseph II (r. 1780–1790), drew on Enlightenment ideals, earning the title of "revolutionary emperor."

Emerging from the long War of the Austrian Succession in 1748 with the serious loss of Silesia, Maria Theresa was determined to introduce reforms that would make the state stronger and more efficient. First, she initiated church reform, with measures aimed at limiting the papacy's influence, eliminating many religious holidays, and reducing the number of monasteries. Second, a whole series of administrative renovations strengthened the central bureaucracy, smoothed out some provincial differences, and revamped the tax system, taxing even the lands of nobles, previously exempt from taxation. Third, the government sought to improve the conditions of the agricultural population, cautiously reducing the power of lords over their hereditary serfs and their partially free peasant tenants.

Joseph II, coregent with his mother from 1765 onward and a strong supporter of change from above, implemented reform rapidly when he came to the throne in 1780. Most notably, Joseph abolished serfdom in 1781, and in 1789 he decreed that peasants could pay landlords in cash rather than through labor on their land. This measure was violently rejected not only by the nobility but also by the peasants it was intended to help, because they lacked the necessary cash. When a disillusioned Joseph died prematurely at forty-nine, the entire Habsburg empire was in turmoil. His brother Leopold II (r. 1790–1792) canceled Joseph's radical edicts in order to re-establish order. Peasants once again were required to do forced labor for their lords.

Despite differences in their policies, Joseph II and the other absolutists of the later eighteenth century combined old-fashioned state-building with the culture and critical thinking of the Enlightenment. In doing so, they succeeded in expanding the role of the state in the life of society. They perfected bureaucratic machines that were to prove surprisingly adaptive and enduring. Their failure to implement policies we would recognize as humane and enlightened—such as abolishing serfdom—probably reveal inherent limitations in Enlightenment thinking about equality and social justice, rather than deficiencies in their execution of Enlightenment programs. The fact that leading philosophes supported rather than criticized absolutist rulers' policies thus exposes the blind spots of the era.

## Jewish Life and the Limits of Enlightened Absolutism

Perhaps the best example of the limitations of enlightened absolutism is the debates surrounding the emancipation of the Jews. Europe's small Jewish populations lived under highly discriminatory laws. For the most part, Jews were confined to tiny, overcrowded ghettos, were excluded by law from most professions, and could be ordered out of a kingdom at a moment's notice. Still, a very few did manage to succeed and to obtain the right of permanent settlement, usually by performing some special service for the state. Many rulers relied on Jewish bankers for loans to raise armies and run their kingdoms. Jewish merchants prospered in international trade because they could rely on contacts with colleagues in Jewish communities scattered across Europe.

In the eighteenth century an Enlightenment movement known as the **Haskalah** emerged from within the European Jewish community, led by the Prussian philosopher Moses Mendelssohn (1729–1786). (See "Individuals in Society: Moses Mendelssohn and the Jewish Enlightenment," page 490.) Christian and Jewish Enlightenment philosophers, including Mendelssohn, began to advocate for freedom and civil rights for European Jews. In an era of reason and progress, they argued, restrictions on religious grounds could not stand. The Haskalah accompanied a period of controversial social change within Jewish communities in which rabbinic controls loosened and interaction with Christians increased.

Arguments for tolerance won some ground. The British Parliament passed a law allowing naturalization of Jews in 1753, but it later repealed the law due to public opposition. The most progressive reforms took place under Austrian emperor Joseph II. Among his liberal edicts of the 1780s were measures intended to integrate Jews more fully into society, including eligibility for military service, admission to higher education and artisanal trades, and removal of requirements for special clothing or emblems. Welcomed by many Jews, these

---

■ **Haskalah** The Jewish Enlightenment of the second half of the eighteenth century, led by the Prussian philosopher Moses Mendelssohn.

# INDIVIDUALS IN SOCIETY

## Moses Mendelssohn and the Jewish Enlightenment

I n 1743 a small, humpbacked Jewish boy with a stammer left his poor parents in Dessau in central Germany and walked eighty miles to Berlin, the capital of Frederick the Great's Prussia. According to one story, when the boy reached the Rosenthaler (ROH-zuhn-taw-lehr) Gate, the only one through which Jews could pass, he told the inquiring watchman that his name was Moses and that he had come to Berlin "to learn." The watchman laughed and waved him through. "Go Moses, the sea has opened before you."*

In Berlin the young Mendelssohn studied Jewish law and eked out a living copying Hebrew manuscripts in a beautiful hand. But he was soon fascinated by an intellectual world that had been closed to him in the Dessau ghetto. There, like most Jews throughout central Europe, he had spoken Yiddish — a mixture of German, Polish, and Hebrew. Now, working mainly on his own, he mastered German; learned Latin, Greek, French, and English; and studied mathematics and Enlightenment philosophy. Word of his exceptional abilities spread in Berlin's Jewish community (the dwelling of 1,500 of the city's 100,000 inhabitants). He began tutoring the children of a wealthy Jewish silk merchant, and he soon became the merchant's clerk and later his partner. But his great passion remained the life of the mind and the spirit, which he avidly pursued in his off-hours.

Gentle and unassuming in his personal life, Mendelssohn was a bold thinker. Reading eagerly in Western philosophy since antiquity, he was, as a pious Jew, soon convinced that Enlightenment teachings need not be opposed to Jewish thought and religion. He concluded that reason could complement and strengthen religion, although each would retain its integrity as a separate sphere.[†] Developing his idea in his first great work, *On the Immortality of the Soul* (1767), Mendelssohn used the neutral setting of a philosophical dialogue between Socrates and his followers in ancient Greece to argue that the human soul lived forever. In refusing to bring religion and critical thinking into conflict, he was strongly influenced by contemporary German philosophers who argued similarly on behalf of Christianity. He reflected the way the German Enlightenment generally supported established religion, in contrast to the French Enlightenment, which attacked it.

Mendelssohn's treatise on the human soul captivated the educated German public, which marveled that a Jew could have written a philosophical masterpiece. In the excitement, a Christian zealot named Johann Casper Lavater challenged Mendelssohn in a pamphlet to demonstrate how the

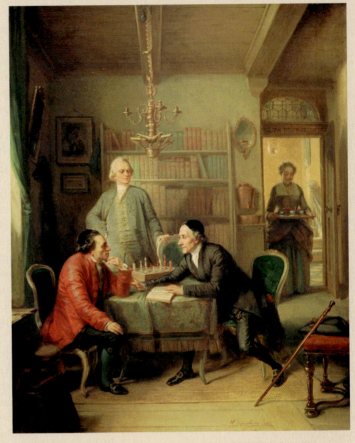

Lavater (right) attempts to convert Mendelssohn, in a painting by Moritz Oppenheim of an imaginary encounter. (The Magnes Collection of Jewish Art and Life, Berkeley, California/akg-images)

Christian faith was not "reasonable" or to accept Christianity. Replying politely but passionately, the Jewish philosopher affirmed that his studies had only strengthened him in his faith, although he did not seek to convert anyone not born into Judaism. Rather, he urged toleration in religious matters and spoke up courageously against Jewish oppression.

Orthodox Jew and German philosophe, Moses Mendelssohn serenely combined two very different worlds. He built a bridge from the ghetto to the dominant culture over which many Jews would pass, including his novelist daughter Dorothea and his famous grandson, the composer Felix Mendelssohn.

### QUESTIONS FOR ANALYSIS

1. How did Mendelssohn seek to influence Jewish religious thought in his time?
2. How do Mendelssohn's ideas compare with those of the French Enlightenment?

*H. Kupferberg, *The Mendelssohns: Three Generations of Genius* (New York: Charles Scribner's Sons, 1972), p. 3.

[†]David Sorkin, *Moses Mendelssohn and the Religious Enlightenment* (Berkeley: University of California Press, 1996), pp. 8ff.

**The Pale of Settlement, 1791**

reforms raised fears among traditionalists about the possibility of assimilation into the general population.

Many monarchs rejected all ideas of emancipation. Although he permitted freedom of religion to his Christian subjects, Frederick the Great of Prussia firmly opposed any general emancipation for the Jews, as he did for the serfs. Catherine the Great, who acquired most of Poland's large Jewish population when she annexed part of that country in the late eighteenth century, similarly refused. In 1791 she established the Pale of Settlement, a territory including parts of modern-day Poland, Latvia, Lithuania, Ukraine, and Belarus, in which most Jews were required to live. Jewish habitation was restricted to the Pale until the Russian Revolution in 1917.

The first European state to remove all restrictions on the Jews was France during the French Revolution. Over the next hundred years, Jews gradually won full legal and civil rights throughout the rest of western Europe. Emancipation in eastern Europe took even longer and aroused more conflict and violence.

## NOTES

1. Quoted in H. Butterfield, *The Origins of Modern Science* (New York: Macmillan, 1951), p. 47.
2. Quoted in Butterfield, *The Origins of Modern Science*, p. 120.
3. Quoted in John Freely, *Aladdin's Lamp: How Greek Science Came to Europe Through the Islamic World* (New York: Knopf, 2009), p. 225.
4. Quoted in Jacqueline Broad, *Women Philosophers of the Seventeenth Century* (Cambridge: Cambridge University Press, 2003), p. 17.
5. Quoted in L. Schiebinger, *The Mind Has No Sex? Women in the Origins of Modern Science* (Cambridge, Mass.: Harvard University Press, 1989), p. 64.
6. Quoted in G. L. Mosse et al., eds., *Europe in Review* (Chicago: Rand McNally, 1964), p. 156.
7. D. E. Mungello, *The Great Encounter of China and the West, 1500–1800*, 2d ed. (Lanham, Md.: Rowman & Littlefield, 2005), p. 98.
8. Quoted in Emmanuel Chukwudi Eze, ed., *Race and the Enlightenment: A Reader* (Oxford: Blackwell, 1997), p. 33.
9. See E. Fox-Genovese, "Women in the Enlightenment," in *Becoming Visible: Women in European History*, 2d ed., ed. R. Bridenthal, C. Koonz, and S. Stuard (Boston: Houghton Mifflin, 1987), esp. pp. 252–259, 263–265.
10. Aurora Wolfgang, *Gender and Voice in the French Novel, 1730–1782* (Aldershot, U.K.: Ashgate, 2004), p. 8.
11. Jean Le Rond d'Alembert, *Eloges lus dans les séances publiques de l'Académie française* (Paris, 1779), p. ix, quoted in Mona Ozouf, "'Public Opinion' at the End of the Old Regime," *The Journal of Modern History* 60, Supplement: Rethinking French Politics in 1788 (September 1988): S9.
12. Cited in Giles McDonough, *Frederick the Great: A Life in Deed and Letters* (New York: St. Martin's Griffin, 2001), 341.

# LOOKING BACK  LOOKING AHEAD

Hailed as the origin of modern thought, the Scientific Revolution must also be seen as a product of its past and of the interaction between Europeans and non-Europeans. Medieval translations of ancient Greek texts from Arabic into Latin spurred the advance of scholarship in western Europe, giving rise to universities that produced and disseminated knowledge of the natural world. Natural philosophers following Copernicus pioneered new methods of observing and explaining nature while drawing on centuries-old traditions of Christian faith as well as astrology, alchemy, and magic. In expanding their knowledge about the natural world, Europeans drew on traditions of observation and practice among indigenous peoples of the New World.

The Enlightenment ideas of the eighteenth century were a similar blend of past and present, European and non-European; they could serve as much to bolster absolutist monarchical regimes as to inspire revolutionaries to fight for individual rights and liberties. Although the Enlightenment fostered critical thinking about everything from science to religion, the majority of Europeans, including many prominent thinkers, remained devout Christians. Enlightenment ideas were inspired by contact and exchange with non-Europeans in Asia, Africa, and the Americas.

The achievements of the Scientific Revolution and the Enlightenment are undeniable. Key Western values of rationalism, human rights, and open-mindedness were born from these movements. With their new notions of progress and social improvement, Europeans would embark on important revolutions in industry and politics in the centuries that followed. Nonetheless, others have seen a darker side. For these critics, the mastery over nature permitted by the Scientific Revolution now threatens to overwhelm the earth's fragile equilibrium, and the Enlightenment belief in the universal application of reason can lead to arrogance and intolerance of other people's spiritual, cultural, and political values. Such vivid debates about the legacy of these intellectual and scientific developments testify to their continuing importance in today's world.

## Make Connections

Think about the larger developments and continuities within and across chapters.

1. How did the era of European exploration and discovery (Chapter 14) affect the ideas of the scientists and philosophers discussed in this chapter? In what ways did contact with new peoples and places stimulate new forms of thought among Europeans?

2. What was the relationship between the Scientific Revolution and the Enlightenment? How did new ways of understanding the natural world influence thinking about human society?

3. Compare the policies and actions of seventeenth-century absolutist rulers (Chapter 15) with their "enlightened" descendants described in this chapter. How accurate is the term *enlightened absolutism*?

# 16 REVIEW & EXPLORE

## Identify Key Terms

Identify and explain the significance of each item below.

natural philosophy (p. 463)

Copernican hypothesis (p. 464)

law of inertia (p. 465)

law of universal gravitation (p. 467)

Cartesian dualism (p. 469)

Enlightenment (p. 472)

rationalism (p. 473)

sensationalism (p. 473)

philosophes (p. 474)

deism (p. 475)

salon (p. 482)

rococo (p. 482)

public sphere (p. 485)

enlightened absolutism (p. 485)

cameralism (p. 486)

Haskalah (p. 489)

## Review the Main Ideas

Answer the section heading questions from the chapter.

1. What revolutionary discoveries were made in the sixteenth and seventeenth centuries? (p. 462)

2. What intellectual and social changes occurred as a result of the Scientific Revolution? (p. 468)

3. How did the Enlightenment emerge, and what were major currents of Enlightenment thought? (p. 472)

4. How did the Enlightenment change social ideas and practices? (p. 479)

5. What impact did new ways of thinking have on politics? (p. 485)

## Suggested Resources

### BOOKS

- Bevilacqua, Alexander. *The Republic of Arabic Letters: Islam and the European Enlightenment.* An engaging study of the origins of scholarship on Islam in the West and the central role of this scholarship in inspiring the Enlightenment.

- Curran, Andrew S. *The Anatomy of Blackness: Science and Slavery in an Age of Enlightenment.* 2013. Examines how Enlightenment thinkers transformed traditional thinking about people of African descent into ideas about biological racial difference.

- Dear, Peter. *Revolutionizing the Sciences: European Knowledge and Its Ambitions, 1500–1700,* 2d ed. 2009. An accessible and well-illustrated introduction to the Scientific Revolution.

- Delbourgo, James, and Nicholas Dew, eds. *Science and Empire in the Atlantic World.* 2008. A collection of essays examining the relationship between the Scientific Revolution and the imperial expansion of European powers across the Atlantic.

- Ellis, Markman. *The Coffee House: A Cultural History.* 2004. An engaging study of the rise of the coffeehouse and its impact on European cultural and social life.

- Jardine, Lisa. *Ingenious Pursuits: Building the Scientific Revolution.* 1999. A lively and accessible account of how the Scientific Revolution emerged from intellectual exchange and competition among scholars.

- Massie, Robert K. *Catherine the Great: Portrait of a Woman.* 2012. Recounts the life story of Catherine, from obscure German princess to enlightened ruler of Russia.

- McMahon, Darrin M. *Happiness: A History.* 2006. Discusses how worldly pleasure became valued as a duty of individuals and societies in the Enlightenment.

- Portuondo, María. *Secret Science: Spanish Cosmography and the New World.* 2009. Examines the role of natural scientists in providing useful knowledge for Spanish imperial expansion in the Americas and the impact of their work on the overall development of science.

- Robertson, John. *The Case for the Enlightenment: Scotland and Naples, 1680–1760.* 2005. A comparative study of Enlightenment movements in Scotland and Naples, emphasizing commonalities between these two small kingdoms on the edges of Europe.

- Sorkin, David. *Moses Mendelssohn and the Religious Enlightenment.* 1996. A brilliant study of the Jewish philosopher and of the role of religion in the Enlightenment.

### MEDIA

- *Catherine the Great* (A&E, 1995). A made-for-television movie starring Catherine Zeta-Jones as the German princess who becomes Catherine the Great.

- *Dangerous Liaisons* (Stephen Frears, 1988). Based on a 1782 novel, the story of two aristocrats who cynically manipulate others, until one of them falls in love with a chaste widow chosen as his victim.

- *The Encyclopedia of Diderot & d'Alembert Collaborative Translation Project.* A collaborative project to translate the *Encyclopedia* edited by Denis Diderot and Jean le Rond d'Alembert into English, with searchable entries submitted by students and scholars and vetted by experts. **quod.lib.umich.edu/d/did/**

- *Galileo's Battle for the Heavens* (PBS, 2002). Recounts the story of Galileo's struggle with the Catholic Church over his astronomical discoveries, featuring re-enactments of key episodes in his life.

- *The Hermitage Museum.* The website of the Russian Hermitage Museum founded by Catherine the Great in the Winter Palace in St. Petersburg, with virtual tours of the museum's rich collections. **http://www.hermitagemuseum.org/wps/portal/hermitage**

- *Longitude* (A&E, 2000). A television miniseries that follows the parallel stories of an eighteenth-century clockmaker striving to find a means to measure longitude at sea and a modern-day veteran who restores the earlier man's clocks.

- *Mapping the Republic of Letters.* A site hosted by Stanford University showcasing projects using mapping software to create spatial visualizations based on the correspondence and travel of members of the eighteenth-century Republic of Letters. **republicofletters.stanford.edu/**

- *Newton's Dark Secrets* (PBS, 2005). Explores Isaac Newton's fundamental scientific discoveries alongside his religious faith and practice of alchemy.

- *Ridicule* (Patrice Leconte, 1996). When a provincial nobleman travels to the French court in the 1780s to present a project to drain a malarial swamp in his district, his naïve Enlightenment ideals incur the ridicule of decadent courtiers.

# GLOSSARY

**al-Andalus** The part of the Iberian Peninsula under Muslim control in the eighth century, encompassing most of modern-day Spain. (Ch. 8)

**anticlericalism** Opposition to the clergy. (Ch. 13)

**Antigonid dynasty** Dynasty of rulers established by General Antigonus in Macedonia after Alexander's conquests, which ruled until 168 B.C.E. (Ch. 4)

**apostolic succession** The doctrine that all bishops can trace their spiritual ancestry back to Jesus's apostles. (Ch. 7)

**aqueducts** Canals, channels, and pipes that brought freshwater into cities. (Ch. 6)

**Arianism** A theological belief that originated when Arius, a priest of Alexandria, denied that Christ was co-eternal with God the Father. (Ch. 7)

**Assyrian Empire** An empire that originated in northern Mesopotamia and expanded to encompass much of the Near East in the tenth through the seventh centuries B.C.E. (Ch. 2)

**Aztec Empire** A large and complex Native American civilization in modern Mexico and Central America that possessed advanced mathematical, astronomical, and engineering technology. (Ch. 14)

**Babylonian Captivity** The period from 1309 to 1376 when the popes resided in Avignon rather than in Rome. The phrase refers to the seventy years when the Hebrews were held captive in Babylon. (Ch. 11)

**baroque style** A style in art and music lasting from roughly 1600 to 1750 characterized by the use of drama and motion to create heightened emotion, especially prevalent in Catholic countries. (Ch. 15)

**barracks emperors** The emperors of the middle of the third century, so called because they were military commanders. (Ch. 6)

**bishops** Christian Church officials with jurisdiction over certain areas and the power to determine the correct interpretation of Christian teachings. (Ch. 6)

**Black Death** Plague that first struck Europe in 1347 and killed perhaps one-third of the population. (Ch. 11)

**boyars** The highest-ranking members of the Russian nobility. (Chs. 8, 15)

**Bronze Age** The period in which the production and use of bronze implements became basic to society. (Ch. 1)

**caliph** The chief Muslim ruler, regarded as a successor to the Prophet Muhammad. (Ch. 8)

**cameralism** View that monarchy was the best form of government, that all elements of society should serve the monarch, and that, in turn, the state should use its resources and authority to increase the public good. (Ch. 16)

**canon law** Church law, which had its own courts and procedures. (Ch. 9)

**caravel** A small, maneuverable, two- or three-masted sailing ship developed by the Portuguese in the fifteenth century that gave them a distinct advantage in exploration and trade. (Ch. 14)

**Cartesian dualism** Descartes's view that all of reality could ultimately be reduced to mind and matter. (Ch. 16)

**cathedral** The church of a bishop and the administrative headquarters of a diocese. (Ch. 10)

**chivalry** Code of conduct in which fighting to defend the Christian faith and protecting one's countrymen were declared to have a sacred purpose. (Ch. 9)

**Christendom** The term used by early medieval writers to refer to the realm of Christianity. (Ch. 9)

**Christian humanists** Northern humanists who interpreted Italian ideas about and attitudes toward classical antiquity and humanism in terms of their own religious traditions. (Ch. 12)

**civilization** A large-scale system of human political, economic, and social organizations; civilizations have cities, laws, states, and often writing. (Ch. 1)

**civitas** The city and surrounding territory that served as a basis of the administrative system in the Frankish kingdoms, based on Roman models. (Ch. 8)

**Code of Justinian** A collection of laws and legal commentary issued by the emperor Justinian that brought together all existing imperial laws into a coherent whole. (Ch. 7)

**college of cardinals** A special group of high clergy with the authority and power to elect the pope and the responsibility to govern the church when the office of the pope is vacant. (Ch. 9)

**Columbian exchange** The exchange of animals, plants, and diseases between the Old and the New Worlds. (Ch. 14)

**comitatus** A war band of young men in a barbarian tribe who were closely associated with the chief, swore loyalty to him, and fought with him in battle. (Ch. 7)

**comites** A senior official or royal companion, later called a count, who presided over the civitas. (Ch. 8)

**commercial revolution** The transformation of the European economy as a result of changes in business procedures and growth in trade. (Ch. 10)

**common law** A body of English law established by King Henry II's court that in the next two or three centuries became common to the entire country. (Ch. 9)

**communes** Sworn associations of free men in Italian cities led by merchant guilds. (Ch. 12)

**conciliarists** People who believed that the authority in the Roman Church should rest in a general council composed of clergy, theologians, and laypeople, rather than in the pope alone. (Ch. 11)

**confraternities** Voluntary lay groups organized by occupation, devotional preference, neighborhood, or charitable activity. (Ch. 11)

**conquistadors** Spanish for "conquerors"; armed Spaniards such as Hernán Cortés and Francisco Pizarro, who sought to conquer people and territories in the New World for the Spanish crown. (Ch. 14)

**constitutionalism** A form of government in which power is limited by law and balanced between the authority and power of the government, on the one hand, and the rights and liberties of the subjects or citizens on the other hand; could include constitutional monarchies or republics. (Ch. 15)

**consuls** Primary executives in the Roman Republic, elected for one-year terms in the Senate, who commanded the army in battle, administered state business, and supervised financial affairs. (Ch. 5)

**Copernican hypothesis** The idea that the sun, not the earth, was the center of the universe. (Ch. 16)

**Cossacks** Free groups and outlaw armies originally comprising runaway peasants living on the borders of Russian territory from the fourteenth century onward. By the end of the sixteenth century they had formed an alliance with the Russian state. (Ch. 15)

**courts** Magnificent households and palaces where signori and other rulers lived, conducted business, and supported the arts. (Ch. 12)

**Covenant** An agreement that the Hebrews believed to exist between themselves and Yahweh, in which he would consider them his chosen people if they worshipped him as their only god. (Ch. 2)

**craft guild** A band of producers in a town that regulated most aspects of production of a good in that town. (Ch. 10)

**Crusades** Wars sponsored by the papacy for the recovery of Jerusalem and surrounding territories from the Muslims in the late eleventh to the late thirteenth centuries. (Ch. 9)

**cuneiform** Sumerian form of writing; the term describes the wedge-shaped marks made by a stylus. (Ch. 1)

**debate about women** Debate among writers and thinkers in the Renaissance about women's qualities and proper role in society. (Ch. 12)

**deism** Belief in a distant, noninterventionist deity; common among Enlightenment thinkers. (Ch. 16)

**Delian League** A military alliance led by Athens whose aims were to protect the Aegean Islands, liberate Ionia from Persian rule, and keep the Persians out of Greece. (Ch. 3)

**democracy** A type of Greek government in which all citizens administered the workings of government. (Ch. 3)

**diocese** An administrative unit in the later Roman Empire; adopted by the Christian Church as the territory under the authority of a bishop. (Ch. 7)

**Domesday Book** A general inquiry about the wealth of his lands ordered by William of Normandy. (Ch. 9)

**Edict of Nantes** A document issued by Henry IV of France in 1598, granting liberty of conscience and of public worship to Calvinists, which helped restore peace in France. (Ch. 13)

**encomienda system** A system whereby the Spanish crown granted the conquerors the right to forcibly employ groups of Indians in exchange for providing food, shelter, and Christian teaching. (Ch. 14)

**English Peasants' Revolt** Revolt by English peasants in 1381 in response to changing economic conditions. (Ch. 11)

**enlightened absolutism** Term coined by historians to describe the rule of eighteenth-century monarchs who, without renouncing their own absolute authority, adopted Enlightenment ideals of rationalism, progress, and tolerance. (Ch. 16)

**Enlightenment** The influential intellectual and cultural movement of the late seventeenth and eighteenth centuries that introduced a new worldview based on the use of reason, the scientific method, and progress. (Ch. 16)

**Epicureanism** A system of philosophy based on the teachings of Epicurus, who viewed a life of contentment, free from fear and suffering, as the greatest good. (Ch. 4)

**excommunication** A penalty used by the Christian Church that meant being cut off from the sacraments and all Christian worship. (Ch. 9)

**Fertile Crescent** An area of mild climate and abundant wild grain where agriculture first developed, in present-day Lebanon, Israel, Jordan, Turkey, and Iraq. (Ch. 1)

**feudalism** A term devised by later scholars to describe the political system in which a vassal was generally given a piece of land in return for his loyalty. (Ch. 8)

**fief** A piece of land granted by a feudal lord to a vassal in return for service and loyalty. (Ch. 8)

**First Triumvirate** The name later given to an informal political alliance among Caesar, Crassus, and Pompey in which they agreed to advance one another's interests. (Ch. 5)

**Five Pillars of Islam** The five practices Muslims must fulfill according to the shari'a, or sacred law, including the profession of faith, prayer, fasting, giving alms to the poor, and pilgrimage to Mecca. (Ch. 8)

**flagellants** People who believed that the plague was God's punishment for sin and sought to do penance by flagellating (whipping) themselves. (Ch. 11)

**friars** Men belonging to certain religious orders who lived not in monasteries but out in the world. (Ch. 9)

**Fronde** A series of violent uprisings during the early reign of Louis XIV triggered by growing royal control and increased taxation. (Ch. 15)

**Gothic** An architectural style typified by pointed arches and large stained-glass windows. (Ch. 10)

**Gracchi reforms** Land reforms proposed by the Gracchi brothers to distribute public land to the poor of the city of Rome. (Ch. 5)

**Great Famine** A terrible famine in 1315–1322 that hit much of Europe after a period of climate change. (Ch. 11)

**Great Schism** The division, or split, in church leadership from 1378 to 1417 when there were two, then three, popes. (Ch. 11)

**gynaeceum** Women's quarters at the back of an Athenian house where the women of the family and the female slaves worked, ate, and slept. (Ch. 3)

**Hammurabi's law code** A proclamation issued by Babylonian king Hammurabi to establish laws regulating many aspects of life. (Ch. 1)

**Hanseatic League** A mercantile association of towns begun in northern Europe that allowed for mutual protection and trading rights. (Ch. 10)

**Haskalah** The Jewish Enlightenment of the second half of the eighteenth century, led by the Prussian philosopher Moses Mendelssohn. (Ch. 16)

**Hellenistic** A term that literally means "like the Greek," used to describe the period after the death of Alexander the Great, when Greek culture spread. (Ch. 4)

**Hellenization** The spread of Greek ideas, culture, and traditions to non-Greek groups across a wide area. (Ch. 4)

**helots** Unfree residents of Sparta forced to work state lands. (Ch. 3)

**heresy** A religious practice or belief judged unacceptable by church officials. (Ch. 6)

**Holy Office** The official Roman Catholic agency founded in 1542 to combat international doctrinal heresy. (Ch. 13)

**Holy Roman Empire** The loose confederation of principalities, duchies, cities, bishoprics, and other types of regional governments stretching from Denmark to Rome and from Burgundy to Poland. (Ch. 9)

**hoplites** Heavily armed citizens who served as infantry troops and fought to defend the polis. (Ch. 3)

**Huguenots** French Calvinists. (Ch. 13)

**humanism** A program of study designed by Italians that emphasized the critical study of Latin and Greek literature with the goal of understanding human nature. (Ch. 12)

**Hundred Years' War** A war between England and France from 1337 to 1453, with political and economic causes and consequences. (Ch. 11)

**imperator** Title originally given to a Roman general after a major victory that came to mean "emperor." (Ch. 6)

**Inca Empire** The vast and sophisticated Peruvian empire centered at the capital city of Cuzco that was at its peak from 1438 until 1533. (Ch. 14)

**indulgence** A document issued by the Catholic Church lessening penance or time in purgatory, widely believed to bring forgiveness of all sins. (Chs. 9, 13)

**infidel** A disparaging term used for a person who does not believe in a particular religion. (Ch. 8)

***Institutes of the Christian Religion, The*** Calvin's formulation of Christian doctrine, which became a systematic theology for Protestantism. (Ch. 13)

**Iron Age** Period beginning about 1100 B.C.E., when iron became the most important material for tools and weapons. (Ch. 2)

**Jacquerie** A massive uprising by French peasants in 1358 protesting heavy taxation. (Ch. 11)

**janissary corps** The core of the sultan's army, composed of slave conscripts from non-Muslim parts of the empire; after 1683 it became a volunteer force. (Ch. 15)

**Jesuits** Members of the Society of Jesus, founded by Ignatius Loyola, whose goal was the spread of the Roman Catholic faith. (Ch. 13)

**Junkers** The nobility of Brandenburg and Prussia, who were reluctant allies of Frederick William in his consolidation of the Prussian state. (Ch. 15)

**Kievan Rus** A confederation of Slavic territories, with its capital at Kiev, ruled by descendants of the Vikings. (Ch. 8)

**Kush** Kingdom in Nubia that adopted hieroglyphics and pyramids, and later conquered Egypt. (Ch. 2)

**law of inertia** A law hypothesized by Galileo that states that motion, not rest, is the natural state of an object, and that an object continues in motion forever unless stopped by some external force. (Ch. 16)

**law of universal gravitation** Newton's law that all objects are attracted to one another and that the force of attraction is proportional to the objects' quantity of matter and inversely proportional to the square of the distance between them. (Ch. 16)

**ma'at** The Egyptian belief in a cosmic harmony that embraced truth, justice, and moral integrity; it gave the kings the right and duty to govern. (Ch. 1)

**Magna Carta** A peace treaty intended to redress the grievances that particular groups had against King John; it was later viewed as the source of English rights and liberty more generally. (Ch. 9)

**manorialism** A system in which peasant residents of manors, or farming villages, provided work and goods for their lord in exchange for protection. (Ch. 8)

**mercantilism** A system of economic regulations aimed at increasing the power of the state based on the belief that a nation's international power was based on its wealth, specifically its supply of gold and silver. (Ch. 15)

**merchant guild** A band of merchants in a town that prohibited nonmembers from trading in that town. (Ch. 10)

**Messiah** In Jewish belief, an anointed leader who would bring a period of peace and happiness for Jews. (Ch. 6)

**millet system** A system used by the Ottomans whereby subjects were divided into religious communities, with each millet (nation) enjoying autonomous self-government under its religious leaders. (Ch. 15)

**Minoan** A wealthy and vibrant culture on Crete from around 1900 B.C.E. to 1450 B.C.E., ruled by a king with a large palace at Knossos. (Ch. 3)

**monotheism** Worship of a single god. (Ch. 2)

**Mycenaean** A Bronze Age culture that flourished in Greece from about 1650 B.C.E. to 1100 B.C.E., building fortified palaces and cities. (Ch. 3)

**mystery religions** Belief systems that were characterized by secret doctrines, rituals of initiation, and sometimes the promise of rebirth or an afterlife. (Ch. 3)

**natural law** A Stoic concept that a single law that was part of the natural order of life governed all people. (Ch. 4)

**natural philosophy** An early modern term for the study of the nature of the universe, its purpose, and how it functioned; it encompassed what we would call "science" today. (Ch. 16)

**Neolithic era** The period after 9000 B.C.E., when people developed agriculture, domesticated animals, and used tools made of stone and wood. (Ch. 1)

**New Christians** A term for Jews and Muslims in the Iberian Peninsula who accepted Christianity; in many cases they included Christians whose families had converted centuries earlier. (Ch. 12)

**Nicene Creed** A statement of belief written by a group of Christian church leaders in 325 that declared God the

Father and Jesus to be of the same "substance"; other interpretations were declared heresy. (Ch. 7)

**oligarchy** A type of Greek government in which citizens who owned a certain amount of property ruled. (Ch. 3)

**open-field system** System in which the arable land of a manor was divided into two or three fields without hedges or fences to mark individual holdings. (Ch. 10)

**Orthodox Church** Eastern Christian Church in the Byzantine Empire. (Ch. 7)

**pagan** Originally referring to those who lived in the countryside, it came to mean those who practiced religions other than Judaism or Christianity. (Ch. 6)

**Paleolithic era** The period of human history up to about 9000 B.C.E., when tools were made from stone and bone and people gained their food through foraging. (Ch. 1)

**pastoralism** An economic system based on herding flocks of goats, sheep, cattle, or other animals beneficial to humans. (Ch. 1)

**paterfamilias** The oldest dominant male of the Roman family, who held great power over the lives of family members. (Ch. 5)

**patriarchy** A social system in which men have more power and access to resources than women of the same social level, and in which some men are dominant over other men. (Ch. 1)

**patricians** The Roman hereditary aristocracy; they held most of the political power in the republic. (Ch. 5)

**patronage** Financial support of writers and artists by cities, groups, and individuals, often to produce specific works or works in specific styles. (Ch. 12)

**patron-client system** An informal system of patronage in which free men promised their votes to a more powerful man in exchange for his help in legal or other matters. (Ch. 5)

**pax Romana** The "Roman peace," a term invented by the historian Edward Gibbon in the eighteenth century to describe the first and second centuries C.E., which he saw as a time of political stability and relative peace. (Ch. 6)

**Peace of Utrecht** A series of treaties, from 1713 to 1715, that ended the War of the Spanish Succession, ended French expansion in Europe, and marked the rise of the British Empire. (Ch. 15)

**Peace of Westphalia** The name of a series of treaties that concluded the Thirty Years' War in 1648 and marked the end of large-scale religious violence in Europe. (Ch. 15)

**Persian Empire** A large empire centered in today's Iran that used force and diplomacy to consolidate its power and that allowed cultural diversity. (Ch. 2)

**Petrine Doctrine** A doctrine stating that the popes (the bishops of Rome) were the successors of Saint Peter and therefore heirs to his highest level of authority as chief of the apostles. (Ch. 7)

**pharaoh** The title given to the king of Egypt in the New Kingdom, from a word that meant "great house." (Ch. 1)

**philosophes** A group of French intellectuals who proclaimed that they were bringing the light of knowledge to their fellow humans in the Age of Enlightenment. (Ch. 16)

**Phoenicians** Seafaring people from Canaan who traded and founded colonies throughout the Mediterranean and spread the phonetic alphabet. (Ch. 2)

**Platonic ideals** According to Plato, the eternal unchanging ideal forms that are the essence of true reality. (Ch. 3)

**plebeians** The common people of Rome; they were free but had few of the patricians' advantages. (Ch. 5)

**polis** Generally translated as "city-state," it was the basic political and institutional unit of Greece in the Hellenic period. (Ch. 3)

**politiques** Catholic and Protestant moderates who held that only a strong monarchy could save France from total collapse. (Ch. 13)

**polytheism** The worship of many gods and goddesses. (Ch. 1)

**popolo** Disenfranchised common people in Italian cities who resented their exclusion from power. (Ch. 12)

**Praetorian Guard** Imperial bodyguard created by Augustus. (Ch. 6)

**predestination** The teaching that God has determined the salvation or damnation of individuals based on his will and purpose, not on their merit or works. (Ch. 13)

**primogeniture** An inheritance system in which the oldest son inherits all land and noble titles. (Ch. 9)

**principate** Official title of Augustus's form of government, taken from *princeps*, meaning "first citizen." (Ch. 6)

**Protectorate** The English military dictatorship (1653–1658) established by Oliver Cromwell following the execution of Charles I. (Ch. 15)

**Protestant** The name originally given to followers of Luther, which came to mean all non-Catholic Western Christian groups. (Ch. 13)

**Ptolemaic dynasty** Dynasty of rulers established by General Ptolemy in Egypt after Alexander's conquests, which ruled until 30 B.C.E. (Ch. 4)

**Ptolemy's *Geography*** A second-century-C.E. work that synthesized the classical knowledge of geography and introduced the concepts of longitude and latitude. Reintroduced to Europeans about 1410 by Arab scholars, its ideas allowed cartographers to create more accurate maps. (Ch. 14)

**public sphere** An idealized intellectual space that emerged in Europe during the Enlightenment, where the public came together to discuss important issues relating to society, economics, and politics. (Ch. 16)

**Punic Wars** A series of three wars between Rome and Carthage in which Rome emerged the victor. (Ch. 5)

**Puritans** Members of a sixteenth- and seventeenth-century reform movement within the Church of England that advocated purifying it of Roman Catholic elements such as bishops, elaborate ceremonials, and wedding rings. (Ch. 15)

**Qur'an** The sacred book of Islam. (Ch. 8)

**rationalism** A secular, critical way of thinking in which nothing was to be accepted on faith and everything was to be submitted to reason. (Ch. 16)

**reconquista** The Christian term for the conquest of Muslim territories in the Iberian Peninsula by Christian forces. (Ch. 9)

**regular clergy** Men and women who lived in monastic houses and followed sets of rules, first those of Benedict and later those written by other individuals. (Ch. 7)

**relics** Bones, articles of clothing, or other objects associated with the life of a saint. (Ch. 7)

**religious orders** Groups of monastic houses following a particular rule. (Ch. 9)

**Renaissance** A French word meaning "rebirth," used to describe the rebirth of the culture of classical antiquity in Italy during the fourteenth to sixteenth centuries. (Ch. 12)

**representative assemblies** Deliberative meetings of lords and wealthy urban residents that flourished in many European countries between 1250 and 1450. (Ch. 11)

**republicanism** A form of government in which there is no monarch and power rests in the hands of the people as exercised through elected representatives. (Ch. 15)

**rococo** A popular style in Europe in the eighteenth century, known for its soft pastels, ornate interiors, sentimental portraits, and starry-eyed lovers protected by hovering cupids. (Ch. 16)

**Romanesque** An architectural style with rounded arches and small windows. (Ch. 10)

**sacraments** Certain rituals defined by the church in which God bestows benefits on the believer through grace. (Ch. 7)

**salon** Regular social gathering held by talented and rich Parisians in their homes, where philosophes and their followers met to discuss literature, science, and philosophy. (Ch. 16)

**satraps** Administrators in the Persian Empire who controlled local government, collected taxes, heard legal cases, and maintained order. (Ch. 2)

**Scholastics** University professors in the Middle Ages who developed a method of thinking, reasoning, and writing in which questions were raised and authorities cited on both sides of a question. (Ch. 10)

**Second Triumvirate** A formal agreement in 43 B.C.E. among Octavian, Mark Antony, and Lepidus to defeat Caesar's murderers. (Ch. 5)

**secular clergy** Priests and bishops who staffed churches where people worshipped and who were not cut off from the world. (Ch. 7)

**Seleucid Empire** Large empire established in the Near East by General Seleucus after Alexander's conquests, which remained in power until 63 B.C.E. (Ch. 4)

**Senate** The assembly that was the main institution of power in the Roman Republic, originally composed only of aristocrats. (Ch. 5)

**sensationalism** The idea that all human ideas and thoughts are produced as a result of sensory impressions. (Ch. 16)

**serfs** Peasants bound to the land by a relationship with a manorial lord. (Ch. 8)

**signori** Government by one-man rule in Italian cities such as Milan; also refers to these rulers. (Ch. 12)

**simony** The buying and selling of church offices, a policy that was officially prohibited but often practiced. (Ch. 9)

**Socratic method** A method of inquiry used by Socrates based on asking questions, through which participants developed their critical-thinking skills and explored ethical issues. (Ch. 3)

**Sophists** A group of thinkers in fifth-century-B.C.E. Athens who applied philosophical speculation to politics and language and were accused of deceit. (Ch. 3)

**Spanish Armada** The fleet sent by Philip II of Spain in 1588 against England as a religious crusade against Protestantism. Weather and the English fleet defeated it. (Ch. 13)

**stadholder** The executive officer in each of the United Provinces of the Netherlands, a position often held by the princes of Orange. (Ch. 15)

**Statute of Kilkenny** Law issued in 1366 that discriminated against the Irish, forbidding marriage between the English and the Irish, requiring the use of the English language, and denying the Irish access to ecclesiastical offices. (Ch. 11)

**Stoicism** A philosophy, based on the ideas of Zeno, that people could be happy only when living in accordance with nature and accepting whatever happened. (Ch. 4)

**Struggle of the Orders** A conflict in which the plebeians sought political representation and safeguards against patrician domination. (Ch. 5)

**sultan** The ruler of the Ottoman Empire; he owned all the agricultural land of the empire and was served by an army and bureaucracy composed of highly trained slaves. (Ch. 15)

**sumptuary laws** Laws that regulated the value and style of clothing and jewelry that various social groups could wear as well as the amount they could spend on celebrations. (Ch. 10)

**Test Act** Legislation passed by the English Parliament in 1673 to secure the position of the Anglican Church by stripping Puritans, Catholics, and other dissenters of the right to vote, preach, assemble, hold public office, and teach at or attend the universities. (Ch. 15)

**tetrarchy** Diocletian's four-part division of the Roman Empire. (Ch. 7)

**Torah** The first five books of the Hebrew Bible, containing the most important legal and ethical Hebrew texts; later became part of the Christian Old Testament. (Ch. 2)

**Treaty of Tordesillas** A 1494 treaty that settled competing claims to newly discovered Atlantic territories by giving Spain everything to the west of an imaginary line drawn down the Atlantic and giving Portugal everything to the east. (Ch. 14)

**Treaty of Verdun** Treaty signed in 843 by Charlemagne's grandsons dividing the Carolingian Empire into three parts and setting the pattern for political boundaries in Europe still in use today. (Ch. 8)

**tribunes** Plebeian-elected officials; tribunes brought plebeian grievances to the Senate for resolution and protected plebeians from the arbitrary conduct of patrician magistrates. (Ch. 5)

**troubadours** Poets who wrote and sang lyric verses celebrating love, desire, beauty, and gallantry. (Ch. 10)

**tyranny** Rule by one man who took over an existing government, generally by using his wealth to gain a political following. (Ch. 3)

**Union of Utrecht** The alliance of seven northern provinces (led by Holland) that declared its independence from Spain and formed the United Provinces of the Netherlands. (Ch. 13)

**vassal** A warrior who swore loyalty and service to a noble in exchange for land, protection, and support. (Ch. 8)

**vernacular literature** Writings in the author's local dialect, that is, in the everyday language of the region. (Ch. 10)

**viceroyalties** The name for the four administrative units of Spanish possessions in the Americas: New Spain, Peru, New Granada, and La Plata. (Ch. 14)

**virtù** The quality of being able to shape the world according to one's own will. (Ch. 12)

**wergeld** Compensatory payment for death or injury set in many barbarian law codes. (Ch. 7)

**Yahweh** The sole god in the Jewish religion. (Ch. 2)

**Zoroastrianism** Religion based on the ideas of Zoroaster that stressed devotion to the god Ahuramazda alone and that emphasized the individual's responsibility to choose between good and evil. (Ch. 2)

# INDEX

Catholic Church (*continued*)
    in southern Germany, 371, 382
    in Spain, 358, 436(*i*)
    state and, 247(*d*)
    Thirty Years' War and, 428
    on usury, 277
Catholic Counter-Reformation. *See*
    Counter-Reformation
Catholic Enlightenment, 478
Catholic League, 428
Catholic Reformation (Counter-Reformation).
    *See* Counter-Reformation (Catholic
    Reformation)
**Cati, Pasquale,** 381(*i*)
**Catiline** (Rome), 132–133
**Cato the Elder** (Marcus Cato), 126–127
**Cauchon, Pierre,** 307(*d*)
**Cavendish, Margaret,** 472
Cave paintings, 6
Cayenne, 409
Celebrations, Christianity and, 192
Celibacy
    Christian, 179
    clerical, 244, 361, 365, 371
    Luther and Zwingli on, 361, 365
Celtic peoples, 181, 182, 186(*i*). *See also* Gaul
    and Gauls
    Christianity of, 192
    in Gaul and Britain, 187–191
    mythology of, 188
    religion of, 186
    Rome and, 114, 159, 189(*i*)
Cenobitic monasticism, 178
Censors (Rome), 127
Central Asia. *See also* specific locations
    alphabet in, 36
    nomads from, 189–190
Central Europe. *See also* specific locations
    Black Death in, 297–298
    Christianity in, 257
    in High Middle Ages, 235–236
    lifestyle in, 426
    Magyars from, 218, 224
    plague in, 297–298
    Roman Empire and, 144
Centralization
    Hellenistic, 94
    in High Middle Ages, 258
    state-building and, 230, 232–240, 429,
    439
Centuriate Assembly (Rome), 117
*Ceremonies and Customs of all the
    Peoples of the World* (Picart),
    477(*i*)
**Cerialis** (Rome), on Pax Romana, 149(*b*)
Ceuta, Morocco, 398
Chain mail, 189(*i*)
Châlons, battle at, 190
**Champlain, Samuel de,** 408
*Chansons de geste,* 285
Chapels, Renaissance wealth and,
    341, 344
Chariots, 24, 78, 156, 158, 196(*b*)
**Charlemagne,** 209, 211–214
    Carolingian Renaissance and, 214–215
    conquests by (768–814), 211(*m*)
    coronation of, 212–214

feudalism after, 225
Hildegard of the Vinzgau and, 213(*b*)(*i*)
marriages of, 212, 213(*b*)
successors to, 218
**Charles I** (England), 449, 450–452, 450(*d*),
    451(*i*)
**Charles I** (Spain). *See* Charles V (Holy
    Roman Empire; Charles I of Spain)
**Charles II** (England), 453–454
**Charles II** (Spain), 316(*i*), 436, 436(*i*)
**Charles III** (Spain), 409
**Charles IV** (France), 302
**Charles V** (Holy Roman Empire; Charles I
    of Spain)
    abdication by, 371, 384, 410, 413, 419
    empire of, 353, 369(*m*)
    exploration and, 402
    Henry VIII and, 371
    Luther and, 361
    Netherlands under, 384
    papacy and, 370
    sack of Rome under, 330
**Charles VII** (France), 305, 306, 350
**Charles VIII** (France), 330
**Charles XII** (Sweden), 444–445
**Charles Martel,** 210
**Charles the Bald** (Franks), 180(*i*), 218
**Charles the Great.** *See* Charlemagne
**Charles the Simple** (Franks), 218–219
Charters. *See also* Magna Carta
    of Medina, 202–203
Chartres Cathedral, female donor to, 242(*i*)
**Chaucer, Geoffrey,** 320, 320(*i*)
Chemistry, 470
*Chess Game, The* (Anguissola), 347(*i*)
Chieftains, of barbarian tribes, 182
Childbearing
    in Middle Ages, 267–268
    in Roman Empire, 151
Childbirth. *See also* Births and birthrate;
    Midwives
    Hellenistic medicine and, 103
    in Middle Ages, 266, 270–271
    in Renaissance, 325(*i*)
Children. *See also* Families
    abandonment of, 268
    in Egypt, 23–24
    Hellenistic, 94
    in Jewish society, 39–42
    literacy of, 320
    in Middle Ages, 266, 267–268, 267(*i*)
    in Rome, 122, 155
    Spartan, 64
**Chilperic** (Merovingian), 210
China
    Columbus and, 401
    economy in, 392
    Enlightenment attitudes toward, 480
    exploration by, 392
    Hellenism and, 89
    navigation technology from, 397
    papermaking in, 339
    plague in 1890s, 296
    Roman trade and, 162
    silver and, 414
    trade and, 275, 392
**Chinggis Khan,** Crusades and, 253

*Chinos,* 415(*b*)
Chivalry, 240–241
Choir monks, 248
Cholula, Mexico, 403
**Chrétien de Troyes,** 287
**Christ.** *See* Jesus of Nazareth
Christendom, 210, 257. *See also* Christianity
**Christian III** (Denmark-Norway), 371
Christian Church. *See* Christianity; Protestant
    Reformation; Reformation; specific
    churches
Christian humanists, 337–338, 356, 363, 379
Christianity. *See also* Cathedrals; Church(es);
    Jesus of Nazareth; Missions and mis-
    sionaries; Orthodox Church; Refor-
    mation; Saint(s); specific groups
    in 16th century, 358
    Arian, 175, 191
    of barbarian peoples, 186, 190
    Black Death and, 299
    Carolingians and, 214–215
    Charlemagne and, 211
    childbirth and, 271
    church hierarchy in, 165, 176, 373
    classical culture and, 178–179
    Columbus and, 400, 401
    conversion to, 164, 165, 417–419, 418(*d*)
    in Crusades, 230, 251–257, 254–255(*d*)
    in eastern Europe, 222
    in England, 191–192, 371–374, 453
    expansion of, 256–257
    Great Schism and, 308–310
    growth of, 162–166, 176–180
    in Iberian Peninsula, 206, 237–238,
    351–352
    institutions of, 165
    in Ireland, 191
    Islam and, 203, 207–208
    marriage and, 179, 417
    in Middle Ages, 268–272
    Muslims and, 207–208
    Nestorian, 175
    Nicene, 175
    Ottoman Turks and, 379, 447
    reconquista and, 237
    reforms of, 356, 358
    rise of, 140
    in Roman Empire, 162–166, 170, 172,
    174, 356
    saints and sacraments in, 180, 358, 361,
    367, 379
    schisms in, 175, 308–310
    in Spain, 206, 207, 208
    spread of, 163–164, 174(*m*), 382, 418(*d*)
    usury and, 270
    views of Muslims and, 208
    women and, 164, 165, 178, 179, 215, 385
**Christine de Pizan,** 348–349
Church(es). *See also* Christianity; Religion(s);
    specific religions
    in High Middle Ages, 287–288, 288(*i*)
    in medieval villages, 263, 268
    in Middle Ages (High), 308
    Protestants vs. Catholics on, 361
    state and, 176, 309, 365
Church councils. *See* Councils; specific
    councils

**Enlil** (god), 11, 13
**Ennion** (Rome), glass beaker by, 161*(i)*
Enslaved peoples. *See* Slaves and slavery
Entertainment
    in Middle Ages, 280, 280*(i)*
    in Rome, 156–158, 159–160, 159*(i)*
Environment and environmentalism
    climate change and, 294–295, 426
    in Paleolithic period, 6
Ephors (overseers), 64
Epic literature. *See also* Philosophy; specific
      works
    *Beowulf* as, 215–217, 217*(d)*
    *Epic of Gilgamesh*, 14, 47
    of Hesiod, 56
    of Homer, 56, 59–61, 60*(d)*
**Epicurus** and Epicureanism, 99
Epidemics. *See also* Disease; specific condi-
      tions; specific diseases
    Columbian exchange and, 411
    Justinian plague as, 197, 296
    population and, 411
Epirus, 114, 115
Epitaphs, in Rome, 155
*Epitome of Military Science* (Vegetius), 147*(d)*
Equality. *See also* Rights; Women
    in barbarian society, 183
    in Sparta, 64
**Equiano, Olaudah,** 481
Equites class, in Roman Empire, 142
Eras. *See* specific eras
**Erasistratus,** 103
**Erasmus, Desiderius,** 338–339, 356, 379
**Eratosthenes,** 101
Eremitical monasticism, 178
**Esarhaddon** (Assyria), 35*(b)*
*Essay Concerning Human Understanding*
    (Locke), 473–474
Essays, of Montaigne, 420–421
Estates (land)
    in Rome, 128, 159
    women managers of, 242
Estates (assemblies), Dutch, 449, 454
Estates General (France), 432
Estates of Burgundy, 434*(d)*
Estonia, Russia and, 445
**Ethelbert** (Kent), 192
Ethics. *See also* Morality
    of Jewish monotheism, 39
Ethiopia, Hellenistic geographers and, 101
Ethnic groups. *See also* specific groups
    barbarian, 181–182
    in Europe, 319
    in Middle Ages, 319–320
    mixing of, 419
Etruria, 114
Etruscans, 109*(i)*, 110, 111–112, 111*(m)*,
    112*(i)*, 113, 114
EU. *See* European Union
Euboea, 56
Eucharist (Lord's Supper), 165, 269, 361, 364*(b)*
**Euclid,** 101, 462
"Eulogy for Murdia, The," 124*(d)*
Euphrates River region, 10, 15, 32, 48
**Euripides,** 72, 73*(b)*
Europe and Europeans. *See also* European
    Union (EU); specific locations

Africa and, 409
    barbarian migrations and, 187–191
    Black Death in, 296–298, 298*(m)*
    Carolingian Empire in, 210–217
    Christianity and, 176–179
    Columbian exchange and, 411
    in early Middle Ages, 200
    ethnic diversity and, 319
    expansion of, 390, 396, 398, 417–421
    exploration and conquest by, 395–403,
      399*(m)*
    humans in, 6
    invasions and migrations in, 218–224
    Islam and, 218, 224
    Jesuits in, 381, 382
    North American claims by, 403, 406–409
    after Peace of Utrecht, 436, 437*(m)*
    political and economic decentralization in,
      224–226
    religious divisions of (ca. 1555), 380*(m)*
    Renaissance in, 324
    after Thirty Years' War, 428, 429*(m)*
    trade in, 276*(m)*, 390
    unions with indigenous peoples and, 410,
      411
    voyages of discovery by, 395–403, 399*(m)*
    West and, 4
    witches and witchcraft in, 382, 384–386
European Union (EU), Charlemagne and,
    211
Eurymedon (Kopru) River region, 159
**Eurysaces, Marcus Vergilius** (Rome),
    128*(i)*
**Eusebius** (bishop), 174
Evolution, human, 6
Exchange. *See* Culture(s); Trade
Exchequer (England), 232, 258
Excommunication
    Gregory VII on, 244
    of Henry IV (Holy Roman Empire), 244
    of Luther, 361
Exodus (Hebrew), 37, 37*(m)*
Expansion. *See also* Exploration; Imperialism;
      specific countries
    Assyrian, 44
    of Christianity, 256–257
    Crusades and, 256
    English, 402
    Etruscan, 112
    European, 390, 396, 398, 417–421
    French, 302, 350, 350*(m)*, 402–403, 436
    Greek, 62, 110
    Hittite, 27
    Muslim, 202–203, 437, 480
    political, 232
    Prussian, 440, 486, 488*(m)*
    of Rome, 119, 120*(m)*, 122–127,
      144–150, 145*(m)*
    of Russia, 441, 442*(m)*, 443, 444, 488–489
    Spartan, 63, 64*(m)*
Expeditions. *See also* Exploration
    scientific, 467–468
Experimental method, 464, 469, 470, 472
Experimentation, in Scientific Revolution,
    461*(i)*, 464, 470
Exploration. *See also* Expansion; Voyages
    in Atlantic Ocean region, 394–395, 398

    by China, 392
    by Columbus, 396, 399–401, 400–401*(d)*,
      401*(m)*
    by England, 402
    Enlightenment and, 480
    European, 395–403, 399*(m)*
    by France, 402–403, 438
    Genoese, 394–395
    Greek, 62
    by Portugal, 393, 396, 398–399
    reasons for, 396
    by Spain, 396, 399–402
    technology and, 396–397
    by Vespucci, 402
Exports. *See also* Trade
    Phoenician, 34
Extinction, of hominids, 6
Extreme unction, 271

Fairs, after Hundred Years' War, 306
Faith. *See also* Religion(s)
    reason and, 309, 320, 478
    salvation by, 359, 361
Families. *See also* Marriage
    in 17th century, 426
    ancient, 9
    barbarian, 182
    Carolingian, 212
    in Egypt, 23–24, 24*(i)*
    Hammurabi on, 18
    Jewish (Hebrew), 38–43, 43*(d)*, 477*(i)*
    in Middle Ages, 266
    Puritan, 453*(i)*
    Roman, 122–125, 128, 151–152, 155
    Spartan, 64–65
*Family of Henry Chorley, Haberdasher of
    Preston, The* (painting), 453*(i)*
Famine
    in 17th century, 426
    in Middle Ages, 266, 292, 294*(i)*, 295
    population and, 426
Far East. *See* Asia; specific locations
Farms and farming. *See also* Agriculture;
      Manors and manorialism; Peasants;
      Serfs and serfdom
    ancient, 9
    barbarian, 182
    in Egypt, 23, 23*(d)*
    in Hammurabi's code, 18
    Hellenistic, 93–94
    in Mesopotamia, 10
    Roman, 123, 167, 172
Fascism, Etruscan fasces and, 113
**Fastrada** (wife of Charlemagne), 213*(b)*
Fathers. *See also* Families
    Roman, 122
Fealty, oaths of, 234*(b)*
**Fedele, Cassandra,** "Oration on Learning,"
    335*(d)*
**Ferdinand I** (Holy Roman Empire), 371
**Ferdinand II** (Holy Roman Empire), 439
**Ferdinand III** (Holy Roman Empire), 439
**Ferdinand and Isabella** (Spain), 351–353,
    353*(b)*, 396, 402
    Columbus and, 400*(d)*, 401
    Holy Roman Empire and, 368
Ferrara, as city-state, 328

Fertile Crescent, 7. *See also* Mesopotamia; Middle East; Near East; Sumer and Sumerians; specific peoples
    cultural exchange in, 18
    Egypt and, 22–23
Fertility, in Middle Ages, 266
Fertilizers, 123
Feudalism, 225. *See also* Middle Ages
    barbarian society and, 183
Feudal law, 186
**Ficino, Marsilio,** 331, 337
Fief, 225
Finance(s)
    in Crusades, 253
    in England, 232, 239
    in France, 234
    Merovingian, 209–210
Finland, Christianity in, 257
Fire
    in medieval cities, 278
    in Roman cities, 156
First Crusade, 252–253, 252(m), 256
First Intermediate Period (Egypt), 21–22
First Messenian War, 63
First Punic War, 119
First Triumvirate (Rome), 133–134
Fish and fishing industry
    in Canada, 403
    in Mesopotamia, 11
    in Middle Ages, 267
    in Spain, 201(i)
Five good emperors (Rome), 153
Five Pillars of Islam, 204
Flagellants, 299
Flanders. *See also* Holland; Low Countries
    business in, 278
    France and, 303, 436
    peasants in, 295, 312, 316
    Renaissance painters in, 342
    towns in, 273, 316
    trade and, 275, 303
Flavian Bill, Cicero on, 131(d)
Flavian dynasty (Rome), 152, 153, 153(f), 154
Fleas, plague spread and, 296
Flemish language and people. *See* Flanders
Floods
    in Mesopotamia, 11
    of Nile, 20, 20(d)
Florence
    banks in, 326
    as city-state, 326, 328, 328(d)
    growth of, 326, 330
    judicial inquiry of labor organizer in, 315(d)
    Medici family in, 329, 330, 337, 345
    plague in, 297, 300(d)
    Renaissance arts in, 341, 345
    republic in, 329
    same-sex relations in, 318, 330
    Savonarola in, 330, 330(i)
*Florentine Codex,* 405(d)
Food(s). *See also* Agriculture; Diet (food); Grain; Population; Spice trade
    ancient, 6
    of Columbian exchange, 411
    in Egypt, 23

in Middle Ages, 266, 312
population and, 8, 62
riots over, 427
in Rome, 123, 125, 156
Foragers, 2–3, 6, 8, 9
Force. *See* Violence; Weapons
Forests, on manors, 263
Fortuna (fate), 337
Foundation myths, Roman, 112
Foundlings, 342
*Four Apostles, The* (Dürer), 363(i)
"Four Horsemen of the Apocalypse," 292
Fourth Crusade, 252(m), 253
Fourth Lateran Council (1215), 245, 246(i), 269
France. *See also* Paris; specific leaders and wars
    absolutism in, 428, 431–433, 434–435(d), 474
    Africa and, 409
    Albigensians and, 245
    Alsace and, 436
    architecture in, 287
    armed forces in, 350, 430, 433, 435(b), 436, 449
    Austria and, 436, 437(m)
    Black Death in, 297, 350
    Burgundy and, 182, 190, 306, 350, 434(d)
    Calvinism and, 374, 383
    Catholic Church in, 383, 432
    Charlemagne and, 211
    Christian humanism in, 337
    civil war in, 350, 431
    colonies of, 408, 409
    economy in, 426, 431, 436–438
    England and, 436
    enlightened absolutism and, 485
    Enlightenment in, 474–475
    expansion of, 302, 350, 350(m), 402–403, 436
    exploration by, 402–403, 438
    Flemish peasants and, 312
    government of, 233–234, 235(m)
    Great Schism and, 308
    Greece and, 62
    guild system in, 437
    Habsburgs, Burgundy, and, 368
    Habsburg-Valois wars and, 330, 370, 382
    Henry II (England) and, 232–233
    Hundred Years' War and, 302–308, 304(m)
    after Hundred Years' War, 306–308, 350
    Italy and, 330
    Jews in, 270, 300, 491
    judicial system in, 238
    kingdom of, 235(m)
    literature in, 285–287
    manors in, 263
    as modern state, 350
    monarchy in, 350, 474
    Muslims and, 202
    nationalism in, 307–308
    nobility in, 432
    Normandy and, 233–234, 305, 306
    papacy vs. monarchy in, 245–246
    peasants in, 316, 431
    Protestantism in, 383, 431, 432, 473

Prussia and, 436, 486
religion and, 382–384, 431, 432
Roman Catholic Church in, 383, 432
royal court in, 425(i), 432–433
Seven Years' War and, 486
Sicily and, 236
Spain and, 382, 436, 438
tariffs in, 437–438
textile industry in, 437
Thirty Years' War and, 428, 429(m), 431
trade and, 275
Vikings in, 218–222
Visigoths and, 190
wars under Louis XIV, 433, 436
**Francesco di Bernardone.** *See* Francis of Assisi (Saint)
Franche-Comté, 436
**Francis I** (France), 350, 382
Franciscans, 250, 417, 417(i), 418(d)
**Francis of Assisi** (Saint), 250
Frankish kingdom, 190–191, 209–214, 225. *See also* Carolingian Empire; Charlemagne; Franks
**Franklin, Benjamin,** 482
Franks, 182, 209–214. *See also* Frankish kingdom
    Agathias on, 181(d)
    Salian, 183–186
**Frederick I** (Barbarossa, Holy Roman Empire), 235–236, 245
**Frederick I** (Prussia), 441
**Frederick II** (Holy Roman Empire), 236, 236(m), 237(i)
**Frederick II** (the Great, Prussia)
    Enlightenment and, 485–486
    Jews and, 491
    on partition of Poland, 488(m), 489
    War of the Austrian Succession and, 486
**Frederick III** ("the Ostentatious") (Elector of Brandenburg). *See* Frederick I (Prussia)
**Frederick III** (Holy Roman Empire), 368
**Frederick William** (Great Elector, Brandenburg), 440–441
**Frederick William I** (the "Soldiers' King") (Prussia), 441, 441(i), 485
Freedom(s). *See also* Serfs and serfdom; Slaves and slavery
    for serfs, 262
    for slaves, 123–125
Freemasons, 485
Free people of color, in American colonies, 411
French and Indian War. *See* Seven Years' War
French Empire, Canada in, 438
French language, 158, 433, 474
French phase, of Thirty Years' War, 428
Frescoes
    Christian (England), 165(i)
    Croatian, during Black Death, 301(b)(i)
    Minoan, 58(i)
    Renaissance, 325(i), 344
    Roman, 114(i)
    women and, 346
Friars, 246, 250–251, 357(i), 359, 417–419
Frisians, Carolingians and, 210
**Frobisher, Martin,** 402

**Nicholas V** (Pope), 398
Nicias, Peace of, 67
Nigeria, iron smelting in, 32
Nike (goddess), 90*(i)*
Nile River region. *See also* specific locations
    Egypt and, 19–21, 20*(d)*, 21–22, 23
    Kushites in, 34
Nîmes, France, 157*(i)*
"Ninety-five Theses on the Power of
    Indulgences" (Luther), 360–361, 368
Nineveh, 15*(i)*, 44, 47
    battles at, 45*(i)*
**Noah** (Bible), 11
Nobility. *See also* Aristocracy; Counts
    in 17th century, 426
    in ancient societies, 9
    in armed forces, 445
    in barbarian society, 183
    Carolingian, 215, 218
    cathedral donation by, 242*(i)*
    chivalry and, 240–241
    Crusades and, 251
    in France, 432
    German, 365
    in High Middle Ages, 240–242
    in Holy Roman Empire, 244
    Hungarian, 379, 439
    in Italian Renaissance, 326–327, 341
    papacy and, 244–245
    peasants and, 365
    power and responsibility of, 242
    Prussian, 440, 441, 486
    in Renaissance, 326–327, 348
    Russian, 223, 442, 443, 445, 446,
        487–488
    Spartan, 64
    trade and, 275
    women in, 433
Nomads
    Bedouins as, 202
    Hebrews as, 36–37
    Huns and, 189–190
    Persians and, 50
Nongovernmental organizations (NGOs),
    Western Christian Church as, 177
Nonwhites. *See* Race and racism; White
    people
Norman Conquest (1066), 187, 302
Normandy
    England and, 230*(i)*, 232
    France and, 233–234, 305, 306
    in Hundred Years' War, 305, 306, 308
    Vikings in, 222
Normans, 206, 222, 224, 232*(i)*. *See also*
    Normandy; Vikings
    Sicily and, 236, 236*(m)*
North Africa
    Islam in, 202, 203, 205
    Justinian and, 194
    Phoenician colonies in, 34
    Rome and, 135
    trade in, 393, 395
    Vandals in, 190
North America. *See also* America(s); New
    World
    European claims in, 403, 406–409
    slaves in, 408

Vikings and, 224, 399
War of the Spanish Succession and,
    437*(m)*
Northern Europe. *See also* Christian humanists
    blacks in, 347
    Christianity in, 256
    exploration by, 402–403
    Great Famine in, 295
    Renaissance and, 342
    Roman expansion into, 159
Northmen. *See* Normandy; Vikings
Northumbria, learning in, 215–217, 216*(b)(i)*
Norway. *See also* Scandinavia
    Christianity in, 256–257, 371
    Protestant Reformation in, 371
    Vikings from, 218
Notre Dame Cathedral (Paris), 287, 288*(i)*
    fire in (2019), 288*(i)*
    school of, 282
Nova Scotia, 436
Novels. *See* Literature
Nubia
    cylinder sheath from, 32*(i)*
    Egypt and, 22, 33
    Hellenistic sculpture and, 92*(i)*
    Persia and, 49
Numerals, Arabic, 208
Numidia, Rome and, 121, 129
Nuns (Christian). *See also* Convents; Monks
    and monasteries
    Carolingian, 214–215
    Catholic Reformation and, 381
    Gregorian reforms and, 244
    in Ireland, 191
    lifestyle of, 248
    monastic revival and, 246
    Protestant Reformation and, 368
    Scholastica and, 178
Nursing. *See* Breast-feeding
Nutrition. *See* Diet (food); Food; Health

Oaths of fealty, 234*(b)*
Obsidian, 10
**Occam.** *See* William of Occam
Occult, astronomy and, 468
Occupations (work). *See also* Labor
    of Puritans, 452*(i)*
    status of, 348
Oceans. *See* specific ocean regions
**Octavia** (Antony's wife), 136*(b)*
**Octavian.** *See* Augustus
**Odoacer** (Ostrogoths), 190
*Odyssey* (Homer), 60, 61
*Oeconomicus* (Xenophon), 76*(d)*
*Oedipus at Colonus* (Sophocles), 72
*Oedipus the King* (Sophocles), 72
"Of Cannibals" (Montaigne), 420–421
*Of Natural Characters* (Hume), 481
**Olaf II** (Norway), 257
Old Babylonian period, 15
Old Church (Delft), 378*(b)(i)*
Old Kingdom (Egypt), 21, 22
Old Stone period. *See* Paleolithic (Old Stone) era
Old Testament, 36, 183*(i)*. *See also* Bible
    Assyrians in, 47
    Vulgate Bible and, 179
**Oleg** (Varangian), 223

Oligarchy
    in Dutch Republic, 454
    in Greece, 62, 68
    in Italian government, 327
    in Venice, 328
**Olivares, Count-Duke of** (Gaspar de
    Guzmán), 438
Olives, 93, 411
Olympic games, 66, 78
Olympus, Mount, 61, 75
*On Christian Liberty* (Luther), 362*(d)*
*On Crimes and Punishments* (Beccaria), 479,
    479*(i)*
*On Floating Bodies* (Archimedes), 102*(b)*
*On the Different Races of Man* (Kant), 481
*On the Immortality of the Soul* (Mendelssohn),
    490*(b)*
*On the Revolutions of the Heavenly Spheres*
    (Copernicus), 464
*On the Structure of the Human Body* (Vesalius),
    470, 471*(b)(i)*
Open-field system, 263–266
**Oppenheim, Moritz,** 490*(i)*
Oppian Law (Rome), 126
Optimates (Rome), 129
Oracles
    at Delphi, 49, 78, 90
    at Siwah, 85
"Oration on Learning" (Fedele), 335*(d)*
"Oration on the Dignity of Man" (Pico della
    Mirandola), 335*(d)*
Ordeal, trial by, 239
Orders. *See* Clergy; Estates (classes); Nobility;
    Peasants; Religious orders
Ordinances
    in Calvin's Geneva, 376*(d)*
    in Malmø, Denmark, 376*(d)*
    school, from Württemberg, 376–377*(d)*
*Oresteia, The* (Aeschylus), 72
Orient, 392. *See also* Asia
Original sin, 180
Orléans, battle at, 305–306, 308
**Orlov, Gregory,** 486
Orthodox Church, 258. *See also* Christianity
    Byzantine church as, 197
    Catholic Church and, 251
    monasteries in, 197
    in Russia, 442, 444
    Serbs and, 222
Oseberg ship, 221*(i)*, 222*(i)*
**Osiris** (god), 23, 50, 97, 97*(i)*
Ostia, 111
Ostrogoths, 182, 183, 188–189, 190, 191
**Oswiu** (Northumbria), 192
*Othello* (Shakespeare), 421
**Otto I** (Germany), 235, 256, 257
Ottoman Empire. *See also* Ottoman Turks;
    Turkey
    Egypt and, 392
    in 1566, 446*(m)*
    government of, 447
    Hungary and, 449
    military in, 447, 449
    religion and, 442, 447
    Russia and, 444, 488–489
    trade and, 393–394, 396, 449
    Transylvania and, 439, 449

# A History of Western Society: A Brief Overview

| | Government | Society and Economy |
|---|---|---|
| **3000 B.C.E.** | Emergence of first cities in Mesopotamia, ca. 3800<br>Unification of Egypt; Archaic Period, ca. 3100–2600<br>Old Kingdom of Egypt, ca. 2660–2180<br>Dominance of Akkadian empire in Mesopotamia, ca. 2331–2200<br>Middle Kingdom in Egypt, ca. 2080–1640 | Neolithic peoples rely on settled agriculture, while others pursue nomadic life, ca. 7000–3000<br>Expansion of Mesopotamian trade and culture into the modern Middle East and Turkey, ca. 2600 |
| **2000 B.C.E.** | Babylonian empire, ca. 2000–1595<br>Code of Hammurabi, ca. 1755<br>Hyksos invade Egypt, ca. 1640–1570<br>Hittite Empire, ca. 1600–1200<br>New Kingdom in Egypt, ca. 1570–1075 | First wave of Indo-European migrants, by ca. 2000<br>Extended commerce in Egypt, by ca. 2000<br>Horses introduced into Asia and North Africa, by ca. 2500 |
| **1500 B.C.E.** | Third Intermediate Period in Egypt, ca. 1070–712<br>Unified Hebrew kingdom under Saul, David, and Solomon, ca. 1025–925 | Use of iron increases in western Asia, by ca. 1300–1100<br>Second wave of Indo-European migrants, by ca. 1200<br>"Dark Age" in Greece, ca. 1100–800 |
| **1000 B.C.E.** | Hebrew kingdom divided into Israel and Judah, 925<br>Assyrian Empire, ca. 900–612<br>Phoenicians found Carthage, 813<br>Kingdom of Kush conquers and reunifies Egypt, ca. 800–700<br>Roman monarchy, ca. 753–509<br>Medes conquers Persia, 710<br>Babylon wins independence from Assyria, 626<br>Dracon issues law code at Athens, 621<br>Solon's reforms at Athens, ca. 594<br>Cyrus the Great conquers Medes, founds Persian Empire, 550<br>Persians complete conquest of ancient Near East, 521–464<br>Reforms of Cleisthenes in Athens, 508 | Phoenician seafaring and trading in the Mediterranean, ca. 900–550<br>First Olympic games, 776<br>Concentration of landed wealth in Greece, ca. 750–600<br>Greek overseas expansion, ca. 750–550<br>Beginning of coinage in western Asia, ca. 640 |
| **500 B.C.E.** | Persian wars, 499–479<br>Struggle of the Orders in Rome, ca. 494–287<br>Growth of the Athenian Empire, 478–431<br>Peloponnesian War, 431–404<br>Rome captures Veii, 396<br>Gauls sack Rome, 387<br>Roman expansion in Italy, 390–290<br>Philip II of Macedonia conquers Greece, 338<br>Conquests of Alexander the Great, 334–324<br>Punic Wars, 264–146<br>Reforms of the Gracchi, 133–121 | Growth of Hellenistic trade and cities, ca. 330–100<br>Beginning of Roman silver coinage, 269<br>Growth of slavery, decline of small farmers in Rome, ca. 250–100<br>Agrarian reforms of the Gracchi, 133–121 |

| Religion and Philosophy | Science and Technology | Arts and Letters |
|---|---|---|
| Growth of anthropomorphic religion in Mesopotamia, ca. 3000–2000<br><br>Emergence of Egyptian polytheism and belief in personal immortality, ca. 2660<br><br>Spread of Mesopotamian and Egyptian religious ideas as far north as modern Turkey and as far south as central Africa, ca. 2600 | Development of wheeled transport in Mesopotamia, by ca. 3000<br><br>Use of widespread irrigation in Mesopotamia and Egypt, ca. 3000<br><br>Construction of Stonehenge monument in England, ca. 2500<br><br>Construction of first pyramid in Egypt, ca. 2600 | Cuneiform and hieroglyphic writing, ca. 3200 |
| Emergence of Hebrew monotheism, ca. 1700<br><br>Mixture of Hittite and Near Eastern religious beliefs, ca. 1595 | Construction of first ziggurats in Mesopotamia, ca. 2100<br><br>Widespread use of bronze in ancient Near East, ca. 1900<br><br>Babylonian mathematical advances, ca. 1800 | *Epic of Gilgamesh*, ca. 1900 |
| Exodus of the Hebrews from Egypt into Palestine, ca. 1300–1200 | Hittites introduce iron technology, ca. 1400 | Phoenicians develop alphabet, ca. 1400<br><br>Naturalistic art in Egypt under Akhenaten, 1367–1350<br><br>Egyptian *Book of the Dead*, ca. 1300 |
| Era of the prophets in Israel, ca. 1100–500<br><br>Beginning of the Hebrew Bible, ca. 950–800<br><br>Intermixture of Etruscan and Roman religious cults, ca. 753–509<br><br>Growing popularity of local Greek religious cults, ca. 700 B.C.E.–337 C.E.<br><br>Introduction of Zoroastrianism, ca. 600<br><br>Babylonian Captivity of the Hebrews, 587–538 | Babylonian astronomical advances, ca. 750–400<br><br>Construction of Parthenon in Athens begins, 447 | Homer, traditional author of *Iliad* and *Odyssey*, ca. 800<br><br>Hesiod, author of *Theogony* and *Works and Days*, ca. 800<br><br>Aeschylus, first significant Athenian tragedian, ca. 525–456 |
| Pre-Socratic philosophers, ca. 500–400<br><br>Socrates executed, 399<br><br>Plato, student of Socrates, 427–347<br><br>Diogenes, leading proponent of cynicism, ca. 412–323<br><br>Aristotle, student of Plato, 384–322<br><br>Epicurus, founder of Epicurean philosophy, 340–270<br><br>Zeno, founder of Stoic philosophy, 335–262<br><br>Emergence of Mithraism, ca. 300<br><br>Greek cults brought to Rome, ca. 200<br><br>Spread of Hellenistic mystery religions, ca. 200–100 | Hippocrates, formal founder of medicine, ca. 430<br><br>Building of the Via Appia begins, 312<br><br>Aristarchos of Samos, advances in astronomy, ca. 310–230<br><br>Euclid codifies geometry, ca. 300<br><br>Herophilus, discoveries in medicine, ca. 300–250<br><br>Archimedes, works on physics and hydrologics, ca. 287–212 | Sophocles, tragedian whose plays explore moral and political problems, ca. 496–406<br><br>Herodotus, "father of history," ca. 485–425<br><br>Euripides, most personal of the Athenian tragedians, ca. 480–406<br><br>Thucydides, historian of Peloponnesian War, ca. 460–440<br><br>Aristophanes, greatest Athenian comic playwright, ca. 445–386 |

| Government | Society and Economy |
|---|---|
| **100 B.C.E.** | |
| Dictatorship of Sulla, 88–79 B.C.E. | Reform of the Roman calendar, 46 B.C.E. |
| Civil war in Rome, 88–31 B.C.E. | "Golden age" of Roman prosperity and vast increase in trade, 96–180 C.E. |
| Dictatorship of Caesar, 45–44 B.C.E. | |
| Principate of Augustus, 31 B.C.E.–14 C.E. | Growth of serfdom in Roman Empire, ca. 200–500 C.E. |
| "Five Good Emperors" of Rome, 96–180 C.E. | Economic contraction in Roman Empire, ca. 235–284 C.E. |
| "Barracks Emperors'" civil war, 235–284 C.E. | |
| **300 C.E.** | |
| Constantine removes capital of Roman Empire to Constantinople, ca. 315 | Barbarian migrations throughout western and northern Europe, ca. 378–600 |
| Visigoths defeat Roman army at Adrianople, 378 | |
| Bishop Ambrose asserts church's independence from the state, 380 | |
| Odoacer deposes last Roman emperor in the West, 476 | |
| Clovis issues Salic law of the Franks, ca. 490 | |
| **500** | |
| Law code of Justinian, 529 | Gallo-Roman aristocracy intermarries with Germanic chieftains, ca. 500–700 |
| Spread of Islam across Arabia, the Mediterranean region, Spain, North Africa, and Asia as far as India, ca. 630–733 | Decline of towns and trade in the West; agrarian economy predominates, ca. 500–1800 |
| **700** | |
| Charles Martel defeats Muslims at Tours, 732 | Height of Muslim commercial activity with western Europe, ca. 700–1300 |
| Pippin III anointed king of the Franks, 754 | |
| Charlemagne secures Frankish crown, r. 768–814 | |
| **800** | |
| Imperial coronation of Charlemagne, Christmas 800 | Invasions and unstable conditions lead to increase of serfdom in western Europe, ca. 800–900 |
| Treaty of Verdun divides Carolingian kingdom, 843 | |
| Viking, Magyar, and Muslim invasions, ca. 850–1000 | Height of Byzantine commerce and industry, ca. 800–1000 |
| Establishment of Kievan Rus, ca. 900 | |
| **1000** | |
| Seljuk Turks conquer Muslim Baghdad, 1055 | Decline of Byzantine free peasantry, ca. 1025–1100 |
| Norman conquest of England, 1066 | Growth of towns and trade in the West, ca. 1050–1300 |
| Penance of Henry IV at Canossa, 1077 | *Domesday Book* in England, 1086 |
| **1100** | |
| Henry I of England, r. 1100–1135 | Henry I of England establishes the Exchequer, 1130 |
| Louis VI of France, r. 1108–1137 | Beginnings of the Hanseatic League, 1159 |
| Frederick I of Germany, r. 1152–1190 | |
| Henry II of England, r. 1154–1189 | |

| Religion and Philosophy | Science and Technology | Arts and Letters |
|---|---|---|
| Mithraism spreads to Rome, 27 B.C.E.–270 C.E.<br>Life of Jesus, ca. 3 B.C.E.–29 C.E. | Engineering advances in Rome, ca. 100 B.C.E.–180 C.E. | Flowering of Latin literature: Virgil, 70–19 B.C.E.; Livy, ca. 59 B.C.E.–17 C.E.; Ovid, 43 B.C.E.–17 C.E. |
| Constantine legalizes Christianity, 312<br>Theodosius declares Christianity the official state religion, 380<br>Donatist heretical movement at its height, ca. 400<br>St. Augustine, *Confessions*, ca. 390; *The City of God*, ca. 425<br>Clovis adopts Roman Christianity, 496 | Construction of Arch of Constantine, ca. 315 | St. Jerome publishes Latin *Vulgate*, late 4th c.<br>Byzantines preserve Greco-Roman culture, ca. 400–1000 |
| *Rule of St. Benedict*, 529<br>Life of the Prophet Muhammad, ca. 571–632<br>Pope Gregory the Great publishes *Dialogues, Pastoral Care, Moralia*, 590–604<br>Monasteries established in Anglo-Saxon England, ca. 600–700<br>Publication of the Qur'an, 651<br>Synod of Whitby, 664 | Using watermills, Benedictine monks exploit energy of fast-flowing rivers and streams, by 600<br>Heavy plow and improved harness facilitate use of multiple-ox teams; harrow widely used in northern Europe, by 600<br>Byzantines successfully use "Greek fire" in naval combat against Arab fleets attacking Constantinople, 673, 717 | Boethius, *The Consolation of Philosophy*, ca. 520<br>Justinian constructs church of Santa Sophia, 532–537 |
| Bede, *Ecclesiastical History of the English Nation*, ca. 700<br>Missionary work of St. Boniface in Germany, ca. 710–750<br>Iconoclastic controversy in Byzantine Empire, 726–843<br>Pippin III donates Papal States to the papacy, 756 | | Lindisfarne Gospel Book, ca. 700<br>*Beowulf*, ca. 700<br>Carolingian Renaissance, ca. 780–850 |
| Foundation of abbey of Cluny, 909<br>Byzantine conversion of Russia, late 10th c. | Stirrup and nailed horseshoes become widespread in combat, 900–1000<br>Paper (invented in China, ca. 150) enters Europe through Muslim Spain, ca. 900–1000 | Byzantines develop Cyrillic script, late 10th c. |
| Schism between Roman and Greek Orthodox churches, 1054<br>Lateran Council restricts election of pope to College of Cardinals, 1059<br>Pope Gregory VII, 1073–1085<br>Theologian Peter Abelard, 1079–1142<br>First Crusade, 1095–1099<br>Founding of Cistercian order, 1098 | Arab conquests bring new irrigation methods, cotton cultivation, and manufacture to Spain, Sicily, southern Italy, by 1000<br>Avicenna, Arab scientist, d. 1037 | Muslim musicians introduce lute, rebec (stringed instruments, ancestors of violin), ca. 1000<br>Romanesque style in architecture and art, ca. 1000–1200<br>*Song of Roland*, ca. 1095 |
| Universities begin, ca. 1100–1300<br>Concordat of Worms ends investiture controversy, 1122<br>Height of Cistercian monasticism, 1125–1175 | Europeans, copying Muslim and Byzantine models, construct castles with rounded towers and crenellated walls, by 1100 | Troubadour poetry, especially of Chrétien de Troyes, circulates widely, ca. 1100–1200<br>*Rubaiyat of Umar Khayyam*, ca. 1120<br>Dedication of abbey church of Saint-Denis launches Gothic style, 1144 |

| Government | Society and Economy |
|---|---|
| **1100 (CONT.)** Thomas Becket, archbishop of Canterbury, murdered 1170<br><br>Philip Augustus of France, r. 1180–1223 | |
| **1200** Spanish victory over Muslims at Las Navas de Tolosa, 1212<br><br>Frederick II of Germany and Sicily, r. 1212–1250<br><br>Magna Carta, charter of English political and civil liberties, 1215<br><br>Louis IX of France, r. 1226–1270<br><br>Mongols end Abbasid caliphate, 1258<br><br>Edward I of England, r. 1272–1307<br><br>Philip IV (the Fair) of France, r. 1285–1314 | European revival, growth of towns; agricultural expansion leads to population growth, ca. 1200–1300<br><br>Crusaders capture Constantinople (Fourth Crusade) and spur Venetian economy, 1204 |
| **1300** Philip IV orders arrest of Pope Boniface at Anagni, 1303<br><br>Hundred Years' War between England and France, 1337–1453<br><br>Political disorder in Germany, ca. 1350–1450<br><br>Merchant oligarchies or despots rule Italian city-states, ca. 1350–1550 | "Little ice age," European economic depression, ca. 1300–1450<br><br>Black Death appears ca. 1347; returns intermittently until ca. 1720<br><br>Height of the Hanseatic League, 1350–1450<br><br>Peasant and working-class revolts: Flanders, 1328; France, 1358; Florence, 1378; England, 1381 |
| **1400** Joan of Arc rallies French monarchy, 1429–1431<br><br>Medici domination of Florence begins, 1434<br><br>Princes in Germany consolidate power, ca. 1450–1500<br><br>Ottoman Turks under Mahomet II capture Constantinople, May 1453<br><br>Wars of the Roses in England, 1455–1471<br><br>Establishment of the Inquisition in Spain, 1478<br><br>Ferdinand and Isabella complete reconquista in Spain, 1492<br><br>French invasion of Italy, 1494 | Population decline, peasants' revolts, high labor costs contribute to decline of serfdom in western Europe, ca. 1400–1650<br><br>Flow of Balkan slaves into eastern Mediterranean, of African slaves into Iberia and Italy, ca. 1400–1500<br><br>Christopher Columbus reaches the Americas, 1492<br><br>Portuguese gain control of East Indian spice trade, 1498–1511 |
| **1500** Charles V, Holy Roman emperor, 1519–1556<br><br>Habsburg-Valois Wars, 1521–1559<br><br>Philip II of Spain, r. 1556–1598<br><br>Revolt of the Netherlands, 1566–1598<br><br>St. Bartholomew's Day massacre in France, 1572<br><br>English defeat of the Spanish Armada, 1588<br><br>Henry IV of France issues Edict of Nantes, 1598 | Consolidation of serfdom in eastern Europe, ca. 1500–1650<br><br>Balboa discovers the Pacific, 1513<br><br>Magellan's crew circumnavigates the earth, 1519–1522<br><br>Spain and Portugal gain control of regions of Central and South America, ca. 1520–1550<br><br>Peasants' Revolt in Germany, 1524–1525<br><br>"Time of Troubles" in Russia, 1598–1613 |

| Religion and Philosophy | Science and Technology | Arts and Letters |
|---|---|---|
| Aristotle's works translated into Latin, ca. 1140–1260<br>Third Crusade, 1189–1192<br>Pope Innocent III, height of the medieval papacy, 1198–1216 | Underground pipes with running water and indoor latrines installed in some monasteries, such as Clairvaux and Canterbury Cathedral Priory, by 1100; elsewhere rare until 1800<br>Windmill invented, ca. 1180 | |
| Founding of the Franciscan order, 1210<br>Fourth Lateran Council accepts seven sacraments, 1215<br>Founding of Dominican order, 1216<br>Thomas Aquinas, height of scholasticism, 1225–1274 | *Notebooks* of architect Villard de Honnecourt, a major source for Gothic engineering, ca. 1250<br>Development of double-entry bookkeeping in Florence and Genoa, ca. 1250–1340<br>Venetians purchase secrets of glass manufacture from Syria, 1277<br>Mechanical clock invented, ca. 1290 | *Parzifal, Roman de la rose, King Arthur and the Round Table* celebrate virtues of knighthood and chivalry, ca. 1200–1300<br>Height of Gothic style, ca. 1225–1300 |
| Pope Boniface VIII declares all Christians subject to the pope in *Unam Sanctam*, 1302<br>Babylonian Captivity of the papacy, 1309–1376<br>Theologian John Wyclif, ca. 1330–1384<br>Great Schism in the papacy, 1378–1417 | Edward III of England uses cannon in siege of Calais, 1346<br>Clocks in general use throughout Europe, by 1400 | Paintings of Giotto mark emergence of Renaissance movement in the arts, ca. 1305–1337<br>Dante, *Divine Comedy*, ca. 1310<br>Petrarch develops ideas of humanism, ca. 1350<br>Boccaccio, *The Decameron*, ca. 1350<br>Jan van Eyck, Flemish painter, 1366–1441<br>Brunelleschi, Florentine architect, 1377–1446<br>Chaucer, *Canterbury Tales*, ca. 1387–1400 |
| Council of Constance ends the schism in the papacy, 1414–1418<br>Pragmatic Sanction of Bourges affirms special rights of French crown over French church, 1438<br>Expulsion of Jews from Spain, 1492 | Water-powered blast furnaces operative in Sweden, Austria, the Rhine Valley, Liège, ca. 1400<br>Leonardo Fibonacci's *Liber Abaci* popularizes use of Hindu-Arabic numerals, important in rise of Western science, 1402<br>Paris and largest Italian cities pave streets, making street cleaning possible, ca. 1450<br>European printing and movable type, ca. 1450 | Height of Renaissance movement: Masaccio, 1401–1428; Botticelli, 1444–1510; Leonardo da Vinci, 1452–1519; Albrecht Dürer, 1471–1528; Michelangelo, 1475–1564; Raphael, 1483–1520 |
| Machiavelli, *The Prince*, 1513<br>More, *Utopia*, 1516<br>Luther, *Ninety-five Theses*, 1517<br>Henry VIII of England breaks with Rome, 1532–1534<br>Merici establishes Ursuline order for education of women, 1535<br>Loyola establishes Society of Jesus, 1540<br>Calvin establishes theocracy in Geneva, 1541<br>Council of Trent shapes essential character of Catholicism until the 1960s, 1545–1563<br>Peace of Augsburg, official recognition of Lutheranism, 1555 | Scientific revolution in western Europe, ca. 1540–1690: Copernicus, *On the Revolutions of the Heavenly Bodies*, 1543; Galileo, 1564–1642; Kepler, 1571–1630; Harvey, 1578–1657 | Erasmus, *The Praise of Folly*, 1509<br>Castiglione, *The Courtier*, 1528<br>Baroque movement in arts, ca. 1550–1725: Rubens, 1577–1640; Velasquez, 1599–1660<br>Shakespeare, West's most enduring and influential playwright, 1564–1616<br>Montaigne, *Essays*, 1598 |

| Government | Society and Economy |
|---|---|
| **1600** | |
| Thirty Years' War begins, 1618 | Chartering of British East India Company, 1600 |
| Richelieu dominates French government, 1624–1643 | English Poor Law, 1601 |
| Frederick William, Elector of Brandenburg, r. 1640–1688 | Chartering of Dutch East India Company, 1602 |
| English Civil War, 1642–1649 | Height of Dutch commercial activity, ca. 1630–1665 |
| Louis XIV, r. 1643–1715 | |
| Peace of Westphalia ends the Thirty Years' War, 1648 | |
| The Fronde in France, 1648–1660 | |
| **1650** | |
| Anglo-Dutch wars, 1652–1674 | Height of mercantilism in Europe, ca. 1650–1750 |
| Protectorate in England, 1653–1658 | Agricultural revolution in Europe, ca. 1650–1850 |
| Leopold I, Habsburg emperor, r. 1658–1705 | Principle of peasants' hereditary subjugation to their lords affirmed in Prussia, 1653 |
| English monarchy restored, 1660 | Colbert's economic reforms in France, ca. 1663–1683 |
| Ottoman siege of Vienna, 1683 | Cossack revolt in Russia, 1670–1671 |
| Glorious Revolution in England, 1688–1689 | |
| Peter the Great of Russia, r. 1689–1725 | |
| **1700** | |
| War of the Spanish Succession, 1701–1713 | Foundation of St. Petersburg, 1701 |
| Peace of Utrecht redraws political boundaries of Europe, 1713 | Last appearance of bubonic plague in western Europe, ca. 1720 |
| Frederick William I of Prussia, r. 1713–1740 | Growth of European population, ca. 1720–1789 |
| Louis XV of France, r. 1715–1774 | Enclosure movement in England, ca. 1730–1830 |
| Maria Theresa of Austria, r. 1740–1780 | |
| Frederick the Great of Prussia, r. 1740–1786 | |
| **1750** | |
| Seven Years' War, 1756–1763 | Growth of illegitimate births in Europe, ca. 1750–1850 |
| Catherine the Great of Russia, r. 1762–1796 | Industrial Revolution in western Europe, ca. 1780–1850 |
| Partition of Poland, 1772–1795 | Serfdom abolished in France, 1789 |
| Louis XVI of France, r. 1774–1792 | |
| American Revolution, 1775–1783 | |
| French Revolution, 1789–1799 | |
| Slave insurrection in Saint-Domingue, 1791 | |
| **1800** | |
| Napoleonic era, 1799–1815 | British takeover of India complete, 1805 |
| Haitian republic declares independence, 1804 | British slave trade abolished, 1807 |
| Congress of Vienna re-establishes political power after defeat of Napoleon, 1814–1815 | German Zollverein founded, 1834 |
| Greece wins independence from Ottoman Empire, 1830 | European capitalists begin large-scale foreign investment, 1840s |
| French conquest of Algeria, 1830 | Great Famine in Ireland, 1845–1851 |
| Revolution in France, 1830 | First public health law in Britain, 1848 |
| Great Britain: Reform Bill of 1832; Poor Law reform, 1834; Chartists, repeal of Corn Laws, 1838–1848 | |
| Revolutions in Europe, 1848 | |

| Religion and Philosophy | Science and Technology | Arts and Letters |
|---|---|---|
| Huguenot revolt in France, 1625 | Further development of scientific method: Bacon, *The Advancement of Learning*, 1605; Descartes, *Discourse on Method*, 1637 | Cervantes, *Don Quixote*, 1605, 1615<br>Flourishing of French theater: Molière, 1622–1673; Racine, 1639–1699<br>Golden age of Dutch culture, ca. 1625–1675: Rembrandt van Rijn, 1606–1669; Vermeer, 1632–1675 |
| Social contract theory: Hobbes, *Leviathan*, 1651; Locke, *Second Treatise on Civil Government*, 1690<br>Patriarch Nikon's reforms split Russian Orthodox Church, 1652<br>Test Act in England excludes Roman Catholics from public office, 1673<br>Revocation of Edict of Nantes, 1685<br>James II tries to restore Catholicism as state religion, 1685–1688 | Tull (1674–1741) encourages innovation in English agriculture<br>Newton, *Principia Mathematica*, 1687 | Construction of baroque palaces and remodeling of capital cities, central and eastern Europe, ca. 1650–1725<br>Bach, great late baroque German composer, 1685–1750<br>Enlightenment begins, ca. 1690: Fontenelle, *Conversations on the Plurality of Worlds*, 1686; Voltaire, French philosopher and writer whose work epitomizes Enlightenment, 1694–1778<br>Pierre Bayle, *Historical and Critical Dictionary*, 1697 |
| Wesley, founder of Methodism, 1703–1791<br>Montesquieu, *The Spirit of Laws*, 1748 | Newcomen develops steam engine, 1705<br>Charles Townsend introduces four-year crop rotation, 1730 | |
| Hume, *The Natural History of Religion*, 1755<br>Rousseau, *The Social Contract* and *Emile*, 1762<br>Fourier, French utopian socialist, 1772–1837<br>Papacy dissolves Jesuits, 1773<br>Smith, *The Wealth of Nations*, 1776<br>Church reforms of Joseph II in Austria, 1780s<br>Kant, *What Is Enlightenment?*, 1784<br>Reorganization of church in France, 1790s<br>Wollstonecraft, *A Vindication of the Rights of Woman*, 1792<br>Malthus, *Essay on the Principle of Population*, 1798 | Hargreaves's spinning jenny, ca. 1765<br>Arkwright's water frame, ca. 1765<br>Watt's steam engine promotes industrial breakthroughs, 1780s<br>Jenner's smallpox vaccine, 1796 | *Encyclopedia*, edited by Diderot and d'Alembert, published 1751–1765<br>Classical style in music, ca. 1770–1830: Mozart, 1756–1791; Beethoven, 1770–1827<br>Wordsworth, English romantic poet, 1770–1850<br>Romanticism in art and literature, ca. 1790–1850 |
| Napoleon signs Concordat with Pope Pius VII regulating Catholic Church in France, 1801<br>Spencer, Social Darwinist, 1820–1903<br>Comte, *System of Positive Philosophy*, 1830–1842<br>Height of French utopian socialism, 1830s–1840s<br>List, *National System of Political Economy*, 1841<br>Nietzsche, radical and highly influential German philosopher, 1844–1900<br>Marx, *Communist Manifesto*, 1848 | First railroad, Great Britain, 1825<br>Faraday studies electromagnetism, 1830–1840s | Staël, *On Germany*, 1810<br>Balzac, *The Human Comedy*, 1829–1841<br>Delacroix, *Liberty Leading the People*, 1830<br>Hugo, *The Hunchback of Notre Dame*, 1831 |

| | Government | Society and Economy |
|---|---|---|
| **1850** | Second Empire in France, 1852–1870<br>Crimean War, 1853–1856<br>Britain crushes Great Rebellion in India, 1857–1858<br>Unification of Italy, 1859–1870<br>U.S. Civil War, 1861–1865<br>Bismarck leads Germany, 1862–1890<br>Unification of Germany, 1864–1871<br>Britain's Second Reform Bill, 1867<br>Third Republic in France, 1870–1940 | Crédit Mobilier founded in France, 1852<br>Japan opened to European influence, 1853<br>Russian serfs emancipated, 1861<br>First Socialist International, 1864–1871 |
| **1875** | Congress of Berlin, 1878<br>European "scramble for Africa," 1880–1900<br>Britain's Third Reform Bill, 1884<br>Dreyfus affair in France, 1894–1899<br>Spanish-American War, 1898<br>South African War, 1899–1902 | Full property rights for women in Great Britain, 1882<br>Second Industrial Revolution; birthrate steadily declines in Europe, ca. 1880–1913<br>Social welfare legislation, Germany, 1883–1889<br>Second Socialist International, 1889–1914<br>Witte directs modernization of Russian economy, 1892–1899 |
| **1900** | Russo-Japanese War, 1904–1905<br>Revolution in Russia, 1905<br>Balkan wars, 1912–1913 | Women's suffrage movement, England, ca. 1900–1914<br>Social welfare legislation, France, 1904, 1910; Great Britain, 1906–1914<br>Agrarian reforms in Russia, 1907–1912 |
| **1914** | World War I, 1914–1918<br>Armenian genocide, 1915<br>Easter Rebellion, 1916<br>U.S. declares war on Germany, 1917<br>Bolshevik Revolution, 1917–1918<br>Treaty of Versailles, World War I peace settlement, 1919 | Planned economics in Europe, 1914<br>Auxiliary Service Law in Germany, 1916<br>Bread riots in Russia, March 1917 |
| **1920** | Mussolini seizes power in Italy, 1922<br>Stalin comes to power in U.S.S.R., 1927<br>Hitler gains power in Germany, 1933<br>Rome-Berlin Axis, 1936<br>Nazi-Soviet Non-Aggression Pact, 1939<br>World War II, 1939–1945 | New Economic Policy in U.S.S.R., 1921<br>Dawes Plan for reparations and recovery, 1924<br>Great Depression, 1929–1939<br>Rapid industrialization in U.S.S.R., 1930s<br>Start of Roosevelt's New Deal in U.S., 1933 |
| **1940** | United Nations founded, 1945<br>Decolonization of Asia and Africa, 1945–1960s<br>Cold War begins, 1947<br>Founding of Israel, 1948<br>Communist government in China, 1949<br>Korean War, 1950–1953<br>De-Stalinization of Soviet Union under Khrushchev, 1953–1964 | Holocaust, 1941–1945<br>Marshall Plan enacted, 1947<br>European economic progress, ca. 1950–1970<br>European Coal and Steel Community founded, 1952<br>European Economic Community founded, 1957 |

| Religion and Philosophy | Science and Technology | Arts and Letters |
|---|---|---|
| Decline in church attendance among working classes, ca. 1850–1914 | Modernization of Paris, ca. 1850–1870 | Realism in art and literature, ca. 1850–1870 |
| Mill, *On Liberty*, 1859 | Great Exhibition in London, 1851 | Flaubert, *Madame Bovary*, 1857 |
| Pope Pius IX, *Syllabus of Errors*, denounces modern thoughts, 1864 | Freud, founder of psychoanalysis, 1856–1939 | Tolstoy, *War and Peace*, 1869 |
| Marx, *Das Capital*, 1867 | Darwin, *On the Origin of Species*, 1859 | Impressionism in art, ca. 1870–1900 |
| Doctrine of papal infallibility, 1870 | Pasteur develops germ theory of disease, 1860s | Eliot (Mary Ann Evans), *Middlemarch*, 1872 |
| | Suez Canal opened, 1869 | |
| | Mendeleev develops periodic table, 1869 | |
| Growth of public education in France, ca. 1880–1900 | Emergence of modern immunology, ca. 1875–1900 | Zola, *Germinal*, 1885 |
| Growth of mission schools in Africa, 1890–1914 | Electrical industry: lighting and streetcars, ca. 1880–1900 | Kipling, "The White Man's Burden," 1899 |
| | Trans-Siberian Railroad, 1890s | |
| | Marie Curie, discovery of radium, 1898 | |
| Separation of church and state in France, 1901–1905 | Planck develops quantum theory, ca. 1900 | Modernism in art and literature, ca. 1900–1929 |
| Hobson, *Imperialism*, 1902 | First airplane flight, 1903 | Conrad, *Heart of Darkness*, 1902 |
| Schweitzer, *Quest of the Historical Jesus*, 1906 | Einstein develops theory of special relativity, 1905–1910 | Cubism in art, ca. 1905–1930 |
| | | Proust, *Remembrance of Things Past*, 1913–1927 |
| Keynes, *Economic Consequences of the Peace*, 1919 | Submarine warfare introduced, 1915 | Spengler, *The Decline of the West*, 1918 |
| | Ernest Rutherford splits atom, 1919 | |
| Emergence of modern existentialism, 1920s | "Heroic age of physics," 1920s | Gropius, Bauhaus, 1920s |
| Revival of Christianity, 1920s–1930s | First major public radio broadcasts in Great Britain and U.S., 1920 | Dadaism and surrealism, 1920s |
| Wittgenstein, *Essay on Logical Philosophy*, 1922 | First talking movies, 1930 | Woolf, *Jacob's Room*, 1922 |
| Heisenberg's principle of uncertainty, 1927 | Radar system in England, 1939 | Joyce, *Ulysses*, 1922 |
| | | Eliot, *The Waste Land*, 1922 |
| | | Remarque, *All Quiet on the Western Front*, 1929 |
| | | Picasso, *Guernica*, 1937 |
| De Beauvoir, *The Second Sex*, 1949 | U.S. drops atomic bombs on Japan, 1945 | Cultural purge in Soviet Union, 1946–1952 |
| Communists fail to break Catholic Church in Poland, 1950s | Big Science in U.S., ca. 1945–1965 | Van der Rohe, Lake Shore Apartments, 1948–1951 |
| | Watson and Crick discover structure of DNA molecule, 1953 | Orwell, *1984*, 1949 |
| | Russian satellite in orbit, 1957 | Pasternak, *Doctor Zhivago*, 1956 |
| | | "Beat" movement in U.S., late 1950s |

| | Government | Society and Economy |
|---|---|---|
| **1960** | Building of Berlin Wall, 1961 | Civil rights movement in U.S., 1960s |
| | U.S. involvement in Vietnam War, 1964–1973 | Stagflation, 1970s |
| | Student rebellion in France, 1968 | Feminist movement, 1970s |
| | Soviet tanks end Prague Spring, 1968 | Collapse of postwar monetary system, 1971 |
| | Détente between U.S. and U.S.S.R., 1970s | OPEC oil price increases, 1973, 1979 |
| | Soviet occupation of Afghanistan, 1979–1989 | |
| **1980** | U.S. military buildup, 1980s | Growth of debt in the West, 1980s |
| | Solidarity in Poland, 1980 | Economic crisis in Poland, 1988 |
| | Unification of Germany, 1989 | Maastricht Treaty proposes monetary union, 1990 |
| | Revolutions in eastern Germany, 1989–1990 | European Community becomes European Union, 1993 |
| | Persian Gulf War, 1990–1991 | Migration to western Europe increases, 1990s |
| | Dissolution of Soviet Union, 1991 | Former Soviet bloc nations adopt capitalist economies, 1990s |
| | Civil war in Yugoslavia, 1991–2001 | |
| | Separatist war breaks out in Chechnya, 1991 | |
| **2000** | Vladimir Putin elected president of Russian Federation, 2000 | Same-sex marriage legalized in the Netherlands, 2001 |
| | Terrorist attacks on U.S., Sept. 11, 2001 | Euro enters circulation, 2002 |
| | War in Afghanistan begins, 2001 | Voters reject new European Union constitution, 2005 |
| | Iraq War, 2003–2011 | Immigrant riots in France, 2005, 2009 |
| | Angela Merkel elected chancellor of Germany, 2005 | Worldwide financial crisis begins, 2008 |
| | Barack Obama serves as U.S. president, 2009–2017 | European financial crisis intensifies, 2010 |
| | Growing popularity of anti-immigrant, far-right political parties across Europe, 2010s | Anti-austerity protests across Europe begin, 2010 |
| | NATO intervenes in Libyan civil war, 2011 | Arab Spring uprisings in the Middle East and North Africa, 2011 |
| | Al-Qaeda leader Osama bin Laden killed, 2011 | France legalizes same-sex marriage, 2013 |
| | Vladimir Putin re-elected, 2012; again in 2018 | Occupy Movement begins in the United States, spreads to Europe, 2011 |
| | Ex-NSA contractor Edward Snowden leaks classified U.S. government information, 2013 | Greek debt crisis, 2015 |
| | Russia annexes Crimea (southern Ukraine) and supports pro-Russian Ukrainian rebels, 2014 | Massive influx of refugees from the Middle East, 2015–2016 |
| | Growth of Islamic State, 2014–2015 | Refugee crisis undermines European unity, 2016 |
| | Terrorist attacks in Paris organized by Islamic State kill 130 people, 2015 | Austria legalizes same-sex marriage, 2019 |
| | Brexit referendum, 2016 | European Union home to about 500 million citizens, 2019 |
| | Terrorist attacks in London, Barcelona, St. Petersburg, and other European cities, organized by Islamic State, kill at least 115 people, 2017 | |
| | Donald Trump serves as U.S. president, takes hard line against NATO and European Allies, 2017– | |
| | Anti-immigrant, anti-EU conservative political parties control governments in Poland, Hungary, Italy, elsewhere, 2018 | |
| | United Kingdom receives extension on date of Brexit, 2019 | |

| Religion and Philosophy | Science and Technology | Arts and Letters |
|---|---|---|
| Second Vatican Council announces sweeping Catholic reforms, 1962–1965<br><br>Pope John II, 1978–2005 | European Council for Nuclear Research founded, 1960<br><br>Space race, 1960s<br><br>Russian cosmonaut first to orbit globe, 1961<br><br>American astronaut first person on moon, 1969 | The Beatles, 1960s<br><br>Solzhenitsyn, *One Day in the Life of Ivan Denisovich*, 1962<br><br>Carson, *Silent Spring*, 1962<br><br>Friedan, *The Feminine Mystique*, 1963<br><br>Servan-Schreiber, *The American Challenge*, 1967 |
| Revival of religion in Soviet Union, 1985–<br><br>Growth of Islam in Europe, 1990s<br><br>Fukuyama proclaims "end of history," 1991 | Reduced spending on Big Science, 1980s<br><br>Computer revolution continues, 1980s–1990s<br><br>U.S. Genome Project begins, 1990<br><br>First World Wide Web server and browser, 1991<br><br>Pentium processor invented, 1993<br><br>First genetically cloned sheep, 1996 | Consolidation and popularization of postmodernism in fine arts and literature, 1980s<br><br>Solzhenitsyn returns to Russia, 1994; dies 2008<br><br>Author Salman Rushdie exiled from Iran, 1989<br><br>Gehry, Guggenheim Museum, Bilbao, 1997 |
| Number of Europeans who claim to be religious continues to decline, 2000–<br><br>Sexual abuse scandal challenges Catholic Church across the globe, 2000–<br><br>UN announces first World Philosophy Day to "honor philosophical reflection" across the globe, 2002<br><br>Ramadan, *Western Muslims and the Future of Islam*, 2004<br><br>Pontificate of Benedict XVI, 2005–2013<br><br>Jorge Mario Bergoglio elected as Pope Francis, 2013<br><br>Noted Slovenian philosopher Slavoj Žižek critiques contemporary Western notions of freedom, 2014 | Google emerges as popular Internet search engine, 2000s<br><br>Growing concern about global warming, 2000s<br><br>First hybrid car, 2003<br><br>Facebook founded, 2004<br><br>YouTube founded, 2005<br><br>iPhone introduced to consumers, 2007<br><br>Copenhagen summit on climate change, 2009<br><br>Paris summit on climate change sets Paris Agreement to limit $CO_2$ emissions, 2015<br><br>UN Climate Control conference in Katowice, Poland, updates Paris Agreement, 2018 | Middle East conflict leads to looting and destruction of archaeological sites and museums, 2000–<br><br>Growing importance of artists and art centers outside of Europe: in Latin America, Africa, and Asia, 2000–<br><br>Digital methods of production and display grow increasingly popular in works of art, 2000–<br><br>Movies and books exploring clash between immigrants and host cultures popular: *Bend It Like Beckham*, 2002; *The Namesake*, 2003; *White Teeth*, 2003; *The Class*, 2008; *Brooklyn*, 2015<br><br>Memorial to the Murdered Jews of Europe opens in Berlin, 2005 |

# CONTEMPORARY EUROPE

**NORWAY**
Bergen
Oslo

**SWEDEN**
Göteborg
Stockholm

SCOTLAND
Edinburgh
Glasgow

NORTHERN IRELAND
Belfast

IRELAND
Dublin

*North Sea*

Aarhus
**DENMARK**
Copenhagen

*Baltic Sea*

**RUSSIA**
Kaliningrad
Gdańsk

UNITED KINGDOM
Liverpool
Birmingham
WALES
ENGLAND
*Thames R.*
London

**NETHERLANDS**
Amsterdam
Rotterdam

Berlin

*Elbe R.*

**POLAND**
Warsaw

*Vistula R.*

Antwerp
Brussels
**BELGIUM**
Luxembourg
**LUXEMBOURG**

Paris
*Seine R.*

*Loire R.*

*ATLANTIC OCEAN*

W  N  E  S

**GERMANY**
Frankfurt

*Rhine R.*

Prague
**CZECH REP.**
Brno

Kraków

**SLOVAKIA**
Vienna
Bratislava
Miskolc

*Oder R.*

*Bay of Biscay*

**FRANCE**
Lyons

*Rhône R.*

**LIECHTENSTEIN**
Zürich
Bern
Vaduz
Innsbruck
**SWITZERLAND**
A L P S
Munich
**AUSTRIA**
Graz

*Danube R.*

Budapest
**HUNGARY**

Milan
*Po R.*

**SLOVENIA**
Ljubljana

Zagreb
**CROATIA**

Belgrade
**BOSNIA AND HERZEGOVINA**
Sarajevo
**SERBIA**

Oporto

**PYRENEES**
**ANDORRA**
Andorra la Vella

Marseilles
**MONACO**

San Marino
**SAN MARINO**
**APENNINES**

Split
*Adriatic Sea*

Podgorica
**MONTENEGRO**

**PORTUGAL**
Lisbon
Madrid
**SPAIN**

Barcelona

*Corsica*

Rome
**ITALY**

Tiranë
**ALBANIA**

Seville

Naples

*Sardinia*

*Balearic Is.*

*Tyrrhenian Sea*

*Ionian Sea*

Gibraltar (Gr. Br.)

Algiers

Palermo
*Sicily*

Rabat

Tunis

Valletta
**MALTA**

**MOROCCO**

**TUNISIA**

*Mediterranean*

Tripoli

**ALGERIA**

**LIBYA**

### Elevation

| Feet | Meters |
|---|---|
| Over 13,120 | Over 4,001 |
| 6,561–13,120 | 2,001–4,000 |
| 1,641–6,560 | 501–2,000 |
| 661–1,640 | 201–500 |
| 0–660 | 0–200 |
| Below sea level | Below sea level |

⊛ National capital
• Major city

0   150   300 miles
0   150   300 kilometers

THE CONTEMPORARY WORLD

PACIFIC OCEAN

ATLANTIC OCEAN

ATLANTIC OCEAN

Alaska (U.S.)

CANADA

UNITED STATES

Greenland (Den.)

ICELAND

UNITED KINGDOM

IRELAND

FRANCE

SPAIN

PORTUGAL

Azores (Port.)

Bermuda (U.K.)

MOROCCO

Canary Is. (Sp.)

Western Sahara (Mor.)

MAURITANIA

Hawaii (U.S.)

MEXICO

BAHAMAS

DOMINICAN REPUBLIC

HAITI

CUBA

JAMAICA

BELIZE

HONDURAS

GUATEMALA

EL SALVADOR

NICARAGUA

COSTA RICA

PANAMA

VENEZUELA

COLOMBIA

Puerto Rico (U.S.)

ST. KITTS AND NEVIS

ANTIGUA AND BARBUDA

Guadeloupe (Fr.)

DOMINICA

Martinique (Fr.)

ST. VINCENT AND THE GRENADINES

ST. LUCIA

BARBADOS

GRENADA

TRINIDAD AND TOBAGO

GUYANA

SURINAME

French Guiana (Fr.)

CAPE VERDE

SENEGAL

GAMBIA

GUINEA-BISSAU

GUINEA

BURKINA FASO

SIERRA LEONE

LIBERIA

CÔTE D'IVOIRE

GHANA

MALI

Galápagos Is. (Ec.)

ECUADOR

PERU

BRAZIL

BOLIVIA

PARAGUAY

CHILE

URUGUAY

ARGENTINA

SAMOA

TONGA

Easter I. (Chile)

Falkland Is. (U.K.)

Equator

N
W E
S

0          1,500          3,000 miles
0     1,500     3,000 kilometers

80°N

60°N

40°N

20°N

0°

20°S

40°S

60°S

80°S

160°W  140°W  120°W  100°W  80°W  60°W  40°W  20°W

ARCTIC OCEAN

NORWAY
SWEDEN
FINLAND
DEN.
NETH.
BEL.
LUX.
GERMANY POLAND
ESTONIA
LATVIA
LITHUANIA
BELARUS
RUSSIAN FEDERATION
CZ.
SLK.
UKRAINE
AUS.
HUNG.
SLN.
CR.
ROMANIA
MOLDOVA
SWITZ.
ITALY
SE.
B.H.
BULGARIA
KAZAKHSTAN
MONGOLIA
MO. KO.
ALB.
GREECE
N. MAC.
TURKEY
GEORGIA
ARMENIA
AZERBAIJAN
UZBEKISTAN
KYRGYZSTAN
TAJIKISTAN
TURKMENISTAN
TUNISIA
MALTA
CYPRUS
SYRIA
LEBANON
ISRAEL
IRAQ
West Bank
Gaza Strip
JORDAN
KUWAIT
AFGHANISTAN
IRAN
N. KOREA
S. KOREA
JAPAN
CHINA
ALGERIA
LIBYA
EGYPT
SAUDI ARABIA
QATAR
UNITED ARAB
EMIRATES
BAHRAIN
OMAN
PAKISTAN
BHUTAN
NEPAL
BANGLADESH
INDIA
MYANMAR
(BURMA)
Taiwan
PACIFIC OCEAN
NIGER
CHAD
SUDAN
YEMEN
DJIBOUTI
ERITREA
VIETNAM
LAOS
THAILAND
CAMBODIA
PHILIPPINES
Mariana Is.
(U.S.)
Guam
(U.S.)
MARSHALL
IS.
NIGERIA
BENIN
TOGO
CAMEROON
CENTRAL
AFRICAN REP.
SOUTH
SUDAN
ETHIOPIA
SOMALIA
MALDIVES
SRI
LANKA
BRUNEI
PALAU
FEDERATED STATES
OF MICRONESIA
EQ.
GUINEA
GABON
CONGO
RWANDA
UGANDA
KENYA
DEM. REP. OF
THE CONGO
SINGAPORE
MALAYSIA
NAURU
KIRIBATI
SÃO
TOMÉ
& PRÍNCIPE
BURUNDI
TANZANIA
COMOROS
SEYCHELLES
INDIAN OCEAN
INDONESIA
PAPUA
NEW
GUINEA
SOLOMON
IS.
TUVALU
ANGOLA
ZAMBIA
MALAWI
ZIMBABWE
MADAGASCAR
MAURITIUS
TIMOR
LESTE
VANUATU
FIJI
NAMIBIA
BOTSWANA
MOZAMBIQUE
ESWATINI
SOUTH
AFRICA
LESOTHO
AUSTRALIA
New Caledonia
(Fr.)
NEW
ZEALAND
Tasmania
(Aust.)

| ABBREVIATIONS | |
|---|---|
| ALB. | ALBANIA |
| AUS. | AUSTRIA |
| BEL. | BELGIUM |
| B.H. | BOSNIA AND HERZEGOVINA |
| CR. | CROATIA |
| CZ. | CZECH REPUBLIC |
| DEN. | DENMARK |
| HUNG. | HUNGARY |
| KO. | KOSOVO |
| LUX. | LUXEMBOURG |
| MO. | MONTENEGRO |
| NETH. | NETHERLANDS |
| N. MAC. | NORTH MACEDONIA |
| SE. | SERBIA |
| SLK. | SLOVAKIA |
| SLN. | SLOVENIA |
| SWITZ. | SWITZERLAND |

ANTARCTICA

20°E  40°E  60°E  80°E  100°E  120°E  140°E  160°E

# About the Authors

**Merry E. Wiesner-Hanks** (Ph.D., University of Wisconsin–Madison) taught first at Augustana College in Illinois, and from 1985 to 2018 at the University of Wisconsin–Milwaukee, where she is now Distinguished Professor of History emerita. She is the Senior Editor of the *Sixteenth Century Journal,* one of the editors of the *Journal of Global History,* and the author or editor of more than thirty books, including *A Concise History of the World.* From 2017 to 2019 she served as the president of the World History Association.

**Clare Haru Crowston** (Ph.D., Cornell University) teaches at the University of Illinois, where she is currently Professor of history and department chair. She is the author of *Credit, Fashion, Sex: Economies of Regard in Old Regime France* and *Fabricating Women: The Seamstresses of Old Regime France, 1675–1791,* which won the Berkshire and Hagley Prizes. She edited two special issues of the *Journal of Women's History,* has published numerous journal articles and reviews, and is a past president of the Society for French Historical Studies.

**Joe Perry** (Ph.D., University of Illinois at Urbana-Champaign) is Associate Professor of modern German and European history at Georgia State University. He has published numerous articles and is the author of *Christmas in Germany: A Cultural History* (2010). His current research interests focus on issues of consumption, gender, and popular culture in West Germany and Western Europe after World War II.

**John P. McKay** (Ph.D., University of California, Berkeley) is professor emeritus at the University of Illinois. He has written or edited numerous works, including the Herbert Baxter Adams Prize–winning book *Pioneers for Profit: Foreign Entrepreneurship and Russian Industrialization, 1885–1913.*